THE WORLD OF FASHION

THE WORLD OF FASHION

SECOND EDITION

JAY DIAMOND

ELLEN DIAMOND

FAIRCHILD PUBLICATIONS

NEW YORK

With love to Alex, Michael, Matthew, and Amanda

Editor: Chernow Editorial Services
Interior Design: Rebecca Lloyd Lemna
Cover Design: Lisa Klausing
Cover Illustration: Liselotte Watkins

Second Edition, Copyright © 1997
Fairchild Publications, a division of ABC Media, Inc.

First Edition, Copyright © 1990
by Harcourt Brace Jovanovich, Inc.

Library of Congress Catalog Card Number: 96-85742

ISBN: 1-56367-075-5

GST R 133004424

Printed in the United States of America

Contents

Extended Contents

PART THREE *The Fashion Merchandise Industries*

Preface

The excitement, coupled with the significant monetary rewards offered to its participants, makes the fashion industry one of the more appealing career arenas. Each participant has an opportunity to change the course of fashion. Whether the task involves design, merchandising, sales, or some phase of the many promotional endeavors subscribed to by the industry, the challenges are numerous. Many of those in the field have achieved fortune as well as fame. Some have even gained the global recognition usually reserved for entertainment celebrities. Whatever a person's goal, the fashion world is a place where individuals can both express themselves and carve out a niche in the marketplace. For those who choose careers in the industry, *The World of Fashion* provides the fundamental information needed for success. For others who merely want to learn more about the industry, it is a basic introduction.

The book has five parts that are divided into nineteen chapters. Part One, Introduction to Fashion, begins with the evolution of fashion, moves on to study the consumer, explores fashion in the global marketplace, and concludes with a look at the exciting careers the field offers. Part Two, The Producers of Raw Materials, examines the textiles, fur, and leather segments of the industry and addresses the various roles they play in fashion. Part Three, The Fashion Merchandise Industries, presents an overview of women's, men's and children's apparel, wearable accessories, trimmings, cosmetics and fragrances, and fashions for the home. Part Four, Designing and Manufacturing of Fashion Apparel and Accessories, discusses the role of the fashion forecasters, designers, and manufacturers as well as processes and procedures used to produce fashion merchandise. Part Five, Merchandising Fashion, speaks of the importance of fashion advisory and information services, explores all of the important fashion retail environments, and examines the many aspects of advertising and promotion undertaken by industry participants.

A wealth of industry sources are featured throughout the text, including designers, manufacturers, materials suppliers, and fashion promoters. The text has two features of particular interest. They are "The World of Fashion Profiles" and "A Point of View." The former examines many of the people and companies whose presence and talents have contributed significantly to the fashion world. The latter includes articles that have been either written especially for this text by leaders in a particular area of the fashion industry or published articles from a variety of sources.

Each chapter contains a number of different pedagogical elements, such as Chapter Highlights, Important Fashion Terminology and Concepts, questions For Review, Exercises and Projects, and Case Problems.

To bring *The World of Fashion* "to life," the authors have developed a video series, *The Business of Fashion*, that closely parallels the written text. An instructor's manual provides additional exercises and projects and a set of exams for each chapter.

Acknowledgments

We wish to acknowledge the following people and organizations who have significantly contributed to *The World of Fashion,* 2nd edition.

Allen Edmond Shoes; American Apparel Manufacturer's Association; *American Demographics* Magazine; American Fiber Manufacturers Association Inc.; American Fur Industry; American Wool Council; Amity Leather; Bloomingdale's; Christopher Thomas Agency; Fran Coleman, Tickle Me!; Color Association of the United States (CAUS); Committee for Color Trends; Council for Fashion Designers of America; Joanne Criscione and Karen Cohen, Criscione; Bill Dadd, Cotton Incorporated; Allan Ellinger, Marketing Management Group; Lou Epstein, Hong Kong Trade Development Council; Marlene Eskin, Market View; Fashion Group; Fragrance Foundation; Carey Greber, Saint Laurie Ltd.; Haysun Hahn, Promostyl; Scott Houston, The Fashion Association; International Silk Association; Lili Kasdan, Leather Apparel Association; Steve Keenan and Bonnie Dredd, King Casey; The Larkin Group; Linen Promotion Commission; Prof. Tanya Lowenstein, Nassau Community College; Macy's; Gae Marino, Coleen Triggs, and David Wolfe, Henry Doneger Associates; Monarch Knitting Machines; NAMSB; National Cotton Council of America; Rosenthal China; Sawgrass Mills; Seidel Tanning Corp.; Seventh on Sixth; Wool Bureau.

Readers selected by the publisher were also very helpful. They included: Laura Bliss, Stevens College; Carolyn Blount, Shoreline Community College; Suzanne Coil, Baker University; Judith Everett, Northern Arizona University; Yvette Hays–Logan, University of Rhode Island; Pam Kuchenmeister, Illinois State University; Rosemary Leach, Skyline College; Pam Norum, University of Missouri–Columbus; Beverly Olsen, Dakota County Technical College; Christine Pratt, Fashion Institute of Technology; Teresa Robinson, Middle Tennessee State University; George Sproles, GES Associates; Janice Threw, Southern Illinois University–Carbondale; Diann Valentini, Fashion Institute of Technology; Stella Warnick, Seattle Pacific University; Debbie West, Draughons Junior College; Helen Xenakis, Fashion Institute of Technology

THE WORLD OF FASHION

Introduction to Fashion

Part One discusses the evolution of fashion from the days of couture designers, who created fashions for the few, through the twentieth century. Chapter 1 explores this evolution from the beginning of couture through the various inventions of the Industrial Revolution that made fashion available to all classes. Chapter 2 takes a decade-by-decade approach to twentieth-century fashion, presenting the historial events that influenced fashion; fashion highlights for men, women, and children; and the designers and their influences on fashion.

The success or failure of a fashion product depends upon its acceptance or rejection by the consumer, who is the focus of Chapter 3. To create and produce fashion that will meet with success, the industry studies the consumers, their motives, social classes, and other characteristics to determine which type of merchandise is important to each group. A variety of research tools, such as questionnaires, personal observations, and focus groups are used for the analyses of prospective customers.

As with other professions, fashion has its own vocabulary, and those who participate in the industry must be familiar with these terms. Chapter 4 discusses fashion language, as well as the ever-changing nature of fashion and the potential for each style to remain popular. For example, certain styles may become popular because an "influential" person wears them. These people are the fashion leaders, and can have a significant influence on consumers.

Unlike many industries, fashion occurs in a global environment. As discussed in Chapter 5, fashion is designed and manufactured in a global marketplace. To make American fashion businesses more competitive with businesses in other parts of the world, the United States government has enacted specific legislation that every industry participant should know. To improve their global marketing success, fashion companies belong to international trade associations, and attend trade expositions throughout the world.

The fashion arena thus offers careers in design, manufacturing, retailing, and promotion. Each affords the individual different monetary rewards and different challenges and is discussed fully in Chapter 6.

CHAPTER 1

The Evolution of Fashion

After you have completed this chapter, you will be able to discuss:

- The evolution of fashion and some of the factors that played a role in its development.

- The impact of the Industrial Revolution on the fashion industry.

- The role of unionization in the garment industry.

- Various components of the fashion industry.

The world of fashion began with individual **couturiers** and evolved, as a result of the Industrial Revolution, into a mass-market industry. By studying this evolution, we will be better equipped to understand the organization of the fashion industry and the directions in which it is moving.

THE BEGINNING OF COUTURE

Although the history of fashion may be traced back hundreds of years, it was not until the late 1700s that individuality of design began to emerge. Styles were set by royalty and carried out by the dressmakers who served them. Only the upper class could afford what was fashionable and finely produced. The poor made their own clothing or wore the castoffs of the rich.

By the end of the eighteenth century, one name had emerged in fashion design—*Rose Bertin.* Initially a milliner's apprentice, she became France's premier designer. As a result of the recognition she received from the Princess de Conti, Bertin was appointed court milliner in 1772. In that position, she was introduced to Marie Antoinette. She soon became the Queen's confidante as well as her official designer. Eventually, Bertin became the minister of fashion for the French court. As her reputation grew, she was commissioned to design hats and dresses for the aristocracy. Her fame spread to other countries, and she soon started to export her merchandise.

Garments for the wealthy class were elaborately tailored and trimmed. Each piece was hand sewn, embroidered, jeweled, and embellished to perfection. Aside from Bertin, the names of the dressmakers to the royal families and the aristocracy were generally unknown. Those who employed them jealously guarded their identities to avoid losing them to other families.

During the early nineteenth century, the opulent designs that dominated the wardrobes of the rich began to disappear; less elaborate dress became the order of the day. It was not until after 1845, when the Englishman *Charles Frederick Worth* emigrated to Paris, that the world would come to know another designer. In Paris, he first worked for a fabric dealer, whom he convinced to open a dress department. In 1858, Worth was the first to open a couture house on the rue de la Paix. Along with a list of private clients in Europe and America, he was court dressmaker to Empress Eugènie of France. His success would soon motivate others to establish their own couture businesses.

Fed by the magnificent textiles and trimmings of nearby Lyon, it was natural for Paris to establish itself as the world's leading center for couture. The names that followed Worth are legendary, and will be discussed in Chapter 2.

THE INDUSTRIAL REVOLUTION

Until about 1770, man worked in much the same manner as did his ancestors. Products were slowly made by hand. Cloth was handwoven, and a cobbler still used only a hammer, knife, and awl to make a shoe over a last, or form.

During this time, the Western world witnessed the growth of the middle class, which prospered from new avenues of trade and industry, and spent money on such luxuries as fine clothing. As the middle class grew in importance, its members created new fashion directions. The business suit, for example, became an important element in a man's wardrobe. Before long, fine tailor shops were opened in London's Savile Row to provide this new business attire.

Charles Frederick Worth was the first couture designer. His designs were worn by Empress Eugenie of France and other wealthy patrons.

Changes, however, were taking place in the methods of production. In large part, they could be attributed to the growth of the textile industry, which was revolutionized by a series of time-saving inventions. In 1733, John Kay received a patent for his **flying shuttle,** which resulted in the manufacture of a loom that produced materials more rapidly. Similarly, spinning was a slow process until 1764, when James Hargreaves, a British spinner, invented the **spinning jenny.** He placed eight spindles on a frame, which could be turned by a single wheel. As a result, one spinner could simultaneously produce eight threads instead of producing one thread at a time. Hargreaves later created a machine that could spin sixteen threads at a time. Ultimately, even a child

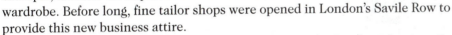

TABLE 1.1

INVENTIONS OF THE INDUSTRIAL REVOLUTION THAT CHANGED FASHION		
Year	**Inventor**	**Invention**
1733	John Kay	Flying Shuttle
1764	James Hargreaves	Spinning Jenny
1785	Edmund Cartwright	Power Loom
1793	Eli Whitney	Cotton Gin
1846	Elias Howe, Jr.	Sewing Machine

could run the machine and turn out work that had previously required one hundred spinners. Then, in 1785, Edmund Cartwright invented the **power loom,** which wove cloth so rapidly that the hand loom was quickly reserved for limited runs of special fabrics.

The increased speed of the spinning machine resulted in demands for large supplies of cotton fiber. This problem was solved by an American, Eli Whitney. In 1793, he invented the **cotton gin,** which separated the cotton seed from the fiber so quickly and expertly that one man was able to turn out the work that once required 300 men.

Because of the competitive advantage these inventions gave to manufacturers, England was very protective of its discoveries, and forbade the emigration of textile workers and the exportation of its textile machines. Some workers, however, memorized the details of each machine's construction. These workers left England in disguise, and were able to reproduce the machines in other countries. For example, Samuel Slater left England after learning the construction details for many textile machines. He opened a spinning mill in Rhode Island in 1790, where he introduced the factory system to the United States. During the Civil War, the demand for fabrics to manufacture uniforms helped the growth of American mills, most of which were in New England. By the end of the war, the mills were capable of mass producing textiles. Fashion was now on the way to becoming a major industry in the United States, but one more step was necessary.

Although fabrics were being produced faster than ever before, it was not until the development of the first sewing machine that the world would be treated to a new generation of fashion.

The sewing machine was developed by Isaac Singer and changed the course of fashion.

The Sewing Machine

Although Walter Hunt invented a **sewing machine** in 1832, he did not apply for a patent until 1854, when it was denied on the grounds of abandonment. On September 10, 1846, however, Elias Howe, Jr. did receive a patent for his sewing machine. As a result, he is generally regarded as its inventor. His failure to market the machine successfully led to attempts by others to further develop the machine. Finally, in 1858, Isaac Singer designed a machine that worked by the use of a foot treadle, thereby freeing the hands to manipulate the fabric. That year, the Singer Sewing Manufacturing Company was incorporated and sales reached 3,000 units. With this invention, women began to sew professional-looking clothes at home, and factories experienced the birth of ready-to-wear apparel.

UNIONIZATION AND THE GARMENT INDUSTRY

These new inventions created what is now known as the garment industry. Coupled with the significant growth of the American population, they led to an increase in the production of apparel. At first, factories were located primarily

The fire at the Triangle Shirtwaist factory was used by the garment industry to make the public aware of sweatshop conditions.

in Boston and Baltimore. Later, they opened in significant numbers in New York City, the gateway to the new world. Immigrants from Eastern Europe became the mainstays of the sewing industry, as immigrants from Asia and Latin America are now. Their willingness to work long hours for low wages made them extremely desirable workers. As the demand for mass-produced goods increased, more and more workers were used to fill every available inch of space in the factories. Working conditions deteriorated and employees were trapped in unsanitary and dangerous environments.

In an effort to improve working conditions and wages, seven local unions amalgamated to form the International Ladies' Garment Workers Union, known as the **ILGWU,** in 1900. Unfortunately, it was not until tragedy struck that the union made inroads in cleaning up the factories. In 1911, fire broke out at the Triangle Shirtwaist Company in New York City. With the door to the main entrance bolted to keep workers from leaving, and a fire escape leading to nowhere, the inferno became a deathtrap for more than one hundred people. As a result of this tragic incident, many Americans came to support the garment workers in their struggle against the **sweatshops.** Through the years the union gained significant strength, successfully upgrading working conditions and negotiating fringe benefits and better salaries for its members.

The men's wear industry also experienced the same sweatshop conditions. The successful strike at the Hart, Schaffner & Marx manufacturing plant in Chicago in 1910 led to the eventual formation of the Amalgamated Clothing Workers Union of America in 1914. Later, the **Amalgamated,** as it was known, merged with the shoe and textile workers to form the **ACTWU** (Amalgamated Clothing and Textile Workers Union).

Today, the garment industry's unions face a new problem—that of decreasing membership. Their numbers have been significantly eroded by the advent of offshore production. To counteract this problem, unions are trying to create

At the turn of the century, John Wanamaker's of Philadelphia was a major retailer.

Sears Roebuck & Company began its business in Chicago in 1893 selling its goods through catalogs.

jobs by encouraging consumers to buy domestically produced goods. One example is a television commercial that reminds viewers to **"look for the union label."**

RETAILING'S RESPONSE TO MASS PRODUCTION

Until the middle of the nineteenth century, merchandise, especially wearing apparel, was in short supply. The privileged few had quality clothing that was custom made by tailors. Others made their own clothing at home, with little concern for questions of fashion.

As a result of the Industrial Revolution, merchandise was produced in quantity in the United States. New facilities were needed to sell this large assortment of apparel and accessory items to the masses. The first were **limited-line stores,** or **specialty stores,** that restricted their merchandise to a narrow classification. Joseph Lowthian Hudson started a small men's and boy's haberdashery store (Hudsons) in 1881 in the old Detroit Opera House, and Nordstrom opened its doors in 1901 as a shoe emporium. With the immediate success of these stores, the same companies opened new facilities. This phenomenon started the trend toward **chain store** retailing.

At the turn of the twentieth century, the merchandise assortment was becoming more abundant and varied than ever before. Some merchants decided to open new operations that sold more than one type of merchandise, or to expand their limited-line stores to full-line **department stores.** George Dayton built a six-story multiuse building in Minneapolis in 1902, called Daytons, which eventually merged with Hudsons to become Dayton Hudson. Henri Bendel, established in 1912, started as a small millinery business and eventually evolved into a specialized department store operation, featuring women's apparel and accessories. Other important major retailers who began their businesses during this time were Macy's in New York City, Filene's in Boston, Wanamaker's in Philadelphia, and Neiman Marcus in Dallas.

Although these stores flourished in the major cities, consumers in rural areas had little access to these retailers. In response, companies began to sell merchandise through the mail. The early **mail-order** merchants were both located in Chicago: Montgomery Ward, which began its business in 1872, and Sears Roebuck & Co., in 1893. Each published a **catalog** offering a wide variety of products that could be ordered through the mail.

Retailing continued to expand throughout the country with branch operations. Although many of the early participants are still in operation, many of those who began the industry, such as Gimbels and B. Altman & Co., are no longer in business.

SEGMENTS OF THE FASHION INDUSTRY

Today the numerous segments of the fashion industry include textiles, manufacturers, retailers, licenses, franchises, fashion communications, and market consultants. Although these areas will each be explored later in the text, the following is a brief outline of their roles in bringing the goods from the point of production to consumption. **Designers** whose talents drive the industry will be explored separately in the next chapter.

Textiles

Before any garment may be designed, the most important materials used in their manufacture—**textiles**—must be created. The production of these fabrics involves a variety of different participants as well as processes.

Raw cotton undergoes numerous processes before being made fibers and then fabrics.

Fibers must be selected to meet the fabric requirements of designers, manufacturers, and the consumers. In addition to the natural fibers cotton, flax, wool, and silk, chemical companies have developed numerous manufactured fibers. Companies such as DuPont, Hoechst-Celanese, and BASF, are constantly researching and developing new fibers, improving existing ones, and responding to the demands created by their customers.

The fibers are then transformed into fabrics at the textile mills, which are located all over the globe. Some limit their responsibilities to one aspect of production, such as weaving yarns; others are vertical operations that perform all of the processes necessary for complete production. Burlington Mills is an example of a **vertical company.**

A converter is the segment of the textile industry that finishes goods according to the specifications of its clients. Brittany and Erlanger are two such companies.

For more detailed discussion of the textiles industry, see Chapter 7.

Manufacturers

As evident by their very name, this segment of the industry is responsible for production. Many manufacturers participate in every phase of the construction operation, including designing the line, purchasing fabrics and trimmings, making patterns, cutting and sewing garments, and ultimately marketing the goods to the retailers. Today, many manufacturers, such as Nine West and Liz Claiborne, have even opted to do their own retailing.

Although some run complete operations from the point of production to consumption, others function in a more specialized manner. They might hire free-lance designers to create their collections, or even fashion consultants, such as The Fashion Service in New York City or Design Intelligence in London, to design the entire line. Some companies design and do their own cutting, such as Criscione, an apparel company, and use outside contractors to sew the garments. Others use contractors for all of the operations.

Whatever the approach, manufacturers are responsible for all phases of production. Many find the benefits of outside contracting so attractive that they are only directly involved in developing the line and distributing it to retailers.

Some of the smaller manufacturers do not even sell their own lines. Instead, they employ **manufacturer's representatives** to sell for them. Known as "reps" or "jobbers" in the industry, they sell a number of noncompeting lines in their own showrooms. They receive remuneration in the form of commissions from the manufacturers they represent. They are technically classified as **limited-function wholesalers,** but do not take title to or physically handle the goods as **full-service wholesalers** do in most fields.

The typical wholesale component of other industries is conspicuously absent in the fashion industry. Because the goods are short lived, they must get to the retailers as quickly as possible and not sit on a middleman's shelves.

An important form of manufacturing in the apparel industry is **licensing.** Licensing is an agreement in which individuals and businesses (the *licensors*) give others, (the *licensees*) such as fragrance or home fashions manufacturers, permission to use their names on products and companies for a fee or commission. The practice has grown enormously and has enabled well-known designers to expand their influence and gain worldwide recognition. Celebrities, entertainers, and corporations are also involved in licensing agreements.

The practice of designer licensing was initiated in the mid-1960s, with such designers as Pierre Cardin, John Weitz, and Ralph Lauren. Licensing arrangements differ from designer to designer. Some demand complete control over the individual designs and the right of refusal for substandard offerings; others merely allow their names to be placed on products without significant personal involvement.

Pierre Cardin, one of the world's most famous fashion designers, used this method to capture the attention of consumers all over the world. He began with men's wear but now has more than 800 licensing arrangements all over the world, covering such products as children's wear, eyeglasses, home fashions, hats, shoes, and lingerie. Other famous designers who enjoy licensing agreements include Bill Blass, Calvin Klein, Christian Dior, and Donna Karan.

Retailers

Once the manufacturers have met their responsibility in the fashion chain, they sell their products to an assortment of **retailers,** who market these goods to customers. Although traditional retailers, such as department or specialty stores, long had a monopoly on fashion merchandise, there is now a great deal of competition from nontraditional retailing formats, such as direct-mail companies, home shopping on cable television, and on-line computer services.

In examining retailing, we run the gamut from the industrial giants to the smallest entrepreneurs. More and more restructuring is occurring because of mergers and acquisitions. In 1994, Federated Department Stores, which had already acquired such companies as Bloomingdale's and Stern's, acquired Macy's. As a result it became a giant in the industry. In 1995, Federated expanded even further, with the purchase of the Broadway stores on the West Coast.

Even the methods of conducting business are constantly changing. For example, Sears, once a pioneer in the catalog business, has eliminated its gen-

Macy's — the largest store in the world — is a division of Federated Department Stores.

eral catalog in order to expand its in-store fashion merchandise business. It is also de-emphasizing its private labels in favor of more nationally recognized brands.

The field has also experimented with several new concepts. They include the **spinoff stores,** which are specialty shops featuring a specific collection of the parent department store. Examples of these separate shops include Macy's Aeropostale, and subspecialty units, exemplified by the Knot Shop that feature a defined or limited merchandise assortment. Other types of retailing include manufacturer's and designer **outlets.** Originally intended as an alternative for designers and manufacturers to dispose of the leftovers such names as DKNY, Ralph Lauren, Gucci, Alexander Julian, and Anne Klein now use these outlets to sell additional merchandise. **Off-price discounters,** such as Marshalls, Kids "R" Us, and Syms offer manufacturers' irregulars, seconds, closeout goods, canceled orders, overruns, and goods returned by other retailers. These outlets also offer branded apparel and accessories at a fraction of their regular selling prices.

The majority of fashion merchandise carried by the retailer is purchased from manufacturers. Today, however, stores manufacture their own goods or have manufacturers produce goods exclusively for them. These products are known as **private label merchandise.** Private-label merchandise sometimes carries the name of the retail store in which it is sold, such as The GAP or The Limited, which includes Lerner New York, Lane Bryant, Structure, Express, and Victoria's Secret. It can also carry a name used by the retailer exclusively, such as SFA Collections by Saks Fifth Avenue or Erica Taylor of the May Department Stores. The exclusivity gives retailers an edge on the competition and offers the potential for greater profits, better gross margin, and image enhancement.

The retail business is conducted in a host of venues. The most conventional are downtown central districts, where most department stores operate their **flagship** or main stores, and the suburban **shopping malls,** which continue to increase in size. Some, such as the Mall of America in Bloomington, Minnesota, are combinations of shopping and entertainment centers. Another shopping arena is the **festival marketplace,** which is usually a location once used for other purposes, but now has been transformed into shopping centers that feature unique surroundings. Examples are Union Station in St. Louis, South Street Seaport in New York City, and Quincy Market in Boston. Still other venues include **vertical malls,** such as Water Tower in Chicago, which reaches skyward because of the limited space in the downtown area, **enclosed outlet centers,** such as Gurnee Mills outside of Chicago and Sawgrass Mills in Ft. Lauderdale, and **fashion streets,** such as Worth Avenue in Palm Beach, Madison Avenue in New York City, and Rodeo Drive in Beverly Hills, where the most fashionable shops cater to the richest consumers. Power centers, where such giants as T.J. Maxx and Marshalls dispose of fashion as well as other merchandise at rock bottom prices in stores that span several thousand feet, complete the types of venues used for fashion retailing.

The Mall of America is a megamall combining shopping and entertainment.

Benetton

Founded in Treviso, Italy, in 1964 by a sister and three brothers, the Benetton Company has become the most important of the globally positioned fashion franchises. It all began when the sister sold her bicycle to buy a knitting machine on which she could develop unusual patterns. Few could then have imagined that this would be the beginning of a company that would have a sales volume of close to $2 billion by the mid-1990s.

Initially, the family sold sweaters to local merchants. When the demand increased dramatically, the family decided to enter the retail business. Ten years after their first store opened in 1968, Benetton was operating 1,000 retail outlets in Italy. Today, the product line, which is designed by 200 designers who produce 2,600 styles in 250 different colors, is marketed through 7,000 stores in 100 countries around the world, with the majority in Italy and other European nations. Others are in the United States, Canada, South America, Japan, India, Turkey, Egypt, and Mexico. The stores are either company owned or franchised.

To keep up with the demand for its products, the company has equipped its facilities with state-of-the-art technology. In addition to completely computerized cutting procedures, the company employs a robot packing system in its warehouses that can ship 35,000 boxes in a single day. Seamless knitting is the method used in knitwear construction, eliminating the need for any sewing in these garments.

To quickly respond to the demands of its retail network, Benetton can ship orders within eight days of their receipt. To guarantee the availability of the colors needed by the stores, their merchandise is produced as *grey goods* and dyed in any of the 250 colors they feature.

Benetton has made certain that its appeal is globally appropriate by studying the cultures of every country in the world and producing items that would fit within these cultures. The prices charged by the franchisees are suggested by the Benetton organization, but may be adjusted as the individual franchisees wish.

The company's advertising campaigns continue to attract attention throughout the world. Its magazine and television advertisements touch many social issues in a controversial way. Photographs of AIDS patients at their last stages of life and the faces of starving children are just a few of the images used.

Given the worldwide success of its lines, Benetton has demonstrated that international franchising can be successfully accomplished in the fashion industry.

Retailing formats also include *leased departments* and *franchises*. Although they will be explored fully in Chapter 18, their definition and importance should be mentioned briefly in this introduction.

Leased departments, owned by outside companies, are operated as departments within another retailer store. Leased departments includes restaurants, shoe shops, and fine jewelry departments. An example includes Revillon Furs of New York, which operates in Saks Fifth Avenue.

Franchising is a contractual arrangement that permits an individual (**franchisee**) to operate a business under the recognizable name of an individual or company (**franchisor**). Franchising plays a significant role in the fast-food industry, where companies such as McDonald's and Burger King sell the rights to use their names to individuals. The franchisee pays a fee to the franchisor. In addition to the monetary requirement, the franchisees are required to purchase all products and supplies developed by the franchisor. In the fast-food industry, for example, everything from the meat patties to the paper plates on which they are served is specified in the franchise contracts. In the fashion arena, there are franchised units under names such as Ralph Lauren, Yves Saint Laurent, and Lady Madonna. International franchising is growing in the fashion industry. One of the global leaders in franchising—Benetton—is explored in a World of Fashion Profile.

Diana Vreeland

It was the outbreak of World War I that brought eight-year-old Diana Vreeland from Paris to the United States. In Paris, she had lived in a world in which art, culture, and fashion played dominant roles. Her parents were friends with such people as Diaghilev and Nijinsky. As a result Vreeland felt comfortable mingling in a society that was open to only a few.

In 1924 she married Thomas Vreeland. When they moved to New York City in 1937, she accepted a position at *Harper's Bazaar* that was offered to her by then fashion editor, Carmel Snow.

Although most people outside of the industry believe that a sure ticket to the inner circles begins with "natural beauty," Vreeland often regarded herself as an ugly duckling. Lacking the conventional beauty often associated with those in fashion, she chose to create a persona that epitomized individuality and style. She had short black hair, rouged cheeks, and bright red lips

that set her apart from the rest. Her writing style was as unique as her dress. In 1939 she became fashion editor, working with Mrs. Snow and art director, Alexey Brodovitch. In 1963 she left *Bazaar* to work as associate editor at *Vogue;* she became editor-in-chief, a position she held until 1971.

Unlike those who merely reported on the fashion scene, Vreeland was a significant promoter. Whenever she felt something was important, she prominently placed it in her columns.

From 1972 to 1989 she served as consultant to the Costume Institute of the Metropolitan Museum of Art. Exhibits such as "Balenciaga," American Women of Style," "Yves Saint Laurent," and "The Glory of Russian Costume," to name a few are among the fashion subjects covered during her tenure at the museum. She was considered to be one of the leading players ever to work in the fashion industry.

Diana Vreeland was one of the most influential people in fashion history.

Retail organizations and methods of operation are constantly being restructured to meet the challenges of today's demanding consumer. The methodology employed by today's retailers will be fully explored in Chapter 18.

Fashion Communications

Designing the most exciting collection or operating the most fashion-forward retail enterprise in no way guarantees recognition and success. The messages about the creative new designer, a revolutionizing breakthrough in fiber development, or a new approach to personalized shopping by a retailer only reach the appropriate markets if the **media** chooses to pass them on.

Every company in the fashion industry uses either its own advertising or public relations department or outside resources to get its name into print or broadcasting outlets. Publicists write scores of press releases, articles that extol the virtues of those they represent, and prepare media kits consisting of releases, photographs, and any other material that might motivate the editorial staffs of the media to convey their messages.

Fashion magazines help dispense fashion news to the consumers of fashion.

The targets of these publicity releases are consumer magazines, such as *GQ, Elle, Harper's Bazaar,* and *Vogue,* trade periodicals such as *Women's Wear Daily* and *California Apparel News,* and television programming, ranging from the daily broadcasts of a fashion editor to programs like Elsa Klensch's *Style* on CNN, which focuses on collections of apparel, accessories and home furnishings, or MTV's *House of Style,* which offers news about fashion, lifestyles, and celebrities to a younger market.

In the fashion industry, there are those whose endorsements often catapult designers into the limelight. Currently some of the most powerful names include John Fairchild of *Women's Wear Daily,* Liz Tilberus of *Harper's Bazaar,* and Anna Wintour of Condé Nast. Former media giants who are worthy of mention here include Carmel Snow, fashion editor of *Harper's Bazaar* from 1932 to 1957, and Diana Vreeland, who was fashion editor at *Harper's* from 1937 until 1962 and at *Vogue* from 1962 to 1971. Vreeland's background and influence on fashion is the subject of a World of Fashion Profile.

The entire subject of fashion communications is explored in depth in Chapter 17.

Market Consultants

A host of different businesses interact with designers, manufacturers, and retailers to assist with the decision-making process. They include *fashion forecasters, resident buying offices,* and *reporting services.* All of these market consultants provide their own expertise and help lead their clients in the right direction.

Briefly, the **fashion forecaster** is someone who, like a weather forecaster, makes predictions long before the designer sets out on the path to creating a new collection. These professionals work as far as eighteen months in advance of a season and provide information that helps their clients develop merchandise. By thoroughly investigating some of the primary markets, such as textiles, the forecaster is able to guide designers and manufacturers in their selections of color, texture, styles, and so on. Visiting and analyzing the worldwide fashion centers also enables the fashion forecaster to predict what styles will more than likely appeal to the consumer. David Wolfe, a leading forecaster, regularly visits St. Tropez to study what is being worn on the streets.

Resident buying offices (RBOs) are companies located in the wholesale fashion markets, such as New York City's Garment Center. They are the eyes and ears of store buyers who, because of their distance from the wholesale markets, cannot make the frequent visits necessary to assess what is new in the industry. RBOs provide everything the retailer needs to make the appropriate purchasing decisions.

Reporting services are similar to RBOs in that they provide pertinent information to retailers. However, they do not purchase merchandise, as does the resident buying office. Their forte is mainly information.

Each of these marketing consultants will be discussed in detail in Chapter 17.

Regular interaction among the various industry components assures greater success for each of them. Their cooperative efforts foster a better image for the field of fashion, and generally assures a more productive future for those who produce the merchandise.

THE FUTURE OF FASHION

As the twenty-first century approaches, the world of fashion continues to change. Traditional rules of the game, which included faithfully following the dictates of specific designers on such issues as appropriate dress length, are finally being broken. Although globally renowned designers are still crowding the runways with outrageous styles at prices that only a few can afford, new designers are showing fashions that reflect what is taking place on the streets, in the political arenas, in the entertainment field, and in movements to protect the environment.

From 1922 to 1991, the USSR was dominated by the Communist Party. In 1985, Mikhail Gorbachev began a campaign for the country to improve the economy and lessen social constraints. Finally, in 1991, Communism collapsed. In Germany, the years of East/West separation came to a sudden halt, as symbolized by the tearing down of the Berlin Wall in 1989/1990. In the United States, people are turning away from the excesses of the 1980s. They are spending money more cautiously, and no longer emphasize extravagance in dress, dining, and living. Instead of boasting about purchases made in upscale boutiques, many who still follow high fashion are heading to "off-price" merchants and letting their peers know about the bargains they found.

The new freedom in Russia allows citizens to shop in other countries as these women are doing at a Wal-Mart in Anchorage, Alaska.

Designer's secondary collections far outsell their designer lines.

Those in the fashion business are no longer concerned just with silhouette trends and whether short or long hem lengths will be accepted. They are studying people more closely, in every part of the globe, to learn about their style preferences and needs. The streets are providing unlimited ideas to the manufacturers of apparel and accessories for their collections. Consider, for

Designs illustrating the cultural diversity of today's designers: Malaysian designer, Yuki (left) and Japanese designer, Rei Kawakubo (right).

example, the biker's leather jacket that turns up as the top of an evening dress; the baseball cap still worn by men, but now with ponytails peeking through the back opening; the exercise clothing that has shifted from the gym to the street; the baggy pants worn very low on the hips and originated by the rappers; the permanent and temporary tattoos that men and women of every age are sporting; and the piercing of parts of the body, in addition to the ears, for the insertion of ornaments. These developments signal that fashion may be born anywhere.

Because designers recognize that fashion is not only for the affluent, they are generating a greater number of **secondary collections.** In America, Donna Karan's DKNY line far outsells her designer line and Isaac Mizrahi's less formal collection, "Isaac," was preceded by considerable press coverage. In Europe, the United Kingdom's John Galliano markets a less costly collection, "Galliano Girl," and Italy's Franco Moschino produces a line called "Cheap & Chic." Others who have taken this road include Bill Blass, Calvin Klein, Sonia Rykiel, Giorgio Armani, and Jean Paul Gaultier.

Fashion continues to expand its horizons with the recognition of a new breed of designers who have emerged from a variety of ethnic backgrounds. Each brings his or her own experiences to the collections. Rei Kawakubo from Japan has captured the attention of fashion's editorial press and the public with avant-garde designs marketed by her own company, *Comme des Garçons.* Yohji Yamamoto, also from Japan, specializes in oversize clothing in a variety of textures. African American designer Tracy Reese's lively interpretations reflect her interest in theater, dance, and music. In addition, new corners of the globe are having an impact on fashion. Yeohlee Teng, from Malaysia, uses clear lines and geometric forms for better-priced apparel. Teng and another Malaysian, Yuki (Gnyuki Torimaru), whose designs often feature bias-cut, dramatic silhouettes, are making that part of the world better known to fashion. Gemma Kahng, from South Korea, employs unusual ornamentation and detailing in her collections. Each of these designers has demonstrated that fashion creativity no longer resides exclusively within traditional boundaries.

To enhance the fashion designer's creative instincts, the fiber manufacturers have provided a host of new products. Lycra spandex is being used in conjunction with natural and manufactured fibers to enhance function as well as beauty, and Teflon, once reserved for the coating on pots and pans, is applied to textiles earmarked for ski parkas, raincoats, and sportswear, as well as to textiles slated for home fashions. Microfibers are challenging the luxurious feel of silk, and polyester, in general, is losing its bad reputation, and becoming a more popular fiber in the apparel industry. New durable press treatments to textiles now permit apparel products to be labelled as "wrinkle-free," "wrinkle resistant," "no-iron," or simply "WR."

Technology has risen to new heights in the world of fashion. Every segment of the industry, from the production of raw materials to the final distribution to the consumer, takes advantage of ever-improving technological discoveries. The most notable are the **CAD systems,** which eliminate the need for endless paper patterns and the time spent by the designer creating them at the drafting table. Other electronic applications, however, are moving the fashion industry into areas that not long ago seemed like fantasy.

For example, providing **on-line computer services** has enormous implications for fiber producers, end-product manufacturers, market consultants, retailers, and promoters of fashion. Such commercial on-line services as CompuServe, America OnLine, and Prodigy, as well as the Internet, offer a new vehicle to communicate, advertise, and sell to suppliers and customers. Information about companies such as Spiegel, Lands' End, and Brooks Brothers are currently available on-line. Individuals can download pictures of merchandise over their modem lines and place orders or ask questions via e-mail. Further examples and explanations of the applications will be covered in the appropriate chapters throughout the text.

Another time and money saving invention is the fax machine, which disseminates information in a matter of seconds, enabling a design that originates in one country to be quickly copied in another. By transmitting the design electronically, the time and effort needed for traditional transmission is eliminated.

In 1995, the film *Unzipped*, which carefully scrutinized the fashion industry, was heralded by movie critics as a filmmaking success. The film depicts one year in the life of fashion designer Isaac Mizrahi, and his trials and tribulations in mounting a successful collection after the previous season's collection was less than enthusiastically received. From Mizrahi's thoughts to the backstage madness of the supermodels about to enter the runway, the audience is treated to the often chaotic atmosphere that surrounds fashion.

No one can predict the future of fashion, whom the major players will be, or how successful styles will become. By examining the past, one may begin to understand what this industry is all about and the number of variables that interact in the marketplace. Fashion forecasters research consumer prefer-

The film Unzipped *provides an insight to the trials and tribulations of Isaac Mizrahi (center) planning a collection.*

ences and motives. The results of these studies influence the entire fashion industry. This process begins with the textile producers, who generate the fabrics that will be used by the designers and manufacturers to produce apparel and accessories. These decisions influence the trimmings industry, which creates the little "extras" that change a conventional product into one with more appeal; the market consultants, such as the resident buying offices that help retailers with their purchasing decisions, the store buyers who must make the selections, the visual merchandisers who display fashion to its best advantage, the fashion promoters who create special events for professionals and consumers, and the editorial press, which may help to arouse interest in or destroy a particular fashion.

Many people—some famous, some unknown—impact the industry. For example, anyone with an interest in fashion knows the names of such contemporary designers as Donna Karan, Ralph Lauren, and Calvin Klein, and such past legends such as Chanel, Balenciaga, and Dior. But who can name a well-known patternmaker, sewer, or trimmer? Although the former group steals the fashion headlines, the designers alone do not create fashion.

Chapter Highlights

- The evolution of fashion began with the individual dressmaker, who designed clothing for the nobility.

- Fashion reached its present state only after the invention of time-saving machines that made the mass production of ready-to-wear apparel practical.

- The industry grew by employing immigrants who worked for low wages under poor conditions. In the early 1900s, conditions led to the formation of unions, notably the ILGWU and the Amalgamated.

- Increased output led retailers to expand their operations in order to reach more consumers. In addition to limited line stores, consumers could now shop in chain stores and department stores, as well as through mail-order catalogs.

- Fashion is now influenced by social and political developments, as well as by the preferences of fashion leaders.

- To meet the demands of economically cautious consumers, designers are developing less expensive secondary lines.

- The fashion industry is composed of textile producers, manufacturers, retailers, media, and market consultants.

Important Fashion Terminology and Concepts

ACTWU	franchising	outlets
Amalgamated	full-service wholesalers	power loom
CAD systems	ILGWU	private label merchandise
catalog	leased departments	reporting service
chain store	licensing	resident buying office
cotton gin	limited-function whole-	retailers
couturier	salers	secondary collections
department store	limited line store	sewing machine
designers	look for the union label	shopping malls
enclosed outlet centers	mail-order	specialty stores
fashion forecaster	manufacturer's represen-	spinning jenny
fashion streets	tative	spinoff stores
festival marketplace	market consultant	sweatshops
flagship stores	media	vertical company
flying shuttle	off-price discounters	vertical malls
	on-line computer services	

For Review

1. Who was the first person in fashion design with a specific clientele?
2. What were five inventions of the Industrial Revolution that led to mass production of apparel?
3. Who were the first workers in New York City's garment center? How did they manage to improve the sweatshop conditions?
4. Which segment of the fashion industry is represented by the Amalgamated?
5. Discuss the concept of licensing and how it has helped some designers prosper.
6. Name an important international franchise operation. Describe how it can react to orders as quickly as it does.
7. List some retailing formats.
8. What are the new rules of the fashion game?
9. What benefits do on-line computer services provide to the fashion industry?
10. Discuss the role of the media in the fashion world.
11. How do market consultants assist those in the fashion world?

Exercises and Projects

1. Write to the Singer Sewing Machine Company requesting photographs and information on the history of sewing machines. Using the information, prepare a written report on the various advances in the field from the first machine to the most recent.
2. Select a specific type of retailer such as an off-price discounter or manufacturer outlet, and trace its history. Concentrate on a well-known store in the selected category.

3. Write to one of the on-line computer companies mentioned in the chapter and obtain examples of the type of information it provides to one component of the fashion industry, such as designers or retailers.

The Case of the Successful Designer

Nancy Park, a young South Korean designer, received positive reviews from the fashion press for her collections designed under the Bravo label. In just four years, Park had worked her way up from design assistant to head designer. In that position, she has been responsible for the company's offerings for the past two years. With a flair that is both whimsical and fluid, she is steadily gaining popularity in America. As a result, Bravo's competitors have made offers for her services. In addition, a financial backer has offered to finance Park in her own fashion business. Although Bravo has offered to match the salaries offered by the competitors, it would give Park a merchandise line with her own name. Unable to come to terms with her employer, Park has submitted her resignation and is now weighing numerous offers being presented to her.

Didier Ltd., a dress manufacturer, offered to make her the head designer at a guaranteed salary plus 20 percent of sales. Her name would be on a label that reads "Didier Ltd., designed by Nancy Park."

Signal Fashions is a company that manufactures under its own label, but also produces lines that bear the names of well-known designers via licensing agreements. Signal offered a contract to Park that would create a separate division that would have only her name on every label. She would have complete design control, a salary triple her already excellent income, and the potential for part ownership in the company if the line was successful for two years.

Invest Associates, a financial backer with investments in five well-known couture operations, has offered capital that would establish Park in her own first-class fashion business. The deal promises to finance two collections, make available contracting facilities enjoyed by its other interests, and give park 50 percent of the profits. The label would feature Park's name, and she would have ultimate control over the company's design approaches.

With time drawing near for a decision, Nancy Park is still weighing the merits of each offer.

Questions

1. What are the advantages and disadvantages of each offer?

2. Which offer do you think Park should accept? Why?

point of view

Ralph Does the Deal

Janet Ozzard with contributions from Rich Wilner

NEW YORK—"I have built my own domain, my own conglomeration. I have very strong feelings about how to build a business." So said Ralph Lauren, a few hours after buying back his women's wear license from the bankrupt Bidermann Industries Wednesday. Details of the deal could not be learned, but sources said the price Lauren paid was $40 million to $45 million.

Sources claim the price was slightly above book value, adding that Bidermann would likely hold the license for only three more years at best. The Lauren women's business, sources noted, was "not hugely profitable," and profit projections over the next three years amounted to less than the sale price.

In addition, Bidermann faced the possibility that Lauren could wrestle the license away through an arbitration proceeding. In a recent filing before the American Arbitration Association, Lauren claimed Bidermann violated terms of their licensing agreement, primarily by not hitting projected sales levels, according to sources.

Lauren has had plenty of time to think about what he'd do differently in women's—22 years, to be exact. That's how long Bidermann has held the license to manufacture and distribute the designer's women's apparel.

Now, with a month of negotiations behind him, Lauren is ready to build the women's business, which includes the Collection, Ralph Lauren Sport and Ralph lines. Lauren said he'll likely add to that group with new labels in the near future. Currently, he's rumored to be shopping for a denim license.

But first, he's just savoring the feeling.

"It hasn't even sunk in yet," he said. "It's terrific. It's been a long time in coming."

Retailers are eager to see Lauren take the reins. The men's business, which Lauren has run since he started his company 27 years ago, is now hitting about $550 million in annual wholesale sales—more than four times the women's business. The stores would clearly like to see those kinds of numbers in women's.

"We have a very big Ralph business, the biggest in any store," said Kal Ruttenstein, senior vice president and fashion director of Bloomingdale's. "The women's business is substantial, but the men's business is bigger. I have to assume that when Ralph gets back his license, we will see great growth. Nobody does it better. When Ralph wants to pump something up, he really pumps it up. The design is great."

"We have a fabulous Ralph Lauren business, which continues to grow from strength to strength, and we're very optimistic about the line and the future," said Stephen Bock, senior vice president and general merchandise manager at Saks Fifth Avenue. "We have barely scratched the surface. We think we have a long way to go and haven't nearly reached our potential with him." "We carry the collection in a small way," said Butch Mullins, senior vice president and general mer-

chandise manager at Neiman Marcus. "Ralph Lauren is a very recognizable label, and there is certainly always a need for new fresh product in the bridge market.

"Everything, though, hinges on product. If the product is great and management of the business in terms of deliveries is good and the marketing program is good, there's the opportunity to do business. But in the past, we have had our difficulties, which is basically why we don't carry the Ralph label now. Our success with the collection has been just modest."

In a telephone interview from his Montauk home Wednesday, the designer said he has a team in place to start working the Polo formula on women's wear.

First, he said, he won't be looking for another women's license. While Lauren said he's not bitter about the experience with Bidermann, he emphasized he wants to keep the line in-house.

"I have other licenses around the world. Some are very good and go way beyond what I could ever do. Others are okay. I think what has been the issue for me is to have control of my own domain," Lauren said. "I have my own concepts about what I want to do. I think I can control my destiny a lot more."

Lauren has named Cheryl Sterling president and chief operating officer of the Polo Ralph Lauren retail and licensing company. Following that move, Lauren said he'll put together a team in-house to run the business. But Lauren noted that Stuart Kreisler, who had been a consultant to his women's business at Bidermann, won't be part of the new management.

"Stuart has always been a good friend," he said. "I'm not sure what will happen there."

The new team will focus solely on women's apparel.

While Lauren said that the negotiations with Bidermann were "very good, very straightforward," he did say that the company "had a lot of other irons in the fire."

"It wasn't a personal conflict," said Lauren. "It was a theoretical conflict. [Maurice] Bidermann has always been very nice to me and tried to be very cooperative. But I'm in the Ralph Lauren business, while he's got many different labels, products, factories. Ralph Lauren, Polo—that's my name and my life."

The negotiations with Bidermann picked up speed a month ago, fueled by Bidermann's Chapter 11 filing July 17, roughly one month after the company brought turn-around specialists Alvarez & Marsal on board to run the operation. Creditors had choked off shipments to the firm, and cash flow was insufficient to meet high debt payments.

By the time Bidermann filed, Bryan Marsal, a founding partner in Alvarez & Marsal and Bidermann's new chief executive, had already started on a long-range operating plan for the company's three units: Gold Toe, Arrow Shirt and Ralph Lauren Womenswear.

But Lauren, long eager to recapture the women's apparel license, whose $120 million in sales paled in comparison to Lauren's men's business, forced an early decision on the future of Bidermann's Ralph Lauren Womenswear unit by filing a "notice of termination" proceeding

with the American Arbitration Association.

"I built the Polo business to be a $550 million company, and I've run that all my career, with my own team," Lauren said. "I believe in my ability to do that with my own team," Lauren said. "We are going to expand [the women's business] and build it to a very strong business."

Lauren would not give a dollar figure for what he thought the women's business could be.

"It was licensed 22 years ago," said Lauren. "Women's wear was a real infant. I licensed it because that seemed to be the appropriate thing to do at that point. Now, I have the experience and the business knowledge."

And with that experience, Lauren said he plans to create "a much broader scope," with growth in the existing women's divisions as well as some new labels.

Lauren is also looking for sales growth from existing accounts, rather than expanded distribution. "I don't think that's an answer to building a business. It goes totally against how I work. I want to stay focused on the stores that want my product, that understand me and want to build with me."

Retailers are also hoping that the business will not only grow, but will run more smoothly.

One East Coast department store executive said the store has been getting good results from Lauren's women's collection this fall, but acknowledged it's been an up-and-down ride, depending on the season. The executive noted that the women's line, compared with the men's, has a lot of catching up to do. "There's enormous breadth

in the men's wear," the executive said, adding that women's jeans could also be a major opportunity for Lauren. "Just look how successful Calvin Klein is. There's no reason why Ralph couldn't be."

And another retailer said that new management might result in "earlier deliveries and better reorders."

Bringing in the women's business won't cause that much disruption to his company, Lauren stated.

"There's definitely a different philosophy" to the men's and women's businesses, he said. "The women's business is much more changeable, and faster, although the men's business is moving faster and faster.

"The women's business is faster, it's very alive. But I go through some of that in terms of design. When Collection goes down the runway, "I'm there, and I'm connecting with some of the biggest names. But a business is not always developed by fashion shows. It's built by a team that's focused on the business and on the customer."

Will this new business, which will almost certainly lead to greater revenues, pave the way for a public offering?

"I've thought about it, certainly," said Lauren. "But it's not in the near future. I can't say it won't happen, and it's very possible it would. It depends on where I am in my career. But I like doing what I'm doing—running my own thing, not having a public company that goes up and down with every breath of air. If that were not the case, I would have gone public a year ago, or two years ago."

Fashions of the Twentieth Century

During the twentieth century, fashion changed significantly. Previously, style and silhouette were dictated by the wealthy. Seamstresses and tailors carried out their client's wishes regardless of their own taste and expertise. It was Charles Frederick Worth who first showed clothing on a mannequin. In 1858, he and his wife opened the first couture house. Other designers who were groundbreakers in the early 1900s will be discussed in this chapter.

Although these designers created new and influential styles, their promotion by the fashion industry did not guarantee their success. Other influences include attitudes of the people, social and political issues, technological advances, and world events. Many designers were aware of the social influences and news events of the times in which they worked and produced fashions that reflected these periods. Such events as women's suffrage, World War I, World War II, and the women's rights movement, as well as developments in the world of entertainment, had an impact on women's clothing. For example, women working in factories during World War II wore pants for comfort, a fashion that was adopted for everyday life. Female executives of the 1980s preferred broad-shouldered suit jackets, copied from men's styles, to project the image of equality and power. Finally, the tattoos of the 1990s on women's bodies are an expression of individualism.

This chapter discusses the fashions for each decade of the twentieth century beginning with 1900 and concluding with 1990 in the following manner:

- *The News of the Times* outlines the various newsworthy events and changes that affected fashion.
- *The Fashions of the Times* examines the specific fashion trends and highlights.
- *The Designers Who Influenced Fashion* provides an overview of those individuals who created the fashions.

After you have completed this chapter, you will be able to discuss:

· Important historical events of the twentieth century and how they influenced fashion.

· Different fashion highlights for men and women of the twentieth century.

· Important designers of each decade in the twentieth century, and their influences on fashion.

· Some of the retro looks that surfaced in the 1990s and their sources.

1900–1910

The News of the Times Focused Attention on . . .

the changing role of women. Although wealthy women from New York City, London, Vienna, and other cities made their way to the Paris salons of such designers as Paul Poiret to enhance their wardrobes, a new breed of women was emerging. They entered politics, joined clubs, played sports, and went to college. With the expansion of retailing to accommodate the mass production of merchandise that resulted from the Industrial Revolution, many women went to work in the stores and the factories that made the goods as well as continuing to serve the needs of their families. Henry Ford produced his first Model T in 1908.

The Fashions of the Times Were . . .

delicate and still impractical for the changing role of women. Although representing a new era, fashions were a throwback to the late 1800s. A lady's costume was by no means simple. Pinched-in waistlines, exaggerated by tight-fitting corsets, were shown off in one-piece dresses made of chiffon and lace fabrics with leg-of-mutton sleeves and necklines that were characteristically high. The **Gibson Girl look,** born in the 1890s was still very much in evidence, consisted of floor-length skirts and **shirtwaist blouses.** Hats were an integral part of fashion in the 1900s. They were enormous creations, profusely ornamented with ribbons, feathers, birds, and other elaborate embellishments. Shoes did not play an important role in this decade because the fashions were floor-length. Handbags were small and feminine. Gloves were a significant part of each outfit. Whether it was summer or winter, properly dressed ladies were never without them.

Men had numerous types of outfits, each designed for specific occasions. Upper class men wore **frock coats** for formal wear and **suits** for less-formal situations. The cuts were straight but rather loose-fitting. Laced-up boots were part of every wardrobe, as were **spats** (fabric coverings) worn over regular shoes. Hats were an important part of every costume; the type was dictated by the particular function or event. Sportswear as we know it had not yet appeared on the fashion scene. For casual situations, men wore **knickers, blazers** of tweeds and flannels, and less formal hats and shoes.

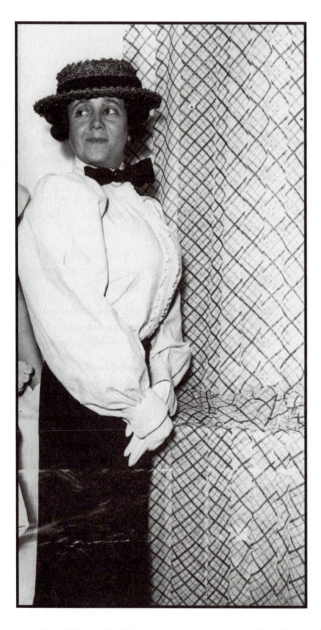

The Gibson Girl look featured shirtwaist blouses and floor-length skirts.

Paul Poiret designed in Paris and attracted women, such as actress Joan Crawford, from all over the world to his salon.

Children's clothing, however, were adaptations of their parents dress. Girls looked like miniature women in their frilly dresses, while boys were small clones of their fathers in their suits, stiff shirts, ties, and hats.

Although there were fashion changes dictated by Poiret throughout this decade, not many chose to shed the formal look of the earlier periods.

The Designers Who Influenced Fashion Include . . .

Paul Poiret reigned between 1903 and World War I. He freed women from corsets and designed loose-fitting clothing, but he later designed skirts so narrow at the hem women were unable to walk. *Mme. Paquin,* whose claim to fame was that she never made two dresses alike, was the first woman to achieve importance in couture. She designed glamorous evening wear and suits that were adorned with lavish fur. *Jeanne Lanvin* began as a milliner and ultimately branched out into couture that underscored a youthful look as well as styles that were fashioned from costumes worn in her native Brittany. Wedding gowns were one of Lanvin's specialty, as were metallic embroidered garments and other fashions that featured intricate stitching.

1 9 1 1 – 1 9 2 0

The News of the Times Focused Attention on . . .

the events that resulted in the outbreak of World War I. Women continued to gain more independence and were entering universities in greater numbers than ever before. However, all attention was focused on World War I, which the United States entered in 1917. With the large number of men participating in the action, women performed domestic jobs that were once the exclusive domain of men. This set the stage for women to become a force in industries which they had never been allowed to enter. Silent movies offered a new form of entertainment. A particularly controversial film was D.W. Griffith's film, *Birth of a Nation.*

The Fashions of the Times Were . . .

a mix of the fashionable and functional. For those whose attention was fashion forward, Poiret's design for a show called *Le Miraret* in 1912 set a trend. His **hobble skirts,** many with slit fronts, revealed women's legs for the first time. It was worn with a wide tunic. The narrow shape led to the abandonment of petticoats. Other skirts were straight and lines were simpler than ever before. Tailored suits were extremely popular for daytime wear, and skirt hemlines were very narrow. With these designs, shoes and hosiery became important fashion elements. A side-buttoned shoe was very popular. Ensembles were very much in vogue, with coats that matched the dresses underneath. Furs were used to line coats and trim hemlines.

Fortuny's Delphos gowns are composed of narrow pleats and are in costume collections in many of the world's museums.

Madeleine Vionnet's bias-cuts featured cowl and halter necklines. Her designs continue to influence fashion.

The decade began with millinery that echoed the earlier years, but was quickly replaced with less ornate, smaller styles. Parasols became important accessories, as did small handbags.

While many men continued to embrace the styles of the previous period, a new breed opted for the natural shoulder look. Devoid of heavy padding with narrow lapels and straight trousers, a new silhouette was capturing attention. A simpler form of dress, save for the special occasion, was now the more popular approach.

Children continued to be dressed as scaled-down replicas of adults. Their clothing was fancy, impractical, and anything but functional.

As the decade moved towards its conclusion, the impact of World War I on everyday life and a sense of practicality pervaded dress. The period ended with a "uniformness" of fashion, with easy and basic forms as the order of the day. What would follow in the next decade was quite a contrast.

The Designers Who Influenced Fashion Include . . .

Fortuny, whose designs were worn by wealthy women and are now collected by museums all over the world. The most famous of his designs is the **Delphos** gown which is a patented design composed of columns of many narrow, irregular, vertical pleats that are permanently set in silk by a secret process. The shape was enhanced by silk ties fastened at the waist. Another designer of this decade was: *Nina Ricci,* who designed graceful, elegant fashions that kept pace with the times, but did not break new ground. On the other hand, *Madeleine Vionnet*'s innovations included the bias cut, eliminating the need for fastenings of any kind on dresses, and cowl and halter necklines that still influence fashion. She opened her own couture house in Paris in 1912, which closed during World War I and reopened in 1918. It is also said that she rather than Poiret was the first to eliminate the need for corsets.

1 9 2 0 s

The News of the Times Focused Attention on . . .

many different things. In the United States, the decade was greeted with the prohibition amendment to the constitution, which brought about an era in which alcoholic beverages were forbidden. Illegal speakeasies—nightclubs that sold illegal liquor—were commonplace in the major cities. The music of the decade was jazz. The end of the silent film era was signalled by the release of *The Jazz Singer,* the first film with spoken lines and the prototype for Mickey Mouse was developed Disney. In 1919, another constitutional amendment gave women the right to vote. Their vote counted in the election of Herbert Hoover as President in 1920. Women continued to work, but it was their increased participation in sports that led to a casual type of dress. In 1925 F. Scott Fitzgerald's novel *The Great Gatsby* was published and B.F. Goodrich registered the trademark for zipper. America had its first female senator. Charles Lindbergh traveled by air across the Atlantic Ocean in 1927. By the end of the 1920s, all of the frivolity, glamour, and excitement was replaced with the anxiety and fear created by the Wall Street crash in 1929.

The Fashions of the Times Were . . .

The flapper wore knee-length, flounced hemlines and layers of chains.

entirely different from the previous decade, with elegance playing a significant role. They reflected the optimism that followed the end of World War I. Fashionable women quickly forgot the functional wear of the previous decade and embraced innovative new styles. As the decade advanced, skirts became shorter. The day of the **flapper** dawned, with knee-length hemlines, long-torso silhouettes with ruffled flounces, layers of chains adorning necklines, and close-fitting hats called cloches covering short hairstyles. Beading and fringes of every type decorated evening wear, and fur wraps lavishly covered them. Stylish women wore silk dresses for daywear under straight woolen coats, and ensembles featured jacket linings matching the blouses that were worn with them. **Sportswear** was introduced, and women wore knickers, **culottes,** and blazers to spectator events.

Men of the 1920s were also introduced to a new look. Bell-bottomed and flared trousers replaced the straight-legged models, jacket waistlines were nipped-in, and shoulders were softer. Men, like women also began to wear sports clothing. Knickers were fashionable, and the polo shirt was introduced. An air of informality was everywhere.

Children's clothing continued to echo adult styles. Girls wore shorter, less-restrictive silhouettes, while the boys donned baggy tweed pants ranging from shorts for the very young to full-length pants or knickers for the older set.

THE WORLD OF FASHION PROFILES

Coco Chanel

Chanel remains a legend for her taste, personal style, and dedication to perfection.

Considered by most fashion connoisseurs to be the century's most important couturiere, Chanel was born in France in 1883. As mistress of a sportsman and horse breeder, she was determined to project a fashion image of simplicity and elegance.

Chanel's career began inauspiciously when she started to trim hats for her own use. As people admired them, she began to produce and sell hats at home, eventually setting up a small shop. Her millinery business expanded to include dresses, which became equally successful. A brisk business prompted the opening of boutiques in fashionable Deauville and Biarritz and, then, an expanded headquarters in Paris. Her clothing was casual but smart, and her followers were quick to embrace these new style concepts. Her collections were simpler and more practical then anything else then produced.

Chanel achieved success not only as a couturiere, but as an integral part of the social scene. With simplicity as key to her inventiveness, her collections became broader. Evening wear consisted of simple chemises translated from daytime dresses, but with exquisite fabrics and intricate detailing.

She was a fashion influence from the 1920s until the beginning of World War II, when her presence in fashion collapsed. She closed her couture house, and except for her legendary fragrances, nothing else was produced under the Chanel label. In 1954, however, at the age of 71, Chanel was once again ready for the challenge. Although her new designs were considered "tired" by the press, fashionable women quickly embraced them again. The suit she perfected was now produced in a host of new materials and trims, employing color in innovative ways. Pants often replaced suit skirts, and brocades, velvets, and satins were used to create glamorous, understated evening apparel. Simplicity was still manifest in the shape or silhouette of the garments.

Chanel's styles continue to influence fashion and many of today's designers. Whenever the little black dress resurfaces, or when tweed suits embellished with pockets and interesting trim are shown, we are reminded of the genius of Chanel.

The Designers Who Influenced Fashion Include . . .

Jean Patou, whose flapper dress created a sensation in 1925 with shorter skirts, dropped waistlines, and uneven hems. He was a real master at change. In 1929, he was the first designer to bring the waistline back to its normal position and design skirts that were longer. *Captain Edward Molyneux* had couture houses in Paris, Monte Carlo, and London, where his clientele included royalty and theatrical personalities. His clothing was fluid, elegant, uncluttered, and never seemed to go out of fashion. Of course, one of the world's greatest innovators, *Gabrielle "Coco" Chanel,* reigned during this decade. The World of Fashion Profile of Chanel outlines her lifestyle and design inventiveness.

1930s

The News of the Times Focused Attention on . . .

the economic depression caused by the Wall Street stock market crash. The election of Franklin Delano Roosevelt as President in 1932 and his New Deal philosophy offered hope for relief from the effects of the Depression. Prohibition was repealed. In 1936, the Prince of Wales abdicated to marry Wallis Simpson. The poor economy and growing concerns about developments in Europe particularly Hitler's increasing popularity and aggressive behavior created a more serious outlook. At the beginning of the decade, relatively few could afford the extravagances of the 1920s. Some women tried to make do with what they had by "camouflaging" their old clothing. By the middle of the decade, however, Roosevelt's New Deal generated some optimisim, and fashion once again was on the move. Nylon was developed by DuPont. The film industry reached new heights, concentrating on musicals and comedies that provided vicarious pleasure to Depression America. It was the era of Fred Astaire and Ginger Rogers' madcap comedies and epic films such as *Gone With the Wind* (1939). When Clark Gable appeared in *It Happened One Night* (1934) without an undershirt, sales of undershirts dramatically dropped. However, by the end of the decade the threat of World War II hovered over people.

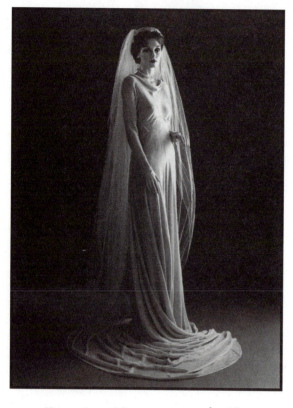

Vionnet's wedding gown with its sweeping train was high fashion of the thirties.

The Fashions of the Times Were . . .

quite different from the 1920s. Gone were the flappers and the gaudiness of the 1920s. When the country began to lift itself out of the Depression, an era of elegance emerged.

The short hemlines now dropped to midcalf for daytime and to the floor for evening wear. The **bias cut,** popularized by Vionnet, was an important silhouette; strapless necklines were favorites for the evening and back-sweeping trains adorned many gowns. Suits, out of favor in the 1920s, made a comeback—this time with padded shoulders and shorter jackets. Colors were subdued, with black, gray, green, and brown the most popular. Fabrics were soft with crepes, jerseys, satins, and soft wools being the favorites.

Men's clothing took on a looser look. Shoulders were broadened and padded; trousers were loose, straight, pleated, and cuffed; and many suits were double breasted, with wide lapels or revers.

The biggest news of the decade was the growing acceptance of the **spectator sportswear** introduced in the 1920s. Both men and women embraced this leisure wear. Tweed suits, navy blazers worn with white pleated skirts, simple hats, shorter cotton dresses, and even pants found their way into women's wardrobes. While these new styles would eventually be worn for any occasion, in the 1930s they were appropriate only when attending the races or watching other sports events. For the same occasions, men chose the newly introduced knit sport shirts and slacks that were worn with contrasting colored sport coats.

Men's wear in the 1930s featured padded shoulders, double-breasted suits, and spectator sportswear.

Mainbocher designed the wedding dress worn by Wallis Simpson for her marriage to the Duke of Windsor.

Children's styles were similar to those of the previous decade, with simplicity of design the important factor.

By the end of the decade, lavish clothing gave way to more practical designs. The world turned to more functional dress that would last well into the forties.

The Designers Who Influenced Fashion Include . . .

Chanel, who was still in the forefront of couture. *Mainbocher,* an American, who had great success at home and in Europe, appealed to those in the highest social circles. His design of the Duchess of Windsor's wedding dress in 1936 became the most copied style of the decade. *Jean Desses* was noted for the flowing chiffon evening gowns that echoed his Greek ancestry, and *Madame Grès* brought draping to new heights working with chiffon and silk jersey. *Elsa Schiaparelli* changed the shape of the figure by using broad padded shoulders fashioned after the uniforms of London's guardsmen. She also used ornaments of unique shapes to enhance her designs, and designed avant-garde sweaters with unusual motifs. She used the first zipper on pockets in 1930. Schiaparelli's collections were always considered elegant and chic. American designer, *Vera Maxwell,* designed a **weekend wardrobe** in 1935 consisting of a collarless tweed and gray flannel jacket, a flannel tennis skirt, a longer pleated tweed skirt, and cuffed flannel trousers.

1940s

The News of the Times Focused Attention on . . .

the war against Germany, Italy, and Japan. In the United States, women again worked in factories replacing the men who went off to war. Food rationing added to the discomfort of citizens and residents of many European nations. Because fabric was in short supply, the government regulated its use. *General Limitation Order L-85* restricted, for example, the amount of fabric used for a garment as well as the number of pockets and buttons it could have. Nylon was diverted from clothing to use in the production of parachutes, tents, and ropes for the war effort. Other scarce products included wool, silk, and rubber. As a result, civilian use of these materials was limited. The famous fashion houses of Paris closed their doors. As a result, American designers were given their first major opportunity in fashion. They were featured in magazines, such as *Vogue* and *Harper's Bazaar*, more frequently. Dorothy Shaver, the president of Lord & Taylor, gave American designers an opportunity to feature their garments in the famous retail organization she headed. At the end of the 1940s, clothing manufacturers in the United States were expanding. The ready-to-wear industry significantly grew.

As the war came to an end in 1945, the world faced the difficult process of recovery. Movies began to flourish with the release of *The Outlaw*, delayed for three years because of its sexual connotations. Television began to emerge as a leading medium.

Textured handknit like an abstract crusader — in handspun yarns

Sportswear by Bonnie Cashin could be mixed and matched.

The Fashions of the Times Were . . .

simple at the beginning of the decade because of the dictates of war. Popular styles included padded shoulders that exceeded those of the 1930s and shorter skirts. American designers, such as Bonnie Cashin and Claire McCardell, designed sportswear and **separates** that could be mixed and matched. The air of casualness lasted well into the 1950s and beyond.

When the war ended, Paris repositioned itself as fashion's standard-bearer. The **New Look**—rounded shoulders, full bustlines, tiny waists accentuated by full skirts—dominated Dior's collection and it was soon adapted by fashion manufacturers everywhere. Skirts grew longer—fifteen inches off the ground—jackets were short and fitted. The swimsuit took a new direction as **bikinis** made their debut.

Basics dominated men's wear. The suit silhouette most favored was the single-breasted style. By the end of the decade, lapels were narrower. A casual approach to fashion with contrasting sport coats and trousers quickly became popular.

Fashions for the young were more casual. Carefree styles for girls, included puffed sleeves and flared skirts. **Jeans** were slowly being accepted, but only for riding bicycles or leisure activities. Oversized sweaters—called **sloppy joes**—were the hot items of the day. Boys wore T-shirts, sport shirts, and styles that were inspired by the military.

The Designers Who Influenced Fashion Include . . .

Americans who joined the ranks of the French as world leaders in fashion. *Adrian,* who had gained a reputation as a designer for films, designed ready-to-wear collections from 1941 to 1952. Tailored suits with large-square shoulder pads were typical of his sophisticated designs. *Bonnie Cashin* was not at all influenced by the dictates of Paris. Her specialty was comfortable clothing for country weekends and travel, made of such fabrics as wool jersey, knits, leather, suede, and tweeds. Hoods, toggle closures on coats and jackets, and leather trim on garments were her trademarks. The toga and kimono were standards. *Claire McCardell* developed casual wear and is credited with what is known as the *American Look.* Simple, clean lines in functional, comfortable clothing were her strengths. She adapted the large pockets, topstitching, and sturdy fabrics of men's clothing to women's wear. *Norman Norell* used simple lines, rich fabrications, and exquisite workmanship for his garments. His evening wear designs consisted of sequined gowns and his sportswear-look of sweaters worn over long skirts. He also designed jumpsuits and pantsuits. *Pauline Trigère* used luxurious fabrics, rich tweeds and artistic prints in very simple, but intricate cuts. *Christian Dior's* New Look in 1947 was met with wild enthusiasm. Year after year, his creations captured the fashion world's attention—**A-line** and **Y-line** silhouettes in the next decade. *Balenciaga* was the master tailor and dressmaker. His sculptural creations are the embodiment of cut and fit, with each garment architecturally built to mold perfectly to the figure.

Claire McCardell shown here with her separates.

Dior's New Look featured tiny waists accentuated by very full skirts.

1950s

The News of the Times Focused Attention on . . .

the Korean War from 1950 to 1953. In the United States, Dwight D. Eisenhower became president and in England Elizabeth became queen in 1952. Acrylic and polyester fibers became available. The term *teenager* came into general use in the mid-1950s. Teen idols included movie stars James Dean and Marlon Brando, who rose to fame in their respective movies, *Rebel Without a Cause* (1955), and *On the Waterfront* (1954). A new generation of music took hold with the beginning of rock 'n' roll. Elvis Presley's popularity soared. With the publication of *On the Road* by Jack Kerouac, the terms **Beat Generation** and **beatnik** were coined. The economy boomed and America dominated world manufacturing. Money was available again for discretionary and luxury purchases. Men became increasingly interested in fashion, opening up new markets for manufacturers and designers. Americans, who suffered from discrimination, demanded their rights. The Civil Rights movement was sparked by demonstrations in Montgomery, Alabama, and Little Rock, Arkansas, in 1955. Sputnik, the first space satellite, was launched by the Russians in 1957. Television became more widely available in homes. More and more women began to enter the job market in careers such as finance, which were once reserved for men.

The Fashions of the Times Were . . .

extremely diverse. Hemlines were alternately long to short depending on the year and the designer. The first half of the decade was dedicated to elegance, symbolized by the couture collections. Tailored clothing was important for daytime wear; full-skirted strapless evening dresses were appropriate for special occasions. Sportswear, including slacks, **pedal pushers,** shorts, and hal-

Elvis Presley popularized a new style of music and influenced dress.

Full-skirted strapless dresses were worn for such special occasions as proms.

ters, was a favorite. Mixing and matching different pieces to create new outfits gained in popularity. Increasingly, apparel was created from the newly developed manufactured fibers.

By the middle of the 1950s a new style developed on American college campuses that reflected a laid-back, nonaggressive way of life. The beatnik look had been born. **Leotards** and tapered pants were topped by hooded knits and overshirts, black stockings were the rage. Young men sported beards. **Unisex fashions** began, with men and women sharing the same styles.

Styles that were exclusively for men included charcoal gray suits that featured narrow lapels and natural shoulders and bore the **Ivy League** label. Pants were narrow—many with buckle closures at the back. The standard white shirt was joined by pale pink, which was also considered appropriate for business. Madras was a popular material for sport coats, and shorts were being worn for casual wear. Leather jackets were very popular, especially for the younger set who were enthralled by film stars and rock 'n' roll idols.

Teenage girls began the decade wearing the fullest skirts, often made of felt emblazoned with *poodles,* over stiffened crinolines, and ended with many switching to a more relaxed look. Saddle shoes and white bucks were everywhere.

As the 1960s approached, styles never seen before would surface and gain immediate acceptance.

The Designers Who Influenced Fashion Were . . .

sometimes those who had been popular in the 1940s such as Balenciaga, Dior, and Bonnie Cashin. New faces also emerged. *Hubert de Givenchy* was noted for a masterly cut, something that he learned from Balenciaga. His peasant blouse also won him great admiration, as did his collections of elegant evening wear. Intricate cuts, precise seaming, batwing styles, and asymmetrical shapes were among American designer *Charles James'* many innovations. The stage was set for the 1960s and the emergence of such designers as Mary Quant and Yves Saint Laurent, who first designed for the house of Dior in the 1950s.

1 9 6 0 s

The News of the Times Focused Attention on . . .

the election of John F. Kennedy as President of the United States in 1960. America gained in the race for space. Alan Shepard was the first man in space, John Glenn the first man to orbit the moon, and Appollo III the first capsule to land on the moon in 1969. After Kennedy's assassination, President Lyndon Johnson guided the Civil Rights Act of 1964 through Congress, along with significant antipoverty legislation. A second Civil Rights Act, passed in 1965, guaranteed every citizen the right to vote. Despite the passage of these bills, inequalities persisted and riots occurred in Los Angeles (Watts), Chicago, Cleveland, Newark, and Detroit. Both Martin Luther King and Robert Kennedy were assassinated in 1968. America's involvement in a war in Vietnam—a small country in southeast Asia—dominated the news, as did antiwar demonstrations on college campuses and city streets. Continuing hostilities between Israelis and Arabs erupted in the Six Day War. The Beatles quickly extended their popularity to American audiences with hit after hit; the term *Beatlemania* was born. In upstate New York, the 1969 Woodstock festival attracted **hippies** from all over the nation, who came to hear their favorite musicians. The *New York Times* supplement, *Fashions of the Times,* was the first fashion magazine to put an African American model on its cover. The National Organization for Women (NOW) was founded in 1966.

Beatlemania resulted in record-breaking crowds at concerts.

The Fashions of the Times Were . . .

no longer dictated by a few designers. Instead, a variety of styles and choices swept the world. The **mod style** was definitely in. Originally a term applied to tailored youth fashions of the period, it was rivaled by the **Rockers,** who dressed in leathers and crash helmets.

Probably the greatest fashion controversy of the 1960s centered around skirt lengths. At the beginning of the decade, skirts hovered around the knee, rising steadily until the shortest **miniskirts** were the order of the day. By 1970 **midi** and **maxi** lengths were introduced. The midcalf length quickly flopped as women still were uncertain about which direction to take. A new fashion capital was born in London, where minis were the popular items. Boots became a standard complement to the miniskirts. Many women discarded their shoes and built complete boot wardrobes. First Lady Jacqueline Kennedy became an important fashion role model for women, inspiring the **Chanel suit** and popularizing the **pillbox hat.** So popular was the Chanel suit that it was produced at every price point and worn by every segment of the population. Dress silhouettes included an **empire waistline** and **A-line** or straight-cut shapes that were loose from shoulder to the hem. A popular design by Yves Saint Laurent was inspired by *Mondrian* paintings and constructed of several blocks of color.

The confusion about skirt lengths led many women to wear pants for all occasions. *Pantsuits,* which were introduced in the mid-1960s, were increasingly accepted by women by the late 1960s. Denim and jeans were no longer reserved for the young and those outside the mainstream. What was once considered appropriate only for leisure activities was now making the fashion scene for every type of function.

The phrases "Black is Beautiful" and "Black Pride" expressed the new feeling of self-confidence and self-worth among African Americans. Traditional African garments, such as **dashikis,** which were often made of **kente cloth** fabrics, were worn. **Afro** hairstyles and **corn-row braids** were widely adopted by both men and women in the late 1960s.

On the beach, Rudi Gernreich's **topless bathing suit** made its debut. Swimwear was dominated by one-piece loosely fitted blouson styles and two-piece bathing suits, including the bikini model.

Men's fashions were equally exciting. With the popularity of long sideburns to match longer hair lengths, jacket lapels became exaggerated and pants were flared or bell bottomed. Men wore boots, used jewelry as accents, and shed anything with a traditional look.

The campus set dressed more informally than ever. Torn jeans, ragged T-shirts, army boots, and long hair became the uniform. Based on rejection of uniformity—an anti-fashion expression—these styles represented the unkempt hippie look. All types of clothing were acceptable—long and short, new and old. The materials were all natural, and **psychedelic designs** and imagery affected clothing's color and fabrics. Unisex styles continued to gain in popularity.

The miniskirt was the rage of the 1960s.

The Designers Who Influenced Fashion Were . . .

from all over the world. London emerged as a fashion capital with *Mary Quant's* unique designs. Using the **Mod look** of miniskirts to capture the youth market, her materials included denim, vinyl, and colored flannels, all paired with tights. In Paris, *Courrèges* also featured the mini and designed the now famous **go-go boots** that revolutionized the shoe industry. *Yves Saint Laurent* opened his own couture house and treated the world to endless fashion innovations from ballgowns to pantsuits and everything in between. He presented his first ready-to-wear collection, *Rive Gauche,* that would have wider appeal than his higher-priced couture. *Pierre Cardin* showed his **nude look** in 1966, followed by metal body jewelry, and astronaut suits and helmets. He also brought designer fashion to a wider consumer market through licensing agreements. All over the world, clothing and accessories for men, women, and children bore his signature. In America, *Anne Klein* was a pioneer in the junior clothing category, transforming juniors into more sophisticated styles. Skirts

Mondrian's geometric paintings influenced a collection of Yves Saint Laurent dresses.

and blazers were popular items in her collections, as were jersey dresses, pants, and sweaters. *Geoffrey Beene* was winning accolades and awards from the fashion industry. His specialty was simplicity of design, emphasizing cut, line, and detailing. *Halston,* who began as a milliner at Bergdorf Goodman and eventually gained popularity with his famous pillbox hat design for Jackie Kennedy, shifted to apparel. *Rudi Gernreich* designed more comfortable, unstructured swimwear, including a topless model in 1964. He specialized in sport clothes in dramatic cuts and color combinations.

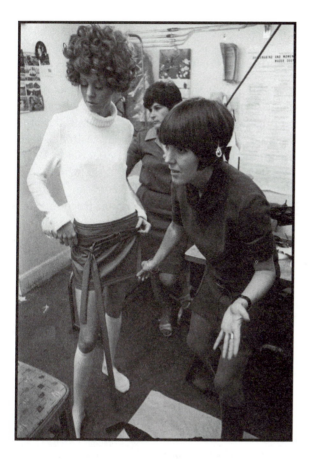

Mary Quant and her mod miniskirt designs launched London as a fashion capital.

Two fashion trends set by First Lady Jacqueline Kennedy, a fashion role model, were the pillbox hat and Chanel suits.

1970s

The News of the Times Focused Attention on . . .

President Richard Nixon's visit to China in 1972 and his resignation as president in 1974. Oil prices skyrocketed and the first Earth Day was celebrated in 1970. Jimmy Carter was elected president in 1976, the year the United States celebrated its Bicentennial. Egyptian President Anwar Sadat visited Israel, opening the door to negotiations that led to the Camp David Accords in 1979. The same year the Shah of Iran fled to the United States, after which Iran became an Islamic Republic. The Iranian seizure of 63 American hostages caused anxiety in America. The movie industry achieved greater freedom with such films as *A Clockwork Orange* (1971). While fashions inspired from *Saturday Night Fever* (1977) and *Annie Hall* (1978) were quickly copied.

The Fashions of the Times Were . . .

more individual then ever before. People were given choices instead of having fashion dictated to them. The designers who had reigned supreme relinquished their holds on the consumer. With the rejection of the midi, designers quickly realized the need to satisfy the likes and dislikes of their customers. Women were not ready to rid their closets of comfortable pantsuits, which they continued to wear for all occasions. Manufacturers responded by turning

The Peacock Revolution made men as conscious of fashion as women.

them out at every price point. Some minis caught fire, as did form-fitting **hot pants** and the **platform shoes** with which they were worn. While young people wore them successfully, the more mature market opted for flared-legged trousers. Granny clothing was in, as was second-hand clothing for those interested in punk rock. Designs by Zandra Rhodes were inspired by the new music. Evening pants were seen everywhere, topped by sheer silks, jerseys, and other dressy fabrics. The preferred blouse was the tunic worn over pants.

Unisex clothing, carried over from the 1960s, was still a favorite. Both men and women wore new, relaxed, and comfortable **leisure suits.**

For men, who had become as fashion conscious as women, the new **peacock look** was the choice. The broad upturned padded shoulders, fitted waistline, long jacket, and flared pants created the excitement.

Denim garments were available for all members of the family. Jeans became extremely fashionable, many sported visible labels to indicate the maker's name. **Designer jeans** became a status symbol.

The **layered look** was a fashion innovation that prompted women to buy several pieces of clothing that could be worn one on top of the other.

By the end of the decade, a casualness pervaded the fashion world. Clothing was functional as well as stylish. Knits were in great abundance, in a variety of weights and textures. Those seeking comfort quickly embraced these fabrics. Evening clothing became less important and was worn only by a few. The tailored, less dressy look was now appropriate for most occasions.

Ralph Lauren

"I stand for a look that is American," states Ralph Lauren, who is a master at marketing lifestyles. "It is an attitude, a sense of freedom. I believe in clothes that last, that are not dated in a season. They should look better the year after they are bought." These few words summarize beautifully what Lauren and his clothing are all about.

His creative talents were first recognized when he was associated with Beau Brummel neckties. The field was full of narrow, Ivy League ties, and Lauren thought Americans were ready for a new look. He introduced the four-inch wide tie made of opulent materials; soon it became the status tie to wear. Lauren then began to design a full line of men's wear, and soon become an international force in the fashion industry.

In 1968, he established Polo, a name taken from a sport that depicted style and grace, and pro-

Ralph Lauren here with his designs.

duced a total men's wardrobe. Using fine fabrications in a natural shoulder silhouette, along with expertly crafted shirts, knitwear, outerwear, accessories, and shoes, he quickly achieved a place of importance in men's wear. His line has become one of the industry's most distinctive looks.

In 1971, Lauren expanded his empire to include women's clothing. For the active, independent woman, he created an understated elegance that plays equally well in all parts of the country. Beautiful fabrics and attention to well-tailored construction make his suits, dresses, sportswear, knits, and jackets wardrobe mainstays. He soon introduced boy's wear, and later girl's wear of comparable quality. To round out his fashion empire, Lauren added a line of home furnishings, fragrances, luggage, handbags, belts, wallets, scarves, sunglasses, and hats.

Not only does Lauren create beautiful designs, but he markets them as well. From his Madison Avenue flagship housed in the former Rhinelander mansion to a network of stores throughout the world, he markets everything he creates.

The Designers Who Influenced Fashion Were . . .

from both sides of the Atlantic. **Prêt-à-porter,** which was established in France in the 1960s, began to thrive. In Italy, *Giorgio Armani* was recognized as a masterful designer, who created both men's and women's clothing. His unconstructed blazer in fine Italian fabrics was his specialty and was copied at every price point. *Gianfranco Ferré,* another Italian, became famous for his sculptured designs and beautiful pleating that appeared on comfortable, fluid clothing. In America, *Calvin Klein* made simple designs for both men and women, and became a household name with his designer jeans. *Betsey Johnson's* creations were unique. T-shirts in all lengths, vinyl dresses with paste-ons, spandex knits, and tight pants were characteristic of her work. *Norma Kamali* distinguished herself with unusual use of fabric—parachute nylon for jumpsuits and sweatshirt material from gymnasiums to the streets for a variety of ready-to-wear styles. Her innovative use of fabrics carried over into the 1980s and were copied by many manufacturers. *Mary McFadden* used fine pleating in dresses and tunics. *Ralph Lauren* has remained a leading designer since the 1970s. His philosophy and contributions to the industry are outlined in The World of Fashion Profile.

Designer jeans created by such designers as Calvin Klein became status symbols for the wearer.

1980s

The News of the Times Focused Attention on . . .

the election of Ronald Reagan as President in 1980. His presidency ushered in an era of conspicuous consumption that his reelection four years later reinforced. The marriage of Diana Spencer and Prince Charles in 1981 supplied the bridal industry with a design that would be significantly copied. Women's role in the workplace grew, as some rose to executive positions once reserved for men. A new term, **yuppie,** was coined to describe the upwardly mobile young professional. The space program was set back with the Challenger disaster in 1986.

The bridal industry quickly copied the wedding gown of Lady Diana.

The stock market crash in October 1987 sent the economy into a tailspin. George Bush won the election for President in 1988. The Berlin Wall came down, symbolizing the reunification of Germany. China sent shockwaves throughout the world with the Tianamen Square Massacre. MTV began and brought new stars, such as Prince and Madonna into homes. Night clubbing emerged as an important part of the life of the young. The television show, *Dallas,* reached an international audience of more than 300 million, re-popularizing the **ten gallon hat.** AIDS, which would have a profound effect on the fashion industry, was recognized as a worldwide epidemic. By 1990, a number of top designers (Halston, Perry Ellis, Willi Smith) as well as colleagues who worked in supporting roles in the fashion industry were known to have died of AIDS. Animal rights activists began their campaign against fur apparel. Global concern for the environment continued, with a growing preference for natural fibers.

The Fashions of the Times Were . . .

a revival of earlier styles, with an emphasis on elegant evening wear. The **pouf skirt** started in the Paris couture shows, was soon adapted by manufacturers all over the world. Miniskirts returned to the forefront of fashion, as they were accepted first by the youth and later by more mature women who chose to shed the longer hemlines for a newer, younger look.

At the beginning of the decade, licensing arrangements blossomed. As a result designer label merchandise, sporting the signatures of the world's best couturiers, began appearing on a variety of apparel and accessory products.

New trends in fashion were inspired by the physical fitness craze. The film, *Flashdance,* which starred Jennifer Beals and featured torn sweats and aerobic dancing had a major impact on fashion. Warmup suits and sneakers (now called **athletic shoes**), previously reserved for sports activities were now worn as streetwear. By the end of the decade the number of athletic shoe styles stocked by stores was often larger than their stock of traditional shoe styles. Day-time casual shoes were replaced by a wardrobe of athletic shoes; many teenagers never purchased a regular pair of shoes. The uniform of the youth market consisted of a pair of Levi's jeans, a shirt and sweater, and athletic shoes. Before long, adults donned the same outfit. At the same time, the growth in the number of women executives created a need developed for women's business suits—suits that would be equal in design and quality to men's wear. The **power suit,** with its medium-length skirt and tailored jacket, hung in the closets of these new executives. A tailored blouse was usually worn underneath.

By the end of the decade, the fashion world was not in one particular mode. Freedom of choice dominated. Skirts were worn at all lengths and pants

Lacroix's pouf skirt was the sensation of the Paris runway and soon adapted by many manufacturers.

The women's movement lead many to dispose of their bras.

were shown in a variety of silhouettes. The Madonna-inspired **bustier** was being worn by the young. Lycra spandex was not only used in exercise wear, but in many types of garments. Torn jeans, once ready for disposal, became a fashion statement.

The Designers Who Influenced Fashion Were . . .

Donna Karan, who started under the tutelage of Anne Klein and was responsible—along with *Louis Dell'Olio*—for maintaining the classic sportswear designs established by Klein. In 1984, Karan opened her own company with backing from a Japanese firm. Her sportswear was characterized by blazers and pants that echoed men's fashions. Sarong skirts and easy, wearable dresses were her signatures. *Perry Ellis* captured the fashion world with both men's and women's designs beginning in the mid-1970s. His influence continued until his death in 1986. Hand-knitted sweaters played an important role in his collections. Japanese designers showed their fashions at the Paris prêt shows in 1983 and immediately stimulated interest with their loose unconstructed and oversized silhouettes. *Rei Kawakubo's* clothes were described as bag lady styles, but throughout the 1980s Japanese designers gained attention in both men's and women's wear. *Christian Lacroix,* the first couturier to emerge in

Torn sweats worn in Flashdance inspired clothing for physical fitness activities.

many years, captivated the fashion world in 1987 with his extravagant pouf design. *Gianni Versace* created imaginative styles that were sensuous for women and avant-garde for men. *Claude Montana* introduced biker's leathers to high fashion. *Adrienne Vittadini* used knits in unusual colorations and patterns to establish a niche in the marketplace. *Tommy Hilfiger* produced men's wear collections that would be comfortable for both mature and younger consumers.

1990s

The News of the Times Focused Attention on . . .

the collapse of the Soviet Union in 1991. The emergence of the European Economic Community led to the expansion of companies overseas. The Gulf War between the United States and Iraq ignited a feeling of patriotism that led to numerous styles that sported designs with flags. The economic recession at the beginning of the decade made consumers more cautious and led to the failure of many businesses. The bankruptcy of Macy's and its takeover by Federated Stores was one major indicator of the economy's downward turn. Bill Clinton was elected President of the United States in 1992. New trade pacts such as NAFTA and GATT, promised to improve trade among nations. The Disney Company produced several animated movies, including *The Lion King* and *Pocahontas*. The O.J. Simpson trial was the biggest media event from mid-1994 to 1995. Americans waited to learn more about the impending changes in health care, and to see if the first Republican-controlled Congress in forty years would change the course of events.

The grunge look for the youth market and Jean Paul Gaultier's designs were attention-getting highlights in the nineties.

Vintage shops feature resale clothing of the top designers.

The Fashions of the Times Were . . .

at first a carryover from the previous decade, but with a strong inclination toward individuality that has led to many new styles. Platform shoes reappeared and young people increasingly replaced their athletic footwear with **Doc Martins.** The **grunge look** appealed to many in the youth market. A very casual air was evident in daytime wear. Baggy pants and T-shirts exemplified the **hip-hop style** popularized by movies such as *Boyz 'N the Hood.* As the middle of the decade approached, the look was definitely **retro.** Designers were influenced by every period of the twentieth century and inspired by silhouettes of the most famous classic designers. There were Jacques Fath-inspired peplum suits and the mixing of vintage clothing from shops that carried **resale merchandise** with contemporary pieces. Once again, consumers were attracted to updated versions of padded and fitted jackets from the 1950s; pointed pumps and the wrapdress from the 1970s; narrow suits worn with wedgies; the sheath dress reminiscent of Audrey Hepburn's character, Holly Golightly, in *Breakfast at Tiffany's;* the **Kelly bag,** named for and worn by Grace Kelly in the 1950s; and suits that echoed those worn by Jackie Kennedy in the 1960s. Of course, only time will tell how long styles will last and what will still be popular at the turn of the century.

For men, a more casual look came into vogue as companies established **dressing down Fridays.** It became commonplace for executives to wear **khakis** and **button-down shirts,** without ties, to the office. For the rest of the week, however, the traditional American classic cut suit and European models were still preferred. Leisure wear now consists of jeans, work shoes, leather jackets,

Jil Sander specializes in clean design without ornamentation.

and active apparel that can be worn to work out or on the street.

Children continued to wear less formal attire, such as jeans and sweatshirts. The baseball cap is king and crowns most young people's heads.

The Designers Who Influenced Fashion Were . . .

those who had made their mark in previous decades such as Lagerfeld, Karan, Blass, Gaultier and Lauren. Others, however, who came into their own include American designers: *Richard Tyler,* winner of the CFDA's Perry Ellis Award for New Fashion Talent in 1993, creates inventive, perfectly tailored clothing; *Anna Sui,* who designs imaginative and adventurous clothing for a younger market; *Isaac Mizrahi,* who produces everything from raincoats to evening wear with a young, inventive air; *Todd Oldham,* who creates simple shapes. often in bold colors and embellishes them with beading or embroidery; *Tracy Reese,* who creates young designer sportswear including separates and dresses earmarked for career women; *Nicole Miller* specializes in unique prints for scarves, men's ties, and garment linings; *John Galliano* specializes in bias-cut evening wear and was selected as Givenchy's replacement following the great master's retirement; *Joseph Abboud* excels in men's wear with a blend of European styling and American practicality. New European designers include *Herve Leger,* with sensuous and seductive designs and *Jil Sander,* Germany's premier designer, who specializes in clean design without decoration and cuts that were once out of the ordinary.

Chapter Highlights

- 1900–1910

  FOR WOMEN:
  Pinched-in waistlines, tight-fitting corsets, leg-of-mutton sleeves, floor-length skirts, shirtwaist blouses, ornate hats.

  FOR MEN:
  Frock coats, laced-up boots, spats, knickers, blazers.

  FOR CHILDREN:
  Duplicates of adult clothing.

- 1911–1920

  FOR WOMEN:
  Narrow silhouette, straight skirts, hobble skirts, matching ensembles, fur trims, smaller hats and handbags.

FOR MEN:

Natural shoulder look, narrow lapels, straight pants, simple styling.

FOR CHILDREN:

Duplicates of adult clothing.

- 1920s

FOR WOMEN:

Shorter skirts, flapper styles, long-torso silhouettes, ruffled flounces, beading and fringes, fur wraps for evening wear, some spectator sportswear.

FOR MEN:

Bell-bottomed and flared trousers, nipped-in waistlines, softer shoulders, knickers, polo shirts.

FOR CHILDREN:

Duplicates of adult clothing.

- 1930s

FOR WOMEN:

Midcalf hemlines for day and floor-length for evening, bias cuts, strapless necklines, suits with padded shoulders and short jackets.

FOR MEN:

Broadened and padded shoulders, loose trousers with pleated waist and cuffed bottoms, double-breasted suits, spectator sportswear.

FOR CHILDREN:

Simple styles.

- 1940s

FOR WOMEN:

Padded shoulders, short-to-long skirts, tiny waistlines, full skirts, short-fitted jackets, bikinis, jeans, oversized sweaters.

FOR MEN:

Single-breasted suits, contrasting sport coats and trousers, narrow lapels.

FOR CHILDREN:

Girls wore "Sloppy Joes" and boy's wore T-shirts and sport shirts.

- 1950s

FOR WOMEN:

Diverse fashions included long and short hemlines, elegant and tailored clothing, sportswear, the beatnik look for the young.

FOR MEN:

Dark gray suits, narrow lapels and shoulders, narrow pants, Ivy League look, dress shirts in colors.

FOR CHILDREN:

Girls wore full skirts over crinolines and mother-duaghter lookalike outfits. Boys wore plaid vests and miniature gray flannel suits like their fathers.

- 1960s

  FOR WOMEN:
  Youth-oriented styles, the Mod Look, miniskirts, hot pants, Chanel suits, chemise dresses, midis and maxis, pantsuits, unconstructed swimsuits.

  FOR MEN:
  Exaggerated lapels, flared or bell-bottomed pants, boots, jewelry, and long hair.

  FOR CHILDREN:
  Torn jeans and T-shirts.

- 1970s

  FOR WOMEN:
  Pantsuits, hot pants, platform shoes, granny clothing, evening pants and tunics.

  FOR MEN:
  Broad, upturned padded shoulders, fitted waistlines, long jackets, flared trousers.

  FOR WOMEN AND MEN:
  Unisex dressing.

  FOR WOMEN, MEN, AND CHILDREN:
  Designer jeans.

- 1980s

  FOR WOMEN:
  Elegant evening wear, miniskirts, signature merchandise, warm-up suits, athletic shoes, and bustiers.

  FOR MEN:
  Physical fitness attire worn for most occasions.

  FOR CHILDREN:
  Teenagers wore athletic shoes instead of traditional shoes, Levi's, and a shirt or sweater.

- 1990s

  FOR WOMEN:
  Platform shoes, Doc Martins, grunge casual wear, retro styles and silhouettes borrowed from previous decades.

  FOR MEN:
  Dressing down with khaki's and button-down shirts, jeans, work shoes, leather jackets.

  FOR CHILDREN:
  Jeans, sweatshirts, and baseball caps.

Important Fashion Terminology and Concepts

Afro
A-line
athletic shoes
beatnik look
bias cut
blazers
button-down shirts
Chanel suit
corn-row braids
culottes
dashikis
Delphos gown
designer jeans
Doc Martins
dressing down Fridays
empire waistline
flapper
frock coat
Gibson Girl look
go-go boots
grunge look

hip-hop style
hippies
hobble skirt
hot pants
Ivy League
jeans
khakis
Kelly bag
kente cloth
knickers
layered look
leisure suits
leotards
midis
miniskirts
Mod Look
New Look
nude look
pantsuits
peacock look
pedal pushers

pillbox hat
platform shoes
pouf skirt
power suit
prêt-à-porter
psychedelic designs
resale merchandise
retro look
separates
shirtwaist
sloppy joes
spats
spectator sportswear
sportswear
ten gallon hat
topless bathing suit
T-shirts
unisex
weekend wardrobe
Y-line
yuppie

For Review

1. Who were the major designers in the first decade of the twentieth century?

2. Contrast the fashions for women during the second and third decades of the twentieth century.

3. Discuss the styles of Coco Chanel, and the impact they continue to have long after her death.

4. Which two American designers of the 1940s were credited with popularizing women's sportswear?

5. What was considered to be the greatest fashion controversy of the 1960s?

6. How did Mary Quant change the look of fashion for the young?

7. Describe the peacock look in men's wear that was popular in the 1970s.

8. In what way did the jeans of the 1970s differ from those that came earlier in the century?

9. Discuss how Ralph Lauren first impacted men's fashions.

10. What types of merchandise were introduced for street wear during the 1980s that had previously been reserved for sports activities?

11. Give examples of retro looks during the mid-1990s.

Exercises and Projects

1. Select apparel from two consecutive decades of the twentieth century and compare them. To locate the apparel, use historic costume books, lifestyle books, fashion and lifestyle magazines, and family photo albums. You can also contact companies for archival photos and press kits. Make copies (or use original photos when available) of the apparel and affix the visuals from each decade on one foamcore board. Identify and label garments and accessories.

2. Collect copies of photographs of the retro styles of the mid-1990s from current fashion and lifestyle magazines. Match them to the original styles from which they were adapted. Use your library for reference materials.

The Case of the Insecure Designer

Rick Waters has always been told that he has a "good eye" for fashion. In pursuit of a career in the industry, he enrolled in a four-year college that offered a wide range of fashion majors, including merchandising and design. Although he liked design, he thought that other students in the program had a much greater natural ability than he did for the creation of original designs. As a result, he decided to become a fashion merchandising major.

After graduation, he became an assistant buyer for a major department store. As he combed the markets for merchandise, he always thought that his ideas were better than many he saw. He felt he had the talent necessary to produce merchandise that would sell, even if it was not in the couture category. Generally, he was right on target with the suggestions he made for his department's fashion direction.

Questions

1. Where would you suggest he look for his inspiration?

2. How might he go about creating styles without drawing upon original ideas?

Dissatisfied with his career as a merchandiser, he decided to turn to some level of apparel design. After looking for a more creative position, he was hired by Sanders & Smith, a department store that was moving in the direction of private label fashions. His initial responsibility was to research sources that would enable him to style a youthful collection that would retail at moderate price points.

Excited with the opportunity to bring a new line to the market, he enthusiastically set out on his assignment.

Why Women Designers Really Matter, 1930–1995

Marylou Luther

For this discourse, the fashion heroines are women designers. Female designers who changed the course of fashion during the last 65 years. Some of them were better than male designers of the same period. Some were not. All left or are leaving their mark, many of them changing our psyches along with our clothes.

When The Fashion Group was first becoming a presence on the international fashion stage in the 1930s, the two most important female designers were Madeleine Vionnet and Coco Chanel. Both made their mark by molding the dress to the woman rather than molding the woman to—and into— the dress. Both closed their doors in 1939—Vionnet never to return to fashion, Chanel reopening in 1954.

Vionnet's legacy is the bias cut. By designing in the round and cutting fabric on the diagonal, Vionnet took her mannequins out of their corsets into a dress that could be worn without fastenings and underpinnings. Hers was the first true body dress. In her book, *Couture,* Caroline Rennolds Milbank reported that the first nipple ever shown in the pages of Vogue was through a bias-cut white satin of a Vionnet design in 1932—a hint at her modernity and the impact she would have on a whole century."

Chanel brought the *c* word to fashion—*c* for comfort, *c* for casual. She was the first designer to use jersey in women's clothes, the first to be influenced by the street, the first to turn an English sailor's sweater into a high fashion pullover for women, first to translate a felt Tyrolean jacket worn by Alpine

yodelers into the longest lasting fashion of the 20th Century, first designer to create a fragrance, first to use costume jewelry in haute couture, first to mix real jewels with fake, first to invent the little black dress, the rope of pearls, the shoulder bag and the sling-back pump.

The 1940s belonged to Hollywood, and the most important women costume designers were Irene and Edith Head. Irene, who replaced the legendary Adrian as supervising designer at MGM, created Lana Turner's sweater-and-skirt look (think Prada, 1995, and you've got it) in *The Postman Always Rings Twice,* 1946. Her favorite leading lady was Ginger Rogers, whom she dressed in her signature mitered stripe suits in *Weekend at the Waldorf,* and those amazing dance dresses in *The Barkleys of Broadway* and *Lucky Partners.*

While Edith Head was to reach her greatest acclaim in The '50s, '60s, and '70s, she first made her name with the glamour dresses she designed for Barbara Stanwyck in *The Lady Eve,* 1941; Ginger Rogers' mink dress for the first fashion psychodrama, *Lady in the Dark,* 1943; and Dorothy Lamour's sarongs in *The Road to Rio,* 1947.

Both Edith and Irene predicted that skirt hems would go down when wartime shortages and the infamous L85—the War Production Board's restrictive code on use of fabric for apparel—were lifted, but it took Christian Dior's New Look at 1947 to send skirts plummeting.

In New York, Claire McCardell, Bonnie Cashin, Tina Leser, Clare Potter and Anne Klein were beginning to carve out the first truly

"American" look, defined by the easy, comfortable, casual looks that were later to become known as American sportswear.

In the 1950s, the above-mentioned designers, joined by Vera Maxwell, Carolyn Schnurer and Jane Derby, continued to define the American concept of easy, colorful, simple dressing, totally uninfluenced by Paris design and totally supported by New York's legendary retail guru, Dorothy Shaver of Lord & Taylor. It is noteworthy that these originators of French-free American design were all women with the exception of Rudi Gernreich and Tom Brigance.

Anne Fogarty's petticoated dresses with fitted bodices became something of a national uniform with the young, and Edith Head's strapless full-skirted tulle dress for Elizabeth Taylor in *A Place in the Sun* (1951) and her strapless ballgown for Grace Kelly in *To Catch a Thief* (1955) became the prototype for prom dresses from Los Angeles to New York.

In Paris, Chanel reopened her doors in 1954, and "the Chanel suit" became an American status symbol, thanks to the Davidow copies.

In Los Angeles, Margit Felligi was pioneering inventive new swimwear for Cole of California, who signed Hollywood swim diva Esther Williams to promote them, and Rose Marie Reid was making waves with her own swimwear company. In The 1960s, the mega-trend was the mini, mothered in London by Mary Quant. It was the decade of the Youthquake, the Pill, ecumenics, drugs, rock 'n' roll, Woodstock and the Age of Aquarius. Paraphernalia was the groovy boutique of this groovy era, and Betsey Johnson was its grooviest in-house designer.

Norma Kamali discovered Swinging London and brought its artifacts to her fifty-third street boutique, later adding her own award-winning designs, and in the 70s, becoming the first American to bring real design to inexpensive fabrics—sleeping bags and sweats.

The most important woman of the decade, Jacqueline Kennedy, was not a designer, but her influence on fashion is still being felt—as it was then with her input in Oleg Cassini's clothes for her.

The 1970s brought us the women's movement and pants—pants first as a social protest against mini skirts, later as a sign of sexual equality. Sonia Rykiel invented a new fit—high armholes, shrunken tops, pants with no pleats and round legs—and a new fashion religion, bohemianism.

In London, three women owned the decade. Thea Porter created what came to be known as the rich hippie look—a rags-to-riches idea of getting the rich folks to wear what the poor folks had worn for centuries, but translated into the world's most opulent fabrics. Her fashion seraglio on Greek Street was the quintessential expression of that fashion era's ethnic mode.

Zandra Rhodes, the queen of fashion fantasy, made the most extraordinary dream clothes of the decade, bringing such print motifs as a Las Vegas billboard to gossamer chiffon and an Australian rock to matte jersey—these at a time when evening gown prints were veritably limited to florals and dots. Her "Conceptual Chic" collection, celebrating the safety-pinned punk styles of London's Kings Road, was one of the first examples of high fashion being influenced by the street.

In a decade that became famous for re-issuing ideas from the past,

Jean Muir proved that modernity was alive and well, at least in her hands. She also promulgated the at-the-time strange idea that it is dishonest to tear up everything every six months just because it's time for a new collection.

The best-selling dress of the decade was Diane von Furstenberg's printed jersey wrap dress with bust darts (male designers had stopped using them). The dress that had sold more than 300,000 models at around $70 each earned her the cover of *Newsweek* in 1976, where she was called "the most marketable female in fashion since Coco Chanel."

The 1970s was also the decade of designer jeans, with best-sellers coming from heiress Gloria Vanderbilt.

Body dressing became a nation-wide fashion urge, thanks in part to the disco rage and its celebration of the bodysuit with tie-on skirt in *Saturday Night Fever.* Credit Norma Kamali and Danskin designer Bonnie August for forwarding this fashion cause.

Diane Keaton's vests, ties, chino pants and men's fedoras in the 1977 Woody Allen movie, *Annie Hall,* (many from Ralph Lauren, but all assembled and styled by Keaton) influenced millions of young working women to put together similar getups in a fashion move that became known as gender bending. A few years later, Giorgio Armani called it androgyny.

The message of the 1980s was the emergence of the woman executive as reflected first by fashion androgyny, then shoulder pads, followed by minimalism and comfort-dressing.

Rei Kawakubo was the most powerful woman designer of the 1980s.

She did not, of course, invent black. She just took it from a little black dress to a big black force in global style, creating a look, a mood and a powerful movement that

shook the very foundations of fashion. She continues to see the role of artist as provocateur, and her clothes provoke real passion. Her strong feeling for asymmetry, whereby the right side of her clothes seldom know what the left side is doing, has had a global impact.

The bodysuit gained new fashion status at the hands of Donna Karan, who made it the base garment of her collections, teaching women its slenderizing, sex-arising virtues. And the jumpsuit jumped into high fashion with its most famous advocate, Pauline Trigère.

The 1990s are mid-way as we go to press, and so far the woman designer of the decade is Donna Karan. Her DKNY collection, her menswear, her pantyhose, her leathergoods, her New York frame of mind, her fragrance, her treatment line, her London shop, her advertising—all have broken new ground. And her signature collection is one of the few today that looks to the future rather than the past. (In 1994 she presented the first interactive fashion show, with the audience flashing miners' headlights on the models so the reflective fiberglass-coated fabrics would glow. And for spring 1995 she offered prom dresses made from the paper-like fabric used in Federal Express envelopes.)

London's Vivienne Westwood is helping define the decade with her quirky, cartoon-like take on retro. Her post-punk revelations began with the crinoline, which petticoated its way around the fashion world, and she was the first to bring real, Victorian-inspired corsets and bustles to the runways, the first to show platforms with 6-inch heels—the forerunners (fore-walkers?) of today's teetering sandals.

Like Karan, Germany's Jil Sander does not believe in putting off the future by putting on the past. Her modern, streamlined clothes are making a definite impact on fashion in the 90s—first with impeccably cut suits and pantsuits, now with more complete collections notable for their fabric invention (the first metallized organzas, the first cotton tweed) and artistic use of color.

Five years from the 21st century, it is interesting to note that while some of the most famous male designers are looking back in a rage of retro, the women continue to forge ahead.

Miuccia Prada is a modernist/minimalist who has created a kind of deluxe bohemian for the fashion intelligentsia. She has made the Prada bag the status symbol of the 90s to date. Rei Kawakubo continues to make waves for Comme des Garçons, reminding everyone that the 21st century is Asia-bound. Rykiel, Muir, and Rhodes evolve their now-famous fashion handwriting. Kamali rediscovers the gym and stakes out new claims on Hollywood

glamour. Yeohlee surges ahead as a futurist, her fluid, architectural designs as sane as they are urbane. Cynthia Rowley is Generation X-ercising fashion with wit and fantasy. Betsey Johnson's Youthquake never stops stirring things up. And von Furstenberg is busy reinventing home shopping.

The Fashion Group International®, Inc.

Fashion's New Establishment

Katherine Betts

About three months ago, Marc Jacobs was walking through JFK airport on his way to Milan when he spotted something familiar at the duty-free counter. Two of the scarves in the glass display case looked like his, but Jacobs was so surprised to see them that he asked a saleswoman to take them out of the case for closer inspection. Yup, they were his.

For any fashion designer, landing in the duty-free shop can mean only one of two things: Either his name has been soiled by reckless licensing deals-turning up on everything from umbrellas to cigarette lighters-or he has arrived in fashion's "establishment," that firmament reserved for household names like Calvin Klein, Yves Saint Laurent, and Karl Lagerfeld. Jacobs may not be on that level yet in terms of recognition, but he and his seven other designers—Helmut Lang, John Galliano, Stefano Gabbana, Domenico Dolce, Tom Ford, Isaac Mizrahi, and Michael Kors—might as well start scanning the duty-free displays. They may not have all of

the mega-licensing deals lined up yet, but they are well on their way to becoming as established as their predecessors. When we look back on this decade, we will remember their names.

Every ten years or so a shift occurs in fashion that has nothing to do with declarations like "Long!" or "Short!" and everything to do with the people making those declarations. Usually it also has to do with a generational succession: When Saint Laurent inherited the couture crown from Balenciaga, he was dressing a woman who met the rigors of daily urban life, as opposed to pampered socialites who changed four times a day. When Mary Quant captured the attention of London in the 1960s, she was not only introducing the miniskirt, she was responding to the rebellious nature of a new youth culture. And when Armani created his signature soft power suit in the eighties, he was inventing a uniform for a new generation of women who wanted to show that they had the salaries—but not the silhouettes—of men.

Like Saint Laurent and Quant and Armani before them, fashion's new establishment is at the center of a shift. What characterizes them is their placement between two highly defined generations. Neither Gen-Xers nor boomers, the new-establishment designers—all 40 or under—possess the ambivalence and the irony of the 20-year-olds who sometimes inspire them but none of the self-aggrandizing narcissism of the boomers who came before them. They are building their own empires by responding to the needs of clients who are like them: more casual about fashion than sensible. They realize that designer labels no longer have the potential to command the kind of blind devotion they inspired in the seventies and eighties. They know that on the street, where images move product, the idealism of, say, a Ralph Lauren ad campaign has been superseded by the irony of a Diesel jeans campaign. In fact, jeans, sunglasses, and sneakers have replaced perfume, watches, and furs as the fetish items of the decade. And the kids who are buying those products, the kids who are scotch-taping Calvin Klein CK One perfume ads to their walls, are computer literate, sports oriented, androgynous, and still logo obsessed. All of this—along with the influence of the new establishment—has changed the way women dress.

"The pageantry has changed," explains Jacobs. "In the eighties the attention was not on spare fashion. What seemed correct was the beading and poufs and extravagance. But the silhouette, the shapes of people's bodies, the way people wear clothes has changed. Today the idea of coming out of a department store looking like you just spent $4,000 is not attractive."

The emphasis on originality and personality in fashion now doesn't jibe with the idea of highly visible names. If Armani mastered the art of the subtle signature, and Prada introduced the idea of the invisible status symbol, then what designers like Galliano, Lang, and Jacobs are insisting on is no status at all, and a signature that is recognizable only in the proportions and finish of the clothes. Lang and Jacobs are fans of the high, tiny armhole; Galliano has perfected the bias-cut dress; Dolce & Gabbana practically own the rights to constructed lingerie. While they all owe an enormous debt to the designers who vanquished brand-name fashion (Miuccia Prada and Jil Sander), the new establishment has seized the moment by creating fashion that is malleable in a way that the clothes of their predecessors weren't.

Nonetheless, within the group, their distinct styles reflect extreme differences in personality. Where Lang is a hard-edged minimalist with a raw, subversive sensibility, Galliano is a whimsical romantic who morphs fairy-tale imagination with sexy shapes. He is the irreverent storyteller to Lang's rough-edged cynic; Galliano is given to giddy pro-

nouncements, while Lang's conversation is punctuated with halting indecisiveness. Galliano's references can run a fantastical gamut from Vionnet to flamenco or from Louis Brooks to the Cherokee Indians; Lang sticks to everyday street references like jeans, T-shirts, and perforated nylon football jerseys.

If Lang and Galliano are the two extremists, Jacobs and Mizrahi are the clean American purists with approachable, witty personalities to match. With an eye for the street and the flea market, Jacobs casually mixes Halston references with a twenties beaded flapper dress. He is an expert stylist who scours New York clubs for ideas, sizing up the hodgepodge mix of the fashion crowd and honing it into a sexy, refined silhouette. But where Jacobs is "enamored of the present," Mizrahi is in live with movies and television and retro glamour. He likes to say that the movies are about the promise of glamour and that's why he became a designer. "I can't imagine the two apart. Fashion is ultimately a form of entertainment." Jacobs, on the other hand, likes to say that fashion is "whatever" and that his inspiration comes from "wherever."

In the middle are the four more commercial-minded personalities: Ford, the American-born creative director of Gucci; Kors, the most minimal of the three Americans; and Dolce and Gabbana, who in ten years have turned their sexy, Sicilian tailoring into an international trademark. Ford, the newcomer in the group, is probably the most visible right now simply because he has single-handedly-and triumphantly reinvented Gucci. Apart from pinstripes and funky shoes, his trademark has become his keen marketing sense (he controls the company's image on the runway, in the adds, and in store windows) and his ability to graft his own style

onto that of a 73-year-old company in three quick seasons. "Being a designer," Ford likes to say, "is an ego thing. It's a controlling thing, so of course you want to impose your image on the world."

Like Ford, Dolce and Gabbana present collections that are both trendy and commercially viable. In ten years, the designers have gone from being soulful underdogs obsessed with Sicilian shrouds and lingerie to clever businessmen who know how to walk the fine line between trendiness and accessibility. They comb nightclubs for ideas which they then apply to their sexy tailored suits and fifties-film-star dresses. And like Ford and Kors, Dolce and Gabbana are slick, savvy, and seductive in person. Kors doesn't have the advertising budget of Gucci and Dolce & Gabbana, but he knows his customer and peppers his conversation with business statistics he's garnered from relentless cross-country trunk shows. His reputation for extreme luxury and his devotion to his customers ("75 percent of them have second homes") have catapulted him into the new establishment after fifteen years in business.

Although some—Kors, Jacobs, and Galliano—have flirted with bankruptcy, all of the new-establishment designers are on their way to building solid fashion empires. Ford, a Gucci stockholder, now oversees eleven different product categories for Gucci and has even entertained thoughts of starting his own name and, more important, proved he can produce wearable, commercial clothes for Givenchy. Lang, who recently opened three new shops in Europe for men and women, just signed a license for jeans, and is currently discussing licensing deals for underwear, eyewear, and perfume.

Jacobs, who is planning to open his first New York shop next month, has had great success with licensed shoes, scarves, and his less-expensive Look line. And Mizrahi, Kors, and Dolce & Gabbana all have successful second lines underway.

Building a name in the nineties involves a broader vision than it did in the past, though. Where establishment names—Cardin, Saint Laurent, and Perry Ellis—were marketed in a way that brought cachet to an economic group that couldn't afford luxury products (e.g., a lipstick for someone who could never buy a Saint Laurent dress), Lang and his colleagues are aiming at a broader market from the get-go. They're building their names to compete with one another at the luxury end and with the bigger-brand logos that dominate the street. They have to keep one eye on Calvin Klein and Tommy Hilfiger and the other on Nike, Reebok, the Gap, Nautica, Ray-Ban, and Timberland.

In the case of Mizrahi, recognition has come from beyond the fashion world, too. The release of the documentary *Unzipped* gave him much wider recognition than the runway ever could. "For me now, maybe an empire means a TV show, too, or maybe some sort of movie deal," he explains. "Today fashion is different. Armani invented something, and then he became the king of the country he invented. We can't be inventors the way Vionenet or Poiret were. We have to be inventive and have ambition and drive and luck."

They also have to be completely global, traveling constantly for inspiration, licensing deals, fashion shows, fabric fairs, and production meetings. Instead of holing up in an ivory tower and waiting for the fashion world to come to them, this generation migrates to the fashion action. Lang just bought an apartment in New York, but he works in Vienna and shows in Paris. Jacobs lives in New York but does a lot of his work in Milan and frequently travels to Tokyo for the Japanese license of his Look line. The day I talked to them, Isaac Mizrahi was dashing off to London for the premiere of Unzipped, and Michael Kors was already engrossed in a fabric meeting for his new, less-expensive KORS line.

"There's this idea that after the fashion show the designer is cosseted away in some divine house in Marakech," Kors muses. But *no*. It's like *hello,* I'm in a production fitting."

"We aren't interested in mansions and Porsches," adds Jacobs. "I don't think success is about money anymore. I really love what I do, and every penny I make goes right back into it." Even their dreams are different. Although Galliano always wanted the couture house he finally got, Lang recently turned down an offer to design deluxe ready-to-wear for the house of Balenciaga. "The idea of re-creating Balenciaga is exciting. But it doesn't work with jeans and sunglasses and everything I'm doing now. You can't have it all, you know." Lang pauses then adds, "Anyway, it's about America. It's not about couture."

"I think maybe our generation is different because we have dreams," Mizrahi adds, "but we don't want to presume anything. I was watching Charlie Rose interview Cecilia Bartoli, and he asked her what her future was, and she said, 'I want to sing more Haydn.' I mean, she's a diva, but not because she went by anybody else's formula."

Similarly, the members of this new establishment have created their own rules. And they apply to everything—from the way a runway show is produced to the way a pant leg is cut. But there are still certain old rules, left over from the previous generation, that they would never break. One is the value of the consumer's trust. "There's been a lot of confusion," says Jacobs. "People are so conditioned to buy the wrong thing because it's the 'hot' thing. People are told it's all about this, it's all about that. With designers like YSL and Armani, women trusted them because they didn't change every season. They evolved."

So ten years down the road, when Jacob's initials and Kors's cashmere are all over the display case in the duty-free shop at JFK, women will immediately recognize them. But more important, they will recognize other women wearing the new establishment's designs.

Vogue, July 1996.

CHAPTER 3

The Powerful Consumer

After you have completed this chapter, you will be able to discuss:

- The terms demographics and psychographics.

- Different buying motives of emotional and rational purchasers.

- Categories of consumers by social classes and explain their differences.

- Differences between observation and questionnaire methods for consumer research.

- How focus groups help businesses learn about consumer wants and needs.

- Some of the legislation that has been enacted by the Federal government for the protection of the consumer.

Does the designer or the consumer determine the direction fashion will take? Both approaches have advocates in the business environment. During some periods, a designers' direction, no matter how impressive his or her accomplishments, is totally ignored. At the beginning of the 1970s, for example, the industry "mandated" the midi as the proper skirt length. Across the country, however, customers rejected this new length, and retailers who stocked the midi suffered considerable losses. Rather than accept the style they did not want, many women opted for an alternative—pants. As a result of that experience, many manufacturers and retailers began to be more aware of the wants and needs of consumers.

The close of the twentieth century appears to be a time of freedom of choice. Designers have acknowledged that they alone cannot decide what their customers want, and are offering a smorgasbord of fashion to capture their attention. In fact, the look of the mid-1990s fostered the "retro" look— designs that were adapted from the most successful silhouettes, fabrications, and colors of the world's greatest fashion creators. Was it that designers were playing it safe, or were they judging the wants and needs of consumers by past successes?

To understand what the consumers want, it is necessary to understand what motivates them to buy. The study of market segments and various sociological analyses also contribute to consumer assessment. The more attention the producers and retailers of fashion pay to the consumer, the better prepared they will be to meet the challenges of the world of fashion.

MARKET SEGMENTS

To ascertain the wants and needs of the fashion consumer, one must differentiate among the many types of fashion consumers. Income, lifestyle, age, occupation, and other characteristics create different fashion needs. The demands of young, urban business couples certainly differ from those of more conservative members of our society. By separating their clients into segments—or groups—based on these various criteria, professionals in the fashion world better understand what to offer their clients. We will examine this consumer market in terms of its demographics and psychographics.

Demographics

Demographics is the study of various objective characteristics of the population, such as population size, geographic concentration, age, occupation, family life-cycle, education, and income. Market researchers can find this information in governmental sources, such as the publications of the Census Bureau and the Commerce Department, and from original research studies companies sponsor to assess their markets. The importance of each demographic factor is discussed below.

Consumers must be broken down into different categories such as age and lifestyle to address their fashion needs.

Population

Population size and location are important considerations. A company does not study an entire population, only that portion directly related to the prod-

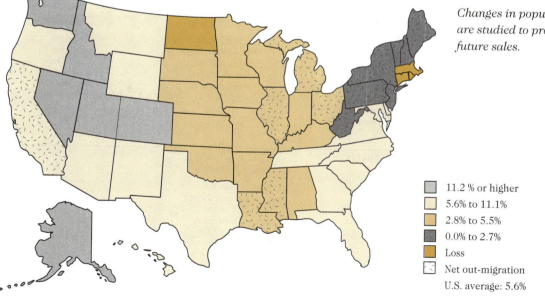

Changes in population are studied to project future sales.

▨	11.2 % or higher
▫	5.6% to 11.1%
▨	2.8% to 5.5%
▨	0.0% to 2.7%
▨	Loss
▨	Net out-migration

U.S. average: 5.6%

uct being considered. For example, a children's wear manufacturer is concerned with the number of children in the general population. An infants' wear producer, however, needs more specific information about the birth rate to determine the size of the potential market. In addition to sheer numbers, the geographic concentration of people also plays a vital role. For example, the population shifts to the South in the 1980s had positive implications for manufacturers of swimwear. Similarly, the great movement to the mountain states in the 1990s created greater needs for hiking gear.

Different lifestyle categories account for different needs.

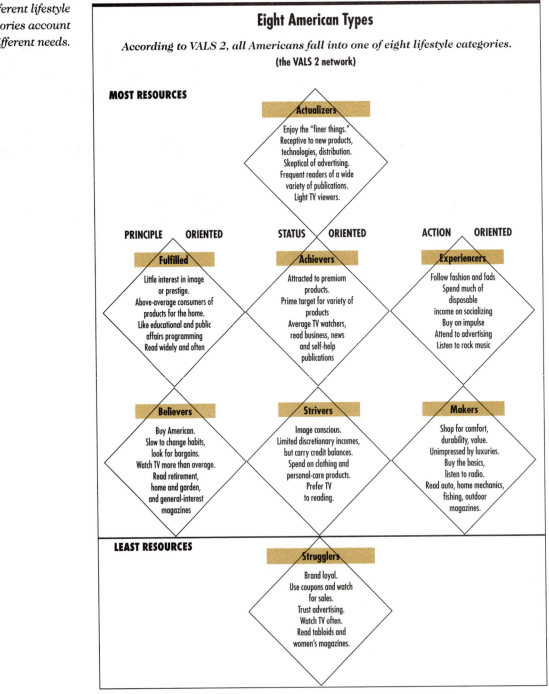

Eight American Types

According to VALS 2, all Americans fall into one of eight lifestyle categories.
(the VALS 2 network)

MOST RESOURCES

Actualizers
Enjoy the "finer things."
Receptive to new products,
technologies, distribution.
Skeptical of advertising.
Frequent readers of a wide
variety of publications.
Light TV viewers.

PRINCIPLE   ORIENTED   **STATUS   ORIENTED**   **ACTION   ORIENTED**

Fulfilled
Little interest in image
or prestige.
Above-average consumers of
products for the home.
Like educational and public
affairs programming
Read widely and often

Achievers
Attracted to premium
products.
Prime target for variety of
products
Average TV watchers,
read business, news
and self-help
publications

Experiencers
Follow fashion and fads
Spend much of
disposable
income on socializing
Buy on impulse
Attend to advertising
Listen to rock music

Believers
Buy American.
Slow to change habits,
look for bargains.
Watch TV more than average.
Read retirement,
home and garden,
and general-interest
magazines

Strivers
Image conscious.
Limited discretionary incomes,
but carry credit balances.
Spend on clothing and
personal-care products.
Prefer TV
to reading.

Makers
Shop for comfort,
durability, value.
Unimpressed by luxuries.
Buy the basics,
listen to radio.
Read auto, home mechanics,
fishing, outdoor
magazines.

LEAST RESOURCES

Strugglers
Brand loyal.
Use coupons and watch
for sales.
Trust advertising.
Watch TV often.
Read tabloids and
women's magazines.

Age

Fashion manufacturers and retailers may emphasize styles that cater to a specific age group. Therefore, to market their product effectively, they need to know what proportion of the overall population fits into each age group. The continued growth of the sixty-five and older market makes them a group more and more important to the fashion industry. This is reflected in the growth of large-size women's clothing, as women in that age group may wear clothes in that size range. This, added to the continuing demand for large sizes in all age groups, signals the specialized size producer and merchants to expand their offerings. The Limited took heed of these developments and expanded its Lane Bryant division, which specializes in larger sizes.

Occupation

Most fashion industry professionals agree that the single greatest factor affecting the women's market is their growing presence in the work force. Not too long ago, the majority of women did not have professional careers. Today, women are participating at every level of the economy and as a result, their clothing needs have changed. More and more manufacturers are producing fashions suitable for the workplace. Many retailers have expanded their "career dress" departments and have developed personal shopping services that cater to women who have less time to shop because of professional commitments.

Another occupation-related factor—**dress-down Friday**—resulted in an increase in the production of casual clothing for work. Many major companies have instituted relaxed dress requirements for all their employees one day a week. This enables even executives to shed their traditional business clothing and wear casual attire. Although this trend has given the suit manufacturer cause for concern, other manufacturers have gained by making more relaxed, but professional, attire to accommodate this change.

Family Life Cycle

Categorizing individuals by groups according to their life cycles is another way to determine fashion needs. Each group has its own special requirements and a knowledge of them can help those in fashion businesses. The following classifications, which are typical segments of the **family life-cycle**, are explored in terms of their potential fashion needs.

YOUNG UNMARRIED   Whether they live with their parents, their friends, or on their own, the members of this group are responsible only for themselves. With the exception of such basic costs as rent, food, and utilities, most of their **discretionary income** is spent on recreation, entertainment, and clothing. On the whole, they are a very fashion-conscious group, eager to accept style changes. Teenagers fall into this group, and they swing with fashion trends. If the mini is in vogue, they purchase it; if next season the lengths are longer, they quickly accept that change. A great number of designers and manufacturers try to cater to this group. Buying clothing and accessories for work as well as play is an ongoing process.

NEWLY MARRIED   Typically, this family unit has two wage earners. They are sometimes called *dinks,* which stands for "dual income, no kids!" Because

Those with money to spend and time to shop are considered power shoppers.

these couples have two incomes and share household expenses, they can increase their discretionary spending on clothing as well as other purchases. The manufacturer of quality fashions and designer labels find it important to cater to this group.

FULL NEST I   The arrival of children typically causes a temporary reduction in real and discretionary funds. Many women stay home when a child is first born, resulting in a short-term reduction in income. When they return to work, however, the cost of child-care significantly diminishes the family's discretionary income. This group's fashion purchasing also radically changes. Less money is spent on clothing for the parents and more on the younger set.

FULL NEST II   In this classification, the children are teenagers. Women who stayed home to raise their children now often return to the workplace. Those women who opted for careers are still on the job, but may now earn substantial incomes. With their increased income, a great deal of money is again spent on fashion merchandise. As more mature women, their tastes are generally more sophisticated and not as easily influenced by trends. They look for better quality merchandise, and manufacturers of both men's and women's higher-priced merchandise target this group. The teenage offspring of this family typically enjoys "trendy" merchandise and is among the best customers for anything new on the fashion scene. These teenagers, for example, were the ones captivated by the grunge look of the early 1990s, and they quickly shed their sneakers when the "Doc Martin" shoes arrived on the scene. Anything new is apt to attract them! With many teenagers working part time, they have their own spending money and are able to buy more expensive items.

FULL NEST III   In this classification, both the husband and wife usually work, and the children, 17 and older, are still dependent on their parents. Family income is usually higher than ever before, and the spending on fashion merchandise is significant for all members of the family. Bearing this in mind, many manufacturers have directed their efforts towards **bridge** merchandise— goods that are well below couture, but above what is best described as "better" sportswear and dresses. Examples of these labels are Jones New York, and Ellen Tracy. Designer merchandise is directed to a large segment of the group.

Increasingly, however, the traditional **full nests** have been replaced with **single-family households.** In this nontraditional classification, there is often a single parent raising the children. In these cases, purchasing fashion merchandise is not the same priority it is in *nested families*. Because total income is lower, less money is earmarked for fashion items.

EMPTY NEST I   With the children on their own, much of the parents' financial responsibility has diminished. Although, some women retire from their jobs, the number that remain working continues to increase. Income for this classification is generally higher than for the others. Manufacturers and retailers direct quality fashion products for both work and play at this market. Resort wear is also targeted toward this group, because its members now have the funds necessary for travel and for the clothing required for these vacations.

EMPTY NEST II   Members of the family have retired. As a result, there is a significant decrease in income. Except for a small group whose financial investments guarantee a "good" life style, the majority in this classification is faced with cuts in spending. Thus, less is spent on fashion merchandise. Clothing for the workplace is not necessary and purchases are usually for leisure wear.

SOLE SURVIVOR I   In this classification, the survivor remains on the job. Business-oriented clothing is still important. Many in this position eventually seek a new relationship, which puts new demands on fashionable dress. Because financial responsibilities are less demanding and a regular paycheck is ever present, this group is responsible for quality purchases. Manufacturers of more mature styles find this market has little competition.

SOLE SURVIVOR II   More and more people who have lost their mates are retired. Many change their life styles as well as their places of residence; they may move to retirement communities. With all of the social activities provided for senior citizens in these communities, there is more emphasis on dress than if one lived in a more diverse community. These people become purchasers of leisure merchandise. Others in this group are constrained by lower incomes. They buy little for themselves, but continue to make purchases for family members.

Geographic Concentration

Where people live also determines the clothing and accessories they need. Obviously, a shift in population to warmer climates signals a greater need for lightweight merchandise; a shift northward would necessitate the reverse. Fashion producers must carefully study geographic concentrations, not only to determine the extent of the markets for their particular products but also the market's potential for growth. California's significant population growth in the 1970s and 1980s signaled fashion designers to create styles oriented to the casual attitudes prevailing on the West Coast. Because of this shift in population, California became an important fashion resource both for its own retailers and for those merchants all across the nation catering to the needs of relaxed dressers.

Education

The college campus is an important arena for dress-down clothing. Here are examples of students from campuses across the U.S. wearing T-shirts, shorts, and baseball caps.

Money alone does not account for the style and quality of merchandise preferred by consumers. Although many with little or no formal higher education earn substantial salaries, educational level often determines income levels and merchandise needs. As the level of education increases, so does the number of people entering business or becoming attorneys, investment bankers, accountants, and physicians. Each profession sets its own dress standards. Individuals need apparel appropriate to their careers. A study of the educational goals of consumers will help reveal how extensive the market will be for fine-tailored clothing and accessories. Stores such as Burberry, Barney's, and Bergdorf Goodman, have capitalized on the rewards of education by targeting this rapidly growing group as their primary customers.

Income

A person's income determines the quality and price of the fashion merchandise they purchase. Producers and retailers of fashion must be constantly aware of income shifts in their potential markets to determine the price points they will offer for sale. With the two-income family now commonplace, there is more discretionary spending. Many fashion businesses have capitalized on this increase in disposable income by offering additional lines to meet the needs of this group. Designers, such as Donna Karan and Giorgio Armani, who relied on the upper classes for their business have added lower-priced lines—DKNY and Mani respectively. They have captured a share of the market that has moved toward quality merchandise but still cannot afford the price points of the couture collections. Most of the major couture houses feature prêt-à-porter, or ready-to-wear, that is often more profitable than their higher-priced offerings.

In America, fashion is available at every price point from high-end couture to mass-produced, popular-priced lines. Later in the text, we will focus on the various fashion merchandise classifications according to their price structures.

Psychographics

A more sophisticated approach to the study of market segments is to narrow the groups into even more narrowly defined categories. For example, while age is a factor in determining consumer needs, obviously not all thirty-year-old females are the same. Some are at home raising families, while others pursue professional careers. Their fashion merchandise needs are distinctly different. Two men earning $60,000 annually have different needs depending upon their marital status, career, and type of residence. Perhaps one earns his $60,000 as a plumber, is married, and owns a home, while the other is single and lives in an apartment. Their needs are obviously different.

Psychographics is the subjective study of characteristics, which describe motivations to buy, such as personality, life style, ethnicity, attitudes, interests, and opinions. The results offer a more complete look at consumers. By identifying particular characteristics, companies can better match their products to the needs of potential customers. Instead of trying to appeal to all thirty-year-old women, psychographic segmentation narrows the field to those with similar characteristics so that specific marketing tactics can be more effectively directed.

Table 3.1 is a study by the Newspaper Advertising Bureau, based on a psychographic questionnaire, which categorized males into specific psychographic groups. The essence of the study defines consumption patterns, along with commentaries on his fashion purchasing potential.

A company that manufacturers men's apparel and wishes to find a specific market could make meaningful use of the breakdowns in Table 3.1. For example, a designer of men's leather pants and bomber jackets would immediately eliminate several groups based on this study, such as the quiet family man, the traditionalist, the discontented man, and the ethical highbrow. The remaining groups, most notably the pleasure-oriented man, the achiever, and the he-man, would be targeted by this company, as might the sophisticated man.

Although psychographic studies are being used more than ever, they alone should not guide fashion producers and retailers in their pursuit of the best

TABLE 3.1

CATEGORIES OF MALES IN SPECIFIC PSYCHOGRAPHIC GROUPS

The Quiet Family Man

A self-sufficient, shy individual with little community involvement, who spends much of his free time with his family. He has less interest in consumer goods than most men. He would not be a chief target for the fashion industry.

The Traditionalist

Security and esteem are essential to this follower of conventional rules. He perceives himself as altruistic and considers other people's welfare to be important. He is a conservative shopper and prefers well-known manufacturer's brands. Most likely he is at home wearing classic clothing from manufacturers such as Ralph Lauren, if his income affords him quality merchandise, or lines such as Botany 500 if he is inclined to buy more moderately priced clothing.

The Discontented Man

Dissatisfied with his career, his goals are for a better job, more money, and security. As a purchaser, price consciousness is his characteristic. He is a good candidate for off-price merchants, such as Syms.

The Ethical Highbrow

This man is characterized by sensitivity to other's needs, satisfaction with life and work, and interests in culture, religion, and social reform. Quality is an important consideration and is often a sufficient justification for spending greater sums on a purchase. He would probably be a good customer for lines like Tommy Hilfiger, where understated, quality merchandise is available at higher than average prices.

The Pleasure-Oriented Man

The "macho" type, he rejects anything that gives the impression of femininity. He is self-centered and a seeker of instant gratification who buys impulsively. His purchases are more likely centered on clothing with a masculine image. He is the perfect customer for athletic apparel such as muscle shirts, that show off his physique.

The Achiever

A hard-working man who is interested in social prestige, power, and money. He likes adventure and social activities that revolve around good food and entertainment. He is totally status conscious. A perfect market for designers like Giorgio Armani and stores like Barney's.

The He-man

Action and excitement pervade this man's life. He is a bachelor type, and even if marriage becomes a reality, he continues to conduct himself more as a dominant, single individual. High fashion leather apparel is what would attract his attention.

The Sophisticated Man

An intellectual who admires people of artistic and intellectual achievement. He is the epitome of those whose images are socially cosmopolitan. His tastes in clothing are both unique and fashionable. He would be at home wearing Ralph Lauren and Bill Blass creations and shopping in upscale specialty stores like Paul Stuart.

consumer market. They should be used in conjunction with other considerations, such as demographics and such factors as social issues, and class structure, which will be examined in the remainder of this chapter.

Buying Motives

Do price and quality motivate a customer to buy designer merchandise? Does the prestige of the label stimulate purchasing? Does the polo pony logo on a Ralph Lauren shirt make it a better product, or does the name increase its desirability? Consumers are motivated to buy for different reasons—some emotional, other rational. To better satisfy the consumer, those in the fashion industry also evaluate potential markets on the basis of motives.

Emotional Motives

Status and prestige are often involved in the purchase of consumer products. Fashion merchandise, in particular, often appeals to **emotional motives.** Throughout history, many people have selected apparel based on the designer's name. A Dolce & Gabbana creation or an Isaac Mizrahi suit is sure to attract the attention of many fashion enthusiasts. Often, fabrics used by designers capture the consumer's senses. Denim, for example, prior to the 1970s was an important fabric in the manufacture of jeans. This durable, practical material gave the wearer many years of service. The product was not fashion oriented, but was worn primarily by teenagers and workers who wore them for practical purposes. Along came Sasson and Calvin Klein, and the designer jeans market was born. Labels were no longer hidden inside the garment, but were displayed for everyone to see. Jeans became a status fashion and prices quickly escalated. Were the enormous sales due to fine construction, durability, and fair pricing, all rational reasons for purchasing, or was the customer motivated by the prestige associated with a fashion designer?

Standard gear for the youth market include T-shirts and backpacks.

While the geniuses of fashion often provide creative styling, expert tailoring, and exquisite fabrication, would their sales be as great if their garments were not identified with world-famous labels? Designers, manufacturers, and retailers are not in business to teach people about product quality and price, but to give customers what they want. If the polo pony logo provides greater profitability for the producer and retailer, then they should market these products as long as customers purchase them. The creations and more notably the "labels" identifying Pierre Cardin in the 1960s and 1970s emotionally motivated shoppers to purchase designer clothing and accessories. In the home furnishings industry, sales have skyrocketed since apparel designers have signed licensing agreements with those manufacturers. Gianni Versace, Bill Blass, Ralph Lauren, Adrienne Vittadini, and Calvin Klein have had a great deal of success by affixing their labels to bed linens and china. The quality is not necessarily better, but the motives for purchasing have changed.

Pierre Cardin

Pierre Cardin was a major force behind licensing.

Whether it was restlessness, aggressiveness, compulsiveness, or just good business sense that drove Pierre Cardin to involve himself in so many enterprises, all must certainly agree that no one has had his hand in as many fashion ventures.

His name was not necessarily as famous as some of the other couturiers at the middle of the decade, when he designed haute couture. He never had achieved the stature of the likes of Chanel, Dior, and Schiaparelli. Then he recognized that there was a fashion world of consumers who would love designer creations but simply could not afford the extravagant prices.

Some of his designs, such as the *bubble dress* of the 1950s, caught the public's attention and was quickly copied by manufacturers at many price points. Cardin understood that consumers would eagerly buy designer merchandise if the design would bear a couturier's name, but would be priced below the cost of original designs.

He was certainly the major force behind the licensing of designer labels. For a fee, Cardin allowed a manufacturer of his choice the right to affix the Cardin label to merchandise that the manufacturer would produce. Cardin did not necessarily

have a hand in creation of the merchandise, but he had the right of approval before it could be marketed. With this move, the Cardin label was everywhere—on women's, men's, and children's clothing, as well as on watches, jewelry, handbags, belts, wallets, active sportswear, and swimsuits. His name was in every country with a fascination for designer clothing. Cardin's

licenses numbered several hundred.

He set the stage for others like Geoffrey Beene, Bill Blass, Dior, Donna Karan, and Emanuel Ungaro. In some cases, the labels were affixed to the outside of the garments on sleeves, collars, pockets, and cuffs for all the world to see. Licensing provided the average person with status and prestige clothing once reserved for only the privileged.

A World of Fashion Profile of Pierre Cardin reveals how his business astuteness helped the world to become more conscious of designer labels.

Rational Motives

Other consumers base their purchases on careful examination of the products. Is the quality good? Is it competitively priced? Is the material durable? Are all questions considered by the rational buyer. The rational female consumer is not motivated to buy simply because everyone is wearing a new, fashionable skirt length. Her decision is based on whether or not it is appropriate for her figure. Designer names do not play a major role in the rational purchaser's decision-making. Consumers who use **rational motives** when making purchases constitute a sizable segment of the fashion market.

Many retailers who offer private label merchandise that compares in style and quality to the designer lines, but costs less, have found that rationally motivated shoppers will purchase these products. Manufacturers who specialize in knockoffs of designer styles also reach an audience comprised of rational shoppers.

The number of off-price merchants, such as Loehmann's, Marshalls, Filene's Basement, and T.J. Maxx, who carry well-known items, but sell them for less, are satisfying the needs of the shopper who likes the notion of wearing designer merchandise but considers price first and foremost.

By knowing their clientele, fashion professionals can move in either direction. Their marketing strategies might include all of the elements that motivate emotional purchasing or those that stimulate rational considerations. Many fashion retailers make this decision by offering a merchandise mix oriented toward both emotional and rational buyers.

SOCIOLOGICAL CONSIDERATIONS

Other factors to consider in addressing consumer needs are sociologically based. Life style, for example, necessitates changes in clothing design. Students of all ages once dressed more formally. Some dress codes for kindergarten through high school required ties and shirts for boys and dresses for girls. Even footwear was regulated. Today's younger generation generally wears fashionable clothing such as jeans, often intentionally torn, T-shirts, and athletic shoes. This has become standard dress for attending class. The producers of proper school attire quickly found their market severely limited. However, currently in some schools, there is a movement to require students to wear uniforms. One of the major issues is to eliminate the clothing competition. This trend is being supported by legislation.

Wearing uniforms to schools is an issue gaining in popularity and supported by President Clinton.

Casual dress is a part of every age group's life style. With the emphasis on relaxation and physical fitness, some merchandise classifications have grown. Sweatshirts and pants, warm-up suits, athletic shoes, running shoes, etc., have taken dollars away from other product groups. The trend toward dressed-down Friday, as discussed earlier, has made casual attire appropriate even in the boardroom. President Clinton has given greater credibility to activewear every time he appears on television in his running apparel. When did presidents of the United States appear before their public so casually dressed? Going to a restaurant for a casual dinner at one time required somewhat more formal dress. Today, a sweatsuit and athletic shoes can often be appropriate attire.

Another social phenomenon being addressed by the fashion world is the change in the status of women. As already explored, women are in many instances a major bread-winner in the family. They earn their own money and spend more than ever before on discretionary purchases. Fashion producers, recognizing this change, have redirected their marketing efforts. Many now approach women as intelligent, independent, educated individuals whose interests are not solely home centered. Merchants and producers specializing in career dress for women are finding this to be a lucrative market.

Those in the fashion industry are best served when they address the social changes in our society and market merchandise that best suits these changes.

SOCIAL CLASSES

We often hear about the various **social classes** into which our society is divided. In terms of income, goals, and attitudes, the American population is generally categorized into upper, middle, and lower classes, and then into subdivisions of each. By studying these various groups, fashion merchandisers have yet another barometer by which to judge how best to target their customers.

Upper Class

These are the wealthiest people in our society, about three percent of the population, Although money is the primary factor for inclusion in this group, there is a difference in purchasing practices among the different levels within the upper class.

UPPER-UPPER CLASS   Those in the upper-upper class have inherited wealth and are the socially elite members of our society. Their purchases tend to be conservative, with quality an important factor; trendiness is not an important consideration. Cost is unimportant to the members of this class. Understated elegance is probably the best way to describe their fashion preferences.

LOWER-UPPER CLASS   Although their wealth may exceed that of the upper-upper class, they do not have the appropriate family history to join that group. This group is made up of the *nouveau riche* (new rich). They, too, do not consider cost to be important, and their fashion purchases are usually made in the finest shops featuring the best of European and American couture. The label is everything. Many in this level tell the world of their success, and do it through material extravagances, such as expensive, recognizable wearing apparel.

Middle Class

Approximately forty-two percent of the population is considered middle class. Segmentation of the middle class is also important, because the top and the bottom behave quite differently in terms of purchasing.

UPPER-MIDDLE CLASS Although they prefer designer labels and fashion-forward merchandise, this group is a little more cautious about the money it spends than are the members of the upper class. Recognizing this group as an excellent market for designer labels, many of the top fashion producers manufacture separate lines for its consideration. Donna Karan and Perry Ellis, for example, whose couture lines were priced too extravagantly for the middle class, satisfied the needs of those consumers with lines like DKNY and Perry Ellis Portfolio. These lines were lower priced, but satisfied customers with their status labels. So successful were these innovators, that others, such as Isaac Mizrahi, with the Isaac label, and Giorgio Armani with Mani, followed suit.

Many in this class are the regular shoppers at off-price stores such as Loehmann's, T.J. Maxx, and Filene's Basement, where they purchase designer labels at lower prices than those charged at traditional department and specialty stores.

LOWER-MIDDLE CLASS Unlike the upper level of the middle class, this group's merchandise selections are geared to lesser quality merchandise. They are often the purchasers of trendy merchandise copied down to lower-price points that they can afford. Stores like Contempo Casuals, Express, and Pants Place are where they typically shop for fashion merchandise.

Lower Class

This class constitutes the largest segment of the American population, accounting for approximately fifty-five percent of the total number. Although they are extremely price conscious, they do account for the purchase of a significant amount of the merchandise produced by the industry.

UPPER-LOWER CLASS Price is very important to this group, and purchases are generally made at stores that sell budget merchandise. Most purchasing is done at specialty chains that offer merchandise at minimum prices, such as Lerner New York. They seek fashion items, but their purchases are made when the styles have reached their lowest prices. In addition to the lower-priced specialty chains, they patronize the value discount retailers such as Kmart and Wal-Mart, and off-price stores like Marshalls and Hit or Miss. They are also the

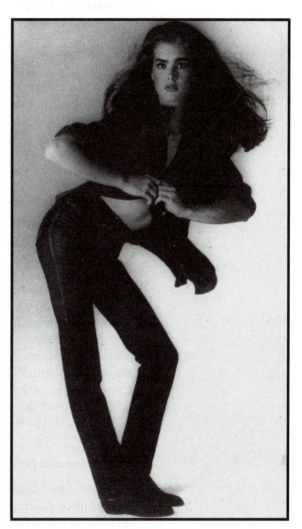

The middle class embraced designer jeans as their fashion status symbol.

targets of the cable shopping networks where inexpensive, low quality merchandise is available.

LOWER-LOWER CLASS More concerned with survival than fashion, these individuals purchase clothing and accessories as necessities.

FASHION AND CONSUMER RESEARCH

The study of market segments, buying motives, sociological considerations, and social classes will provide general information with which the fashion professional can evaluate the potential consumer market. Some producers, retailers, market consultants, or trade associations prefer to learn even more about their prospective customers. Many, therefore, conduct research studies dealing with specifics rather than generalities. They sometimes use investigative techniques, such as observations, questionnaires, and focus groups to gather information to evaluate the wants and needs of consumers. Examples of issues can include what styles are the people wearing, where do they like to shop, would personal shopping present a plus for a retailer trying to reach their markets, which fashion magazines are best suited to promote a collection, and at what price points are their targeted customers likely to spend.

The Research Procedure

When those in the fashion industry decide that they must make important decisions concerning their businesses, they sometimes engage in formal research. The majority of companies go to outside sources for these projects. The giants of the industry, such as DuPont, which might want to investigate consumer acceptance of fibers, or The Limited, which constantly needs to assess new locations for expansion, sometimes have in-house staffs to conduct research on an on-going basis. Whichever approach is followed, the methodology for studying the problems is the same. The following represents the steps used for successful research.

Identifying and Defining the Problem

Among the problems that might be considered are: a designer who wants to change price points, a retailer who is considering the introduction of a new division, or a trade association that is toying with the idea of moving its sales exposition to another geographic area. Research studies can help define the problems that might result from these changes.

To make certain that the research concentrates on the specific problem, a further refinement of the problem might prove necessary. For example, a fashion designer who wants to see if other merchandise classifications might warrant future manufacturing considerations must also study "how large is the market for men's active sportswear, and is the timing right to enter such an arena."

Once the problem to be studied has been sufficiently focused, the research project can move forward.

Gathering Data

The next step is to gather the data on which a decision can be based. The data is available from two sources—secondary and primary. Secondary sources are examined first, because they are more readily available, inexpensive to collect, and might satisfy the needs of the research team without the necessity of entering the arena of original or primary research.

Secondary data are available from a variety of places, including these listed below:

1. Company Records. Companies offer a great deal of information, including sales reports, product returns, price point analyses, and so forth. Because this is on-hand at most companies, it is easy to retrieve and examine for decisions that might have to be addressed in the research study. A women's fashion manufacturer, for example, who is studying the possibility of adding a companion men's line, might study the nature of the retail outlets they already serve to determine if enough of them also sell men's wear.

2. Governmental Agencies. The Federal government, in particular, investigates and publishes information that could be beneficial to a fashion merchant. For example, if a merchant is considering entering the import market, the U.S. Government Printing Office publishes a tariff schedule for imported merchandise that lists the rates of duty as well as the rules of importing. Other regular studies that have implications for fashion business include the various census reports. The Monthly Catalog of U.S. Government Publications produces a wealth of materials on business conditions that provide invaluable information to fashion companies.

3. Trade Associations. Many associations in the fashion industry deal with matters that could help those in need of research assistance. The Fashion Association (TFA), for example, regularly prepares reports on the status of the men's wear industry. It might serve a designer who wants to learn about a particular direction for fiber use or price points. Other associations include the National Retail Federation (NRF) that covers the retailing field and the Leather Association that covers the leather industry. The reports that they generate could help investigators with their projects.

4. Periodicals. Numerous trade papers and magazines regularly engage in research projects or publish stories that cover the fashion industry. Publications such as *Women's Wear Daily* (*WWD*) and *Daily News Record*

Gathering data with personal interviews is an early step in a research procedure.

(*DNR*) are full of such information. Other publications such as *Stores* magazine and *Visual Merchandising and Store Design* (*VM&SD*), both retail-oriented, are excellent sources.

Primary data are pursued when secondary research proves insufficient for the needs of the investigators. The data must be obtained by original research. The information is gathered from customers, potential product users, employees, vendors, market representatives, and the media. The major techniques employed in the gathering of data for primary studies are: questionnaires, observations, and focus groups.

1. Questionnaires. By asking a series of questions, fashion companies may be better able to satisfy consumers. This **questionnaire method** makes inquiries by personal interviews, telephone, or mail. The choice depends on such factors as the size of the market, its location, and how quickly the responses are needed.

   No matter which type of collection procedure is followed, a number of details must be considered, in terms of questionnaire preparation, before the researcher may begin to gather the data. They are:

   - The length of the form must be as brief as possible—limited to one page in most cases. A longer questionnaire could easily discourage the respondent.

   - The language should be appropriate to the respondents. If the questionnaire is directed to industry practitioners, then the language of the trade is perfect. If consumers are the targets, avoid technically oriented terminology. If the form will be mailed, the rule of simplicity is even more important. The interviewer, who might have helped consumers interpret difficult questions, will not be present.

   - The questions should be arranged sequentially so that a smooth transition is made from one to another.

   - Every question should be specific, with words such as "generally" and "usually" avoided. Such words might have different meanings to different respondents.

   - Wherever possible, choices should be given for possible answers. In this way, the data will not require interpretation and will be compiled easier.

   An example of a typical questionnaire used by a fashion retailer is on page 75.

2. Observations. By merely observing a group of people, one can make some judgments about their fashion preferences. Reporters from *Women's Wear Daily,* for example, often use this **observation technique.** They attend most of the affairs frequented by those most likely to wear high-fashion merchandise. At the annual presentation of Council of Fashion Design Awards, for example, those who make and wear the most creative designs are assessed without having a single question thrown at them. As each attendee enters the event, photographers and reporters quickly record what they are wearing. The news is often reported on the pages of *WWD,* in other publications, and on television newscasts.

Dear Preferred Customer:

In all the years of our existence, we have tried to provide you with fashionable merchandise that is timely and represents the creations of the world's major designers and manufacturers. In an effort to offer you even greater exclusivity, we are considering the inclusion of merchandise that will be designed by our own team of product developers. They have had a great deal of expertise in the fashion world. The merchandise, classified as **private label** will have a fashion-forward emphasis, and will be priced to suit the needs of many of our customers.

If you would answer the following questions, not only will it help us in our new direction, but we would be delighted to offer you a certificate entitling you to a 20 percent discount on your next purchase.

You may be assured the information you have provided will be confidential and used only for this research.

1. What percent of your fashion purchases are made at one of our stores?
    __ up to 10%
    __ over 10% to 25%
    __ over 25% to 50%
    __ over 50%

2. What percent of your purchases are designer labels?
    __ up to 10%
    __ over 10% to 25%
    __ over 25% to 50%
    __ over 50%

3. When you shop in stores that offer their own brands (private labels), what percent of the merchandise is of that nature? _____

4. Would you consider purchasing our own brands? _____

5. Could you suggest a name for our new children's private label merchandise?

    _____

6. What is your family income?
    __ under $30,000
    __ from over $30,000 to $40,000
    __ from over $40,000 to $50,000
    __ from over $50,000 to $70,000
    __ from over $70,000 to $100,000
    __ over $100,000

7. What is your family status?
    __ Single, living alone
    __ Single, living with roommate
    __ Newlywed
    __ Married with children under five years
    __ Married with children from six to twelve
    __ Married with teenagers
    __ Married with older children
    __ Empty nester (still employed)
    __ Empty nester (retired)
    __ Divorced or separated (with family)
    __ Divorced or separated (no family)

8. What is your occupation? Include "working at home" if you are a homemaker.

    _____

Suit Style	Color	Lapel
single breasted/plain	black	notched
single breasted/vest	dark blue	peaked
double breasted/plain	white jacket	shawl
double breasted/vest	printed jacket	none
other	other	other
_____	_____	_____

Survey Site _____

Fashion count used by a manufacturer of men's formalwear.

Instructions: Circle one selection in each category, or write-in those that do not fit any of the preselected choices.

More formal observations or *counts* are sometimes conducted to provide specific data on just about any fashion category. These **fashion counts** theoretically determine which styles people are wearing. Thus, if a large percentage of men in the study wore suits that were more form-fitting than traditional styles, it might be a signal that men were ready to move into that silhouette.

The fashion count is particularly important in times of radical fashion change. When skirt lengths are being shifted from one extreme to the other, it is prudent for fashion retailers to take a look at what the people are wearing, and not necessarily at what the designers are touting. Stocking the wrong length, of course, could be detrimental to the store's profit.

The observation has a distinct advantage over the questionnaire in that it does not require the participation of those being studied. It merely involves the selection of a site in which the people needed for observation purposes congregate. For a look at formal wear, the choice might be the opening night at New York's Metropolitan Opera, where those inclined to show off the latest couturier designs will be present. The beach of a winter resort would be a perfect setting for the swimsuit manufacturer to observe popular styles, so that those with great appeal might be included in the company's next summer collection.

Once the location for counting has been selected, a simple form is used to record the observations. Teams are sent out to do the recording and report back with the collected data.

Above is a typical example of a fashion count that a men's formal wear manufacturer might want to use to assess wearer preferences.

3. Focus Groups. This technique, which involves a small group of people and a moderator, seems to be used more and more. The information is recorded and videotaped. It produces excellent results for fashion producers and retailers. Businesses invite representative members of potential markets to join a panel to evaluate their offerings, methods of advertising, promotional endeavors, services, and so on. Typically, the **focus group** is comprised of

from ten to fifteen people on a one-time or regular basis. Through active participation, the recorder is able to note the various opinions about what is being studied. A retailer might form a group to determine whether or not a new level of fashion items should be added to the store's merchandise mix. A manufacturer might convene a focus group to consider the expansion of its present couture operation to include prêt-à-porter.

What is extremely important in the use of focus groups is the selection of those in the study and the choice of a competent recorder who will be able to note even the smallest subtleties offered.

Sampling and Collecting Data

After determining the appropriate methodology for collecting data, it is necessary to determine how many responses are needed for the survey to be meaningful. It is neither necessary or practical to involve every relevant individual or company in the study in order to come to a meaningful conclusion. A fashion manufacturer with a potential retail market of 1,500 stores, for example, need not gather information from all of those retailers. They need only to investigate a representative portion of that population. The segment that is selected is known as a sample. In order for the results to be effective, the sample must be truly representative of the group.

Among the different **sampling** techniques employed by researchers are the following:

Marketers use focus groups to develop design ideas, advertising plans, etc.

RANDOM SAMPLING   In **random sampling,** each individual or business in a predetermined group has an equal chance to be selected. If, for example, a designer wanted to know how retailers would react to his or her line, a list of all of the stores in the market would be needed, but only a small percent would be surveyed.

NONRANDOM SAMPLING   **Nonrandom sampling** is similar to random sampling, except that the sample is restricted to, perhaps, one price point. Thus, depending on the criterion, only stores with merchandise price points of more than $200 might be considered.

AREA SAMPLING   In situations where a particular area is being studied, the **area sample** would be restricted to those stores that fall within a predetermined boundary. The actual number of those to be included is determined by statistical formula.

Once the sample has been decided on, the data are collected. The mail, telephone, personal interviews, or other methods may be conducted by professionals from marketing research organizations, in-house staffs, or college students who have been sufficiently trained.

Processing and Analyzing Data

Once the data have been collected, it must be processed. In the case of questionnaire or observation techniques, careful preparation of the forms used will make processing easier. If open-ended questions have been avoided and every conceivable response was given a separate category for simple checking-off, the task will be accomplished faster. With the use of computers, the data can be quickly tallied.

Once the data have been summarized, analysis can take place. Some studies, such as those looking for color directions from fashion counts, can be easily assessed. Those that cover more complicated issues will need greater interpretation.

This phase of the research is the most important, because it will encourage management to move in a particular direction. Therefore, seasoned marketing analysts evaluate all of their client's potential options and make recommendations as to which will be most beneficial. Those who conduct research in-house must make certain that their assessments are not biased and are the results of input from many members of the management team.

The final step is a written report that outlines all of the stages of the study. This report, along with charts, graphs, and other materials, will help to explain the research team's suggestions.

The power of the consumer is what makes one store, designer, or business profitable and others unsuccessful. That consumers do make conscious choices is evident from the fact that some products sell in enormous quantities and others fail miserably. So powerful are the consumers that only the inexperienced fashion professional ignores their wishes and fails to plan for them.

CONSUMER SAFEGUARDS

Although the consumer is powerful in terms of accepting and rejecting merchandise, he or she may not always be aware of industry practices that diminish the value of their selections, making them impractical or even dangerous. The Federal government has enacted legislation designed to protect consumers from unnecessary harm. Some fabrics, for example, are flammable and can cause severe burns. Many of these fabrics were used in children's clothing, such as pajamas. To protect the consumer, the Federal government passed the Flammable Fabrics Act of 1953, which restricted the use of the more dangerous of these fabrics. An explanation of this act and other pieces of legislation will indicate the government's role in protecting the consumer.

Wool Products Labeling Act of 1939

This act protects consumers as well as product manufacturers from the presence of wool fiber substitutes. Under the jurisdiction of the Federal Trade Commission, the act has been amended several times. It requires that the label must indicate the percentage of fiber content by weight, and the wool category used in the product. The categories include:

- Wool, new wool, or virgin wool for fibers that have never been previously manufactured.
- Recycled wool for fibers used in a woven or felted material that was never worn by the ultimate consumer, and turned back into a fibrous state.

Fur Products Labeling Act of 1952

Amended several times in 1961, 1967, 1969, and 1980, the act was passed to enable consumers to identify the actual fur used in the garment. Before passage of this legislation, consumers were regularly confused with such "furs" as mink-dyed muskrat or seal-dyed rabbit. Both of these were actually misrepresentations, because the first was not mink and the second not seal. The act requires that a label must indicate the country of origin if other than the United States, the English name of the animal, if the fur has been dyed, and if the garment is made of "waste" pieces. The act also requires the same information to be used in all advertisements.

Flammable Fabrics Act of 1953

Initially, the main purpose of the act was to prohibit the use of highly flammable fabrics in the manufacture of articles of clothing transported in interstate commerce. Fabrics were required to pass a 45 degree angle rate-of-burning test. The government later concluded that the burning rate alone was an insufficient test. Factors such as molten fiber drippings, smoke intensity, and temperature of ignition were also important. In 1967, therefore, the act was amended to include fabrics used for interior furnishings, as well as such related materials as paper, plastic, rubber, and synthetic foam. On May 14, 1973, enforcement of the Flammable Fabrics Act was transferred to an independent regulatory agency, the Consumer Product Safety Commission.

Textile Fiber Products Identification Act of 1960

This act requires that certain fiber content information be clearly indicated on labels that are securely affixed and conspicuously placed on textile products. Enforced by the Federal Trade Commission, which is a regulatory agency, the items included are the generic names of the fiber, the percentage of fiber content by weight listed in descending order of dominance, the country where the textile product is manufactured, and the manufacturer's name or a registered identification number.

Care Labeling of Textile Wearing Apparel Act of 1972

Enacted in 1972, it was amended in 1984. Administered by the Federal Trade Commission, it requires that care labels be affixed to most textile apparel products used to cover the body, and most fabrics sold to the consumer for home sewing. The label must be conspicuously and securely placed, as well as indicate one care method, such as washing, and give instructions for doing so.

Chapter Highlights

- People in the fashion world approach their consumer markets in one of two ways. Some try to dictate fashion, while others try to satisfy consumer wants or needs.

- Marketing research studies both demographic and psychographic factors to determine what products consumers want depending on a variety of characteristics.

- Consumers buy goods for emotional reasons and/or rational reasons.

- Every social class has specific characteristics that influence its purchasing patterns.

- To determine how to market products most successfully, manufacturers, designers, and retailers conduct market studies.

- In these marketing studies, data are gathered through secondary and primary sources. Secondary sources include company records, publications by government agencies, and the activities of trade associations. Primary sources include questionnaires, observations, and focus groups.

- After data are collected, they are processed and analyzed to determine consumer preferences.

- The Federal government has enacted legislation designed to protect the consumer.

Important Fashion Terminology and Concepts

area sample	Flammable Fabrics Act of 1953	questionnaire method
Care Labeling Of Textile Wearing Apparel Act of 1972	focus groups	random sample
	full nest	rational motives
demographics	Fur Products Labeling Act of 1952	sampling
discretionary income		single-family households
emotional motives	market segment	social classes
empty nest	nonrandom sampling	Textile Fiber Products Identification Act of 1960
family life-cycle	observation technique	
fashion count	psychographics	Wool Products Labeling Act of 1939

For Review

1. Aside from the designer's own decisions, who else is important in determining which styles will become popular?

2. Define the term demographics.

3. What is meant by the term market segment?

4. Differentiate between the terms *full nest* and *empty nest*.

5. Explain how the geographic concentration of consumers plays an important role in the manufacture of fashion merchandise?

6. Define the term psychographics.

7. Which emotions play a more important role in the purchase of designer merchandise that has easily seen identifiable labels or logos?

8. What is the major difference between the upper and lower segments of the upper class in terms of how they purchase merchandise?

9. How does the observation method differ from the questionnaire technique?

10. Describe the role of the participants in a focus group.

11. Is it necessary to survey every potential member of a group to come to a conclusion about the group?

12. What is meant by random sampling?

13. What are some of the features of the Fur Products Labeling Act?

14. Why was the Flammable Fabrics Act enacted into law?

Exercises and Projects

1. Prepare a questionnaire form that explores consumer thoughts on private label merchandise. After the form has been developed, use it as the basis for a research project. Methodology for data collection should be determined and carried out by the class.

2. Develop an observation form that could be used to determine customer preference for a particular fashion product. Swimsuits, for example, would be excellent for warm weather climates, and coats for the colder regions. The form should list as many styles of the selected category as possible. The information could be easily obtained from photographs in fashion magazines.

   Once the form has been completed, teams should be assigned to places where the merchandise is worn and counts of the different styles should be recorded. By tabulating the results, a customer preference determination can be made.

3. Write to a regulatory agency, such as the Federal Trade Commission, for information on the different legislation they oversee that protects the consumer. With the information, prepare an oral report for delivery to the class.

The Case of the Disloyal Customer

Granvilles is a specialized department store that is located in the northeastern part of the United States. It has been in operation for the past fifty years, opening first its flagship store. With significant success, it opened twelve branch operations. Except for the flagship store, which is located in a busy downtown area, the other units are located in upscale, regional malls.

The store has always restricted its merchandise mix to men's, women's, and children's apparel and accessories. The price points are at levels that appeal primarily to upper middle class families. Until three years ago, Granvilles had been extremely profitable. Sales continued to increase, and management was totally satisfied with the showing.

During the last three years, however, there has been a noticeable decline in sales volume and profits. After carefully assessing its method of operation, management concluded that it was not doing anything different now then it had in the past. The only possible explanation for the decline in sales was competition from a major off-price retailer who was carrying some of the same designer labels at lower prices. Although Granvilles appealed to the manufacturers to stop shipping to its rival, the request was ignored. By selling to the off-price retailer, the manufacturers were able to dispose of leftovers at the season's end.

After numerous meetings, management decided that it could bring back some customers by adding private label merchandise to its inventory. Recognizing that the customer was important to the success of Granvilles, management decided to scientifically study the problem before making any final decision.

Questions

1. Has Granvilles properly defined its problem?

2. What type of research would you suggest that Granvilles undertake to solve its problem? Why?

Whatever Happened to Customer Loyalty?

As the retail wars intensify and as the markets of the 90's continue to be reshaped by more value-conscious consumers and radically new systems of retail distribution, a new debate is emerging regarding "customer loyalty". At its nucleus, the issue is the age-old question of what drives consumer purchases the most. Is it price, quality, service, image or convenience?

The outcome of this debate is of no small consequence since it forms the core selling philosophy of today's retail industry. For manufacturers, customer loyalty has been sought through the development of "brand equity" and "power brands". This is what is achieved, purportedly, through sustained, high quality, national and global advertising. Such positioning enabled a product or manufacturer to be "top of mind" as consumers considered their purchase needs.

At the retail end, power brands have also been important in a variety of key ways. Retailers initially drew people into their stores by featuring power brands. In so doing, many retailers developed into "brands" themselves and the strongest became the "anchors" that determined the success of shopping malls.

For manufacturers and stores alike, it is clear that the customer loyalties of the past are gone and that there is a new set of dynamics driving consumer purchasing patterns. Several events occurred to destroy the conditions that had built customer loyalty.

Power Brands Are Everywhere

The days when power brands were the primary drawing cards for department stores have been replaced by ubiquitous availability. Because of a variety of factors—overcapacity in manufacturing, for one—power brands began appearing in mass merchandisers and then discounters and then through the mail and then in factory outlets.

As this occurred, the role and value of "power brands" changed. Not only were they no longer something any outlet could claim to carry with exclusivity, the price consumers had to pay for them varied all over the lot.

The New Category Killers

To capitalize on the changing conditions, "category killer" retailers have emerged, purchasing power brands in specific categories, concentrating on making them available to consumers with the greatest selection at the lowest price.

Intelligent, Value-Conscious Consumers

Over the past decade, consumers have gotten a whole lot smarter about their purchasing and are now naturally attracted to the option that allows them to buy what they need at the "low price".

A sustained period with little growth in disposable income has naturally led consumers toward a position where price has become a more significant component of the overall purchase decision.

These and such developments as product parity, lower disposable income, time pressures, and so on, have eroded both traditional brand loyalty and store loyalty to a large degree. Both still exist, but the lines between brand, store, price and "service" as the key selling points are blurring.

Brand Loyalty Sways

One of the first victims of these shifts has been brand loyalty. Throughout the consumer product spectrum, few brands have remained unscathed despite their prior levels of loyalty. And, this is not an issue that just affects consumers in the lower income brackets; indeed, this lack of purchasing commitment has affected those in the $50,000-plus range.

A national poll conducted by New York advertising agency Warwick Baker & Fiore last March found that 90% of shoppers who go to the store for frequently purchased items go with a specific strategy for saving money. And they are paying careful attention to just how much they save. What is more, this shopping behavior crosses age groups and sexes. Among those "most likely" to believe they save money by using coupons and sales are men, consumers aged 35 to 54, college graduates, working women and married women.

Shifts In Store Loyalty

Where people are shopping is clearly driven by options that are offering the greatest value relative to price. This has produced the dramatically successful factory outlet malls. The loyalty to regional malls has changed profoundly over the past decade.

Nearly three hundred factory outlet malls have opened nationwide since 1990. Why do people go? Is it because of the prices, the brands or the mall itself? Are these the people who used to go to department stores because they carried the power brands? Or are these people who always wanted power brands but couldn't afford them? Total Research (Princeton, New Jersey) says its research indicates that the typical customer "is a person enamored with brands and saving money". And the average customer seems to be more than satisfied with the outlet shopping experience. A recent survey of 2,100 shoppers in 13 of these centers revealed that the average customer visits them 10 times a year and that one in six visits them four times a month.

How about strip malls? These are opening at the rate of 2,000 a year. Who shops there? These malls are patronized by 89% of adult Americans, with 24% shopping there exclusively (compared to the 5% who shop only at regional shopping centers). The average customer shops seven times a month compared to the two trips a month experienced by the regional malls.

The profile of the people who shop at these places show a full range of income and education levels. And, with more than half in the $50,000-plus income bracket, strip centers are attracting the group sought after by the more upscale regional malls.

And what is a Bloomingdale's, Macy's or Nordstrom's clearance center? A discount outlet or a downscaled department store?

Some Answers Surface

Behind all this lies the most important structural change in the economy—perhaps the most significant we have experienced in our lifetime. It goes way beyond any particular format or pricing strategy. To view it as one or the other is a mistake for anyone in the business.

What is going on is akin to the management/organizational strategy of the day, "re-engineering": a process that re-aligns all of the elements within a system so that there is the least possible waste and the highest possible quality outcome.

This re-structuring has been generated by the recognition that modern technology is not just a tool to allow us to do what we have always done faster, or cheaper, or better. It is, instead, a powerful tool that enables us to accomplish our objectives in new ways—if we organize the entire system of production, distribution and sales to maximize the contribution all these technologies can make.

Wal-Mart, Home Depot, Kmart, JC Penney, Levi Strauss, Proctor & Gamble, Taco Bell, Dell Computer, outlet malls and others are not engaged in some form of pricing competition. They are engaged in innovative attempts to significantly improve the efficiency and quality of getting a product to the consumer through the implementation of systems that utilize the best of modern computer and telecommunications technologies. Retailers are forced to confront and challenge a wide range of "business as usual" aspects within the retail system. *The resulting sales mechanics are so new that many of the traditional powers in our economy are having serious difficulty understanding and responding to what they perceive to be some form of pricing or marketing strategy.*

Knowing about the many discount options mass merchandisers and discounters provide, consumers want it all: rock-bottom prices, the highest possible quality, the greatest service and the least hassle. Consumers will, then, reward those places where this set of demands is most reliably met.

Smart retailers have worked hard to create systems that can accommodate this new marketplace reality. They are essentially striving to achieve "store loyalty and enthusiasm" capable of attracting and keeping "smart" customers.

Indeed, retailers need to ensure that they are able to obtain the products their customers want, at the lowest possible cost; they also know this is one buying group that won't stay around long if disappointed. *This has created a new type of vendor who will work in partnership with retailers to reduce the time and the costs throughout the entire "system" associated with finally putting the goods in the customers' hands.*

Another key to the changes is the renewed importance of the salesperson, whose knowledge and behavior must sustain, rather than contradict, this dedicated effort toward higher customer satisfaction.

What is evolving, then, is an integrated, seamless process from the point-of-sale all the way through to the raw material purchases of the vendors. This opens a whole new set of opportunities and a need to re-think the brand-store-image-price-service equation.

Mapping *Real* Consumer Behavior

In every retail outlet, a unique set of consumers enter a particular selling environment created by the net result of retailer decisions on such things as lighting, placement, music, signage, facings, and so on. Solid intelligence about what is really going on in the store can best be gained not by asking people questions or by bar code analysis, but by actually observing how people move through the store, where they stop, what they do, what choices they make, etc. Then, any change that is introduced among any of the designated variables can be assessed based on its impact on the changes in movement and behavior patterns.

It was impossible to do in the past and difficult to do five years ago, but it is a piece of cake today if one applies modern video technologies to the task of observation.

Hi-Tech Sharpens Focus

Modern technology is making cameras increasingly more sophisticated and capable of being digitally managed: more importantly, they are getting smaller and can be placed almost anywhere in a nonob-trusive manner. This makes it possible to record what really goes on in a retail environment at any time. The resulting data can then be evaluated in terms of what has indeed occurred. The actual impact of change in any aspect of the merchandising strategy can be weighed; strategic alterations in the retail setting can be addressed and implemented as deemed necessary.

Envirosell Tracks Consumer Footprints for Clues

Sounds so simple, perhaps, and it is! It is successfully being implemented in several environments. One of the pioneers in this new technique is Envirosell, a New York-based firm which has spent several years getting in the trenches with the consumer through these video-based observations. "By actually observing the behavior of real customers in a real store, we have learned some important lessons, many of which are contrary to common wisdom," says Paco Underhill, Managing Partner, Envirosell. "For example, dramatic end-cap displays for some items are totally dysfunc-tional. A quiet part of the store is much better for anything which the customer actually wants to spend some time handling or thinking about. Not everything can be effectively sold in a nano-second."

The experiences with this approach have underscored important aspects of consumer behavior. For example, it has been shown that consumers actually approach the majority of items at an angle as they walk down an aisle. This has profound implications for packaging, display and signage. Great graphics which do not get readily observed within the actual display have little real value.

To be sure, technology will continue to transform the way we all do business: by increasing the speed, volume and efficiency with which we can accomplish things, by making "close to the customer" a reality instead of a slogan, and also by allowing us to gain true insights into what occurs in the moments leading up to a purchase decision. That's precious information for tomorrow's marketing plans.

Retail Futures, Vol. I, No. 2.

Consumer Infidelity

Robin Lewis

Women are fickle, if not downright promiscuous, when it comes to where they buy their intimate apparel and hosiery. She'll buy a bra in Wal-Mart, Penney's, Nordstrom, or Victoria's Secret, according to whatever tickles her fancy at the moment. She'll buy sleepwear in Saks, panties in Kmart and hosiery at Ann Taylor, depending on the mood that moves her.

Cross-shopping, or the purchase of different apparel items in different stores or retail channels, is here. Store loyalty for the lifetime apparel needs of any one consumer appears to be a thing of the past.

While department stores once had the lion's share of intimate apparel, their position has been under constant fire, mainly by the discounters and specialty stores, which have been steadily taking chunks of their business.

Discounters, in fact, now control the largest share of the intimate apparel category. In hosiery, the discounters and food/drug outlets dominate and, along with direct mailers, continue to capture more share. Department store share continues to slip.

These shifts are clearly consumer-driven, as consumers exploit virtually unlimited shopping options.

If it's a rush to save time, a consumer might seek the convenience of a specialty store nearby. If the goal is spending less, she might pursue discount store options. Or, if her value requirement is for a more fashion-forward item, the consumer may shop across several department and specialty stores.

This is a consumer who is loyal to no one, who has different value needs at different times and is clearly taking advantage of an overabundance of choice.

However, while the consumer may appear to be promiscuous about where she shops, she's actually more discerning than ever. They buy for very specific reasons. They're also smarter and have a clear idea of what an item is worth. Finally, they know precisely where they can get the best value for the least amount of time and effort.

None of this has to do with having a favorite store, although a shopper may have six favorite stores across all distribution channels. In fact, what some see as promiscuity is really polygamy: the new consumer is discriminately married to many different stores for many different occasions and needs.

The same polygamy exists when choosing between the national brands and private label (which includes store brands). Indeed, in every category except bras, private label is growing in market share while the brands are losing. This indicates both a discerning and more intelligent consumer; she makes a purchase decision based on her own specific value equation, as opposed to being lured simply by the lowest price or the more ephemeral promises of a brand's advertising.

The apparent loyalty to the national brands in the bra category, in addition to the fact that women are willing to pay regular price, merely reinforces the concept of the discriminating consumer. Part of this loyalty obviously stems from the consumers' requirements for fit, function and comfort. However, it also points to the fact that the branded suppliers long ago focused on learning what their consumer wanted in a bra and then painstakingly designed, merchandised and marketed their product. Apparently, they are still doing so today. The bra experience provides a clear example of successful strategies that might well be employed by the suppliers and retailers in the other product categories, in order to court the cross-shopper.

As with bras, hosiery brands apparently provide added value over private label. Although the consumer's product requirements are somewhat different than for bras, if she can find those values more conveniently, and at prices she perceives as fair, the type of store she buys from is not a major concern. This is clearly a product category in which the knowledgeable and discerning consumer has a specific set of value requirements and knows the retail outlets that can deliver them.

In many cases, the stores she chooses are brand names themselves, such as Victoria's Secret, which, from the consumers' perspective, provide value equal to the "national brands." Therefore, this form of private labeling will continue to grow. It provides the consumer with branded value and provides the retailer with greater pricing and margin flexibility.

So, as they improve their sourcing skills, retailers will increasingly compete with the national brands. In effect, they will be marketing their stores as brands. And for those that have outlets nationwide, their sheer physical presence is equivalent to a powerful advertising campaign.

Another indication of a more knowledgeable and discerning consumer is the fact that she is increasingly willing to pay regular price in retail channels that are generally recognized for their lower prices. This describes a consumer who has a clear idea of what something is worth, relative to where she's buying it. It also describes a store that understands this consumer's value equation and knows how to deliver it. Therefore, the consumer will seek the product in that store and happily pay what's asked. These discerning shoppers are also increasing their purchases in these stores at the expense of other retailers who have not responded to the value demands of the consumer.

While the largest share of shoppers across all channels spans the 30-to-64-year-old age group, the 30-to-44 segment is growing at a faster clip. There are also higher incomes across almost all channels, which again signals a heightened selectivity, regardless of traditional perceptions of what a store may have represented in the past. In fact, in the discount tier, consumers with incomes over $60,000 comprise the fastest-growing share. This dramatically illustrates that cross-shopping for different values, across all store types, will be with us well into the next century.

Shopping Amid TV Lounges, Fax Machines and Espresso Bars

Evelyn Nieves

The sun worshippers are absorbing their last rays of the summer. Soon, the beaches will close. Then, inexorably, the chill will come and time for a sweater, preferably a cotton argyle with a touch of chocolate brown.

Major clothes-shopping season is here, the most wonderful time of the year for major clothes shoppers. What's not to love? The Sunday papers are fat with back-to-school circulars, white shoes will soon be gone from sight and all the other hardcore shopping buffs are out of their closets, running around the stores to bring home new stuff.

It's something to see when the shoppers are out in force, as they are here at the Mall at Short Hills. Since the mall opened a new $100 million wing last week—it has three new department stores and 35 new smaller stores—it's become a hardcore shoppers' happening. The major leaguers are clamoring to compare the Neiman Marcus with the Nordstrom, the Nordstrom with the Saks. Not to mention the espressos at Dean & DeLuca and Au Bon Pain. It's inspiring, in a way, to know one great American pastime is in no danger of becoming stale.

"Gangway," said Keila Johnson, making a beeline for the directory of new stores the minute she walked in the mall's south entrance. "I've got some serious shoe shopping to ponder."

Tyra O'Neill was looking for a jacket and skort ("a skirt that's really shorts") set. "In the vintage style." Sara Rosenzweig was aiming for Gucci, Fendi and Louis Vuitton (she loves Europe). Gary Titus

wanted to see the brown loafers at Bruno Magli. "Brown is finally the new black," he said. His friend, Rog Q. Landers wanted a suit from Barneys New York. "I know it's not a new store," he said. "But we're from Manhattan. I love not paying tax for expensive clothes."

Most of the stores here are not for the timid of wallet. There is an unspoken "Don't ask, don't tell" policy; you don't ask prices, no one tells you. That's what price tags are for. But the mall has come up with new services, gimmicks to excite the "been-there, bought-that" suburbanite. Shopping colleagues can pick up beepers at information counters, to page one another if they decide to split up for some solo shopping.

Phyllis Castellano, a frequent shopper, got a real kick out of the Frequent Parker Card that Neiman Marcus offers at its valet parking pad. "One free park for every 10," she said. "That's cute."

At Nordstrom's concierge desk, you can ask for someone to carry your bags to your car or send a fax. The store also has a lounge with a television. ("Who needs that when they're shopping?" Ms. Castellano said.) There are also new lounge areas in the mall to park yourself in after shopping until you drop, with dried flower arrangements and leather 30's-style sofas, like the kind that Ralph Lauren sells for a zillion dollars.

Taylor Johnson, a shopaholic ("capital S") sat herself down on one, unimpressed. "We have one in the den," she said. But she almost hyperventilated with delirium when she saw the mall's new Guess? store.

"I can't breathe!" she said, clasping her hand to her 14-year-old heart. She seemed pleased at the performance, but was quickly outdone by her best friend, Rae Horowitz.

"I've already died," Rae said. "I've died! Died and gone to heaven right here."

The pair had traveled all the way from Monmouth County ("near Rumson, where Bruce Springsteen lives," Rae said) for this new shopping experience. ("We used to live close by when I was young," Taylor said.)

They are preparing for the new school year, which starts in, like, less than two weeks. "I've got so much shopping to do," Rae said. Her shopping muscles are well toned after a summer spent collecting baby T-shirts and vintage Levi's cutoffs. But now she and Taylor want clothes like those Alicia Silverstone's character wears in "Clueless." "You've seen the movie, haven't you?" Rae asks, as if everybody that matters has. "It takes a lot of coordinating to get those outfits."

Like most master shoppers, they arrived early (10 A.M.) with Rae's mother and younger sister and plotted their strategy. Rae and Taylor would go to Guess? (heaven in denim), while Rae's mom and sister would go next door to Baby Guess? Whichever pair finished first would wait for the other in Guess? Home Collection. Then to the directory to map out the rest of the day. "Real shopping," Rae said, "is a serious time."

The New York Times, August 25, 1995.

CHAPTER 4

Ever-Changing Fashion and Its Acceptance

After you have completed this chapter, you will be able to discuss:

- Various terms that comprise the *language of the trade*.

- Different stages of the fashion cycle.

- Influences on the fashion industry created by individuals and/or groups.

- Practices of copying and adapting fashion.

As we reviewed each decade of the twentieth century in Chapter 2, it was clear that fashion is ever changing. Styles come into and go out of favor. Sometimes the success of an item is extremely short-lived; other times its success survives from one season to the next. Designers need to understand what motivates consumers to change, because success in the fashion industry means encouraging consumers to discard something old for something new. If everyone wore the same garments year in and year out, the industry would generate far fewer sales.

Designers are the leading players in the field. They must use their creative talents to produce merchandise that captures the consumer's attention. Other players include product developers, merchandisers, and the media. In the end, however, the consumer makes the final decision. If the consumer is not ready to change, they will reject new styles. Consumers may choose to wear what is in their wardrobes, rather than succumb to a style change that does not reflect their needs.

In some cases, a new style can be rejected in the development process or at the manufacturer's sample stage. Buyers regularly pass over some items in favor of others. Those items that are rejected are withdrawn from the line and sold as **designer's samples** in showroom **sample sales** or to retailers who successfully merchandise such items. Although this is often disheartening to the creators of the merchandise, it is less costly to reject the item at this stage than to sell it to the stores, only to have it become a markdown. Retailers absorb considerable losses from markdowns and often remain distant from the designers and manufacturers who created them.

THE LANGUAGE OF THE TRADE

As with any industry or profession, the fashion business has its own language of the trade. To participate in the field or even just to comprehend what the world of fashion is all about, it is necessary to be familiar with the basic terminology. The most frequently used terms are defined below in alphabetical order.

Adaptation

A garment that uses the main elements of another's design, with variations on such elements as fabric, trim, and ornamentation.

Classic

An item that has staying power in the fashion industry. Although some styles fall in and out of favor, classics become staples or integral parts of wardrobes. A navy blue blazer is an example of a classic.

Collection / Line

A designer's or manufacturer's offerings for a particular season. Although line is often used interchangeably with collection, some industry participants reserve the word collection for more expensive merchandise, and line for the lower-price points.

Couturier (m) / Couturiere (f)

French terms for male and female designers of original styles that are made of expensive fabrics using fine sewing and tailoring techniques and materials. Collections are shown twice a year—spring/summer and fall/winter.

Dress-down Fridays

Days on which casual attire is accepted as proper dress in the office. Studies have found that workers are just as productive—if not more so—when they are comfortably attired. Companies such as Levi Strauss, Dayton/Hudson, Marshall Field's, and Neiman Marcus have created brochures and help lines to answer questions on what is appropriate to wear on these casual days. John Molloy's revision of his book, *Dress for Success,* will include information on dressing down.

Fad

A style that is enthusiastically accepted for a short period of time. A fad tends to gain popularity and acceptance at a brisk pace only to fall rapidly into dis-

This high-fashion design, shown on the runway, will hopefully capture the attention of the consumer.

use. *Nehru jackets,* with abbreviated collar and no lapels, were fashioned after the silhouette worn by India's prime minister, Nehru. They swept in and out of the fashion scene of the 1960s. Their quick demise cost millions to both manufacturers and retailers. In the early 1990s, however, a completely collarless style appeared on shirts. A large segment of the younger market bought these shirts in great quantities. The shirt fit perfectly with the casual direction men's wear has been taking.

The main street in New York City's garment district has been appropriately re-named Fashion Avenue.

Fashion

A style accepted by the majority of a group. The mini will always be considered a style, as will flared pants, chemise dresses, and turtleneck sweaters. They will only be considered a fashion when a majority of the consuming public accepts and purchases them.

Haute Couture

Literally it stands for fine dressmaking, but in America it has come to mean high fashion.

Knockoff

A garment that has been copied from the design of some expensive item of clothing. The silhouette and details of the more expensive model are retained, but lower costs are achieved with less expensive fabrication and construction. The knockoff is sometimes called a **copy.**

Prêt-à-porter / Ready-to-Wear

French for *ready-to-be carried* and used to describe garments that are mass-produced rather than custom-made, i.e., ready-to-wear.

Sample Sales

Periodic clearance sales that manufacturers hold to sell the styles that did not make it into production.

Seventh Avenue

The main street of New York City's garment center, but also used to refer to the entire garment district. Also called *Fashion Avenue.*

Silhouette

A garment's shape or outline. Although there are numerous variations of silhouettes in fashion, there are five basic shapes in women's apparel. They are: the tubular silhouette that falls straight; the bouffant that flares out in fullness; the A-line silhouette that falls from the shoulder extending to the hem; the wedge silhouette, which has greater width in the upper body than the lower body; and the hourglass silhouette, which has equal shoulder and hip width and exagger-

A-line Silhouette

Hourglass
Silhouette

Wedge Silhouette

Tubular
Silhouette

ated waist indentions. In men's tailored clothing, silhouettes are the American or classic-cut jacket, which employs a fullness to the garment, and the European model, which accentuates a tapering at the waistline and broad shoulders.

Style

The characteristic appearance of the garment or accessory. Skirts, for example, are a style, as are dresses, shirts, and sweaters. Sometimes there is so much variation within a style that the style actually becomes a classification, with many styles in each. For example, skirts may be flared, straight, pleated, or gored. Styles do not change, although their acceptance by customers changes periodically. Platform shoes, for example, were popular in the 1960s, and again in the early 1990s. Between those two periods, there was little interest in platform shoes, but it was still a style. A simple definition for style is "the characteristics that distinguish one garment or accessory from another."

Bouffant Silhouette

These basic women's silhouettes reappear regularly in designer collections.

Taste

A personal feeling about a particular style. When people speak of good taste, they are referring to the appropriateness of a style for a particular use or occasion. What really constitutes taste is often the opinion of some and not adhered to by everyone.

FASHION CYCLES

The term **fashion cycle** refers to a style's introduction, growth, maturity, and decline. Styles move through the cycle at different rates. Short-lived styles are called **fads** and are the industry's nightmare. With the money spent on design, fabric selection, color decision-making, garment production, and marketing, the losses from a fad's quick demise can be significant. Styles that last for at least one season are considered fashion. There is no exact time frame for each style to move through the fashion cycle; each lasts as long as there is customer acceptance. The grunge look in the early 1990s lasted a few seasons, while acceptance of the athletic shoes as fashion footwear continues.

Whatever the duration of a style's popularity, all styles go through the same stages of the cycle.

Introduction Stage

During this period, the designer's new styles are shown to the public with limited exposure. Those with the greatest success potential, as determined by such professionals in the field as fashion forecasters and the editorial press, are often hyped in the pages of the consumer fashion magazines, whose readers eagerly seek out these styles. Fashion spreads in such publications as *GQ, Elle, Seventeen, Town & Country, Essence, Vogue,* and *Harper's Bazaar* usually arouse the interest of their readers. Other styles may reflect on what is current for the new season. Some styles bear labels of distinction and are eagerly awaited by the followers of a particular collection.

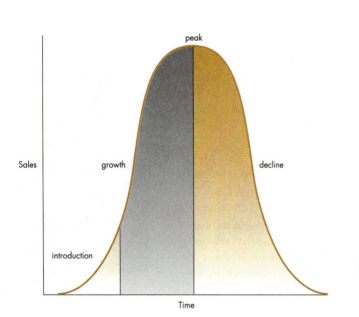

The fashion cycle.

The introduction stage is the phase of the cycle at which the styles are most expensive. Take for example a couturier's creation. It is painstakingly developed using the finest fabrications and hand workmanship, and may sell for several thousand dollars. Its introduction is risky and expensive. If it is too radical for acceptance, the designer's reputation may suffer. Of course, if the style finds acceptance at this highest price point, adaptations or copies will move into the marketplace and find wider consumer acceptance.

Growth Stage

Once the style seems to catch fire, lower priced variations and copies are marketed. Those consumers who were attracted to the new silhouettes, shapes, or fabric innovations, but were unable to afford the extravagantly high prices charged for the originals, can now avail themselves of the less-costly models. During the growth stage, the style may be available at a variety of price points. There is, however, a tendency for sales to decline at the highest levels once the market has been saturated with the copies.

Maturity Stage

At this stage, sales achieve their highest potential. The original style is shown at every retail level in many fabrications and adaptations. Stores such as Neiman Marcus, Saks Fifth Avenue, and Henri Bendel might still be featuring the original versions, with the specialty chains selling the lower-priced copies. How long the style remains at the height of its popularity depends upon whether consumers will continue to buy more than just one model of the style. In some cases, shoppers make a single purchase of a style, while in other cases more than one purchase may be made. The bell-bottomed and flare-legged pants of the 1970s were bought over and over again and, at that time, became **staples** in fashion wardrobes. The knickers, however, introduced in the early 1980s, generally became a one-time purchase.

At some time during this stage, the style's acceptance peaks, sales level off, and the decline stage is reached.

Decline Stage

Usually the decline stage is shorter than the introduction phase. Manufacturers of the style at the higher price level have abandoned production before this period, recognizing that less expensive copies are taking over the market. They are busy at work, with new styles as another fashion cycle begins. This point in the cycle finds the items drastically reduced in the traditional stores and at very low selling prices at the off-price retailers, who have bought manufacturer leftovers at greatly reduced prices.

When a style has completed the fashion cycle, it does not mean that the public will never again see it. Without question, most styles find their way back into favor, oftentimes as more modern interpretations of past designs. It may take anywhere from ten to fifty years or more for this to happen. Usually only one style recurs at a time. At the beginning of 1995, however, numerous reoccurring styles made the rounds from a number of previous decades. The styles, shapes, and silhouettes that were once in favor—such as the belted suit of the 1940s, padded jackets and pointy pumps of the 1950s, and the wrap dress of the 1970s—were all resurrected, but in a slightly different way. Good styles do not generally die, they just wait long enough in the wings for someone to bring them back into the mainstream of fashion.

Thus, styles recur or are reinvented, sometimes reappearing as a more accepted fashion than when it was first offered to the consumer.

FASHION TRENDSETTERS AND LEADERS

When the fashion designer creates his or her collections, there is no guarantee that acceptance will follow. A great deal of promotion and fanfare generally surrounds the introduction of the new merchandise, but that only helps get the attention of the prospective market.

One sure-fire way to assure acceptance of a particular style is to have it worn by an admired member of society. These people are **trendsetters** and **fashion leaders.** In America, they are generally from the fields of entertainment and sports. Others include members of European royalty and the American first families. The common denominator of these trendsetters and fashion leaders is wealth—a necessity for participation in acquiring new and innovative fashion.

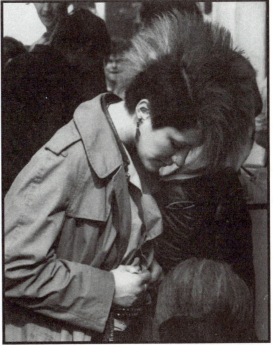

Punk fashions, exemplified by this haircut, were created on the streets.

Although we are all aware of the fashion innovations that trickle down to the masses after being created by such legendary designers as Saint Laurent, Lagerfeld, Ralph Lauren, and Calvin Klein, we often overlook *street styles,* which are creatively assembled and altered by rappers, ravers, home girls, skaters, dead head bikers, drag queens, and punks. Many of the fashions created on the street, such as creative buzz cuts, Dr. Seuss inspired hats, doorknocker earrings, cut-offs, hair extensions, nameplate chains, men's pajamas worn as baggies, tie-dyed T-shirts, neo-hippie patchwork, ethnic jewelry, truckers wallets on chains, tattoos, extreme theatrical makeup, unusually colored hair, body piercing, and latex gear, have achieved significant recognition from the fashion world. These trends all owe their appearance to concrete streets, not runways. Designers such as Todd Oldham, Anna Sui, Jean Paul Gaultier, and even the House of Chanel are continuously revitalized and energized by the street/club scene.

An examination of people from the entertainment world, the sports scene, and the important families of Europe and America shows how important these people are as trendsetters, from both **top down** as well as **bottom up fashions.**

The Entertainment World

People all over have a fascination with the stars of stage, screen, and television. They have influenced clothing, hairstyles, and makeup. Some celebrities have influenced fashion through their own style of dress, while others have started trends based upon the attire worn by the characters they have portrayed.

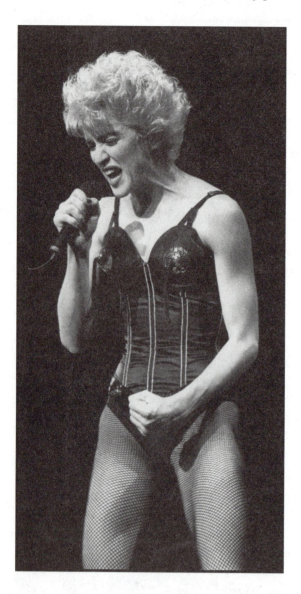

Madonna in her attire by Jean-Paul Gaultier caused a great stir in the fashion world.

One of the most popular movie stars of the 1940s was Joan Crawford. Her followers often imitated the styles she wore on and off the screen, particularly the exaggerated, broad-shouldered jacket. Women everywhere wore them. The broad shoulder favored by Joan Crawford, as well as other styles that became important in fashion, were designed by Adrian, one of Hollywood's legendary designers. See a World of Fashion Profile focusing on the talents of Adrian.

Other stars were also considered fashion leaders. Marlene Dietrich wore suits that resembled those worn by men, and soon had a rash of followers dressing that way. Katharine Hepburn, who never wore a dress in her personal life, helped make pants standard and appropriate dress for every occasion. Cary Grant favored the drape suit worn by the Duke of Windsor and helped bring it into prominence for men.

When rock 'n' roll took the world by storm, not only was the music new, but so were the styles worn by the famous groups. The Beatles quickly influenced the world with their hit tunes and their fashions. Their mod suits became the rage, and their famous haircuts were soon seen on a great number of their youthful followers.

Today's stars also influence the way consumers dress. Two stars recently imitated have been Madonna and Michael Jackson. She popularized sexy dressing and wore undergarments as outerwear, with a widespread use of lace and a bustier. Michael Jackson's preference for the single glove had teenagers all over the world wearing the solo glove as part of their dress.

T A B L E 4 . 1

FASHION LEADERS AND THE STYLES THEY POPULARIZED

Fashion Leaders	Styles Popularized
British Royalty	
Duke of Windsor	Knickers, patterned sweaters, drape suit, glen plaids, the "Windsor" knot.
Lady Diana	Wedding dress, slicked hairstyle.
First Families	
Jackie Kennedy	Pillbox hat, A-line skirts, empire-waist gowns, low-slung pumps, bouffant hairstyle, oversized sunglasses.
John Kennedy	Hatless and coatless appearances led to decline in sales of hats and overcoats; Izod knit shirt worn under sport coat.
Nancy Reagan	Chanel-type suits, the color red.
Barbara Bush	Faux pearls
Bill Clinton	Nylon running shorts.
Entertainers	
Joan Crawford	Broad shoulders.
Marlene Deitrich	Male-inspired suits.
Cary Grant	The drape suit.
The Beatles	Mod suits, long hair.
Madonna	Sexy dressing, lace fabrics, the bustier.
Michael Jackson	One glove.
Bruce Springsteen	Jeans, T-shirts, earring.
Cindy Crawford	Face mole as a "beauty mark."

The Beatles' mod attire and hairstyles influenced fashion in the 1960s.

Adrian

A graduate of New York City's School of Fine and Applied Arts, Gilbert Adrian, who dropped his first name when he was discovered by Hollywood, continued his studies in Paris. There he met one of America's foremost composers, Irving Berlin, who assisted him in getting the costuming assignment for Broadway's *Music Box Revues,* *Greenwich Village Follies,* and George White's *Scandals.*

In 1923, Adrian went to Hollywood to design costumes for Rudolf Valentino, one of the most important early movie stars. From that time until 1939, he was the studio's chief designer. In addition to creating costumes for Joan Crawford, he also designed for such greats as

Katharine Hepburn and Rosalind Russell.

His signature designs were sleek, long jackets accentuated by broad shoulders and narrow waists. This silhouette would become Joan Crawford's favorite. For evening wear, his clothing for the films was generally of the "romantic" look, often using flowing organdy as the fabric. His *Letty Lynton gown,* designed for Crawford was the rage of the day. It was reported that Macy's alone sold more than 500,000 pieces!

He ultimately left the world of entertainment and opened his own studio, where he created both couture and expensive ready-to-wear.

Adrian, primarily known as costume designer for films, also designed couture and ready-to-wear.

a .Women in the 1970s were influenced by the Annie Hall *film. b. It didn't take long for the public to don the Ray-Ban sunglasses worn by Tom Cruise in* Risky Business. *c. Young men wore a T-shirt and sport jacket combination emulating the wardrobes worn on* Miami Vice. *d. Television shows like* Melrose Place *set the fashion preferences for its viewing audience.*

Even more influential than the stars themselves were the characters they played in films or on television. Annie Hall, a character created by Woody Allen, not only become a memorable film role, but also a major look for the late 1970s. Women all over America were wearing the Annie Hall outfit, replete with oversized men's shirts, very long skirts, baggy khaki pants, and men's hats.

As soon as John Travolta wore his white disco suit in *Saturday Night Fever,* young men everywhere adapted the style as their own. It was one of the most popular suits ever worn by the young.

The curly hair faze was popularized by Barbra Streisand in the movie, *A Star is Born.* The movie *Grease,* filmed in the late 1970s, quickly brought leather motorcycle jackets into fashion; *Flashdance,* one of the hottest films of the 1970s helped to popularize gray sweatshirt fabric as a fashion material; *Risky Business* and Tom Cruise popularized Ray-Ban's Wayfarer® sunglasses; and *Urban Cowboy* brought the western-look to urban America.

The live-to-shop image created by characters in the film Clueless, *made it the fashion movie of the summer of 1995.*

The summer of 1995 was witness to a movie that brought teenage fashions to a new level. Unlike the typical grunge dress of the time, *Clueless* brought fashions to the screen that would hopefully impact the junior market. Parading around in glamorous styles designed by Anna Sui, Dolce & Gabbana, Martine Sitbon, and Donna Karan, the characters were dressed more for Rodeo Drive than the traditional malls. Only time will tell if it will redirect teenage fashion.

On television, Western wear fashioned after the men in the nighttime soap, *Dallas,* was quickly the rage. All over the country, men were wearing jeans, boots, and western shirts, all topped with Stetsons, or cowboy hats. Don Johnson was being groomed as a star in *Miami Vice,* and his mode of dress included the T-shirt worn under an Armani sportcoat in pastel colors, a look that soon became popular with young men. Sockless feet in loafers were also a Johnson trend. Over on the *Dynasty* set, designer Nolan Miller was creating the widest shouldered silhouettes for Linda Evans and Joan Collins, which soon became one of fashion's styles of that decade. Jennifer Aniston's hairstyle in the television series, *Friends,* as well as the clothes worn by the entire cast, is a recent influence.

(left) Elegant fashions, inspired by the costumes of Nolan Miller for Dynasty, *became one of fashions hottest trends of the 1980s.*
(right) The hairstyles and clothing worn by the cast of Friends *greatly influenced the youth market in the 1990s.*

In the 1980s, rock 'n' roll stars, such as Bruce Springsteen, helped make T-shirts and jeans standard dress for the younger crowd. Rap took center stage in the early 1990s and brought with it the low rise, baggy pants that soon were worn by many teenagers.

The Sports World

Every sport requires a particular mode of dress for its participants. With the rising popularity of sports and the growing number of spectators, it is easy to understand why many fans have adopted their styles of dress from their favorite sports and athletes.

Basketball, for example, has given the athletic footwear industry an enormous boost by popularizing certain models worn by the stars. Michael Jordan and the Air Jordans became the favorite of most teenage boys. Even at prices that approached $200 a pair, they became top sellers. Companies such as Nike manufacture and distribute a whole host of athletic footwear and apparel in stores all over the world, as well as in their own superstores, Nike Towns.

Golf, with its fashion oriented colors and designs worn by the major players, has encouraged the fashion industry to produce the same styles for streetwear. The wide-brimmed hat popularized by golf star Greg Norman has become a favorite on and off the links. Designers such as Giorgio Armani and Ralph Lauren have designed golfwear, which is influenced by their signature looks.

Aerobic sports, bicycling, and boxing have also influenced fashion, with leotards, double-layer shorts, bicycle pants, and aerobic shoes.

Football and hockey jerseys, sporting the names of teams and the player numbers, are common among young and old. As soon as a new team surfaces or a new star emerges, the gear worn on the field is quickly translated into wearing apparel.

Greg Norman, the golf legend, popularized the wide-brimmed hat for golfers.

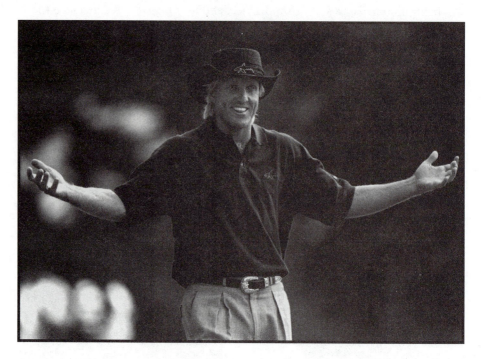

Skiing, of course, has introduced the world to a whole new wardrobe. Initially, ski apparel was designed of functional fabrics that maintained warmth. The fashion industry, however, immediately benefitted when people of all ages embraced the styles for everyday wear.

Even the fishing vest, with its host of pockets, has been embraced by fashion enthusiasts, and the bandanna worn by Andre Agassi on the tennis court has become a fashion staple for many.

As soon as a new sports figure receives the attention of the fans, the fashion industry is sure to follow with apparel that mimics his or her choices.

British Royalty

Although the members of royal families are generally not known for their fashion acumen, some have left their marks as fashion leaders. Most notable have been the Duke of Windsor and Lady Diana, the Princess of Wales.

The Duke of Windsor, a member of the British royal family, was the heir to King George V. After the King's death, the Duke became Edward VIII, but abdicated before his coronation to marry Wallis Simpson, an American divorcee. He began a private life that made him a fashion celebrity. Wherever he went, he was immediately recognized for his keen sense of fashion. He helped to popularize knickers, which he wore for casual dress, and the patterned sweaters that accompanied them. He also wore the English drape suit, which was more comfortable because it had more fabric in the shoulders and chest and fell softly on the wearer to form a wrinkle or drape. Finally, he sported glen plaid woolens, which men all over the world were soon wearing, and the Windsor knot—a wider knot than the traditional tie knot. Not only were his choices popular during his day, but the popularity of some have remained constant.

Lady Diana has also emerged as a royal family member to watch. Her youth and regal beauty enabled her to break from the more conservative traditions of dress favored by the British royals. Her choices sometimes have caused some consternation among other members of the royal family. Her wedding dress was quickly copied and was worn by brides all over the world. In 1995, she was a presenter at the Council of Fashion Designer's Awards extravaganza. Her appearance was recorded by every important fashion publication and television news broadcast. Her now-famous hairdo was greeted with enthusiasm and was copied by women all over the world.

America's First Families

Ever since television started to play a prominent role in American politics, we have been able to inspect our leaders more closely. Not only are we able to judge their political strengths and weaknesses, but we may immediately evaluate their appearances.

The influence of television became clear with the election of John Kennedy as President in 1960. For the first time Americans had a closeup view of a first family that was unlike those that came before them. The Kennedys were young, vital, and charismatic. We recognized that the family was different in stature and dress from the Eisenhowers, Trumans, and Roosevelts. A World of Fashion Profile focuses attention on the Kennedys and how they influenced fashion.

The Kennedy's

John Kennedy was a member of the famous Kennedy family of Boston. As he climbed the political ladder that would eventually bring him to the presidency, he married Jacqueline Bouvier, a young socialite. Increasingly, their pictures were featured in newspapers, magazines, and on television, and on the fashion pages of industry publications, such as *Women's Wear Daily*, that were earmarked for those in the world of fashion.

Jackie would quickly begin to set some of fashion's newest trends. For her husband's inauguration in 1961, she wore a pillbox hat designed by Halston. The style quickly caught fire and was worn by women all over America. Before long, whatever she wore was copied. Attending Sunday mass, she often covered her bouffant hairstyle with a mantilla. Both the bouffant hairstyle and black lace mantillas became the rage, as did A-line skirts and low-slung pumps. When she appeared at a ball wearing an empire-waist gown, that too quickly became a mainstay in evening wardrobes. Even the oversized, wraparound sunglasses that

The Kennedy's were the most emulated political family.

framed her face were copied by eyewear manufacturers at every price point.

John Kennedy was also watched by the public, and immediately received negative publicity from the

men's hat industry when he went bareheaded to his inauguration. The hatless Kennedy was held responsible for the decline of hats worn by men. He soon, after much persuasion, carried a hat to show that he still used one. He was also criticized by overcoat manufacturers, because he was regularly seen without one. He often appeared only in a suit, no matter how inclement the weather. Men followed his lead and shed their coats.

In a more positive vein, John Kennedy had some responsibility for moving the Izod® knit shirt, emblazoned with the famous alligator, from relatively limited use to new fashion heights. He and the rest of the male Kennedy clan wore the shirt as a favorite under sport coats for many social events—not just for activewear. It soon became standard dress for many men.

After Kennedy's assassination, Jackie remained a favorite of fashion enthusiasts. At the time of her death, she was still considered one of the most influential fashion leaders of the century.

Nancy Reagan was another First Lady whose interest in and attention to fashion was carefully reported by the press. She was especially fond of James Galanos evening gowns and Adolfo's Chanel-type suits. She favored the color red and American women soon chose red as their favorite color.

Barbara Bush, although an unlikely candidate for fashion distinction, made her own mark on the industry. She was not what fashion enthusiasts would consider the perfect model-type. Her matronly figure, was, however, one to which older, more mature women could relate. When she wore the now famous royal blue gown to her husband's inauguration, and later used the color in many other outfits, it was quickly adopted by those women who normally were not considered to be fashion plates. Her preference for oversized, faux pearls quickly caught the attention of manufacturers of costume jewelry. The accessory became one of the most purchased of the decade.

The Clintons were also carefully studied for their personal preferences. Whenever Hillary changed hairstyles—and it was often—they were quickly criticized. Bill Clinton, regularly seen jogging in nylon shorts, unintentionally has become a fashion influence on active sportswear.

Once designers finish their creations and send them down the runways, their success or failure depends on their acceptance or rejection by the consumer markets for which they were designed.

In the world of fashion, acceptance at the highest level comes at the hands of those who influence fashion—those whose choices are imitated by admirers, known as **fashion followers.** As we have seen, many of the fashion influencers and leaders are from royalty, the political arena, and the entertainment world. When an individual has a large following, their clothes are often emulated by their fans. Most people have neither the time, the confidence, nor the money to create their own fashion direction. Thus, they rely on those they admire for direction.

COPYING AND ADAPTING STYLES FOR EVERY PRICE POINT

It should be understood that for the vast majority of consumers to embrace a style, it must be copied or adapted at lower price points. At one time, a style originated at the couture level and eventually made its way down to ready-to-wear. What remained constant was the style; the fabrics, construction, and details changed to fit the different price structure. Today some fashions originate in the street, and then make their way into manufacturer's lines.

A style that originates at the couture level, and becomes an accepted fashion generally follows this route:

1. The design originates at the highest price point and is first introduced on the runway.

2. At fashion shows, editors of consumer magazines and trade publications critique the collections and report their opinions. The audiences also include wealthy private clients, invited celebrities, and retail fashion directors.

3. Some retailers purchase the actual couture styles or copies from manufacturers.

4. At this higher price level, the fashion innovators are the purchasers. They wear their selections to places where they will be seen by the press, which will often show pictures of them in their publications or will write about them in their columns.

5. Those styles that seem destined for popularity will be copied or adapted by manufacturers at every price point.

Faux pearls worn by First Lady Barbara Bush were an important fashion accessory.

6. The copies are then sold in department and specialty stores to those who follow fashion, but are unable to buy at the higher price points.

7. At the end of the cycle, the styles lose their appeal and are often found in off-price and discount stores.

8. As the particular style bottoms-out, the couturier is ready to dazzle the fashion trendsetters with a new collection.

Chapter Highlights

- People in fashion speak a particular language. In order to be a professional in the field, you need a working knowledge of that jargon.

- The fashion industry is cyclical in nature. A design moves through the various phases of the fashion cycle, from its creation through its eventual decline.

- Although the designer is credited with creating the latest styles, much of today's fashion originates in the streets.

- No matter where the styles are born, success comes only after they are worn by fashion leaders and trendsetters. The individuals who influence fashion are generally affluent and come from such visible segments of society as the entertainment world, royalty, and politics.

- Once a particular fashion has been created and popularized it filters down to fashion followers.

Important Fashion Terminology and Concepts

adaptation	fashion follower	Seventh Avenue
bottom up fashion	fashion leader	silhouette
classic	haute couture	staples
collection	knockoff	style
couturier (-iere)	language of the trade	taste
dress-down Fridays	line	top down fashion
fad	prêt-à-porter	trendsetter
fashion	ready-to-wear	
fashion cycle	sample sales	

For Review

1. Define the term sample sale.

2. Differentiate between the terms fashion and fad.

3. Describe the stages of the fashion cycle.

4. From what walks of life do most fashion trendsetters and influencers come? Give some examples.

5. How did the Kennedy family influence fashion?

6. Give examples of styles that were popularized by entertainment celebrities.

7. Where can consumers purchase the styles that have reached the bottom of the fashion cycle?

8. As styles are "bottoming-out," what is happening to make the cycle begin again?

Exercises and Projects

1. Find pictures from consumer fashion magazines, newspapers, and trade periodicals that visually describe each term defined in the section "The Language of the Trade." Create an illustrated table. Under each picture list the term.

2. Using a history of fashion text or magazine articles as sources, select a memorable apparel or accessory design that was first successful, died from popularity, and was then resurrected. Indicate the style, its years in original favor, when it was reintroduced, and the length of time it lasted for each period. Obtain photographs of the original style and describe how it was marketed in later years.

3. Prepare a list of motion picture films and television programs in which the garments worn by characters were considered fashion innovations (include classic and current films). Refer to texts on the history of costume for information. For each film indicated, find a photograph to depict the styles popularized.

4. Compile an illustrated table that features five rock stars and the fashions they were responsible for bringing to their fans. Each style should be shown worn by the entertainer.

The Case of the Calculated Risk

Every year since her company began, fashion designer Tracey Gordon has been a success. Creating apparel collections for women at the better price points catapulted her into the forefront of the fashion industry. Season after season, her collections featured styles that pleased her followers. Her designs were often worn by people from the entertainment industry. They include actresses of stage and screen and several of the more successful hosts on talk shows and television news magazines. With well-known women wearing her garments, her styles are regularly seen on the pages of fashion publications, which cover the events attended by her famous clientele.

As with every designer, Tracey is always at work creating next season's line. For her to continue her successful path, new styles are always in the works. Not only will the newer items generate business, but they will be there, ready for sale, when the older styles start to decline in popularity. Being aware of the cycles through which fashion moves and understanding that even the most successful items will eventually fall from favor, she stops the old style's production as soon as it shows signs of lower sales. Rarely

Question

Should Tracey go against the traditional fashion cycle used as a barometer for her company and try to "stretch" the cycle for another season with the company's hot item? Defend your answer using the discussion in the chapter on fashion cycles and the route taken by successful styles.

does she carry the same design from one season to the next. This is an effort to lower the losses that occur when styles stop selling. She is fully aware of the fact that her best designs will be copied at lower price points, making the originals less likely to sell.

This past season, Tracey created the best-selling item ever produced in her workrooms. It caught fire as soon as it was shown to the public and continues to sell well. With the new season approaching, it is time to abandon the old and concentrate on the new. The aforementioned style, however, is still at the maturity stage, and does not appear to be slowing down. Even with copies at lower prices, her original item is still hot in the upscale stores.

She and her management team have been holding discussions for the last three weeks to decide whether or not, for the first time in the company's history, to carry the item over to the next season.

point of view

Street Style

David Wolfe

Street style is an important fashion force today and likely to remain so. Yet for centuries the term would have been considered oxymoronic and the concept unthinkable. In reality, there was a style in the streets, in that the general population always adhered to some sort of a social dress code. Tinkers, tailors and candlestickmakers all wore clothing of a set mode depending upon the century and the geographical location in which they happened to find themselves. Primitive tribes the world over all conformed to their own style codes. Fashion, such as it was, was formulated by necessity, availability of materials, level of craftsmanship accessible and of course, affluence. The style of those fashions was not ever created by the masses who wore them. They were most often interpretations of those in a higher social strata; royalty, religious leaders, tribal chiefs or other such process whereby those less fortunate emulated their betters.

Setting the Scene for the Emergence of Street Style

That theory, a fashion filtration system from high to low, remained a secure system until the last half of the 20th century. Until then, those with money and leisure, the guardians and patrons of culture, were responsible for creating changes in style. When Marie Antoinette, on a whim, stuck feathers in her already towering coiffure, courtiers followed suit and set a style that remained until the English Court was disbanded at the advent of World War II. That same fashionable monarch also provided fashion history with one of the first examples of street style when she fantasized about being a milkmaid and had luxurious versions of peasant garb made. That small glitch aside, the trickle down system remained intact until the 1950s. Even then, most of the Western world's style was still a watered-down version of the deluxe custom made haute couture which was shown to great fanfare twice a year in Paris, a city that had long held a monopoly on fashion. However the seeds of a fashion revolution were being planted and they thrived in the fertile soil of social discontent that came on the heels of two world wars in quick succession.

Modern Street Style, Born of the Beatniks and Living in Blue Jeans

"Beatniks" as they came to be called were the first of the rebellious style setters that came from a strata of society other than the privileged echelons. They were writers, poets and artists known as "The Beat Generation" whose work expressed the disillusionment and sense of disenfranchisement that intellectuals were feeling in the midst of the economic boom that followed the end of the World War II. In blue denim jeans and black turtleneck sweaters, the Beatniks lived a lifestyle outside the rigid rules of their time and they spawned groups with similar attitudes who soon developed similar styles. "Hell's Angels" are direct style descendants of Beatniks. Such style rebels have existed before in fashion history, but usually without affecting the mainstream and certainly seldom changing the entire system. (The Aesthetic movement of the 19th century sought to bring about clothing reform, but without much success.) One item of apparel moved up from the bottom of the fashion food chain to a position of eminence unparalleled in history. The blue denim jeans pants originally made for California miners had become a "uniform" for the agricultural and lower class. When stars like James Dean and Marlon Brando flaunted their humble roots by wearing jeans, a major movement was set in place. Blue denim jeans moved up and up until they became high profile status items in the 1970s, when designers cashed in on their low-brow (and therefore sexual) image. Calvin Klein, Guess?, Jordache and surprisingly, socialite Gloria Vanderbilt all became famous as names on the labels of blue jeans.

Yves Saint Laurent Sees Style in the Streets

In 1960, one influential designer elevated the street look of the beat generation to the very heights of high fashion and in doing so, he reversed the order of the fashion system. Yves Saint Laurent had succeeded Christian Dior following his untimely death and the young genius was viewed as a powerful force. When he created a "street" inspired collection, the traditional chasm between street and style was bridged. He said, "Motorcycle jackets in alligator, mink coats with sweater sleeves, turtleneck collars under finely cut flannel suits . . . those street inspirations all seemed very inelegant to a lot of people sitting on the gilt chairs of a couture salon. But this was the first collection in which I tried hard for poetic expression in my clothes. Social structures were breaking up. The street had a new pride, its own chic, and I found the street inspiring as I would often again." That statement, a veritable manifesto, has been echoed over and over again by designers ever since.

Demographics and Electronics Explain the Rise of Street Style

Demographics must be studied in order to understand why underground style surfaced and became a major force in fashion. Military men returning from the long duration of World War II simultaneously fathered a generation of babies whose vast numbers added up to a population well known as "The Baby Boom". That generation is responsible for many economic, social and cultural changes simply because there were so many of them. But their influence cannot be accounted for by mathematics alone. As young people often had done in the past, they questioned the values of their parents and created a new society of self-indulgence that looked attractive to the older generation who felt that wartime deprivations had cheated them of their own youthful good times. So the young generation, which became known quite aptly as "The Youthquake" assumed leadership of mass culture, redefining art, music and of course, fashion.

Another revolution was occurring that made it possible for street style to emerge. Television spread popular culture to the most remote corners of the world and suddenly everyone, everywhere was exposed to the same fashion forces. The fact that advertisers were often hawking products to the emerging youth market meant that visualization had to be broad enough to penetrate a vast audience. There was no room for elitism. There were more middle and lower class kids watching TV than aristocrats, so the fashion images sent forth were targeted far, far below high fashion taste levels. "American Bandstand" was a phenomenally successful fashion vehicle although its chief purpose was the promotion of the rock and roll music emerging from the African-American subculture during the 1950s. Young men and women all over America wanted to dress exactly like the Philadelphia kids they saw dancing every afternoon on TV. It is not surprising that singers and musicians soon came to be seen as fashion role models. They were usually not from the upper strata of society and their style came from non-traditional sources. And it was embraced and emulated around the world.

Anti-Establishment Rebellion Hits the Streets

The next important chapter in American street style was written by the hippies who were the cultural descendants of the beatniks. The rigid social structure that was in place in the 1950s crumbled under the pressure of a youthful population disenchanted by the older generation's death grip on financial stability and security which the hippies came to view as stifling. They believed in "free love", in mind altering drugs and total self expression in terms of a style based upon second-hand and antique clothing, thereby making a big anti-consumerism statement.

The American post-war economy was fueled by the consumption of goods with a very short life span, whether automobiles, hit records or fashion. The hippies refuted that economic system and in doing so, they led street style into a fondness for nostalgia which lasted for decades and decades. Until that time, no one except those in dire straits would wear something old and no one would have dreamed of making something new to look as if it were old. But thrift shop style became chic and wave upon wave of nostalgia washed over fashion. In the '60s, Victoriana was in style again. In the '70s, there came revivals of the '30s and '40s and '50s. By the middle of the '90s, it was the '60s being revived. Along the way which seemed to be going backwards much of the time, there were some new developments too. In an effort to make blue denim look old and worn-out, French designers Marithe & Francois Girbaud pioneered "stone-washing", a process that broke down fabric fibers and led to years of fashions that were "distressed" and "laundered", all in an effort to make them look used.

Britain Assumes Leadership with a Little Help from the Beatles and the Punks

Music led street style across the Atlantic to England, to London and Liverpool, when the British pop music scene exploded early in the 1960s. The Beatles and other groups worked as hard on their fashion images as on their music. Having suffered far greater deprivations during the war years, it took Britain longer than the United States to recover economically and when that recovery occurred, pop culture boomed in an atmosphere of affluence and freedom. Designers such as Mary Quant (credited as the inventor of the miniskirt) and Barbara Hulanicki of Biba produced colorful, youthful and sometimes shocking designs that found immediate favor with the girl on the street. At the same time, young men paraded up and down Carnaby Street in the most outrageous outfits seen since the time of the dandy more than a century earlier.

How is it that a society usually seen as stodgy could become a breeding ground for outrageous fashions? Perhaps it is simply politeness that keeps Brits from laughing at the eccentrics who have always been accepted and cherished in the United Kingdom, everyone from Dame Edith Sitwell to Quentin Crisp and Zandra Rhodes. Only in such a tolerant environment could the Punk style of the early 1980s have been allowed to flower. It was the most rebellious, most intentionally obnoxious fashion statement that had ever been (intentionally) made. Young Britains, feeling deprived of opportunity in the work force while being supported by a socialist government, became furious and bored at the same time. They drew attention to their emotional angst with an incredibly offensive self-presentation. Heads were partially shaved and the remaining patches of hair were dyed bright colors and made to stick straight up. Safety pins were used to embellish both raggedy clothes and the flesh. T-shirts were partly burned away and pants often featured "bondage" straps to bind the legs together. Vivienne Westwood and Malcolm Maclaren visualized the style which

was sold from a shop at World's End, the area at the end of London's Kings Road in Chelsea. A musical expression plaintively shrieked by Sid Vicious went hand-in-hand with the fashions of course. Amazingly enough, the punk street style showed staying power and held sway over some young people for several decades.

MTV Broadcasts Street Style to the World

The cross-pollination of music and style became stronger still with the advent of "music videos" in the 1980s. To promote their recordings, artists began to make very complex and visually sophisticated visualizations of their music. A new television network, MTV, began in a small way but soon became a world-wide cultural institution. And the clothes the musicians wore while performing in the music videos which were repetitiously broadcast were seen by millions around the world, in time almost usurping the influence of fashion magazines in communicating style information. Again, the presentations were aimed at a low taste level because of widespread music distribution and sales. Madonna, Boy George, Cyndi Lauper and Michael Jackson styled themselves in distinctive and exciting images which were imitated everywhere. As music goes, so goes street style. When rap and hip-hop swept the music charts suddenly a new street style emerged, that of the black inner city young man in hugely oversize jeans (there is no escaping the union of denim and street style).

Is Street Style at the End of the Road?

Street style has become a victim of its own success. Now it is so influential that it is almost instantly swept up-market to more sophisticated and expensive areas. When Karl Lagerfeld picked-up the hip-hop influence for a Chanel collection, it became a sign of the times that street style had become a mainstream fashion influence. No longer does it belong solely to the young man or woman on the street. It has become difficult to define, to fence into an identifiable arena. It is, and always has been, the most accurate reflection of society at large and as the 20th century draws to an end, street style has become fragmented, almost tribal. Instant electronic communication has made every style rebellion into a mainstream, marketable commodity immediately, thus de-fusing its appeal to the young person in the street who is forced to discard it quickly and move on. Therefore, it is possible that the end of street style as a universal fashion influence is drawing to a close. Whereas once it represented an attractive, youthful, sexually charged rebellious mode of self-expression, now it can be seen as an insular and segmented reflection of a small, and often unattractive sector of modern society. Then again, perhaps that very perception will allow street style to remain on the street, the sole property of the young rebels who use self-presentation as self-expression, the ultimate aim of fashion, whether haute or low.

David Wolfe, Creative Director DE Doneger Design Direction, the Color and Trend Forecasting Division of The Doneger Group

Flip-Flop: The Runway Leads the Street

Amy M. Spindler

Like a professional virgin, street style has always claimed to resent the attention of designer suitors.

Punks in London fought against having their attire appropriated and charged to have their photographs taken. Grunge rockers satirized the designers who borrowed their thrift-shop look and gave it four-digit prices.

Yet, as designer attention has turned away from street style, there is the sense that existing outside that spotlight has made street style irrelevant. Worse, the tiny street-style houses now seem to be following designers they once led.

Whether you were a high-end designer company, a jeans manufacturer or a fast fashion factory set up to regurgitate new trends each week, you once looked to one source for inspiration: kids.

There was a time when trend forecasters, and the manufacturers who relied on them, could stay ahead of changes by watching the streets of London and New York. But now, fashion seems to be in a becalmed state of harmonic convergence. At the International Jean-swear and Sportswear show at the New York Coliseum, which closed on Sunday, that convergence was represented by one item: the lean, low-slung trousers epitomized by Gucci's fall 1995 collections.

It is a great source of consternation to magazines and store buyers who have long counted on the street to keep fashion fresh, on the edge and subversive.

"Just yesterday we were having this conversation in our office," said Ernie Glam, a fashion writer for Project X, a New York-based alternative youth-culture magazine, who was covering the show. "Before,

European designers were appropriating from the streets. What's happening now is that the street is appropriating from the designers."

The realignment first happened a year ago, when Gap basics, preppy hip-hop staples and clean rave dressing mirrored the sort of clean clothes being shown on the runway.

In the midst of those basics, Tom Ford, designing for Gucci, took fashion in a new direction. Gucci's impact was so unexpected and powerful because large companies, with the money to promote a look the way the 12-page Gucci advertisements have been able to, rarely make such radical changes. The style also had a quality that street fashion often does but that designer clothes almost never do: cool. Street-wear companies were in the strange position of following, even if some claim the look is straight from the vintage stores.

"This isn't the classic 70's cut," said Todd Resnick, the president of Vision Sales, which represents several street-wear labels. "In the 70's, everything was tight. It wasn't so lean and low riding. It's coming from the European influence—I never thought I'd be saying it, but the Gucci influence."

When big design houses were looking to street fashion for ideas, it was partly because the looks were always road-tested in a smaller market. Big design houses knew the clothes were salable because they were already being worn. That relationship changed when street wear hit a holding pattern; like most of its expensive designer counterparts, it is not evolving.

"Basically people in the street aren't wearing fashion anymore the

way they were," said Mr. Ford, who was recently in London observing the club scene. "If you look to the street for fashion, you're going to walk away with a T-shirt and jeans for inspiration. In London, especially, to make sure there wasn't a clue I wasn't picking up on, I went to three or four clubs. The only thing I could pick up on was a slight retro punk thing."

Since most recent street-wear sweeps of dress—punk, hip-hop, grunge and rap—have been tied to a new musical style, it could be that street style is somber because the sophistication of the newest music comes without a dress code.

Mr. Ford said that he listened to bands like Menswear and the Cranberries—"bands that sound like Blondie singing the Beatles"—while designing the collection but that he was imagining what people going to hear such music might wear. In clubs, the fashion wasn't mirroring the music.

"It wasn't a real-life nightclub, but an imaginary nightclub, because at the real-life nightclub I didn't see anything," he said. When there is a music hook to a look, he said, "These things are so packaged into trends, the music and the looks, and exploited to death so no one wants to see them." He added. "I don't think anybody wants to read another mod story, do you?"

Music videos, so often directors of street fashion, are providing few new ideas. The more wealthy and successful that even the most subversive bands get, the more they are photographed for fashion magazines, the more they are on video and the more they become conscious of their dress. Trent Reznor, whose Nine Inch Nails is one of the edgiest acts around, has even hired stylists. It took Madonna all of nine months to get into the newest Gucci collection for the MTV Video Music Awards show.

"The group Salt-n-Pepa is really a good indicator of the direction fashion might be going, and I've noticed they're wearing more designer clothes," Ernie Glam said. "Perhaps that's why the street is appropriating looks from the runways. You see all these successful rock groups and rap artists wearing European runway clothes. Streetwear labels are responding to that."

Eric Azagury, the designer for a line called Free, Paris, said that when he first started his company, he looked to Azzedine Alaia's fitted look for inspiration. Then, for several years, he looked to the London and New York street scenes.

"Now I'm back again to the 80's," he said, adding that he was drawing from high-end designers for inspiration, including Gucci.

The looks are no more knockoffs, he stresses, than Chanel's hip-hop looks were knockoffs of hip-hop fashion.

In fact, the business of the original hip-hop houses like Phat Farm and Cross Colours hardly suffered from Chanel's attentions; they rose to prominence in the street, but were also legitimized when they were appropriated by major design houses.

The shift back to the power of the designer to make fashion change is illustrated best by the jeans business.

The basics and classics booms of the last five years have meant the reign of the most basic, classic jean: the five-pocket version. But with the comeback of 70's clothes like designer jeans, even Sergio Valente and Gloria Vanderbilt are in demand.

Recent controversy over the Calvin Klein jeans campaign has popularized his new designer jean, but Mr. Klein himself said he has seen kids wearing the original Brooke Shields version bought at vintage stores.

The designer Helmut Lang has made the stiffest denim hip, giving jeans one big rolled cuff on his runway.

What is still a powerful force in American street style is the logo-ridden, discordant-colored, utilitarian-cut clothes popularized by snow-boarders, surfers and skateboarders. That look has been expertly appropriated by Diesel, a huge jeans company that markets itself with satirical images.

It is a style that is dominant even among the young in Belgium, which is why Oliver Rizzo, a recent graduate of the Royal Academy of Fine Arts in Antwerp (the alma mater of Martin Margiela, Ann Demeulemeester, Dries van Noten and Walter van Beirendonck), is specializing in the look. His company is called Keystone, after a California surfer's spot, and his was the most interesting work at the jeans-wear show.

But since surf and skateboard style is based on 1950's classic sportswear, only the colors look rebellious; the shapes are classic.

"That is the new look on the street, a smart sweater and khaki pants," Bill Mullen, the creative director of Details magazine, said of the magazine's September issue. "We're clocking that, so in essence we are covering street fashion. It's funny when street fashion is taking it from the runways, but it's something in the air."

He views the trend with more than a little skepticism, however.

"Rock-and-roll and youthful fashion should be about things your parents would hate," he said.

The New York Times, September 19, 1995.

Should Public School Kids Wear Uniforms?

Charol Shakeshaft

When I was a kid in school, we didn't wear uniforms. In junior high, I argued for school uniforms, believing they would save students—especially girls—time and hassle. Thirty-five years later, as a parent of a 10-year-old, I still think uniforms would improve the quality of life for students.

Uniforms in public schools are legal, as long as the uniform does not infringe upon students' political speech or impose different standards for males and females. Although the Supreme Court has not addressed the legality of uniforms in schools, lower courts have upheld the right of public schools to require uniforms. California went so far as to pass a law explicitly making it legal for public schools to adopt uniform requirements, an action designed to reinforce the legality of this kind of local decision.

President Bill Clinton, in his State of the Union address in January, added uniforms to the national debate on schooling—applauding the benefits of a standard dress code. Later, Clinton instructed the federal education department to distribute manuals advising school districts on how to require uniforms.

From Seattle to Phoenix to Charleston, praise of uniform policies is profuse. One of the most often cited benefits of requiring uniforms is economic. Uniforms generally cost less than do most clothes that students want to wear. For instance, the yearly cost of uniforms in Long Beach, Calif., is $70 to $90 for a set of three. Compare that to a trip to the Gap!

Uniforms also can diminish the display of material wealth among students. If expensive jackets, shoes and outfits aren't allowed, students are relieved of anxiety over their attire. Uniforms provide a time when economic privilege seems equalized.

Uniforms promote individuality. Yes, individuality. If students are judged by what they think and how they perform, rather than on how they dress, they are more likely to develop and value diversity of thought. In most school districts, kids already wear uniforms by social category—jocks, phreaks (sic), preppies, Gangsta'—often without articulating what values and lifestyles these uniforms represent.

Long Beach, Calif., offers impressive evidence that schools where students wear uniforms are safer than those where students don't. Since Long Beach adopted a uniform requirement for its 83,000 students in 1994, there are a third fewer assault and battery cases, student fights have been cut by half and student suspensions are down by 32 percent.

What compels me to urge school districts to adopt uniforms are the data I've collected during the past three years in nine middle and high schools on Long Island. In those schools, the girls report they spend as much as two-and-a-half hours each day selecting their clothes and "getting ready" for school. These girls describe great anxiety about their appearance, particularly their clothes, and report harassment from both males and females about how they look. Appearance and image for girls is big business and high pressure. I long for a safe space for girls that diminishes such pressure and decreases their anxiety. Schools that expect all students to wear the same type of dress offer support to girls in their fragile adolescent years.

Studies tell us that nearly all parents welcome uniforms. Students are not so quick to approve of wearing the same dress as their classmates every day. But many students who first balk at uniforms change their minds once they have tried them.

Uniforms honor the occasion of school. They help students separate what is expected in school from what they do in malls or on beaches or at movie theaters. Uniforms help create a climate that fosters learning and puts it at the center of students' lives.

Newsday, March 10, 1996.

Fashion in the Global Marketplace

The fashion industry has changed considerably. The fashion capitals of the world were Paris, where couturiers introduced designs to the world, and New York City, where the industry focused on ready-to-wear. It was not until after the end of World War II that other fashion centers began to emerge. By the 1950s Italian designers such as Emilio Pucci and Mila Schoen were distinguishing themselves in Florence, Rome, and Milan with imaginative creations that rivaled the greats of Paris. London was also waking up to fashion with the designs of Jean Muir, and later, in the 1960s, with Mary Quant. It was not long before the fashion world spread to Tokyo, Germany, Spain, Scandinavia, Canada, and Hong Kong. Fashion and its creation is now global.

After you have completed this chapter, you will be able to discuss:

- How governmental legislation affects the importation of merchandise.

- The relationship of NAFTA and GATT to the fashion industry.

- Why the United States imposes quotas on imports.

- The most important international fashion centers and their significance to the industry.

- The selling arrangements in the industry that move goods from the producer to the retailer.

Where styles are physically designed is only one aspect of the fashion industry. The textile mills that supply the fabrics, the sewers who make the garments, the trimmings houses who create the enhancements all contribute to bringing the finished product to the ultimate consumer. Each of these industry segments can be based in any part of the world. In fact, many American companies, while based in the United States, do little other than design and distribute the merchandise from these shores. Once the individual styles have been created, most often they are produced offshore, and completed with materials and trimmings that have been purchased in yet another part of the world. It is the exception, rather than the rule, when a garment and all of its elements come from one region.

To understand the complexities of this **global marketplace,** it is necessary to learn about the role of the American government in the fashion industry, the major international centers, the **trade expositions,** the **trade organizations,** and the ways in which the products are sold to merchants.

Off-shore centers, such as Hong Kong, account for significant fashion production.

GOVERNMENT INVOLVEMENT IN FASHION IMPORTING

When American fashion manufacturers confine their production to the United States, there are no restrictions placed on how much they may produce, the prices they may charge, or to whom they sell the goods. With the global nature of the fashion business today, however, domestic producers are likely to interface with other countries in the manufacture of their merchandise.

Once a company decides that it would be more favorable for its operation to use materials from foreign shores or to have the garments constructed **off-shore,** the federal government becomes a major player in that organization's business.

The major reason for government's intervention is to ensure that imported goods will not provide unfair competition for goods produced at home. Because foreign labor costs are often lower than labor costs in the United States, the final prices for offshore products will be significantly lower than for domestic products. The government tries to protect American business in a number of ways. These include establishing quotas on imported goods, imposing tariffs, enacting trade pacts with other nations, and using particularly high standards as a restraint measure.

Quotas

A quota is the set amount of merchandise that a country's government allows to be imported in a specific category. Quotas are generally established in numbers of units rather than in dollar amounts. To protect U.S. manufacturers from unfair competition, the Federal government has established very specific quotas.

There are two classifications of quotas, **absolute** and **tariff rate.** With absolute quotas, any merchandise that exceeds the established limit must be disposed of through a variety of means established by the U.S. Customs Service. If goods are subject to tariff-rate quotas, any merchandise exceeding the

TABLE 5.1

ABSOLUTE QUOTAS

Each of the following types of cotton has its own quota:

- Cotton having a staple length under $1\frac{1}{8}$ inches, except harsh or rough cotton having a staple length under $\frac{3}{4}$ of an inch, and other than linters.
- Cotton, other than linters, having a staple length of more than $1\frac{1}{8}$ inches.
- Cotton card strips made from cotton having a staple length under $1\frac{3}{15}$ inches and comber waste, lap waste, sliver waste, and roving waste, whether or not advanced.
- Fibers of cotton woven but not spun.

specified limits may enter at a higher rate of duty or remain in a bonded warehouse until the opening of a new quota.

Those in the fashion industry must have a complete understanding of the quota system and which merchandise is subject to such restrictions. Silk, for example, does not have a quota restriction, because the United States is not a silk-producing nation. Cotton, however, which is a fiber produced on U.S. shores, is subject to quotas. The specificity of the restriction is best understood by examining Table 5.1, which has been excerpted from the Custom Services' listing.

Duty

Fashion merchandise imported into the United States is subject to **duty.** The duty rate levied on each item is a percent of its appraised value. The rates vary according to the individual product and the country of origin. Some fashion items, such as those considered to be antiques, are imported duty free.

In addition to merchandise classification, the amount of a duty is determined by American relations with that country. The majority of countries enjoy Most Favored Nation status (MFN), which rewards them with lower rates than countries with which we have no formal trade agreement. Some countries, such as emerging nations, are able to ship their goods to the United States duty free to help improve their economic situations.

Table 5.2 excerpts the tariff schedule of the U.S. Customs Service. Note that there is a considerable difference in tariff rates for preferential countries (MFN) and those that are considered nonpreferential. Stated rates also change from time to time.

Trade Pacts

The American government over the years has enacted legislation that affects the manner in which we trade with other nations. Two of the strongest of these **trade pacts** were approved in 1994. They are **GATT** and **NAFTA.**

GATT

The **General Agreement on Tariffs and Trade (GATT)** slashes worldwide tariffs on a variety of products by approximately 40 percent. It establishes new trad-

New York City's garment district attracts buyers from all over the world.

points are the likes of the Liz Claiborne empire, which boasts several lines for men and women and scores of others that do not have the immediate name recognition, but nonetheless play an important role in New York City's fashion center.

Since the 1980s some fashion businesses in New York City have moved from the garment center south to Soho. Competitive rents, availability of large space on a single floor, and an art-and-loft type of environment have lured such avant-garde designers as Maria Snyder, Todd Oldham, and Marc Jacobs away from the more traditional, uptown locations.

Regional Markets

The fashion industry is not confined to New York City. In cities such as Los Angeles and San Francisco, for example, scores of manufacturers operate apparel and accessories companies for all merchandise classifications and every price level. In addition to those companies that are based in these **regional markets,** many feature permanent showrooms that are maintained by New York's manufacturers or showrooms in apparel centers that function primarily during the market weeks.

Los Angeles ranks second as a domestic fashion capital. Its principal offering is sportswear with a casual orientation, although it does feature other types of merchandise. A look at the pages of the *California Apparel News,* the major trade paper for the fashion business on the West coast, immediately reveals the scope of its industry. Bob Mackie, of film industry fame, and James Galanos, at the couture level, are headquartered in Los Angeles, as are less pricey lines such as Karan Kane, Nancy Heller, Cherokee, Carole Little, Barry Hunter, Miss Liberty, Barocko, and L.A. Gear.

In the northern part of California, the San Francisco region is enjoying its status as the nation's third largest fashion center. Its several hundred manufacturers include The Gap, Banana Republic, Old Navy, Esprit, Levi Strauss, and Jessica McClintock.

Throughout the country, there are other fashion markets. There are approximately 2,000 showrooms in the Atlanta Apparel Mart. In Miami, for example, there is considerable growth. Companies cater not only to the retailers in the south, but also to those from South America. Their specialty is sportswear and swimsuits. Dallas is home to designers Victor Costa, Julie and Leonard, Bonnie Boynton, and Jo Hardin. The city also serves as home of the Dallas Apparel Mart, an important center for selling to retailers. Chicago is known primarily for men's wear, with companies such as Hartmarx. Its famous Apparel Merchandise Mart houses showrooms for manufacturers from all over

1996 Market Weeks

The 1996 general women's and children's apparel market weeks at the various regional marts and in New York are listed below. In addition to these general markets, various specialized events are held throughout the year at some of these venues. Dates are subject to revision, and individual marts should be contacted for confirmation and more information.

LOCATION	SUMMER	FALL I	FALL II	RESORT	SPRING
ATLANTA (Atlanta Apparel Mart)	Jan. 25-29	April 11-15	June 13-15	Aug. 22-26	Oct. 24-28
BIRMINGHAM (Birmingham Jefferson Civic Center)	Jan. 21-22	March 24-25	June 9-10	Aug. 18-19	Oct. 13-14
BOSTON (Bayside Expo Center)	Jan. 14-17	April 14-17	June 16-19	Aug. 18-21	Oct. 13-16
CHARLOTTE (Charlotte Merchandise Mart) (children's market)	Jan. 19-23 Jan. 19-22	March 22-26 March 22-25	June 7-11 June 7-10	Aug. 16-20 Aug. 16-19	Oct. 11-14
CHICAGO (Chicago Apparel Center)	Jan. 26-30	March 29-April 2	May 31-June 4	Aug. 16-20	Oct. 25-29
DALLAS (International Apparel Mart)	Jan. 18-22	March 21-25	June 6-10	Aug. 15-19	Oct. 17-21
KANSAS CITY (Kansas City Market Center)	Jan. 13-15	April 13-16	June 22-24	Aug. 24-27	Oct. 26-29
LOS ANGELES (California Apparel Mart)	Jan. 12-16	April 19-23	June 21-25	Aug. 9-13	Nov. 1-5
MIAMI (Miami Merchandise Mart)	Jan. 14-17	March 16-19	May 31-June 3	Aug. 9-12	Oct. 12-15
MINNEAPOLIS (Hyatt Merchandise Mart)	Jan. 21-24	March 10-12	April 14-17	June 9-11 Aug. 11-14	Oct. 20-23
NEW YORK (For New York updates, contact Fashion Calendar, 212-289-0420)	Jan. 8-19	Feb. 19-March 1	March 25-April 12	July 29-Aug. 9	Oct. 28-Nov. 15
PITTSBURGH (Monroeville Expo Mart)	Jan. 21-23	April 14-16	June 9-11	Sept. 8-10	Nov. 3-5
SAN FRANCISCO (The Fashion Center)	Jan. 6-9	April 13-16	June 15-18	Aug. 17-20	Oct. 19-22
SEATTLE (Seattle International Trade Center)	Jan. 20-23	March 30-April 2	June 8-11	Aug. 3-6	Oct. 26-29

This schedule for market weeks appeared in an issue of WWD.

the nation. Milwaukee is a center for leather with one of the country's most prestigious shoe manufacturers, Allen Edmonds, and wallets producer, Rolfe, based there.

European Fashion Capitals

All over the continent, designers produce collections that are earmarked for their own populations, as well as for export to the rest of the world. Paris, Milan, and London are Europe's leading fashion producers, with Germany, Spain, and other countries beginning to attract international attention.

This design by Emanuel Ungaro is typical of the creativity identified with Paris.

Paris, France

With the likes of Saint Laurent, Lacroix, Ungaro, Galliano, Gaultier, and Lagerfeld headquartered in Paris, it is no wonder that it remains the fashion capital of the world. With the support of the French government and the resources necessary for design, Paris attracts fashion creators from all over the world.

At one time, Paris was predominantly concerned with **haute couture**—fine dressmaking—or by American definition, **high fashion.** Today, however, **prêt-à-porter (ready-to-wear)** takes its place alongside the much higher priced merchandise. Because only a fraction of the market can afford couture designs, it is the ready-to-wear that actually brings the profits to the designers.

Although we are immediately familiar with the names of elite designers, hundreds and hundreds of creative talents work in the Paris fashion industry. Those who have achieved the highest status are accepted as members of the prestigious **Chambre Syndicale de la Couture Parisienne,** a branch of the larger organization—*Federation Française de la Couture.* The prestigious organization is included in a World of Fashion Profile.

In addition to the Chambre Syndicale, there are two more branches of the Federation. *Chambre Syndicale de Prêt-à-Porter,* which represents the ready-to-wear branches of the couture as well as other French prêt designers and *Chambre Syndicale de la Mode Masculine,* which represents couture men's wear designers. With its rigid rules and regulations, the Chambre Syndicale de la Couture Parisienne recognizes only a handful of designers for membership to the *Couture-Creation.*

The customers of couture are wealthy people who purchase original designs for their own wardrobes, retailers who purchase them for their inventories or have them translated into less costly models, and manufacturers who use the designs for inspiration when designing their own lines. Attendance at the fashion premieres, which take place twice a year, requires an entrance or **caution fee** for people in the industry. The amount, established by each house, may come to several thousand dollars, but is deducted from purchases made. If a buyer or manufacturer fails to find something to purchase, the fee is for-

Chambre Syndicale de la Couture Parisienne

In 1868 the Chambre Syndicale de la Couture Parisienne was organized to stabilize and coordinate the activities of the French couture industry. Throughout the years, its position and role in fashion has been strengthened, and it is recognized worldwide as a major fashion trade organization.

Membership is restricted to those who meet the group's stringent requirements. Those requirements include having a workroom, employing a minimum of twenty workers, each capable of providing precision workmanship, completing all work in-house and without contracting out to other factories, custom-making all clothes entirely, and presenting a collection twice a year, as determined by the Chambre, in a live fashion show format.

The services afforded the membership are numerous, including one that offers protection against the copying of designs, a practice commonplace in the United States. To guard against fashion piracy, every design created by a member is photographed and registered. If the design is copied in France, it is punishable by law. With so many couture houses eager to show their collections at a specific time, the group avoids conflicts by establishing a schedule that specifies days and hours when each designer may present his or her line. In this way, buyers have time to view each collection. The Chambre issues appropriate credentials for buyers and the Press. It requires that couture houses deliver merchandise within thirty days of purchase. It also provides a training program for everyone in France who demonstrates a talent for sewing. It also negotiates with the government on matters affecting the fashion industry, making certain its membership abides by the established rules.

Nowhere in the world is couture so completely protected by a trade organization.

feited. Private customers attend these fashion shows, as does the press, by invitation and are not charged a caution fee.

With its flair for innovative styling, Paris is likely to remain the world's most famous fashion capital. Its interesting to note that American designers have been contracted to design for well-known French designer houses. In the 1990s, designers from all over the world have been named to perpetuate the French fashion industry. American notable, Oscar de la Renta, has been responsible first for designing couture and later ready-to-wear for the House of Balmain. British-born John Galliano has taken over the design responsibilities for Dior. And for the first time since 1968, when couturier Balenciaga retired, the spring ready-to-wear collection designed by Dutch-born designer Josephus Melchior Thimister has received favorable reviews.

Milan, Italy

Once known primarily as a source for quality leathers and fabrics, Milan has emerged as a leading fashion center for both men's and women's clothing. While some designers, such as Valentino and Galitzine, have remained faithful to Rome, others have opted for headquarters in Milan. Names such as Armani, Gianfranco Ferré, Gianni Versace, Krizia, and Missoni design garments earmarked for worldwide distribution. Some, for example Armani, feature both couture and ready-to-wear collections.

Gianni Versace's vivid and wide ranging designs make him one of Milan's most popular apparel and home fashions designers.

London, England

Traditional, conventional ready-to-wear and fine tailoring was the hallmark of British fashion before the 1960s. At that time, a youth-oriented look, spearheaded by Mary Quant, emerged on London's streets. Her freshness captivated the hearts and pocketbooks of the young, and she, along with other talented designers, prepared Great Britain and the rest of the world for mod clothing.

Although the Quant miniskirts and hot pants caught fire, Quant's popularity declined as did the excitement over British fashion. Today, however, after many years of neglect by the rest of the fashion world, London is enjoying its status as a fashion center. Vivienne Westwood, Zandra Rhodes, Betty Jackson, Maxfield Parrish, Wendy Dagworthy, Victor Edelstein, Jeremy Howitt, David Davies, and David Reiss are just some of the talents who have restored London's ready-to-wear market.

Fine-tailored men's wear has always been a British specialty, and Savile Row is London's famous locale for fine classic clothing. Turnbull & Asser, Henry Poole, Burberry, and Gieves & Hawkes are some of the leading purveyors of British men's wear.

Designs, such as this one by Zandra Rhodes, keeps London in the forefront of fashion.

Spain

Always known for leather shoes and apparel, Spain has made important strides in women's and children's sportswear. Through its trade association, **Camara de la Moda Española,** more than five hundred firms market their lines. It is through this affiliation, that the Spanish fashion manufacturers have been able to gain some recognition outside of the country. The bulk of the companies, headed by such designers as Marce Manuel, Adolfo Dominguez, Marguerita Nuez, and Antonio Alvarado are centered in either Madrid or Barcelona.

Germany

Scattered all over the country, Germany has more than 2,000 manufacturers of fashion-oriented merchandise. Many of its designers enjoy reputations that reach all over the globe, with the United States a significant market. Leading companies include Hugo Boss, Escada, Mondi, and Jil Sander.

Scandinavia

Denmark, Sweden, Finland, and Norway comprise the important manufacturing countries of that region. The industry is coordinated by the **Central Scandinavian Clothing Council,** which is headquartered in Copenhagen. The best-known merchandise comes from Finland's Marimekko, which produces both ready-to-wear and a full line of home fashions. Although these countries are recognized collectively, each has a distinctive approach to fashion. Sweden's and Norway's contributions are more moderately priced, youth-oriented designs; Denmark's forte is expensive, high fashion merchandise; and Finland is the leader in original Scandinavian design.

Eastern Europe

With the abundance of inexpensive, skilled labor in countries like Poland and Hungary, they are becoming important centers of apparel production. American manufacturers, such as Liz Claiborne, are manufacturing some products there. Macy's has also produced some of its private labels, such as Alfani, in Poland. These nations used to send most of their production output to the former Soviet Union. Now, the Eastern European nations are exporting to countries throughout the world.

South America

South America lags behind the rest of the world in fashion merchandise. The one product, however, that has importance is leather. Garments and accessories, such as shoes and handbags, are produced relatively inexpensively and exported all over the world. Brazil, in particular, is a leader in leather products.

Retailers, such as JCPenney, are opening stores and selling their private label merchandise in Mexico.

Asia

At the beginning of the 1960s Asia entered the fashion arena. Japan and Hong Kong were the first to become international players. They were later joined by Korea, Singapore, China, and Taiwan. Although these countries collectively account for a significant amount of the world's fashion production, China, Taiwan, and Korea are primarily involved in textile manufacturing and garment construction, with original design occurring mainly in Japan and Hong Kong.

Japan

Although there are fashion businesses dotting the map of Japan, Tokyo is the principal producer. Japan's role in the fashion industry is in both original design and manufacture of merchandise for foreign companies. Not only does the region produce Japanese designs under their own labels, but Renown, one of the world's leading manufacturers, holds the rights to produce such prestigious American labels as Perry Ellis in Japan for that country's consumption.

Designers of Japanese descent have had an influence in the international fashion industry since the mid-1960s. Hanae Mori was one of the first Japanese designers to capture the attention of the global fashion market, with an aesthetic touch inspired by her Japanese background. Kenzo has worked in Paris since the mid-1960s. His licensing arrangement with The Limited in the 1970s made his designs available to the less affluent consumer. Issey Miyake combines Japanese attitudes towards fashion, such as wrapping and layering, with exotic fabrics of his own design. One of the more widely acclaimed designers from that region is Rei Kawakubo, who creates collections for Commes des Garçons. Her asymmetrical shapes in cotton, canvas, or linen fabrics are draped and wrapped over the body.

Japanese corporations also provide financial backing for U.S. design firms. In 1984 Takihyo Corporation helped Donna Karan to open her company Donna Karan New York, which it currently half owns. Anne Klein & Co. is also a wholly owned subsidiary of Takihyo. In 1996 Takihyo decided to discontinue the designer line, which this season was designed by Patrick Robinson. The company will continue to back the bridge collections—Anne Klein II and A line.

Hong Kong

Although Hong Kong has made significant strides in bringing its own apparel collections to the world of fashion, it is their ability to produce garments at low prices that makes them an important part of the field. Famous internationally based companies, such as Armani, Calvin Klein, and Liz Claiborne, often manufacture their goods in Hong Kong. Few countries can offer such expert tailoring at such modest costs.

In the field of original design, companies such as Toppy, Episode, Girdano, G2000, and Goldlion are gaining in international importance. Designers who are emerging as creative forces in the industry include William Tang, Lulu Cheung, Ben Yeung, and Allan Chiu.

This fashion excitement is, however, balanced by the unpredictable implications of Hong Kong's return to China in 1997. This transition from a government that believes in free enterprise to one that has a history of tight control on business, leaves many unanswered questions. The joint declaration

In Hong Kong, fashion is introduced in the Convention and Exhibition Center at the harbor front.

between the United Kingdom and the People's Republic of China spells out the following stipulations:

- Hong Kong will enjoy a high degree of autonomy as a Special Administrative Region (SAR) of the People's Republic of China, with socialist policies applied in the mainland not to be applied to Hong Kong. It will maintain its previous capitalist system and lifestyle for fifty years after 1997.

- The Hong Kong SAR will have autonomy in economic, financial, and monetary matters.

- The Hong Kong SAR will determine its own shipping policies.

- There will be the continuing right of free entry and departure from Hong Kong.

There is, however, no way to effectively enforce these stipulations, and China has always acted independently in international matters. Whether China will allow Hong Kong to function autonomously is a subject of great controversy.

Canada and Mexico

Although Canada and Mexico have participated in the fashion industry as both producers of goods for their own countries and exporters to the United States, NAFTA, which eliminates tariffs, promises to expand their fashion industries.

Canada

With its chief market in Montreal and a second one in Toronto, Canada has more than 2,000 apparel and textile manufacturers. They produce a diverse range of apparel from the highly sophisticated and expensive to the more moderately priced. Among the better known collections are those of Denis Desro, Jean Claude Poitras, Judy Cornish, Roger Edwards, Zapata, and Lida Bada.

TABLE 5.3

U.S. IMPORTS OF MFA* APPAREL
FROM SELECTED COUNTRIES—1964–1994

*(Millions of SME)***

Countries	1964	1974	1984	1988	1992	1993	1994 SME	1994 Dollars	% Chng 1994/93
PRC	0	7	421	635	948	936	934	$3,589	0%
Hong Kong	140	309	848	743	820	772	864	4,205	12%
Taiwan	36	353	808	726	687	652	651	2,154	0%
Korea	9	246	635	600	419	428	410	1,842	−4%
Subtotal	185	915	2,712	2,704	2,874	2,788	2,859	$11,790	3%
% Total Imports	39%	57%	63%	51%	41%	37%	34%	38%	
Japan	165	137	120	46	10	9	7	$64	−22%
% Total Imports	35%	8%	3%	1%	*	*	*	*	
Phillippines	37	85	197	266	381	393	411	$1,351	5%
Bangladesh	0	0	20	142	341	355	430	741	21%
Indonesia	—	—	108	150	227	260	281	1,025	8%
India	—	23	112	147	218	232	257	1,105	11%
Sri Lanka	0	1	91	116	192	237	254	832	7%
Thailand	—	—	89	63	186	228	234	897	3%
Singapore	—	75	107	141	149	116	96	470	−17%
Malaysia	—	—	54	95	144	140	147	637	5%
Pakistan	—	—	53	73	125	124	145	437	17%
Macau	—	—	54	69	91	85	111	604	31%
Subtotal	—	—	885	1,262	2,054	2,170	2,366	$8,099	9%
% Total Imports	—	—	21%	24%	29%	29%	28%	26%	
Dominican Republic	—	5	79	186	419	488	546	$1,574	12%
Mexico	—	76	72	158	267	321	482	1,597	50%
Costa Rica	—	—	28	75	207	241	265	685	10%
Jamaica	—	—	8	80	130	158	199	454	26%
Guatemala	—	—	2	32	128	157	161	591	3%
Haiti	—	34	57	93	36	49	16	29	−67%
Subtotal	—	—	246	624	1,187	1,414	1,669	$4,930	18%
% Total Imports	—	—	6%	12%	17%	19%	20%	16%	
All Others	—	—	329	640	954	1,165	1,521	$6,510	31%
% Total Imports	—	—	8%	12%	13%	15%	18%	21%	
TOTAL IMPORTS	469	1,619	4,292	5,276	7,079	7,546	8,422	$31,393	12%

* Less than 1/2 of 1%

* Multifiber arrangement — Includes all fibers except silk

** Square meters equivalent

SOURCE: US Department of Commerce, Office of Textiles and Apparel

Avon manufactures virtually all of its Mexican products in Mexico; here the president of the Mexican and Central American divisions inspects the product.

Although they produce a wide variety of women's and men's apparel, they are particularly noted for men's clothing, and are the second largest supplier to the United States after Italy.

Mexico

With its ability to produce apparel and accessories at modest cost and with the new conditions set forth by NAFTA, Mexico has the potential to become a leader in the production of merchandise for American companies. Many businesses in the United States are setting up shop in Mexico to take advantage of the new regulations. One of the problems that has plagued Mexico in the past has been poor-quality construction. With new American interests in the region and quality control a priority, better quality can be expected.

Caribbean Basin Countries

With some of the lowest labor costs in the world and tax and quota exemptions established for them by the United Sates under the Caribbean Basin Initiative, many countries in that region have become important producers of fashion products. Countries such as El Salvador, the Dominican Republic, Haiti, Jamaica, Costa Rica, and Honduras continue to show significant increases in their exports. They are not the originators of fashion, but serve global fashion businesses by producing merchandise for them.

Table 5.3 features United States imports from selected countries from 1964 to 1994.

SELLING FASHION PRODUCTS AROUND THE WORLD

With the size and scope of the fashion industry growing all over the world, designers and manufacturers in the United States use a variety of means to distribute them.

TABLE 5.4

INTERNATIONAL TRADE EXPOSITIONS

COUNTRY	Trade Exposition	Merchandise	Location
UNITED STATES	INT'L TRIMMINGS EXPO	trimmings	New York
	INT'L BOUTIQUE SHOW	women's wear	New York
	THE KID'S SHOW	children's wear	New York
	NAMSB	men's wear	New York
	PRIVATE LABEL EXPO	private label	New York
	FFANY	shoes	New York
	NADI	display materials	New York
	INT'L JEANSWEAR & SPORTSWEAR	sportswear	Miami
	WOMEN'S & CHILDREN'S MARKET	women's and children's wear	Dallas
	INT'L TEXTILES SHOW	textiles	Los Angeles
	MAGIC	men's wear	Las Vegas
	BOBBIN SHOW	technology	Atlanta
SPAIN	MOSTRA DE TEJIDOS	textiles	Barcelona
	FERIS	costume jewelry	Barcelona
	BARNAJOYA	jewelry	Barcelona
	EXPOCALZADO	shoes	Madrid
	IBERPIEL	furs, leather	Madrid
ITALY	SPOSAITALIA	bridal	Milan
	MODA-IN	shirting fabric	Milan
	LA MODA MILANO	ready-to-wear	Milan
	PRATO EXPO	textiles	Florence
	PITTI BIMBO	children's wear	Florence
	IDEABELLA	textiles	Cernobbio
FRANCE	PREMIERE VISION	textiles	Paris
	INDIGO	home textiles	Paris
	SEHM	men's and boy's wear	Paris
GERMANY	GDS	shoes	Dusseldorf
	INTERSTOFF	textiles	Frankfurt
PORTUGAL	PORTUGUESE OFFER	textiles	Lisbon
SINGAPORE	INTEX	textiles and trimmings	Singapore
	FASHION FORUM	fashion merchandise	Singapore

time going from showroom to showroom in many different geographical locations. With the considerable expense involved in reaching all of the markets, buyers often miss out on lines that they do not have the time to pursue.

Walking through a trade show quickly gives the buyer an overview of the current season's offerings and the ability to quickly compare the offerings of competing companies.

Some of the larger fairs include **NAMSB,** for the men's wear industry. It presents three shows a year in New York City, where more than 1,000 lines are exhibited and more than 30,000 retail organizations of every size come to make their purchases for the following season. **The Kids Show** and **International Boutique Show,** both sponsored by the Larkin Group, cater to vendors and sellers of children's wear and women's wear respectively. **NADI** is a fair of the display industry, and **SEHM,** held in Paris twice yearly, attracts approximately 40,000 buyers of men's and boy's fashions from all over the world.

Table 5.4 lists many of the world's fashion-oriented trade expositions.

Chapter Highlights

- Fashion, once an industry with limited boundaries, seems to have lost all of its borders.

- Although the majority of the ready-to-wear industry is based in the United States, many of its producers have opted for off-shore production facilities to reduce the costs of making the goods. With the design teams based in America, the assembling processes accomplished overseas, and the ultimate customers served all over the world, fashion now is part of the global marketplace.

- To minimize the competition that comes from foreign-produced goods, the Federal government places restrictions on imported merchandise by tariffs and quotas.

- At the same time, the government recognizes that international trade can be beneficial to U.S. citizens. Thus it has also enacted legislation to make us a better trading partner. Pacts known as GATT and NAFTA solidify these efforts in the global marketplace.

- In addition to Paris, the world leader in couture fashion, and New York City, chief producer of ready-to-wear, other locations have emerged as fashion capitals. Some, such as Italy and London, have become leaders in original design, while others, like Hong Kong, excel as producers of fashion for other nations.

- The selling of the merchandise guarantees a profit for the companies. Vendor sales are accomplished in a number of ways, including the use of trade expositions.

- Other selling arenas include manufacturer's showrooms and the facilities of manufacturer's representatives.

Important Fashion Terminology and Concepts

absolute quota

Camara de la Moda Espanola

caution fee

Central Scandinavian Clothing Council

Chambre Syndicale de la Couture Parisienne

duty

garment district

GATT

global marketplace

high fashion haute couture

International Boutique Show

The Kids Show

manufacturer's representatives

market shows

market week

NADI

NAFTA

NAMSB

offshore production

prêt-à-porter

ready-to-wear

regional market

reps

road staff

SEHM

Seventh Avenue

trade exposition

trade pacts

tariff rate quota

For Review

1. Why do American manufacturers utilize off-shore production facilities?

2. Differentiate between absolute quotas and tariffs.

3. What benefits does a country derive from favored nation status?

4. What is the ultimate goal of the GATT pact?

5. Which countries are affected by NAFTA?

6. Distinguish between the fashion strengths of New York City and Paris.

7. Define the term regional market.

8. In what way does Hong Kong serve the world of fashion?

9. Why have trade expositions become so popular with vendors and buyers?

10. How does a manufacturer's rep's showroom differ from one that is company owned?

Exercises and Projects

1. Using the schedule established for absolute quotas by the U.S. Customs Service, prepare a table of quotas for ten fashion-oriented products. The schedule is available in most libraries.

2. Visit or write a regional wholesale mart, such as the Chicago Merchandise Mart or the Dallas Apparel Mart, and identify the types of companies they lease space to, the expenses involved in acquiring space, the market they serve, and anything else of interest concerning wholesale marts. Prepare a report based upon the information you have received for oral presentation to the class.

3. Visit a fashion retailer and examine the merchandise assortment in one classification to determine the country of origin. List each of the countries in the order of overall importance to the store's inventory. Indicate the percentage of foreign-made to domestically produced goods.

4. Using the list in the chapter as a reference source, select a trade exposition and obtain information about it. Find out how often each fair is held, the types of vendors featured, the markets served, the expense of participation, and so on. The information may be obtained through a visit or by writing to the sponsor.

The Case of the Underpublicized Collection

For the past five years, Sheri Litt was employed as an assistant designer of children's clothing. Her initial experience was with a traditional line that specialized in infant's wear. After two years with that company, she became an assistant designer, working for Fun in the Sand, a business that manufactured stylish play togs and beach wear for the small set. While working there, she met Caryn Gallop, who started in sales and eventually became national sales manager. The two had an excellent working relationship, and together, helped the company gain industry-wide attention.

Three months ago, Sheri became increasingly interested in starting her own business. She always wanted to be the head designer for a company, but could not advance because one of the Fun in the Sand's partner was the lines creator. She considered moving on to another organization, but always felt self-employment was her dream. Not being able to afford the start-up costs on her own and lacking marketing expertise, she approached Caryn about a potential partnership. The two grew increasingly excited about the prospects of ownership and joined forces to open a new venture, Togs for Tots.

With savings of their own and capital obtained from a lending institution, they organized the company. They took a small space in an off-the-beaten-path location, where the designs would be created and an office would be in place for billing. Although it had only a small area to serve as a showroom, its location in the garment district was sufficiently good to gain the attention of many buyers. With a limited advertising budget, they did all they could to promote their new enterprise.

The first line was ready to be shown, but they were still not satisfied that their sales approach was reaching the maximum number of potential buyers.

Question

What route would you suggest that Gallop and Litt take to guarantee that their line will be seen by the industry's important buyers without the expense of their own showroom in a better location?

Penney's Long Haul in Mexico

Joanna Ramey

With the intensity of a Christmas rush, the new new J.C. Penney store here on a recent Sunday evening was packed with an upscale crowd eagerly trying on fashions and scrutinizing price tags.

Opened in May in the Plaza St. Agustin, which is situated against the backdrop of the El Cerro del Cielo mountain range, Penney's has created one of its most elegant stores, with marble floors, a luxurious beauty salon with 24 stations and Doric pillars in the jewelry department.

However, one thing appeared missing from an otherwise perfect retail picture: steady sales.

"We do have the traffic," responded Luis Serafin, manager of the Penney's Monterrey store and a 23-year veteran of the chain. "Now what we want to do is turn this traffic into sales."

He declined to specify how much volume the store has taken in so far, or provide a projection for the unit, though he did point to several hot items to demonstrate how some Mexicans, even in an economic crisis, are finding pesos to spend in the store.

For example, from Penney's private label Worthington line, 75 short-sleeved knit shells, made in the U.S., priced at 128 pesos ($21) sold during the first 10 days of business.

During another 10-day period, 76 cotton crewneck T-shirts, under Penney's Cabin Creek label, priced at 86 pesos ($14), were sold.

Two Tag Heuer watches sold in the first month of business for 6775 pesos ($1,117) and 1190 pesos ($198), Serafin noted.

For Penney's in Mexico, it's been a long haul. Plans for the company's debut here and in nearby León were laid years before the country's retailing climate turned sour.

After delaying its debut by two months, the store opened on the revised date even though much of its imported merchandise still hadn't arrived. Imports comprise 75 percent of the store's inventory and the paperwork and logistics required to comply with Mexico's new certificate of original rules greatly slowed deliveries.

No less of a challenge has been the Mexican economy. Although it's stabilized since its Dec. 20, 1994 crash, consumer spending remains greatly diminished, even in Pedro Garza Garcia, one of the wealthiest neighborhoods in the country, where Penney's Monterrey unit is located. "We're targeting the upper class and the emerging middle class," Serafin said. "They are probably the least affected by the economic crisis."

The store is part of an expanded portion of the mall, next door to a Sears de Mexico that opened in March.

In addition, Dillard Department Stores is planning to open its first Mexican unit in the mall. It was originally scheduled for a fall opening, but has been postponed due to construction delays caused by the economy. Dillard's now hopes for a 1997 opening.

"We are on such a learning curve here," Serafin said, during a recent interview.

Because of Mexico's state of flux, Penney's has put on hold its plans to open five more stores in the next two years, and an undetermined number of others before the end of the decade.

"We have been forced to readjust our timetable," said a Penney's spokesman, noting how interest rates of upwards of 100 percent have halted new construction and revised plans.

Nevertheless, he said Penney's executives remain bullish about Mexico as fertile grounds for expansion. "We'll go forward with those plans when feasible," he said.

Wall Street analysts view Penney's presence in Mexico favorably and consider it part of a long-term strategic move, rather than a grab at immediately increasing sales. The share the retailers' long-term view of Mexico as a growing market, but are quick to note how, particularly in the next two to three years of economic recovery, competition in the growing Mexican department store niche will be fierce. Penney's leading competitors in Mexico are seen as Sears and the Mexican-owned Liverpool chain.

"Their stores in Mexico aren't going to be material to their sales growth or their earnings, particularly over the next couple of years, but strategically, it gives Penney's the opportunity to explore waters outside of the U.S.," said Steve Kernkraut, a Bear Stearns analyst, who follows Penney's stock. "Even if they open 20 stores in Mexico, it will still be a small piece of their business. But if you add up Mexico, Chile [where Penney's opened a store in March] and other countries they might go into, it could amount to something significant."

"It is an investment," said Bernard Sosnick, a retail analyst for Oppenheimer & Co., noting that Mexico and Chile provide testing grounds for Penney's private label merchandise in Latin America. "The stores may be profitable, but the opportunities are not nearly what they were before the de-evaluation."

In picking northern Mexico to open its first two stores, Penney's is courting customers who for years have routinely made the two-hour trek to Texas to shop Penney's or other stores in McAllen or Laredo.

While Serafin said prices at Penney's in Mexico now range 10–15 percent higher than at Penney's border stores, customers should view prices in both countries to be on par when transportation and tariffs are taken into account.

The economic crisis may be helping Penney's since it seems to be changing the shopping patterns of Mexicans. Several who were interviewed at the Monterrey store said they have virtually stopped their twice-monthly shopping trips to Texas, and that they are apt to look for bargains in Mexico.

"This J.C.Penney has beautiful merchandise," said Jesus Jaime, though he left the store empty-handed after his first visit with his teenage daughter. "The prices look the same as their McAllen store," added Jaime, who owns a small business and counts himself among this industrial city's large middle class. No one in his family has bought any apparel since the crisis began.

Teenager Raquel Oviedo, who attends private school, said before the economy went sour she would go to McAllen to shop at Penney's and Dillard's, spending as much as $200 a month on apparel. Her only purchase since the crisis is a blouse bought in a Mexican flea market. "Things are cheaper there," she said. "Most of the stores are now too expensive."

Despite the drought in disposable income, Serafin said Penney's Mexican merchandise strategy isn't based solely on price and aims to recreate the U.S. store merchandising. This is a costlier approach compared to Sears stores in Mexico, which sell Mexican-made apparel whenever possible.

"Sometimes, we look at these consumers and think they are only driven by price," Serafin said. That's wrong, he explained, noting there's a need to emphasize fashion when making merchandising choices, which can mean importing more. "You need to look at the Mexican consumer as being sophisticated," he said. "They want quality and they want fashion."

While the store carries many of the same women's brands, such as Melrose and Chaus, and private labels sold in its U.S. doors, there is other merchandise carried in Mexico that isn't available in the U.S. This is largely due to the fact that distribution in these lines is available to Penney's only outside the U.S., much like what the chain has seen with its Puerto Rican stores.

For example, the Mexican store's cosmetic and fragrance department is 20-25 percent larger than the U.S., accommodating additional brands like Clarins, Dior, Chanel, Givenchy, Nina Ricci, Borghese and Elizabeth Arden.

In the jewelry department, also larger than a typical Penney's, Mont Blanc, Tag Heuer and Fossil brands are carried. In hosiery, Anne Klein and Liz Claiborne pantyhose are stocked.

Mexican brands are represented in women's accessories and apparel, including Ivonne apparel, a major moderate-priced line known for a broad assortment of classic fashions. It offers double-breasted gabardine jackets, assembled in Mexico from Italian fabrics, selling for 417 pesos ($69) and a sleeveless cotton gingham dress of Mexican fabric, selling for 330 pesos ($55).

Serafin, who most recently managed Penney's stores in the border town of Nogales, Ariz., said Penney's wants to send a message of consistency to its customers. For example, the store won't raise prices on merchandise already in the store, even when inflation rises or the peso's value slides against the dollar. During previous economic downturns, Mexican retailers commonly upped the price of existing inventory, sometimes on a daily basis, to outpace inflation. This practice has become less evident in the industry during the current crisis, indicating that retail competition is heating up in Mexico.

Another way Penney's courts devaluation-weary customers is by charging purchases paid with a Penney's credit card issued in the U.S. at U.S. interest rates. That's a big incentive for customers to buy, given that U.S. rates on cards are hovering around 20 percent, compared to Mexican rates upward of 100 percent. So far, these credit card sales have amounted to 20 percent of all credit sales in the two Mexican stores. Total credit sales are accounting for 40 to 50 percent of total sales.

"We are trying to be sensitive to the fact that this is a difficult time economically," Serafin said. "It is a reward to those customers we have had for a long time."

Women's Wear Daily, July 12, 1995.

Hong Kong Fashion—Setting the Pace in Asia

Mimi Yeung

In Hong Kong, people involved in the apparel business are intensely proud of past achievements—and equally positive about future opportunities. In just forty years the territory's clothing industry has established itself as a world leader in garment producing, exporting and sourcing, and has increasingly made a name for itself as a home of design—a creative fashion capital mounting a new Asian challenge to the traditional "big five" of New York, London, Paris, Milan and Tokyo.

Hong Kong's textile and garment operation improved quality through the '50s and '60s and by the '70s the territory was already attracting orders to produce for some of the top U.S. and European labels.

Against a backdrop of quotas restricting the quantity of Hong Kong's apparel exports to major markets, the territory's manufacturers continued their steady move into higher quality production throughout the '80s.

They excelled in "quick response" production, while keeping costs competitive through the strategic use of offshore production in China, S.E. Asia but as far as the Caribbean, Ireland, Spain and Madagaacer.

In 1984, for the first time, Hong Kong's total exports of garments exceeded in value those of any other producer in the world. Throughout the decade annual growth averaged 10 percent, and by 1989 Hong Kong's domestic exports of garments reached a value of US$9.2 billion (compared with US$4.4 billion in 1983).

The '90s have seen a new and important development in Hong Kong's garment industry. Much of the labour intensive production has moved away, whilst Hong Kong has concentrated its attention on design, high-tech CAD/CAM production, marketing and managing. The territory has emerged as a leading international fashion centre in its own right, creating stylish clothing not only for the world's favorite labels, but increasingly nurturing its own designers and brandnames of international renown.

Labels such as Toppy, Episode, Theme, Bossini, Giordano, G2000, Crocodile and Goldlion are already well established in international markets, especially in Asia, while designers such as Vivienna Tam, Walter Ma, Allan Chin, William Tang, Ben Yeung and Lulu Cheung have made their own individual mark overseas.

They are achieving in their collections a distinctive blend of East and West; of their cosmopolitan Hong Kong way of life and their Chinese cultural heritage.

Few are better qualified to understand and interpret through fashion the Asian economic dynamo and the rise of important new markets with distinctive Asian tastes and sizing.

Today, Hong Kong fashion competes at the highest level, and is found in department stores, boutiques and chain stores in leading markets around the world.

Hong Kong's total exports of garments topped US$21.2 billion in 1994—and the recent trend toward greater trade liberalization promises even more opportunities for our local entrepreneurs.

Markets are today highly diversified. Although the USA remains the largest, Germany, Japan, the UK and China are also significant, and Hong Kong's trading reach extends to markets in all five continents. Product range is also immense, including women's and men's and children's wear, sportswear, leather and fur products.

Such is the capability of Hong Kong's garment industry to produce good quality at reasonable cost, and to offer the best in cutting, making up, quality control and speed of delivery, that some of the top international names in designer couture now produce in the territory, in addition to international labels.

For the future the goal of Hong Kong's fashion industry leaders is to strengthen the territory's capabilities and status as a fashion centre. We have a firm foundation on which to build, there is a close and long-standing alliance between Hong Kong's garment industry and the Hong Kong Trade Development Council in developing markets for Hong Kong apparel and raising awareness about the quality of its design.

Hong Kong Fashion Week, which the Hong Kong Trade Development Council organizes on a biannual basis, has developed into a major international fashion event, attracting a total of more than 1,000 exhibitors and 41,120 buyers in 1994.

Another positive trend further underpinning Hong Kong's role as an established fashion centre is regional growth. The territory, on account of its sophisticated infrastructure and modern business culture, is a prime purchasing and sourcing centre as well as marketing base from which to tackle Asia's booming economies. It lies at the centre of the region's trade network; it boasts an ultra-modern exhibition centre, due to more than double in capacity by 1987; and it is a gateway to China, the world's most exciting new market.

Major trade fair organizers from Europe are also establishing a presence in the territory, to tap the potential of Asia's new consumers—IGEDO, Prêt-à-Porter and Semaine de Cuir, are just three to have forged partnerships or initiated their own events.

In four decades Hong Kong has enjoyed a remarkable rise to prominence in the world of fashion, development from a manufacturer of humble products into a leading player on the international scene. This success has depended on a number of factors—the territory's free trade economy, entrepreneurial flair, a hard-working and skilled labour force with the flexibility to adapt and upgrade advanced financial and transportation systems.

These factors will remain firmly a part of the Hong Kong matrix as it approaches the new century, in which the economies of the Asia-Pacific will provide a key stimulus to global economic growth. In this context, we can foresee Hong Kong strengthening its role as a leading force in the world of fashion design—and assuming an even higher profile than it enjoys today.

Assistant Executive Director, Editor-in-Chief, Hong King Apparel and Hong Kong Fashion.

Despite Higher Costs, No Place Like Home for Some U.S. Firms

Rosemary Feitelberg, Arthur Friedman and Anne D'Innocenzio

The lure of cheap labor keeps taking chunks out of domestic production, but for many companies, U.S. manufacturing remains a key strategy.

Makers say hands-on quality and production control and the Quick Response capabilities offered by local manufacturing keep them from turning to imports. Some industry executives even see signs of growth in U.S. manufacturing.

Proponents of domestic manufacturing range from moderate-price sportswear firms, such as Norton McNaughton, to top-price designer ready-to-wear houses, such as Oscar de la Renta Ltd.; each says it does 75 percent of its manufacturing in the U.S.

Among the apparel giants, VF Corp.—which has made QR a cornerstone of its marketing strategy—sews in the U.S. 85 to 90 percent of everything it produces, according to Lawrence R. Pugh, chairman and chief executive officer.

"We have expanded offshore in the Caribbean and Mexico, but we have also been maintaining our domestic manufacturing," he said.

"In total, we have not downsized our domestic manufacturing. I am not suggesting to you that we will be downsizing. I think that over a period of time—the next three to five years—domestic manufacturing will go down to 75 percent, but I am hopeful we will not have to downsize any U.S. employment, and all of this will come about because of growth."

VF, which employs more than 50,000 people in production in the U.S., also has been expanding its international business.

Others are skeptical about the long-term prognosis for domestic production. The crucial issue in the recent strike at The Leslie Fay Cos. was the proposal to shut down domestic production in favor of off-shore sourcing, which the company said it had to do to remain competitive. The six-week strike ended in July with a compromise that will keep half of its 1,200 Pennsylvania production workers employed until July 31, 1995.

Industry groups, organized labor and contractors say that while some feel job losses have slowed, they face an upward battle.

"There is a growing awareness that maintaining the manufacturing base is important, but we have a long way to go. Persuading people in this industry to believe in that is very difficult, but we're working hard," said Jay Mazur, president of the ILGWU.

Nationwide, apparel production jobs fell to 800,000 in 1993 from 1.26 million in 1973.

Eli Elias, president of the New York Skirt and Sportswear Association, added, "Unless there is significant change in government trade policy, [U.S.] production in the apparel industry will not exist 20 years from now. The theory I grew up with was that production was the source of all wealth, and maybe

that's why our trade deficit keeps on growing, because we're becoming production-poor."

Nevertheless, a number of vendors on SA are ready to cite the advantages of domestic production.

"We never would have been able to get the goods in the stores as fast as we have if we were doing it offshore," said David Mercer, president of Expo, a contemporary dress manufacturer that produces all of its garments domestically. The strategy has enabled the firm to react quickly to such trends as slip-dresses and jumpers.

Mercer said he expects domestic manufacturing to strengthen in the years ahead.

"Once labor costs go down, it will be more cost-effective to manufacture in the States," he said. "I think that will happen because our labor force is anxious to get more business."

For the past eight years, Cynthia Rowley Inc., a designer dress resource here, has produced all its garments in the U.S., according to Erica Mays, production manager. By maintaining all elements of production in the same area, there is little room for error, she said.

"Quality control is the greatest advantage. Everything is within a four-block radius of my office," she said. "It makes it easy to check on how things are being done."

The "Made in the USA" label is a real selling point, according to Mays, who worked in retail for a number of years. She said shoppers routinely asked where goods were made.

With a relatively small scale of production, the company would lose money by manufacturing overseas, Mays said. However, the company investigates the possibility twice a year, even though Mays feels

cost and quality control issues should keep Rowley here.

"It goes back to quality. That American-made label used to symbolize quality," she said. "It certainly still does for Cynthia Rowley."

All of Chetta B's garments are produced domestically, according to Howard Bloom, president and chief executive officer. Having manufactured a limited amount of dresses overseas, he said the language barrier was a problem.

"I always had an unsettling feeling with the communication," he said. "If you're doing work in the Far East and they don't feel like talking to you, they won't pick up the phone. Or they'll pick up and speak in Chinese."

In addition to better quality control and faster turn time, Bloom said domestic production is an advantage because retailers are buying closer to the season.

"Stores don't want to buy as far in advance as they used to," he said. "It's not that fashion is changing so fast."

With a growing number of retailers placing orders closer to season, Datiani, a contemporary dress firm here, produces 95 percent of its goods domestically—as opposed to 80 percent three years ago, according to Ben Dash, president. To maintain the bulk of production here, the company continually aims to lower overhead and looks for less-expensive fabrics, he said.

Domestic fabric resources are offering better quality and prices, but Dash said that has not inhibited him from investigating outlets overseas.

"For us to give stores new things, we have to shop the market all the time. Vendors are always going to want goods to be cheaper," he said. "People still don't want to spend. The economy isn't too good in a lot of areas."

Scarlett Nite, a junior dress division of Dalil Fashions here, produces 95 percent of its garments in New York, according to Holly Thorner, executive vice president. Last year, when the company produced 20 percent of its goods in Central America, the amount of damaged merchandise increased, she said, since chiffons and other delicate fabrics do not ship well.

The "Made in the USA" label makes a difference in Texas, Michigan and other areas with strong labor forces, Thorner said.

"In New York and other big cities, you're accustomed to seeing a lot of imports in the stores," she said. "In a lot of places, the economy is tough. People recognize the 'Made in USA' label."

Oscar de la Renta manufactures 75 percent of its merchandise in six factories in the New York area, according to Gerald Shaw, president and ceo. The issue is control, not price, said Shaw, adding that lower-priced vendors venture overseas to be price-competitive.

"We prefer to manufacture in our own backyard, where everything is under our nose," he said.

Greater communication between politicians and apparel manufacturers might improve domestic manufacturing and other issues affecting the industry, he said.

"The government needs to be better informed and more cooperative. This is an enormous industry, but there's no pulling together," Shaw said. "They need to know what the problems are and how to solve them. The worst thing that could happen is nothing. The best

thing that can come out of it is that we solve a few things."

With production evenly split between imports and domestic manufacturing, Halmode Apparel, a dress firm here, plans to maintain that balance in the years ahead, according to Robert Adler, president and ceo. The company could not have doubled its volume from $80 million to $160 million in the past five years without manufacturing overseas, Adler said.

To respond to fashion trends quickly, Vintage Blue, a junior dress line the company acquired in 1991, is produced entirely in the U.S.

"The future of the junior business and the fashion business is in the States or close by," Adler said.

Halmode began sourcing dresses out of China in 1977, because of lower labor costs for embroidery and other handwork embellishment, he said.

Searle Blatt Ltd. manufactures its coats and sportswear in the U.S. and plans to do so for as long as possible, according to Steve Blatt, president and chief executive officer. The company could save 20 percent by manufacturing in Ukraine, as some coat makers are doing, he said.

"I would prefer to remain here, but I'm not sure I'll always have that luxury," Blatt said. "We used to investigate options every three years. Now it's becoming more urgent."

Unlike a growing number of outerwear manufacturers, Searle has avoided manufacturing overseas by producing a limited number of garments at higher price points, Blatt said.

Part of the demise of domestic manufacturing might be attributed to the lack of skilled workers and

the inability of factories to do short runs, he noted. With more American factories closing each year, Blatt said he expects domestic manufacturing to weaken in the next five to 10 years.

"I don't think it has anything to do with loyalty or anything else. There are very few factories with skilled workers," he said, "I looked for a domestic factory to manufacture sportswear for two years, and it went out of business almost as soon as I got in."

Outerwear maker Larry Levine produces 45 percent of its items here, and the remainder in Honduras and China. Silk anoraks, microfiber rainwear and other specialty items are developed overseas since the fabrics are sourced there. Although the company is always looking for new sources for fabrics, wool outwear will continue to be sourced in the U.S. even though many competitors are working in Eastern Europe, Levine said.

"As soon as the Russian fabric market is depleted, the prices will rise again," he said. "I'm opposed to go-ing because I think it's dangerous to put all your eggs in the same basket."

When Harvé Benard was started 27 years ago, all its coats and suits were made in the U.S., but now only 25 percent are produced domestically, according to Benard Holtzman, president and chief designer.

By sourcing overseas, the company has grown from $46 million to $100 million in the past five years, he said.

"Everyone would prefer to be here," Holtzman said. "We began working overseas 18 years ago as a defense mechanism. Now the product is more competitive at retail."

While sportswear firms in particular have turned to importing for better pricing and profits over the past two decades, some companies have stayed home.

"We have better control over quality, and we get a quicker turnaround," said Norty Sperling of Norton McNaughton. The exception to its U.S. production is handknit sweaters, which are done offshore.

"The lead time is critical these days," said Michael Kipperman, chief executive officer at Gotham Apparel Corp., which under the Turtlebeck label sells to such mass chains as Caldor, Kmart and Wal-Mart. "We can design something by 10 a.m. and have the sample in our hands on the same day."

Kipperman noted that from 1980 to 1983, the company tried producing shetland sweaters in Taiwan, but was disappointed.

"We are learning how to work with a gun pointing at our heads," he said, adding that 60 percent of his sample merchandise has a 24-hour turn time from when it is designed. He is aiming to have all of his products meet those standards by 1995.

"We don't want any surprises," said Barry Cohen, executive vice president at Ellen Figg, a maker of moderate-price apparel that produces its line here. "All of our production facilities are 45 minutes away from the showroom, and because of that, we can keep a close tab on production and quality, which are the two major demands from retailers."

Cohen said manufacturing in the U.S. allows the company to pick up on a hot trend, such as the pleated skirt last spring and the liquid metal looks in blouses for holiday shipping.

"We were able to design, produce and deliver to stores within a couple of weeks," Cohen said. "If we produced overseas, it would have taken us six months."

"The main reason makers have been going overseas was because of price, and now that is becoming less of an issue," said Cohen, noting that his U.S. production costs have stayed flat over the past three years. "I am doing bigger programs with retailers, who are willing to pay a premium for American-made products—and this is producing economies of scale."

"Mills are hungry for work, and I am better able to negotiate," said designer Cynthia Steffe, who started producing overseas in 1988, but switched when stores started buying closer to season.

For industry groups, organized labor and contractors, the fight to maintain production in the U.S., is a tough one.

Bruce Herman, president of the Garment Industry Development Corp., said there the losses in apparel manufacturing jobs have leveled off.

"We are seeing a greater interest in domestic sourcing and a potential for some growth," he said. "A lot of importers are bleeding rather badly, and more companies are coming to realize that a balance of domestic production and importing can play a strategic role in sourcing and delivering a well-priced product in a timely manner to retailers."

Lower real estate prices have brought some new factories to the Midtown garment center, particularly along Eighth Avenue, and in Chinatown, Herman said. Other important areas for manufacturing are the Williamsburg and Sunset Park sections of Brooklyn.

Founded in 1984, the GIDC is a nonprofit consortium of business, government and labor helping apparel firms with marketing, technology assistance and training, and real estate. It is supported by New York City, New York State, trade associations and the ILGWU. Its funding has grown from $120,000 in its first year to more than $1 million this year.

Herman said one of the most important of GIDC's programs and services is a Quick Response Supplier Network, which stemmed from a study called "Keeping New York in Fashion," published in 1992. The report's chief recommendation was that apparel firms should turn to QR technology.

The QR program helps companies reorganize production, marketing and inventory management systems to create links with retailers, contractors and suppliers.

In 1991, the GIDC also created Fashion Exports New York to help apparel companies become exporters. Another key program that's being expanded is a Quality Control Network, which helps manufacturers establish formal quality control guidelines and systems for their own factories and contractors. It also has training programs for upgrading worker skills.

"There is a future for apparel manufacturing here. The question is under what conditions," Herman said. "It's a matter of whether the industry will revert back to sweatshop conditions, or whether it will upgrade itself through technology.

Cheap labor and sweatshop conditions exist all over the world, so we shouldn't try to compete on that level. We should make New York a Quick Response center and that's what can separate us from the rest of the world."

Jay Mazur of the ILGWU agrees. "New York manufacturing offers an opportunity for competitive advantage if a company is willing to modernize its production."

"That's the future of the industry here," Mazur said. "There has been a recognition and participation on the part of the city and state in recent years in support of the industry. Through the Council for American Fashion, the GIDC and the work of the union, we are bringing home the message that companies can strike a balance between importing and domestic production and be competitive and successful."

The CAF is a labor-management partnership aimed at promoting the New York apparel industry.

Mazur said another key to keeping manufacturing in the U.S. is improved labor-management relations. He points to General Motors' Saturn division, whose employees have a say in running the company.

According to the ILGWU, there are 100,000 apparel manufacturing workers in the city, 58,000 of whom are union members. Each figure is about half of what it was in 1973. Back in the Fifties, New York had as many as 350,000 workers.

The largest concentration of jobs—60,000—is in Manhattan. Brooklyn is next with 22,000, followed by Queens with 15,000, the Bronx with 2,500 and Staten Island with 500. In addition, the ILGWU estimates there are another 80,000 jobs in New York in support industries.

Mazur points to FENY's progress in promoting exports as important to the industry's future here. "There is demand for American products overseas," he said.

Meanwhile, he contended, "If price is the only bottom line in a company, it's destructive in the long run. There's got to be a sense of balance where price and maintaining jobs are figured in. What's the point of getting the best possible price if people can't pay for the product because they don't have a job?"

Women's Wear Daily, September 8, 1994.

China on Front Burner for Retail

Elaine Underwood

With Western markets saturating, loosening trade restrictions are reviving marketers' interest in China, whose 1 billion-plus population has long tantalized them. An outcoming, exclusive survey of the Chinese market, to be officially unveiled by consulting giant Coopers & Lybrand at the National Retail Federation's annual convention in New York City this month, will reveal Chinese consumers as markedly similar to those in the U.S.

Mass marketers such as Kmart and others are exploring options in China. There they would join U.S. retailer Wal-Mart, which is developing stores in China through a joint venture with Thai conglomerate Charoenpokphand, a host of fast-food restaurants and such brands as Nike, Disney (licensed apparel) and Lee, which will start selling and advertising its jeans in Guangdong province in February.

Globalization has long been a rallying cry in the retailing and apparel manufacturing industries. The passage of NAFTA and GATT in 1994 is putting global expansion plans on the frontburner in 1995. And the country's affluent consumers (those earning at least $1,000 a year) will almost quadruple by the millennium to some 200 million, McKinsey & Company estimates.

Coopers & Lybrand staged three focus groups in Shanghai, one of the more prosperous cities, with young women in their late teens and early twenties, and middle-aged women and men. The groups had average disposable income of some $4,000 a year.

"They were very quality and value conscious," said Mark Kingdon, managing associate at Coopers & Lybrand. "They defined quality as something that stood up well and delivered on its promise."

The respondents preferred foreign brands to domestic, but the price of imports was sometimes too intimidating.

"I went to a very high-end department store in Shanghai, which sold Bally shoes and Burberry's raincoats, and it was dead," said Kingdon. "That's where the quality/value trade-off begins."

Chinese men cared little about clothing brands, but said they prized home electronics and would spend $1,200 for a TV and VCR. Younger women, unsurprisingly, were the most primed for the pitch.

"They were highly aspirational and said they liked to spend money on electronics and clothing," said Kingdon. "They were also cavalier about spending more money than they could afford. You can see the consumer economy coming."

Poised for early success in China is Wal-Mart, said retail expert Walter Loeb, president of Loeb Associates in New York.

"Wal-Mart is going to enter China as they announced with value-oriented, quality merchandise," said Loeb. "It's commodity apparel items that will succeed over there."

Brandsweek, January 9, 1995.

The early French designers who impacted fashion were Worth (top left), Poiret (top right), and Chanel (bottom).

4

5

6

7

*Cooperation of many
different industry
professionals
is required from the
initial production
phases to the ultimate
runway showings.*

8

9

10

11

After the long process from creation to completion, only the best of the women's wear collections shows up on the runway.

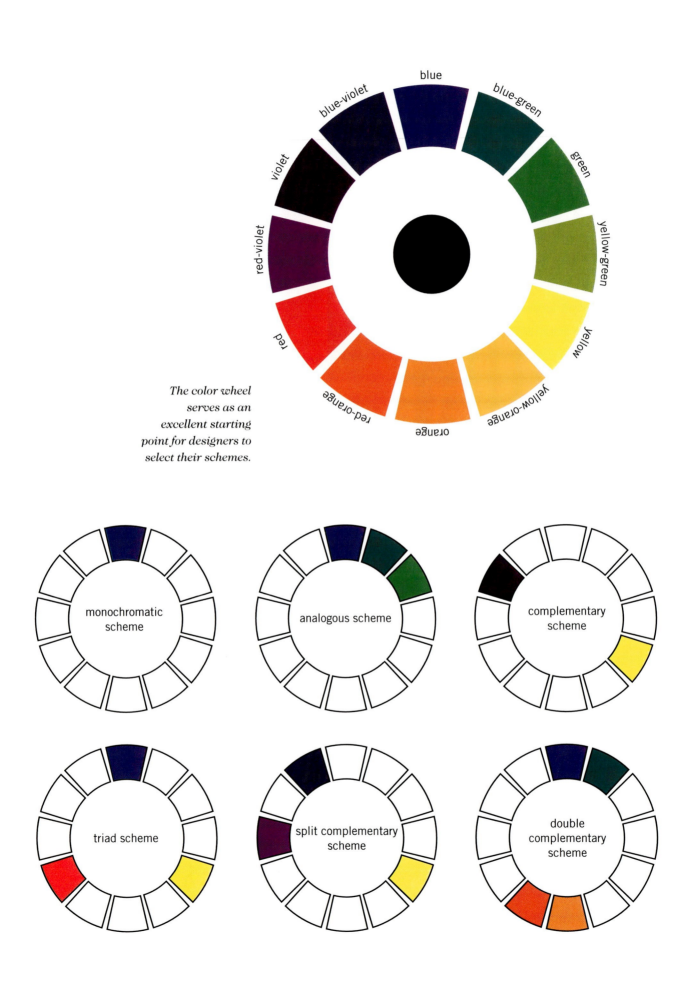

blue

blue-violet

blue-green

violet

green

red-violet

yellow-green

red

yellow

red-orange

yellow-orange

orange

The color wheel serves as an excellent starting point for designers to select their schemes.

monochromatic scheme

analogous scheme

complementary scheme

triad scheme

split complementary scheme

double complementary scheme

CHAPTER 6

Careers In Fashion

The world of fashion offers challenging, exciting, and financially rewarding career opportunities. The variety of activities involved in fashion results in diverse jobs that attract people with different backgrounds. Unlike other industries and professions, rigorous credentials and licenses are not required. Although formal education and training are beneficial, successful people in fashion may have studied fine arts, marketing, design, textiles, or just a broad based program. Many legends began their careers in other fields before choosing fashion. Giorgio Armani studied medicine, as did Geoffrey Beene, Gianni Versace and Gianfranco Ferré studied architecture, and Vivienne Westwood and Bruce Oldfield were teachers.

The types of careers are as numerous as the types of businesses that comprise the industry. The fashion industry is one of the largest employers in the United States. Because of global expansion and offshore production facilities, overseas opportunities are also plentiful. Manufacturers, wholesalers, designers, importers and exporters, retailers, publishers, marketing consultants, and public relations firms are just some of the areas of employment. Classified advertisements in consumer newspapers and in such trade papers as *Women's Wear Daily* and *DNR* present opportunities for those interested in a career in fashion.

SEGMENTS OF THE FASHION INDUSTRY

Some of the positions offered in classified ads are self-explanatory from the job titles; others require more explanation. Trade papers sometimes separate classified ads into two categories—Help Wanted and Sales Help Wanted. Within these classifications, positions are available in all segments of the textile and

After you have completed this chapter, you should be able to discuss:

- Employment opportunities in the various segments of the fashion industry.

- Techniques for a successful job interview.

- How to prepare a résumé and a cover letter.

Designer Fran Coleman of Tickle Me!, a company she started, creating a style.

apparel industries. This chapter discusses the fashion industry in terms of the careers offered in textiles, manufacturing, retailing, market consultants, and fashion communications.

Textiles

The textile industry employs technically skilled individual, whose talents and abilities range from creative and artistic to production and sales.

Textile Designer

Textile designers are artists who create particular patterns and present them in a format that can be translated into fabrics. They paint their designs on paper or fabric and prepare the **repeats** that will be used in the finished products. Their extensive use of computers necessitates a thorough understanding of the available software. Some major companies employ designers who simply develop the design concepts and leave the technical developments to repeat artists and painters. Those who usually enter this aspect of the industry are art and design graduates. Their remuneration is generally high.

Colorist

In companies with a great deal of specialization, the **colorist** is responsible for creating the color combinations that will be used in the production of the designer's patterns. The colorist must be an expert in color theory and must understand all of the technical aspects of color utilization.

Grapher

In knitwear, after an initial design has been completed, the design is graphed and the graphs used in the production process. In addition to requiring a complete knowledge of knitting construction, the **grapher** must also be computer literate. With CAD programs, graphing may be accomplished more quickly.

Converter

The **converter** oversees the change of greige goods (gray goods), which are unfinished fabrics, into finished textiles. Dyeing, printing, and the application of a variety of fabric finishes constitute converting. Some of the finishes enhance appearance, while others are merely functional. The converter's career is a highly technical one that requires a complete knowledge of fibers and fabrics. Additional information on converting will be found in Chapter 7, Textiles.

Dyer

A comprehensive knowledge of dyeing techniques, dye substances, colors, and chemicals is the responsibility of the person who dyes the stock, yarns, or finished fabric. The **dyer** is actually a textile chemist who understands all of the interactions of fabrics and the colors that will be applied. He or she should be a graduate of a textile chemistry program to ably perform the tasks involved in dyeing.

Production Manager

Making certain that every phase of manufacturing textiles is perfect is the job of the **production manager.** A highly paid career, it involves a complete understanding of every aspect of the textile industry. The production manager oversees plant operations and is responsible for coordination of all activities including staff management.

Textiles Sales Representatives (Reps)

Designers, manufacturers, and retailers are customers of textiles companies. Whatever the market they serve, sales reps in textile companies must have a complete understanding of fibers, weaving and knitting, coloring and finishing processes, product care, and fabric end uses. Knowledge is acquired through both formal and on-the-job training. These professionals have the potential to earn substantial incomes.

Manufacturing

At the very core of the fashion industry is the manufacturer. Whatever the products, manufacturing positions cut across all lines.

Designer

Textile reps sell to manufacturers and designers and must understand and know the benefits of each fabric.

Designers are responsible for setting the tone of a line in terms of silhouette, color, fabrication, and trim. The most successful have an educational background that includes sketching, draping, patternmaking, and sewing. They are the mainstays of the industry—without their creations, there would be no lines to sell.

Designers must be both technically and artistically competent. Besides preparing aesthetically appropriate sketches of their designs, they must fully understand the production requirements of each model. Knowing the draping qualities of textiles, patternmaking, construction techniques, and production limitations of their designs is essential. A knowledge of CAD, computer-aided design, is almost a must. In some cases, artists are called on to sketch for designers who use the draping approach or to draw designs when the designer is not able to. Sometimes artists paint textile designs according to the designer's instructions so that they can be translated into fabrics; and still others—especially at the couture level—actually hand-paint designs on fabrics.

Inspiration comes from a variety of events, places, and situations including movies, television, museum exhibitions, exotic travel, and historical events. The designer must adapt these inspirations into a line of merchandise that will excite the consumer.

Designer Joanne Criscione and her assistant discuss details of a new pattern.

Designers are so vital to the company, they are often the principals in the business and have their names on the labels. The major fashion houses are known by the names of their designers; they are equivalent to stars of the entertainment industry.

Occasionally, a designer becomes successful without having followed the traditional path. Sometimes good ideas and good taste are enough—as with Ralph Lauren who was a tie salesman, and Perry Ellis, who was a store buyer. One of the better known children's wear companies, Tickle Me!, was founded by an individual with no formal training but the ability to translate a good idea into a solid business. Fran Coleman, founder of Tickle Me! is featured in a World of Fashion Profile.

Assistant Designer

The unsung heroes of the design industry are the **assistant designers.** Well versed in all aspects of design, these individuals work as part of a team and are rarely recognized outside of their companies. In many companies, teams of assistant designers actually create the lines. The designer, however, has final approval concerning what will be produced and what will be eliminated, and takes credit for all of the work.

The assistants generally supervise the sewing of the sample garments, select trimmings, shop the textile markets for fabrics, and aid the designer in any way necessary. They are usually not highly paid, especially in comparison to the designer, but hope that with experience they will become head designers.

Merchandiser

The responsibilities of this position vary from company to company, but generally include making decisions concerning the company's line and fabric, marketing research, projecting sales, serving as liaison with the sales staff, contacting the mills, reviewing production considerations, and costing the merchandise. In some smaller companies, a **merchandiser** may also serve as designer. In these cases, the merchandiser travels extensively and scouts the market for styles, purchases them, and has adaptations made for the company

Fran Coleman

In the early 1980s, Fran Coleman was busy carrying out the traditional role of most married women. She was raising her family and spending free time participating in a variety of activities, including painting. She showed promise as an artist, but had no particular ambition toward such a career.

Known to be somewhat creative by her friends, Fran was approached to make a trimmed shirt for one of their daughters. It had so much eye appeal that the friend asked if she would like to make them and sell them to stores. At first she declined, but later, with the friend's cooperation, she got up the courage to approach a retailer with the samples. Although initially rejected by the merchant, she prodded him enough to convince him to buy. They sold quickly, with reorders to follow.

Working from her home and selling to local merchants soon became a real business. As luck would have it, her family, which was in the textile screen printing business, was able to provide her with factory space to enlarge her fledgling operation.

Today, with a large staff of designers, colorists, patternmakers, and other talented people, she operates one of the most successful children's wear companies in the country. Her products are sold throughout the United States in such fine stores as Neiman Marcus, Saks, Macy's, and Bloomingdales, and in specialty shops all over the world. She was the first children's wear designer to be recognized with the prestigious Dallas award for fashion design for two years.

Her story indicates that designers do not always follow the traditional paths, but come from every aspect of life.

Fran Coleman began her children's wear company at home and expanded it into an international company.

line. Merchandisers are generally highly paid, especially when product development is within their control.

Assistant Merchandiser

To become a merchandiser, it is necessary to begin as an assistant. This job varies with the needs of the particular merchandiser in a company. Some **assistant merchandisers** are primarily responsible for following and tracking fabric and trimmings orders, initial costing of sample garments, sales projections, and acting as the intermediary between the merchandiser and other company personnel, such as the designer, colorists, stylists, sales manager, production manager, and quality control manager. This position enables one to learn all the aspects of manufacturing.

Stylist

Companies that do not have a designer or do not give the merchandiser total responsibility for style development may employ a **stylist.** Stylists travel extensively, visiting markets to select styles that will fit the company's line. Rather than just copying the originals, the stylist generally translates each style to fit the manufacturer's needs. A thorough knowledge of textiles and color is necessary, so that the stylist can substitute fabrics and colors in the original designs to make the copy cost efficient.

In large companies, stylists assist designers by researching the market and making suggestions on fashion trends and innovations. Designers and colorists translate this information into specific patterns. To carry out their assignments, stylists interface with fashion forecasters and members of color associations, who are knowledgeable about trends in the industry.

Today's pattern-makers prepare their work using CAD systems.

Patternmaker / Grader

Patternmakers use the original design to create the patterns that will be used to produce the finished garments. They must be technically trained in construction, grading of sizes, production, cutting, and fabric utilization. Because most companies now use computers for pattern-making and grading procedures, pattern-makers and **graders** need a working knowledge of computer programs and the use of a **digitizer** for grading patterns.

Salaries for these positions are very high because few people choose to specialize in this area. While it does not afford the glamour of a designer's career, it provides for excellent, steady employment.

Cutter

As the name implies, **cutters** cut the fabrics and other materials into shapes as dictated by the patterns. This career requires considerable technical skill, including familiarity with computerized cutting. Companies that mass produce merchandise most often use the computerized format; those at the upper levels of fashion might still cut one garment at a time. When a natural material such as leather is being cut, it is the skilled operator who knows how to eliminate the blemished parts while producing the necessary pieces. Even though this skill is very important, remuneration is moderate.

Production Manager

Without a proper production team, the manufacturer's efforts can end in disaster. Anyone with experience in the fashion business has had experiences with poor quality construction, damaged merchandise, and late delivery. The **production manager** for an apparel manufacturer must coordinate and direct all aspects of production so that the designs are carefully executed and the delivery is made as requested on the purchase order.

Several market conditions complicate production. For example, manufacturers often perform only one aspect of the production process. For example, a company might prepare patterns and cut the materials into the component parts of a product, but subcontracts sewing to an outside contractor. In these situations, the production manager must accurately assess the abilities of possible contractors, so that appropriate firms are chosen to complete the production. Thus, the manager must supervise outside suppliers, as well as in-house production.

In today's fashion industry, a significant number of companies produce their merchandise offshore. The distance from the manufacturer's headquarters to the production point complicates the production manager's job. Many find themselves commuting between two countries to make certain that the finished products will be satisfactory and that delivery will be on schedule. For these efforts, production managers are very highly paid.

Quality Controller

One problem that often plagues the manufacturer is poor product quality. Many companies employ **quality controllers** to make certain that the merchandise headed for the retailer is in the best condition to guarantee customer satisfaction. Common errors include the wrong trim on a garment, mismatched sizes in two-piece outfits, poor seaming, faulty zippers, and different dye lots for items that are supposed to match.

Without attention to these details, the merchandise may be shipped to the store, but will soon be returned as unsatisfactory. Not only does this create difficulties for the merchant, who now has an inventory shortage, but it is extremely costly to the producer. Such goods are eventually sold at very low prices to closeout retailers resulting in a loss to the manufacturer.

To evaluate production quality, the controller must know all phases of construction, including familiarity with the quality of materials used. Because much of today's apparel and accessories are produced offshore, many companies hire quality controllers to work abroad so that the finished products need not be shipped back to the factory for the correction of errors.

Quality controllers are well paid because their expertise enables the manufacturer to produce the best possible merchandise.

Manufacturers' Sales Representatives (Reps)

Selling a fashion line can be a financially rewarding career. It is not unusual for sales personnel in apparel firms to be among the highest paid on a company's payroll.

Manufacturers' sales reps are paid basically by two methods. Those who work strictly in showrooms generally receive a salary, while those who cover specific territories are paid on commission. Sometimes, the sales rep receives a guaranteed salary plus a small commission on sales made. The straight commission salesperson, however, has the potential for higher earnings.

The customers served fall into several categories, from small retail operations with limited buying potential to the giants that are capable of purchasing larger quantities. Other buyers represent resident buying offices—businesses that represent retailers and purchase for them or recommend specific lines to them for purchase. Whether it is a small account or a large one, the manufacturer's sales rep performs the same functions: showing the line, helping with

Cutters must be skilled in all methods of cutting, including computerized cutting.

situations, the production manager must accurately assess the abilities of possible contractors, so that appropriate firms are chosen to complete the production. Thus, the manager must supervise outside suppliers, as well as in-house production.

In today's fashion industry, a significant number of companies produce their merchandise offshore. The distance from the manufacturer's headquarters to the production point complicates the production manager's job. Many find themselves commuting between two countries to make certain that the finished products will be satisfactory and that delivery will be on schedule. For these efforts, production managers are very highly paid.

Quality Controller

One problem that often plagues the manufacturer is poor product quality. Many companies employ **quality controllers** to make certain that the merchandise headed for the retailer is in the best condition to guarantee customer satisfaction. Common errors include the wrong trim on a garment, mismatched sizes in two-piece outfits, poor seaming, faulty zippers, and different dye lots for items that are supposed to match.

Without attention to these details, the merchandise may be shipped to the store, but will soon be returned as unsatisfactory. Not only does this create difficulties for the merchant, who now has an inventory shortage, but it is extremely costly to the producer. Such goods are eventually sold at very low prices to closeout retailers resulting in a loss to the manufacturer.

To evaluate production quality, the controller must know all phases of construction, including familiarity with the quality of materials used. Because much of today's apparel and accessories are produced offshore, many companies hire quality controllers to work abroad so that the finished products need not be shipped back to the factory for the correction of errors.

Quality controllers are well paid because their expertise enables the manufacturer to produce the best possible merchandise.

Manufacturers' Sales Representatives (Reps)

Selling a fashion line can be a financially rewarding career. It is not unusual for sales personnel in apparel firms to be among the highest paid on a company's payroll.

Manufacturers' sales reps are paid basically by two methods. Those who work strictly in showrooms generally receive a salary, while those who cover specific territories are paid on commission. Sometimes, the sales rep receives a guaranteed salary plus a small commission on sales made. The straight commission salesperson, however, has the potential for higher earnings.

The customers served fall into several categories, from small retail operations with limited buying potential to the giants that are capable of purchasing larger quantities. Other buyers represent resident buying offices—businesses that represent retailers and purchase for them or recommend specific lines to them for purchase. Whether it is a small account or a large one, the manufacturer's sales rep performs the same functions: showing the line, helping with merchandising, making certain goods are delivered on time, handling customer complaints, working with the credit office, bringing customer suggestions to the manufacturer, and fostering better vendor-purchaser relationships.

Divisional merchandiser salaries are high. The actual amount is based upon the division's sales volume and profitability to the store.

Buyer

Most fashion merchandising students interested in retailing as a career hope to become **buyers.** Buying is seen as the glamour career in the store. Although it does offer the excitement of evaluating new merchandise, attending fashion shows, and traveling to foreign markets, it also requires considerable time commitment and technical skills. In today's retail environment buyers are also involved in product development, Buyers are constantly studying computer printouts, planning purchases, figuring markups, taking markdowns, determining their **open-to-buys,** and computing the percentage of goods sold in a specific amount of time. Too many college students think that the only skills successful buyers need are good taste and color sense. This is far from the truth. Although a sense of style and color is a necessity, the ability to make quantitative decisions is the utmost important qualification.

Most executive trainees who are merchandising oriented can become buyers in as few as four or five years. To determine the accessibility of the buyer position, students need only to walk through a large retail organization and count the different merchandise classifications. Each organization has someone who specializes in purchasing one or two classifications.

The salaries are high and are based upon the importance and scope of the specific merchandise to the store.

Buyers attend NAMSB, one of the more important men's wear trade expositions.

Assistant Buyer

Most **assistant buyers** begin their careers in executive training programs. Some may have served as department managers before their promotion to assistant buyers. Whatever the track for achieving this position, the assistant buyer's role is very demanding and the salary is comparatively moderate. Assistants make regular visits to the market to place reorders, check on the status of expected merchandise, accompany the buyer to make recommendations on new merchandise, prescreen lines to assess appropriateness for buyer viewing, take markdowns, act as liaison with department managers, and sell during peak periods. The goal of every assistant is to become a buyer; this stage is the proving ground.

Product Developer

Many retailers now create their own merchandise. To meet this challenge, they employ **product developers** who decide which items will be marketed under the store's private labels. Companies like Macy's, Saks Fifth Avenue, The Limited, and J.C.Penney participate in these programs. The product developers scout the international markets seeking merchandise that might be adapted into styles for their stores. They might choose the sleeve of one garment, the collar of another, and so on until a specific style has been created. Successful product developers must have an understanding of style, silhouette, fashion trends, fabrication, color, and fit. They are most often graduates of fashion merchandising programs and receive high salaries for their work.

Store Manager

Most retail organizations operate their merchandising, control, and promotional divisions from a flagship store or centralized office. Unlike the people in these positions, who perform their activities for the entire organization, each unit in an organization needs its own **store manager.** A large chain requires only one buyer to purchase shirts for 500 stores, but it requires 500 managers.

The store manager's job depends on the size of the unit. In department store flagships and branches, they are often responsible for personnel, service, traffic, security, and maintenance. In the traditional units of chain operations, they are the ones who manage their stores. They hire salespeople, schedule employee hours, handle customer complaints, change displays, keep records, and do anything required to keep the store properly functioning. Many store managers work for a straight salary; others are rewarded with bonuses based on sales volume or profits.

Regional Manager

Most large chains are divided into regions or districts, which are overseen by managers. A **regional manager** may be responsible for as many as fifty stores. His or her job is to make certain that each store is functioning within the policies of the home office by evaluating each store manager's performance, and making recommendations for improvements. In some chains, the regional manager may recommend merchandise transfers. Merchandise that is selling poorly in one unit might be shifted to another where it has better sales potential. The job involves making periodic visits to each unit and reporting back to management with a performance assessment.

Regional managers come from the ranks of store managers. They are straight salaried or salaried plus a bonus for profitability.

Department Manager

In major retail operations, a store is divided into merchandise departments. The head of each is a **department manager,** who is responsible for inventory control, record keeping, sales management, employee scheduling, and selling. The department manager receives only average monetary rewards and aims for a promotion to store manager or merchandiser.

Fashion Director

This high-level position in most major department stores often carries the title of vice president. The **fashion director** studies the fashion industry day to day, so that the store is prepared to accommodate any fashion innovation.

In the major flagship store, the fashion director works closely with the buyers and merchandisers, alerting them to such details as changing hemlines,

The fashion director often coordinates and plans a fashion show.

color preferences, silhouette trends, and new fabrications. Although each buyer is ultimately responsible for the actual purchases, the fashion director often supplies the information upon which these buying decisions are based. To be successful, directors must work as much as a year in advance of a season to gather information. They travel abroad to assess foreign design trends and textile mill offerings, make regular visits to domestic mills for fabric and color research, scout the tanners for leather information, constantly stay abreast of the trade paper forecasts, and are involved in all activities that provide market insights. After all of this detailed study, the fashion director presents to the store's merchandising team an analysis of the upcoming season's offerings and how each buyer's merchandise can be coordinated into a specific, total fashion image.

Many stores use fashion shows to promote their merchandise. Often it is the fashion director who plans the show's format, pulls the merchandise from the different departments, hires models and musicians, prepares the program, and arranges the seating plans. In some stores, the fashion director is called on to select the accessories that will be used to enhance apparel in window and interior displays.

The job is an exciting one. It provides an opportunity to work with many segments of the store and the fashion industry and gives the individual the chance to help mold the store's fashion image.

Advertising Manager

Those with artistic and creative talent might head for a career in retail advertising. Having studied all aspects of graphic design, the **advertising managers** must shape the image of the store's advertising campaigns. They write copy, create artwork, prepare layouts, and direct the specialists.

The advertising manager shapes the image of the company's campaign.

Department Manager

In major retail operations, a store is divided into merchandise departments. The head of each is a **department manager,** who is responsible for inventory control, record keeping, sales management, employee scheduling, and selling. The department manager receives only average monetary rewards and aims for a promotion to store manager or merchandiser.

Fashion Director

This high-level position in most major department stores often carries the title of vice president. The **fashion director** studies the fashion industry day to day, so that the store is prepared to accommodate any fashion innovation.

In the major flagship store, the fashion director works closely with the buyers and merchandisers, alerting them to such details as changing hemlines, color preferences, silhouette trends, and new fabrications. Although each buyer is ultimately responsible for the actual purchases, the fashion director often supplies the information upon which these buying decisions are based. To be successful, directors must work as much as a year in advance of a season to gather information. They travel abroad to assess foreign design trends and textile mill offerings, make regular visits to domestic mills for fabric and color research, scout the tanners for leather information, constantly stay abreast of the trade paper forecasts, and are involved in all activities that provide market insights. After all of this detailed study, the fashion director presents to the store's merchandising team an analysis of the upcoming season's offerings and how each buyer's merchandise can be coordinated into a specific, total fashion image.

Many stores use fashion shows to promote their merchandise. Often it is the fashion director who plans the show's format, pulls the merchandise from the different departments, hires models and musicians, prepares the program, and arranges the seating plans. In some stores, the fashion director is called on to select the accessories that will be used to enhance apparel in window and interior displays.

The job is an exciting one. It provides an opportunity to work with many segments of the store and the fashion industry and gives the individual the chance to help mold the store's fashion image.

Advertising Manager

Those with artistic and creative talent might head for a career in retail advertising. Having studied all aspects of graphic design, the **advertising managers** must shape the image of the store's advertising campaigns. They write copy, create artwork, prepare layouts, and direct the specialists.

More and more stores are using **desktop publishing programs** to save money by producing their merchandise catalogs and ads in-house. Therefore, the advertising director must be totally familiar with computer software pro-

*In-store demonstrations
generally result in
significant sales.*

Interpreters

With the increase in international travel, travelers often shop in places where a different language is spoken. To cater to this clientele, many retailers who are based in cities that attract significant tourism employ interpreters to assist these people. At Macy's in New York and Harrod's in London, for example, individuals who speak many different languages are available to accompany shoppers who seek assistance with their selections. The retailers find that these are excellent customers, who often buy quickly and in significant amounts. The basic requirement for such a position is the ability to speak at least three languages fluently. Interpreters are paid a regular wage, and sometimes a commission on the merchandise they sell.

Market Consultants

Retailers, manufacturers, and designers are always interested in having as much information as possible so that both short- and long-term goals are satisfactorily achieved. Throughout the fashion industry consulting companies function specifically to help such clients. Resident buying offices, reporting services, and fashion forecasters make up the majority of these **market consultants.** For fees, percentages, and/or commissions, they supply the information needed to achieve success. Each market consulting organization employs a variety of specialists who are responsible for serving their clients' needs. The resident buying offices, the most numerous of the group, assist store buyers with their purchasing requirements; the fashion forecaster predicts long-range trends; and the reporting services prepare press releases concerning every aspect of the fashion industry.

The resident buyer helps a client plan the new season.

Since all of the marketing consulting companies disseminated materials to their subscribers, this segment offers a great opportunity to those individuals with skills in drawing and writing. For example, flyers containing drawings of the merchandise suggested for the buyer's store must be drawn in a manner that will motivate the retailer to consider purchasing. Individuals are also needed to prepare written promotional pieces describing resources, best-selling items, and fashion notices. Such a position requires the ability to express ideas clearly and simply.

The following positions are just some of the important ones found in many consulting companies.

Resident Buyer

Although the title indicates purchasing, the resident buyer is an adviser rather than a purchaser. The major responsibilities are locating new resources, suggesting hot items, handling complaints about vendors, and supplying general fashion information that might help the store buyer formulate purchasing plans. Some buying, specifically reorders and special orders, is part of the job, but not the major part.

Unlike the store buyer, who has countless store responsibilities and works long hours to accomplish them, the resident buyer works regular business hours. In cases such as market week, a hectic period when the store buyers visit the wholesale markets, the hours are generally longer. Although the typically short hours may be attractive to some people, the salary levels are much below those of retail buyers. It is easier to become a buyer in a resident buying office than at the retail level, and the formal educational requirements for entry into this career are much less rigorous.

Many people take positions as resident buyers to learn about the fashion industry. Once satisfied that their expertise has been heightened, they transfer to the better paying, more challenging career of retail buying.

Assistant Resident Buyer

An entry-level position, **assistant resident buyers** spend considerable time in the market "following up orders." They check delivery dates and the merchandise status of orders placed by the stores they represent. The job is extremely low paying and serves only as an initiation into the fashion world.

Fashion Forecaster

Resident buying offices and fashion forecasting companies predict fashion trends. **Fashion forecasters** visit the textile mills to assess the fabrics and colors that will be featured in clothing approximately twelve to eighteen months later, study haute couture designs that will probably be translated into more affordable priced models, and analyze social, political, and economic events that could become the basis of future fashion trends. Often, they travel to foreign countries to observe the ways in which the people dress—this is sometimes the inspiration for new designs. A fashion forecaster's career requires good verbal and writing skills, a keen understanding of fashion fundamentals, and the ability to participate in research endeavors.

The salaries for such individuals are high, because their forecasts often become the basis for future business decisions.

Fashion Communications

Both print and broadcast media provide exciting careers in fashion. Trade papers such as *Women's Wear Daily,* consumer newspapers and magazines, and television are arenas in which people with communication skills can seek employment. In addition to a complete knowledge of fashion, each participant must be capable of writing about or illustrating fashion concisely and excitingly, to communicate ideas in a meaningful manner, and to be able to successfully relate to all segments of the industry.

Fashion forecasters predict trends so that their clients can plan for the future.

Unlike the store buyer, who has countless store responsibilities and works long hours to accomplish them, the resident buyer works regular business hours. In cases such as market week, a hectic period when the store buyers visit the wholesale markets, the hours are generally longer. Although the typically short hours may be attractive to some people, the salary levels are much below those of retail buyers. It is easier to become a buyer in a resident buying office than at the retail level, and the formal educational requirements for entry into this career are much less rigorous.

Many people take positions as resident buyers to learn about the fashion industry. Once satisfied that their expertise has been heightened, they transfer to the better paying, more challenging career of retail buying.

Fashion photographers must be able to capture the tone and style of fashion designs.

Assistant Resident Buyer

An entry-level position, **assistant resident buyers** spend considerable time in the market "following up orders." They check delivery dates and the merchandise status of orders placed by the stores they represent. The job is extremely low paying and serves only as an initiation into the fashion world.

Fashion Forecaster

Resident buying offices and fashion forecasting companies predict fashion trends. **Fashion forecasters** visit the textile mills to assess the fabrics and colors that will be featured in clothing approximately twelve to eighteen months later, study haute couture designs that will probably be translated into more affordable priced models, and analyze social, political, and economic events that could become the basis of future fashion trends. Often, they travel to foreign countries to observe the ways in which the people dress—this is sometimes the inspiration for new designs. A fashion forecaster's career requires good verbal and writing skills, a keen understanding of fashion fundamentals, and the ability to participate in research endeavors.

The salaries for such individuals are high, because their forecasts often become the basis for future business decisions.

Fashion Communications

Both print and broadcast media provide exciting careers in fashion. Trade papers such as *Women's Wear Daily,* consumer newspapers and magazines, and television are arenas in which people with communication skills can seek employment. In addition to a complete knowledge of fashion, each participant must be capable of writing about or illustrating fashion concisely and excitingly, to communicate ideas in a meaningful manner, and to be able to successfully relate to all segments of the industry.

Richard Avedon

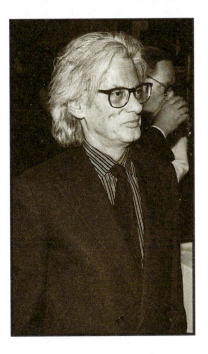

Starting in an unlikely environment—the merchant marine—Richard Avedon went on to achieve fame as a fashion photographer. After taking an experimental photography class at the New York School for Social Research, given by the art director of *Harper's Bazaar*, he was invited to join the staff of the magazine in 1945. His tenure at *Harper's* lasted twenty years. In 1966, he moved to *Harper's* rival fashion publication, *Vogue*, where he remained until 1990. Since leaving *Vogue*, he has been staff photographer for *The New Yorker*.

Avedon's photography had a style all its own. He incorporated freedom and drama into his works.

Those in the industry are always able to recognize his work even if it is untitled.

Avedon's numerous awards include the Art Director's Show (1950) highest achievement medal, the Pratt Institute citation of dedication to fashion photography (1976), the Art Director's Club Hall of Fame (1982), and the Council of Fashion Designers of America Lifetime Achievement Award (1989).

Retrospectives of his photographs have been displayed in one-person shows at the Museum of Modern Art (1975), the Metropolitan Museum of Art (1978), the Whitney Museum (1994), and the National Portrait Gallery in London (1995).

Richard Avedon's photography is noted for its freedom and drama.

Commentator

In television, fashion information is delivered both visually and orally to the viewer. Although the major emphasis is on the visual, commentary often follows the action. The commentary is, however, generally written in advance by retail or designer fashion coordinators when lines are shown to potential customers. Because most television stations rely upon their own regular journalists to read commentary that has been written by someone else, there is little career opportunity for being a commentator. One exception to this is *Style,* a fashion feature on cable television with Elsa Klensch. She is one of the very few fashion commentators for television.

Shopping Network Host

Throughout the United States there are several cable channels that bring merchandise into the homes of the viewer. The programs use a variety of hosts to present the merchandise, the majority of which is fashion apparel and accessories, in a way that motivates the viewer to purchase. They have the looks and personalities necessary to gain rapport with their audiences.

Wardrobe Consultant

The credits at the end of film and television productions, often list the names of designers or stores whose clothing was worn by the casts. Most programs use a **wardrobe consultant** whose job is to scout the market for the right merchandise to outfit its stars and then to make arrangements for the loan of the merchandise in exchange for the displayed credit. The consultant must have a full knowledge of the fashion industry, the resources where apparel is available, and the expertise necessary to select the best styles to enhance the wearer's figure. Graduates of fashion programs are best suited for these highly paid positions.

Fashion Educator

A career sometimes associated with the field of fashion communications is that of the *fashion educator*. Many schools from post-secondary to the two- and four-year college level include programs in fashion design and/or merchandising. Some schools offer a full range of fashion subjects such as retailing, merchandising, designing, and so on; others specialize in just one segment of the fashion industry.

Those with a desire to teach the practices and procedures needed to enter the fashion industry may find employment as instructors. Typically, the requirements for such a career include a masters degree and hands-on experience in the industry.

THE INTERVIEW

Securing the Interview

After studying the career choices and selecting those appropriate to one's educational background and practical experience, the route to a job interview should begin. Interviews may be secured in many ways, but the best is networking. Nothing works better than a recommendation from a friend, relative, or acquaintance who knows someone in the field. That is not to say that a recommendation guarantees a job. It usually just helps gain an interview; the rest is up to the candidate.

A second technique is to carefully review classified advertisements. Candidates can also research the fashion industry at trade shows, in fashion periodicals, and through trade associations and organizations. They can obtain information about specific companies that could be potential employers.

Contacting an employment or recruitment agency is still another road to take. Agencies that specialize in finding employment in the fashion industry are easily found in newspapers and in the yellow pages. They often have leads for positions where fees are paid by the prospective employer.

Whatever approach serves the applicant's needs, specific materials must be prepared before the interview. They are the:

- Résumé
- Cover letter
- Portfolio (to show the applicant's special talents)

The Résumé

Those responsible for hiring rarely want to interview every prospective candidate for the job. To determine which individuals have the necessary qualifications for employment, most business executives or human resources managers

SAMPLE RÉSUMÉ

JENNIFER MURRAY
3930 Stanton Street
Chicago, IL 60616
312-555-6098

EDUCATION: Bradley Community College   Chicago, IL
AAS Fashion Merchandising, June 1996
Honors: Magna Cum Laude

SPECIAL EXPERIENCE: I was one of ten students selected from a group of
95 to participate in an internship with Printemp in
Paris as a personal shopper. Being fluent in French
helped me considerably.

COLLEGE ACTIVITIES: Fashion show coordinator
President, Retailing club
Freshman orientation adviser

EXPERIENCE:

6/94 -present   LORD & TAYLOR   Chicago, IL
Personal shopper and interpreter

- Assist customers with their selections.
- Interpret for French and Italian visitors.
- Select merchandise for corporate accounts.
- Choose accessories for fashion shows.

5/93 - 9/93   THE GAP   Chicago, IL
Selling and visual merchandising

- Arranged inventory.
- Installed visual presentations.
- Responsible for cashdraw tally.
- Prepared in-house signage for displays.

6/92 - 8/92   BOOGIE'S DINER   Chicago, IL
Selling and inventory management

- Supervised inventory control.
- Handled customer returns.
- Prepared vendor returns.
- Reordered merchandise as per manager's
request.

INTERESTS: Travel, theater, skiing, aerobics.

REFERENCES: Will be furnished upon request.

prefer to have some initial information concerning the applicant's achievements. This personal and professional background is presented in a **résumé,** a historical compilation of a candidate's education and employment record.

Résumés may be professionally written by specialists, for a fee, or may be created by the individual. Many books on résumé writing are available in libraries and bookstores and through local government employment agencies.

dising. Some schools offer a full range of fashion subjects such as retailing, merchandising, designing, and so on; others specialize in just one segment of the fashion industry.

Those with a desire to teach the practices and procedures needed to enter the fashion industry may find employment as instructors. Typically, the requirements for such a career include a masters degree and hands-on experience in the industry.

SAMPLE COVER LETTER

3930 Stanton Street
Chicago, IL 60616
312-555-6098
December 19, 1996

Ms. Emily Winters
Human Resources Manager
Lord & Taylor
1525 Fifth Avenue
New York, NY 10007

Dear Ms. Winters:

At the suggestion of Mr. Anthony Finch, Director of Executive Development at Lord & Taylor in Chicago, I am writing to you about possible employment as a personal shopper in your New York City flagship store.

I completed my two-year degree in Fashion Merchandising, in June, 1995, and am currently anticipating enrollment at New York's Fashion Institute of Technology for a bachelor's degree. The program is given in the evening, which will allow me to work full time.

The time spent at your company's Chicago store enabled me to apply what I learned in college to the real world of retailing. It was an excellent experience.

Enclosed is a copy of my resume, which gives you some background information about me.

Sincerely,

Jennifer Murray

Jennifer Murray

cover letter. Whatever the motivation, the letter should simply ask the reader to examine the enclosed résumé and arrange for an interview.

Common errors in preparing cover letters are including information that duplicates what is found in the résumé, including so much information that there will be little to discuss at the interview, and addressing the letter Dear Sir or Dear Human Resources Manager. This indicates that the writer spent no time learning the name of the individual responsible for hiring. A telephone call to the company will certainly provide the name and appropriate title of the person to whom the résumés and cover letters should be addressed. It is also imperative to correctly spell the individual's name. Any mistake with this simple matter might indicate a sloppy or lazy approach.

Finally, the paper or stock on which the letter is written, as well as the envelope, should be the same as that of the résumé. This package is the only means of getting the interviewer's attention. Because each letter might be one of hundreds received by a particular company, it must make a professional impression.

Portfolios

Many positions in the fashion world require creativity. Individuals interested in careers as designers, stylists, product developers, colorists, illustrators, writers, photographers, and visual merchandisers will need to prepare a **portfolio.** At the time of the interview, it will show your artistic and creative abilities.

The portfolio, which will quickly give an impression of your accomplishments, should be presented in a professional format. This may be achieved by employing the services of an expert or by your own careful preparation. A design portfolio should include sketches with color and fabric swatches for all of your designs and any other materials illustrating your creativity. For a writing position, articles in trade or consumer publications should be carefully organized and displayed. Notice of any prizes should also be highlighted.

With a perfectly executed package, you are ready to prepare for the interview.

Preparing for the Interview

Once an interview is arranged, prepare to sell yourself to the organization by dressing appropriately and learning something of the company's background and goals.

Researching the Company

All too often candidates are rejected because they know little about the organization to which they are applying for a job. By researching the company, an individual demonstrates that he or she is not merely applying for any job, but is being selective.

Major companies, such as DuPont, Calvin Klein, Ralph Lauren, The Limited, and Macy's, for example, are the easiest to learn about. They prepare annual reports for their stockholders, in which the company's assets, specialties, and goals are generally summarized. These are available just for the asking. Major businesses are often the subjects of articles in the trade papers and consumer newspapers, all of which are easily obtainable in libraries. Sometimes a firsthand glimpse of a company may be achieved through a "look" at it. When applying to a major retailer, for example, a visit to one of its stores will immediately reveal its inventory emphasis and the code of dress demonstrated by its employees. When the career choice is editorial in nature, familiarize yourself with that company's periodicals to learn about the style of writing and the areas of interest.

As much research as possible will benefit the applicant by making him or her feel more comfortable and confident during the interview.

Role Playing

Many career hopefuls show up at an interview totally unprepared for the questions that may be asked. While researching the company will provide information, it will not provide the questions or techniques that might be employed during the interview. **Role playing** is a technique that might help. It involves two people, one who plays the part of the interviewer, the other the interviewee. Although this will not be identical to the actual interview, it can usefully simulate the meeting between the business executive and the job applicant.

Ideally, role-playing could involve a friend or relative with business experience or a teacher with interviewing experience. If these sources are unavailable, another student could perform the interviewing task. Whoever the participants might be, it is necessary to provide the mock interviewer with any company information gathered during the research stage.

Having participated in this role playing, the applicant is better prepared to handle the real thing.

Appearance

All too often, hopes for a position are dashed by having worn the wrong outfit for an interview. While the terms *good taste* and *appropriate dress* are bandied about, many people simply do not understand their meanings. A good method for choosing the right interview outfit is to visit a retailer that specializes in corporate dress or business attire, or a service, such as personal shopping where individual attention is provided. Another approach is to visit the company to which you are applying and observe the type of clothing worn by their staffs. For a fee, there are specialists who will help you with your total appearance, including personal grooming and wardrobe selection. Many books written on the subject are available in the library.

Whatever resources are used to determine the appropriate dress, its importance cannot be overemphasized. When the door is opened to the interviewer's office and the applicant enters, it is this first impression that may make or break the interview.

Postinterview Practice: Letter of Appreciation

After the interview is concluded, the candidate should send a letter that expresses appreciation for the time spent with the applicant and indicates continuing interest in the company. Emphasis should be placed on what was learned during the interview, as well as the enthusiasm the applicant has to work for the company. It might also be beneficial to relate how, if successful in obtaining the job, one would be an asset to the organization.

SAMPLE LETTER OF APPRECIATION

3930 Stanton Street
Chicago, IL 60616
312-555-6098
January 8, 1997

Ms. Emily Winters
Human Resources Manager
Lord & Taylor
1525 Fifth Avenue
New York, NY 10007

Dear Ms. Winters:

Our meeting on Friday with you and your assistant made me realize that working for your company would be an exciting and rewarding experience. Not only did you both make me immediately feel at home, but your enthusiasm for Lord & Taylor has made me believe working for the company would be a wise choice. I believe that I can certainly fit comfortably in your organization and would like to have the opportunity to do so.

While I was told that others were being considered for the position, I believe, if chosen, my contributions would be at the highest level.

If you have any other questions you would like answered, please feel free to contact me.

Sincerely,

Jennifer Murray

Jennifer Murray

Chapter Highlights

- The fashion industry offers a variety of career opportunities in textiles, manufacturing, designing, retailing, marketing, and communications.
- The fashion industry accommodates people with diverse educational backgrounds. There are, however, some technically oriented careers that necessitate a mastery of particular skills.
- Because the fashion world is global in scope, employment opportunities are not limited to one geographic location.
- Candidates for jobs in the fashion field should prepare a résumé, cover letter, and, if appropriate, a portfolio.
- Prepare for the job interview by researching the company background, role playing, and assembling an appropriate wardrobe.

Ideally, role-playing could involve a friend or relative with business experience or a teacher with interviewing experience. If these sources are unavailable, another student could perform the interviewing task. Whoever the participants might be, it is necessary to provide the mock interviewer with any company information gathered during the research stage.

Having participated in this role playing, the applicant is better prepared to handle the real thing.

Appearance

All too often, hopes for a position are dashed by having worn the wrong outfit for an interview. While the terms *good taste* and *appropriate dress* are bandied about, many people simply do not understand their meanings. A good method for choosing the right interview outfit is to visit a retailer that specializes in corporate dress or business attire, or a service, such as personal shopping where individual attention is provided. Another approach is to visit the company to which you are applying and observe the type of clothing worn by their staffs. For a fee, there are specialists who will help you with your total appearance, including personal grooming and wardrobe selection. Many books written on the subject are available in the library.

Whatever resources are used to determine the appropriate dress, its importance cannot be overemphasized. When the door is opened to the interviewer's office and the applicant enters, it is this first impression that may make or break the interview.

Postinterview Practice: Letter of Appreciation

After the interview is concluded, the candidate should send a letter that expresses appreciation for the time spent with the applicant and indicates continuing interest in the company. Emphasis should be placed on what was learned during the interview, as well as the enthusiasm the applicant has to work for the company. It might also be beneficial to relate how, if successful in obtaining the job, one would be an asset to the organization.

Chapter Highlights

- The fashion industry offers a variety of career opportunities in textiles, manufacturing, designing, retailing, marketing, and communications.
- The fashion industry accommodates people with diverse educational backgrounds. There are, however, some technically oriented careers that necessitate a mastery of particular skills.
- Because the fashion world is global in scope, employment opportunities are not limited to one geographic location.
- Candidates for jobs in the fashion field should prepare a résumé, cover letter, and, if appropriate, a portfolio.
- Prepare for the job interview by researching the company background, role playing, and assembling an appropriate wardrobe.

3. Using the classifieds in a trade paper such as *Women's Wear Daily* or *DNR,* chose a career opportunity that motivates you to seek further information. Research the company in terms of size, geographical location, merchandise specialization, etc. The information can be obtained from the sources outlined in the chapter.

The Case of the Successful Job Candidate

Stacey Peters will graduate from college in two months with a degree in fashion merchandising. In addition to the required liberal arts courses, she has studied a number of fashion-related subjects, such as retail management, textiles, advertising, fashion coordination, and fashion publicity. Her cumulative grade point average is 3.7 out of a possible 4.0, which will enable her to graduate with honors. Because she comes from a family that has been in the fashion industry at various levels, Stacey brings a great deal of enthusiasm to a prospective employer.

Like any diligent prospective graduate, she has done her investigative homework. She has researched numerous manufacturing companies and retail organizations, preparing a résumé appropriate to each. To her credit, her time and effort have paid off. She was invited to interview with three prestigious fashion-oriented retail organizations and five manufacturers. The interviews resulted in three firm offers:

1. Smith and Campbell, a department store with fifteen branches, offered her admission to their executive training program, which could lead to either a merchandising or management career. The starting salary is $25,000 with future raises based upon her ability to perform.

2. Design Images, a high-fashion chain organization, offered her a position as an assistant store manager in one of the company's 35 units. For a starting salary of $21,000, Stacey would assist the store manager and have such decision-making responsibilities as employee scheduling, visual merchandising, handling customer complaints, and inventory replenishment. Within two years she could become a store manager.

3. The Male Image, a men's wear designer and manufacturer, has agreed to hire Stacey as a sales representative. Initially she would sell the company's line in the showroom for a salary of $27,000 and eventually become a "road" salesperson with compensation based on straight commission.

Each of the companies is based in Stacey's general geographic area and provides potential for a successful career.

Questions

1. What aspects of each job should Stacey investigate before making a decision?

2. What are the disadvantages, if any, of each job?

3. Which position would you suggest she accept? Why?

The Designers' New Palette

Alison Grudier

Textile designers are trading in paint and paper for a faster, more flexible medium: the computer. The move lets them turn out multiple variations on a design in record time.

"The design groups I produce on the computer are the best that I'm capable of because I can revise and rework a design, going over every square inch of detail until it's perfect," commented Bernice Mast of New York-based design studio Mastmedia.

Mast is just one of many printed-fabric designers logging on to computer-aided textile design. And the desire to experiment with multiple variations on a design has a strong precedent in the development of art. Monet, for instance, painted the Rouen cathedral well over a dozen times, recording the play of light on its gothic facade at different hours of the day.

But while Monet made the time to explore his artistic vision at Rouen, textile designers have felt compromised by the time and expense involved in reworking patterns on paper. Computer-aided design, they contend, allows freedom of experimentation while ensuring production integrity.

For most textile designers, the first encounter with computers generally involves scanning in paintings and altering colors on screen, but that is changing. CAD technology is improving to where designers can create right on a computer screen. Developments such as faster processors, drawing tablets and pens, and paint simulations have encouraged designers to go beyond merely processing and altering painted images.

Computer processing speed doubles about every 18 months, for about the same price. For computer artists, that increase in processing power translates to a larger drawing area and faster color changes. Any artist who's sat counting the seconds while the computer saves her work will attest to the importance of increased processing speed.

Jakim Notea of Cadtex Corp. explains. "Four years ago, the maximum drawing size on a PC was 512 x 800 pixels [7" x 11" at low resolution]. Today, a PC can be equipped with 192 MB of RAM, which will give an unlimited drawing area."

The jagged edges common in earlier computer-generated designs resulted from a compromise by artists. Textile designers often worked low-resolution, sacrificing image clarity to produce a normal-sized design.

Sigrid Olsen designs her signature collection on a Computer Design Inc. [CDI] system that was purchased several years ago.

"When I first started creating designs on the computer, the buyers complained that the designs looked too blocky," she said. "So I went back to painting."

Olsen now plans to upgrade her CDI system to run that vendor's new U4IA [Euphoria] software. She said the upgrade will let her create the brightly colored, nature-inspired prints she is known for. Drawing tablets and pressure-sensitive pens are making working with computers more neutral for artists. The Wacom pen and tablet has become a standard option offered by most CAD software vendors. To get maximum benefit form the pen and tablet, software must respond like lead-based pencils, charcoal or other media. For example, with Desitex software from NedGraphics Prints, a designer can use the pressure-sensitive pen to layer on color just as she would with watercolors, or simulate a variable-density airbrush by varying the pressure of programs like Fractal Dabbler or Fractal Painter, artists using the pen can shade drawings in successive motions, making computer drawing remarkably similar to traditional drawing.

Beyond even the tablet is the Graphic Instinct product from Lectra Systems. With a projection device mounted behind a drawing table, the user has a computerized workstation that resembles a normal drafting table. A cordless pen has the look and feel of a marker, but the design created can be endlessly changed and recolored using the one computerized marker rather than dozens of felt-tip markers.

Programs from Cadtex, CDI, Sophis and Designer Software use the existing colors in a design and rotate through all the possible color placements, giving the designer the chance to scroll through hundreds of colorways in a few minutes, stopping and saving the ones that look the best. In a five-color design, the total number of possible colorways is 720.

"The designers are experimenting with more colorways because they don't have to pay $100 for each new painting," commented Alyse DeMaria, a designer at P. Kaufman Inc., which supplies fabric to home furnishings companies.

One of the most important parts of textile designs is the spacing of motifs within a design repeat. True design software enables the user to move motifs and layer them behind or in front of other elements until the desired effect is achieved. Adobe Photoshop version 3.0 creates floating selections, CDI uses an image clipboard and Athena Design creates vector-defined objects to give designers the freedom they have been demanding. These functions, once only available on high-end graphics workstations, are now possible on desktop PCs.

For pure creation, designer Mast likes Fractal Painter.

"The program simulates papers and textures that really add depth to my designs," she said. "The filters allow me to brainstorm—I can come up with five more ideas than I would have if I had to use paints."

Designers are quick to point out that it's not the computer that is doing the work, but the artist who uses the computer.

"An artist can't be the best at traditional design one day and contemporary patterns the next just because he has a computer," remarked Anthony Aiello, design director for Fieldcrest Cannon's blanket division. "It still takes a skilled hand and a creative eye."

Because of the high cost of most CAD systems, the pressure to get the most return on the investment has led companies to employ them for preparing designs for production, or to replace service work paintings. However, as the cost of the technology comes down and improvements in software and hardware make using computers more natural, designers will increasingly turn to computers to create, experiment and present original design concepts faster and in greater detail than possible with traditional materials.

Daily News Record, April 6, 1995

Advice to Aspiring Designers: Get Smart Before Getting Started

Valerie Seckler

Talented designers too often underestimate the importance of business skills when seeking financing for their young businesses.

This was the consensus of factors, the most common source of funding for designers whose companies are in early growth stages. These entrepreneurial ventures are often rich in design and sales talent, said factors interviewed by WWD, but sorely lacking in crucial backroom support like production proficiency, accounting expertise and sales organizations.

Such shortcomings typically undermine a designer's efforts to obtain

financing and often explode the fledgling enterprise, factors noted.

Miles Stuchin, president of Access Capital, a factor that counts apparel designers among its clients, said, "We sometimes see design expertise but weak production skills. Often a company can produce, but is weak on bookkeeping. In smaller companies with limited funds, these can be big problems."

Observed Walter Kaye, president of Merchant Factors, "We don't see lots of designers going into business as we did in the past. Many who try don't know how to go beyond line development."

"They're not as able to market themselves and find funding as their predecessors," added Kaye, who founded Merchant 10 years ago at age 57.

In order to win the confidence and financing of factors, a young designer firm must build the proper business foundation and get at least one successful retail season under its belt.

After sinking $10,000 to $15,000 of their own money into their businesses, designers' next infusion of funds can come from a variety of sources, factors explained. They include family members, investors

to my designs," she said. "The filters allow me to brainstorm—I can come up with five more ideas than I would have if I had to use paints."

Designers are quick to point out that it's not the computer that is doing the work, but the artist who uses the computer.

"An artist can't be the best at traditional design one day and contemporary patterns the next just because he has a computer," remarked Anthony Aiello, design director for Fieldcrest Cannon's blanket division. "It still takes a skilled hand and a creative eye."

Because of the high cost of most CAD systems, the pressure to get the most return on the investment has led companies to employ them for preparing designs for production, or to replace service work paintings. However, as the cost of the technology comes down and improvements in software and hardware make using computers more natural, designers will increasingly turn to computers to create, experiment and present original design concepts faster and in greater detail than possible with traditional materials.

Advice to Aspiring Designers: Get Smart Before Getting Started

Valerie Seckler

Talented designers too often underestimate the importance of business skills when seeking financing for their young businesses.

This was the consensus of factors, the most common source of funding for designers whose companies are in early growth stages. These entrepreneurial ventures are often rich in design and sales talent, said factors interviewed by WWD, but sorely lacking in crucial backroom support like production proficiency, accounting expertise and sales organizations.

Such shortcomings typically undermine a designer's efforts to obtain financing and often explode the fledgling enterprise, factors noted.

Miles Stuchin, president of Access Capital, a factor that counts apparel designers among its clients, said, "We sometimes see design expertise but weak production skills. Often a company can produce, but is weak on bookkeeping. In smaller companies with limited funds, these can be big problems."

Observed Walter Kaye, president of Merchant Factors, "We don't see lots of designers going into business as we did in the past. Many who try don't know how to go beyond line development."

"They're not as able to market themselves and find funding as their predecessors," added Kaye,

who founded Merchant 10 years ago at age 57.

In order to win the confidence and financing of factors, a young designer firm must build the proper business foundation and get at least one successful retail season under its belt.

After sinking $10,000 to $15,000 of their own money into their businesses, designers' next infusion of funds can come from a variety of sources, factors explained. They include family members, investors with roots in the apparel business, contract manufacturers seeking to boost production to cover overhead and joint ventures established with apparel companies that are looking to segment or trade up.

"All too often designers lose their initial investment because the new company doesn't have staying power," cautioned Kaye. "We've seen budding designers with lots of ideas but little capital, and we discourage them. They need adequate capital to develop their samples line, buy supplies and stay afloat until the money from their first season comes in."

A joint venture is one of the best ways for young designer firms with limited capital to get started, according to Kaye. The joint venture partner gets "very big leverage" in exchange for its business and financial support, resulting in "many deals that work out very well," he noted.

"Existing Seventh Avenue companies tend to be frequent and good sources of money," Stuchin agreed, assessing the joint venture route. "Complementary businesses and players tend to know and trust each other."

$50 million in volume with clients making $1,000 garments," said Wassner.

Nevertheless, Merchant's Kaye insisted, "It isn't necessarily harder for younger designer companies to get financing, but they often lack the business acumen to secure the funds.

"Many times they get bad advice," he added. "They can only get started seeking loans from factors after their first season of orders are in from good retailers."

Women's Wear Daily, March 27, 1995.

Buying Style

Gail Gilchriest

Most days, I dress for success in a T-shirt and shorts. I usually work alone, at home; when I'm expecting the FedEx guy, I wash my hair and put on a bra.

Lately, however, I've had meetings. And even with clean hair and proper undies, my customary work clothes don't afford me that talent-to-be-reckoned-with authority a writer needs to score the really juicy jobs. At a business appointment one day, the secretary mistook me for a delivery person. (She said, "Ten more minutes and we'd have gotten the pizza for free, right?") Clearly, the time had come for some serious big-girl clothes: I needed a suit. Since I shop so infrequently, and since I wanted something spectacular for an unspectacular price, I sought professional help.

The wealthy have been hip to personal shoppers since the free-spending '80s, but now many department stores extend the service of these "wardrobe consultants" to their ordinary customers, free of charge. Daniel Barry, a retail analyst for Merrill Lynch, says high-end department stores, unable to build their business with ever lower prices, lure shoppers instead with above-and-beyond service. "The main customer," he notes, "is the working woman with more money than time." Lynn Henderson, president of the Association of Image Consultants International (AICI), says membership has grown from fewer than 100 members in 1990 to 500 in 1995; many are independents who cull merchandise from a variety of retailers and charge an hourly rate for their taste and time.

Personal shoppers' skills vary. You find good ones, bad ones and some who are just so-so. But almost all excel at making the cash register ring, especially those employed by department stores. Staff shoppers usually achieve their position as a reward for their high sales volume. Those numbers then zoom even higher. "The personal shopper's average sales check is eight times higher than in other areas of the store," explains Susan Finkelstein, vice president of special services for Macy's West/Bullock's. "That's because they aren't selling single items, but entire wardrobes." It's not unusual for a personal-shopping customer to spend $1,000 to $3,000 during a seasonal wardrobe spree, on which the personal shopper receives a better commission (say, 6% to 7%) than a regular salesperson (3% to 5%). A pro can build a clientele of 300 or more good customers and earn a six-figure annual salary, according to one personal-shopper division head.

I didn't need a whole wardrobe, just a suit. But I wanted something more than a suit. I wanted to establish a long-term relationship with someone who would help me decide what to pack on my journey from rags to riches. I imagined that these first new threads would lead to a big book or movie deal, and then I could buy another, more expensive outfit, and another, and another. Ultimately, my personal shopper would join my lawyer, my agent and my accountant as part of the stable of professionals retained as testimony to my success.

Ultimately is the key word here. The ideal candidate for a personal shopper is someone with money and no time, or money and no taste. If you have no money, no time and no taste, it's unlikely that a personal shopper will develop your look, on a budget, quickly. I interviewed five in my search. I found one sympathetic to my budget, but she didn't share my taste. Another had great taste, but didn't take my budget seriously (neither did I, since I eventually allowed myself to go way over it). But it is possible to find a consultant with whom you can develop an efficient, financially responsible relationship—you just need time to shop around for her.

My first foray into wardrobe consultation was with Linda at a Los Angeles Bullock's. During a get-acquainted phone call, I outlined my quest: a year-round suit that would work as well at dinner as at meetings. And, I stressed, I wanted to spend about $400, more than I could comfortably afford but what I thought would get the style and quality I desired.

Linda asked me to name my favorite designers. A pop quiz! I choked. Assuming the Gap didn't count, I sputtered the first few names that came to mind. Calvin Klein, Donna Karan. And yeah, Bob Mackie rolled off my tongue before I could stop it.

I met Linda on Saturday afternoon. I loved the first outfit she showed me. It was an Anne Klein II, black, a wool blend with a tiny, textured stripe. It looked great and felt luxurious. She waved a brown Tahari jacket with matching pants at me and breezed me past a Jones New York skirt and jacket. It was too late, I was smitten with Anne Klein. The moment I put it on, I

morphed from short and goofy to sleek and smart. I studied my reflection in the mirror, noticing for the first time that I looked just a little like Catherine Deneuve. The shirt Linda paired with the suit—a shimmery, man-tailored gray number—didn't work for me. It pushed the whole look over the edge, right past Deneuve and all the way to k.d. lang. I wanted to play ball with the big boys, I explained, but I didn't want to look like one. Linda understood. She fetched some delicate but stylish T-shirts. I stood taller. I shook my hair. I struck a pose. *Bonjour.*

Linda said I could "do" a skirt or a different "pant" with the "look"— that Seventh Avenue lingo made me feel secure. She scurried away and returned with said skirt, another pant and a snappy white cotton vest. "This is all within my price range, right?" I asked. Her eyes rocketed to the ceiling. She said nothing as I groped for the tag— $430. Wow, I thought, this suit must be on sale! Linda seemed perturbed that I needed time to think about it, but she agreed to hold my selections for a few days. Linda knew her stuff.

Andrea at a Nordstrom store served me a soda before I even had my shoes off. Every outfit she selected was squarely in my price range, and I do mean squarely. Not one of them particularly excited me. She showed a black wool gabardine suit by Nordstrom, an anonymous gray pinstripe and two nice Dana Buchman outfits she described as being "like Ellen Tracy, except taking more risks." The Dana Buchmans fit nicely but weren't my style. I finished the soda, thanked Andrea and moved on.

After speaking to two independents who were too busy to shop right away, I called Lisa, whom I

found through the AICI (800-383-8831). (A recommendation from a friend is another way to find an independent.) Lisa works in Irvine, the suburbs, quite a hike for me. She suggested I meet her at a mall in that area, where she knew the merchandise. Big mistake, I decided during the half-hour freeway jaunt. But once I met her, the long haul seemed almost worth it. She'd really done her homework. After our initial chat, she had phoned friends in the movie industry to ask what writers wear to meetings. Then she'd pre-shopped, pulling outfits at several stores for me to look at. Her fee was $75 per hour, typical for an independent shopper in Los Angeles. "I usually also charge $150 for pre-shopping," she said, "but since I want you as a long-term client, I'll waive that this time." I was grateful.

At Nordstrom we tried several suits, some Christian Dior, a few with three pieces, all priced under $400. We stopped by a First Issue store to see some mock turtlenecks on sale. We swung through Liz Claiborne. At Robinsons-May I tried on a brown wool suit marked down from $200-plus to $119.

I liked Lisa. She was thorough and enthusiastic, and seemed challenged rather than bored by my budget. She'd seen me in my underwear and mentioned Heather Locklear. I'm not saying she compared me to her, but I took it as a compliment just the same. Still, the distance was an inconvenience, and I didn't particularly like the clothes Lisa selected. Our tastes didn't jibe. That seemed a considerable danger sign for the future of a fashion-based relationship. I wrote a check for $150 for our two hours together and went home empty-handed.

Although there were other stores and other independents I could have called, I was tired of shopping already. If I had more time to shop, I wouldn't need a personal shopper, right? Besides, I couldn't get over that Anne Klein II suit Linda had shown me—first love and all that.

I walked back into Bullock's feeling downright cocky about my decision. I was even considering shoes. Linda rang up the sale. The total, with tax, came to $993.

"There must be a mistake," I squeaked. Linda's eyes zoomed skyward. "The suit was $430, right?"

"The *jacket* is $430," Linda sniffed. "These are separates, I thought I mentioned that. The pants are $260, the vest is $200 and the little shirts are $10 each. A fantastic value."

My palms turned clammy. Looking well-dressed seemed to have gone to my head. I knew better than to think the tag on the jacket reflected the cost of the suit. I deep-sixed the vest—that brought the damage down to $700 and some serious change. Linda took my credit card. "Would you like it hanging or in a bag?" my very own personal shopper asked with a smile. The next thing I knew, I found myself roaming the shoe department. I was destitute—but confident, and damned attractive.

Later, when I'd recovered, I called Bullock's to ask why their professional shopper hadn't stayed within my price range. Linda, I was told, was supposed to, and was still learning. A few minutes later, Linda called me and said the little vest had been marked down 40%. Now *that's* the kind of caring I'd hoped to find. Maybe I'll stick with her. I like her taste, and perhaps, better dressed, I can earn enough to afford it.

Working Woman, February 1996.

PART TWO

The Producers of Raw Materials

Before a designer can finalize plans for a new collection, all of the available raw materials that go into making the various products must be explored. Of particular importance is the variety of fibers and fabrics that might be used. The appropriate choice is based on construction, methods of coloring and decoration, and the decorative and functional finishes that enhance appearance and use. A complete knowledge of the textile industry is necessary to assure the selection of the most appropriate fabrics.

Another raw material is fur. By themselves, furs are used for coats, other outerwear, and trimmings. There are numerous types, each providing a different look and price point. Today's fur manufacturers, while still producing products in record numbers must confront animal rights protesters, who believe that animals should not be killed for their skins. The fur producers have expended great energy in efforts to convince consumers about the humaneness of the industry.

Leather is another raw material that receives a lot of attention from designers of fashion merchandise. It is used in the construction of garments, as well as for such accessories as shoes and handbags. As with other materials, leather comes in a wide range of qualities and prices.

Having learned all of the technical aspects of these materials, the reader should be ready to explore each of these components of fashion merchandise.

CHAPTER 7

The Textile Industry

After you have completed this chapter, you should be able to discuss:

• Natural and manufactured fibers.

• Major fiber classifications and the advantages of each.

• Various dyeing and printing techniques used in textile coloration and the advantages of each method.

• The importance of the finishes that are applied to fabrics.

• Some of the methodology used by the industry in the marketing of textiles.

Exciting fashion design is not simply the result of a creative mind sketching innovative silhouettes. The professional apparel and home fashions designer must completely understand the raw materials that will be incorporated into the final product to best serve the consumer's needs.

The major raw material for the fashion industry is textiles. Today's market is so vast, with centers globally based and operations so complex because of technological advances in production, that fabric users must constantly check that their final choices are appropriate. A designer developing a garment intended for extensive wear while traveling, for example, must consider the fiber's ability to shed wrinkles. The wrong choice of fiber content could quickly result in an unsuccessful product.

Although the United States leads the world in textile production, considerable competition comes from other countries. Just as apparel producers have gone offshore to manufacture their garments, many designers regularly scout foreign markets for fabrics. In an effort to curtail imports and protect domestic production, the United States impowers a quota on those fibers, such as cotton, that pose the greatest threat to domestic production. With such new trade agreements as GATT and NAFTA, there are even more serious considerations for American producers. Only time will tell if these pacts will help or hinder the domestic textile industry.

SCOPE OF THE TEXTILE INDUSTRY

As far back as 5000 B.C. individuals made fabrics from fibers found in nature. By contrast, present day manufacturers operate in a technologically advanced environment that affords more accurate production at incredible speed. In the United States alone, more than 700,000 people are employed in the textile industry, producing enough yardage to travel round trip to the moon and back twenty-three times and circle the globe fourteen times! Procedures that once took several months now take as little as a few minutes. The sophisticated looms

(left) Today's textile industry employs enormous sales staffs to cover the needs of the marketplace.
(below) Color cards and swatches are used to sell fabrics to manufacturers and designers.

can turn out as much as one hundred yards of cloth in an hour. According to the American Textile Manufacturers Institute, the industry is capable of producing enough yardage in one minute to make 2,000 dresses, twenty-four hours later there will be a sufficient yardage for three million dresses. The industry invests more than $2.37 billion on new plants, equipment, and computer systems that monitor all of the processes. According to ATMI statistics, of the total amount of fabric output, thirty-eight percent is used for women's, men's, and children's apparel; twenty-seven percent for home furnishings; eight percent for floor coverings; twenty-three percent for industrial and miscellaneous consumer products; and four percent for export.

Few industries are as carefully scrutinized by the government. Numerous legislative acts under which the industry operates include the Wool Products Labeling Act of 1939; the Flammable Fabrics Act of 1953; the Textile Fiber Products Identification Act of 1960; and the Permanent Care Labeling Ruling of the Federal Trade Commission of 1972. They have been put in place primarily to protect the consumer (see Chapter 3).

PRIMARY AND SECONDARY SOURCES OF FABRIC

The textiles industry is made up of primary and secondary sources. Primary sources, such as mills or converters, make or create the materials; secondary sources, such as jobbers and retailers, are merely responsible for selling fabric.

Mills

Mills are the giants of the industry. They are **vertically integrated,** which means that they not only manufacture the fabrics, but also produce the yarns and apply the necessary finishes (functional and decorative enhancements) to improve the fabrics. These operations produce woven and/or knitted fabrics. The larger American mills are primarily located in the south, with the major ones in North and South Carolina.

The major vertically integrated mills include Burlington Industries, Inc., Collins & Aikman Corporation, Cone Mills Corporation, Dan River, Inc., Milliken & Company, and WestPoint Stevens.

The mills sell their goods to a variety of users including converters, manufacturers and designers of apparel and home fashions, jobbers or wholesalers, and retailers.

Converters

Converters are the intermediaries between the mills and their customers. These companies buy **greige (gray) goods** (unfinished fabrics) from the mills and then have them dyed, printed, and finished according to the specifications and directions of designers and manufacturers of apparel and home fashions. Their flexibility allows them to address the current needs of the fashion industry in terms of colors, patterns, and finishes.

Importers

As with finished garments, fabrics are being produced in many parts of the globe and are then imported into the United States. There are two types of textile importing companies: the **direct importer** and **import mill.** Direct importers buy finished fabrics or manufactured textile products, such as clothing or soft luggage, and bring them into the United States. An import mill is a foreign company that owns textile machinery and makes the fabric (or yarns) that is then exported to the United States.

Although the greatest amount of fabrics are imported from the Far East, fabrics are imported from other parts of the world as well.

Jobbers

This industry segment buys fabrics primarily from the mills and converters, with occasional purchases from garment manufacturers who no longer have the need for goods that were purchased. **Jobbers** deal in small quantities and are able to dispose of **mill overruns,** a term used to describe more fabric than was originally specified, fabric no longer needed by garment producers, discontinued fabrics, and some current materials. Their customers are the custom tailors whose needs are limited, furniture upholsterers, and manufacturers who produce very small quantities. Jobbers are primarily located in large textile and garment centers such as New York City, Atlanta, Chicago, Dallas, and Los Angeles.

Retailers

Although the home sewing business has declined in recent years, there is still a need for stores that sell to the ultimate consumer. They buy in small quantities that include mill overruns, closeouts, and the newest fabrics. Many of these retailers are mom and pop stores, with some chain operations found in the industry.

FROM FIBER TO FABRIC

Five elements are involved in the production of fabrics: **fibers, yarns, structure, color, finish.** Fibers are usually twisted together and spun into yarns. Yarns are either woven or knit to form a fabric. Color is added to enhance the fabrics's appeal and a finish is applied to make the fabric suitable for its intended use.

It is important for a designer to understand that each of these elements provides the fabric with certain basic characteristics or properties. If any part is changed, the result would be a different fabric—perhaps making it unsuitable for the specific end use. For example, by blending or combining two or more fibers, characteristics of each may be achieved in a single fabric. A blend of cotton and polyester provides the wearer the coolness of cotton and the ease of laundering of the polyester. Table 7.1 includes the four classifications of properties: aesthetics, durability, comfort, and safety.

Fibers

Fibers are the basic ingredients of fabrics and are classified into two broad categories: **natural** and **manufactured.** Natural fibers are derived from plants, animals, or minerals, and include cotton, flax, wool, or silk. Manufactured fibers are chemically produced through petroleum-based cellulosic or rubber and mineral bases. Each fiber has characteristics that make them suitable for various uses. Their popularity at any given time is determined not only by their inherent characteristics but also by demand.

TABLE 7.1

CATEGORIES OF FIBER PERFORMANCE PROPERTIES

Aesthetics	Durability	Comfort	Safety
Properties relating to visual effects as well as those perceived by touch	Properties relating to resistance to wear and destruction in use	Properties relating to physical comfort	Properties relating to danger or risk of injury
Flexibility	Abrasion Resistance	Absorbency	Flammability
Hand	Chemical Effects	Cover	
Luster	Environmental Conditions	Elasticity	
Pilling	Strength	Wicking	
Resiliency			
Specific Gravity			
Static Electricity			
Thermoplasticity			

Leading producers of cotton include the United States, the People's Republic of China, India, and Egypt.

Natural Fibers

Cotton and **flax** are the major vegetable fibers used in the production of apparel and home fashions. **Wool** and **silk** are the two most important fibers derived from animals. Other natural fibers include **hemp, ramie,** and **jute. Specialty hair** fibers, such as cashmere, alpaca, vicuna, camel's hair, angora, and mohair play less important roles because of their high cost.

COTTON   Consumer purchases of cotton merchandise continue to increase at record levels. Once threatened by the manufactured fibers, consumer demand has made it today's most widely used fiber. Most cotton comes from the southern part of the United States, but significant amounts are being produced in other countries. China ranks second in the world, and Russia third. India, Egypt, Mexico, and Brazil are also important cotton-producing nations.

Seedlings emerge about one week after planting and flower in approximately four to six weeks. The flowers ripen and fall off the plants in a few days, leaving a small ovary that matures into a cotton boll. Once the boll expands, it splits and produces a fuzzy, puffy substance. When the cotton is ready for picking, it is mechanically harvested. Ginning, the next stage, separates the fiber from the seeds. After ginning, the fiber is classified and graded. The class of fiber depends upon its length, which runs anywhere from $\frac{3}{8}$ to $2\frac{1}{2}$ inches, quality, and fineness. The fiber is then turned into fabric using many of the various techniques discussed below.

FLAX   The long fibers taken from the stems of flax plants are processed and made into fabrics called **linen.** Unlike cotton, linen is not produced in the United States, but the United States is a chief user of the fiber. Russia, France, Belgium, Ireland, Egypt, Poland, and Italy are the major linen-producing countries. The oldest known fiber, it was only rivaled by the introduction of cotton, which was less expensive and more versatile.

The flax fiber is removed from the stalk through a process that is called **retting.** Retting is achieved by natural means, such as placing the stalks on the grass (dew retting), submerging them in water, or using chemicals. Once loosened, the stalks are broken and skutched, a term used that describes taking

Flax comes from the stem or stalk of the flax plant and is harvested by pulling the entire plant from the ground.

the flax from the stalk. They are then separated according to fiber lengths by a hackling process that combs and straightens the fiber, which is then spun into yarn.

Even though it wrinkles easily, linen remains a favorite for clothing worn in warm climates because it is extremely cool and lightweight.

WOOL The Wool Products Labeling Act defines wool as "the fiber from the fleece of sheep or lamb or the hair of the angora or cashmere goat." The most significant quantity of wool comes from domesticated sheep. Wool is particularly easy to produce because approximately one year after shearing, the sheep is again ready to deliver a brand new crop of raw material.

Sheep are raised all over the world, with Australia, South Africa, Great Britain, Russia, and the United States as major wool producing countries.

After the fleece has been sheared and is ready for processing, it is graded according to the length of its staple, which generally ranges from 1 to 16 inches, and fineness. It is then sorted and separated into grades, cleansed by a

The best quality wool comes from the sides and shoulder of the sheep, the poorest comes from the lower legs.

Silk is a continuous strand of two filaments cemented together forming the cocoon of the silkworm.

scouring process, and combed to increase smoothness and strength. Any wool that is sheared at 8 months or earlier is classified as lamb's wool, an extremely soft and lustrous fiber.

Properties such as absorbency, elasticity, and density help to provide warmth and make wool a favorite cold-weather fiber.

SILK   The only natural fiber that is several hundred yards long is silk. It is a filament fiber produced by the silkworm during the building of the cocoon. Strands measuring as long as 1600 yards can be unwound or reeled and used to produce fine silks. A coarser, short-fiber silk, which must be spun to produce yarn comes from a wild species and is called *tussah silk.* By far the greatest amount of silk is cultivated, and its vast production is carefully controlled to ensure fine yarn. Other varieties of silk include *douppioni,* a rough, uneven textured fiber, and *waste silk,* short fibers that come from damaged cocoons and must be spun into yarn like cotton or flax.

Properties of silk fabrics include a *hand* like no other. Silk fibers are extremely strong, have a high lustrous appearance, and provide elegance to any garment designed for a silk fabric.

Japan continues to be the world's leading silk producer, followed by China, Korea, Italy, and India. It is one of the few fibers not produced in America.

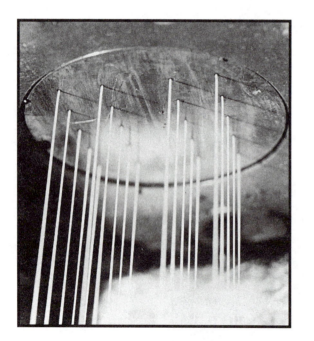

Manufactured fibers are produced by forcing liquid through a device called a spinnerette.

Manufactured (or Man-Made) Fibers

As early as the mid-1800s the quest for laboratory-created fibers had begun. Hilaire de Chardonnet, a native of France, experimented and ultimately developed an **artificial silk** known as **rayon.** Through the purification and breaking down of wood pulp and cotton linters, the fuzzy by-products of cotton, into liquid form, scientists formed this new, cellulose-based fiber.

Manufactured fibers are made when a thick chemical substance is forced through tiny holes in a metal device, which resembles a shower head, called a

The DuPont Company

On October 28, 1938, at a *New York Herald Tribune* forum at the soon-to-be-opened New York's World Fair, DuPont announced the name of a new fiber—*nylon*. This discovery soon dramatically changed the world of fashion. Not only did DuPont revolutionize the hosiery industry, but it went on to develop other fibers with major implications for the textile industry.

In 1951, it offered Orlon and Dacron. In 1952, these fibers were successfully blended with cotton to give the world never before known comfort and ease of care. It was not long before French fashion designers began to utilize nylon and Orlon, in combination with high-quality natural fibers. This was the type of recognition that the manufactured fiber industry needed to market its products to the fashion industry.

To demonstrate the benefits of these new fibers, DuPont promoted them in many unusual ways. To convince the men's wear market of the value of Dacron, it had one of its marketing men wear a Dacron polyester suit for sixty-seven days without pressing it. When it was time to launder the suit, DuPont had the man jump, suit and all, into a swimming pool. When he emerged from the pool, the suit was tossed into a dryer from which it emerged wrinkle-free. The rest is history.

Before DuPont's introduction of Lycra spandex, stretch control of fabrics was difficult. With the stretch and recovery characteristics of the fiber, the swimsuit and undergarment industries were revolutionized. Soon, renowned designers were using Lycra fabrics in their collections. Today they are regularly used by Donna Karan, Nicole Miller, and Norma Kamali.

Other fiber innovations included Teflon, used not only for cookware but as a coating on rainwear, and Micromatique, a fiber that most closely resembles silk.

DuPont's pioneering discoveries in the fiber field has led the way for fashion producers to utilize manufactured fibers in their collections and to treat them with the same "dignity" afforded natural fibers.

---

spinnerette. The fine streams of liquid are extruded into a bath and solidified into filament fibers. The number of holes in the spinnerette range from as few as ten to as many as 10,000. The shape, number, and size of the holes in the spinnerette vary with the desired filament fiber and yarn.

As the filament emerges from the spinnerette, the fibers are solidified. Three methods are used to extrude and harden the fibers, depending on the chemical composition of the solution. These methods are called: **wet spinning, dry spinning,** and **melt spinning.** As the filament hardens, it is stretched to reduce its diameter. This also increases the strength of the fiber and stabilizes its ability to stretch without breaking.

One of the trail blazers in the production of manufactured fibers is E.I. DuPont de Nemours & Company, Inc. Its development of nylon and other fibers revolutionized the textile industry. A profile of the company is included in a World of Fashion Profile.

Manufactured fibers are referred to by the **generic name** established by the **Federal Trade Commission.** The fiber manufacturer identifies a **trademark** in order for its fibers to be distinguished from generic fibers produced by other fiber manufacturers. Acetate, acrylic nylon, rayon, and spandex are examples of generic names. Creslan® is the registered trademark for acrylic produced by American Cyanamid Company and Lycra® is the registered trademark for spandex produced by E.I. DuPont.

Table 7.2 lists trade names, generic class, and manufacturers.

MICROFIBERS During the 1990s, technological advancements made it possible to produce fibers, such as polyester, nylon, and acrylic, in diameters finer than

TABLE 7.2

SELECTED FIBER TRADE NAMES

Trade Name	Generic Class	Producer
A.C.E.	polyester	AlliedSignal Fibers
Acrilan	acrylic	Monsanto Chemical Company
Anso	nylon	AlliedSignal Fibers
Antron	nylon	E.I. DuPont de Nemours & Company, Inc.
Biokryl	acrylic	Mann Industries, Inc.
Caprolan	nylon	AlliedSignal Fibers
Celebrate	acetate	Hoechst Celanese Corporation
Chromspun	acetate	Eastman Chemical Products, Inc.
Cordura	nylon	E.I. DuPont de Nemours & Company, Inc.
Crepeset	nylon	BASF Corporation
Creslan	acrylic	American Cyanamid Company (Cytec Industries, Inc.)
Cumuloft	nylon	Monsanto Chemical Company
Dacron	polyester	E.I. DuPont de Nemours & Company, Inc.
Estron	acetate	Eastman Chemical Products, Inc.
Fortrel	polyester	Wellman, Inc.
Glospan	spandex	Globe Manufacturing Company
Golden Glow	polyester	BASF Corporation
Golden Touch	polyester	BASF Corporation
Hollofil	polyester	E.I. DuPont de Nemours & Company, Inc.
Hydrofil	nylon	AlliedSignal Fibers
Lurex	metallic	Metal Film Company
Lycra	spandex	E.I. DuPont de Nemours & Company, Inc.
Micromattique	polyester	E.I. DuPont de Nemours & Company, Inc.
MicroSpun	polyester	Wellman, Inc.
MicroSupreme	acrylic	American Cyanamid Company (Cytec Industries, Inc.)
Modal	rayon (HWM)	Lenzing Fibers Corporation
Nega-Stat	polyester	E.I. DuPont de Nemours & Company, Inc.
Pa-Qel	acrylic	Monsanto Chemical Company
Pil-Trol	acrylic	Monsanto Chemical Company
Resistat	nylon	BASF Corporation
SEF	modacrylic	Monsanto Chemical Company
Silky Touch	nylon	BASF Corporation
Softglow	nylon	BASF Corporation
Stainmaster	nylon	E.I. DuPont de Nemours & Company, Inc.
Supplex	nylon	E.I. DuPont de Nemours & Company, Inc.
Tactesse	nylon	ICI Fibers, Inc.
Timbrelle	nylon	ICI Fibers, Inc.
Trevira Microness	polyester	Hoechst Celanese Corporation
Ultron	nylon	Monsanto Chemical Company
WearDated	nylon	Monsanto Chemical Company
Worry Free	nylon	AlliedSignal Fibers
Zefkrome	acrylic	Mann Industries, Inc.
Zefran	acrylic	Mann Industries, Inc.
Zeftron	nylon	BASF Corporation

(left) Yarns being processed for use in fabrics.
(above) Manufactured yarn is placed on spools ready for further processing.

silk. The fine fibers are called **microfibers.** Fabrics made from microfibers are extremely soft and drapable and are almost indistinguishable from silk.

Yarns

Yarns are groups of fibers twisted together to form a continuous strand. All textile fabrics are produced from yarns. The process is called **spinning.** Yarns are woven or knitted to form a textile fabric. Before the actual spinning takes place, the fibers must be cleansed and refined to rid them of impurities or oils that will affect appearance and durability. Once the fibers have been cleansed and refined, they may be spun into yarn.

There are two main categories of yarns: **spun** and **filament.** Spun yarns are short lengths of fiber twisted or spun to hold them together. Filament yarns are composed of continuous strands of fiber that may be miles long. Manufactured fibers can be produced in any length desired.

Various spinning methods are used, with ring spinning the most common in the United States. Open-end spinning is a newer system that is three to five times faster, with air jet the fastest at a rate that is seven to ten times that of the conventional ring technique.

Constructing Fabrics

There are two major methods used in the process of turning yarn into fabric: **weaving** and **knitting.** For some fabrics, known as **nonwovens,** the fiber or stock is turned into a fabric without first producing the yarn. The most important of these processes are called **felting** and **bonding.** The former matts fibers into a web that is held together with additives; the latter forms webs from either filament fibers that are then layered, or loose staples that are plied together by numerous means.

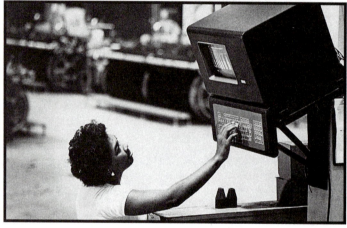

(top) Textiles being handwoven on a simple loom. (bottom) Today, the computer plays a major role in weaving textiles

Weaving

Interlacing two or more sets of yarns at right angles produces woven fabrics. The stronger set of yarns are called **warps** and are placed lengthwise on the loom. The **fillings,** or cross-wise yarns, also called **wefts** are then interlaced with the warp yarns. The range of weaves runs from the plain weave, which is the simplest, to the **jacquard,** from which the most intricate patterns are created.

The different techniques not only produce fabrics that have different appearances, but also impart different characteristics.

PLAIN WEAVE The most often used weave—the **plain weave**—produces fabrics that range from sheer to heavy. Well-known fabrics include gauze, gingham, taffeta, burlap, and canvas. Each warp yarn passes alternately over and then under one filling yarn. A variation of the plain weave is the **basket weave,** which interlaces two or more sets of yarns as one yarn. If a two-by-two basket is desired, two sets of yarns are interlaced with two sets of fillings. This variation of the plain weave imparts a decorative effect in the fabric. Because of the frequent interlacings of the yarns, plain woven fabrics tend to wrinkle more.

TWILL WEAVE When the need for durability is important, such as for work clothes, the **twill weave** is often the choice. The construction produces a diagonal line that runs upward to the right or left. This creates a **herringbone pattern.** Denim is produced using the twill weave.

SATIN WEAVE If a smooth, shiny surfaced fabric is desired, it may be achieved with the satin weave. By floating one yarn over as few as four or as many as twelve yarns before interlacing them, a lustrous surface is the result. Satin is the name of the fabric woven by this method using filament yarns. It is lustrous and smooth. Sateen is a durable cotton fabric made with spun yarn, but not as lustrous. Although the shiny surface has been achieved, long floats of the yarn create a fabric with inferior wearing quality. In addition, the use of filament yarns create a rough surface and contribute to filaments breaking. Satin-woven fabrics are used in apparel, where durability is not important, such as evening wear and dresses.

PILE WEAVE When a plush surface is desired, the pile weave is used. Its production requires three sets of yarns: a regular set of warps, a regular set of fill-

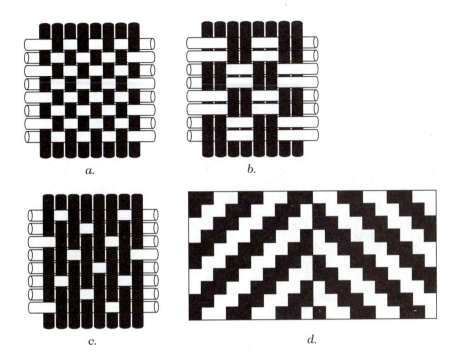

a. b.

c. d.

a. The plain weave is the simplest method of weaving. b. The basket weave is a variation of the plain weave. c. The satin weave is used when a shiny fabric is desired. d. The twill weave produces a diagonal design.

ing yarns, and an additional set—either warps or filling yarns—that form the dimensional surface. The raised surfaces are either left alone, leaving a looped appearance as in terry cloth, or are cut as in the case of velvet.

DOBBY WEAVE   If the desired fabric is to feature a small, geometric pattern, the **dobby weave** is the construction choice. Using a dobby loom, fabrics such as birdseye piqué, found in some cotton apparel, is produced.

JACQUARD WEAVE   The most intricate weave is the **jacquard.** It is a complicated procedure that requires a special loom called the **jacquard loom,** originally invented in 1805. A series of punched cards were laced together to control the warp yarns and achieve the desired pattern. The jacquard loom required a large space and very high ceiling. Today, the computer has simplified production. Although computerized jacquard looms are faster than the original, they still operate more slowly than other looms. As a result, fabrics produced, such as brocades and damasks, are generally quite expensive.

Knitting

Interlooping yarns produces a knitted fabric. Specifically, loops are formed and new loops are then drawn through the preceding ones. The continuous addition of loops creates a knitted fabric. Knitting may be accomplished by hand or machine, each producing a different type of knitted material. Unlike weaving, which requires

The Jacquard loom produces intricate patterns.

Sophisticated machines knit fabrics quickly and efficiently.

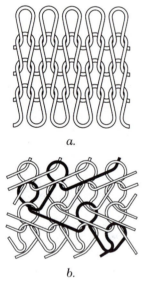

a. Weft knitting produces a horizontal material. b. Warp knitting involves producing fabric in which loops are vertically attached.

two or more sets of yarns, knitting is accomplished by using one continuous, single yarn. The appearance of a knitted fabric is accomplished by the type of machinery used, the density of the yarns, the size of the needles, and the spacing of the stitches.

Basically, there are two types of knitting techniques: **weft knitting** and **warp knitting.** Knitted goods that are produced horizontally are weft knitted, with the stitches running from side to side for the width of the fabric, and are interlooped with each succeeding row. Examples of weft knits are the fabrics used for sweaters and hosiery. Construction takes place on either flat or circular knitting machines.

In warp knitting, a very large number of yarns are used to make the fabric. Each yarn is looped around a single needle to form loops that are vertically attached to other loops.

The sophistication of today's equipment enables manufacturers to produce a vast array of goods using yarns that run from the finest to the densest. Single jersey, double jersey, and intricate jacquard knits are easily manufactured with state-of-the-art knitting machines. Computer-controlled and electronic machines enable the industry to design a vast array of fabrics within a few minutes.

CAD or Computer-Aided Design

In the fashion industry, a wealth of patterned materials are made available to apparel and home furnishing designers for use in their collections. Often, the fabric's patterns give the garments and home fashions their appeal. To meet the demands of the apparel and home fashions industries' creative forces, the fabric industry is always involved in the development of new designs that would enhance the finished products.

Until recent years, fabric designers painstakingly hand rendered their designs. With pen and ink and a vast array of paints, they produced the patterns on paper. This was a time-consuming task, because the patterns had to

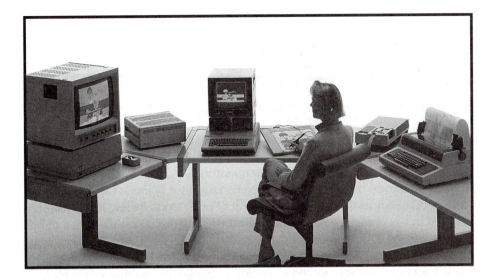

Designs are created on CAD or computer aided design systems in a matter of a few hours.

be depicted as **repeats** on a large board to show how it would look as fabric.

Today, technology enables the process to be significantly shortened. With the use of the computer and a number of different software packages, the designs can be accomplished in a matter of a few hours. These systems, known as **CAD** or **computer-aided design,** have revolutionized the industry. They are available in a broad range of programs, from the simplest to the most sophisticated.

Some of the systems used in the textile industry include Monarch Computex, the leading provider of Macintosh-based CAD systems, Pointcarré Weave, Monarch Design Studio, Primavision, Arabesque, and Weavette. Although they each provide specific features that are unique to their systems, collectively they are used for every aspect of the design process.

Coloring Fabrics

The most important element in a textile product may very well be color. A wrong color could easily hamper sales. Color can sell an inferior fabric or make the most desirable fabric unmarketable. There are two methods of applying color during the various stages of fabric production: **dyeing** or **printing.**

Dyeing Fabrics

Solid-colored fabrics and sometimes multicolored designs, such as plaids, are achieved by dyeing. Today's textile industry has a large number of dyes available to satisfy every company's requirements. Aside from the ability to properly impregnate color with specific intensities, each dye has specific characteristics that determine its most appropriate uses.

The dye selected must be the best suited for the ultimate use of the product by the consumer. For example, when laundering is a chief benefit of a garment, its **colorfastness** must be guaranteed. That is, the color must not bleed or run. Fading is yet another factor to be considered, especially when exposure to sunlight is likely, as with fabrics used for draperies. Without careful attention to the specific end use, customer returns can be assured. Table 7.3 lists some of the general classifications of dyes and their important characteristics to the apparel and home fashion industries.

Dyeing can be accomplished at any stage during textile manufacturing.

- Fibers may be dyed—stock dyeing.
- Yarns may be dyed—yarn dyeing.
- Fabrics may be dyed—piece dyeing.
- Garments may be dyed—garment dyeing.

FIBER OR STOCK DYEING   When short fibers or stock are placed in a dye bath before they are spun into yarn, they are being **fiber-** or **stock-dyed.** This process is generally restricted to woolen materials. Its advantage is the degree of color penetration that can be achieved. The color is locked into the yarns, making them **colorfast.** One problem with fiber or stock dyeing is that color is selected in the earliest stages of manufacturing, before consumer demand has been assessed.

Adding color directly to the chemical solution used to produce manufactured fibers is a special method of coloring fibers called **solution dyeing.** Fabrics made from solution-dyed yarns are practically fade proof and are therefore suitable for draperies. However, because solution-dyed materials are available in only a limited range of colors, the method is not widely used on fabrics slated for fashion apparel.

YARN DYEING   Color can also be added after the fibers have been spun into yarn. This allows a little more time for fashion considerations to influence selection. **Yarn dyeing** is less expensive than stock dyeing, but more costly than piece dyeing. Examples of yarn-dyed fabrics are gingham, madras, and brocade.

Occasionally solid-colored fabrics are yarn-dyed instead of piece-dyed because yarn dyeing results in better dye penetration and improved colorfastness. A good example is fabrics used for upholstery.

PIECE DYEING   Adding color to a fabric is called **piece dyeing.** Coloring at this stage eliminates some risk because you are dyeing the piece goods to order for a definite sale. Its advantage is to postpone the color decision as long as possible, but the penetration of the dye is not as dense as in the techniques discussed above.

When a fabric is made of two or more different fibers and two color effects are desired, the results may be achieved by a process called **cross-dyeing.** Because dyes react differently with different fibers, the dyes can be put into the same dyebath so that one dye will color one fiber and another the second fiber. In a fabric that is rayon and polyester, for example, one dye in the dye bath will have affinity for the rayon, the other for the polyester. The major advantage of cross-dyeing is that it is an inexpensive technique when compared with yarn dyeing, which would have otherwise been used to achieve the various patterns.

Fabric from the dye bath is ready for additional finishing.

TABLE 7.3

GENERAL CLASSIFICATIONS OF DYES AND THEIR IMPORTANT CHARACTERISTICS

Type of Dye	Dye Characteristics
Acid	Excellent for bright colors, not fast to washing, withstands dry cleaning.
Basic	Good to achieve bright shades, generally colorfast to laundering and light, crock resistant.
Chrome	Excellent colorfastness, dull color.
Direct	Poor colorfastness to light and washing, generally dry cleanable.
Disperse	Colorfastness varies according to fiber used, colorfast to crocking, generally dry cleanable.
Fiber reactive	Perfect for bright colors, good fastness to color except when used in chlorine.
Napthol	Bright colors, color fastness to light varies, colorfast to sunlight and laundering.

GARMENT DYEING   When it is necessary to apply color as late as possible, entire garments may be dyed. In this way when a retailer wants a specific color within a modest time frame, the manufacturer can dye the garments to order. For example, Benetton stocks its inventory, void of color, and within a matter of three weeks or less, can accommodate any color asked for by their stores. By using garment dyeing, Benetton avoids the possibility of being left with colors that do not sell.

Printing Fabrics

Patterns may be applied to fabrics by a number of printing processes. Artists carefully prepare designs on paper or with the aid of computer programs, which must then be adapted for use on fabrics.

The oldest technique for pattern application is painting designs directly on fabric. While it is not frequently used, it is found in the collections where limited quantities are produced. Maria Snyder, a New York based designer of couture quality merchandise, is known for her hand-painted applications. Each one is painstakingly reproduced on silks and other fibers by craftspersons who follow her original design.

The majority of patterns that appear on fabrics are printed by one of three commercial methods: screen printing, roller printing, and heat-transfer printing.

SCREEN PRINTING   Although it is one of the oldest printing processes, **screen printing** is still extensively used today in the production of fashion-oriented fabrics. The goods may be hand or roller-screen printed, the latter providing the speed necessary to accommodate large-scale fabric production. At Tickle Me!, a children's wear manufacturer that extensively uses screen-printed materials in its garments, the automated roller-screen method is used when production requirements are significant. Hand-screening is the choice when limited quantities are ordered.

Fabric being hand screen-printed.

In both cases, an artist designs the print and transfers it onto one or more screens made of nylon, polyester, or metal tightly mounted on a wooden or metal frame. Because screens were originally made of silk, the process was called **silk screening.** A film that adheres to the screen is cut away wherever the color must penetrate. Print paste is poured into the frame and forced through the screen onto the fabric passing under each screen. This is repeated until all of the colors have been applied. The number of screens depends on the different colors in the pattern. For a six-color job, six screens would be needed.

There are three ways of making screen prints: **hand-screen printing, automatic-screen printing** (flat-bed screen printing), and **rotary screen printing.**

Rotary screen printing, which is used today, is capable of printing more than 100 yards of cloth in one minute. Dye is fed inside the screens and forced through tiny holes onto the fabric. Each cylinder on a printing machine adds a different color and a different part of the pattern. Modern technology enables the textile industry to print high-quality fabrics in this manner and, with carefully selected dyes, colors will not fade.

ROLLER PRINTING   In **roller printing,** copper-plated rollers are engraved with patterns for each color. If eight colors are to be used in the design, eight different rollers will be engraved, each representing a different part of the pattern. The rollers, which have been etched with a photoengraving process, rotate through a dye bath and transfer dye onto the fabric. After all of the colors have been applied, the print is complete. It is best suited for long production runs of the same pattern. It is used primarily for woven fabrics and not for knits because of the resulting fabric tension.

HEAT-TRANSFER PRINTING   With **heat-transfer printing,** patterns are first printed onto paper and then transferred onto fabric. The paper and the fabric are rolled together under pressure at high temperatures to achieve the transfer.

For large production needs, rotary screen printing is employed.

The main advantage is cost. It is less expensive to use than the other techniques because it requires a considerably smaller investment in equipment. Heat-transfer printing involves printing designs on fabrics and garment parts or garments. Individuals who have purchased patterns and have transferred them onto T-shirts at home with an iron have basically performed heat-transfer printing.

Finishing Fabrics

Finishing is the final treatment of the fabric that will enhance both its performance and aesthetics and make it suitable for its intended end use. Fabrics can be made shrinkproof, softer, water repellent, or wrinkle resistant. Finishes can be grouped as either chemical or mechanical.

A chemical finish can be bleaching or mercerization for cotton. Mercerization of cotton will improve luster and add strength to the fabric. A mechanical finish includes brushing or napping to produce a fuzzy surface.

Shrinkage resistant finishes, such as Sanforization, provide comfort by helping to maintain the fit of a garment. Scotchguard® is the name of a soil resistant finish for upholstered furniture and Zepel® is the name of a water-repellent finish for raincoats. Some finishes, such as glazing, polishing, or embossing improve the aesthetics of a fabric.

Table 7.4 represents some of the finishes that enhance appearance.

Finishes provide the consumer with easy-to-care-for fabrics that require a minimum amount of ironing or pressing after the garment is worn and cleaned. Durable press or permanent press is a well-known care finish. Table 7.5 identifies finishes to improve or increase function.

Computers are used to apply functional and fashionable finishes to fabrics.

TABLE 7.4

FINISHES TO ENHANCE APPEARANCE

Finish	Process
Calendering	An ironing process that produces a smoother, stiffer, polished fabric.
Delustering	Removing unwanted sheen with chemical treatment.
Embossing	Creating a dimensional design with engraved rollers.
Flocking	With the use of adhesives, short fibers are applied to fabrics giving them a plush effect.
Fulling	Scouring and laundering wool to make it more compact.
Mercerization	Using sodium hydroxide to increase sheen, strength and absorbency in cotton fabrics.
Moireing	Achieving a watermarked effect by using etched rollers.
Napping	Brushing the surface of the fabric to raise the surface.
Plisseing	Adding a crinkled effect by pasting sodium hydroxide onto fabric results in shrinkage, and thus a crinkled look.
Shearing	Evening pile-woven fabrics through the use of a machine that resembles a lawn mower.
Singeing	Smoothing a fabric's surface by carefully passing it over a gas flame to burn off tiny fibers.

TABLE 7.5

FINISHES TO IMPROVE OR INCREASE FUNCTION

Finish	Processes
Antistatic	Chemical application that prevents clinging.
Durable press	The use of resins and heat help keep the garment's shape, even after laundering.
Flame retardency	Chemical treatment to make fabrics resistant to burning.
Permanent press	An application of heat, resins, or liquid ammonia permanently holds creases or pleats.
Preshrinking	Different processes used to reduce shrinkage; best known is Sanforizing.
Sizing	Applying starches to add stiffness, body, and weight to fabric.
Water repellent	A special finish that helps fabric repel water but still lets air flow through.

MARKETING TEXTILES

As with any other segment of the fashion world, textiles must be marketed to capture the attention of fabric buyers and designers, and the ultimate user of the product—the consumer. Of significant importance to the textile industry are the trade associations and trade expositions. They each assist the producers in reaching appropriate markets.

The International Wool Secretariat

In 1937, the wool growers of the southern hemisphere founded the International Wool Secretariat (IWS). Its goal is to promote and improve the performance of wool all over the world. Headquartered in London, the organization has fully staffed offices in thirty-two countries. It is the broadest based international fiber network supplying technology to the industry.

The American branch, the Wool Bureau, Inc., is headquartered in New York City, with a technical research facility in Woodbury, New York. Other centers are found in Italy, Holland, Japan, and Great Britain. The IWS uses computer links to rapidly disseminate information on new wool developments and to address processing problems.

In addition to technical research centers, the IWS maintains an International Wool Men's Wear Fashion Office in London, an International Wool Fashion Office for Women's Wear in Paris, and a Knitwear Styling Service in Delft, Holland. These offices offer significant information for fashion designers who use woolens.

The Woolmark symbol was created in 1964 to identify for the consumer wool yarn and wool products that meet high standards for strength, colorfastness, mothproofing, shrink resistance, and other qualities. More than 14,000 manufacturers in more than fifty countries are licensed to use the symbol. It has become an international standard of quality.

By working with spinners, weavers, knitters, and manufacturers, the IWS helps to expand public knowledge and use of wool, to develop new products and processes, to encourage the economical production of high quality wool goods in apparel and home furnishings, and to coordinate the marketing of wool and wool products.

Trade Associations

Trade associations are groups that are responsible for publicizing the efforts of their industries and providing research materials for their members. A complete list of trade associations is included in the appendix.

Cotton Incorporated and the National Cotton Council are concerned with the American cotton industry. The former organization is responsible for increasing the retail market share of American cotton fiber, with its goal of enhancing the American consumer's preference for cotton and cotton-containing fabrics. The latter is the unifying force of the American cotton industry's seven segments: producers, ginners, warehousemen, merchants, cottonseed crushers, cooperatives, and textile manufacturers.

The Wool Secretariat, on the other hand, is an internationally based organization that promotes wool all over the world. Some of the group's activities are outlined in a World of Fashion Profile.

Trade Expositions

With the vast number of fiber producers, fabric manufacturers, and wholesalers in the world, the need to bring them together for the purposes of showing and selling their lines has become increasingly more important. Because they are located throughout the world, it is generally too costly and time-consuming for purchasers to visit all of the important textile centers. The trade exposition has become an important vehicle for enabling the various components of the fashion industry to interface with each other. At these shows, row after row of vendors are housed in booths that feature their sample lines. Sales representatives benefit from this centralized meeting place by reaching prospective customers they might not have ever known to be potential users of their products. The buyers, on the other hand, can, in a short time, compare the offerings of several competing vendors.

a.

b.

c.

d.

a. Yarn cards show availability of colors and are used for marketing. b. Boards suggest ways in which fabrics can be used by potential purchasers for their collection. c. Presentation boards make dramatic statements for fabric usage. d. Line drawings, accompanied by fabric swatches, show end uses for fabrics.

The number of textile expositions that are held all over the world continues to grow. A look at Table 5.3, International Trade Expositions, immediately reveals that these events are held in every conceivable corner of the globe. In cities like Barcelona, Singapore, Florence, Paris, Frankfurt, and New York, the textile expos are in full swing.

ADVERTISING AND PROMOTING TEXTILES

Advertising and promotional endeavors are directed toward both the industrial purchaser and the consumer. The efforts put forth by the industry are numerous and include both print and broadcast advertising.

In terms of advertising, the fiber producers regularly develop campaigns that are found in both the trade and consumer newspapers. In the trades, such as *Women's Wear Daily, Daily News Record,* and the *California Apparel News,* the targeted audiences are the designers, who select the fabrics to be used in their creations, and the retailers, who merchandise fashion items. Fiber producers are also advertising on television. By showing their fibers in television commercials, they are reaching the consumer market that might seek a particular fiber if sufficiently motivated. Cotton Incorporated, for example, regularly runs commercials using their slogan, "The Fabric of Your Life," in the hope that it will be remembered when consumer purchasing takes place.

Many companies also participate in cooperative advertising, in which they share the expense of a designer's ad, for example, when the fiber producer's name is mentioned. In this way, the fiber producer can "ride the coattails" of a famous designer or manufacturer.

Many promotions are also part of the fiber's producer's marketing plan. DuPont, for example, produces a runway show featuring their Lycra® spandex fiber and invites the designers to see how they can work it into their apparel collections. Cotton Incorporated regularly presents a fashion show at the

Council of Fashion Designer's Seventh on Sixth event, in which they feature full lines of clothing especially designed for the show. The attending designers and manufacturers are then able to see the potential for the fiber in their own lines. Not only do they reach those in attendance, but the publicity received through media coverage gives them even more coverage.

The major fiber producers maintain their own staffs for advertising and promotion. When special events are planned, they often use outside resources.

Chapter Highlights

· The textile producer is the primary supplier of the fashion industry.

· The textile industry is comprised of industrial giants that perform all the processes necessary to produce fabric and are vertically integrated. The smaller organizations specialize in one specific aspect of textile development.

· Fibers are natural, such as cotton, flax, wool, and silk, or manufacturerd, such as microfibers, polyester, and spandex.

· Fibers are spun into yarn or made into filaments.

· Yarns are primarily woven or knitted into fabric through a variety of means, the most widely used of which is weaving.

· Fibers, yarns, fabrics, or garments are then dyed; some fabrics are printed with designs that have been created by textile artists.

· A variety of finishes may be employed to improve the fabric's durability and attractiveness.

· To successfully market its offerings, the textile industry has established trade associations, each one representing a specific subdivision of the field and trade expositions, where vendors and purchasers meet to buy and sell textiles.

Industry advertisements are directed at manufacturers, designers, and consumers.

Important Fashion Terminology and Concepts

artificial silk	Federal Trade Commission	heat-transfer printing
automatic-screen printing	felting	hemp
bonding	filament yarn	import mill
CAD (computer-aided design)	fillings	jacquard weave
colorfastness	finishes	jobbers
converting	flax	jute
cotton	garment dyeing	knitting
cross dyeing	generic name	linen
direct importer	greige (or gray) goods	manufactured fibers
dry spinning	hand-screen printing	melt spinning
		mill overruns

microfibers	screen printing	warp knitting
natural fibers	silk	warps
nonwovens	silk screening	weaving
piece dyeing	solution dyeing	weft knitting
ramie	specialty hair fibers	wefts
rayon	spinnerette	wet spinning
repeats	spinning	wool
retting	stock dyeing	yarn dyeing
roller printing	trademark	yarns
rotary screen printing	vertical integration	

For Review

1. Discuss the concept of vertical integration in textiles.
2. Where is the textile industry located in the United States?
3. Differentiate between spun and filament yarn.
4. What type of loom is used when a large intricate pattern is needed for a fabric?
5. Why does the satin weave produce a fabric that is less durable?
6. Distinguish between weft and warp knitting.
7. At which stage will dyeing provide the greatest amount of penetration for fibers?
8. What is cross-dyeing?
9. Describe the procedure used in screen printing.
10. Why are finishes applied to fabrics?
11. What is the major advantage of linen to the wearer?
12. Why does the textile industry use trade expositions to sell its offerings?
13. How does Cotton Incorporated make use of the Seventh on Sixth promotion for its industry?

Exercises and Projects

1. Using narrow strips of paper, 1/4 inch wide and 6 inches long, construct a plain weave, a twill weave, and a 5-float satin weave.
2. Scan the pages of fashion magazines, such as *GQ, Vogue, Elle,* and *Harper's Bazaar,* and find five fashion-oriented cooperative ads that feature the fiber producer's name.
3. Write to one of the many textile trade associations to learn about the specifics of its group. Prepare a report featuring the services it offers.

The Case of the Fiber with an Image Problem

The rayon industry has always spent a great deal of money promoting its fiber. In its early years, the trade association responsible for building rayon's image concentrated on the product's appeal to the industrial market. Through extravagant theatrical productions, fashion manufacturers, designers, and retail merchandisers were made aware of the advantages of the rayon fiber. Many fashion producers and store buyers jumped on the bandwagon and included rayon in their merchandising plans.

While the industrial market has accepted the merits of rayon, many household consumers still consider rayon a low-cost fiber used only to imitate natural fibers in the production of inexpensive garments. The industry is thus faced with an image problem.

At its last major conference, the association's membership had as its prime agenda item, "The Selling of Rayon to the Consumer." If top designers use the fiber and understand its advantages, how can the message be delivered to the public? There was a general agreement that the approach used to motivate market professionals could not be employed to attract consumer attention. There is simply no arena large enough to house the masses for such industrial extravaganzas. By the meeting's end, a solution to the problem had not been found.

Question

How can the household consumer be motivated to consider rayon as a quality fashion fiber?

point of view

An Improved Quality of Life Through Fiber Innovation

Jerry Blumberg

The substitution of synthetic fiber for natural fiber has been underway for more than 50 years. It has been driven over this period by the application of rapidly expanding technical knowledge in polymer science and the engineering sciences, particularly chemical and mechanical engineering.

In the industrialized world, this substitution is virtually complete, especially in the traditional apparel, home furnishings, and carpet markets. In the developing world, the substitution is well along, although there is room for growth into the next century.

That does not mean that fiber innovation has ended. Research and development continues. But the goal now is to add higher value functionality to the fiber targeted at specific market needs. There are many examples.

Micro-denier fibers give textiles aesthetic properties previously attainable only with high-priced natural fibers while maintaining the synthetics' ease-of-care. Producer-colored fibers eliminate increasing waste management costs at the mills. Fibers modeled after biological systems provide breathability, thermal comfort, and different natural appearances like suede and fur.

For example, examination of a highly-tailored cross section of polyester fiber, which goes into DuPont's "Coolmax", reveals four channels running along the fiber. These channels provide paths to move perspiration more effectively from the bodies of people who are exercising to the surface of the garments they are wearing. This results in increased evaporative cooling making the wearer more comfortable during strenuous activity. By contrast, garments of natural fibers and those made from surface-treated fabrics encourage moisture to stay in the fabric. That reduces the cooling effect and results in discomfort to the wearer.

Hollow-core polyester fibers provide effective insulation in "Thermax" fabrics by trapping a layer of warm air next to the skin. The fibers are specially crimped and surface treated to help diffuse more water vapor through the fabric to keep the wearer drier and more comfortable in cold weather.

As people become more aware of safety, health, cleanliness and comfort, there will be an increasing demand for textiles and other fiber systems which improve the quality of life. Fibers, which provide protection from damaging ultraviolet radiation, from bacteria, from unpleasant or harmful odors, from difficult-to-remove stains and spills to name a few, are all technically possible today and will be increasingly fashioned into highly functional, high-value apparel and home furnishing textiles as time goes on.

The result of these developments is to break small, high-value segments away from large markets. Said differently, it is a way to provide a high degree of specific functionality to those who value it in synthetic fibers.

The most dramatic advances in fiber material systems will come when some level of intelligence can be imbedded into the system itself. These systems will actively respond to changes in their environments.

Ultimately, fiber systems, which can actively take part in their own design, manufacture and in-use survivability, have the potential to substantially lower total system life cycle costs. For example, fiber-reinforced bridge components give warning when they need to be replaced, lowering the cost of bridge maintenance. Intelligent material systems such as this will be a reality within the next 30 years.

Taken as a whole, the new knowledge in material science, biology, and electronics are causing a fundamental change in the way we work with materials. We are moving from adaptation, refinement and shaping of what is available to designing and producing material systems to specification. Rather than inventing new materials and seeing where their balance of properties allows them to be used, success in the future will be dependent on designing, producing, and delivering a specific solution to order.

It is a future full of change and opportunity for our industry. It is a future that demands the integration of nontraditional technologies and diverse perspectives to realize its full potential.

Jerry Blumberg, Senior Vice President, DuPont Company.

Quality CAD Output on Fabric Inches Closer to Reality

Matt Nannery

Textile companies salivate over the prospect of printing directly from their computers onto fabric. But concerns over color integrity and printer maintenance are just two of several issues keeping that forbidden fruit just out of reach for many.

A handful of textile companies and designers are already producing CAD output on fabric, but few are satisfied with the results. The process, nonetheless, remains extremely seductive to textile companies. The reason: It allows them to produce samples instantaneously—without going through the considerable expense and added time of having the design engraved and printed in the traditional manner.

"Getting a strike off now takes four to eight weeks, and if the customer doesn't like it we've gone through that time and expense for nothing," commented Rich Riley, manager of CAD services at Jantzen, the swimwear division of V.F. Corp. Riley said Jantzen hopes to begin producing fabric CAD samples sometime next month.

Richard Malachowski, director of research and engineering at Cranston Print Works, agreed with Riley that the technology is inviting.

"You don't take the risk of having something engraved that turns out not to be what the customer wanted," he said. "Printing directly on fabric from a CAD system would be a tremendous time saver because you could do all samples, proofing, coloring and strike-offs via that system."

Malachowski said the process would give companies like Cranston an economical way to produce numerous fabric samples for cus-

tomers to choose from. Currently, printers narrow their options before going through the expense of producing strike-offs.

"Currently, we do six or eight different color combinations before deciding on two that we'll send to be engraved. And coloring is much easier to do right on the CAD system. Small batches of color don't have to be mixed for a sample."

Malachowski, however, is far from bowled over by the current state of the technology. "I've looked into it a lot and what I've seen doesn't look bad, but I'm not completely satisfied," he said.

Despite a laundry list of reservations ranging from printer maintenance to color integrity to limited sample size, textile companies and textile designers continue to dabble in the technology. Though many textile companies sell designs based on ink-jet output on paper, textile companies say apparel makers are often hesitant to place orders based on paper samples—hence, the push to print directly on fabric.

"This is still a very tactile market where people want to touch and feel something before they commit to a purchase," commented Alison Grudier, a Boston-based CAD consultant. "With paper output we can simulate a finished product, but what we want to do is produce a sample as close to the actual finished product as possible."

"Buyers don't seem to be as respective to ink-jet paper output," added Katy Chapman, CAD system supervisor at the Springmaid/Performance division of Springs Industries. "What they really want to see is fabric."

Some textile companies— Springs included—say they've

secured orders based on paper CAD simulations; however, most of those sales are to sophisticated customers who understand that the actual printed fabric will look considerably different from the paper representation. Furthermore, most of these customers have longstanding, trusting relationships with the textile companies with which they place orders based on paper output.

"The more sophisticated customers will buy off the paper sample because they can visualize the finished fabric," Malachowski said. "These are customers we have a history with. We do a lot of business with Wrangler, for example. They have a feel for what the final product will look like."

For new clients and many small manufacturers, however, CAD output on paper just doesn't cut it. Cathy Chow, president of Kick Design, a small New York-based textile design company, explains.

"A lot of our customers aren't apparel people, so it's difficult for them to visualize what the fabric will look like," she said. "CAD output on fabric gives them more confidence in making a decision. Fabric drapes, paper doesn't. Customers like to see what a fabric looks like when it falls in folds."

Chow said her company produces commissioned work under Disney and Warner Bros. licenses. The designs are produced on the fairly standard desktop publishing program Adobe Illustrator and disks are sent out to Great Neck, N.Y.-based Supersample, a fledgling third-party service that produces strike-offs on ink-jet printers.

"The fact that there is a service out there that can give us quick and inexpensive CAD strike-offs on fabric lets us make the strike-off part of the fabric design process rather than the first step in the manufacturing process," Chow explained.

Cranston's Malachowski said most textile companies looking into CAD fabric output will purchase their own printers, rather than use third-party services, "to better control scheduling." He said Cranston is waiting for newer models to become available before making future purchases. He added, however, that printer companies eyeing the textile design market may hold introductions of new machines for next fall's ITMA show in Milan.

"Printer makers are saving up for a big splash in October of '95," Malachowski said. "I would wait until ITMA before I made a new purchase."

There are barely a handful of printers currently on the market capable of printing on fabric, and all were designed for desktop publishing. Printing of CAD samples was an afterthought.

"We have a printer from Iris Graphics that's great at producing paper prints for proofing," Malachowski explained. "But when I put fabric on it, the colors are kind of dull."

The few textile companies currently experimenting with fabric output are using ink-jet printers from Stork or Iris, though Canon Corp. is said to be working on a printer specifically designed for fabric.

John Ingram is manager of color technology for Iris, which produces three continuous ink-jet printers capable of printing on fabric. Two are manual-feed systems, where the fabric must be taped to the printer drum. The third and newest model, the 4012 SmartJet, is automatic. It was commercially available in 1990.

"The original purpose of these machines was in pre-press proofing," Ingram said. "And that's still the dominant use, but we are selling the machines to textile design firms and textile printers too. The ultimate goal of these companies is to use color fabric output as a digital strike-off."

Ingram said Iris is upgrading its printer in response to the demand in the textile industry, and Malachowski said Stork will likely offer a new unit next year. "Stork is building a better ink-jet printer that has more jets and can produce bigger samples," he said.

The types of fabrics the printers can accept are limited also, and carriage widths make it tough to produce enough fabric to sew an actual sample garment. The fabric most often printed directly from a CAD system is either all-cotton or poly/cotton sheeting, though silk and flat-surfaced synthetics are also used. Hairy and nubby-surfaced fabrics are unsuitable because they can clog printer heads.

Supersample's Kushner said he has successfully printed on linen, silk, wool, cotton sheeting, rayon and cotton knit. He admitted that hairy fabrics are a problem. "When I put flannel on my printer, it looks great for six or eight inches—then the jets start to clog."

Though Springs does not print on hairy fabrics, Chapman said Springs has been having clogging problems because of airborne lint rising from the fabric during the printing process. The ink jets don't actually touch the fabric when printing on flat-surfaced fabrics.

"We were having trouble with the amount of fiber getting into our Iris printer," she said. "We are trying to cut down on the lint."

Inks remain a problem also.

Water-soluble soy-based inks tend to run, while "fabric-reactive" inks tend to wick. Both can result in unclear images.

Malachowski prefers the fiber-reactives to the soy-based inks. "The best colors are the fiber reac-

tives, but you still don't get quite the depth and vibrance you get in production printing."

He described fiber-reactive colors synthetic dyes that bond with cellulose. As such, he said they are especially useful with natural fibers. The Stork printer Cranston uses for paper output accepts fiber-reactive dyes.

The Iris printer Chapman uses at Springs uses soy-based dyes, but she said her company has found a way around the problem of weak colors. "We've developed a coating in June so the ink wouldn't sink into the fabric. We want it to sit on top of the fabric and maintain its vibrancy. Now we are producing crisp and clean floral patterns off an ink-jet printer."

Still, Springs prints fabric CAD sample in two passes to ensure that the colors are strong.

"You really need to print it in two passes to get the color saturation," she said.

Subtle variations in color are difficult to produce as the color palette on an ink-jet printer is minuscule when compared to that available through conventional fabric printing.

"When you do a production print, you have a 12- or 14-color palette," Malachowski added. "With ink-jets, a four-color process is used to make up all visible colors. You miss something in the orange and turquoise ranges."

"With an engraving, we can really fine tune the color and get exactly the look we want," Springs' Chapman added.

Grudier said CAD fabric output is better suited to well-defined prints rather than more subtle effects.

"For certain fabrics, those used in children's wear for instance, ink-jet output provides a very good simulation," she said. "These are clean, well-defined designs—but with watercolor looks, you are not seeing true output on an ink-jet.

"Also, a digital printer cannot duplicate some of the 'fall-on' colors possible in the production process—the layering effect that is produced when you lay a red over a yellow."

Printer makers are addressing the complaints. Iris' Ingram said that company's printers can now vary the size of the droplets that hit the fabric. He said the feature lets users produce variations in shading.

Grudier said both Iris and Stork are making improvements in their offerings.

"Stork was printing on wool jersey at the CAD Expo in New York in August," she said, "and Iris makes the most wonderful color printer for cotton broadcloth. There is defi-nitely a market in textile printing for these kind of printers."

Despite problems with CAD output, textile companies and independent designers remain hopeful that technology will catch up to their needs. As a swimwear maker, Jantzen is especially interested. Even though printer carriage limits the size of a CAD strike-off, Jantzen is in the unique position of being able to produce enough material on an ink-jet printer to sew an actual sample garment.

"This would be a great asset to our sales reps when they go on calls," Riley said. "When our sales reps show a CAD simulation or sketch of a garment alongside a paper representation of a design, it's up to the buyer to visualize them together. If we get this up and run-ning, our sales reps will be able to say 'here's the suit.'"

Springs' sales reps are already putting CAD fabric output to use in the field.

"We don't generally use it for presentations, but it's good that the option is there when we need it," she said. "If we have a very important preview for a big customer and the plates haven't been engraved yet, this is a lifesaver."

Kick Design's Chow said the technology has allowed the apparel makers that contract with her for designs to plan their production much more efficiently.

"My clients are very often selling off an ink-jet fabric sample," she said. "They can go directly to a retailer and secure an order before the fabric is even sourced."

Daily News Record, December 1, 1994.

Patagonia: Only Organic Cotton From Now On

Joyce Barrett

Outdoor clothing manufacturer Patagonia Inc., Ventura, Calif., is shifting its entire spring 1996 cotton line to organically grown cotton, because of what it says are the environmental hazards of conventional upland cotton, charges that were immediately denied by cotton growers.

The decision, called a permanent one in a statement by Patagonia founder Yvon Chouinard, will include all-cotton products and cotton blends.

Sixteen new fabrics will be used for the 66 cotton-using styles in the spring line, primarily sportswear. Patagonia first offered organic cotton apparel in fall 1992 and has increased its organic line each subsequent year.

"The assumptions a lot of us made about cotton, in part because of its natural feel, were wrong," Chouinard said. "Given what we now know about conventional cotton, there is no going back on this decision, regardless of its impact on the company's sales or profits."

Patagonia's decision to use organic cotton was made by the company's board of directors in 1994 and is based on concerns about the toxification of soil, air and groundwater caused by conventional cotton, which is grown with chemicals, according to Chouinard.

David Guthrie, manager, cotton agronomy and physiology at the National Cotton Council, disputed Chouinard's claim that conven-tional cotton is toxic to the environment.

"[Conventionally grown cotton] doesn't use more pesticides than any other commodity," Guthrie said, acknowledging that more than 20 years ago pesticides for cotton, as well as for other crops, were toxic. However, stringent standards implemented by the Environmental Protection Agency have eliminated those toxics, he said.

"Historically, cotton used chemicals damaging to the environment, but they have long since been eliminated from the arsenal," Guthrie said.

Guthrie went on to say that organic cotton is more expensive than conventional cotton, primarily because yield per acre is lower and manual labor often is required to cut weeds in the field.

"We knew when we came out with this announcement that we would get that type of reaction from the National Cotton Council," said a Patagonia spokesman. "But we're standing by what we believe."

Guthrie predicts that the use of organic cotton could hike prices at least 10 percent.

The Patagonia spokesman said the average price increase per garment would be "between $4 and $5, with a range of $2 to $10."

For instance, he said a pair of Standup walking shorts, a Patagonia benchmark product, which retails for $40 this year, will sell for $45 in spring 1996.

Chouinard did note that costs associated with using organic cotton are more at each of the production steps. While the company plans to lower profit margins on the organic styles, the products will still cost more, Chouinard said.

"We're asking our customers to split the difference: to pay a little extra now to save on the clean-up bill later," he said. Organic cotton comprises a minute portion of all cotton grown in the U.S.

Some 19.7 million bales of upland cotton were produced in 1994, with not more than 50,000 bales of organic cotton produced, Guthrie said. A bale of cotton weighs 480 pounds.

In an effort to avoid shortage problems, Patagonia will work with growers to insure delivery to mills and garment factories. Most organic cotton is grown in Arizona, Texas and parts of California, primarily because those regions aren't as plagued by insects as Southeastern regions, Guthrie said.

Patagonia distributes its merchandise through 12 company-owned stores and 600-plus specialty retailers and catalogs. It also distributes its products throughout Europe.

Organic production has flattened in the past several years, and now, Guthrie predicts that sustainable growth is developing. He predicted that growers would welcome Patagonia's approach to contracting before the growing season to reduce their risks at market.

"One of the biggest problems with organic cotton apparel is that it costs more," Guthrie said. "Studies have shown that consumers aren't willing to pay more than 10 percent more for organic cotton. It's limited to a small niche in the upscale market where price is not a consideration."

Environmental consciousness at Patagonia is not limited to cotton. The company introduced the fleece garments made from recycled soda bottles in fall 1993 and has eliminated packaging materials from one underwear line.

Women's Wear Daily, August 14, 1995.

CHAPTER 8

Furs and Leather

Like the textile industry, the fur and leather industries are primary markets. By themselves, their products serve no purpose in the consumer market. However, when manufactured into apparel, accessories, or home fashions or when used as trimmings for fashion items, they achieve popular appeal.

These two industries serve the tastes of people at many income levels. Leather shoes are available at both expensive and inexpensive price points, the wide range being the result of variations in quality, styling, and construction, and sometimes the inclusion or omission of a designer name. Once reserved for the affluent members of our society, furs are now within reach of a larger number of consumers. The price differential for this product depends on the availability and quality of the skins, the intricacy of construction, the color popularity, the designer signature, and the importance of the fur as a fashion statement.

Both furs and leather must undergo extensive treatment before they can be manufactured into garments or accessories. In addition to designers, technical experts are necessary. Whereas textiles are relatively easy to transform into fashions, leather and fur products require painstaking craftsmanship.

Both industries will be explored in terms of

- Market scope
- Production procedures
- Materials
- Style
- Marketing

FURS

Often, the gala social events covered by print and broadcast media attract attention, in part, because of the apparel worn by attendees. Whether it is the opening night festivities for The Metropolitan Opera or the annual award presentations of the Council of Fashion Designers of America, what the people

After you have completed this chapter, you should be able to discuss:

- Changes in the consumer market for garments made of fur.

- Stages involved in the processing of furs.

- Various techniques of fur construction.

- Furs such as mink, ermine, sable fox, rabbit, muskrat, and persian lamb.

- The necessity for the Fur Products Labeling Act of 1952

- The process by which leather hides are transformed into usable materials.

- The origins of leather and its uses.

wear is often bigger news than the events themselves to the editorial press and photojournalists. Because the photographers are often restricted to locations outside of the arenas where the galas are held, their pictures often show the guests arriving in their evening wraps. If the events take place during the colder times of the year, fur garments receive the camera's attention.

Although fur has long been associated with special occasions, it is not exclusively used for such occasions. Today, while style and fashion are often foremost in the minds of consumers, function is also a consideration. The warmth a fur garment provides, along with its long-term use, makes fur a practical purchase. Women rushing to their offices or shopping in their favorite stores may be seen wearing anything from a sweeping mink to a casual raccoon coat.

However, some individuals feel that the taking of skins from animals for the purpose of adornment is inappropriate—in part because it is endangering some animal species; in part because of the perception of how these animals are raised and killed. **Animal rights activists** and environmentalists have made their cause known throughout the world with a variety of demonstrations. They have assaulted wearers of fur garments and picketed fur salons. An attack on the Fifth Avenue offices of Karl Lagerfeld is an example. A well-funded organization, **PETA, People for the Ethical Treatment of Animals,** spent $11.5 million in 1994 to discourage the purchase of furs. Supporters, led by vocal celebrities such as Bob Barker, Ricki Lake, and Cindy Crawford, have caused significant setbacks in the industry. Some consumers are not buying any furs, others are only buying furs from animals that are not endangered. Several

(left) Luxury furs are used primarily for special occasions. (right) Casual furs are worn for shopping, to business, and for everyday use.

The animal rights activists demonstrate to deter the use of furs for garments.

fashionable retailers with global recognition, such as Harrods in London, have closed their fur salons as the efforts of these groups succeeded in reducing demand of fur garments. Others have been forced into bankruptcy. With the adverse press initiated by these demonstrations, the industry has decided to take a stand and publicize its right to freely sell furs. Through position papers developed by trade associations and advertisements by individual fur manufacturers that respond to the arguments of animal rights activists, the industry has continued to market furs. It no longer concentrates merely on the beauty of the product and the prestige given to the wearer, but it makes every effort to allay the fears of those who might abandon the idea of a fur purchase because of the controversy that surrounds the industry.

Components of the Fur Industry

Before a fur garment is offered for sale, it passes through the hands of different specialists. The process begins with those who raise or trap the animals, then moves to the processors who transform the skins of the animals with the hair intact, and finally ends with the designers and manufacturers who create the finished products.

Farmers and Trappers

Fewer than one-quarter of the furs produced in North America comes from animals that run in the wild. The majority of the furs come from animals raised on fur farms. The vast majority are centered in Wisconsin, Minnesota, and Utah in the United States and Ontario and Quebec in Canada. Cumulatively, there are 3,700 family farms selling more than six million pelts annually at a price tag of $230 million.

To produce the pelts in a humane way for garment use and to dispel any arguments about mistreatment of animals, the farmers have developed standards that are administered by the Fur Farm Animal Welfare Coalition in the

Fendi

Five sisters—Paola, Anna, Franca, Carla, and Alda—direct one of the world's major fashion houses that emphasizes leather and furs. The business was opened in 1925 by their parents—Edoardo and Adele Fendi—as a small leather and fur workshop.

A new boutique on the Via Pave in Rome, Italy, and the entry of the five sisters into the business paved the way for its ultimate recognition. In 1965, Karl Lagerfeld, joined forces with the Fendi family and combined his creative genius with their business expertise. Their collaboration gave a particular style to fur coats. Stitches, inlays, interwoven fabrics, and lacquering changed the furs from the traditional, functional item to a more creative and fashion-oriented item. Beginning with made-to-order fur garments, the company strengthened its position with a ready-to-wear fur line in 1969.

Their leather goods underwent a similar evolution. Handbags were printed, interwoven, dyed, and tanned. In 1977, the company expanded its efforts to include ready-to-wear. By 1984, Fendi became an international name.

In 1985, the Gallery of Modern Art of Rome celebrated Fendi's sixty years as a fashion house and its twenty-year collaboration with Karl Lagerfeld with an exhibition. In that same year, the company launched its first fragrance.

In 1987, the third Fendi generation, sensitive to market needs, created the Fendissime line of fur and sportswear. In 1989, Fendi opened its first American flagship store on New York City's Fifth Avenue. During the same time the company launched the *Fendi Uomo* fragrance to accompany its newest endeavor, the Fendi Uomo line, a collection of men's wear.

By 1992, the Fendi company was headquartered in one central building in Rome, which also housed all of the fur workrooms. Today, in addition to fur and leather products, Fendi licenses many items throughout the world. Sixty percent of its production is exported all over the globe. There are more than one hundred Fendi boutiques, worldwide, as well as six hundred in-store shops.

Fendi furs are always lighthearted and fun.

United States and by the Mink Breeders Association in Canada. Every aspect of these farms' activities including methodology, nutrition, veterinary care, and humane harvesting procedures are outlined in their guidelines. Those who raise the animals today are a different breed from those of the past. More and more often they are young farmers with college degrees in agriculture, biology, or business, who serve apprenticeships on established farms to learn the complete fur-production cycle.

When the pelts are obtained by trapping, a great effort has been made to guarantee humane treatment. Endangered species are no longer sought and captured in the United States. Wildlife managers oversee the operations, establishing quotas and trapping seasons when necessary. In addition to learning about trapping from their predecessors, current trappers take specific educational courses learning the latest methods of trapping.

Trappers sell the **pelts**—undressed skins with the hair intact—to agents who auction to wholesalers, manufacturers, and designers. In contrast, fur farmers usually omit the agent stage and sell directly to the garment producers.

Global **fur auctions** are held in such major areas of the United States as New York City, Minneapolis, St. Louis, and other world centers such as St. Petersburg, London, and Montreal.

Processors

After the auction, the pelts are brought to processing companies that transform them into skins that can be turned into garments. Many different processing stages must be undertaken. They include dressing, dyeing, bleaching, and glazing the pelt, all of which will be fully discussed later in the chapter.

Designers and Manufacturers

Once the pelts have been processed, craftspersons turn them into garments. As with other apparel and accessories, the designer creates the styles that will be marketed. In the past, there was little creative styling for furs. The designs were basic or classic, with the fur itself being the most important element in the construction. Today, however, fur styling is as varied as any other garment. No longer are consumers limited to purchasing just one fur, which by necessity was generally simple and long-lasting, but many have several furs in their wardrobes. With style and silhouette now so important, notable designers have come to the forefront and are creating complete lines of furs. Glancing at fur advertisements immediately reveals names that once were associated only with the women's apparel industry. They include Valentino, Fendi, Yves Saint Laurent, and Oscar de la Renta for "high chic" designs and Michael Kors, Marc Jacobs, and Dolce & Gabbana for "cool" fur designs. The use of these and other famous names on labels is usually the result of licensing agreements between the designers and fur manufacturers. By marketing furs with such recognizable fashion names, the industry has been able to more easily justify the high prices to these garments. One of the most successful fur designers is Fendi, who is profiled in a World of Fashion Profile.

Once designers have fashioned the styles, the next stage involves matching the skins to the designs and turning them into salable garments.

Fur auctions are held globally to sell pelts to manufacturers.

Processing of Fur

The three operations necessary to prepare the pelts or skins for construction are:

- Dressing
- Dyeing
- Bleaching

Dressing

Pelts are initially soaked or mechanically treated to render themselves soft. The inside skins are fleshed to remove any unwanted substances. To make the "leather" portion of the pelts more workable, they are tanned or aged by means of chemicals. The tanning process tends to remove some of the natural oils from the skins, which must be replaced through **kicking.** This involves beating the furs against each other. If too much excess oil remains, the furs are placed in a drum filled with sawdust until some of the oil has been removed. After this stage, some fur pelts are further processed. The long **guard hairs** may be removed by a shearing process, as is done with sheared beaver, or by plucking, as is sometimes done with raccoon. After a final cleaning, they are ready to be used naturally or to be color enhanced.

Dyeing

Fur pelts are dyed for a variety of reasons and by several means. Sometimes the purpose is to improve the natural color or to give the bundle of skins a uniform appearance. If there is the slightest variation of color among the skins to be used in a garment, the final product will not have a perfectly matched look. Other times, furs are dyed to give them a fashion flair. It is not unusual for some of the more avant-garde designers to use the fashion colorations of the season for their furs, as they do in their apparel collections. If the fashion industry is touting purple, then purple it might be for some fur garments.

The dyes can be applied most easily by totally immersing the bundle in a dye bath; this is called **dip dyeing** and can be recognized, at once, because both the fur and the leather side will receive the color. If the choice is to color enhance or deepen the natural shade, brushing the edges of the fur with dye, or **tip dyeing,** is the method used. In cases where a pattern might be the designer's decision, as is the case when imitating other fur markings is desired, **stencil dyeing** is used. No matter how the furs are dyed, the fact that they have been colored must be indicated on the tag. This protects the consumer from purchasing a fur that he or she thinks is natural, but has been actually enhanced with color.

Bleaching

White furs are often tinged with yellow, which detracts from their appearance. To eliminate this unpleasant coloration, the pelts are **bleached.** In other cases, just to guarantee the even distribution of dyes, the furs might first be bleached. This is particularly true for dark furs that will ultimately be lightened. Excessive bleaching, while producing the desired light color, however, may be harmful to the fur and could shorten its life.

Glazing

The last process before manufacturing is **glazing.** The fur is sprayed with water and chemicals and pressed with special irons to improve luster and smoothness.

Constructing Fur Garments

Pelts are now sent to the manufacturer to be made into garments. The stages of construction vary according to the inherent characteristics of the fur, the intended appearance of the garment, and the eventual price at which it will be sold.

Matching the Skins

Skins are carefully arranged on the pattern to conform with the designer's plan and to the customer's measurements if the garment is to be custom made. It should be noted that most furs are being mass-produced, rather than customized for each purchaser. Only in cases where expense is not of primary concern is the garment made to exact customer measurements. The stock sizes enable stores to carry a wider assortment, giving the shopper wider selection and immediate wearability.

To achieve the best appearance, the skins are matched and placed according to length and texture of hair, color, and other characteristics. Of course, if the skins have been dyed, there is no color-matching. So subtle are the markings and features that only a trained craftsperson can satisfactorily perform the task of matching.

Cutting and Sewing the Skins

After placement of pelts has been determined, the skins are cut to fit the pattern. Fine garments are hand cut; inexpensive ones may be cut by machine. The method of cutting depends on the characteristics, price, and the ultimate appearance of the fur.

There are several techniques used to cut and sew the pelts into a fur garment.

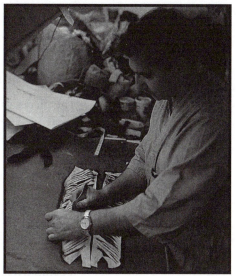

SKIN-ON-SKIN CONSTRUCTION   Producers of inexpensive furs often use the method called **skin-on-skin construction,** in which each skin is placed and sewn next to subsequent skins to form a garment. Unless the furs are long-haired or naturally curly, as in the case of persian lamb, it is almost impossible to conceal the resultant seaming.

LETTING-OUT CONSTRUCTION   Fine furs, such as mink, are generally constructed by the **letting-out method.** This is a costly technique that requires time and skilled craftsmanship. Its purpose is to elongate the fur to the full length of the desired garment, eliminating horizontal joining marks, a characteristic of the less-expensive joining methods. The process involves cutting

(top) The letting-out process elongates fur and avoids cross-seamings.
(bottom) A technician re-sews skins that have been let-out.

each skin vertically down the center of the dark stripe and then cutting the strips diagonally $\frac{1}{8}$ of an inch wide. The narrow strips are then resewn to form the longer skin. After the lengthening procedure, the skins are rematched, sewn to fit the pieces of the design, dampened, stretched, and stapled onto a board until dry. The expert takes care not to stretch the furs too much because they might eventually split if overstretched. The various components are then sewn to complete the garment.

SPLIT-SKIN CONSTRUCTION Although female minks are generally favored because of their silkier appearance and lighter weight, they cost considerably more than male skins. For less expensive garments, the male skins might be manipulated to resemble the female skins by using **split-skin construction.** The operator slices the skin down the center, creating two pieces of fur. Each piece is then let-out and elongated for use in the garment. Although this construction technique is still costly, it reduces the ultimate price of the garment because it requires fewer skins and uses less-costly male skins.

WHOLE-SKIN CONSTRUCTION In cases where smaller garments, such as jackets, are to be produced, elongation of the fur is unnecessary. A full skin will have the length needed without resorting to skin-on-skin joining. The full skin is merely cut to fit the pattern. This is known as **whole-skin construction.**

LEATHERING In cases where bulky furs, such as fox, are used, it is sometimes desirable to insert strips of leather or other material between the rows of skins to eliminate bulkiness. Each skin is sewn to a strip, which is then sewn to another skin until the process is completed. If the skins are very bushy, the inserted strips will not be seen. In addition to eliminating bulkiness, **leathering** also reduces the number of skins necessary to make a garment. Sometimes, the inserts are intentionally visible as part of the designer's styling.

Assembling Fur Garments

The pieces that have been assembled from the skins are then sewn together by hand in an operation called **closing.** This requires expert workmanship by expert technicians.

Finishing Fur Garments

At this point, the lining is sewn to the coat or jacket. Snaps, buttons, hooks and eyes, or zippers are sewn in place. The garment is now finished except for a possible lining monogram that identifies its owner.

Types of Furs

The many different types of furs used in the manufacture of coats, jackets, and enhancements are classified according to specific families. The weasel family group represents some of the world's most desired and costliest furs, including ermine, sable, and mink.

A look at the vast amount of fur advertising reveals that mink is the most popular fur among consumers and that it is available at many price points. Although quality and construction contributes to the price variation, it is the color that often accounts for the biggest difference. Considerable cross-breeding has produced a great number of mutations with many different colors. A

A variety of fur coats are shown on the runway.

garment in a color that is rare, or promoted by the fashion industry as the newest, garners the highest prices. Thus, when a color loses its popularity, garments in that color will probably fall in price.

The cat family is characterized by specific markings and patterns. It is a favorite of fur designers who create the unusual and includes lynx and leopard. The family of furs known as rodents offers a wide range of prices, from the most expensive to the very inexpensive. This family includes chinchilla, beaver, nutria, muskrat, and rabbit. The canine group is primarily dominated by the fox. It is easily distinguished by the long guard hairs and lush fur fibers. It is a showy fur that is often used for special occasions The density generally calls for leathering to eliminate some of the bulkiness. The varieties of fox include red, white, blue, silver, and gray. The ungulate or hoofed-animal family produces fur that is tightly curled and includes persian and South American lamb. See Table 8.1 for a more complete list and description of types of furs.

Regulations in the Fur Industry

Before 1952, the fur industry was less than truthful in describing its furs. Inexpensive pelts such as muskrat were sometimes misrepresented as a type of mink, and advertisements heralded mink-dyed muskrat as a popular fur. In an effort to protect the consumer, federal legislation now requires proper identification of fur garments. The Fur Products Labeling Act of 1952, which has been amended many times, requires the following:

1. Furs must be advertised and labeled using their English names.
2. The name of one fur may not be used to describe another.
3. The country of origin, if not the United States, must be clearly stated in ads and on labels.
4. Garments made of waste or scraps must be labeled as waste or section furs.
5. Furs that are dyed must be noted as such in ads and on labels.

TYPES OF FURS CLASSIFIED ACCORDING TO SPECIFIC FAMILIES

Family	Types of Furs	Description
Weasel	Mink	Finest variety comes from the northern part of the United States where it has been farmed. Female skins are more desirable than males because of their suppleness and lightweight quality.
	Sable	The coldest part of Russia produces the finest sables. It is the intensity of the weather that causes the animal to grow the densest fur. Similar in appearance to mink, but its fuller, longer guard hairs give it a bushier look. One of the world's rarest furs, a prized Russian sable coat can cost in excess of $100,000.
	Ermine	Extremely expensive; a white fur accentuated by natural black-tipped markings on its tail. Rarely used commercially any longer. Seen as part of dress for royalty in state processions. Occasionally, pieces are used as apparel enhancements.
	Stone Marten, Kolinsky, Fitch Wolverine, Otter Skunk	Lesser known furs; found occasionally in designer collections.
Cat	Lynx	Easily recognized by long, bushy guard hairs and slightly spotted markings. Best quality is from the coldest parts of Russia and Canada. While it often plays a role in fashion, its tendency to shed makes it a problem for wearers.
	Leopard	Once the favorite fur of the cat family, no longer used for garments because it is on the endangered species list.
	Lynx Cat	Slightly less costly than lynx.
	Ocelot	Similar to leopard, but not as strikingly marked.
Rodent	Chinchilla	Most expensive fur in this family. Extremely rare as well as extremely perishable. Generally has a gray coloration, but through mutation fur farming other colors have been achieved.
	Beaver	Often the consumers who want this fur ask for "sheared" beaver. The reason for this is that during the processing of the pelts, the long guard hairs are sheared leaving the soft, downy fur fiber undercoat. Available as a natural fur in shades of brown, many fashion designers include beaver dyed in a host of shades in their collections.
	Nutria	May be sheared as is beaver, but more often shown with the guard hairs intact. Extremely serviceable and provides years of wear.
	Muskrat	One of the most widely used furs to imitate the look of more costly skins. Resembles mink when it is dyed and let-out; resembles beaver when sheared. To produce this fur as inexpensively as possible, the typical method of construction used is skin-on-skin.
	Rabbit	Inexpensive and processed to imitate other furs. Often dyed the latest fashionable colors or bleached white. While rabbit garments have a luxurious appearance when new, the phenomenon is short lived because of significant shedding and low durability.
Canine	Red Fox	Orange–red color; caught in the wild. Generally reserved for trimming on coats and suits.
	White Fox	Often the choice for a dramatic entrance. Whitest species from the northernmost parts of the United States and Canada.
	Blue Fox	Actually brownish with a blue cast. Fox with a real blue color is Norwegian blue fox, a mutation developed in fur farming.

(continued)

TABLE 8.1 (*continued*)

	Blue Fox	Actually brownish with a blue cast. Fox with a real blue color is Norwegian blue fox, a mutation developed in fur farming.
	Silver Fox	Silvery guard hairs and blue-black fur fibers. Most silvery variety is called platinum fox, a mutation of the silver fox.
	Gray Fox	Least desirable of the family; relatively inexpensive; often dyed to imitate silver fox.
Ungulate	Persian lamb	Raised on farms; fur is tightly curled and lustrous. Majority are black, but some are available in natural gray and brown.
	Broadtail	Pelts from newborn Persian lamb; characterized by a flat, watermarked pattern. More expensive than Persian lamb.
	South American lamb	Inexpensive and durable; used to produce mouton-processed lamb. Fur is sheared and electrified to relax the pattern.

The **Endangered Species Conservation Act** was passed to protect animals from extinction. If an animal species is threatened because of declining numbers, it cannot be hunted for its pelts. These restrictions are intended to help the species continue to breed and increase its population. Leopards and tigers are among these endangered groups.

Selling Furs to the Consumer

Furs are sold in a variety of places, such as fur manufacturer's facilities, retail establishments, and temporary sales arenas.

Fur Manufacturer's Facilities

Many fur manufacturers open their doors to the public. Individuals are invited to purchase from an inventory that has already been produced or to avail themselves of the company's designer who will custom-tailor a coat or jacket. It is the latter approach that patrons of furriers generally prefer. They are shown a variety of styles or may have one made from their own design, choose from the many bundles of skins on hand, have a muslin made to their exact measurements, and select the lining that would finish the garment. Buying this way, of course, is more expensive than off-the-rack purchasing.

The fur salon at Bloomingdale's is one of retailing's most prestigious.

Retail Establishments

Throughout the world, retailers have long sold furs directly to their customers. Some stores belong to a chain that carries only furs, such as The Fur Vault, while others are department stores with fur salons, which are most often leased departments. The retailer invites a fur manufacturer to open a department in the store and to completely merchandise and manage it. The store charges for the space and often receives a percentage of the sales. Maximillian Furs is such an operation in the Bloomingdale's stores.

Temporary Sales Arenas

One of the ways manufacturers attract large crowds of potential fur purchasers is to lease temporary space in a hotel or convention center. There, for a few days, consumers can examine merchandise and make their purchases. Large print advertisements and television commercials are used to announce these events, which are most often touted as special sales. Sometimes a group of fur manufacturers will combine their efforts, and bring together the merchandise from their respective factories. By doing this, they share in the expense of such an operation.

Leather is intricately used in ready-to-wear as shown here.

LEATHER

Consumers are more interested in leather today than ever before in fashion history. Once utilized primarily as a fashion accessory for shoes, handbags, and small purses, designers from around the globe now use leather to create suits, coats, jackets, and sportswear for every member of the family in a variety of styles and price points. One need only to walk through regional malls to find such stores as Tannery West and Wilsons, which feature significant assortments of leather garments.

As with furs, different skins have different characteristics. Calfskin is unlike pigskin or sheepskin in appearance, and nothing like rawhide. The variety of skins available to producers is large, and the methods of production are numerous. As a result, the finished products are quite varied. Although often imitated by synthetic materials, nothing yet available has the natural feel and beauty of leather.

Characteristics of the Leather Industry

Each year, the industry makes technological advances in the production and processing of leather, including the application of silk-screen designs, and the creation of textures that are softer than ever. With these and other innovations, the industry continues to expand. For the five-year period beginning in 1990, retail sales of leather garments exceeded $3 billion!

The major centers of cattle production for the leather industry are the United States, the countries that formerly made up the Soviet Union, and Western Europe. Other producers include Argentina, Brazil, India, and Mexico. The United States, alone, accounts for more than $1.5 billion. American tanning activities are concentrated in the Northeast, Midwest, Middle Atlantic states, and California. The shoe and leather goods industries alone in America employ more than 200,000 workers.

Processing of Leather

The processing of leather involves twenty individual stages. Once the hides and skins are removed from the dead animals, they must be pretanned or

Andrew Marc

While the fashion industry has heralded its major designers for many centuries, the emphasis has been on names that design a whole host of apparel and accessories. Recognition is generally reserved for those who present apparel collections for women and, less frequently, for men. Rarely is an individual who is associated with one basic material singled out for special attention. In the leather industry, however, this has been the case for relatively few individuals.

Andrew Marc has achieved fame through the exclusive design of leather apparel for men and women. Although most shoppers merely look for a particular leather style and quality, few ask for a specific designer name. The exception is Andrew Marc.

In 1981, the Andrew Marc label rose into prominence under the umbrella company founded by Fred Schwartz, the famous chairman of The Fur Vault. He combined form and function for his signature style—and a classic—the leather bomber jacket. The garment featured a leather outer shell that was lined with fur. It quickly became the industry's leading seller. From this unique concept evolved a collection of diversified silhouettes including motorcycle styles, anoraks, crop styles, and leather sportswear. All of the items are designed with clean understated lines and authentic detail.

Today, the company is owned and operated by Marc and his wife Suzanne. Their commitment is to bring to the public a superior quality product with unsurpassed craftsmanship. By consistently updating their styling and by designing garments with customers' lifestyles in mind, Andrew Marc has become one of the leading leather outerwear companies in the United States.

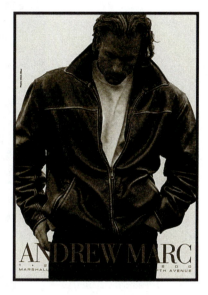

An Andrew Marc design from his 1995 collection.

cured. Hides are the pelts taken from large animals, such as horses and cows, and skins, the pelts taken from the smaller animals such as calves, sheep, and goats. After curing, which involves the use of salt as a primary agent, the pelts begin the twenty stages of processing.

1. Receiving and Storage. The pelts are received, sorted according to size and weight, and packed in bundles that will travel to the tannery as a unit.

2. Soaking. To restore moisture that is lost during the curing stage, the pelts are soaked for eight to twenty hours. The process makes them softer as well as cleaner.

3. Unhairing. Most hair removal is accomplished by the use of chemicals that have little effect on the leather itself. Manufacturers who wish to sell the hair for use in other products remove the hair mechanically.

4. Trimming and Siding. This next stage removes the unusable perimeter areas of the pelt. The process is accomplished with a circular blade.

5. Fleshing. This process removes excess flesh from the underside of the pelt by a mechanical operation employing sharp, rotating blades.

6. Bating. After the hair and flesh have been removed, it is necessary to remove the chemicals used in earlier stages. This removal is accomplished by washing the hides and skins in large cylindrical drums filled with chemicals.

a.

a. Leather processing
involves making pelts
uniform in thickness.
b. Pelts are set out to
dry after they have
been made uniformly
thick. c. Pasting
of skins and hide to
vacuum them dry.

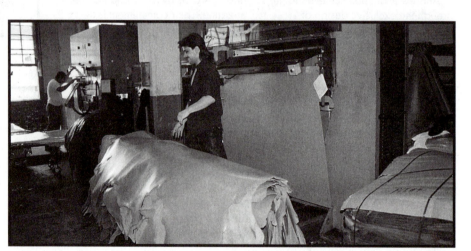

b.

c.

7. Pickling. Prior to the actual tanning operation, the pelts are salted and acid bathed to make them more susceptible to tanning. This is actually a preserving operation.

8. Tanning. Preserving or **tanning** leather can be accomplished in a number of ways. Most leather is now chrome tanned, a four- to six-hour process that produces leather best suited for the majority of product uses. Other tanning agents include barks, roots, oils, and minerals. Each takes longer than chrome tanning and each produces leathers with unique characteristics.

9. Wringing and Sorting. Excess moisture is removed during this stage. Pelts are then sorted according to thickness.

10. Splitting and Shaving. Pelts vary in thickness, and must be **split** or sliced for uniformity. To do this they are fed into a splitting machine that slices off the underneath or flesh layer. If a large area of the flesh layer or split is thick enough, it can be further processed for product usage. The remaining pelt is then fed into a shaving machine that levels the overall thickness to exact specifications.

11. Retanning, Coloring, and Fat Liquoring. Retanning is actually a second tanning done to impart desirable properties to the leather not accomplished through primary tanning. Coloring of leather is now achieved by applying water-soluble dyes. Hundreds of dyes are available today, each with different properties. Factors such as penetration and color density must be considered in dye selection. **Fat liquoring** lubricates the leather's fibers and makes them softer and more flexible.

12. Setting Out. The first of the drying processes involves smoothing the leather grain and removing any excess moisture before the actual drying phase is begun.

13. Drying. A variety of techniques can be chosen to dry leather. The simplest, *hanging,* is a procedure similar to that of clothesline drying; *toggling* is a means of stretching with clips; *pasting* is the most popular method. Skins and hides are actually pasted on six- by eleven-foot plates and vacuum dried, a process in which water is extracted by machine.

14. Conditioning. After drying, some pelts are too hard for use in merchandise production and require conditioning—the introduction of controlled moisture.

15. Staking and Milling. To make the leather soft and pliable, machines stake the leather by pounding it with "fingers" or pins.

16. Buffing. To improve its appearance by removing scratches or blemishes, the grain or surface of the leather is lightly buffed. The operation involves a sanding cylinder that is rotated against the leather.

17. Finishing. The natural beauty of the leather is protected by means of a finishing system. The leather might be coated with transparent materials allowing the grain to show through or covered with opaque powders to achieve a coloring effect. Surface coatings are achieved through polyurethanes and other chemicals. The finishing department carefully selects the right ingredients for specific, desired results.

18. Plating. The final appearance-improving step is plating. Leathers are smoothed to improve their feel or grained through embossing.

T A B L E   8 . 2

TYPES AND USES OF LEATHER

Types of Leather	Uses
Cow and Steer	Used extensively in shoe production for parts such as uppers, soles, insoles, and linings; coats and jackets; gloves, belts, and handbags; luggage and upholstery.
Calf	Shoe uppers; handbags, wallets, gloves; garments.
Sheep and Lamb	Sueded for use in shoes and garments; extremely soft, also used for gloves and linings.
Goat and Kid	Apparel, shoe uppers, gloves, and handbags.
Pig and Hog	Fancy leather goods, such as shoes and billfolds; different types come from the peccary and carpincho pigs.
Deer	Softness makes deerskin a favorite for dress gloves and moccasins.
Horse	Shoe uppers and soles; gloves, and sometimes garments.
Reptile (alligator, most costly to use.	Handbags, shoes, and belts; reptile skins are among the crocodile, lizard, snake)

19. Grading. Unlike fabrics, which are uniformly produced, leather quality differs from pelt to pelt. Leather is graded according to such factors as color, thickness, and defects. The better the quality, the more expensive the ultimate products.

20. Measuring. Since leather hides are irregularly shaped and since price is based upon area, it must be measured.

Origins and Uses of Leathers

Each type of leather is suited to particular uses. Because of their suppleness, some are used extensively for gloves, others, because of their durability, are headed for use in upholstery and shoes. Table 8.2 identifies the types of leathers and uses.

Characteristics of Leather

Just as different fibers have specific characteristics and properties, so do the hides and skins of animals. In addition to the beauty offered the wearer, leather also is functional.

Leather has extremely high tensile strength—it can withstand a great deal of stress without tearing apart. It is also extremely flexible, thereby avoiding the potential for cracking because of cold and heat. Because it also absorbs moisture, breathes easily, and has the ability to conform to specific shapes, it is the perfect material for shoes.

Its versatility makes it a much sought after material by the consumer.

Fashion Leathers

A look through the large assortment of leather merchandise immediately shows that there are many different fashion-oriented leathers. They are basi-

(left) The men's wear industry is a major consumer of leather. (right) Leather pants are easy to wear and are a practical luxury.

cally derived from the categories described in Table 8.2, but have been specially treated or finished to impart different looks. The following alphabetical list is composed of the more popular fashion leathers.

ANALINE LEATHER   A product that is colored with transparent dyes and shows the natural characteristics of the leather.

DISTRESSED LEATHER   A material with a weathered appearance.

LAMB LEATHER   The softest leather of the group.

NAPA   A shiny, smooth, or pebbly surfaced material.

NUBUCK   A lightly buffed leather with a fine nap that appears smoother than suede. It is used for shoes, blazers, skirts, and pants.

SHRUNKEN LAMB   Leather with a pebbly, grained surface.

SUEDE   A velvetlike leather that is produced by napping the skin's underside.

Promoting and Marketing Leathers

The widespread use of synthetic leather has provided competition for the leather industry. Large numbers of consumers have been persuaded to purchase less costly products that have characteristics similar to leather.

The leather industry does have trade associations, such as the Tanner's Council, the New England Tanner's Club, Leather Industries of America, and the Leather Apparel Association, to promote the image of leather and its importance to the consumer. Unfortunately, these associations do not have the same recognition as associations in the textile industry. Unlike Cotton Incorporated and The Wool Bureau, which regularly appear in the print and broadcast media and are immediately recognized by the consumer, the names of the leather associations are not readily known.

Recognition is greater when tanners convince major designers to include leather in their collections. The use of designer names in advertising helps to focus attention on a leather product.

Selling is accomplished primarily through trade shows, among which Leather World, the Wolburn Show, the St. Louis Show, and The Accessory and Garment Leather Show are the most popular in the United States. Semaine du Cuir, in Paris, is the world's largest international fair.

Chapter Highlights

- Both the fur and leather industries have continued to increase their presence in the fashion world.

- The fur industry has had to confront opposition from animal right's activists and environmentalists who use a variety of methods to discourage consumer purchasing.

- The leather industry is facing competition from synthetic products that rival its use.

- Fur prices have become much more reasonable because of increases in fur farming and the popularity of less recognized furs.

- To be manufactured into garments, furs undergo several processes from dressing the pelts to various construction techniques and finishes.

- The Federal government continues to play an important role in the marketing of furs through key legislative acts, the most far reaching of which is the Fur Products Labeling Act.

- The fur industry continues to increase sales each year. Marketing efforts include ads that try to allay concerns raised by industry opponents.

- Fur licensing agreements with famous designers have also helped fur sales.

- Leather processing is a painstaking, time-consuming venture that involves twenty different steps.

- The leather industry is promoted through trade associations.

Important Fashion Terminology and Concepts

analine leather
animal rights activists
bleaching
closing
dip dyeing
distressed leather
dressing
dyeing
endangered species
Endangered Species
    Conservation Act

fat liquoring
fur auctions
fur licensing agreements
Fur Products Labeling Act
    of 1952
glazing
guard hairs
kicking
lamb leather
leathering
letting-out

napa
nubuck
shrunken lamb
skin bundles
skin-on-skin construction
splitting
split-skin construction
stencil dyeing
suede
tanning
tip dyeing

For Review

1. What major undertaking in the early 1990s caused considerable difficulty for the fur industry?
2. How has the fur industry fought the accusations of PETA?
3. Why are there such large price differentials in the fur market?
4. Describe the three industry segments in the production of fur.
5. In what way has the Fur Products Labeling Act helped the consumer?
6. Explain how letting-out improves the appearance of some fur skins.
7. Differentiate between skin-on-skin and split-skin construction.
8. What are the three major types of outlets used to sell furs?
9. What is the difference between a leather hide and a skin?
10. What method of tanning is preferred by the leather industry? Why?
11. What is meant by the term "splitting," as it applies to leather?
12. Collectively, which group of leathers is the most costly?
13. In what way does aniline leather differ from other leathers?
14. In what format does the leather industry sell most of its goods?

Exercises and Projects

1. Call or write to a fur manufacturer asking for permission to record the various stages of fur production. The task might be performed with a still camera, in which case slides would be taken, or a video camera. Using the slides or tape, prepare a talk to accompany the visual presentation to your class.
2. Prepare an oral presentation about the furs currently being marketed by the industry. Pages may be used from fashion magazines and mounted on foamcore board for presentation to the class.
3. Take the position of an animal right's activist and prepare a talk that would support your cause.
4. Select three items of leather from your wardrobe such as belts, shoes, apparel, and handbags, and try to determine their animal sources.
5. Write a report on the status of the leather industry. Information may be obtained from the various associations mentioned in the text, as well as from trade periodicals and consumer publications.

The Case of Uncertain Expansion

A & R Furriers, Inc., have been fur manufacturers for the past thirty years. The company, founded by Paul Kim, has always enjoyed a fine reputation and their profits have regularly increased, providing Mr. Kim with a comfortable life style.

Last year, Cathy, Mr. Kim's daughter, joined the company. Fresh out of college, she brought great enthusiasm and a wealth of ideas that could improve the company's present position. She spoke about the possibility of merging with another company that would give the newly expanded organization a greater competitive edge. Because her father was aware of the pitfalls of merging, the proposal fell on deaf ears. She then suggested expanding the business by opening a retail division. By manufacturing their own garments, she proposed, the company could offer furs at a lower price than most stores and still make an admirable profit.

The senior Kim has thus far vetoed all of his daughter's suggestions. He agrees that expansion in some direction might be beneficial, but he is afraid of jeopardizing the company's position. Mergers are not in line with his thinking and retailing requires efforts not within his expertise.

Although the company's products are successfully sold to stores that insert their own labels on the garments and to individuals who come to the company for custom-designed garments, there does not seem to be another route for increasing business. He is still open to ideas for expansion, but the proper direction seems to elude him.

Question

Bearing in mind his daughter's two proposals, how might A & R expand its operation and increase profits?

point of view

Is There a Future for Fur?

Suzy Menkes

The Marc Jacobs shearling coat is traffic-stopping bright—a gaudy sherbet orange, flashy, trashy, on the precipitous edge of bad taste and great fashion, wrapped taut to the body as the model teeters out on high heels.

It is about as far as fur can go from the double-breasted ranch mink walking out of Lincoln Center on a frosty fall evening. This sturdy coat could have been designed and made any time over the past decade—although its wearer appears to be only in her thirties. The coat may have added a few years to her age and a couple of inches to her hips, but it is keeping her warm, while also fulfilling fur's time-honored role of making her broker husband feel that he has made it.

In that crowd at Lincoln Center, dotted among the cloth and down alternatives, is the spectrum of modern fur. There are some classic mink trenches, but mostly the sporty furs that are the current look from Madison Avenue to Avenue Montaigne: shearling duffle coats and parkas in flat sheared mink, muskrat, beaver, or occasionally cloth with sable lining. There are what passes today for evening fur—dark wraps of velvet-soft fur, or maybe even a vintage Oscar de la Renta shawl from 1973, which he describes as "an old Indian challis, slightly quilted, trimmed with sable tails."

"Mostly what I see are capes with fox trim or the big scarves, quilted, looking like velvet, maybe in beaver," says Blaine Trump—although she herself only brings out her "old raccoon coat" in subzero temperatures. "I have the most glamorous thing," says Susan Gutfreund of her Fendi coat made of deliberately unidentifiable fur hidden under mesh. "The outside is veiling; one piece looks like a shawl so that I can let it drip. There is plenty of arm room, like a poncho. It's the opposite of these heavy constructed furs that we used to think were glamorous and wonderful."

Ah, that outdated dream of deluxe. The dilemma for fur now is that its legendary glamour is associated with the past. While a few houses attempt to project it into the future, unless the industry as a whole can find a way of appealing to a new generation, fashion may be even more effective than the animal-rights activists are in turning stylish backs on fur.

For fashion-aware women, even those with no interest in causes and issues, fur at its most classic is often a turn-off. Or as Trump puts it: "There is nothing that is terribly chic in Fur Land." Faced with ads of models draped in glossy pelts—all tumbling blond hair and *Dynasty* lip gloss—potential customers might have a sneaking sympathy for Christy Turlington. In the striking billboard campaign by PETA (Washington, D.C.-based People for the Ethical Treatment of Animals), a clothesless Turlington declares, "I'd rather go naked than wear fur."

Yet fur figures are no longer in free fall. In spite of public perception that business is bad, sales have climbed 19 percent in the past two years, according to the American Fur Industry. (Although there is no escaping the impact of animal-rights activists, the recession seems to have been the main culprit for fur sales slumping from $1.8 billion in 1987 to the current $1.2 billion.) The recent rise is probably due to several factors, including energetic marketing to address the anti-fur sentiment of celebrities such as Kim Basinger, Brigitte Bardot, Naomi Campbell, and Turlington. The Fur Information Council of America (FICA) last year launched the slogan FUR, MORE THAN ANY OTHER FABRIC—an admittedly middle-of-the-road campaign, but one that suggests fur can compete with cloth. Sophia Loren recently joined the pro-fur voices by appearing wrapped in mink in new ads for Annabella Pellicceria, an Italian furmaker. And New York furrier Gus Goodman even spoofed the PETA campaign, using a naked man reclining on a fur blanket.

But what the industry really needs is new designer blood to take it beyond the swingy marmalade mink beloved by southern Europeans, the beaver bathrobes knotted against a Connecticut winter, and the ubiquitous hooded fur parkas. However practical they are, such styles are indelibly associated with 1980s power women and upscale sportswear, and thus démodé for young women today.

"I can't do fur according to rules that belong to a different generation," says Marc Jacobs, who has signed up with Birger Christensen to do fur, including the neon-bright shearlings that he showed in his fall collection. "There is no point doing the fur you see on every other Milanese woman—three tiers of natural fisher or mink. Nor for me to do ranch-dyed mink. It's not that

I'm against it—it's an aesthetic issue."

Karl Lagerfeld agrees that there is no room for safe and stolid fur in a designer line. He says that at Fendi they do "normal, basic mink coats," but not for the runway, because "it's not right in terms of fashion. I have no other philosophy than to make fur modern," he adds. "Young girls don't dream of a fur coat as an image of luxury. That kind of glamour-girl dream relates to their mothers and aunts."

The fashion cycle is always generational: What initially seems daring and innovative later becomes accepted and ultimately deemed bourgeois and boring. First, Marilyn Monroe was a glamour-puss with mink clutched to her breasts—every woman aspired to a mink—and then it became a dowdy benchmark of matronly status. Fur last generated high-fashion excitement in the 1960s, with "fun furs" in lapin and pony and the hippie afghan coats trimmed with Mongolian lamb. They culminated in 1971 with Yves Saint Laurent's Carmen Miranda couture collection—green and white fox chubbies with orange pantyhose and ankle-strapped platforms for a "happy hooker" look. It scandalized society then: "completely hideous" proclaimed the *International Tribune.* But the YSL furs, while shocking the old guard, hit precisely the mood of the young. Even while she slammed the show, fashion doyenne Eugenia Sheppard prophesied: "Not that Yves's silver fox chubbies . . . won't be wonderful camp for the girls who never wore them."

So who are the designers today who are going to come up with something wonderful in fur that announces, "Mother wouldn't like it"? Marc Jacobs could be one, for he sees those 1971 YSL fox chubbies and their on-the-edge sophistication as a reference point for modern times. "A new generation wants

to look chic, and *chic* is a seventies word," he says, adding that "hooker fur is a fad—anything questionable is kind of chic."

More designers than you might think are still working with some kind of pelt. Fur trim or shearling is used by directional designers like John Galliano, Jean Paul Gaultier, Isaac Mizrahi, Gianni Versace, Christian Lacroix, and Richard Tyler. And those treating a wider range of furs include Gianfranco Ferre, Karl Lagerfeld in his own label, Marc Jacobs, and Valentino.

Saint Laurent is still in there, and his current collection shows how to make fur modern. For fall there are the chubbies in black Mongolian lamb with brilliant satin linings. Vivid mohair plaid coats and shawls are edges with matching four-color fox for the essential splash of 1990s doubtful taste.

Although Calvin Klein and Donna Karan have both recently and publicly pulled out of fur, they are still using shearling. "Shearling doesn't scream a luxury thing—it's in the category of a leather belt," says Klein. "I didn't feel good doing something that can be so wildly expensive—and so many young people are passionately against killing animals. It doesn't seem like a modern thing to be doing, because a really, truly modern woman is not wearing fur."

Is it significant that noncontroversial shearling seems to be having all the fun in fur? "Shearling is the public, accepted fur of the 1990s," says Lagerfeld. He used it in his Fendi collection with irreverence, basting it with sampler stitches or stirring it in with rings, rubber covers, mesh, mohair, and Mongolian lamb. Shearling was served up short and sweet when Isaac Mizrahi sent out aqua and bubblegum pink jackets over fluffy sweaters, and Anna Sui's pink and black shearlings even held their own against the flood of fake furs in her fall collection.

Fur aping fake—as opposed to the other way around—is the biggest fur fashion story of the season. Why? Is it just an ironic commentary on modern attitudes to luxury? Or is dyeing fur in the most "unnatural," gaudy colors merely designer camouflage for the woman who could be subjected, as Trump puts it, to "screaming and yelling"? Although Yves Saint Laurent did not do fakes because, according to Jurgen Doering, who works with Saint Laurent in the fur studio, "we've seen so much from designers like Vivienne Westwood," the collection does include a panther-print velvet jacket, a reversed-calf safari jacket, and a could-be-fake Persian lamb duffle.

Fur designers who are at fashion's cutting edge are even going so far as to work real pelt in the image of fake. Jacobs's curly-lamb collar on a satin jacket is that kind of "is it or isn't it?" look, which was the entire spirit of Lagerfeld's Fendi collection, where a typical outfit was a synthetic leather coat trimmed with real chinchilla and lined with fake Persian. Even off the runway you literally could not tell by touching what was what.

The combination of Lagerfeld and Fendi over three decades has made Fendi indisputably fur's high fashion leader. Susan Gutfreund calls this symbiotic relationship, which started in 1965, "their genius and his creativity," resulting in a modern fur that keeps reinventing itself in tune with fashion. The overall Fendi achievement has been to serve up a "fatfree" fur: slim, light, richly worked but never indigestible. Technically, the pelts have been perforated to make them airy and are pieced together with a light hand. The spirit has been irreverent, even funky. Carla Fendi, one of the family's five sisters, explains that the idea was to move fur from a museum piece to a throw-it-on style. (Oscar de la Renta says, "I like what Karl Lagerfeld has done—taken the fur-makers stamp out of fashion.") Together, Fendi and Lagerfeld can claim to have invented fur as we know it: sables slung over blue jeans, fur-lined parkas, fluid shapes, weightless fabrics, and a modern attitude.

But Fendi's recent offerings have gone further still: disguising, destroying, and concealing. The last make-it-fake collection angered traditional furriers, who are concerned that Lagerfeld's tricks destroy the natural beauty of fur and its classy—if boring—image that reassures the regular customer. Carla Fendi does not accept that their recent furs have been part of "destroy" fashion. She claims that it can be "more intriguing" to have something half-hidden—that it is a bonus to have "the softness, and the warmth" on the inside.

But why should modern fur hide its face? Sure, some women are running scared of protesters; but the traditional opulence and luxury of fur may make others uncomfortable. According to Ralph Romberg, a vice president of Neiman Marcus, the "flat" furs like shearling and curly lamb, or sheared mink and dyed chinchilla are in fashion, while longhaired fox is not. In the same vein, Joseph Boitano, senior vice president of Bergdorf Goodman, says that "modern furs are those that don't have a real animal look about them—they are sheared, treated, dyed."

Other fashion luxuries have been reinvented for the 1990s: cashmere in quiet colors or slithering silks for slinky dresses. Isn't there a modern equivalent in fur?

Lagerfeld believes that he has found it. "To me ermine is *the* fur, because of the touch and because it is weightless, fluid. Take a big shawl in ermine, dyed black—people think it's material. You can travel with it, and it does not weigh one pound." (Pursuing modern fur to its luxurious conclusion would be not to wear the ermine but to use it at home. "To sleep under fur is the most refined, elegant thing in the world," Lagerfeld says. "An ermine sheet is refreshing, weightless, better than anything woven.")

Other designers have different ideas about nineties fur.

"What's gone is evening fur per se—the little white mink jacket—that's finished," says Arnold Scaasi, who has been making furs since 1962. "It's a much sportier look worn after five just as well as during the day." His current collection for Mohl Furs includes a gray cashmere duffle coat lined in reddish sable-colored mink. "Furs have to have some humor, there has to be some fun," says Scaasi, picking from his collection a peacoat in navy cashmere lined with mink, and a sheared beaver bolero with a quilted lining.

Scaasi believes the fashion future of fur lies with curly lamb as a natural follow-up to shearling. Kim Major of Birger Christensen sees a growth market in shearling treated to look like wool; Mongolian lamb; astrakhan; and Persian lamb sueded and dyed on the reverse.

Valentino and de la Renta (both doing furs for Alixandre) pick the "warm bathrobe" and the "fantastic sable wrap" as the acme of modern fur. Those might sound conventional, but there is still a market out there for young women who want fur in the traditional way—and maybe that is why the industry is content to stick with a conventional look.

Alexandra Lebenthal, a 30-year-old Wall Street mutual-fund director, is proof that some young women still aspire to fur—but as a symbol of their own achievement, not their husbands' status. She describes the mink coat she bought five years ago as "a very classic style. In a mostly male industry, women want to make themselves look more sophisticated and mature. It is a signal to others that you have attained a certain level—the same as acquiring a Chanel bag or suit." Lebenthal deliberately avoided a "trendy" fur as not appropriate to her own life, because it was "rather a large expense" and because she expects the coat to last for ten to fifteen years.

Romberg says that although mothers still buy furlined raincoats for daughters going off to college, the change in his lifetime has been the rise of professional women clients. "Thirty years ago it was unthinkable to sell a fur to a woman without her husband," he says.

Yet like any other fashion, fur ought to occupy the middle ground between the runway's shocking pink shearling and Wall Street's conservative sheared mink. Although Vera Wang does not design furs, she has worn fur herself and complains that she doesn't "find a lot of things that I feel are contemporary." She now has plenty of ideas about what could be done to make fur young and modern. "There would be a wonderful way to do fur—less ostentatious and fun to wear," she says, suggesting "taking fur more into pieces" rather than the inevitable full-length coats. Her visions for fur include broadtail vests to be worn under a jacket, mink vests to pop over a pair of stirrup pants, and sweaters and jackets done in a sporty way to take the "ladylike edge" off fur.

The most modern-looking women are downtown wearing flea-market furs: close-fitting 1960s kidskin coats worn over thick hose with combat boots; wild-haired chubbies layered over long skirts; and shearlings with narrow shoulders and tiny armholes, which was the silhouette Jacobs reworked.

Eleonora Attolico, 28 who lives and works in New York, says that while "girls from Greenwich, Connecticut, from the best families, want to wear conventional fur," she "would never wear fur seriously." However, she does admit borrowing 1960s fur hats from her mother and frolicking around SoHo in a "ridiculous" New Look fur coat with a tight waist and full skirt.

As with so much current fashion, it is not the clothes themselves but the attitude that is important. Although most women aren't going to wear thrift-shop furs, the flea market offers fur to a new generation that wouldn't wear what

mother currently has in her closet. As Lagerfeld says: "When daughters start to hate it, mothers should forget about it. And what youth does now, the older women want a few years later."

How Trade Associations Benefit Their Membership

Lili Kasdan, LAA Managing Director

A core group of America's most progressive leather garment manufacturers, retailers, tanners and professional leather cleaners founded the Leather Apparel Association (LAA) in 1990, realizing that there was much to be gained by working together. As a non-profit professional service organization catering specifically to industry needs, LAA has been able to create a comprehensive marketing program and sales support system that many businesses would find cost-prohibitive or impossible to do on their own. The goal of LAA is to promote sales of leather apparel in the American market through public relations, education, advertising and market research. By stimulating demand and increasing the size and scope of the market for leather clothing, LAA is helping every company in the leather apparel business grow stronger, broader, and more profitable.

Members are dedicated to fostering cooperation and working together to improve garment quality, durability and customer satisfaction. Membership is open to all businesses wishing to see the leather apparel business grow in the United States. LAA unites buyers, suppliers and industry peers alike.

Members, therefore, also include producers of leather garment accessories, insulations, water-repellent and garment care products, as well as international tanneries and factories who produce for the American market. Membership represents a public commitment to quality and service.

LAA's national marketing campaign has two distinct targets. The first objective is to stimulate consumer demand, utilizing newspaper and TV publicity, and educational brochures. Maintaining that demand is imperative to the success of the second objective, to promote the sales of products and services made by LAA members specifically. Sales for all types of companies dealing with leather apparel are ultimately dependent on consumer demand.

For example, LAA spends thousands of dollars trying to get retailers to buy garments made by its manufacturing members through trade advertisements, catalogues and other industry promotions. Likewise, LAA tries to influence manufacturers to buy skins from its member tanners. If consumers were not interested in buying leather, LAA's efforts to promote its members would have little effect because

retailers would have no incentive to buy garments from leather manufacturers, and consequently, manufacturers' orders to the tanneries would be down as well.

In order to stimulate consumer interest in leather, LAA creates press kits for newspapers and magazines containing photographs and the latest information on leather fashion trends and garment care. This annual national publicity campaign generates an average of 500 stories in the press every year. LAA spokesmen may also appear on TV news and talk shows to promote leather fashions created by members. Keeping leather in the spotlight serves an additional purpose. When retailers see such publicity in their area, it helps build confidence in the product.

Consumer satisfaction with the performance and durability of leather garments is of great importance to the potential for sales. In an effort to improve garment quality, LAA has issued guidelines for manufacturing which identify the sources and solutions to potential problems that often precipitate consumer complaints. Another set of guidelines help prevent garment owners from making mistakes with cleaning and care. Should consumers or businesses have a problem with a garment, or need help finding a cleaner or vendor, LAA serves as a referral service and information center. LAA maintains a state-by-state listing of its professional leather cleaning members in order to assist the public and the trade.

At the trade level, LAA helps members increase their company profile and publicity through participation in seminars, fashion shows and direct mail campaigns. Trade advertisements and brochures publicize the names and products of LAA members. These marketing vehicles tell buyers what LAA is doing to drive sales up, and why buying from LAA members is good for business.

For sales support, the association offers consumer booklets and retail sales training brochures that explain manufacturing, shopping tips and common leather terminology. LAA garment hangtags containing care instructions serve to increase customer confidence with every item shipped, sold or cleaned. Members also make use of the LAA logo in their own ads, in-store and on displays to enhance their company's prestige and credibility.

LAA gives the industry a united, public voice, making it possible to lobby Washington to protect the industry from international trade politics. Since well over 90% of the leather garments sold in the U.S. are imports, preventing damaging tariffs requires constant vigilance. Dealing with the media on these and other issues is another prime responsibility, which the association handles on a daily basis.

Interviews with reporters and researchers run the gamut from industry sales to questions about animal rights extremists. A bimonthly newsletter keeps members abreast of international industry developments, issues, trends, and business opportunities.

The association gets its funding almost entirely from membership dues, unlike other apparel industry groups who are funded through various tariff systems. Therefore, industry support is the key to providing the kinds of programs and services that will build a stronger, broader and more profitable leather apparel business.

Lili Kasdan, Managing Director, Leather Apparel Association, Inc.

PART THREE

The Fashion Merchandise Industries

Women's, men's, and children's wear make up the apparel components of the fashion industry; other components are trimmings, wearable accessories, cosmetics and fragrances, and fashions for the home.

Each component includes a variety of different products within its lines, and must be aware of specific circumstances that are unique to each, such as size classifications and marketing methods.

The largest of these groups is women's wear. Within this group, manufacturers generally cater to specific product classifications, such as dresses and sportswear, and price categories, such as couture, designer, bridge, moderate, and budget. They market their goods for four or five different seasons, longer than any other segment of the fashion industry.

The men's fashion industry is considerably smaller than the women's. It produces two major lines a season, and companies usually restrict their offerings to one type of merchandise. The goods are most often sold to retailers at trade expositions. One of the latest crazes to hit women's and men's wear is "Fridaywear," a term used to depict a relaxed style of clothing worn to work on

Friday. It has taken some business away from tailored clothing and has added interest to casual merchandise that is worn for this dressed-down day.

The children's wear field closely parallels the women's segment, although it only features two seasons.

Trimmings play an important role in the business of fashion. They are both decorative and functional. The simplest garment may be magnificently enhanced with exciting trim. A wealth of adornments are available for designers to choose from to give their garments and accessories unique looks.

Shoes, handbags, gloves, jewelry, and other accessories are produced all over the world. A complete overview of each is featured so that the fashion professional and consumer will be able to assess the value of each as wardrobe enhancements.

Cosmetics and fragrance sales are skyrocketing all over the globe. Apparel designers have entered the market through licensing agreements and many have made fortunes doing so. The cost to launch a new fragrance may by more than $40 million, but with profits so high, it is considered good business to do so.

One of the fastest growing segments of the industry produces fashions for the home. More and more apparel designers are producing bed and bath products, dinnerware, and other products for the home bearing their famous signatures. Very large specialty retailers are expanding their businesses to handle these home fashion items.

Having studied each of the different fashion merchandise classifications, it is time to move on to the manufacturing of the products.

CHAPTER 9

Apparel: Women's, Men's, and Children's

The apparel business is the most important segment of the fashion industry, accounting for more companies, employees, and sales volume than any other segments. Although it is dominated by the industrial giants, there always seems to be a new company on the horizon ready to make its entrance. Some, through hard work and creative ideas, prove that there is room for a newcomer; others, because of inexperience or undercapitalization, fail. Success depends on the uniqueness of a line, astute buyers, sound financial resources, and creative marketing.

Although there are parallels among women's, men's, and children's wear, there are also distinct differences. Each is available at a wide range of price points, each is produced all over the globe, and each appeals to a variety of consumers. In terms of marketing, they also follow similar paths. But when it comes to designer recognition, the women's wear industry plays the dominant role. While men's wear designers are receiving more attention than ever before, it is the designers of women's wear and their collections that garner most of the press coverage.

By the 1990s, manufacturers of women's, men's and children's wear and their product offerings had changed significantly. Operating in a highly competitive, global environment, all three segments face daily challenges to create the right products for the marketplace.

WOMEN'S WEAR

The hype generated by the women's wear industry is often compared to that of the film industry. Openings of designer collections in Paris, Milan, and New York receive as much attention and press coverage as the release of a major

After you have completed this chapter, you will be able to discuss:

- The major classifications of women's wear.

- The various size ranges of women's wear and their unique characteristics.

- The seasons in women's apparel and the importance of each in the industry.

- A comparison of men's wear before the 1950s with today's fashions.

- Where the major men's wear markets are in the United States.

- The various product classifications in men's wear.

- The effects of Fridaywear on men's and women's apparel.

- How children's fashions have changed since the 1950s.

motion picture. The reigning designers, such as Lagerfeld, Armani, Versace, Saint Laurent, Lacroix, Sui, Klein, and Karan, are treated with the same amount of awe reserved for the world's greatest entertainers. Although the names of the industry are often idolized, most industry employers never receive public recognition.

Women's wear includes merchandise in a number of classifications and price points. Participants in all levels of the industry cater to a specific market segment and must consider a host of factors before embarking on the production of a line. It is an enormously competitive segment of the fashion industry. Those who work in it must understand its goals and how to achieve them.

Throughout the decades, women's wear has undergone more changes than men's and children's wear. From the fashion designs of Poiret and Paquin at the beginning of the twentieth century to Chanel, Dior, Balenciaga, and later to Quant, Courrèges, Lauren, Armani, and Karan, silhouettes were changed, hemlines were raised and lowered, and innovative styling continuously redirected the fashion scene.

Today's designers and manufacturers operate with the same vigor and verve as their predecessors. They must address the needs of potential customers by producing lines that will turn a profit for the industry.

An innovative design from Yves Saint Laurent's spring summer haute couture collection.

Markets

The women's wear industry is truly a global business. Although Paris reigns as the world's leader in haute couture, affluent and sophisticated women also converge on other European capitals to buy the originals of Lagerfeld, Lacroix, Galliano, Westwood, Armani, and the other leading designers. The haute couture business may grow smaller every year, but it still sets the stage for designers' secondary design lines and serves as a source of ideas for American fashion.

In New York City, ready-to-wear holds center stage. From the higher price points of Donna Karan and Calvin Klein to the most modestly-priced lines, no city in the world has as much to offer retail merchants. In its famous garment center, thousands of manufacturers and designers produce new lines, season after season. There are buildings known for specific levels of fashion and buildings housing the newcomers waiting for their companies to be recognized. Regional markets in the United States are in cities such as Chicago, Dallas, Los Angeles, and Atlanta, where apparel centers and marts are filled with branch offices of New York's manufacturers as well the headquarters for those of regional producers.

Product Classifications

The United States apparel industry is composed of those manufacturers who specialize in a particular product line and those whose offerings cut across numerous categories. The bulk of the industry works at what it knows best. Dresses range from the one- or two-piece variety to the fanciest ballgowns, with a range of prices beginning very low and climbing very high. Dress manufacturers concentrate either on daytime dresses or evening wear. Evening wear includes after-five lines, prom and party dresses, and bridal including the mothers of the bride and groom.

The American sportswear market came into its own as early as the 1930s and 1940s. With names like Claire McCardell, Norman Norell, Pauline Trigère, Thomas Brigance, Bonnie Cashin, and Anne Klein, American designers developed a strong following and influenced a unique style of dress. Two-piece dressing that utilized skirts, pants, blouses, and sweaters were the order of the day then and have remained the favorites of women everywhere. The classification includes the separates that enable the wearer to mix and match various elements to form many different outfits.

Coat and suit manufacturers usually restrict their merchandise to this classification, because it requires highly skilled workers and machinery not necessary for other apparel products. There are, however, some manufacturers who cut across other product classifications, such as Jones New York. The market for coats and suits has remained a solid one, with more and more women needing such attire for their careers.

Once identified as active sportswear in the sportswear classification, activewear has become a large classification of the apparel industry. The phys-

Anne Klein (right), shown with her creations in 1974, was an important force in American sportswear.

This mohair jacket and long evening skirt were from Isaac Mizrahi's 1994 designer collection.

ical fitness craze and concerns about weight have caused many women to join exercise clubs, where particular types of apparel are standard. Sweatshirts and sweatpants, nylon shorts, sport bras, bicycle pants, tank tops, and similar apparel are found in every color and pattern. Warm-up suits and jogging outfits complete these wardrobes.

Swimwear is a dominant factor in the fashion industry all year round.

Since the early 1990s, a growing number of women regularly play tennis and golf. This has given manufacturers an entirely new market. Pro shops and specialty stores are filled with assortments that are worn on as well as off the playing fields. One reason for this change has been the television coverage of professional women's sports. Many athletes endorse the apparel they wear and influence the average woman's choice in such items.

Swimwear, once relegated to a short season, now functions year round. Although spring and summer are still the dominant sales periods for swimwear, resort and cruisewear lines have significantly added to profits. Many manufacturers preview their next season's collections at summer's end to get a feel for market changes and a jump on the styling that they will introduce in their resort collections. Swimwear manufacturers are comprised of companies that have been in the industry a long time, such as Jantzen, Catalina, and Gottex. Other swimwear manufacturers have made the assortment more fashion oriented through licensing agreements with famous apparel designers, such as Norma Kamali, Oscar de la Renta, and Calvin Klein. The introduction of this new method of marketing swimwear had caused prices to rise.

One of the fastest growing merchandise classifications is intimate apparel, or lingerie, often called by its new name, innerwear. Merchants such as Victoria's Secret and Cacique operate full specialty stores limited to lingerie. Designers such as Calvin Klein have made undergarments even more appealing. Department stores that once considered lingerie a less important item, are now expanding their operations to carry fuller assortments.

Some of the fashion industry giants diversify their lines and cover a wide range of ready-to-wear items. For example, Liz Claiborne designs sportswear, dresses, men's wear, sunglasses, and shoes within the company and under licensing arrangements.

Whatever the arrangement, collectively the women's apparel market includes the following classifications:

- Sportswear / Coordinated Separates
- Knitwear
- Activewear / Sports
- Coats / Suits
- Daytime Dresses
- Evening Wear
- Intimate Apparel

Table 9.1 lists the various women's wear markets within each classification.

TABLE 9.1

CLASSIFICATIONS OF WOMEN'S WEAR MARKETS

Sportswear / Coordinated Separates

Career
Missy
Junior
Casual / Weekend

Knitwear / Sweaters

Bulky
Pointelle
Intarsia
Jacquard
Novelty
Sweater Sets
Pullovers
Outerwear

Activewear Sports

Golf
Tennis
Ski
Swimwear / Cover-ups
Bicycling
Rollerblading
Exercise / Aerobics

Coats / Suits

Dressy
Casual
Wardrober: Jacket / Skirt / Pants

Daytime Dresses

One- or Two-piece
Dress and Jacket

Evening Wear

After Five / Cocktail
Country-club wear
Gowns
Prom / Party
Special Occasion
Bridal / Mother of the Bride / Bridesmaid

Intimate apparel

Foundations
Daywear (camisole, tap pants, slips, teddys)
Sleepwear (nightgowns and pajamas)
Sleep sets
Sleepshirts / Nightshirts
Robes

Fridaywear

The term **Fridaywear** describes the less traditionally structured clothing that is now acceptable in many offices, particularly on **dress-down Fridays.** Women are dressing more flexibly, with pantsuits and separates forming a larger part of their wardrobes. This more relaxed wear easily makes the transition from work to play. Retailers, such as Banana Republic and Gap, already in the business of merchandising casual wear, are reaping the benefits of this approach to men's fashion. Major retailers, such as Bloomingdale's, Lord & Taylor, and Macy's, have begun to reposition their inventories to address these new needs of women. With the growing popularity of the dress-down Friday concept, more and more companies will have to rethink their merchandise mixes.

Price Points

Fashion merchandise is available in a number of different price points or ranges. In the women's wear industry, manufacturers usually concentrate on one of them—or sometimes two. Donna Karan, for example, produces two collections, one at the designer level, which labels its designs, Donna Karan, and the other at the bridge level, bearing the DKNY label. By doing that, the company is able to reach a segment of the population familiar with the famous signature, but unable to afford its prices.

Intimate apparel is one of the fastest growing merchandise classifications.

At the top of the price ladder is couture, followed, according to cost, by designer, young designer, bridge/better, contemporary, upper moderate/lower bridge, moderate, budget, and private label.

Couture

With prices as high as $2,500 for a jacket or $20,000 or more for an evening dress, couture merchandise is not within the reach of most shoppers. According to some of the more savvy fashion trade periodicals, consumers who purchase an item from a couture collection number only in the hundreds. The merchandise is one-of-a-kind, custom-tailored, and made of the finest fabrications. It is really the only level of fashion where innovative styling is available.

Designer

Even designers who produce couture have turned to prêt-à-porter, or ready-to-wear. Designer merchandise carries labels similar to those at the top price points. Average price points for a jacket is $500 to $1,500 retail. The clothes are generally found in major fashionable department stores such as Saks Fifth Avenue, Barney's, and Neiman Marcus, in spaces described as in-store designer shops.

Young Designer

This price point appeals to a trendy customer, who is very status conscious. The average jacket price at retail is from $300 to $800. Although some department stores have young designer shops, clothing is more likely to be found in specialty stores. Designers includes Gemma Khang, Marc Jacobs, Todd Oldham, Cynthia Rowley, and Anna Sui.

Bridge / Better

The group of sportswear merchandise that falls between the designer levels and the more moderately priced lines are known as bridge collections. This price point also encompasses designers such as Christian Lacroix and Donna Karan, secondary lines; hence the name bridge. Unlike the designer jacket, which retails from $500 to $1,500, a jacket in a bridge collection would sell from $250 to $450. Bridge collections, such as DKNY, RRL, Anne Klein II, and Mani, are recognized by their company's names rather than specific designers. Examples of better lines include Dana Buchman, Adrienne Vittadini, Tahari, and Ellen Tracy.

(left) New York designer Donna Karan's couture label carries very expensive price tags and appeals only to a small market. (right) Her bridge collection - DKNY - with lower price points, has wider consumer appeal.

Contemporary

Sportswear that appeals to the widest audience. Prices for a jacket range from $150 to $225. Sold in department stores and sometimes in their own free-standing stores, examples includes Liz Claiborne, Carole Little, Jones New York, and Evan Picone.

Upper Moderate / Lower Bridge

A price point that is more fashion forward and updated than traditional merchandise. Jackets range from $100 to $120. Clothing with labels, such as Chaus, Karen Kane, and Evan Picone, is sold in department stores.

Moderate

This large, and extremely price conscious, category consists of moderately priced groups of merchandise. They represent the offerings of such leaders as Guess? and Esprit. The prices are more affordable to middle-income consumers. Prices generally range from $70 to $100 for jackets.

Budget

At the lowest level of the price structure are the dresses, sportswear, coordinates, and other apparel items that rarely bear nationally advertised labels. These garments are usually reproductions or adaptations of higher priced goods in low-quality fabrications. Budget merchandise is serviceable, but generally not as well constructed. More and more department stores are disbanding the budget classification leaving it to stores like Target, Kmart, and Wal-Mart.

Liz Claiborne designs are available in several classifications, price points, and special sizes.

Private Label

Private label is a term used to describe merchandise that is manufactured by the retailer themselves in collaboration with a branded manufacturer. Private labels cover all markets from bridge to moderate and cost as much as fifty to one-hundred percent less than if the same item were a brand label. Examples of stores and their private labels include: The Limited, Macy's (Morgan Taylor, Charter Club) Kmart (Jaclyn Smith), JCPenney (Arizona denim, Hunt Club).

Size Specialization

Before the 1950s, the purchase of a dress meant considerable alterations for many customers. Size ranges were dominated by the misses customer, who was generally unable to find anything **off the rack** at sizes smaller than 8, for her junior counterpart, size 7 was the smallest available. Except for some higher priced lines, the size problem cut across most dress styles.

In the 1950s, Anne Fogarty, a designer who dressed the younger figure, broke new ground by promoting the famous Anne Fogarty Five, a dress one size smaller than was normally available. It was an instant success and smaller-figured juniors were able to buy dresses that were better proportioned to their figures. Other manufacturers followed suit. Before long, size 1 became available for the tiniest junior figures and size 2 for the fuller, but small, misses figure.

As more and more women purchased the better-proportioned sizes, fewer alterations were necessary. Today, even more size specialization is in evidence. A female shopper can choose from a variety of size ranges that include misses, juniors, petites, and women's sizes, as well as specialized categories such as maternity and tall sizes.

Misses

The majority of women fall into the misses size range of 6 to 16. The **misses figure** is fuller-figured and longer waisted. Some manufacturers specialize in the smaller figure and begin with a size 2, but only go up to size 12. Other manufacturers begin with size 8, but produce up to 18 for the larger figure. Often, the size range is determined by the particular manufacturer and the specific style.

Juniors

In fashion, the word junior refers to size and not age. Although many manufacturers produce clothing that has a youthful look, junior-sized garments are proportioned to fit those who are slender and shorter waisted. The size range typically found in this category is 5 through 13, although sizes 1, 3, and 15 are generally available.

Petites

Recognition of the specialized needs for a shorter woman has resulted in this smaller-proportioned size range. Typically, petite sizes are manufactured for those women measuring 5'4" and under. The length of the skirt or pants and the proportionate structuring of the sleeves minimize alterations. Petite sizes are odd-numbered, beginning with size 1 and ending with size 13. Some manufacturers have also introduced shorter versions of their misses sizes, which are even-numbered.

Women's

The larger, fuller figures of average heights wear women's sizes. They are even numbered and most frequently available in sizes ranging from 14 to 24. Recent years have seen a tremendous increase in the number of stores that carry this size range. Chains such as Lane Bryant and Lerner Woman, both belonging to the Limited organization, and Elizabeth, part of the Liz Claiborne empire, have many outlets catering to this clientele. What has made the category even more appealing is the styling. Once relegated to "dowdy" looks, the new women's sizes now feature the most fashionable silhouettes.

The shorter, fullest-figured women wear **half sizes.** The clothing is proportioned for the short-waisted heavier figure, and generally comes in sizes from $12\frac{1}{2}$ to $26\frac{1}{2}$.

Tall Sizes

Available in even sizes that begin as small as 8 and range up to 20, tall sizes enable the tallest woman to purchase clothing perfectly proportioned for her figure. Not only are the hemlines longer, but so are the sleeves and waistlines.

Maternity

This size range duplicates the regular misses and junior sizes except that the construction allows for the expansion of the garment. At one time pregnant women had to settle for larger size regular clothing or less fashionable maternity wear. Today, with a vast number of women remaining on the job until

(top)
WWD MAGIC is the world's largest trade show held twice yearly in Las Vegas.
(middle)
Manufacturers such as Sasson purchase space to sell their lines at the trade expos.
(bottom)
Buyers shop the lines at WWD MAGIC in dramatic settings.

their delivery dates, fashionable apparel is a necessity. Business suits and dresses that rival the stylings of regular sized clothing are available in many maternity shops, such as Lady Madonna, Reborn, and Pea in the Pod. Even the most fashionable, narrow-legged jeans and knitted pants, swimsuits, and shorts are available.

Selling Seasons

The women's wear industry has the largest number of selling seasons. Typically, this segment of the industry is represented by four or five collections a year, namely fall, holiday, spring, summer, and—for those who choose to participate—resort or cruisewear. Some fashion leaders, such as Liz Claiborne, break the seasonal norm and introduce new groups of merchandise as frequently as every six weeks. This approach is only appropriate for companies with enormous distribution and production facilities that can keep up with the pace. Some retailers, such as Gap, which manufactures its own merchandise, follow an even faster pace with their fashion items. The use of more than the traditional number of seasons has both advantages and disadvantages. On the plus side, it provides the store with a continuous change of merchandise that can liven the usual slow or down periods. On the minus side, it sometimes adds merchandise to inventories that still need to be disposed of before the new can be successfully merchandised.

Whatever the decision, each season has its own personality and sales potential.

Fall

Generally, this season is the most profitable for the manufacturer. It lasts longer than the others and usually provides a new fashion story or unusual emphasis. It can be a dangerous season, however, if marketing research has indicated a radical change in fashion. The introduction of the briefest miniskirt coming on the heels of the longer length might be greeted with little enthusiasm. At the same time, fashion is a changing business that must take some risks if change is to occur.

Some manufacturers produce two lines at this time, Fall I and Fall II, with the former earmarked for earlier delivery and the latter for later delivery.

Holiday

The so-called **holiday season** is brief and manufacturers offer a new, but abbreviated, line. Some silhouettes that met with success in the fall reappear in more luxurious fabrications. The fall's flannel blazer with pearl buttons might repeat for the holidays as a satin model accented with rhinestone buttons. Companies that concentrate on dressy apparel might receive the greatest attention at this time. As soon as the new year comes, holiday merchandise is marked down to make room for the next season's apparel.

Resort

Sometimes referred to as **cruise wear,** resort wear is a seasonal line that many producers bypass. Those who do invest in these collections often use the line as a barometer for testing fashions that will be shown during the summer. It is traditionally a proving ground for the swimwear industry. As a rule, resort wear belongs to the higher-priced designer and bridge collections, because

The Council of Fashion Designers of America (CFDA)

The purpose of this organization is to promote the image of fashion and the people who are important to the industry. The Council organizes a number of activities, including award presentations, centralized fashion shows, and charity benefits.

Each year, at the New York City's Lincoln Center, celebrities from the world of fashion, entertainment, and the media gather to honor those in the fashion industry who have either made their mark in a specific merchandise classification or who promise to become a leader in the field. Among the awards given are those for continuous outstanding design, the Perry Ellis award for the most promising designer, and achievements in the accessories field.

The CFDA tries to capture the attention of the media and the public with its award's ceremonies. It uses famous people from theater, television, and other walks of life as presenters. The most exciting presenter to date was Lady Diana, the Princess of Wales, whose appearance at the

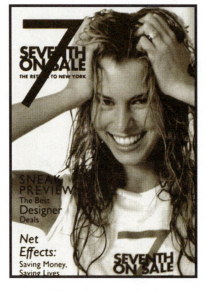

CFDA's promotion for its Seventh on Sale event.

gala was recorded by all the media and shown on television broadcasts all over the world. It is a coup like this that has made the Council a leading publicity agent for the industry.

The CFDA also sponsors the *7th on Sale* event. Leading designers donate merchandise that is sold to raise money to fight AIDS. The items are sold and money is raised in such fashion centers as New York City, San Francisco, and Los Angeles.

One of the most important of the organization's activities is called *7th on Sixth*. With the support of its corporate sponsors and designers, the Council has established centralized fashion shows in New York City's Bryant Park that are similar to those in Paris. Twice a year, enormous tents are erected for use by the designers. Here retail buyers and the press preview collections as well as lines prepared by designers for those in the fiber industry, such as Cotton Incorporated and DuPont.

The CFDA is regularly called upon to promote the fashion industry, and year after year it does so in many innovative formats.

---

their customers are the ones who can afford the luxury of a winter vacation. Manufacturers of lower price points closely follow the high-fashion designers at resort time, using their silhouettes and styles as the basis for their own summer lines.

Spring

The season that often provides the greatest difficulties for manufacturers and retailers alike is spring. At one time, it was a season for lightweight coats, suits, dresses, and sportswear. Fabrics were less bulky than those used in fall apparel, but heavier than the cottons and linens used for the summer lines. Recent years have proved to be a disaster for many manufacturers and merchants who followed this traditional road. Today, most consumers shed the heavy garments of winter and move directly into summer attire. As a consequence, many producers have relegated the once-successful spring season to a partnership with summer. It means heavier, textured linens, cottons, and blends that can easily sell in the summer months if necessary.

Summer

With the traditional spring apparel of yesteryear only a memory, the suits and dresses of fall often step aside to make way for sportswear and swimwear. The season that used to start after Easter in the stores, now begins right after the President's Week clearances. The season slows down in June, with retailers beginning to clear away their summer inventories to make room for fall merchandise. This is often a down time for regularly priced merchandise. Some manufacturers produce interim or transitional collections that sell when summer is waning and fall has not yet begun. The fabrics for these lines are lightweight, but of colorations that are darker and more subdued than the summer items.

Selling Women's Wear

The primary method of selling women's wear is in the manufacturers showrooms. In New York City's Garment Center and the many regional markets throughout the country, the large manufacturers operate their own selling spaces. Smaller organizations often engage a manufacturer's representative to show their merchandise in showrooms that feature several, noncompeting lines. The manufacturers and designers also maintain road staffs that travel designated territories and visit retailers in the hopes of selling the line.

The Council of Fashion Designers of America, the subject in a World of Fashion Profile (see page 242), has been known for its many promotional endeavors, including the now-famous tent shows, Seventh on Sixth, for the women's wear industry in New York City's Bryant Park.

More and more fashion producers are taking their cue from the men's wear industry and are participating in trade expositions. With NAMSB and MAGIC so successful for men's merchandise, expos featuring women's merchandise are becoming increasingly popular. One of the more successful of these events is the International Boutique Show that is held at New York City's Javits Center, which is featured in a World of Fashion Profile on page 244.

Promoting Women's Wear

Promotion is a necessary tool that is used to alert both the industry's professional buyers and the consumers to the season's latest innovations. The ways in which the word is spread are numerous.

Fashion show presentations are the industry's best promotional tool. They start with the much heralded runway shows for the press, stores, and private clientele that take place in Paris, and move on down to the more routine entries that are found in retail operations and mall centers. It gives the attendees firsthand knowledge of what is new for the coming season in a format that generates excitement. Other approaches include designer personal appearances, awards receptions, workshops, contests, fashion clinics, and so forth. A fully detailed exploration of women's wear promotion is offered in Chapter 19.

MEN'S WEAR

While women have been showered with fashion choices for many decades, men have generally been presented with lackluster, traditional attire. Influential designers were preoccupied with enhancing the female figure—camouflag-

The International Boutique Show

Four times each year, the Larkin organization sponsors one of the largest trade expositions in the women's wear industry, The International Boutique Show. In New York City's Javits Center, more than 1,000 vendors from all over the world come together to show their latest lines of merchandise. Row upon row of sales booths, reminiscent of miniature showrooms, line the vast arena, enabling buyers from many countries to shop the lines.

Each individual space is outfitted with writing tables and chairs, at which the buyers are seated to see the merchandise. The items are displayed on racks, with some of the more eye-appealing items featured on the walls. Occasionally, some of the vendors use live mannequins to model clothing from the line.

The advantage of this exposition, as well as others in the fashion industry, is that it affords the sellers and buyers an opportunity to meet on common ground, eliminating the time and effort needed to cover a market that is spread throughout the world. In New York City, the industry's major ready-to-wear market, for example, there are scores of buildings that buyers would have to visit if the trade show was not in operation. This requires more time away from the store than many buyers have available to them.

In addition to the Boutique Show, Larkin sponsors The Kid's Show as well as the Textiles Show. Based on the growth in attendance at all of these venues, it is obvious the needs of both buyers and sellers are being well served.

---

ing it, glamorizing it, and through creative silhouette engineering, reshaping it. The likes of Chanel, Dior, Balenciaga, and other international greats captured all the attention, leaving the men's wear industry in a dull state.

Men's wear has generally been well-tailored clothing; the upper end of the spectrum produced the finest tailoring money could buy. Style simply remained constant—the same suit selling for years and years with no fear of fashion obsolescence. Many, in fact, adopted a "two pairs of pants philosophy" preserving the same suit for even longer periods of time.

Suddenly, in the very early 1960s, men's fashion began to change radically. England was a forerunner in this new movement, with the **mod look** of **Carnaby Street,** where shops attracted the attention of young men with very wide lapels and bell-bottomed trousers. These changes closed the doors on the single-mindedness of men's fashion. European designers, who heretofore concentrated only on female dress, embraced the male's new-found freedom of choice in fashion and began to create new silhouettes for men. Pierre Cardin's **peacock look** was accepted by men who were excited by these innovative stylings. Pierre Cardin, who first made his mark with innovative women's collections, was foremost in the introduction of the newest, high-fashion shapes for men—broad, peaked shoulders, fitted waists, and flared trousers. His entry into men's ready-to-wear helped transform men from the standardbearers of traditional dress to what we see today.

No longer are the gray flannel suit, white shirt, and tie the order of the day for proper business attire. Suits of every texture and coloration in a variety of silhouettes are accessorized with patterned shirts and enhanced with a wide assortment of ties. Today, a more relaxed approach is evident even in the most formal business environments. On Fridays, in particular, companies are opting for more casual dress. Even IBM, for example, has relaxed its dress requirements and accepted a more casual look for every day of the week.

Who wears what and for which occasion, however, still plays an important role in appropriate dress, but the parameters are broader than ever before.

Markets

Although the men's wear industry is internationally based, New York City remains the major player. From the most elegant custom-tailored suits meticulously produced by the fine tailors to the ready-to-wear that accounts for the lion's share of the men's wear business, New York City is the place where it is all available.

Any man interested in a custom-tailored suit that costs more than $1,500 can easily find a small operation that will design, cut, and sew the garment to his exact measurements. Many of the finest merchants who specialize in better **off-the-rack** clothing, such as Barney's, Paul Stuart, and Bergdorf Goodman, will also custom-make clothing for those willing to pay the price. Some designers, such as Alan Flusser, have forsaken the route of ready-to-wear for custom-tailored clothing. Except for Hong Kong, which specializes in hand-sewn suits, few cities, if any, can rival the handcrafted models turned out in New York City.

In addition to New York, with men's wear manufacturers producing at every price point, there are other centers that figure prominently in the industry. In the United States, Chicago, Baltimore, Los Angeles, San Francisco, Boston, Rochester, and Philadelphia are the men's manufacturing centers. Some of the companies are based in these cities, utilizing their facilities for designing, patternmaking, and warehousing. The production, however, is often accomplished offshore in places like Hong Kong and South Korea, where the cost of labor is significantly lower. No matter where the companies are located, most often they maintain showrooms in New York City for the buyers. Unlike the women's industry, which covers New York City's entire garment center, men's wear is more concentrated, with the majority of the major manufacturers having showrooms in one building, 1290 Avenue of the Americas. Later we will discuss the temporary showrooms used by the industry at trade expositions.

Product Classifications

The men's wear industry is made up of several separate classifications. Some manufacturers concentrate on only one apparel group, such as casual wear, or even a subclassification, such as pants; others have various company divisions producing merchandise that crosses several classifications. Hartmarx, for example, is an industry giant that includes numerous merchandise groups under such labels as Jaymar for slacks and Johnny Carson for moderately priced suits.

Tailored Clothing

Collectively, coats, suits, sport coats, and dress trousers comprise the **tailored clothing** category. For many years, this group dominated the industry. Men were expected to wear suits and coats to their places of work and on many social occasions. Other items of apparel were needed to round out their wardrobes for less-formal environments and events.

The Mod look originated in London and took the fashion world by storm.

(left) Men's wear is no longer relegated to lackluster fashions. Layers of different fabrics, as seen here, make exciting designs. (right) Tailored clothing has lost some of its appeal because of relaxed dress codes.

The average businessman owned a number of suits that he rotated throughout the year. With the relaxation of the dress code, many tailored clothing manufacturers are experiencing hard times. Some have redirected their merchandising efforts to include less formal attire; others have been forced to close their doors.

At this time, mergers and acquisitions have resulted in an industry that is controlled by a few giants.

Fridaywear

The men's wear industry has also had to adjust to dress-down Fridays. In addition to the conventional American and European cut suits, more and more casual attire is being worn in the workplace. Casual suits made of tweeds and other sporty fabrications, sport coats and contrasting trouser combinations, and even pants and shirts, alone, have become acceptable for at least one day a week. Often, even the sacred tie has been eliminated during this dress-down period.

Manufacturers like Tommy Hilfiger and Alexander Julian are capitalizing on this concept by featuring comfortable apparel appropriate for both work and leisure activities.

Men's Furnishings

The catch-all category that includes shirts, neckwear, underwear, belts, socks, and pajamas is the furnishings group. It is an important classification that capitalizes on designer licensing agreements. When names such as Pierre Cardin, Bill Blass, Calvin Klein, Yves Saint Laurent, and Geoffrey Beene appear on shirts or undershorts, the price points move upward. Today, even ties that hover around the $85 mark have become staples in some men's wardrobes. With suits often "nondescript in design," it is the tie that distinguishes one man's appearance from another's.

Gloves, scarves, hats, **braces,** and other items round out the men's wear classifications. Gloves remain the dominant item in this group because of their functionality. Hats, once commonplace in a man's wardrobe, are not popular. The only exception are baseball caps, knitted caps worn for skiing and during cold weather, and the tweed and suede sportier types worn with casual attire. Scarves, too, are an insignificant entry. They are generally worn only on the coldest days. The one fashion item that captures a small part of the market is braces, or suspenders. Men with careers in finance, investment banking, and law often choose this accessory as part of their standard dress. Their popularity has resurfaced because CNN talk-show host, Larry King sports scores of different braces. While Larry King will probably not make the lasting fashion impact that some like the Duke of Windsor made, or even Andre Agassi with his bandana, he has given braces a great deal of exposure. Of course, those that actually button-on are considered appropriate, clip-ons are a fashion "no-no."

In addition to all of the brand label furnishings, there is also considerable growth in private labeling in this category.

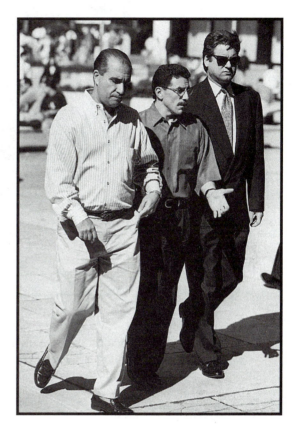

Fridaywear has made office dress less formal.

Casual Wear

This merchandise group came into prominence during the 1970s. The relaxed dress code for some businesses coupled with the requirements of leisure time activities resulted in a tremendous increase in market share for sweaters, knit shirts, jeans, and unstructured sport coats. Although the leisure suits of the 1970s are no longer in vogue, the other items remain in favor.

Active Sportswear

The physical fitness craze that took the United States by storm during the 1980s, has remained very important. Sweatsuits, jogging apparel, running shorts, tank tops, tennis shorts, golf pants and shirts, and athletic footwear have provided comfort both on and off the field. This type of apparel is worn to restaurants, movies, for shopping, on campus, and for leisure activities. Com-

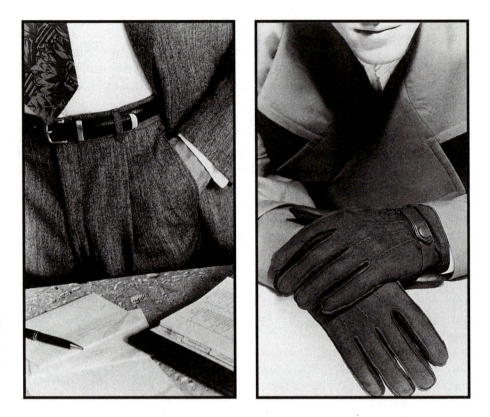

Men's furnishings, such as belts, ties, and gloves have become more important since fashion and functionality have merged.

panies like Reebok and Nike continue to expand their product lines to capture a larger share of this market. Both companies have opened large retail operations that exclusively feature their entire product lines of active sportswear.

Outerwear

Merchandise such as jackets, ski wear, and parkas constitute the outerwear category. Clothing that was once destined only for the coldest climates and for use in winter sports is now being produced with fashion in mind. One need no longer head for the slopes to wear a ski jacket; any casual destination will do. One of the indicators of the change in this once functional merchandise is the choice of colorization. The brightest and boldest color schemes, reflective of the color choices of the times and selected by the fashion designers, are utilized in outerwear. Many miracle fibers, such as Thinsulate®, have helped reduce the bulkiness once associated with these products and made them lighter in weight.

Because the season for this type of merchandise is limited, its manufacture has been assumed in many cases by the producers of active sportswear and rainwear.

Work Clothes

Once relegated for use by those in construction-type jobs, the styles have been adapted for other uses. Jeans, for example, are no longer just functional clothing that affords the wearer long-lasting use (so important for laborers), but are a fashion product on their own. As a separate category, jeans are one of the major classifications of apparel. Worn with denim shirts, sweatshirts, and

Casual wear, especially garments made of denim and leather, came into prominence in the 1970s and has remained a favorite.

workshirts, they have become the uniforms for many, especially students at every educational level.

Jeans first caught the attention of the masses when embraced by companies like Sasson and designers such as Calvin Klein. The name on the back pocket identified the manufacturer of the product and gave prestige and status to the wearer. Although the designer jean has not maintained its popularity, the denim pant is still an extremely important category. This is evident from observing inventory produced by Levi Strauss, the largest of the jeans manufacturers, Lee's, and Wrangler, and the full selections retailed by stores like Gap.

Together with overalls, jeans are the international uniform for people of all ages.

Rainwear

From basic models designed to repel water to the most important classic creations, rainwear has become a significant part of men's wear. Many men choose the all-purpose raincoat, with a zip-out lining, in place of the traditional overcoat. Coats of this nature are not only functional, they are also appropriate for any occasion. Luxury and prestige are also parts of the rainwear market, as seen by the now famous Burberry raincoat. The detachable woolen collar and lining and inner plaid fabrication are symbolic of this raincoat. While styles fall in and out of favor, the Burberry, with a price tag of $700, has helped rainwear achieve a status all its own.

While the raincoat has become a mainstay in most men's wardrobes, its popularity has spelled disaster for the traditional winter coat. So many men have opted for all-weather raincoats that many manufacturers have dispensed with the production of heavy, winter coats.

Size Specialization

Men can choose from a variety of size ranges, particularly in tailored clothing. The vast array enables them to purchase proper-fitting clothing, without the need for major, costly alterations. This not only helps the retailer minimize clothing adjustment, but enables consumers to feel comfortable about the final fit of their purchases.

Although the size variations offer benefits to the purchaser, they often present merchandising problems for the merchant. The need to stock varied size ranges requires a considerable amount of space, as well as large outlays of money.

Tailored Clothing

Coats, suits, and sport coats come in several size ranges to accommodate the tallest to the shortest male, with physiques that range from the athletically fit to the slightly built.

REGULAR The majority of tailored clothing garments are produced for men considered to be of average height—between 5'8" and 5'11". The sizes usually run from 36 to 44, but some manufacturers cut both smaller and larger regulars. The measurement is based on chest size. Typically, the greatest volume is in the 40 to 42 range. Many stores limit their inventories to the even sizes, with some offering only a small number of odd sizes.

LONG For men who are from 6' to 6'3" and are proportionately built. These sizes are most often available from 38 to 46.

SHORT For men who measure from 5'5" to 5'7" and are proportionately built.

EXTRA LONG For individuals who are 6'4" and over. The garments typically range from 38 to 48.

PORTLY These sizes are targeted at men who are in the same group as regulars, but with thicker waistlines.

STOUT Men with heights of 5'5" to 5'7", who wear size 50 or more.

EXTRA LARGE For men who wear size 50 and over and are at least 6'.

ATHLETIC CUT In the past, men with expanded chests and narrow waistlines often required considerable alteration to their clothing. Some manufacturers produce the athletic cut, which addresses this type of physique. The sizes generally are available from 40 to 44 and for heights of 5'8" to 5'11".

Shirts

Shirts are produced in two distinct size designations: one for sport shirts and the other for dress shirts. Sport shirts come in sizes that range from small to extra large, while dress shirts come in sizes that take into account a man's neck measurement and sleeve length.

Dress shirts are the most difficult to merchandise because of the two size requirements they must address. For the average customer, neckband sizes range from 14½ to 17 and sleeve lengths from 32 to 35. Retailers, catering to customers who require special sizes because of their height or weight, carry even broader selections. The complexity of merchandising may be best understood when one considers how many different actual sizes there are for one neck measurement. Size 15, for example is available in sleeve lengths of 32,

33, 34, and 35. If different colors are available, the number of shirts necessary to complete a full size range becomes enormous. Many, manufacturers, especially those who produce at modest price points, have gone to dual sleeve lengths. That is, they produce a 32/33 or a 34/35 to cut down on the amount of inventory. This, of course, does not necessarily suit discriminating purchasers. Those who want specific sleeve lengths must often pay more for the shirt.

In addition to these shirt measurements, there are other variations. Regularly proportioned men wear the regular cut; thin men, the tapered cut; and heavy-chested men, the full cut.

Sweaters

The stretchability of knitwear makes sweaters one of the easier groups to merchandise. Stretchability enables the manufacturer to produce in sizes that range from small to extra large.

Selling Men's Wear

Two seasons, spring/summer and fall/winter, dominate the men's wear industry. Most manufacturers present their major collections for these two seasons, with some adding interim lines if their offerings are more fashion oriented. Spring collections are shown from the middle of July to the end of September; fall presentations take place from mid-January to the end of February. Secondary lines are sold in the March/April period for winter and holiday merchandise and in October for late spring and summer apparel.

President Clinton has helped boost sales in the activewear market.

Although many men's wear companies maintain year-round permanent showrooms in the major markets like New York City, the vast majority of the industry's companies sell their lines at trade expositions.

Trade Association Expositions

The major trade associations sponsor expositions on a regular basis. These expositions bring buyers and sellers under one roof. The most important of these events are those coordinated by the **National Association of Men's Sportswear Buyers (NAMSB)**, the **Men's Apparel Group in California (MAGIC)**, the **Designer Collective, SEHM,** and **IMBEX.**

The largest of the American entries is NAMSB. The organization was founded in 1953 to increase the visibility of the men's sportswear market. Before its formation, tailored clothing received the most attention in the industry. Today, the association's original purpose has been expanded to include all categories of men's wear. Three times a year, NAMSB presents three show weeks in New York City. More than 1,000 men's wear lines are exhibited and more than 30,000 retail organizations of every size come to make their purchases for the following season.

MAGIC is the West Coast version of NAMSB. It was originally established to promote that area's sportswear market, but has grown significantly and features lines from other locations. Like NAMSB, it attracts buyers from all over the country. The exposition, although still using California in its name, is now held in Las Vegas.

As NAMSB grew into an enormous trade show, a small segment of the men's wear industry believed that the format no longer suited its needs. The group consisted of designers whose strengths were quality and originality at a price point above the rest of the market. In 1979, a few of the industry's talented designers formed what has become a showcase for the best in men's wear fashion, the Designer's Collective. Membership is gained only after careful screening of an applicant's work and not by a willingness to pay dues. Those who are selected may exhibit their collections at the group's expositions.

SEHM and IMBEX are European-based groups that market their participant's lines in the same manner as their American counterparts. Designers and manufacturers from all over the world converge on Paris for SEHM and London for IMBEX to show the latest in men's wear.

Promoting Men's Wear

The men's wear industry promotes itself to its retail customers and the editorial press in a number of ways. In addition to using the trade papers, such as *DNR,* a number of different groups have become part of the promotional packages. Two of these are **The Fashion Association (TFA)**, and the Council of Fashion Designers in America (CFDA).

The Fashion Association (TFA)

TFA, formerly known as Men's Fashion Association (MFA), is responsible for promoting men's fashions, as well as some women's fashions, for the industry. The group is comprised of manufacturers, retailers, and fiber and fabrics producers. They meet twice a year to promote the industry, at which time the press is invited to inspect the next season's highlights. Through the use of seminars, slide packages, and award's ceremonies, they present the latest innovations of the industry.

In 1995, TFA introduced its first **electronic press kit.** In a resort location—Scottsdale, Arizona—it videotaped an overview of the trends expected to make men's wear headlines, and sent it to the press. This innovative technology has hopefully helped to spread the association's message.

Council of Fashion Designers of America (CFDA)

The success of selling women's wear encouraged the CFDA to adapt the format for the men's wear industry. In 1995, the CFDA brought together many men's wear collections for runway presentations in various New York City environments, such as the Sony sound center. Designers like Alexander Julian and Tommy Hilfiger presented their collections in productions that rivaled the excitement generated by their women's wear counterparts. The coverage by the press finally brought much needed attention to the industry.

CHILDREN'S WEAR

Early in the twentieth century, children's wear echoed the styles worn by their parents. In fact, children seemed to look like miniature adults. The clothing worn was dictated by the parents, with children having little to say about dress preference.

In the 1950s, a significant change was noted in children's wear. Rock 'n' roll music and television helped to separate the younger generation's tastes from those of their parents. They wanted the right to exercise their opinions in terms of dress and eventually broke away from traditional dress expectations. Girls wore full skirts that were exaggerated by petticoats, as well as loose shirts and oversized sweaters that went with skirts and pants. Boys took to more casual wear that featured knits and jeans. Gone were the days when copies of adult clothing were the only apparel for children's wear. A new world of fashion for the youth of America was born.

Today, some children's wear is again emulating adult clothing. Many manufacturers of adult clothing, such as Tommy Hilfiger and Ralph Lauren, produce little boys items that echo their dads clothing. Stores like Gap, with GapKids, and the Limited's Limited Too, produce lines that resemble their adult offerings.

Product Classifications

Children's wear classifications are as numerous as those for the men's and women's wear markets. For girls, dresses, skirts, pants, blouses, sweaters, suits, swimwear, active sportswear, outerwear, and the like are fashioned to fit specific needs. For boys, the breadth and depth of the product line is just as diverse.

Some manufacturers, such as Healthtex and Tickle Me!, produce a variety of products in their collections. Others restrict their offerings to one classification, such as knitwear. Within both of these merchandise approaches, there is also a need to decide whether to address all children's sizes, from infants to preteen, or to cater only to one or two size categories.

This Tickle Me! ad exemplifies the fun in children's clothing.

Size Classifications

Children's wear has a much broader range of styles than does men's and women's apparel. This is because of the different age groups through which children pass. From the infant stage through the preteen period, many different styles are required.

Infants

Most lines are produced in a range of "month" sizes, beginning with newborn or three months and moving up to twenty-four months. The sizes selected for the individual child do not necessarily reflect the child's true age, because each child experiences a different rate of development. The size is merely directed to an average stature for that particular age.

Toddlers

T2 through T4 is the size range for **toddlers,** children who are crawling and beginning to walk. A large infant can sometimes wear a small toddler size.

all in good fun!

Buster Brown uses extensive advertising to promote its lines.

Children's

Girls' clothing in this classification ranges in size from 3 to 6X and boys' from 3 to 7. Once a toddler has stopped wearing diapers, he or she usually progresses to children's sizes and stays with this range until the first or second year of school.

Girls

Having outgrown the children's classification, girls enter the 7 to 14 sizes.

Boys

When they can no longer wear the children's sizes, boys move into a range from 8 to 20, which serves this group until they are ready to wear some of the specialized student or teen sizes.

Preteen

No longer satisfied with the styles of the girl's range and still insufficiently developed to enter the teen or junior market, girls may wear preteen clothing in sizes 6 to 14. The merchandise generally reflects the styles of the teen market, but is proportioned to fit preteen bodies.

Price Lines

Although the men's and women's industries offer merchandise at all price points, children's price lines are not as diverse. Children's clothing is viewed as a perishable item because of the rapid growth of its wearers, the beating it often takes from just plain wear and tear, and constant laundering. These factors make buying new clothes in larger sizes a necessity. To have greater appeal, most manufacturers stay within a price range that appeals to a wide audience. Of course, there are children's wear manufacturers who deal with a small, upscale market and produce more costly merchandise. An example is Ralph Lauren with his Polo label. Parents who prefer these products for themselves often choose the same labels for their children.

The children's wear market has greater appeal today with its broad fashion offerings.

Selling Children's Wear

The methods of operation parallel those of men's and women's fashions, using individual showrooms, manufacturer's reps, road staffs, and trade expositions. With lines generally produced twice a year, there are two major selling seasons. More and more manufacturers are opting to sell at the trade expos, such as The Kid's Show in New York City, Pitti Bimbo in Florence, and Salon de la Mode Enfantine in Paris.

Promoting Children's Wear

Children's wear requires less expensive promotion than either men's or women's fashions. In addition to fashion shows at trade expositions, manufacturers advertise in children's trade publications, such as *Earnshaws* and Fairchild Publications', *Children's Business*. As with the other segments of the fashion industry, promotion activities will be explored later in the text.

Chapter Highlights

- The men's, women's, and children's wear industries parallel each other in a number of ways. Their merchandise is available at many different price points, it is produced internationally, and the appeal is to very broad markets.

- The women's wear industry receives greater attention from the editorial press than either men's or children's wear.

- Women's fashions come in a variety of price points, classifications, and size ranges.

- The major markets for the women's industry are found throughout the world. Paris, of course is still the center for couture, while no place is a match for New York City's ready-to-wear market. Of course, all over the world other fashion capitols and regional markets coexist and offer merchandise of every style and shape.

- Women's wear has the largest number of seasonal collections.

- Women's apparel is promoted through a variety of endeavors, the most important of which is the fashion show.
- Men's wear styling, after remaining constant for many years, finally came alive in the early 1960s with the mod look from London's Carnaby Street.
- The peacock look, popularized by Pierre Cardin, featured broad, padded shoulders, nipped-in waistlines, and long jackets.
- Men's clothing is available in a range of sizes tailored to fit a variety of physiques without necessitating a great deal of alterations.
- Promotion of men's wear is accomplished through a variety of means, with trade shows and associations playing major roles.
- The children's wear industry came into its own in the 1950s when the youth of America began to express their own opinions about dress.
- Children's sizes range from infants to preteen, with each range featuring appropriate styles for the ages of the wearers. At the preteen level, the styling is similar to those found in junior collections, only the proportions are different.
- In all three apparel classifications, trade expositions play an important role in the selling of the lines.

Important Fashion Terminology and Concepts

athletic cut
braces
bridge collection
budget price point
Carnaby Street
contemporary price point
Council of Fashion
  Designers (CFDA)
couture price point
cruise wear
designer price point
dress-down Friday

electronic press kit
The Fashion Association
  (TFA)
Fridaywear
half sizes
holiday season
IMBEX
Men's Apparel Group in
  California (MAGIC)
misses figure
moderate price point
mod look

National Association of
  Men's Sportswear
  Buyers (NAMSB)
off-the-rack
peacock look
petite sizes
private label
resort wear
SEHM
selling season
tailored clothing
toddlers

For Review

1. Where is the center for women's couture located?
2. Name three classifications of women's wear and the importance of each to the industry.
3. Explain the bridge price point.
4. Is the junior size necessarily directed to the young? Explain.
5. In what way are women's sizes different from half sizes?
6. When and where did the men's wear fashion revolution take place?
7. List five major merchandise classifications in men's wear and indicate one product in each.
8. Describe the differences between regular and athletic cuts.
9. How do dress shirt sizes differ from sport shirts?

10. What are the major seasons in men's wear?

11. Discuss the role played by TFA.

12. What events led to the change in children's clothing styles?

13. Why are children's price lines more restricted than women's and men's?

14. What is the major method used for promoting fashions?

Exercises and Projects

1. Prepare an oral report on a famous apparel designer for presentation to the class. Information is available from the designers or from periodicals available in most libraries.

2. Contact a women's wear buyer to learn about the various seasons in the industry. From the information collected, prepare a table showing the seasons, dates of purchasing, and delivery dates.

3. Visit a men's tailored clothing department in a major store and, through inspection or questioning of the manager, determine the percentages of each subclassification of the category.

4. If you are in a city that hosts a trade exposition, such as NAMSB, MAGIC, the International Boutique Show, or the Kid's Show, write to the sponsor to request tickets for the event. Most organizations will honor student requests. Write a report outlining the various observations made at the event.

5. Prepare a booklet on children's wear for one season utilizing pictures found in mail-order catalogs and magazines. Concentrate on only one size range. Summarize the fashion highlights that are apparent in the selected styles.

The Case of the Disagreeing Partners

Lilliputian is a children's wear company that specializes in infants, toddler's, and children's size ranges. It has been operating successfully for eight years. Unlike most manufacturers, the company began to earn a profit only fourteen months after its doors were opened.

The two-team partnership began with knitted items for infants. The articles were hand constructed by women who worked in their homes. Using this approach, neither a factory nor showroom was needed. Lilliputian sold its goods by calling on better-priced specialty stores.

With significantly favorable reaction, the owners kept expanding. First, they leased a small facility in which they added other lines. A complete line of infant wear was later joined by toddler's and children's groups. In a short time, they gained a national reputation.

As each period of growth proved successful, one of the partners, Donna Barrie expressed a desire to expand once again. This time she feels the preteen market would be an appropriate choice, because mothers would recognize the Lilliputian label and purchase this next size range for their youngsters. Beth Jansen, the other company principal, is opposed to the idea. She believes the new market is significantly different from the one they know, that market is smaller since many stores do not carry as much variety in preteen merchandise, and older children might reject the new line simply because Lilliputian has always meant small children's wear.

The partners are now making a decision.

Question

With which partner do you agree and why?

point of view

Women's Grows at MAGIC

Kristin Young

The sister of MAGIC International, the world's largest men's wear trade show held twice yearly in Las Vegas, is growing up fast.

WWD/MAGIC International—the women's apparel show developed as a joint effort by WWD and MAGIC as a companion piece to the men's wear extravaganza—debuted in February. Now on tap for the second go-round in August are an expanded exhibitor count and more space.

The establishment of the women's show reflected in part the growing magnetism of Las Vegas itself as a trade show capital. In recent years, Las Vegas has traded in its "Sin City" image in favor of family-oriented entertainment spectaculars along with plenty of convention space for business.

In 1994, Las Vegas held 2,662 conventions attracting approximately 2.7 million people. That same year, the Las Vegas Convention Center alone hosted 56 trade shows, which drew over one million people.

"Our growth rates will be curtailed for the time being due to capacity restraints," said a spokesman for the center, adding that the facility plans to expand by 1 million square feet over the next 10 years. In the meantime, the Las Vegas hotels have built huge exhibition spaces hoping to get a piece of the convention action.

WWD/MAGIC is held in the Las Vegas Hilton Hotel Convention Complex, adjoining the convention center, where the men's wear activities hold forth.

With joint registration, the two shows pulled a total of more than 60,000 buyers in February. MAGIC and WWD/MAGIC honor the same registration badges.

Glenn Mounger, MAGIC chief executive officer, and Joe Loggia, chief operating officer, were ready with some big numbers when discussing plans for the upcoming shows to be held Aug. 28–31. They pointed out that retailers will be able to see the latest trends from a total of more than 3,000 exhibitors in some 1.7 million square feet of space spread over the two venues.

Loggia said it was difficult to project buyer numbers, as 50 percent of the attendance comes in to register on the first day of the show. He said he expected that in all—buyers and exhibitor personnel—the show should be visited by over 73,000 people.

Helping to make sure that exhibitors aren't overwhelmed, show management has developed a new customer service agent system. Each exhibitor will be assigned an agent, who will answer questions and be prepared to walk exhibitors through every aspect of the show.

As for WWD/MAGIC alone, the February show had more than 500 exhibitors showing 750 brand names in 871 booths. In August, some 600 exhibitors will be on hand, showcasing 1,000 brand names in over 1,140 booths. The show will cover 250,000 square feet of space, 50,000 more than in February.

Names exhibiting for the first time at WWD/MAGIC in August cover a wide range of categories, such as Anne Cole, Catalina and Jacques Moret in activewear and swimwear; Justin Allen, A.J. Bran-don, Karen Kane, Sigrid Olsen, Generra, Betsey Johnson, Laundry and David Dart in sportswear going from moderate to bridge, and Vanity Fair and Bestform in innerwear.

A hard-walled pavilion, called Promenade, will be constructed to accommodate the new exhibitors. Promenade will be adjacent to the Hilton and directly across from the men's designer pavilion. It's Loggia's hope that traffic will flow easily between the two pavilions and that the group of designers showing in the men's pavilion will be intrigued by the pull of the women's show.

"The men's designer pavilion will house some first-time MAGIC exhibitors—Versace, Valentino Boutique, DKNY, Guess?," said Loggia.

The strength of the retail attendance is seen as a magnet for big-name exhibitors. According to Mounger, a study of MAGIC attendance done during the February 1994 show, the latest available, showed 19 percent of retailers registered were store owners, 21 percent were presidents and 10 percent were vice presidents. Personnel with buyer titles made up the biggest chunk of the retail attendance, at 35 percent, while 4 percent were general merchandise managers and 2 percent divisionals. Various other titles made up the remainder.

As for type of store, 11 percent of the retail attendees were from department stores, 7 percent were from chains and 51 percent were from specialty stores. Rounding out the list were buying offices at 9 percent; discounters, 6 percent; mail order, 3 percent; home shopping, 0.2 percent, and the rest, "other."

"The strength of MAGIC combined, both our women's and men's show, is getting [retail] decision-makers to meet with principals of the exhibiting companies," said Mounger.

Another dimension of the MAGIC shows is international. Some 77 countries, stretching from India to Canada, are expected to be represented at the August edition, either as buyers or exhibitors. "All industries are no longer just regional or even national; you've got to look globally," said Loggia.

Added Mounger: "Where we used to feel our show was an important domestic show, we're in an excellent position to become an important international show."

When retailers aren't shopping the booths, they'll also have opportunities for both trend-spotting and networking at fashion shows, seminars, video fashion reports, golf and tennis tournaments and an opening night concert featuring Earth, Wind and Fire.

As for the long term, Mounger and Loggia are bullish on continued growth for WWD/MAGIC.

"The women's industry is larger than the men's," Loggia said. "So we don't see any reason why WWD/MAGIC shouldn't be as big or potentially bigger than MAGIC International."

Women's Wear Daily, July 19, 1995.

Dress-Down Brings Strategic Shifts

Dianne M. Pogoda

The daytime dress and suit market isn't on the ropes just yet, but the loosening of corporate dress codes and an increase in workers who can do their jobs at home are causing some better and bridge makers to rethink their approach to growth.

To meet the new options in dressing today, some of the strategies ready-to-wear companies are employing include:

- Focusing on eveningwear. Women still have special-occasions and evening events, and if they are dressing down during the day, they will still splurge on something new for evening.
- Maintaining prices to capitalize on value.
- Making tailored apparel with more comfort and better fit.

The work-at-home universe expanded by three million households to 39 million between the second quarters of 1994 and 1995—a 7.6 percent rise, according to IDC/LINK, a market research division of International Data Corp.

The firm projects that telecommuters will be the fastest-growing segment of at-home workers. This group includes employees of outside companies who work at home at least part-time during normal business hours.

The shift in work styles is one reason some women are reevaluating their overall purchasing plans.

Marie Drum Beninati, a partner in the retail practice of CSC, a consulting firm, said there has been a "Europeanization" of the American woman's wardrobe and her attitude about buying.

"People are finding that they don't need 20 of anything, they need one or two really good things, she said. "Europeans will spend a month's salary on a fine designer outfit, and wear it a lot."

There is still a need for a more serious, professional look Monday through Thursday, especially at an executive level. Consequently, dresses and suits continue to do all right, even in these difficult times.

Another plus for the market is that dress-down for women has not been well defined, resulting in as much confusion about the right thing to wear on casual days as there has been about hemlines that see-saw up and down.

If women don't know what to wear, they don't know what to buy, so they stick with the old reliables, according to some observers.

While unit sales of tailored dresses and suits rose 16.2 percent and 17 percent, respectively, in the first nine months of 1995 compared to the same period in 1994, dollar sales were up less—5 percent in dresses and 11.2 percent in suits, according to the NPD Group, a Port Washington, N.Y., research firm.

This indicates that prices not only have not risen, but there has been deflation in the categories, said Beninati.

It spotlights the importance and appeal of value. Dressing from neck to knees for one price with a dress or suit has been one of the category's drawing cards for several years.

"It also means that markdowns occurred much earlier than ever," Beninati noted. "The dress-down and work-at-home trends don't appear to have hurt the day dress and suit markets. This reflects the success of the Talbots of the world."

Beninati suggested that while "business casual" has been well defined for men, the fashion industry still has not come up with a casual workwear uniform for women.

"Tailored clothing also represents the countertrend," she added. "If the consumer sees all these casual clothes in the stores, and she wants to look a little different, what is she going to buy? Tailored."

But business casual is here to stay because people are not going to give up comfort, she said, adding, "The key is making tailored clothes more comfortable and with better fit."

In other parts of the country, the South and West, for example, wardrobes are more casual all week long. In New England and the Midwest, dress is more conservative, she pointed out.

"The shift has strengthened the evening portion of our business," said Alan Geller, president of the **Kenar Dress** division of Kenar Enterprises. "It has redirected women's needs, and manufacturers are prompted to make the dress that much more special. The consumer might be buying fewer dresses, but she's still buying quality."

Geller said the company's established Kenar Dress and Schrader divisions were up about 25 percent in spring bookings, but that hearty new growth was expected from its new AJ Bari line of evening and dinner dresses and suits.

Kenar bought the Bari trademark when its parent, the Gillian Group, was liquidated last year. The collection is hitting stores for spring, and first-year volume is projected at about $10 million.

Richard Elias, president of **Renlyn New York,** said his overall strategy is changing because he is exploring new territories with existing lines and launching new products.

His newer E.R. Gerard suit line, which is less expensive than the bridge-priced Renlyn collection, is selling well—the lower price point has proven to be attractive, he said.

He is also doing more work with catalogs, and is launching a new large-size suit collection through a license with Delta Burke Designs. The suits, as reported, will retail for under $200, and will make their debut in March for fall. First-year sales are projected at $2 million to $3 million.

"We feel we'll avoid some of the effects of that reduced demand," Elias said. "But the key is in restructuring your business to rein in costs and have quick turn. Retailers are holding back on ordering, so you have to be able to turn very quickly. Manufacturers who have foreign production could have a tough time, because they have to work much further in advance."

Tom Murry, president of **Tahari Ltd.,** said the company's sportswear division is being affected by casual Fridays more than its dress and suit division.

It's having a neutral impact in terms of sales, but the sportswear area is changing more in response to the trend.

Murry stressed that Tahari's niche is upscale career clothing, and he said the company's choice has been to remain focused on that area. He said eventually the company will launch a casual division, and that unit will be fully focused on casual apparel.

"There's always a danger in losing your focus," he said. "We've tried to maintain our focus, and we will not do anything that doesn't work with a working woman's wardrobe."

Murry observed that the fashion industry will "no doubt overreact to this trend," then it will subside and finally it will level off.

"I haven't seen a trend yet that didn't cause an overreaction," he stated.

He said there has been an increase in Tahari's pant business, and more sweater sets have been selling. Knitwear has increased to 18 percent of Tahari's business, from 4 percent just two years ago.

There has been some tradeoff with blouses. Sweaters and vests, which are also easy to dress up or down, are alternatives to the jacket.

"Our jacket business is still strong, but when we make a jacket now, we make sure it has multiple uses, that it can be worn for the office with skirt or dress or with casual pants or even jeans," he said.

In the dress and suit area, there is a great emphasis on price, as value is still a key component of this market, he added.

The bridge-rice evening dress business is performing well, and Tahari is going after a solid daytime dress business "at a price."

Rusty Ruster, president of the licensed Mary McFadden Suits collection, said the changes could "put a bit of a crimp" in daytime business, but noted, "People still want to look good and feel good about how they look, so there's room for both."

He said one key to McFadden's suits, which wholesale from $99 to $179 and made their retail debut for spring, is that they are versatile, and can go from the office to dinner or a party.

The main thrust of the line is dressier daytime and evening suits, and the look is achieved through detailing—special buttons, piping, frog closures, novelty zippers and such treatments as petal cuffs—and tex-

hopsack, rayon and acetate piqué.

The wardrobe change that's spreading across the country is "revolutionary, as big as any of the past several hundred years," said consultant R. Fulton Macdonald, president of **International Business Development.**

"'Corporate casual' still calls for clothing Monday through Thursday that commands respect from work-ers, but is not highly tailored and formal," said Macdonald.

He noted that since Latin and European business people still tend to dress more formally, anyone dealing with these groups will be more likely to dress formally.

Traditional suitings, however, are becoming more of an option in all aspects of business.

"Suit and dress makers have an opportunity to respond to this style and tailoring change by reducing the amount of padding, tailoring and formality, lengthening dress skirts so they're not sexy, con-structing lightly padded jackets and designing mix-and-match rather than more formally linked outfits," he said.

Women's Wear Daily, January 30, 1996.

I See London, I See France / I See (Famous Designer's) Underpants

What's seen by few but worn by all? Underwear of course. But that may be changing. Utilitarian garments, once worn only for comfort and modesty, are now being purchased for style as well and intimate apparel may never be the same. As clothes have grown ever more revealing, bras and panties increas-ingly serve more than a supporting role in wardrobing. Aided by racy ads, rap singers and runway shows, fashion has infiltrated the inner-wear market to such a degree that famous designer names now appear as regularly on the waistbands of cotton briefs as they do on dress labels. Why the unprecedented interest in unmentionables?

"It's a new frontier," says Walter Levy, chairman, Levy & Kerson Associates, retail management con-sultants. "Intimate apparel is a divi-sion that has been quiet for a long time so there was a window of opportunity there. It's an area that needed rejuvenation. Plus, designer clothing is not doing as well as it once did because the whole society has turned against conspicuous

consumption, so designers have looked at that and decided to move their names and influence into other merchandise categories."

Levy points out that while the sales volume generated by big ticket apparel items is limited, the market for innerwear is much wider. While an outfit from Calvin Klein's ready-to-wear collection can set you back more than $1,000, a pair of his ath-letic-style sport briefs can be had for less than $15.

"Calvin Klein came in and revo-lutionized women's underwear and others have followed his lead." Levy reasons that Klein's austere, grey and white, cotton interlock, tops and bottoms struck a chord with consumers because the product filled a need that existed for a com-fortable, natural fiber undergar-ment, but also because their androgynous appearance reflected the new role of women in society. "With men and women all wearing jeans and tee-shirts, unisex under-wear was the next logical step." Levy notes that as a result of the line's huge success, the designer is

probably better known for his cot-ton skivvies than he is for his ele-gantly understated suits.

"There's no question that lin-gerie today is quite different from the way it used to be even a short five years ago when the bustier became *the garment* to be seen in," recalls Josie Natori. "Daywear used to be half-slips and tap pants. Now it includes bodysuits, and suit camis for daytime dressing. Lin-gerie in all its forms has truly come out of the closet and is a leading 'must-have' item for the fashion driven customer."

Natori feels the woman of the '90s lives in a high pressure world and considers the acquisition of pretty lingerie to be a well-earned reward for all her hard work both on the job and at home. Capitaliz-ing on the movement toward a more relaxed form of dressing, Natori has created a separate apparel category for herself by challenging preconceived ideas about the nature of lingerie and its functions.

"A dramatic re-shaping of sportswear took place in the '70s and '80s," she explains. "What used to be restricted to clothes you wore to participate in sports has been changed forever by the baby-boomer to the highly segmented and highly diversified business it is today. The same kind of redefinition of intimate apparel is taking place now as the line of demarcation between innerwear and outerwear is quickly blurring."

Richard Martin, curator of The Costume Institute at New York's Metropolitan Museum of Art agrees. In a synopsis of the Infra-Apparel fashion exhibition currently on display there, he writes; "One generation's hidden structures are another's conspicuous designs, one generation's undergarments are another's flaunted outer garments." Martin credits Natori with expanding the horizons of intimate apparel and the exhibition represents her as one of the new league of designers who are taking their designs from the "confidential and personal to the public."

One designer who offers the best of both worlds is Donna Karan. One of the most influential names in ready-to-wear and a powerful presence in almost every other fashion category, Karan now solves the problem of what to wear underneath it all with her new lingerie collection. Donna Karan Intimates combines luxury with comfort via simple but sensual shapes, neutral colors and fine, natural fiber fabrics. As the story goes, Karan decided to try her hand at lingerie design for much the same reason as she began many of her other enterprises. She felt there was something missing. Dissatisfied with the fit and feel of most innerwear, she was

determined to do better. For example: Karan's cotton/spandex underpants are cut full in back, so they won't ride up, high on the leg to allow ease of movement, and reach the waist, thus providing a measure of tummy control.

One of the major retailers that have opened in-store boutiques for Karan's lingerie line is Neiman Marcus. Joan Kaner, senior vice president and fashion director for the store, is enthusiastic about the venture. "Donna Karan has made a brilliant entry into the marketplace," she says. "She brings a lot to the table. First off, she's a woman, so she knows what women want and need and second she's been able to bring to her intimate apparel the same sensibility that one finds in her clothing collection, and this distinguishes her from many of her competitors."

Ira Livingston, vice president, U.S. marketing for Cotton Incorporated, the fiber company of U.S. cotton growers, confirms the trend toward increased comfort in innerwear is growing. He says sales of cotton lingerie are on the rise. "In 1992, cotton held a 46% share of the total intimate apparel market, up from 44% in 1991. Our share of the women's panty market climbed from 63% to 66%, while women's bodysuits saw a 1% increase from 56% to 57% during the same time period."

Eileen West, who has been called "the queen of cotton prints," is at the forefront of the comfortable cotton underwear movement. Best known for her soft, romantic womenswear, the San Francisco-based designer now brings her flowering motifs to a variety of licensed products including intimate apparel. Introduced in 1991, her

line of foundation garments has a distinctively fresh appeal, and features the same buttons, bows, eyelet and other trims that have become a signature trademark.

Peter Sullivan, National Accounts Manager for Vanity Fair Mills, the licensee for Eileen West Innerwear, says the company chose Eileen West to be their first designer lingerie line because she had the prior association with natural fiber products they were searching for. The line is comprised almost exclusively of cotton fabrics, half knits, half wovens. Current patterns include gingham checks, madras plaids, stripes and polka dots. Thanks to imaginative styling, the new label has enabled the manufacturer to expand the audience Eileen West traditionally sold to, bringing in a younger, more contemporary customer.

"Updating lingerie looks with novelty cotton fabrics allowed us to offer a visibly different garment. The woven cotton bras and panties were designed to bring a ready-to-wear feeling to foundations," says Sullivan. But, he maintains good looks aren't the only factor. "This is a comfort-oriented product," he adds. "All the bras and bustiers are fully constructed and shirred in the back to give a perfect fit."

Asked to give a prognosis for the future of intimate apparel Ira Livingston notes; "The innerwear market has turned into a veritable who's who of the fashion industry. Recognizable names like Calvin Klein, Josie Natori, Donna Karan, Eileen West, Adrienne Vittadini, Emanuel Ungaro are on the list of cotton lingerie lovers and others like Guess? are still to come. We are forecasting continued growth for the natural fiber in this arena."

Cotton Incorporated, New York, NY.

CHAPTER 10

Fashion Accessories

Footwear, hosiery, jewelry, gloves, handbags, millinery, belts, watches, scarves, and hair ornaments are the ingredients that lend drama and provide pizzazz to a clothing collection. The excitement generated by a runway designer show is heightened by the accompanying fashion accessories. Once relegated to second-class fashion status, accessories now share the spotlight with apparel designs.

Many American and international creators of fashion apparel collections spend considerable time designing shoes, jewelry, handbags, hats, and other items to coordinate with their lines. Not only do these creations enhance the apparel, but they also bring additional revenue to the companies.

In the accessories market, most of the designers are often the talented but unsung heroes of the back room, recognition goes to the company whose name appears on the items. However, some accessories designers are beginning to receive the recognition they deserve. Robert Lee Morris, for his jewelry designs, and Judith Leiber, for her exquisite handbags, are making fashion headlines just like their counterparts in apparel design. The Council of Fashion Designers of America has helped to promote accessory designers through shows. One is held in facilities adjacent to the tent shows of Seventh on Sixth, which the Council sponsors in Bryant Park, New York City. Awards for outstanding achievement of accessory designs are also given at the annual CFDA ceremony.

The accessories industries are also profiting from a decline in clothing purchases. Whether because of a lack of interest in the new designs or a slow down in the economy, consumers are opting to purchase accessories to spruce up their wardrobes. Often a fashionable necklace or new pair of shoes can transform an old outfit into something new.

The importance of these fashion accessories are highlighted by the increasing number of retailers who are opening accessories-only stores. A walk in any mall or shopping arena immediately reveals the significance of this market to the fashion industry.

After you have completed this chapter, you will be able to discuss:

- The importance of accessories to the fashion industry.

- The functional and decorative importance of accessories to the wearer.

- The considerable price differentials among shoes.

- The impact made on hosiery with the discovery of nylon and introduction of pantyhose.

- The differences between costume and fine jewelry.

- The differences between functional and decorative belts.

- Why watches, previously just functional accessories, have taken on fashion importance.

Many companies dot the domestic map, but a few major operations account for most of the production. U.S. Shoe, for example, produces shoes under such distinctive labels as Calvin Klein, Garolini, Cobbies, Famolare, Amalfi, Pappagallo, and Bandolino; it accounts for a large share of the market.

To combine the best of all worlds, American shoe manufacturers have entered into the international production market by participating in joint ventures. In this way, they can capitalize on cost-efficient production in such countries as Korea and Taiwan.

The leading names in the shoe industry are often the same as those in the apparel industry. Instead of direct participation in a shoe company, many designers are involved through licensing agreements. That is, for a percentage of the sales, they permit companies to market a line of shoes under their signatures. The designer's reputation is protected through an arrangement whereby he or she has the right to reject a style before production begins.

The fitness craze has also caused changes in the shoe industry. An increasing number of men and women have several pairs of athletic footwear in their wardrobes. Before the 1970s, most consumers owned one pair of Keds or Converse sneakers. Today Nike, Reebok, and other companies produce a large number of styles specifically designed for different activities. Although the athletic footwear business is still larger than it was a few decades ago, its popularity has waned in the 1990s. Young people, in particular, have taken to a new breed of shoes inspired by **Doc Martins** and in many instances, have redirected their shoe purchases. This shift proves that with shoes as with any other accessory, fashion often dictates what the consumer will wear.

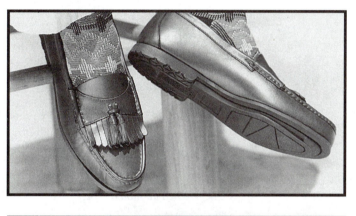

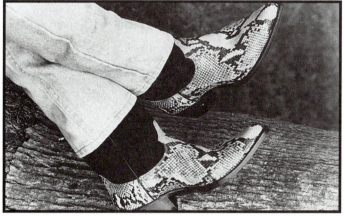

Tassel loafers and boots of every variety are popular items in a man's wardrobe.

Styles

The shoe industry produces a large number of different styles. Some are classics that are popular year in and year out; others make their way through the fashion cycles, reappearing as dictated by the particular apparel styles that are popular.

The men's shoe industry is a little easier to manage, because most of its merchandise is classic. Some men wear the same style business shoes for many years, replacing them with an identical pair only when they are worn out. Women, on the other hand, are more interested in style. With different heel heights needed to accommodate pants and various skirt lengths, a woman's shoe wardrobe seems even greater than before.

Some of the classic and fashion-oriented styles of shoes for men and women are listed in Table 10.1.

TABLE 10.1

CLASSIC SHOE STYLES FOR MEN AND WOMEN

For Men:

bals	Basic style of Oxford with tongue cut in a separate piece from the vamp of the shoe and joined with stitching across the vamp.
brogues	A heavy Oxford, usually with wing-tip decorated with heavy perforation and pinkings.
deck shoes	Canvas shoe that uses lacing through the top and sides of the shoe.
loafers	Slip-on shoe. Popular styles include Gucci® and penny loafer. Also worn by women and children.
sneakers	Canvas or leather athletic wear. Fashion-oriented varieties are generally used for casual wear. Also worn by women and children.

For Women:

Classic Styles

pumps	Slip-on shoe with rounded or V-shaped throat usually low-cut, medium- to high heels. Toe shape varies with current fashion styles.
sandals	Open-type shoe usually held on foot with straps. Also worn by men and children.
slingback	Open-back pump with a strap across the heel of the foot to hold it in place.

When fashion dictates

clogs	Shoes with thick platform soles.
d'Orsay pump	Pumps with low-cut sides, closed heel and toes.
espadrilles	Rope-soled shoe with canvas upper, tied on with long shoelaces threaded through top of shoe and around ankle. Sometimes made without laces as pump cut high and across instep.
ghillie/gillie	Laced shoe usually without tongue and rounded lacer pulling through leather loop fastened around the ankle.
Hush Puppies®	Trade name for casual oxford or slip-on shoe with sueded leather uppers and crepe soles. Also worn by men and children.
jellies	Molded footwear of soft plastic or rubber with cutouts; made in a variety of colors. Also worn by children.
Mary Janes	Shoes that employ a strap across the instep, sometimes buttoned at side, with a rounded front. Also worn by children.
spectators	Two-tone pump made in contrasting colors sometimes with stacked heels.

HOSIERY

One of the largest segments of the accessories industry, hosiery is produced in mills all over the United States. The available products fall into three categories—**pantyhose, stockings,** and **socks.** All three are functional and provide warmth, support, and comfort. However they are designed and dyed based on fashion trends. The fashion industry decides the colors that will be dominant for a particular season. The assortment of colors range from the darkest blacks to the purest whites, in any shade. Hosiery is produced in a variety of **deniers,** or fineness of yarns, and **gauges,** which define the closeness of the knit.

The greatest boom in the hosiery industry occurred in 1938 when DuPont introduced nylon to the world. Crowds immediately gathered anytime a store announced the arrival of nylon hosiery. With such characteristics as strength and elasticity, nylon quickly replaced silk and rayon.

The introduction of pantyhose in the 1960s was another boom to the industry. This garment was designed to accommodate the miniskirts of that decade.

Socks, once the basic staple of the hosiery industry, have taken on an expanded role. Men and women are making extensive use of socks as fashion items. Men can now purchase patterns such as argyles, geometrics, and woven designs instead of just basic dark, solid tones. The color assortment for men includes every point on the color wheel. Women are also making extensive use of socks. From the briefest, finest variety to the longer, bulkier types in wool, cotton, and manufactured fibers—the choices are enormous.

The fitness craze has significantly expanded the athletic sock from the staple white to a variety of tones and decorative patterns. Many organizations, such as Fila, Ellesse, and Ralph Lauren, that produce activewear also produce socks that bear their logos and sell at prices never before dreamed of.

When stores received nylon hosiery shipments in 1938, eager crowds gathered to purchase the "new fiber stockings."

Selling hosiery is different from selling any other accessories. It is sold in department and specialty stores, but can easily be purchased at supermarkets, convenience stores, vending machines, and pharmacies. It is a merchandiser's dream because try-ons are not necessary and not allowed. Fit by each manufacturer is standard and returns a rarity.

JEWELRY

With the addition of a dazzling necklace and bracelet, the simplest, basic black dress can be transformed into an exciting costume. Whether the pieces are genuine diamonds or merely rhinestone, a new look has been created. Available in an assortment of shops ranging from street vendors and flea market stands to the halls of Tiffany & Company, jewelry is available for all.

Jewelry falls into two categories—fine, or precious, and costume, or fashion. Fine jewelry is produced from metals and stones that have intrinsic value. **Fashion jewelry,** on the other hand, has little real value and is purchased more for its usefulness and attractiveness as an accessory.

Fine Jewelry

Fine jewelry has always been looked on as a symbol of achievement. Sometimes a person's importance has been measured in terms of fine jewels. At royal coronations or marriages between aristocratic or celebrity families, the jewels often share the spotlight.

Fine jewelry, like other costly accessories, is available in a wide range of prices. While two diamonds of comparable size might appear similar to the untrained eye, the actual price differential could be staggering.

The cost of fine jewelry is based upon the quality of the precious stones and metals, their size or weight, and the workmanship that goes into its creation. Gemstones include diamond, the hardest natural stone; corundum, more commonly known as ruby; sapphire, emerald, jade, and natural pearl. They are priced according to color, clarity, size, cut, and rarity. Except for pearls, which are measured in millimeters, gemstones are weighed in **carats.** One carat equals 200 milligrams. Precious metals include gold, the most widely used in jewelry, platinum, palladium, and silver. Generally considered too soft

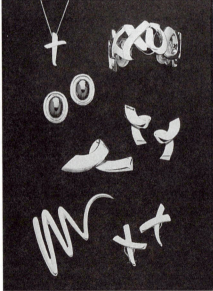

(top and bottom) A dazzling bracelet or several worn together, adds excitement to a basic outfit. These exclusive pieces by Paloma Picasso were designed for Tiffany.

to be used in their pure state, precious metals are combined or alloyed with less expensive base metals for strength. Gold is weighed in **karats.** If jewelry is made from an **alloy** that contains 1/24 pure gold, it can be described as pure gold. The most popular domestic gold is 14 karat; that produced in other countries is usually 18 karat. If the proportion is less than 10 karats, the term karat gold cannot be used.

The most popular silver used in the production of fine jewelry is **sterling silver.** The alloy or combination is 92.5 parts silver to 7.5 parts copper. Not all sterling silver is equal in quality; the thicker the silver, the more valuable the item.

Robert Lee Morris

A self-taught jewelry designer, Robert Lee Morris is a major force in the creation of contemporary jewelry. Whether working in a matte gold finish or shiny sterling silver, he has an unmistakable signature that unifies all of his designs. Pieces are immediately distinguishable by their strong, sculptural shape, in which form and function work together.

Morris' designs appeal to the mind as well as the touch advancing what he calls "Themes of Universal Consciousness." Through powerful allusions to ancient history, religion, myth, and legend, Morris translates timeless symbols into modern forms—daggers, crosses, keys, and fertility symbols. "My recurring theme is the study of man and his artifacts. I want all my work to evoke a warm emotional reaction," states Morris.

After graduating from Beloit College, he established a craft commune in the cornfields of Wisconsin, where he taught himself the basics of jewelry. When the farm in which he lived and worked burned down one winter, he set up shop in Vermont. His work was discovered by Sculpture to Wear, a gallery in New York City's Plaza Hotel. Morris' collection was an instant success amid the work of Picasso, Arp, and Miro. In 1977 he opened Artwear, launching an entire modern jewelry movement.

Design projects by Robert Lee Morris include jewelry, dinnerware, handbags, belts, and containers for Elizabeth Arden.

Through the years he has been bestowed with such honors as the Coty Award, the Council of Fashion Designers of America Award, the International Gold Award, the FAAB Award for best jewelry designer, and the Woolmark Award. In his many endeavors, he has collaborated with such stars of the fashion world as Geoffrey Beene, Kansai Yamamoto, Calvin Klein, Anne Klein, Donna Karan, and Karl Lagerfeld.

His works have been exhibited in such places as the Phoenix Art Museum, the Smithsonian Institution's International Touring Exhibition, and the Harkus, Krakow, Rosen, Sonnabend Gallery in Boston. He is also the subject of a film, *Stripes of a Tiger.*

Today, Robert Lee Morris is busy expanding his designs to handbags, belts, dinnerware, and cosmetics.

In addition to classic designs in fine jewelry, today's fashion world is increasingly interested in contemporary jewelry design. Tiffany & Company, long a leader in exquisite, priceless fine jewelry creation, has carved out a niche for contemporary, fine jewelry. With collections created by Jean Schlumberger, Elsa Peretti, and Paloma Picasso, it has introduced the world of fashion to fresh ideas. The Peretti stylized heart, for example, has become a classic of contemporary design.

Through the imaginative designs of Robert Lee Morris, innovative, fine jewelry is receiving significant attention. Additional information on Robert Lee Morris is discussed in a World of Fashion Profile.

T A B L E   1 0 . 2

FINE AND COSTUME JEWELRY STYLES

bracelet	Ornament that encircles the wrist or arm. Made of metal, chain, plastic, wood, or leather either rigid such as bangle or cuff or flexible with links or chains.
brooch	Synonym for pin. Jewelry made with pin fastener on back, in all types of materials, e.g., gold, silver; may be set with real or imitation gems.
charm	Amulets or pendants that depict a variety of images, such as hearts or disks; may be suspended from bracelets or necklaces.
cuff links	Decorative closures made of metal, sometimes set in real or imitation gems, in a variety of shapes and sizes used to fasten French cuffs on shirts. Originally worn by men, adopted by women.
earrings	Jewelry worn in the ear. Available as clip-on, screwback, or pierced varieties, in designs that range from fitting against the earlobes, or dropping well below the ear.
necklace	Jewelry worn around the neck. Available in many lengths from chokers, which conform to the neck, to ropes, which are often forty-five inches in length. Made of beads, chains, sometimes with real or imitation gems.
ring	Jewelry worn on different fingers and made of many different materials and designs. Sometimes there is special significance for particular rings such as engagement, marriage, or graduation.
studs	Ornamental fasteners used in place of buttons on shirt fronts.
tiara	Curved head ornament worn from ear to ear, resembling a crown.

Costume Jewelry

Costume jewelry ranges from the "fabulous fakes" that simulate fine jewelry to trendy jewelry. Materials that have an appearance similar to precious stones are carefully mounted in gold-filled (thin sheets of gold bonded to a base metal) settings to give the impression of the real thing. Many an unwitting eye has been fooled by the replicas featured at Ciro's, a company that specializes in spectacular imitations. The majority of costume jewelry, however, is not intended to deceive, but to make a fashion statement. The materials used in their production are as varied as the number of artists who create the pieces. Plastic, beads, wood, metal, rope, ceramic, and stones are commonly used by designers. Their works generally follow trends in the apparel industry and are used to augment the consumer's wardrobe.

Styles

Both precious and costume jewelry come in any number of styles. Each serves a decorative or functional purpose. The popularity of a particular style depends on the materials used, the dictates of the fashion world, and whether or not it is considered standard, traditional wear, as is the case with engagement rings. Table 10.2 lists a representative selection of jewelry categories and styles.

TABLE 10.3

GLOVE STYLES

driving glove	Gloves with cut-outs on the back of the hand, or over the knuckles, to increase flexibility. May be knitted or leather, or combination. Originally worn for sports such as golf or race car driving.
gauntlet	Above-the-wrist glove that flares at the wrist.
mittens	Separates the thumb from the other fingers; a favorite for children.
mousequetaire	The longest length glove used for formal occasions. It comes in lengths that measure from eight to sixteen buttons. The glove features a vertical opening above the wrist that allows the wearer to slip her hands out of the glove without the need to remove it.
shorty	A two-button glove that reaches the wearer's wrist.
slip-on	Gloves that slip easily over the hand without fasteners or plackets.

GLOVES

Once a fashion accessory worn primarily for decorative purposes, **gloves** have become more functional. Traditionally, department stores offered a wide assortment of gloves ranging from the longest **mousequetaires** to slip-ons. Women owned many pairs to coordinate with specific outfits. Gloves were worn to dinner parties, luncheons, and other social occasions. Beginning in the early 1970s, however, women abandoned the glove as a decorative statement and wore them mainly for protection against the cold. Except for the few, old-line stores that feature a full assortment of gloves, most stores carry only functional gloves. While leather is still a favorite among wearers, knitted styles are also popular.

There are only a few basic styles of gloves, and of those, only two or three are used frequently. Variations in design comes from the different fabrications and trims that adorn them. **Button** is a term used to refer to the measurement of glove lengths. One button is equal to one French inch (approximately 1/12 of an inch longer than the American inch). Measurements begin at the base of the thumb. A one-button glove is wrist length, a six-button glove is about halfway to the elbow, and a sixteen-button glove is a formal length. Table 10.3 lists important glove styles.

Handbags are not only regarded as a functional accessory but are also "hot" fashion items.

HANDBAGS

The handbag industry continues to change. Before the 1970s, **handbags** served functional rather than fashionable needs. Handbag designers were rarely acknowledged by the editorial press or the consumer. The styles and shapes generally followed the direction of the apparel industry. That is, handbags had little or no identity of their own. All of this has changed in the 1970s, when apparel designers like Dior and Cardin, began to affix their signatures and

TABLE 10.4

TYPICAL HANDBAG STYLES

backpack	Handbag with straps fitting over shoulder to be worn over back.
clutch bag	Handbag free of handles that are held or "clutched."
drawstring bag	Handbag closed by pulling on leather or fabric cord.
envelope	Long, flat, rectangular-shaped bags that have flap closures. Usually of clutch-type without handles.
satchel	Rigid flat bottom shaped sides closed on metal frames. Similar to doctor's medical bag.
shoulderbag	Handbag style in any shape or size with a long strap to place on the shoulder. Some straps are adjustable.
totes	Handbag open on top and held with two straps or handles.

The hat on this runway model attracts as much attention as the suit.

logos to the bags. Fashion-oriented women quickly purchased them with as much excitement as they afforded the buying of apparel. Soon, the handbag industry reached a new level with the acceptance of signature symbols, such as the now-famous LV logo of a Louis Vuitton design. Constructed of vinyl, the bags sold for upwards of $300 and soon became a symbol for status seekers.

The handbag industry is one in which both famous and unknown designers coexist to bring a wide assortment of styles, at many price points, to consumers. Donna Karan and Paloma Picasso are in the forefront of the higher-priced entries, along with the lines produced by Coach and Dooney & Bourke. Judith Leiber produces a collection in which a single style may sell for as much as $5,000. Judith Leiber is discussed in a World of Fashion Profile. Of course, lower-priced lines are also available for those who can only spend more modest sums.

A walk through any major department store reveals the value of the handbag department to the company. Nordstrom and Bloomingdale's feature a wealth of different manufacturers, but also devote designated spaces to certain lines, such as Louis Vuitton, Fendi, Gucci, and Coach, in much the same manner as they do for special apparel collections. The handbag is no longer just a functional product.

There are many styles of handbags available to the shopper. Some styles are classics; others fall in and out of favor. Some of the typical models are included in Table 10.4.

MILLINERY

There was a time when properly dressed men and women wore hats for both social and business occasions. Since the late 1950s, however, the hat has virtually disappeared from the fashion world. A major blow to the men's **millinery** industry was delivered by President John Kennedy, who chose not to wear a hat to his inauguration in 1961. Although Jackie Kennedy revived interest in women's hats, bouffant hairstyles made it difficult for most women to wear them.

Judith Leiber

Judith Leiber handbags are collectors items for her devotees.

Describing herself as a nice lady from Budapest who prefers cooking and rummaging through antiques as her hobbies, Judith Leiber's evening bags are considered art. She began with a $5,000 investment, the price now charged for one of her more elaborate designs. She has received international acclaim and been the recipient of received numerous awards including the Lifetime Achievement Award of the Council of Fashion Designers of America. Her career was the focus of an exhibit mounted at the Fashion Institute of Technology in New York City. The exhibit was titled "The Artful Handbag" and displayed more than 300 individual treasures ranging from the sophisticated to the whimsical. A book, by the same title, about her life and designs is additional proof of her accomplishments.

To underscore the acceptance of Leiber creations, here are some fashion newsworthy facts:

- Barbara Bush wore her "Millie the dog" to state dinners; Hillary Clinton has sported "Socks the cat" with formal evening gowns.

- The Smithsonian Institution, Chicago Historical Society, Dallas Art Museum, and the Los Angeles County Museum of Art include her bags in their permanent collections.
- Beverly Sills, the former international opera star, has a collection of more than seventy.
- Ivana Trump admits she has more than she could count.

Beginning at prices of $1,000 for a modest style and ranging upward of $5,000 for more elaborate designs, Leiber has created more than 3,000 styles since she entered the business in the 1960s. She not only is responsible for creating the patterns, but also for overseeing her business operations on an everyday basis. She advises more than 200 factory workers on such matters as how the thousands of individual stones should be adhered to one frame. The "minaudieres," elegantly jewel-encrusted miniatures, receive the greatest attention. Some of her handbags represent fruits and vegetables, such as tomatoes, eggplants, and watermelon; animals; fairy tale characters; and fans of the Far East. Her patterns include argyle motifs, stained glass designs, and spider webs. Leiber also, however, produces the finest leather handbags.

She and her husband, a fine-arts artist, admit that they take great pleasure in counting the number of Leiber handbags at each of the social galas they attend.

Hats are still seen, however, as ensemble enhancements on the European runways. These are generally unique designs created to lend excitement to the events. Few translate into successful sellers. Occasionally, a style or shape may be adapted for widespread use by the millinery industry.

As with gloves, hats have become functional. Women who wear hats generally prefer such casual types as berets and caps made of knits, leather, and straw materials. Men often opt for the soft cap that fits easily into a coat pocket. Young consumers have embraced the baseball cap as their only head covering.

Hats, absent from the fashion market for several years, have been resurrected and now range from simple to one-of-a-kind models.

BELTS

The belt industry serves both functional and decorative needs. Functional belts are essential components of a garment—the belt that comes with a dress as a trim and those that are used primarily by men for their trousers. The greatest impact on the industry, however, is made by decorative belts. They are available in a variety of widths, from one quarter inch to as much as six inches, and in an assortment of materials, including leather, fabric, straw, elastic, rope, yarn, metal, and plastic. As with other fashion accessories, belt styles are dictated by the silhouettes created by the apparel industry. Prices range from a few dollars to several hundred depending on the materials used and the intricate details of the design.

The New York metropolitan area is the center of all types of belt production. Located within the same geographical area as the apparel industry, manufacturers can quickly and easily respond to the shapes and silhouettes of apparel designers.

Belts with a variety of decoration are considered functional and fashion accessories.

WATCHES

Watches are no longer treated just as necessities. They have become fashion-oriented items. Until a few years ago, the wearer was more interested in performance than appearance, and ownership of more than one timepiece was unusual. While some women had one watch for everyday use and another for evening wear, one watch served all purposes for most men.

During the early 1980s, watches achieved fashion status with the introduction of the Swatch. For a relatively small investment, consumers could purchase various styles to coordinate with different outfits. Changeable watch bands became popular and enabled users to adapt one watch to different fashion needs.

Many watch manufacturers have capitalized on the acceptance of the watch as a fashion accessory and have entered into licensing agreements with designers. In an era when designer status counts, these names help sell products.

At the other extreme of the industry is the fine, jeweled watch. Prices are based on the quality of the instrument, as well as the casing and stones used in its decoration. Timepieces at stores like Tiffany & Company may sell for as much as $50,000!

Watches have become fashion items with many apparel designers creating their own imprint.

SCARVES

For added warmth, men, women, and children don knitted and woven scarves in oblong, square, and triangular shapes. This use, however, is by no means the dominant role of the scarf in fashion. Signature scarves, those featuring the logos and names of world-famous designers, play an important role in women's wardrobes. For many years, women have treasured silk scarves in various shapes that display prints as well as the insignias of Hermès, Dior, Saint Laurent, and Pucci. They are worn draped and tied around the shoulders and neck with dresses, suits, blouses, and sweaters.

VERA, whose design is shown here (left), was the first designer of signature scarves. The scarf by Perry Ellis (right) lends an important accent to this blouse.

During the 1950s, the American accessories market witnessed the introduction of the first designer or signature scarf—this creation by Vera featured bold designs and imaginative colorations. The scarves sold in impressive quantities.

HAIR ORNAMENTS

Accents for the hair are an example of an accessory that fall in and out of favor. One season flowers may be the choice, in another, the oversized clip reminiscent of the clip-board, still another, barrettes in a wide assortment of sizes and shapes.

Small companies manufacture hair ornaments and look to hair stylists for direction in design. The hair design of the time dictates the type of ornament that will be used.

A variety of materials are used for ornaments. Silks and synthetics are used in flower ornaments; velvet, lamé, and mylar are used for bows; hard plastic for combs; metals for clips and barrettes; synthetic stones for decorations; combs for holding ornaments in place; and elastic for attachments.

Hair ornaments are sported by fashionable women.

Chapter Highlights

- The special accents or elements that complement apparel are known as accessories. As with trimmings, they serve as fashion enhancers and functional necessities.

- Accessories include shoes, hosiery, jewelry, gloves, handbags, millinery, watches, belts, scarves, and hair ornaments. Their design and popularity is usually based on the dictates of the fashion apparel they are designed to enhance.

- Accessories provide the wearer with the opportunity to alter an outfit's appearance. Accessories are used to freshen up wardrobes.

- Many apparel designers, such as Donna Karan, Calvin Klein, Ralph Lauren, and Liz Claiborne, are producing accessories through licensing agreements.

Important Fashion Terminology and Concepts

alloy	gauges	mousequetaire
belts	gloves	pantyhose
carats	hair ornaments	scarves
costume jewelry	handbags	shoes
denier	hats	socks
Doc Martins	hosiery	sterling silver
fashion jewelry	jewelry	stockings
fine jewelry	karats	watches
footwear	millinery	

For Review

1. To what extent are fashion apparel designers entering the footwear market and how are they participating?
2. How has the popularity of athletic shoes affected the shoe industry?
3. Describe the reason for the 1938 boom in the hosiery industry.
4. Discuss how the miniskirt affected the hosiery industry.
5. Differentiate between fine and costume jewelry.
6. What is meant by the term sterling silver?
7. What materials, in addition to metals and stones, are used in jewelry designs?
8. What has caused the handbag industry to become a fashion-oriented accessory?
9. How has the market for gloves changed since the 1950s?
10. What contributed to the decline in popularity of men's hats?
11. Which fashion product changed the market for watches?

Exercises and Projects

1. Visit a major department store and evaluate, in terms of space, the importance of each accessories category offered for sale. Begin with the one that occupies the greatest amount of space and conclude with that occupying the least. Square footage occupied should be estimated.

   With this information in hand, compare the amount of attention given to each accessory in the store with the attention it receives from fashion editors.

2. Write to an apparel designer whose name has been associated with a line of accessories. The names can be easily obtained by observing merchandise in a store that carries designer labels. Ask about the merchandising arrangements for the accessories. Are they, for example, owned by the company producing the apparel or are they licensed ventures? Either through the use of a press kit, which many designers publish, or through a company representative, determine the extent of the accessories collections, price points, and methods of promotion.

The Case of the Properly Positioned Accessory

As in all department stores, accessories at N.J. Tompkins are divided into specific departments. Shoes, for example, are in their own department; belts, scarves, and handbags share a department; jewelry and hosiery often share a common area; and so forth.

The major emphasis at Tompkins has been ready-to-wear. Although the accessories they carry are given great attention, until recently, their sales volume paled by comparison to that in the clothing areas. The increased attention being paid to the accessories by the editors of the fashion columns has prompted the company to consider plans that would bolster its sales. One is to rearrange the selling floors and place all wearable accessories on the second floor at a point where the various apparel departments converge. This way, the woman purchasing a dress will be in close proximity to jewelry, handbags, hosiery, and other enhancements. Dissident voices argue that such a move would jeopardize "pure" accessories sales that are traditionally main-floor based.

Another suggestion being considered is to establish small accessories "satellites" within apparel departments. Some shoes, handbags, gloves, and so on would be available for sale in each apparel area. Management has yet to give its opinion on these ideas.

With the accessories market expanding through designer licensing agreements and the fashion forecasters heralding these items as wardrobe "musts," N.J. Tompkins must reach a decision on how to better merchandise its accessories.

Questions

1. What are the advantages and disadvantages of the two suggestions for the repositioning of accessories?

2. What other way might the company motivate greater interest in accessories?

point of view

A Style Is Born

Bonnie Baber

More and more, it seems fashion imitates more than it creates. Footwear design in the '90s has assumed new dimensions. Some call it styling and personalizing the trend of the moment, others defend the art of design. But all in all, isn't the goal to sell a look?

While the fashion spin cycle is forever shortening, and fresh, fast looks are more crucial than ever to spurring consumer fervor, designing is like one big guessing game—timing is crucial. Footwear designers must be adept at assembling all the mixed messages and striking with a look when the time is right.

Many differ on their interpretations of what it means to design. While some insist on designing "freely," ignoring trends, and carving a path as leaders, many others are simply interested less in this, and more in deriving a commercial, marketable look.

Italian designer Ernesto Esposito, Fiesso D'Artico, Italy, perceives a difference between style and creativity in his design philosophy. "Before, we needed creativity, now . . . it's a matter of proposing the right style at the right moment. Fashion was creative when it was born, but now it's a method."

In turn, fashion has gotten specialized, segmented and group-specific. The climate becomes even more treacherous for design as comfort and lifestyle, over couture, become the main concern of consumers.

Fratelli Rossetti, Parabiago, Italy, has believed in maintaining its own style rather than chasing trends. "Not all trends can be followed," Diego Rossetti, president, said.

"Today, fashion is one. For market reasons, the best designers convey a look which grows and matures in time, but which they do not change," he added, mentioning Giorgio Armani and Gianni Versace as examples.

To other designers, it is a question of designing with a special customer in mind. "It is more important for us to create a design, but we never allow ourselves to forget the taste level of the woman we are targeting for our lines," said Charna Garber, president of D'Rossana, New York. "She's never had a name, but we talk about her—her work, her lifestyle, her personal life, her age and her reactions to everything going on in America."

While D'Rossana produces footwear that doesn't seem to stoop to any rules, it is an example of a well-oiled company that niches its product for ease of marketing. Said Garber, "We 'guess right' more than we guess wrong, fortunately because we don't try to be everything, but to fill a niche with this 'wonder woman' we know so well."

For Robert Clergerie, Romans, France, simplicity is key to a unique design. "I keep my collection very simple. When your idea is not strong, your design is always complicated. When your idea is strong, the expression of the idea is simple. So my goal has been to make simple shoes and work on proportion—that gives Clergerie shoes a special look . . . Elegance has to be discreet," he maintained.

Clergerie, however, doesn't agree that simplicity sells more shoes. "The quantity you can sell will always be limited, but some people

will love them enough to buy them. I try not to make a style that will be reserved only for a select few. Not the kind of shoes that you buy and can only wear once."

He thought it was important to know that he has the same line in every country. He feels his shoes are basic enough to appeal to people without changing them to attract more business . . . "Small is beautiful," he said. "If you want a personal collection, you must accept that some people will hate it. If you grow too big in an attempt to get more of the market or a bigger market, you lose your personality."

For Joseph Azagury, London, it is not so much a question of finding a design, but creating a look that will be influential and commercial. "When I have decided on a last shape and heel, the ideas for the actual designs are easy to come up with and are limitless," he said. "At the moment there are many different messages coming from all directions, but at the end of the day I have to go on instinct. I find that when something looks right straightaway, it is generally correct. It is always harder trying to work on something I don't feel good about."

Plotting a salable design is also the goal of Nancy Geist, who designs for Zeitgeist and Cynthia Rowley in New York: "Within my circle, there's a buzz . . . a distinct 'feel' to the moment in fashion . . . I cover myself by presenting "commercial footwear," but I always test one cutting-edge baby."

Guessing Right

In an era where selling shoes is crucial to survival, and when the final judgment lies in the eyes of the consumer, designers must track the pulse of the market now that it is more crucial than ever to "guess right." To do this, they must be, in effect, "street wise"—in sync with trends, plugged into the multitudes and what they want to wear.

"Guessing right on all the trends out there is difficult. I end up doing what I think is right and possible within my constraints," said Amy Buckner, president of Amiana, New York.

Most designers believe that trends are almost always a base on which to build their product. It is information—magazines, television —that often helps them feel prepared when facing the quick changes around them, according to Giuseppe Zanotti of Casadei, San Mauro Pascoli, Italy. "Partly, our work is optimized through market laws. But our instinct allows us to articulate the collections and aim them for women in all their different stages of life."

Paris designer Michel Perry said analysis of all the current influences, mixed with past experiences, is what gives birth to new trends. "Influences and *l'air du temps* are filtered through the personality of each designer. In what concerns me, a note of humor and provocation personalize each of my shoes," he said. "Intuition is very important. It permits me to guess correctly most of the time."

Many designers, though quick to use the words instinct and intuition, hesitate to call it "guessing." Maud de Marco of Ombeline, Fosso, Italy, is one. "Nothing is easy. We swim in a certain ambiance, so it's not really a question of guessing. It's a question of living and what we see, and then adapting.

"We live among all people and with all things, so designs are a mixture of everything," de Marco continued. "One must adapt to trends, but also do what we like."

Since fashion is a market-driven profession, creating for pure pleasure is a luxury few designers can afford. "I have to trust my own talent, instincts and research. I think everything I do is valid, but the consumer is the one who ultimately decides," said Geist. But, she added, "As a designer I feel that I can start the next trend . . . or why create?"

Buckner said she *is* her customer, so she has a good feeling for what will do well. " I don't care if it is not being done anywhere else," she said.

Likewise, the La Gaubretiere, France-based Rautureau brothers, Yvon and Guy, said they, too, create different shoes with the "humility to admit that the consumer is the last to decide the 'rightness' of a creation."

To the Rautureaus, who, unlike Geist, liken themselves to "sponges," "guessing" during the past five years hasn't been too difficult, considering the success of their Free Lance and Pom d'Api lines. But then there's always the next season to worry about.

"It is the consumers who tell us through buying or not buying our shoes. [And we're] lucky to have the best clients in the world. . . . Because it is in having the best, most professional and most difficult that we are the most stimulated to always make the best possible design," said Yvon.

In the end, though, the Rautureaus' unique design is a combination of "savoir-faire, hope and work." Said Yvon: "We are a special case in that we design and produce . . . four recognizable lines that have a certain special 'touch,' a style, a 'bill of sale.' "

Sifting Through Trends

Designer Andrea Pfister usually retires to Positano, Italy, for four months to prepare his shoe collections. He finds it useful to read fash-

ion magazines—of which he collects issues from the 1920s—and watch people walking on the streets, not as a source of inspiration or to copy, but to see what has been done.

"Everything has been done already," said Pfister, who lives in Vigevano. "Our job is to re-interpret the past at the right moment and the right way.

Michaela and Stefano Pancaldi, owners of Pancaldi, Bologna, Italy, also maintain that designers revert to the past for their inspiration. "The Chanel shoe, for example, has been designed by everybody, but each designer changed it through his own style and creativity. As with art movements, each artist interprets the initial idea with his own technique and own spirit. Impressionists, for example, were all different from each other and so were cubists. This happens with designers as well," said Michaela.

Pfister, though, in the end, considers design as "something in the air." Of course, one must be informed, he said, but designers have to think out their ideas before the ready-to-wear clothes collections appear on the runways, so they must be intuitive, and have a feeling for what will be successful.

For Patrick Cox, London, the formula for getting started on a collection begins with a simple silhouette—the loafer. "I usually start by designing Wannabes, which are a weird phenomenon because they seem to go with whatever the latest fashion trend is. Each season I expect it to be the last, but the loafer seems to just always be relevant for some really weird reason.

"Wannabes are so much about color; the stitching and the sole, and they're easy to do. I then do the men's because whatever I design is basically what I would wear. Last comes the women's main collection, and that's where I can go really wild because that's meant to be really cutting-edge."

Spotting ready-to-wear trends early is important for Clergerie, who designs one year before his collection comes out (he is just finishing the design on the next winter collection now). "We just try to imagine how women will be dressed the following season. Will she be wearing a short skirt or a long skirt? Will it be something close to her body or not? Then we try to find a shoe that is close to what we imagine," he said.

Esposito, who has also been designing his own apparel line for the past 20 years, sees his footwear as a "true accessory" that must complement the clothes. Since the clothing is designed far earlier, Esposito said he designs the shoes as a consequence, and knowing the clothes' colors and fabrics makes it easy to adjust and conform to the general trend.

Mixed Messages

Fashion, more now than at any other time, has evolved into a truly global monstrosity. No one designer is immune from the hype surrounding the threads of the moment and the worldwide network of influences. How they cull through a sea of disparate meanings and assemble the jigsaw puzzle of influentials gives birth to a directional fashion trend. So, how do they synthesize all the messages? Pared-down and in classic good taste, Ferragamo is a company that focuses on a common thread running through the industry, and that very marketable, wearable direction is what it aims to express. And yes, ready-to-wear plays a big part in the process, said Fiamma Ferragamo, director of Fer-

ragamo's women's shoe division.

Finding a common ground is necessary for the Rautureaus. "Our collections must 'function' in New York, Milan, Paris, Tokyo. . . . We create our own style which must normally function in different silhouettes in all the different cities," said Yvon.

Esposito believes trends today are universal, and that designers in general are even more popular outside their own country. He attends fashion shows in Paris, Milan and New York, where he believes all trends are synthesized. "The focus is in New York," he said. "There is a gap of a month between the Milan and New York shows. In New York, we see a confirmation and a selection of what was shown on European runways. Designers present the best of all the different trends and it's all simplified."

Perry, meanwhile, claims to not be influenced by runway fashions, since "my shoe collections come out at the same time as the ready-to-wear collections," he said.

Vigevano, Italy-based designer Armando Pollini believes, since his collections are international, fashion messages coming from European cities can coexist. Pollini then merges these messages to create his own modern and personal line. "It's essential for a designer to define an individual and recognizable style," he said.

Pfister believes that, today, there is a new freedom of ideas, but that there is a common thread coming from Milan, Paris, London and especially New York. In fashion, there are returning cycles. "More or less, we all do the same thing."

But ideas that are seen in other countries don't always work for the American consumer, according to Buckner. And likewise with American fashion in other countries. "Only through experience can a designer know what will work and what will not," she said.

Gauging Success

Designers must measure the success of their work. Often they look to each other to decipher whether they are on the right track.

Esposito, who said the best quality in a designer is humility, defines exactly what it means to design in the '90s: "We must look around us and be up to date. We watch other designers, are watched by them and we all compare our work."

Cox had an interesting anecdote to offer on the subject of viewing others' work: "As recently as four or five years ago I was really struggling in business and would look at what other designers had done. I'd inject some element of that into my collection to try to cover every trend and get orders. But as I get more success I just say, 'Forget it, I do what I do.'

"If I find a material someone else is planning to use, I don't. I am now at the stage where I have to lead, not follow. I'm now working with a tannery in Italy to give them color ideas and help with new leathers and that's a tremendous advantage because I'm ending up using a lot of those leathers exclusively in my collection. The whole part of being a designer is to lead the trends and that's what I'm now able to do."

Footwear News, February 5, 1996. With contributions from James Fallon and Ruth Gurevitch (London), Luisa Zargani (Milan) and Christine Eufinger (Paris).

Jewelry & Watches

Wendy Hessen

In a society ever more pressured to pick up the pace, it's clear that time is important to everyone these days.

Watches account for 80 percent of the brands in this category—ranging from Casio, which can be bought on the run at a neighborhood convenience store or pharmacy, to Rolex, which is reserved for the quieter salons of the best jewelers.

Regardless of their age or where they go to purchase a watch, consumers think of Timex first when they think of watches, making its long-standing slogan, "It takes a licking and keeps on ticking," even more appropriate today. Not only is the brand tops in the jewelry and watch category, the name has risen in the overall rankings from seventh position two years ago to the second spot this year.

Increased advertising—up nearly $8 million in the last two years alone—and new technology have paid big dividends for Timex recently. The witty Indiglo campaign and products like its multi-function Ironman series and latest high tech entry, Datalink, have kept consumers coming back to one of the oldest names in the business.

After Timex, the next two names that are best known among all consumers are Seiko and Rolex. Unfortunately for their manufacturers, the reasons these names are known are not always the most optimistic. Seiko ranked in the top three for all age groups, as did Rolex, except among 50-to-64-year-olds, who ranked it fourth.

The Seiko ranking is particularly interesting since it represents a segment of the watch business—with prices generally above $200—that retailers say has been buffeted at retail of late largely by the still-hot fashion watch category. Seiko is hoping to spark some renewed interest in its product and the category with its recently launched Kinetic line, the first quartz watch that doesn't need a battery.

Rolex has been known for nearly a century as the luxury timepiece of the highest quality and is still in demand worldwide. However, even its exceptionally secretive Swiss makers would have to acknowledge that part of its wide visibility is due to the fact that it's one of the most counterfeited brands around. While nearly impossible to gauge what effect the knockoffs have had on the sale of real Rolexes, in the end, they may have only served to boost recognition of the name—and aspiration for the product—more than ever.

Other names that scored with consumers of all ages include Bulova, Casio, Cartier, Citizen and Swatch.

Bulova appeals to an increasingly older customer, and Casio gets the most attention from the 31-to-49-year-old set. Both Cartier and Citizen, however, are on the rise among their established clientele, and Citizen in particular has gained awareness among people under 30. Citizen's rise could be the result of its recent ad campaign which, although hardly hip, does have a younger attitude than its previous campaigns.

According to retailers, in the last several years Swatch hasn't been selling at the furious clip that it did in the Eighties, but with all consumers except the oldest group placing it among the top five, lagging department store sales don't appear to have adversely affected the name. In addition to a recent injection of fashion looks, Swatch will be the official timekeeper at next year's Summer Olympic Games in Atlanta, which the company hopes will put it back on top of consumers' minds here.

Hamilton, Omega and Gruen showed up only among 50-to-64-year-olds. These companies made their mark during World War II and shortly after and may have had their heyday unless they start to focus specifically on the next generation of consumers.

The only two jewelry names making the list, Cartier and Tiffany, are from the high end of the market, giving even more credence to the idea that women are looking for lasting value in their purchases these days. It seems that having "the look of real" may be no substitute for the real thing.

Cartier and Tiffany are also retailers, often with stores in high traffic malls and tourist cities, which further bolsters recognition. Tiffany is in the midst of a long-range expansion plan that calls for several new stores in the U.S. each year, and Simon Critchell, Cartier's president and chief executive officer, recently reported that U.S. sales are running about 30 percent ahead of last year.

The only fashion jewelry line making The Fairchild 100 was Monet, which scored with 10 percent of women in the 31-to-49 age range, a big change from two years ago, when Monet scored with 80 percent of women across the board.

CHAPTER 11

Details and Trimmings

After you have completed this chapter, you should be able to discuss:

• How details are used to differentiate one design from another.

• Five different details that are used in garment construction.

• The differences between details and trimmings.

• Six different types of trimmings used as apparel and accessories enhancements.

• The difference between functional and decorative trimmings.

If apparel and accessories were designed without ornamentation or enhancements, they would lose much of their appeal. A dramatic neckline, intricate pockets, and a smocked or pleated bodice are distinguishing features that give a design its character. These and other artistic treatments are known as **details.** They visually enhance fashion merchandise and sometimes increase functionality.

Trimmings, similarly, play an important role in the creation of fashion merchandise. Decoratively, they provide the pizzazz that often transforms the mundane silhouette or shape into something exciting. The intricate beading that brings individuality to a Judith Leiber evening bag, the appliqués that have become the signature of Tickle Me! children's clothing, and the magnificent flowers that adorn Kökin's millinery creations are just some of the trimmings that help distinguish their designs. These and other adornments provide the fashion designer with "extras" that make the final designs unique.

Some trimmings, known as findings, are also functional elements. This category includes zippers, shoulder pads, interfacings, and threads. Although they generally do not play an important visual role, they are necessary for proper fit and appearance.

Some trimmings are both decorative and functional. Buttons, for example, may be used for closure, but unusual-shaped or oversized versions also become a design feature. Similarly, colored threads may be used to decorate intricate stitching that enhances a garment's eye appeal.

Trimmings can transform this hat into an exciting fashion design.

In the end, it may be the eye-catching quilting, tucks, pockets, buttons, fancy appliqués, braided trim circling the base of a sleeve, little lace collars, rows of colorful ribbons, nailheads, and embroideries that make a particular design successful. Without these tricks of the trade, designs would have less originality.

DETAILS

The designer picks from a variety of numerous decorative and functional elements when creating a garment, including sleeves, necklines, draped effects, flounces, tucks, seams, collars, pockets, and quilting. It is the manner in which these elements are employed that gives individuality to the garment or accessories. Knowing which to choose, how many to use, and applying them in a manner that highlights the other elements of the design is a constant challenge for designers.

Sleeves

Sleeves are both functional and decorative and come in a variety of styles and lengths. Among the most popular sleeve designs are the **bell sleeve** that flares into a soft bell-like shape; the **cap sleeve** that extends on the front and back, covering the shoulders; the **dolman,** featuring a wide armhole that tapers at the wrist; the **kimono sleeve,** cut in one piece with front and back of the garment; the **raglan sleeve** that extends to the neckline, set in by seams slanting from underarm front and back; and the **set-in sleeve,** which is a fitted sleeve sewn into the armhole.

Dropped shoulders and set-in sleeves regularly appear in fashion collections.

Necklines

Necklines are an important element of garment design because they highlight the face and neck. The variations are numerous, ranging from high to low to strapless. One is the basic **jewel neckline,** which is a high, round design. It is an opening at the top of the garment and fits close to the body. Its name is derived from the idea that it is easily adorned with a strand of pearls or other jewels.

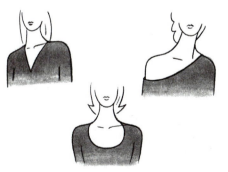

The **bateau neckline** is styled straight from one shoulder to the other. It is sometimes referred to as a boat neckline. Like the jewel neckline, it is collarless.

The **square neckline** employs either a square or rectangular shape that is cut out of the bodice of the garment. It is generally reserved for evening wear or for warm weather attire.

A **surplice neckline** is one in which one piece of fabric wraps over the other to give a dramatic effect.

Necklines come in many styles and variations.

The **turtleneck** is a high rolled-over configuration that fits snugly against the neck and is actually an extension of the body of the garment. It is most often used in knitwear and may be found in apparel worn for daytime and evening. A variation is the **mock turtle.** This is a high neck that simulates the turtleneck, but does not roll over. Sometimes it is considered a collar rather than a neckline.

The **cowl neckline** rolls like a turtleneck, but does not fit snugly. It drapes down in front and gives a more casual appearance.

A **V neck** resembles the letter for which it is named. It is used in varying degrees of openness, with the most daring plunging to the waistline.

The **one shoulder** design adds drama to garments. One shoulder is covered; the other is exposed.

A **halter neckline** is high in the front and open in the back. It is used for evening wear and warm weather apparel. The **keyhole** variety takes its name from a door's keyhole, whose design it imitates.

Designers use these and other types of necklines in a number of ways to emphasize their clothing designs. Necklines may be embellished with a variety of trimmings or left unadorned.

Collars

A collar is a design feature that frames the face and draws attention to it. Unlike the neckline, which is part of the garment, a collar is an extra piece of fabric attached to apparel at the neckline. Although there are many styles to choose from, collars are categorized as either **flat,** like the Peter Pan, **stand-up** like the mandarin, or **rolled,** as in the case of the **cowl.** More specific names are based on their shapes or some costume from which they have been adapted. The **sailor collar,** for example, derives its name from the collar on a sailor's middy.

The following terms are used to describe a collar:

- stand: the part of the collar from the neck edge to the line where it rolls over to the front.
- roll line: the edge at which the stand turns into the front of the collar.

First introduced in the sixteenth century, collars became popular in the nineteenth century on men's coats and shirts. In the twentieth century, a variety of new styles of collars began to adorn men's, women's, and children's apparel.

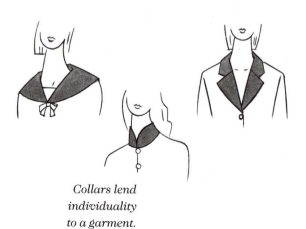

Collars lend individuality to a garment.

A **shawl collar** is a one-piece design that eliminates the seam used on the traditional collar and lapel. It may be single- or double-breasted. It is used in a variety of women's suit and jacket designs, as well as on men's tuxedos. The shawl may be abbreviated and end at the middle of the front of a jacket or extend all the way to the waistline.

The **Mandarin** is a stiff, narrow band that fits close to the neck. As its name implies, it is fashioned after the collar detail of an Asian style jacket. A variation is the Nehru, which derives its name from the jacket worn by India's Prime Minister Nehru.

The **Peter Pan collar** is a small, flat type with rounded edges often used in children's apparel.

The **draped collar** consists of two pieces of soft material that fall in folds from the neckline.

The **Eton** is a large collar that is generally made of a stiff fabric. It is fashioned after the collar worn by students at Eton College in Great Britain.

A **sailor collar** plunges to a "V" in the front, with a tab under the "V," and is square in the back. The collar is finished with an appropriate sailor's tie.

A **convertible collar** can be worn closed at the neck or open. When it is worn open, the finished lapels lie flat against the blouse or shirt. The collar is most often pointed, but sometimes rounded models are used.

Other collars include the **Bertha,** which forms a cape over the shoulders, the **Puritan,** a large collar fashioned after Pilgrim dress, the **Quaker,** a flat, broad collar, and the **funnel,** the shape of which flares out slightly at the top of the neck.

Bows

Although some **bows** may be used as fasteners, their purpose is primarily decorative. They are employed in a variety of sizes and shapes; the choice and placement are left to the creativity of the designer. The result can be "floppy," if a sheer such as chiffon is the fabric of choice, or "stiff," if a crisper fabric such as taffeta is employed.

For blouses, the placement may be high on the neck, or low, just below a plunging collar. In dresses, an oversized bow may be used as a detail on the back that lends drama to the design. Sometimes bows are formed at the waistline of a skirt where the two ends of a sash are tied together. The fabrics used for the bows are often the same as for the garment itself, but may also be of contrasting material or color.

Bows are generally utilized at either the neck or waist, and create a softness to the garment.

Pockets

Pockets are both functional and decorative, and come in a variety of types. They may be constructed as separate pieces and sewn to the garment, or may be created as part of the garment. In the latter case, the pocket is concealed. Some of the more commonly used types include the following.

Patch pockets adorn men's, women's, and children's fashions. They are staples on blazer jackets. The construction involves sewing a separate piece of fabric over a portion of the garment. The piece is stitched on three sides, with the top open. The patch pockets that are found on men's jackets serve as the place in which a silk or cotton handkerchief may be inserted for decorative purposes. There are variations of the patch, including one that has a cuff on the upper edge, the kangaroo type that features an inverted pleat, and the pouch that employs gathers for decorative fullness. Designers often create variations on patch pockets, using such elements as decorative stitching, zippers, draping, welts, button-down closures, and flaps.

The **slash pocket** is merely an opening in a garment that is finished by machine or hand. An "inside" pocket is then suspended from the finished

machine. This pocket is found in pants and garments where attention to the pocket is not significantly important.

Pleats

Basically, there are four types of pleats—the accordion pleat, box pleat, inverted pleat, and knife pleat. Each involves folds of fabric that have been either pressed or stitched to form the desired shape. Pleats may be used as the design of an entire skirt or dress, or as accents on almost any part of a garment. Designers such as Fortuny and Mary McFadden use the **crystal pleat,** the tiniest of all pleats, to capture the fashion world's attention.

More commonly used pleats are the **accordion pleat,** which is often used for an entire skirt. The top is generally stitched to the waistband, with the pleats hanging down. Today's miracle fibers help pleats retain their shapes even after cleaning. The accordion pleat may also be used as neckline accents, in a variety of fabrics. If a stand-up look is required, a stiff material such as taffeta may be pleated.

Skirts that are pleated often use the **box pleat,** which is created with two knife pleats that face in opposite directions. The **inverted pleat,** generally found on skirts and dresses, in varying lengths, involves the placement of two pleats that face each other. The **knife pleat** is folded in the desired width and then left to fall straight. Fabric is available to designers already pleated, in any desired length.

Pleats add elegance to silhouettes.

Cowls

The use of **cowls** is a design detail in which the fabric falls in soft folds. It often adds drama to a design and serves to camouflage the body when it is desired. Certain fabrics, such as matte jersey, chiffon, fine woolen, and velvet, are well-suited for cowls. The draped effect is maximized by cutting the material on the bias, or the diagonal. In this technique, the fabric is cut where the warp or lengthwise yarns intersect with the filling or crosswise yarns.

Cowls may be used in a portion of a garment, such as the neckline, for a skirt, or for a whole dress. The latter is generally reserved for evening wear.

Gathers

Like cowls, **gathers** are used in a variety of places on a garment to achieve extra fullness. For this purpose, the designer must plan for one to two times the usual amount of material. The fuller the gathers, the more fabric required. When a soft material is used, the fabric falls softly. When a stiffer material, such as taffeta, is the choice, the gathers will produce a stand-away effect.

Gathers are produced by sewing the fabric only on one end of the fabric. The remainder is left to fall loosely, to be shirred down the

Supple fabrics are draped to create cowls.

center of a dress at its waistline for a "corseted" fit, to be draped to one side, or to be attached at the top and bottom of the material—such as from the yoke of a blouse to its waistline—to give a dramatic effect. It is the creative designer who employs gathers in interesting ways.

Quilting

Taken from the various techniques used on bed comforters, quilting is used on fashion apparel and accessories. A "puffed up" effect is created by stitching a design on two layers of fabric with padding inserted between them. In quilting, patterned materials often follow a specific design, while solids use different types of motifs. A designer may quilt an entire garment, or may quilt just sections, such as collars and cuffs, to create a detail accent.

Seams

While **seams** are generally used to join two pieces of fabric as unobtrusively as possible, they may also be used as design details. In gloves, for example, **over-seaming** is often used to impart a sporty effect. A **piped seam** is another type of detail that provides design interest. The fabric, cut on the bias, covers a cord, the width of which determines the thickness of the piping. Hand-stitched seams are sometimes used on lapel and collar edges for a casual look.

Tucks

These details, which are both functional and decorative, give specific shape to a garment. A strategically placed tuck can help to accentuate the bustling of a bodice. For decoration, several rows of tucks may run parallel to each other, creating an interesting effect. The width of the tucks vary according to the designer's concept.

Miscellaneous Details

In addition to those details already discussed, others are used in fashion merchandise. **Smocking**, a technique that involves the stitching of small patterns, is used extensively as detail on girl's apparel. **Shirring** is a detail created by using elastic thread that runs row after row on a garment and produces a controlled fullness. **Rouleau** is a decorative detail produced by encircling heavy piping with bias cut fabric and using the piping in interesting patterns around such places as button closures. **Vents** are openings of various lengths that are used at skirt and dress hemlines, and in jackets to provide room for movement. **Jabots** are loosely hanging ruffles at the front of a blouse.

TRIMMINGS

A walk through any well-stocked trimming supplier reveals an endless array of enhancements that can add an extra touch to a designer's creation. Trimmings are so important that many manufacturers and designers have trimmings buyers who scout the market for them. In other companies, where trimmings have become the designer's signature, the designer researches the selections personally. In either case, the final choice concerning the trim is made by the

Trimmings, such as ribbon, are used to accent many garments.

designer. The right choice can certainly add to the attractiveness of the garment and its ultimate success in a collection.

The decorative trimmings most frequently used are fabrics, embroidery, beading, buttons, glitter, belts, appliqués, fringes, and buckles. Trimmings that are also functional include zippers, thread, interfacings, and elastic.

Fabric Trims

Every conceivable type of knitted, woven, or crocheted fabric is produced in narrow strips for application as a trim. The lace edging in lingerie, the bands of velvet and ribbons that circle the sleeves and hemlines of a garment, and the contrasting pipings—strips of fabrics that are rolled and sewn into narrow bands, are just some examples of fabric trims.

Braid

Braiding involves interlacing three or more yarns or strips of fabric to produce a narrow, decorative trim. The process resembles the braiding of hair. Gold metallic braid is a favorite choice when a military look is in fashion.

Appliqué

Small, individual pieces of fabric are often used to create a decoration. When the cut-out pieces are sewn or fastened to larger pieces of fabric to form trim, it is called **appliqué.**

Lace

Dresses, intimate apparel, bridal gowns, and sweaters are just some of the apparel designs that are decorated with lace. Lace is available from markets all over the globe, with choices ranging from the finest, detailed variety to types that are heavily textured. Lace trim is sold on "cards" and is available in widths that usually range from $1/4$ inch to 3 or 4 inches. The use of lace trim varies from season to season. Except for lingerie and bridal wear, it is most popular for summer merchandise.

Embroidery

Various yarns are used to decorate or embroider a garment. **Embroidery** can be hand sewn, or produced by machine. The threads used may be in the same coloration as the fabric it enhances or in a contrasting color to create interest. Intricately embroidered designs are produced with schiffli machines that can apply the most intricate pattern in any direction. Organdy and batiste, two widely used sheer fabrics, are often **schiffli embroidered.**

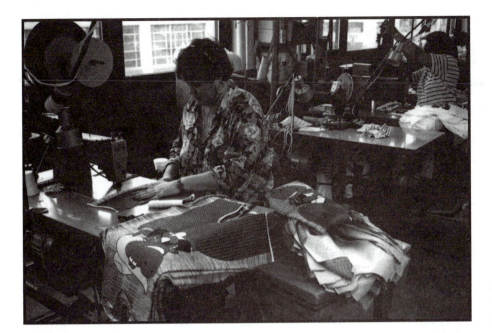

Appliqués are decorative elements to the finished product.

Beading

In seasons when glitter and sparkle are emphasized, **beading** is a popular method of decoration. Glass and metal beads in a variety of sizes, shapes, and colors are applied by hand or machine. The cost of intricate hand-beading has become prohibitively expensive in the United States. As a result, manufacturers may have the entire garment or accessory manufactured offshore. They may also choose to produce the basic garment domestically and then ship it overseas, where labor costs are lower, for beading. The majority of the beading found on evening wear is produced in Asia.

Beading is a favorite attention-getting decoration.

Sequins are often added to designs worn for festive occasions such as holidays and parties. This photo illustrates a worker at a sequin factory checking for imperfections.

Sequins

Small, circular, metallic disks that reflect the light are called **sequins.** They come in a variety of sizes and colors and are used extensively for evening wear. Sequins are a particular favorite for holiday collections.

Rhinestones

Small bits of glass that have been cut to resemble diamonds and other precious and semiprecious stones are called **rhinestones.** Set in "prongs" that are attached to the fabric, they provide a mirror-like sparkle that reflects the light. Rhinestones come in a variety of cuts and sizes. Evening apparel, handbags, and jewelry make extensive use of rhinestone trim.

Buttons

Although buttons serve as decorative and functional design details, they can also be used to trim a garment. They can easily transform a basic design into one of interest. Buttons are available in pearl, wood, metal, glass, leather, bone, and so on, in all sizes and shapes. Fine garments are usually decorated with buttons made of natural materials. In less expensive garments, natural mother-of-pearl is replaced with plastic and leather with vinyl. If a self-covered button is required, the apparel producer usually sends fabric to a button contractor who then covers each button with the supplied fabric. Where exposed buttons are to be used as unobtrusively as possible, a covered button is often the choice.

Threads, in a variety of types, are both functional and decorative components of garments.

Belts

Belts, other than those purchased separately in accessories departments, are used as functional, decorative additions to dresses, suits, pants, and ensembles. Because it is part of apparel design, the belt is usually inexpensively constructed. Many are made of vinyl, inexpensive leathers, or other contrasting materials, such as rope or chain. In cases where self-covered belts are required, the garment manufacturer supplies the fabric to a contractor for final construction.

Belts for trimmings are either stitched or glued to base materials. The stitched variety produces a more durable product.

Zippers

Used primarily as fasteners, **zippers** sometimes add decoration to a design. They come in a variety of lengths and materials. Nylon provides lightness as well as strength, and the major domestic producer is Talon.

Decorative Labels

Labels, usually used on the inside of a garment, came into their own as status-providing identifiers for fashion designers during the 1970s. Designer jeans proudly displayed the creator's name on the back pocket for quick recognition. Today, some companies still use the label on the outside as a means of identifying their garments.

Whether it is used inside or out, the label designs are carefully conceived and produced; woven labels are the choice for quality garments.

Thread

Choosing the appropriate **thread** for a garment or accessory is important to its quality and durability. Thread comes in a variety of yarns and is manufactured by the yarn producer. Before the use of manufactured fibers, threads were made of natural fibers, such as cotton and silk. Today, manufactured fibers offer greater choice and more varied characteristics. In addition, the growing use of manufactured fibers requires use of these more flexible threads. With the elasticity of wovens and knits, for example, thread with a more elastic nature was required. The use of polyester thread supplies that strength necessary to withstand the stretch of manufactured and knit fabrics.

Thread comes in cones for use in manufacturing. The cones hold anywhere from 1,200 to 2,400 yards, come in a variety of thicknesses and basic and fashion colors.

Interfacings

Interfacings are functional trimmings used to give shape and support to garments and accessories. They are not seen by the eye, but are used between the outside layer of the garment and the lining. Collars and lapels on men's suit jackets, for example, are generally enhanced with stable interfacings that can be woven or nonwoven. They may be held in place by sewing them into the garment or by fusing them. The fused method, which is faster and cheaper, is generally employed in less costly products.

When interfacings are needed for knitwear, stretch-knit interfacings are employed because they are less rigid or stable than the other variety.

Elastic

When gathering is needed at the wrist of a blouse or when shirring is the detail on a bodice, elastic is often used by the manufacturer. Once used primarily to keep the tops of socks from rolling down or for form-fitting swimwear, elastic is now used in a variety of forms for many fashion items. Workout clothing that conforms to the body, bicycle pants, and knit leggings, for example, use elastic thread to sew the components of the garment together.

Consumers are often attracted to garments with unusual closures.

Criscione

Joan and Joanie Criscione are the unique mother/daughter team that has made trimmings the signature of their designs. From the day they opened their company in 1995, they have enjoyed great success.

Joanie, who graduated from the Parsons School of Design at age 19, had one goal—to graduate and open her own business the very same day. In collaboration with her mother, they continue to dazzle audiences with their unusual use of enhancements and embellishments. On basic silhouettes, they arrange rhinestones, beads, nailheads, embroideries, and appliqués in patterns that immediately attract attention.

In the late 1980s, the Crisciones achieved significant success in this highly competitive market with their now famous *stone blazer*. Retailers sold the item so quickly and in such large quantities that it was considered a retail phenomenon. Television celebrities, such as Joan Lunden, Kathie Lee Gifford, and Sally Jesse Raphael, wore the blazers on their shows.

Because of the recognition brought by the trimmed blazer, the company was able to sell its collections, six each year, to more than 1,000 retailers in America, Paris, London, Italy, Holland, and Canada. Each season the trimmings become more and more elaborate and more artistically patterned.

Criscione has demonstrated the power of trimmings. When creatively used, they can turn basic designs into smashing apparel.

Joanne Criscione has made her mark as a designer using a variety of trimmings.

Chapter Highlights

- Details and trimmings can transform a basic garment into one with special appeal.
- Details can be decorative or functional; some serving in both capacities. They include necklines, collars, bows, pockets, pleats, drapes, gathers, quilting, seams, tucks, smocking, and shirring.
- Using one basic body, a designer may create two completely different looks by adding different details to each.
- Trimmings, which further embellish garments and accessories, include embroidery, beading, rhinestones, appliqués, fringes, lace, and belts.
- Functional trimmings are called findings and include zippers, thread, interfacings, and elastic.

Important Fashion Terminology and Concepts

accordion pleat	bell sleeve	cap sleeve
appliqué	Bertha collar	convertible collar
bateau neckline	bows	cowl neckline
beading	box pleat	cowls

crystal pleats	lace	seams
decorative labels	Mandarin collar	sequins
details	mock turtleneck	set-in sleeve
dolman	Nehru collar	shawl collar
draped collar	one-shoulder design	shirring
embroidery	overseaming	slash pocket
Eton collar	patch pocket	sleeves
findings	Peter Pan collar	smocking
funnel collar	piped seam	stand
gathers	pleats	stand-up collar
halter neckline	Puritan collar	surplice neckline
interfacings	quilting	thread
inverted pleat	raglan sleeve	turtleneck
keyhole neckline	rhinestones	vents
kimono sleeve	roll line	V neck
knife pleat	rouleau	zippers
jabot	sailor collar	
jewel neckline	schiffli embroidery	

For Review

1. Describe decorative and functional details. Give examples.
2. Differentiate among the bateau, surplice, and jewel necklines.
3. What are the three basic types of collars used in garment design?
4. In what way does the patch pocket differ from the slash pocket?
5. Which two major designers, one past and one present, have used crystal pleating extensively in their garments?
6. To give greater drapability to a fabric, how must it be cut?
7. Describe the quilting process.
8. Are buttons functional or fashionable?
9. What type of machine is used to embroider intricate patterns in any direction?
10. What fashion trimming was visible on designer jeans in the 1970s?
11. Discuss the importance of interfacings in garment construction.

Exercises and Projects

1. Examine the pages of fashion magazines and select photographs of a variety of necklines used on dresses and blouses. Mount each picture on a foamcore board, labeling each neckline. In an oral presentation to the class, describe the "mood" of each selected style.
2. Visit a trimmings supplier to examine the products available to fashion designers. Most major cities have such shops that are open to the public as well as to industry professionals. Ask for permission to photograph the different types of trimmings, so that you may report about them to your class. You might concentrate on just one type, such as buttons, or choose to explore the whole trimmings field.

The Case of the Classic Silhouette

Questions

1. Is Christy wise in staying with the concept that has brought her fashion recognition?

2. How else might she add a freshness to her collections without the risk of losing her place in the market?

In her first two years as a designer of bridge fashions, Christy Daniels, has made a positive impact on the apparel world. Buyers from the major stores have embraced her collections, which have been profitable for them. Her collections use basic silhouettes with many different fabrics and color harmonies.

Now in her third year of operation, retailers are suggesting that Christy introduce new silhouettes and shapes to attract an even wider market. Although most designers subscribe to regular change, Daniels believes that her strength lies with her basic silhouette, and that there will always be enough business for these classic choices. Her sales manager, however, also believes it is time to try something new. Perhaps, he says, a new silhouette or two should be tried to test the waters. Christy is still shying away from such suggestions and is staying with the concept that has brought success.

point of view

Pivot Links Embroidery and Golfwear

Catherine Salfino

Embroidery is often seen as a nice accent to apparel and accessories. At Pivot Sportware, a golf-driven sportswear company here, embroidery is seen as something that's critical to the firm's business.

"The combination of good artwork with embroidery can significantly improve the sale of a shirt, sweater or sweatshirt," explained Ken Seiff, president.

"It allows us to display certain golf lifestyle images in every fine detail. And the ability to use [the] fine detail of our artwork helps distinguish us from other companies," he continued. "It becomes a part of the whole package. And our apparel, to a certain extent, is bought because of the many details we put into our product, embroidery being one."

Seiff said that just about every product Pivot makes exhibits embroidery, whether it's the company's trademark logo of three golfers, or additional, more elaborate artwork or golf scenes. When an item is more sportswear than golf oriented, the visibility of the logo is minimized, perhaps being placed on a sleeve instead of on the chest, Seiff said.

"But it's still there," he said. "One of the really good things about embroidery is it allows us to differentiate our product from someone else's. We can take a solid-blue shirt and distinguish it from a solid-blue Polo or Hilfiger shirt. Embroidery is, in fact, what has led to Ralph Lauren's ability to command the prices he commands. His logo embodies the lifestyle his ads convey. A department store private-

label product can be sold for $20, whereas branded shirts can be sold for $40 or $50 because branded product builds equity on its ads. Consumers are buying into the lifestyle."

To get consumers to buy into the Pivot lifestyle, one that emphasizes golf, the three-year-old company decided to take a younger, fresher approach to golf apparel. Right from the beginning, part of conveying the fun side of the sport came through in the embroidery.

Pivot's signature logo features three golfers who are embroidered on the right side of the chest. One golfer is in full swing, having just hit a ball—to a flag and hole on the left sleeve. Each embroidered golfer is wearing different colored pants, shirts, hats and shoes. The embroidery is not an outline; it's totally filled in, which calls for a lot of work, Seiff reminded. And that's only the company's signature logo. Pivot uses many other embroidered designs, which change seasonally.

The process of creating the logos is both interesting and exacting. First, director of design Courtney Taylor and the rest of Pivot's design staff come up with the graphics. Then the sketches are sent to the Orient, where Pivot's Hong Kong office oversees the embroidery process.

Seiff noted that it's up to the manufacturing facility to find an embroidery factory, which supervises the creation of what's called an embroidery tape. This is a computerized tape that represents all the stitches, actually plotting all the stitches the embroidery machines

will have to take. Next, the embroidery factory uses the tape to run the graphics onto a piece of fabric.

"That sample is looked over by our Hong Kong office and then they send it back to our design department for approval and changes, which there always are," Seiff added. "Simple things like the direction of the stitches often have to be changed. Sometimes when you really look at the design, you can see that the design would have more intensity if the stitch ran diagonally or vertically. Other times the stitches don't fall exactly within the boundaries they're supposed to, so you don't get a clear image. This is a very important stage, commenting on the embroidery proto-sample."

Next, Seiff's staff sends the sample back to the Hong Kong office, where the employees oversee the changes, and then send another sample back to New York for final approval. Upon approval, the Hong Kong office duplicates the tape and sends a copy to each of its factories that's using the artwork. The number of factories can range from 10 to 15, depending on the different pieces of apparel on which the embroidery will appear.

"That's how we maintain control over the quality of our embroidery," Seiff said. "That way, each factory doesn't have to make a different tape. We can take the approved embroidery tape and be confident that it will be reproduced exactly around the world."

Seiff said it takes about two weeks to make the first computer tape, depending on the complication of the artwork. Most of Pivot's embroidery work is done in Hong Kong. He said when an order is put in, the machines typically run 24 hours without rest. Each embroidery machine is controlled by one technician. The machines have either 18, 20 or 24 heads, so they can do 18, 20 or 24 shirts at a time.

Pivot's product is embroidered before the final item, say a shirt, is pieced together. So, before the shirt is made, the garment factory cuts the fabric into the panels used to make the garment. Then, whichever panel requires embroidery—for example, the front of the shirt or sleeve panel—is sent to the embroidery factory. The fabric panel is set on top of the embroidery table and underneath the embroidery head. A 20-head machine can embroider 20 panels at a time. But before the machine can be started, the technician has to prepare a full set of embroidery threads for each table. When the machine is finally started, it will embroider one color at a time.

Timewise, it would take one machine about four or five days to make 1,200 shirts bearing Pivot's three-man golfer and flag logo. And that's after the embroidery factory has received all the fabric panels and the embroidery threads and after the machine has been set.

Seiff said he prefers to use Japan's Tajima machine for Pivot's finer cotton fabrications, like cotton knits and sweaters. The German ZSK Stick Maschinen Gesellshaft machine is used to embroider heavier weight fabrics like denim. Seiff added that most of his product is embroidered on 18- and 20-head machines. And most of the embroidery machines Pivot uses handle eight colors, although there are some new machines that thread up to 12.

The size of the embroidered graphic is the main factor in the cost, since the size determines the number of stitches that will be required. A simple outline is less expensive than filling in the design. But Pivot always fills in its art, Seiff said.

Although the Tajima machines are usually employed, said hand machines are necessary when appliquéing small pieces of fabric that need to be embroidered around the edges. Pivot uses this technique pretty regularly, especially in pieces like a sweater that depicts embroidered golfers wearing shirts that coordinate with Pivot's actual fall or spring collection.

"The differences with the hand-embroidery machine is that there isn't the ability to exert the same control," Seiff said. "It requires a much more skilled laborer to use the hand machine, and therefore costs go up significantly."

Most of Pivot's embroidery plants are stationed in the Orient. The total number of people involved in the embroidery includes two or three designers in the New York office who design and approve the art; three people in Hong Kong who approve the embroidery tape before they send it to New York; the person who makes the embroidery tape; and the people who actually do the embroidering. The number of machine operators varies, depending on how big an order is, how big the embroidery factory is and how many factories are needed.

Seiff said it takes 90 days from the time an order is placed to get the final embroidered product back. But again, the embroidery portion of this time is only four to five days.

"It's not often a delay in getting the embroidery done," he asserted. "There are a lot of embroidery factories in the Orient; it's a very competitive business over there. Which is good for our business."

Daily News Record, Apparel & Home Technology, March 17, 1994.

Cosmetics and Fragrances

Names like Estée Lauder, Clinique, Cover Girl, Prescriptives, and Lancôme dominate the cosmetics industry; others, such as Obsession, White Diamonds, Chanel No. 5, Opium, Giorgio, and Poison do the same for the fragrance industry.

The use of cosmetics and fragrances, however, are not from recent developments. As far back as 1500 B.C., stibium pencils and *kohl,* a forerunner to mascara, were used to paint and accent the eyelids. In Egypt and Arabia, it was long stylish to paint the underside of the eye green and the lid, lashes, and brows black with kohl.

The Roman Empire adopted the use of cosmetics on an unparalleled scale in history. Charlemagne's conquests then spread the use of cosmetics throughout Europe. The ingredients used to make the cosmetics were so precious that whole Arabic dynasties were founded on the spoils of hijacking the caravans that carried them. Chalk and white lead were used to lighten the skin, and pumice stone to whiten the teeth. Deep rouges colored the cheeks, and henna tinted the hair and fingernails. Even men made significant use of cosmetic products. In pre-Revolutionary America, men colored gray hair in beards,

After you have completed this chapter, you should be able to discuss:

- The history of cosmetics and fragrances from ancient times to the present.

- Many of the marketing innovations that helped the cosmetics industry achieve its success.

- The importance of ethnic cosmetics to the industry.

- The role of private branding in the cosmetics industry.

- The various stages of marketing cosmetics and fragrances.

- The distribution of cosmetics.

Cosmetic counters are often the busiest areas for most retailers.

mustaches, and sideburns with a product called Mascaro, the name from which mascara was derived. In the late eighteenth century, the French first manufactured cosmetics for commercial use by introducing *Rimmel,* a mascara that was popular for decades.

Similarly, natural aromatic substances have been used since ancient times to cure ailments, enhance and beautify the ordinary, and appease the gods. This indulgence reached its height in ancient Egypt. As Cleopatra prepared to meet Marc Anthony, she bathed in rare and fragrant essences; the sails of her ship were lavishly sprinkled with perfumes; and precious incense was burned in gold and silver censers.

Because bathing was a luxury of the rich and sanitation only rudimentary, perfumes, composed of flower pomades, balms, or roots, appeared in France during the Renaissance to hide odors.

By the late 1800s and early 1900s, the cosmetics and fragrance industries had introduced a host of new products. Jean-Marie Farina introduced *eau de cologne* in 1820. This marked the emergence of Paris as the center of fine perfumery. Companies like Houbigant and Roger & Gallet made the first synthetic fragrances. In Chicago, a chemist developed a glossy lash darkener in a tube for a company he named after his sister Mabel—Maybelline.

Currently, cosmetics and fragrances are as important to the world of fashion as are the creations of the most famous couturiers. A look at the counters in fashionable retail operations reveal many familiar names including Calvin Klein, Yves Saint Laurent, Chanel, Ralph Lauren, and Donna Karan. This is a signal that these industries are a huge business with impressive profit potential.

COSMETICS

In the early 1920s, cosmetics were used primarily by sophisticated consumers. During that time, a Hollywood makeup artist, Max Factor, packaged and sold a cake mascara (an eye enhancing product that had to be water moistened) that he had created for the movie industry. From the 1920s through the 1950s, movie stars played an important role in influencing consumers to use cosmetics for everyday use. Some of the products that became popular included foundation, face powder, mascara, eyebrow pencil, cheek color (rouge), lipstick, and nail color. Movie fans often imitated the looks developed for the screen, the makeup of Grace Kelly and Doris Day, for example, was often copied.

However, even at the end of the 1950s, many products were still socially unaccepted. In the social climate of that decade, "nice" girls wore very little cosmetics. With so little popular interest in cosmetics, the industry spent very little time developing new products. A list of the major cosmetic brands prior to 1960 is given in Table 12.1.

Highlights of the Cosmetic Industry

1960s

In the 1960s, the cosmetics industry began a major campaign to reach the mass consumer market. With new and improved items in a wide range of pigments, the cosmetics industry was ready to become a major industry.

As cosmetics became easier to apply and colors looked more natural, the cosmetic industry offered consumers a more enticing packaging. Suddenly people became interested.

TABLE 12.1

MAJOR EXISTING COSMETICS BRANDS, PRIOR TO 1960

Aloe Cream	Fabergé	Maybelline
Avon	Fashion Fair	Merle Norman
Bonne Bell	Germaine Monteil	Natural Wonder
Charles of the Ritz	Hard As Nails	Princess Marcella Borghese
Coty	Harriet Hubbard Ayer	Revlon
Cover Girl	Hazel Bishop	Scandia
Cutex	Helena Rubenstein	Tussy
Dorothy Gray	House of Westmore	Ultima
Elizabeth Arden	John Robert Powers	Ultra Sheen
Estée Lauder	Max Factor	Vogue Cosmetics

In the 1960s, women began to use cosmetics on a regular basis. A number of breakthrough products were introduced, including powder blusher, for the healthy look; powder eyeshadow for ease in application; powder brow color for a natural look; liquid eyeliner to emphasize eyes; translucent powder to eliminate streaking; gels for a hint of color; lip gloss for a high sheen look, and applicators to help the inexperienced apply cosmetics.

In addition to these new products, packaging designers and marketers played an important role for the industry. Among the many new techniques they developed to influence the consumer are the following:

- **Kits.** Instead of selling items only in single colors, kits offered multiple shades for eyeshadows, lipsticks, pencils, blushers, and in some cases, false eyelashes.

- **Fun compacts.** Hot color, plastic compacts gave the products a fashion orientation.

- **Megapack Promotions.** Companies packaged total sets of products for eyes, lips, nails, and cheeks, all in a specific color family.

- **Refillable Packaging.** This enabled the consumer to buy a fresh supply of the product without having to spend money on a new package.

- **New Role Models.** Marketers used famous models instead of movies stars in ads.

- **Gift with a Purchase.** Estée Lauder introduced consumers to new products by offering one free item with the purchase of another.

The loveliest glow of all is yours...with this new liquid make-up!

Revlon 'Touch-and-Glow'

Revlon has something new and wonderful for your complexion . . . liquid 'Touch-and-Glow'! It's never masky . . . never heavy . . . this liquid make-up is blended with Lanolite, to beauty-treat your complexion! With 'Touch-and-Glow' there's no made-up look. It's so natural—nobody knows you wear it but you! Find your glow among 8 exquisite complexion colors . . . and wear Revlon 'Touch-and-Glow' for that radiant, youthful look!

'Touch-and-Glow' 1.25 and 1.75 plus tax

The fabulous flattery of candlelight . . . captured in a liquid make-up!

Multi-million dollar ad campaigns have contributed to the extremely profitable cosmetic market. This Revlon ad is from the 1950s.

By the end of the decade, sales in the cosmetics industry reached new heights. Preservative-free products became available. Through sales in health stores, they helped capture a segment of the market that had previously shied away from cosmetics. Fragrance-free items also made headlines with the new Clinique line. The new formulas, coupled with sleek, contemporary packaging, opened up yet another segment of the market.

1970s

In the 1970s, cosmetics adapted to the new freedom of choice philosophy of the apparel industry. Women were no longer coerced into wearing just one look. The cosmetics industry followed suit by offering a wide variety of styles from makeup that emphasized the natural look to more exciting and glamorous selections. Instead of using famous models and movie stars as role models in advertisements, the individual woman became the focus of attention.

Key words were now used to emphasize the qualities of various products. Among them were oil free, nongreasy, waterproof, conditioning, smearproof, smudgeproof, and microencapsulated moisture. Popular products included such new ingredients as NMF, a natural moisturizing factor, hydrolyzed protein, vitamins such as pantheol, ph balancers, and polymers. Although these ingredients did improve the quality of many items, it was the use of these names in the ads that attracted the attention of the shopper.

Unique packaging dominated the decade. The curved wand made mascara application easier. Oversized wand applicators were introduced. All-in-one friction feed or gravity-feed packages for blush were introduced. Roll-on applicators increased the sale of lip gloss. Transparent lip caps allowed the consumer to see the color.

New products also contributed to increases in sales. Matte and brush-on lipsticks, combination lipstick and lip gloss, overnight lash conditioner, face tints for sheer coverage, and lip glosses with fruit flavors increased sales to new levels.

Unique packaging and a variety of promotions often launch new products in the cosmetics industry.

Other factors that generated excitement included the offer of a free gift with a purchase, Norman Norell's pairing designer lipstick with designer fragrance, and Helena Rubenstein's use of an electronic computer to personalize customer selection of cosmetics with appropriate coloring.

1980s

The baby boomers, who came of age in the 1980s, were responsible for a new wave of cosmetics—skin-care products that offered treatment benefits. The 1980s were a decade of increased spending and greater emphasis was placed on cosmetics.

Innovation abounded and new phrases were introduced to capture the market. Claims like irritant-free, environmentally safe, formulated for contact lens users, safe for sensitive skin, long wearing, fadeproof, and doesn't flake were appearing in every form of advertisement. It was not merely a fashion statement that was being made; it was the benefits that the product's use would impart that took center stage. To motivate the educated and affluent market, ads identified specific ingredients in cosmetics, such as diamond dust, sunscreens, mink oil, collagen, aloe, and optical diffusers.

Packaging became more sophisticated, with the introduction of double-ended products that combined nail color and lipstick, self-sharpening, swivel feed pencils for eyelining, super-slim vinyl compacts, and an air-blush system.

New products that made their way to the market included powder pencils, aerosol face powder, multiple purpose items such as an all-in-one nail color formula containing base and top coat, nail kits for French manicures, brush-on powder lipstick, wet-look nail color, and the return of cake mascara.

In addition to new products, new technology resulted in point-of-purchase computers for skin and makeup analysis. Private label lines became prominent. Custom blended colors hit the market for the first time. Price points escalated at the end of the decade. Finally, there were new marketing approaches, such as infomercials. **Infomercials** are used as TV programs that are paid for by sponsors. Celebrities such as Kathie Lee Gifford extol the virtues of the product. Unlike the one-minute commercial, infomercials run thirty minutes.

1990s

Thus far, the look of the 1990s is decidedly retro, following the trend established by the apparel designers. With the aging of the baby boomers, skin products became prominent. Once again, fashion models such as Claudia Schiffer, Kate Moss, and Linda Evangelista are the role models for consumers.

The growth of the cosmetics industry from the 1960s to the 1990s can be seen from the decade by decade list of new brands in Table 12.2.

Ethnic Cosmetics

One of the fastest growing segments of the industry has been cosmetics designed for specific ethnic groups. **Ethnic Cosmetics** have experienced sales increases of between 50 percent and 75 percent per quarter in most chain

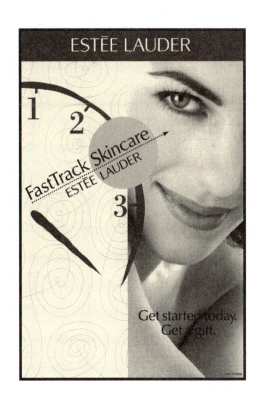

To appeal to a better-informed consumer and compete in a highly competitive market, companies create catchy phrases to sell skin care products.

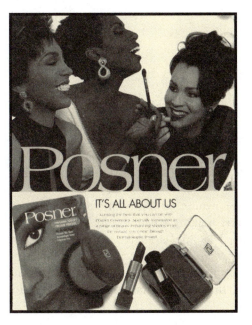

"It's All About Us" targets the American ethnic beauty market.

TABLE 12.2

MAJOR COSMETICS BRANDS INTRODUCED FROM THE 1960S TO THE 1990S

1960s	1970s	1980s	1990s
Almay	Adrien Arpel	Beverly Sassoon	Austin Now
Astarte	Aloette	Biotherm	Beaute Benetton
Biba	Andrea	Chameleon	Black Radiance
Clinique	Baba	Clarion	Bobbi Brown
Clima-Soleil	Calvin Klein	Discipline	Bourjois
Cornsilk	Chanel	Gale Hayman	Clarins
Cyclax of London	Charlie	Gazelle	Colorstyle
Dina Merrill	Christian Dior	Guerlain	Ebone
Eve of Roma	Cosmetiquey	Ilona of Hungary	Erno Laszlo
Eylure	Diane Von	Intelligent	J.F. Lazartigue
Flori Roberts	Furstenberg	Skincare	La Prarie
Germinesse	Halston	Jeanne Piaubert	Linda Mason
Givenchy	Honey & Spice	Jovan	MAC
John and Bee Dee	Il Makiage	Juin Rachel	New Essentials
Kenneth	Indian Earth	Kiehl's	Origins
Lancôme	International	Luminique	Shades of You
Layla	Beauty Club	Naomi Sims	Simply Satin
Lily Daché	Janet Sartin	Orly	Sisley
Longcils	Lancaster	Pola	Tropez
Love	L'Erin	Pupa	
Mary Kay	Lip Quencher	Ralph Lauren	
Mary Quant	L'Oreal	Sothys	
Orlane	Mavala	Tova Borgnine	
Outdoor Girl	Madeline Mono	Trish McEvoy	
Payot	Montage	Victoria Jackson	
Polly Bergen	Norell	Visage Beaute	
Shiseido	Polished Ambers	Yves Saint Laurent	
Stephen Dante	Prescriptives	Zuri	
Viviane Woodard	Redken		
Yardley	Rimmel		
	Rubigo		
	Yves Rocher		

stores. While some attention has been paid to ethnic cosmetics in department stores, such as Fashion Fair Cosmetics, a division of Johnson Publishing Company, little had been done to capture the attention of shoppers through mass merchandising and drug stores. A role model for African-American women is high-fashion model Naomi Campbell.

The Johnson Publishing Company, owners of *Ebony* and *Jet* magazines, have spent considerable time and effort making Fashion Fair Cosmetics the number one line for women of color. The line is sold in more than 2,500 department stores in the United States, Canada, the Caribbean, Europe, and Africa. Because this line is sold mainly in department stores, the company introduced another line called Ebone, that is mass-marketed, at lower-price points.

Apparel Headliners and Cosmetics

Before the 1960s, the cosmetic houses bore names that were associated only with the industry. Famous companies, such as Charles of the Ritz, Estée Lauder, Max Factor, Helena Rubenstein, and Revlon, were strictly involved in producing cosmetics and promoted their names as well as the products they produced.

Beginning in the 1960s, a new trend saw an increased use of famous apparel designer names on cosmetics. Because of the recognition bestowed on these designers, consumers were likely to be attracted to any products that bore their names. Givenchy, the famous French couturier, Lilly Daché, the internationally celebrated milliner, and Mary Quant, the London designer, were the first to cross over into cosmetics. The results were so successful that other apparel designers soon joined their ranks.

In 1970, a host of products were introduced with the names of apparel designers, including Calvin Klein, who gained recognition with his designer jeans collection; Chanel, the world's most famous woman couturiere whose fame skyrocketed even higher with her famous fragrances; Halston, one of America's most creative designers; Christian Dior, one of Paris' notables; and Norman Norell, the leading architect of American fashion. In 1980, the list grew even longer with the addition of Ralph Lauren and Yves Saint Laurent.

By the 1990s, fashion designers who wanted to enter this arena had already done so. Competition in the field was so keen that there was a decrease in the number of apparel designers entering the cosmetics industry.

The trend that is currently generating the most excitement is the establishment of companies headed by makeup artists. The practice is not new. In the 1930s and 1940s, Max Factor parlayed his talents into a major cosmetics company. Today, the makeup artist is taking center stage in the industry.

Bobbi Brown, a leading force in cosmetics, was painting faces as recently as 1990. With her considerable knowledge and support from Bergdorf Goodman, who stocked some of the lipsticks she created, she became a leader in cosmetics. In 1995, her projected wholesale volume was $20 million! Others with similar expertise are getting into the act and blazing new trails for cosmetics.

Bobbi Brown, whose trendy cosmetic line was founded by makeup artists and is owned by Estée Lauder, at work.

Marketing Lines of Cosmetics

With the different brand names and products in the industry, marketing initiatives have become extremely important. Initiatives include new package design, demonstrations of products, personal appearances, samplings, and giveaways.

Packaging

Knowledgeable industry participants freely admit that only a limited number of ingredients can be used to produce cosmetics. With all of the excitement that surrounds advertising campaigns, the only real difference among cosmet-

Marc Rosen

Marc Rosen has been a leading package designer for many years, working for such giants in the industry as Revlon and Elizabeth Arden. After graduating from Carnegie-Mellon and Pratt Institute, he worked for Revlon for four and one-half years. He believes that a "superior, innovative product in beautiful packaging, which can seduce the consumer into wanting to touch it and carry it home is what it's all about." He says that today's global consumer is buying good design and lifestyle, no matter what the product!

After he left Revlon, he further developed his expertise by joining Elizabeth Arden. There he worked closely with such designers as Karl Lagerfeld and the Fendi sisters, for whom he created wonderful packaging. Others for whom he designed unique packaging include Perry Ellis, Oscar de la Renta, Avon, Halston, Princess Marcella Borghese, Chloé, The Limited, and Burberrys.

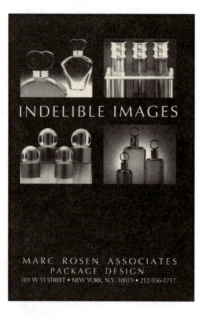

Just one of the many designs for cosmetics packaging by Marc Rosen

His designs have gained international attention. Among the most notable are the fan-shaped crystal decanter for "KL-Women" that won

him the prestigious FIFI Award, the fragrance industry's Oscar, the "Red Door" bottle for the new Arden fragrance, and the glass sphere shaped bottle for "Perry Ellis 360," for which he won another FIFI.

Rosen has also been involved in two highly acclaimed museum exhibitions. In 1979 he created the "Cosmetic Packaging: A 20th Century Art Form" show at the Fashion Institute of Technology in New York City and cochaired the Fragrance Foundation's "Scents of Time" exhibit that traveled nationwide.

For nine years he has written a column for the influential trade magazine, *Beauty Fashion,* and has been associate professor for package design at Pratt Institute's graduate school, where he was presented with the prestigious "Excellence by Design" award.

Today he owns his own company, Marc Rosen Associates, which is responsible for many of the package designs seen in the fragrance industry.

ics are the color palettes that each company designs. Yet even the color ranges and emphases for a particular season are not solely decided by the company. The decision is based largely on information from fashion forecasters—the experts who predict what the apparel industry will be featuring. The cosmetics industry then creates colors that will effectively enhance these garments. Because everyone in the cosmetics field focuses on these fashion forecasts, the result is generally a uniform approach to color.

Given these parameters, how can a cosmetics company distinguish its line from the others. The answer often lies with **package design.** In both cosmetics and fragrances, fashionable and functional packaging continues to play a role in helping the shopper choose a particular product. Often, it is the package, rather than the contents that encourages a consumer to choose one product over another.

In terms of ingredients alone, there is little justification for the price point spread in the industry. Often, the reason for a higher priced product is the cost of the package design. Marketers of beauty products spend enormous sums developing unique packaging that will attract the attention of consumer in this competitive field.

Renowned cosmetics and fragrance package designer Marc A. Rosen is the subject of a World of Fashion Profile.

Demonstrations

The cosmetics departments of most major stores have company cosmetologists, who demonstrate the proper method of makeup application. The **demonstration** usually involves a targeted shopper who will be receptive to and benefit from personalized treatments. After removing any existing makeup from the customer, the cosmetologist professionally applies a range of cosmetics in appropriate colors. This process usually attracts observers who witness the change. Because of the cosmetologist's skill, the customer's appearance is greatly enhanced. As a result, the customer and often the onlookers are motivated to purchase the products that were used in the demonstration.

Personal Appearances

Cosmetics companies attract attention to their products with **personal appearances.** The makeup artists, who achieve recognition by applying cosmetics to models and theatrical personalities, often appear at the counters in the prestigious stores that sell their lines. Such players as Bobbi Brown, Vincent Longo, François Nars, and Carol Shaw regularly make the rounds of stores like Bergdorf Goodman, Saks, Jacobson's, and Nordstrom, drawing crowds eager to hear them tell about their products. Because these artists were responsible for making up the faces of such movie stars as Demi Moore, Angelica Houston, and Geena Davis, customers are eager to learn, firsthand, how to improve their appearances.

Personal appearances by designers, such as Karl Lagerfeld, bring crowds to the stores.

In addition to the name players, company representatives, completely knowledgeable about their lines, also appear on the retail circuit. The announcements in the print ads, telling of their visits, usually draw big crowds.

Sampling

Leading cosmetics producers often introduce their products by **sampling.** To implement this strategy, the company creates a promotional package that contains a sampling of its products. When a customer makes a purchase, he or she can purchase an attractive case of these samples for a small price. Not only does this sampling technique encourage purchasing, but it also introduces the consumer to other products that might lead to future sales.

Premiums

Many companies use **premiums** as a means of encouraging sales. This marketing technique offers the consumer an attractive item with a Christmas purchase. Umbrellas, hand luggage, personalized Christmas ornaments, tote bags, and the like are either given free with a purchase or are available at a modest price. These premiums usually bear the name of the cosmetic company. Thus, when used by the consumer, the premium is a constant reminder of the promotion's product.

Department stores account for the major business of upscale cosmetic lines.

These events usually take place during the Thanksgiving to Christmas season, the time when stores are busiest.

Direct Mail

Many cosmetics companies provide retailers with flyers and brochures to include in monthly statements to customers. Generally, they announce the introduction of a new product, a special price promotion, a sampling opportunity, or any event that might motivate purchasing either at the store or by phone.

Because the flyer is enclosed with monthly statements, there are no additional postage costs. The only investment is the cost of producing the mailer. Most major retailers realize a significant amount of business through such direct mail cosmetics sales.

Joint Merchandising

Cosmetics merchandising differs from typical merchandising practices in retailing because suppliers and retailers **jointly merchandise** the products. Each manufacturer is assigned a specific counter, or area, and is responsible for inventory taking, stock replenishment, and visual presentation. Members of the sales staff, in each area, are trained by the producer of the line they represent and are paid salaries that are shared by both the manufacturer and the store. Sometimes the store pays an hourly wage and the cosmetics company pays a commission on sales.

With the manufacturers supplying point of purchase displays and presenting individual promotions, each counter takes on a personality of its own, setting it apart from the rest of the field.

Retail Distribution

Intensive distribution is the best description of the cosmetics industry's approach to selling. Except for the private brands and a few exclusive arrangements, the same lines are available in most stores. The prevailing belief is that cosmetics are often impulse purchases. The more visible the product lines, the more merchandise the store will sell. Thus, cosmetics counters are located on the main floor, where customers must pass through when entering or exiting the store.

Various types of retail outlets and distribution practices are employed by the industry, including department stores, cosmetics boutiques, mass merchandisers, discount operations, pharmacy chains, and in-home selling.

Department Stores

Department stores sell the vast majority of the better lines of cosmetics including Lancôme, Prescriptives, Clinique, Estée Lauder, Elizabeth Arden, and Ultima II. Because each manufacturer has a separate selling area, each line develops a feeling of individuality. Trained salespersons help solve customers problems by introducing them to the products best suited to their needs.

Cosmetic Boutiques

Beauty salons and individual cosmetic boutiques often carry their own private brands, a topic that will be explored later in the chapter. The success of these operations depends on the service and product knowledge of the cosmetologists. In these environments, an expert usually analyzes the customer's problems and suggests items that will help solve them. They often provide complexion analyses, demonstrations, and makeup applications for special occasions.

Mass Merchandisers

Stores such as Woolworth usually concentrate on lower-priced brands such as Maybelline, and require that customers select their own purchases. The items are usually displayed on peg-board walls or shelves that are clearly marked as to manufacturer and cosmetic category. Point-of-purchase displays are used to draw attention to specific products.

Discount Operations

Companies such as Wal-Mart and Kmart have large sections of cosmetics that are displayed in the same manner as described under mass merchandisers. Their appeal is generally price-oriented, with most items sold below traditional markups. The selections include all price points, with the lower end generating the largest percentage of sales.

Mass-merchandisers concentrate on lower-priced lines of cosmetics.

Avon

Established by David H. McConnell in 1886, Avon is the world's leading direct seller of beauty and beauty-related products, with annual revenues of $4 billion! It markets its products to women in 120 countries through 1.7 million independent representatives. In addition to such renowned products as Anew, Skin-So-Soft, and Avon Style, it is also the world's largest manufacturer of fashion jewelry. Aside from those who represent the company as sellers, Avon employs approximately 30,000 people in other capacities around the world.

Unlike most other cosmetics operations, which sell their goods in a variety of traditional retail outlets, Avon sells only through direct marketing. Through its network of representatives, customers may place orders in their homes or by phone and have them quickly delivered. Catalogs detailing every product in the line are left with customers to assist with more selections in the future. By using this approach, Avon gains the customer's attention without the competition provided by traditional retailing.

The company was one of the first to empower women by using them as direct sellers. In major cities as far away as Guangzhou, China, and in small towns like Bettendorf, Iowa, women are distributing the products and achieving economic independence. Each year, Avon conducts an extensive search to identify candidates for many different awards. Prizes are distributed at a special luncheon.

Avon's innovations have been many. It has on-site day care centers for working mothers, a foundation that extends assistance for women's programs in health, education, community service, art, and culture, and contributes large sums for community activities around the globe.

Pharmacy Chains

All over the country, pharmacy chains account for a large number of cosmetics sales. In general, these chains have two approaches to sales. One features the merchandise in much the same manner as the mass merchandisers and discount operations; the other employs the services of a cosmetologist who assists the customer in the selection of products. Unlike the department stores, where salespeople represent particular lines and are trained by the manufacturers, the pharmacy chain uses one salesperson to assist customers with all of the products sold.

Direct Selling

Companies such as Avon and Mary Kay Cosmetics sell their products directly to the consumer only through individual or group demonstrations. The success of these companies demonstrates that there is a large market for home sales. Representatives carry inventories that are sufficient to satisfy the immediate needs of customers; others carry samples and take orders for future delivery. The keys to success are proper demonstration of the products and personal attention. The direct sales technique eliminates the obvious distractions of the retail store as well as competition from other brands. The customer's attention is focused solely on the product line being shown.

A World of Fashion Profile of Avon discusses its place in the cosmetics industry.

Private Brands

Although national brands continue to dominate the cosmetics market, more and more retailers are focusing their attention on their own brands. Much as with private label apparel, retailers are marketing their own lines of cosmetics alongside such household names as Revlon and Cover Girl. The purpose, of course, is to provide better profit margins, while giving their customers better value.

The success of private branding cosmetics became apparent when the industry's trade shows began to feature displays showing all of the elements needed to create such programs. At these annual expositions, for example, the number of suppliers who developed packaging specifically for private brands increased, as did the manufacturers of complete cosmetics lines who were willing to sell their products under a store's own name.

Sears launched a private cosmetics brand called Beautiful Styles. In partnership with the former president of Lancôme, Pierre Rogers, Sears is planning to promote the new line in 200 of its stores. It features superior products at quality prices. After a ten-year hiatus from cosmetics, Sears reentered the market in 1993 and hopes to make its profit picture even better with the new private brand.

The Global Nature of Cosmetics

Many cosmetics marketers are expanding their horizons and potential for new business by seeking international markets for their products. By spreading out globally, they reduce the financial impact of adverse economic developments such as a recession, in the United States. Thus, if the United States is experiencing an unfavorable business climate, sales in other parts of the world might still earn profits for the company.

Because cosmetics are in great demand all over the world, it is a natural product for globalization. The approach, however, must be carefully executed; different markets require product variations. Lifestyles and personal characteristics in each market can be different. Marketing research is necessary to make certain that these differences will be addressed. Skin complexion, for

Companies like Avon are expanding their operations throughout the world. Here an Avon representative sells the product lines door-to-door in Brazil.

example, is different in northern European countries than those in other regions and must be assessed so that appropriate colors will be properly marketed.

The regulatory policies of each country must also be evaluated. Some ingredients used in cosmetics are prohibited in certain countries. "D & C red number 33," for example, is used fairly extensively in the United States, but is prohibited from use in Japan. Therefore, any product containing that color additive cannot be marketed in Japan. Other colors are more universally accepted and would therefore be better choices for global distribution. If attention is not paid to those details, international marketing will not be successful.

Labeling is another area that must be carefully investigated. Each country has its own rules and regulations governing labels, and they must be studied to avoid problems.

Although these and other issues require investigation, the universal use of cosmetics makes international markets a potentially lucrative source of profits.

In the 1960s fragrances, such as Chanel No. 5 promoted by celebrity Catherine Deneuve, were major money makers.

FRAGRANCES

A fragrance is a product that is literally invisible, available at high prices, and one of the most profitable, international industries. Although it is primarily produced in France and America, its appeal is universal. Women are the primary consumers in this multibillion dollar field, but men purchase a significant number of items for their own use as well as for gift-giving.

For decades, products such as perfume, eau de parfum or toilet water, cologne, and bath coordinates have provided mystery and excitement for its users. Beginning with the essential fragrances extracted from flowers, such as bitter orange, jasmine, and rose, and moving to other ingredients such as grasses, spices, herbs, citrus products, woods, and leaves that come from every corner of the earth, humans have transformed them into products that capture the hearts and minds of most people.

Guerlain and Houbigant were the major players in the fragrance industry until the end of the nineteenth century. In the early twentieth century, the industry then started to slowly expand. It began when François Coty tried to introduce *Rose Jacqueminot* to the public. Discouraged by the refusal of a well-known merchant to sell his new creation, Coty purposely dropped a small bottle of it on the steps in front of the merchant's store. Passersby, intrigued by the aroma, compelled the merchant to place an order for it. From that moment on, Coty established its position in the world of fragrances.

Today, with its promise of tremendous profits, the field has broadened significantly. The famous couturiers of the past—Chanel, Patou, Lanvin, and Schiaparelli—have been joined by many from the current list of apparel designers, who have entered the market with products bearing their famous signatures. The numbers of participants currently make the fragrance industry one of the world's most competitive.

Highlights of the Fragrance Industry

From 1900 to the beginning of the 1920s, there was the possibility of an increase in the type and production of fragrances, but World War I put a stop to development in this area.

After the war ended, designers creating new fragrances—Chanel's "Chanel No. 5," Lanvin's "My Sin" and "Arpege," and Jean Patou's "Amour Amour" and "Moment Supreme." In the 1930s, the industry continued to grow. New products, such as "Je Reviens" by Worth and "Tabu" by Dana, were successfully launched. Elizabeth Arden made headlines with her introduction of "Blue Grass." The world was also treated to what has been billed as the costliest fragrance in the world, "Joy."

The occupation of France by Germany during World War II almost destroyed the fragrance industry. But at the end of World War II, fragrance creators brought a rash of new scents to the public. Carven developed "Ma Griffe," Christian Dior introduced "Miss Dior" to celebrate his New Look in fashion, and Nina Ricci brought out "L'air du Temps," the great classic floral scent.

In the 1950s, the United States finally became a major player in the fragrance game. Led by Estée Lauder and her "Youth Dew," other companies, such as Revlon and Avon, were busy building their empires.

The 1960s witnessed the production and launching of new fragrances in France and America. Designers such as Hermés, Guy Laroche, and Yves Saint Laurent introduced product after product to the public. In 1969, however, the first truly great American **designer fragrance**—Norell—took the country by storm with a licensing agreement with Revlon. It was named after the designer Norman Norell, a leading apparel designer in the United States.

During the 1970s, the use of traditional fragrances started to decline. As a result, the industry began to change. In particular, young people, who were disenchanted with the values of the world, sought basic fragrances to replace the costlier products of past decades. Head shops and other specialty outlets appeared on the scene and sold musks, incense, and patchouli in large quantities. The women's liberation movement also affected the industry. "Charlie" was introduced to augment the masculine pantsuits, ties, and pinstriped fabrics being embraced by the women consumers. At the end of the 1970s, Yves Saint Laurent introduced "Opium," with the first megalaunch. It served as the forerunner of socially controversial fragrance names as "Decadence," "Obsession," and "Poison." By the end of the decade, a record number of new fragrances would be featured. American designers, such as Calvin Klein, Bill Blass, Halston, Ralph Lauren, and Diane Von Furstenberg introduced new fragrances to the consumer. Some became major forces in the field; others had little success.

The 1980s was a decade of comparative ostentation and self-indulgence. Rolex watches, BMW's, designer clothing, and gourmet food were visible everywhere. Status seemed to be the key word, and fragrance producers reacted

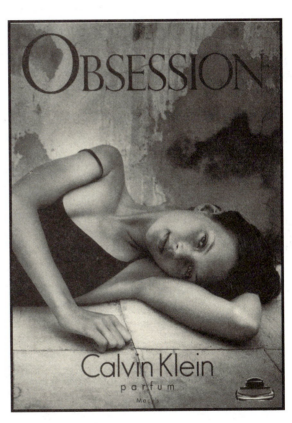

Obsession is just one of Calvin Klein's line of fragrances.

quickly to fulfill the demands of the market. Prestige packaging and celebrity licensing agreements resulted in price increases, but many consumers had little concern for cost. In addition to the designers from the apparel industry, some of the names adorning new fragrances were from the jewelry, television, music, movie, dance, and art industries.

The economic recession at the beginning of the 1990s caused some concern for the industry. Although some new products entered the market, the introductions were fewer than before. Four years after "Passion" took the fragrance world by storm, Elizabeth Taylor lent her name to a new fragrance—"White Diamonds." It became a best seller. Donna Karan ultimately introduced her first fragrance, "Donna Karan New York." Aside from the fragrance itself, the bottle, designed by her husband, sculptor Stephan Weiss, drew a great deal of attention.

By the middle of the decade other new scents were marketed by Victoria's Secret, Talbots, Liz Claiborne, Giorgio Armani, and Todd Oldham.

Fragrance Forms

There are basically four types of fragrances: perfume, eau de parfum, toilet water, and cologne. Each offers the user a different concentration of the scent.

Perfume

Perfume is the strongest, most concentrated, and longest lasting form of fragrance. A blend of natural essential oils and/or aroma chemicals and fixatives make up each perfume. A truly fine product may contain as many as three hundred different elements. Perfume balance is achieved by the addition of alcohol, which also acts as the carrier of the fragrance. The amount of alcohol added to the blend determines the scent's strength.

Perfume may be applied directly from the bottle by "splashing" it on. For the most effective and, even distribution, however, it should be applied with an atomizer.

Eau de Parfum

One of the newest forms of fragrances found in many producer's collections, **eau de parfum** is used as a preparatory base for perfumes. When it is smoothed or sprayed over the body and enhanced with a perfume of the same scent, the overall effect will last longer.

Toilet Water

Used as a base for perfume or by itself, **toilet water** is lighter and more subtle than perfume. It uses more alcohol and fewer scented oils in its mixture than does perfume. Used in spray form, it might also be used as an accent in the hair, creating a long-lasting scent around the body.

Cologne

The lightest of the fragrance forms, **cologne** may be lavishly applied to all parts of the body. It was initially introduced in the seventeenth century in Cologne, Germany—thus its name. It is the least concentrated form of perfume.

In addition to these products, a lost of others, such as soaps, bath oils, bath salts and crystals, bubble bath, hand and body lotions, bath powder, talc, and deodorants, use fragrances.

The Copycats

In the 1980s, while a large segment of the market treated itself to the expensive, designer fragrances, a new breed of product was born. Called **designer impostors,** they mimicked the names that were being heralded by more affluent consumers. In addition to imitating the scents, the packaging was also designed to deliver prestige to the purchaser. The first of these new scents was "Ninja," a copy of Yves Saint Laurent's "Opium." "Ninja" ads featured "Opium" alongside of "Ninja," with a headline that read, "If you like Opium, you'll love Ninja." Its success was so quick and profitable that it was quickly followed by others.

By 1995, the new **copycats** were being vigorously marketed to men and women under age 25, at prices that were about half of the original scents. The leading mimics included "U" from Parfums de Coeur Ltd., "DQI One" by Designer Quality Impressionists, "QK Too," from Deborah International Beauty Ltd., "A Man and a Woman" by Jean Philippe Fragrances, and "Chromosome XX XY" from Parfums Vision International Ltd. Each was designed to compete with the highly successful launch of Calvin Klein's "CK One," which rang up retail sales of more than $50 million in a few months! Other knockoffs with widespread appeal included imitations of Elizabeth Taylor's "White Diamonds," Liz Claiborne's "Sunflowers," and Calvin Klein's "Escape" and "Eternity."

Unlike the prestigious stores that sell the original products, the copycats are sold primarily through such mass merchandisers as Walgreens, flea markets, and off-price retailers.

Marketing Lines of Fragrances

As with cosmetics, marketing involves attractive packaging, demonstrations, personal appearances, sampling, and premiums.

The competition is so keen in the mid-1990s, that the major players often spend enormous sums to launch their new products by a variety of different approaches. Sales for Lancaster Group USA's scent, "Zino Davidoff," were boosted by a James Brown concert. Other techniques include autograph signings and cross-country tours, as that undertaken by Guerlain's Jean Paul Guerlain to promote "Heritage."

The profit potential is so great that some marketing launches, such as those sponsored by Calvin Klein, run as high as $40 million!

Men's Fragrances

Although women's scents dominate the marketplace, sales of men's fragrance are also significant. Men's products were first introduced in the twentieth century. Until the 1930s however, the list focused primarily on hair tonics, shaving soaps, and astringent lotions that were used on shaving niks and cuts.

In the 1930s, some of the products that are still used were introduced. The two major names were "Skin Bracer" and "Aqua Velva." They dominated the market until "Canoe," originally introduced for women, was repositioned as a men's product. It became the best-selling men's scent of the time and is still regarded as one of the classic fragrances.

Men's fragrances are increasing in sales each year.

During the 1950s, additional scents were created for men. For the first time, a French couturier—namely Givenchy—introduced a men's product called "Monsieur de Givenchy," and a women's specialist, Elizabeth Arden entered the field with "Sandalwood."

The widespread introduction of men's fragrances occurred from 1960 to 1970. Estée Lauder's "Aramis," Faberge's "Brut," and Christian Dior's "Eau Savage," became big sellers. From that time on, the race for widespread acceptance included many designers such as Calvin Klein, Hermès, Nina Ricci, Liz Claiborne, Bijan, Chanel, Ralph Lauren, Louis Feraud, and Carolina Herrera.

By the middle of the 1990s, there were several hundred brands competing for men's dollars!

Chapter Highlights

- The use of cosmetics and fragrances goes back to Ancient Egypt and Rome.

- In the early 1920s, cosmetics were used primarily by sophisticated consumers. As late as the 1950s, the industry still had a limited market.

- During the 1960s, cosmetics sales increased dramatically as a result of new products and new marketing techniques.

- Cosmetic sales increased in the 1970s, reaching new heights in the 1980s.

- As the industry grew more profitable, new players entered the arena, including famous apparel designers and cosmeticians from the movie industry.

- Cosmetics are marketed in typical retail outlets as well as through direct sales.

- By the 1990s, one of the fastest growing segments of the industry was ethnic cosmetics.
- The fragrance industry became big business after World War I, with the launch of Chanel No. 5.
- Although World War II brought the industry to a sudden halt, it was resurrected soon after the war's conclusion, as couturiers famous for their apparel designs joined the fragrance bandwagon.
- Until the 1960s, the field was dominated by the French. In 1969, the first American designer fragrance, "Norell" hit the market.
- In the 1980s, fragrance prices began to soar. As demand continued to increase, however, the list of fragrance launches mushroomed, with almost every designer introducing new products.
- Copycat scents also entered the market in the 1980s, offering fragrances at prices that were one-half of the cost of the ones they imitated.

Important Fashion Terminology and Concepts

cologne	eau de parfum	perfume
copycats	ethnic cosmetics	private brand cosmetics
demonstrations	gift with a purchase	sampling
designer fragrance	joint merchandising	toilet water
direct mail cosmetic sales	kits	

For Review

1. When were cosmetics first used?
2. During the 1920s, which group of people served as role models for users of cosmetics?
3. Which decade saw a major increase in the use of cosmetics?
4. With what marketing concept did Estée Lauder help increase cosmetics sales?
5. Who were the first apparel designers to market lines of cosmetics?
6. What role do the fashion forecasters play in the cosmetics field?
7. Describe a "joint merchandising program" as it relates to the cosmetics industry.
8. Discuss the difference between selling cosmetics in department stores and through mass merchandisers.
9. What are private brand cosmetics?
10. What issues must be addressed to successfully market cosmetics?
11. Which fragrance made its mark by billing itself as the world's most costliest?
12. Beginning with the end of the 1970s, what were some of the controversial names given to fragrances?
13. What is the difference between perfume and eau de parfum?
14. What are copycat fragrances?

Exercises and Projects

1. Visit a department store during the Christmas selling period to gather information on the various promotions offered by the different cosmetics companies. Ask for permission to photograph the promotions. Using the information gathered, present a report to the class.

2. Write to a cosmetics or fragrance company to learn about the various marketing techniques it uses to sell its products. Write a report outlining the specifics of each one.

3. Visit a mass merchandiser or other retailer of copycat fragrances. Make a list of the copycat names and the fragrances they imitate.

The Case of the Successful Cosmetician

Michelle Sagan worked for five years at the Clinique cosmetics counter in a large Southern department store. She was trained to help women with the appropriate selection and application of cosmetics. After a few years, she built an impressive personal following. Many customers came to her for makeup applications whenever they had a special occasion. Although her earnings were substantial, she thought that being in her own business would result in even greater rewards.

As luck would have it, Michelle inherited enough money to open her own cosmetics salon. After careful consideration, she selected an appropriate location. She then shopped the market for the proper fixtures and made arrangements for their installation. The only matter she had not resolved was the merchandise assortment she would carry.

One possibility was to carry an exclusive line of name-brand products, from which there were many to choose. Another was to stock a variety of different brands. The third choice was to go the route of private branding and carry only products that bore her own label—Michelle.

Question

Which approach would you suggest Michelle follow? Explain your decision.

Because she had worked for so many years in the department store, she was able to acquire a list of her regular customers. She planned to contact them about her new operation. The rest of her business, she believed, would come from word-of-mouth recommendations.

point of view

Trying to Squeeze 10 Pegs Onto A 5-Peg Wall

Faye Brookman

Mass market cosmetics retailers are doing a new dance: the peg wall shuffle.

They are wondering how to cram more products on the same display wall, a concern triggered largely by Procter & Gamble's decision to begin test marketing its new Oil of Olay color cosmetics line in September in 65 stores in Evansville, Ind.

Although a national rollout has not yet been scheduled, retailers say they must start thinking now about how to squeeze out extra merchandising space for the probability that the new line will go into full distribution. Advanced thinking is required because planograms, or maps of where products will be merchandised, are only updated once or twice a year.

In addition, the introduction of several niche color cosmetics lines has further complicated planning.

Further exacerbating the situation is the fact that many retailers had already parceled out to other brands the space once held by Clarion, a color cosmetics line P&G discontinued two years ago. But also the allocations for Revlon, Maybelline and nail care are being eyed.

That means retailers might have to trim shelf footage from existing brands, in some cases even from P&G sister lines, like Max Factor.

"It is always a challenge to find space on the wall," said Judy Wray, a senior buyer for Revco D.S., based in Twinsburg, Ohio. Revco is among the chains that will be part of the test market for the new line.

Retailers agree that Oil of Olay warrants a home on the merchandising wall, considering its huge name recognition with consumers. Olay has a U.S. wholesale volume of $180 million and a worldwide volume of $650 million, according to industry sources, who added that the new color line could have sales of $110 million. P&G now spends $80 million to $100 million in advertising support behind the Olay brand.

"Oil of Olay is a big name in beauty care, but I wonder how it will translate to cosmetics," mused Steve Lund, category manager for F&M Distributors Inc. of Warren, Michigan.

Lund said he has space for the Olay cosmetics in some of his stores that have been redesigned with roomier cosmetics departments. About 20 of F&M's 115 stores have been redone.

Linda Conway, buyer for Rite Aid Corp. of Camp Hill, Pa., also has stores in the test market.

"We haven't made any decisions yet," she said, "but as we get closer to the test we'll decide where it will go."

Rite Aid, which has 2,829 stores, also has embarked on an initiative in the last year to enlarge its cosmetics departments. As a result, Conway expects to have space available for the new Olay line.

She added that in the ebb and flow of marketing, categories peak out. An area such as nail care, while hot right now, might be ripe for some editing when Olay is tested, she suggested.

Other retailers don't have the same flexibility and said they'll have to steal precious footage from existing lines. For instance, Maybelline's space, devoted to its struggling Revitalizing line, will go under the microscope of many chain store executives, especially since Revitalizing had won some of the space vacated by Clarion.

Revitalizing has done well in some stores but disappointed other retailers. However, many chains have noticed that Maybelline's promotional efforts have had a positive impact on Revitalizing's sales.

Conway at Rite Aid doesn't plan to tamper with Revitalizing.

"It is picking up for us," she said. Revitalizing and Revlon's Age Defying, retailers added, address an audience that Oil of Olay surprisingly is not targeting—mature women.

Still, retailers actually view that as a savvy move.

"They learned with Clarion that you have to start with a young shopper and build loyalty," said Conway.

Olay's positioning will not force it to compete for customers with P&G's Cover Girl.

"They aren't going after Cover Girl's shopper, it is more targeted to department store customers," said Conway. Some buyers, however, see duplication with P&G's Max Factor, a line that has been repositioned over the past three years.

Some buyers have not been impressed with Max Factor's revamped color cosmetics, with its new packaging and in-store fixturing. Other sources, however, said that Max Factor has big plans to support the line, a development that could change minds about the brand.

"From our standpoint, we'll be eyeballing Revitalizing and Max

317

Factor," said Marcia Springer, buyer for Taylor Drug Stores Inc. of Louisville, Ky. "Despite its relaunch," she said of Max Factor, "it has still not done as well as expected."

Others said they'd also be looking at Revlon's footage. One buyer, who asked not to be identified, said she could sacrifice some of Revlon's space, which usually gets eight feet of space.

Buyers added that it was unfortunate that P&G had not introduced Olay at the time of Clarion's demise.

Some of the buyers for the Indiana stores where the line will be tested questioned the validity of the merchandise fixture, since it was imported from Germany and not yet modified for U.S. tastes.

"It is the fixture being used worldwide, but it isn't the fixture that will be part of the rollout, so I don't know why it is being used in the test," said one buyer, who is part of the experiment but asked not to be identified.

She also questioned P&G's plans to illuminate the fixture, considering that many drugstores and discounters do not have electrical outlets along their merchandise walls. There is also the cost of electricity.

P&G executives say that the units are being used only as an experiment and will ultimately help the company devise a more flexible and appropriate fixture for the national rollout. As far as the illumination goes, the executives said, the fixture works just as well without the lights.

P&G is recommending that retailers not take space away from the major beauty players—Revlon, L'Oréal, Cover Girl, Max Factor and Maybelline.

However, many buyers said they have just entered into programs with niche players they want to keep because of the variety the smaller lines provide.

Lines such as Nat Robbins, Prestige, Jane and now Black Opal, a new ethnic line, are often getting space freed up by the discontinuance of Clarion, as well as adjustments based on the performance of existing brands.

"We're testing Nat Robbins and we want to find room for the new Black Opal line because we haven't really served that [ethnic] customer adequately," said Lund.

The niche marketers admitted that the entrance of Olay's new

color line could make space even harder to come by.

"Anytime anyone new comes in, it makes it harder," said Larry Pallini, president of Great American/Nat Robbins in Port Washington, N.Y. But what we offer is a way to add high turns and profits in a small amount of footage."

Because Nat Robbins has come up with a concise fixture design, retailers need as little as one foot of space for a selection of Robbins items, he said.

In fact, the small vendors have become creative at making it easier for mass marketers to add their lines.

"We've become more chain-oriented," said Tom Winarick, vice president of marketing for Prestige Cosmetics of Deerfield Beach, Fla.

Over the last four months, the firm has created a fixture that can easily fit into existing retail peg wall presentations. The number of sku's has been reduced to only those that move the fastest in discount and drugstores.

"When you're smaller," Winarick said, "you have to be more innovative."

Women's Wear Daily, July 28, 1995.

Max Factor: Back to the Movies

Cara Kagan

While makeup artist lines are now the thing in the color market, few companies can lay claim to a 75-year heritage, like Max Factor.

This week, Procter & Gamble began driving home that point through new print advertising, whose theme will extend to the

company's TV image and in-store and promotional campaigns.

The new campaign, called "Makeup That Performs," will feature actual movie makeup artists giving testimonials about the quality and performance of Max Factor products.

"We have decided that our equity lies in the brand's glamorous heritage of both makeup artistry and technology," said Beth Kaplan, group vice president of P&G's cosmetics and fragrance division.

Kaplan was referring to Max Factor, Hollywood's top makeup artist from the Twenties through the Forties, who initially created the line for the special needs of movie makeup artists and then later for consumers.

"After some research we learned that contemporary makeup artists are still using the products in their work," she added. "Incorporating these professionals in our ads seemed like the logical way to demonstrate our point of difference from other lines in the mass market."

Kaplan noted that the company will sign four to six professional makeup artists to appear in both print and TV advertisements.

The first of the series breaks Sunday and will feature Allen Weisinger, the makeup artist for the film *The Age of Innocence.* Print versions broke earlier this month in August issues of women's magazines.

Other makeup artists who will appear in future ads are Gary Liddiard, who did the makeup for *Out of Africa,* and Bob Mills, whose movie makeup credits include *Pretty Woman.*

In addition to singing the brand's praises, the makeup artists will be applying the products to Max Factor models, to demonstrate its effects.

Max Factor's most recent campaign, called Max Factor Impact, focused on the brand's technology and the impact it had on the women while they wore the products.

While company executives declined to comment on sales and advertising dollars, according to industry sources, the firm has increased its ad budget by 10 per-

cent to around $17 million for the 1996 fiscal year, which began June 30.

Jim Stengel, director of marketing for Max Factor International, noted that the company is extending the makeup artist thrust through all aspects of the brand's marketing.

For the next three weekends, starting Saturday, the company is testing a new concept in sampling, called the Max Factor Movie Makeup Artist Studio, which will be held at New York's Lincoln Square Sony Theatre from 2:00 P.M. to 10:00 P.M. each day.

The booth will feature two makeup stations, fashioned after those used on movie sets, with visuals of movie makeup artists at work. Max Factor makeup artists will be on hand to give tips and makeovers to passers-by. There will also be sampling stations so women can try the products. Coupons will be handed out as well.

Max Factor will advertise the booth the weekend prior to each event in The Sunday *New York Times.*

"We ultimately see the kiosk as a traveling forum," Stengel said. "We would like to take it around the country to other appropriate venues."

On a more permanent level, Max Factor will extend the cinematic concept in-store to its permanent display units in mass market doors. Display panels will feature advice and tips from the makeup artists, as well as more information on product technology.

"Visually, we will be taking this image all over the stores," Stengel added. "We will be using it on our wall, on counter top displays and in-aisles."

Throughout August and September, Max Factor will staff its major accounts with trained professionals who will hand out samples, give makeovers and offer tips.

Max Factor finished its last fiscal year, which ended June 30, with 6.6 percent of the $2.2 billion mass cosmetics market or $145 million at retail, according to industry sources. That was up from approximately 5.8 percent, or $127 million, for its fiscal year 1994.

The company is reportedly seeking to raise the brand's share to as high as 8 percent, or $176 million at retail, by the end of this fiscal year.

In addition to its revised advertising and promotional activities, this October the firm will jump on the long-wearing lipstick band wagon with 2-in-1 No Trade Off Moisture Rich Lipstick.

Each of the 36 shades will have a suggested retail price of $5.95.

Company executives maintain that typically lipsticks can be either long wearing or moisturizing since long-lasting formulas usually involve increasing the level of pigment, which can absorb moisture.

Max Factor's new entry contains coated color stabilizers that were designed to help the lipstick stay on longer and absorb much less oil than non-coated colorants, so that moisturizers and conditioners can effectively be added to the formula.

Women's Wear Daily, July 28, 1995.

"Scents of Self" Determine New Roles for Fragrance in the Future

Amanda Green

As the twenty-first century bears down on us, the world of the senses is taking center stage. We've all discovered the importance of the senses of smell and the many indispensable roles of fragrance. The conventional and traditional are, in the main, passe. Women don't want to look or smell like their mothers and grandmothers or even their big sisters.

One of the important trends appears to be a global longing to simplify life. Nothing should be too sweet, too strong, too obvious, too intense. There's a quality of the "Emperor's Clothes" about it all. Nothingness is in the air, Why? What's happening? It seems to me that as life has become more complicated, as we continue to be bombarded with information and change, the response is to "turn down the emotional heat."

This response has found a perfect expression in fragrance. For almost the first time in modern history, men and women are choosing and wearing fragrances for themselves. Sexuality is not a consideration. Elegance is not the question. Country of origin has little meaning. Considerations of chic rarely exist. The idea is to find and wear fragrances that make you feel good about yourself, no matter where they came from.

Everyone is looking for light, bright happy scents. The American fragrance industry, in particular, is inroducing a new variety of fragrances. There are scents to be shared by men and women, new, lighter-than-air versions of famous fragrances, and a category of what perfumes identify as "transparent" which have the clarity of water and the character and subtlety of nature: top of the mountain smells, scents reminiscent of a day near the ocean, fragrances which capture the aroma of a grove of lemon and lime trees. These are fragrances to be worn to modify mood, energize or relax, reduce stress, increase alertness. I call them "behavorial" scents which are inspired not only by societal changes but by the research of the Olfactory Research Fund which The Fragrance Foundation established in 1991 to study the psychological effect of odors.

In the intervening years, the Fund, which was granted tax exempt, charitable status, has spearheaded olfactory research in leading universities and hospitals in the U.S and abroad. The results have scientifically validated the important role of fragrance to our feelings of well-being. At the famous cancer hospital in New York, Memorial Sloan Kettering, a vanilla-type fragrance dramatically reduced stress (67%) for patients undergoing magnetic resonance imaging tests. In a Good Housekeeping Institute study on alertness, a citrus-type scent improved proofreading abilities. At Duke Medical Center Hospital, fragrances administered to women suffering depression during menopause produced a positive mood swing. In similar tests, men suffering from mid-life crisis experienced the same results. All of this is not to say that romantic, sexy scents are not being worn. Of course, they are and will continue to be important. But like fashion in the '90's, everything has its place and time.

In the coming millennium, fragrances will have many more roles to play. They will be a part of virtual reality, will be chosen to remind us of quieter, simpler times, people we knew and loved. Scents will go everywhere. In a study conducted by the French research firm, FACES International, European women were asked: If you were going to outer space, what would be the most important item you would bring with you? Among the responses;

· Perfumes. Perfumes remind me of different situations in life, of different people. . . . Germany
· Perfumes. So I can remember the good moments. France
· My perfume . . . To have memories, a point of reference and a feminine feeling. United Kingdom

In 1997, the French art book publishing house, Flammarion, will publish a book I am writing with Fashion journalist Linda Dyett, entitled *The Secrets of Aromatic Jewelry.* It chronicles the history of jewelry which has held fragrance from antiquity to today. Reports tell us there is a worldwide trend to carry or wear aromatic jewelry like protective amulets much as our ancestors did.

In the October '95 British edition of *Marie Claire,* a fragrance authority indicated, "that ultimately, we could all be taken back to various points in our lives by sniffing an evocative scent. In the future, we may keep our memories in phials rather than photo albums."

The sensory revolution of the 90s has been perfectly captured in the Fragrance Foundation's first public awareness campaign, "Stop and Smell The Memories." "Snapshots" of commonplace and cherished moments, such as school friends sharing the fun of being together, a bride and groom with new memories to treasure, a son imitating his dad splashing on aftershave, and young lovers making beautiful music together promise, "if a picture is worth a thousand words, then your sense of smell is worth a million."

The Fragrance Foundation has long wanted to create a generic public awareness campaign which captures the essence of the fragrance experience throughout each of our lives. Now, through the perserverance and creativity of the Saatchi & Saatchi Advertising Agency and the support of the members of the Board, we are fulfilling our mission to educate and entertain the public with heartfelt messages which everyone can relate to in the most intimate and joyful way.

In preparing for the campaign, Saatchi & Saatchi interviewed people on the street and held a focus group to determine what it was about fragrance that meant the most to the majority. Overwhelmingly, the answer was 'memories' of a person, place or occasion. This made sense since there is an extraordinary amount of scientific evidence to document the fact that odors function as triggers for both intensely personal memories and universal responses.

The campaign reminds us that though scent is fashion's invisible accessory, it never fails to evoke the unforgettable moments, people and places that define our lives and our persona.

Amanda Green, President, The Fragrance Foundation.

Home Fashions

Although the fashion industry focuses on apparel, the home fashions segment is gaining importance. Just as the selection of clothing reflects the mood and personality of the purchaser, so the interior of a home tells the story of the people who live in it.

There are no runway shows or extravaganzas that bring this part of fashion to the public, but many of the world's leading apparel designers are becoming major players in the home fashion field. Significant increases in sales indicate a growing consumer attraction to the products that make up this market.

Home fashions, broadly defined, includes upholstered furniture, case goods, and a host of accessory items that includes bedding, tableware (dinnerware, glassware, flatware), fabrics, floor coverings, decorative accessories, and decorative ornaments.

It is no longer the rule that only fashion apparel changes with great regularity. New and exciting home fashions appear each season, showing unique and creative ideas. Although fashion devotees have followed the lead of apparel designers for years by updating their wardrobes to achieve some level of fashion consciousness, few have paid attention to fashions for the home. With this enormous interest in designer apparel, creating home fashions was the next logical arena for apparel designers to enter. Stephen Earl, style director for the magazine Martha Stewart *Living,* believes, "The way clothing is conceived and sold today is not just about a pair of pants, a shirt, a tie, a dress; it's all about a lifestyle." Mr. Earl, who worked for Ralph Lauren in 1983, says that the Lauren furniture, sheets, and tableware are connected to his clothing; together they create a total picture. In Liz at Home, the Claiborne bedding line, the windowpane plaids coordinate with the floral prints in a manner similar to the fabrications of the company's mix and match clothing. Designers hope that consumers who are loyal to their apparel lines will purchase their home fashions products.

In the past, products were primarily functional. A family furnished its home with necessities. Bed linens were often standard white; sometimes they had a color or pattern. Two types of dinnerware were selected. The "good set of china" was reserved for festive occasions and a less formal set for everyday use. The variety of linens was also limited and except for special occasions, more functional than decorative. As baby boomers began to raise families and furnish their homes, their fascination with designer clothing tempted many to seek the very same names for their home products.

Of course, the *designer label* is no guarantee of success. Even such names as Norma Kamali, Karl Lagerfeld, and Yves Saint Laurent—certain tickets for success in fashion apparel—failed with their lines of home fashions. Success in the home fashions field requires careful planning, not just a name on a label. Ralph Lauren's home fashions business is an excellent example of what it takes to market a profitable line. While some companies merely reassign two or three people from their apparel design team to create household products, Lauren employs approximately 130 people solely in his home fashions operation. His showroom includes a **trial apartment** that is refurbished twice yearly with a full offering of the next season's look. This total home concept enables buyers and merchandisers to understand the collection's concept, and how it should be marketed in the stores. Retail management consultant, Walter K. Levy, says "The look of Ralph Lauren's clothing paves the way for logical extension into the home design." Only those who follow a carefully developed plan will have a better chance to reap the rewards of successful home fashion merchandising.

In addition to the designer phenomenon, two people also had a tremendous effect on the home fashion industry—Martha Stewart and Faith Popcorn. Stewart, publisher, lecturer, and television personality, brought about an awareness of fashions for the home to the baby-boomer population, showing how to beautify homes and gardens. Faith Popcorn named and predicted the rise of **cocooning** (the stay at home syndrome). This was brought about by the desire to leave the corporate rat race in search of a better quality of life.

Home fashions combine elements that are as fashionable and trendy as apparel.

Today, the focus is on variety. Household products are like wearable fashions, changing with great regularity. No longer will one set of sheets suffice for a few years or will the same set of dishes be used on a regular basis.

As with the apparel industry, home fashions also has a fascinating history. Many individuals contributed to the transformation of the industry and the beginning of the twentieth-century movement toward modernism and the styles that evolved from it.

THE EVOLUTION OF DESIGN IN HOME FASHIONS

Elaborate ornamentation in home fashions was characteristic of the Victorian era. The interiors were overcrowded settings with an excessive use of furnishings. The furniture was handcrafted by skilled workers, who designed and produced the items. Although fine homes still featured quality merchandise, the Industrial Revolution resulted in considerable changes in furniture production. Products made in the new factories were no longer designed by craftsmen, but by managerial staffs who knew little about furniture.

During the Victorian era, the middle class was first able to afford the designs that were once available only to the rich. Because these products were inexpensively mass produced in factories, they did not have the quality of the designs from which they were copied. Although the Victorian era offered a blend of Gothic, Renaissance, Moorish, and Oriental designs in cluttered arrangements, many of these elements led to twentieth century modernism.

In the middle to late 1800s, new industrial machinery produced a variety of crudely made home furnishings. Distressed by the poorly crafted offerings, William Morris, a fine craftsman from England, set out to reintroduce quality products for the home. He led a return to hand-made goods that were wrought of fine materials and had a lesser amount of decorative detail. He wrote extensively on his beliefs and lectured about his philosophy on furnishings. It was to be the beginning of the Arts and Crafts movement. His own designs embodied textiles, wallpapers, and other objects. Joining him in the movement were a number of architects and artists who would later be known as interior designers. Simply crafted furniture and accessories were their trademarks. At the turn of the century, another movement emerged to excite the world—Art Nouveau. In Belgium and France, designers Henri Van de Velde, Victor Horta, and Hector Guimard came to the forefront. Their completely new creations featured undulating lines, curved shapes, and oversized flowers. Many of the styles were reminiscent of Japanese design, which featured simple lines and freedom of form. The movement surfaced in America after its introduction in France. Louis Tiffany became the master, with his Art Nouveau designs on iridescent glass. These soon became known as Tiffany glass.

Twentieth-Century Modernism

As the world entered the twentieth century, four designers emerged as the pioneers and eventual leaders of modernism in architecture and design. They were Frank Lloyd Wright, an American, and three Europeans—Walter Gropius, Ludwig Mies van der Rohe, and Le Corbusier. While they were creating modern styles, other designers were following traditional historical patterns.

Although much of the literature discusses Wright's architectural genius, less attention is paid to his design elements that enhanced interior spaces. He also designed furniture, lighting, textiles, and rugs, and introduced materials ranging from natural colored woods to painted steel.

In Germany, Walter Gropius established the Bauhaus school, whose modern designs became primary influences on architecture and interior design. Its popularity continues today with functional products in black, white, neutral, and primary colors. After the closing of the Bauhaus in 1932, Gropius led the architecture department at Harvard University, where he spread his original ideas about modernism.

Mies van der Rohe, also of the Bauhaus school, used an abundance of marble, travertine, steel, and black leather in his modern designs that were void of historical influences or applied ornamentation. Like Gropius, he moved to the United States, heading the Architectural School of Technology in Chicago, where he concentrated on his "less is more" theory of design.

Born in Switzerland, Le Corbusier spent most of his career in Paris where he designed buildings and interior pieces. His approach was cubist, but he used strong primary colors, along with greens and oranges, in a bold new way. His products are characterized by steel tubing, leather cushions, and solid color table tops. Some of his creations have remained popular today and are collectively known as classic modern.

A more fashion-oriented approach to modernism, called Art Deco, originated in France after World War I. It combined primitive art and cubism with modern motifs. Skyscrapers, such as New York City's Chrysler building, theaters, such as Radio City Music Hall, and many exhibition halls were designed in the Art Deco manner. The furniture, textiles, glassware, and ceramics industries were greatly inspired by the this style. Examples of the Art Deco styles include *fiesta* tableware, the famous perfume bottle designed for Coty by Rene Lalique, and Russell Wright American modern dinnerware.

After World War II, Gropius and Mies continued to influence the post modern movement. The most significant styling came from Scandinavia, and was called Danish Modern.

During the 1950s, the atomic age played a role in home furnishings. Sputnik I and II and the testing of the atomic bombs inspired fabric motifs of mushroom clouds and atoms. Asymmetrically shaped tables became popular and formica became a major material for both furniture and accessories.

The freedom of the 1960s brought further changes in design. Psychedelic colors were as prevalent in home fashions as in apparel. Synthetic fibers made their way into homes, where the best seat in the house was the bean-bag chair.

Just as apparel designers look to the past for inspiration so do designers of home fashions. Here, classical shapes are combined with Arts and Crafts colors.

High Tech, and espcially chrome, was popular in the 1970s. The harsh, bright colors of the previous decade were replaced by earth tones. Found objects originally designed for other uses, became standards as home fashions. The orange crate, for example, was now the home's bookcase.

In the 1980s, a new class of consumers evolved. They were the yuppies, whose goal was conspicuous consumption. Evidence of this was the $18,000 price tag for a tea kettle designed by Michael Graves. Lighting took on a new look, with recessed fixtures replacing the traditional lamps in many homes.

As we head for the year 2000, the 1990s is a mixed bag for home fashions. With less money for discretionary spending, the trend for furnishing the home has changed. Although the affluent still avail themselves of the finest, costliest furniture, others are settling for more practical, functional designs. Most consumers are buying furniture through catalogs and megastores, such as IKEA, and accessorizing them to give style and personality. But designer names are still important. Ralph Lauren has not only expanded his home fashion linens, but also added paint to his collection. Alexander Julian, once a leader in apparel design, is also capturing a share of the lucrative home market with a line of furniture. Calvin Klein, Bill Blass, and Liz Claiborne are also making significant inroads into fashion merchandise for the home. Catalogs galore, like the Company Store, Victoria, and Ballard Designs are filling mail boxes with a selection of home fashions for those too busy to shop in stores.

PRODUCTS OF THE HOME FASHIONS MARKET

Products made for the home are more plentiful and varied than ever before. Because a complete discussion of furniture would require several volumes, only the products that enhance the furniture and the rooms in which they are featured are examined.

Bedding

This group includes sheets, pillowcases, blankets, and comforters. As consumers became interested in creating fashion excitement in their bedrooms, the industry addressed their needs with fashion-related items. Ralph Lauren's patterns, for example are influenced by the Victorian era; Calvin Klein's designs, however, by the Arts and Crafts movement.

Different elements are available in a multitude of designs. These include:

- **Bedskirts.** A decorative edging that covers the boxspring and reaches the floor.

- **Duvet cover.** A cover that fits over a comforter and fastens, using velcro or buttons, at one end. It can be described as a giant pillowcase for a comforter.

- **Pillow sham.** A decorative pillow covering that slips over the pillow.

- **Valance.** A free-standing treatment for the top of a window, often used with draperies or blinds as a decorative piece.

The sheets and pillowcases, as well as the accessories, are constructed of fabrics that vary in quality. The patterns, depending on popularity, can be available for long periods. In this growing industry, new designs are introduced every three to six months. Those patterns that sell in limited numbers last for

Designer bedding has revolutionized the industry into one that is more fashion-oriented.

approximately one year. In addition to the sheets being used to cover beds, they are now also adapted for use as window coverings, shades, and other enhancements.

Anyone who has purchased bedding is aware of the wide range of prices. As with apparel, price points are determined by quality and designer label. In terms of quality, sheets come in several different classes.

The most expensive types are produced with materials that have high thread counts. A **thread count** is determined by the number of horizontal and vertical threads per square inch of the cloth. Those classified as percale are made of 180-thread count or higher and are considered fine quality. A coarse type of construction, known as **muslin** has thread counts of up to 160. In luxury bedding, the count usually runs from a minimum of 200 up to 310. The higher the thread count, the more luxurious the hand or feel and the more durable and pill resistant the sheeting. The particular thread count is determined by the manufacturer based upon consumer demand. Most retailers carry a broad selection of designs in each thread count.

The majority of sheets come in either blends of cotton and polyester or 100 percent cotton. Although the blend of cotton and polyester affords the user less wrinkling, easy care applications have now been used to make cottons more resistant to creasing and less dependent on ironing. Sheeting comes in a variety of "textures" that include the standard smooth types, that have an extremely smooth surface that resembles satin and flannel that is made by brushing cotton on one side for softness and warmth.

The price variation is the result not only of the thread count, but also of the color and pattern of the item. Solid color sheets are more costly to produce than white sheets. Prints on white backgrounds are even more costly because the process requires a separate *screen* for each color application. See chapter 6, The Textile Industry, for an explanation of screen printing. Embellishments, such as hems and lace, increase the cost even more.

Tableware

Dinnerware

The dishes we use for our meals are available in a variety of shapes, sizes, and patterns. They come in a range of materials, including **china, stoneware,** glass, and plastics. **Dinnerware** may be purchased as conventional sets, in which the various pieces match, or as individual pieces, which when combined according to an individual's preferences and creativity, lead to more interesting **table settings.** In stores that feature table displays, the latter arrangement seems to be getting significant attention. The user may mix and match different pieces to

Table settings run the gamut from formal to informal.

suit a specific occasion. Octagonal, oval, and square plates have joined the traditional round shape to provide more fashion interest. As with bed linens, dinnerware designs also reflect historical influences. The styles of the Art Deco period and Gianni Versace's elegant motifs that have been translated from classical times, for example, are popular with many people.

One of the most important names in china and **crystal** is Rosenthal. The organization is the subject of a World of Fashion Profile.

Glassware

Two major types of glass are used in the production of **glassware.** They are **soda-lime glass,** which is inexpensive but durable, and **lead glass,** which is more expensive and often hand formed. Steuben and Swarovski are examples of the finest lead and crystal glass. The lead variety is the one that has become more of a fashion item. After the pieces are formed, the glass is shaped into a variety of **stemmed pieces, footed tumblers,** and **tumblers.** Once this has ben completed, the pieces may be enhanced through etching, engraving, cutting, embossing, and sandblasting. Each decorative finish imparts a different appearance.

Flatware

Rounding out the main pieces that are found on the dinner table is **flatware.** As with dinnerware and glassware, there are numerous styles made in a wide range of materials.

Royalty and the upper class have always used sterling silver to set their tables. Today, sterling silver, in patterns from the ornate baroque to the modern designs that are reminiscent of the Arts and Crafts period, is almost always reserved for special occasions in households that are far less affluent. **Sterling silver** flatware and serving pieces are often received by newlyweds as gifts and collected until the desired number of pieces have been reached.

Silverplate, a metal that is made up of a small amount of silver that has been adhered to a base metal, stainless steel, bronzeware, metals adorned with ornamental handles, molded resins, and others are used for daily purposes.

The more expensive flatware is often sold in **place settings,** which include four of five different utensils. Less costly flatware is generally purchased in sets known as service for eight or twelve. Many manufacturers are also selling their products as service for four.

Like many of the other home products, the market is filled with familiar names, such as Gorham and Oneida. New offerings often bear the names of jewelry designers such as Robert Lee Morris.

Fabrics for Home Fashions

One of the most effective ways in which to create a mood or feeling is with fabrics. In every corner of the world, mills are producing patterns and designs in a variety of qualities and price ranges to satisfy everyone's needs. Rich brocades, matalesses, velvets, and other fancy fabrics are in abundance for those with

Fabrics project a mood or feeling in the home fashions market. Here in a fabric showroom, a designer flips through fabric samples while a salesperson waits for the order.

Rosenthal

Classical-traditional designs are a key element of the Rosenthal Company.

Founded in 1879 in Selb, Germany, the Rosenthal Company has emerged as one of the world's finest porcelain (china) and crystal manufacturers. The original focus on classical-traditional designs turned into a whole new movement in 1961, when Philip Rosenthal, Jr., son of the founder, launched the Rosenthal Studio Line. It was a table-top collection that employed the talents of more than 100 famous artists and designers. It gave a day-to-day product that certain sparkle of lifestyle and an appreciation for master quality. Among those who have taken the company to new fashion heights, with magnificent designs, are Gianni Versace, the internationally renowned fashion designer, and also Aldo Rossi, one of the world's leading architects.

The products are internationally marketed. Each country because of its particular taste and style, has different assortments produced for it. Originality is a key element in the production of everything Rosenthal makes. It does not imitate what others have done.

The company has three product lines—Rosenthal Classic, the original concept, Rosenthal-Studio Line, and Thomas by Rosenthal, each featuring an assortment of china, stemware, flatware, and giftware. Each is completely different from the others.

- Rosenthal Classic consists of traditional and elegant products that preserve the value of past decades. Classic shapes are merged with decorative elements and moods of modern times. In this collection, heirloom designs are created and are passed on from one generation to another.
- Rosenthal-Studio Line is design oriented and innovative. Its roster of designers has included the aforementioned Versace, along with Roy Lichtenstein and Dorothy Hafner of the United States, Walter Gropius and Michael Boehm of Germany, Tapio Wirkkala of Finland, Salvatore Dali of Spain, Nina Campbell and Henry Moore of Great Britain, and more than 100 other designers, artists, and architects.
- Thomas by Rosenthal is a functionally oriented line with a fresh and youthful appeal and an emphasis on clear shapes and individual items.

By producing these three different lines, the company has retained its standing as a world-class manufacturer, but one that also embraces today's fashion standards.

Before any product is made available to the stores, it must be approved by an independent jury of specialists. This committee name may be affixed to the item. Because of the painstaking attention paid to design, the company has been awarded numerous prizes and distinctions. Its 1,600 individual design prizes include the prestigious one bestowed by the New York Museum of Modern Art.

The lines are marketed in leading department stores such as Bloomingdale's, Neiman Marcus, and Bergdorf Goodman, in fine specialty stores, and in the company's own "studio-houses." A catalog that features every product in the three lines is available to potential customers so that they may, in the comforts of their home, make their selections before going to the store to make a purchase.

Victorian homes. People with simpler tastes based on more modern styles can choose from geometric and plainer styles. Between these two starkly different types of fabrics are canvas, tweeds, plaids, and others.

Fabrics have many uses in home fashions, including upholstery, curtains, and draperies. The correct fabric selection can immediately transform a mundane room into an exciting one. For example, Missoni, noted designers of elaborate knit fashions, have licensed their patterns for bed and bath products as well as for a line of textiles for interior decorating.

Floor Coverings

Another area of home furnishings in which there are neverending options is **floor coverings.** There are many choices for every room in the house. In areas where warmth is important, **carpeting** is the mainstay. With today's technological advances, mills are manufacturing increasingly durable products in broader color ranges. Joining the standard wools are polyester, nylon, olefin, cotton, and natural fibers, such as sisal.

Recently, the use of **hardwood flooring** has increased. The woods may be simply laid in planks or used to form intricate parquet designs. The boom in the hardwood floor market has given greater importance to the use of area rugs. **Persian** and **kilim rugs,** as well as area rugs in contemporary patterns available in a variety of sizes, are used to cover portions of the hardwood floors. These rugs immediately give a special personality to the room.

Area rugs from every corner of the globe dress wooded or tiled floors.

In kitchens and bathrooms, the floors are usually covered with ceramic tiles. In sizes that range from nine- to eighteen- inch squares and in designs that range from solids to patterns, the product is extremely serviceable and durable.

For more extravagant tastes, marble and granite can be used in just about any room in the house. They too are sometimes covered with area rugs to complete the design concept.

Decorative Enhancements

Ceramics

In addition to ceramic flooring, ceramic accessories can accent any home decor. The costs range from nominal, for pieces mass produced from molds, to costly, for those made individually by craftspersons, who use such methods as a potter's wheel. The glazes, or outer protective coverings, provide the *look* that attracts attention. Large pots for plants, figurines, animals, and table bases are some items that are used as home fashions.

Basketry

Baskets have always played functional roles, such as holding bread and fruit. Today, baskets have become design accents that add interest to almost every room in the house. At stores like Pier 1, row upon row of different styles fill the shelves. At craft fairs, intricate handwoven pieces are featured in an array of natural reeds and other weaving materials. The one-of-a-kind basket often sells for more than several hundred dollars. Many art galleries feature handwoven baskets from around the world at even greater price points, with some selling for approximately $1,000.

The placement of the basketry on shelves, floors, mantels, and window ledges—either by themselves or as holders of plants, towels, accessories—become an important part of interior design.

Accent pillows, in limitless designs and shapes, and beaded frames and mirrors are just some decorative items used to enhance a room's interior.

Accent Pillows

Piled high on sofas, beds, and other upholstered furniture, decorative pillows are providing exciting accents to home furnishings. One of the first to use **accent pillows** on beds was Ralph Lauren. A visit to any Lauren bedding display immediately reveals pillow upon pillow used to create interest.

Pillows come in many designs and shapes. They include needlepoints, scenic brocades, contemporary stripes, velours, velvets, prints, and geometrics. They range in price from twenty to several hundred dollars, depending on workmanship, size, and fabric.

Plants

Home interiors can be an arena to showcase live and artificial plants. In every room, plants are now used as decorative accents. Even in the large bathrooms of today's contemporary home, plants are used to lend design interest. For example, orchids in front of a glass block wall through which diffused light enters allows the plants to thrive and provides a dramatic setting to any interior. Large palms of many varieties stand as high as ten feet tall and majestically create a mood of elegance.

The effect is one of nature brought indoors. For areas in which there is little light, artificial plants of silk and other fibers are used. They require no maintenance and lend the same grace to a living space as do their live counterparts.

Paint

Not too long ago, **paint** was available in a few brands and a limited array of colors. Today, the market has significantly expanded. Augmenting the pre-mixed varieties that bore such labels as Benjamin Moore and Dutch Boy, came new colors that included just about any shade or tint. With the aid of computer matching, the consumer could specify any colors.

In specialty shops around the country, Martha Stewart is marketing paint that costs $110 a gallon! Her concept is to narrow the field of colors to the ones she deems most appropriate. For example, the typical Benjamin Moore line offers so many shades of white that the shopper is often confused. She sells just one white. If the consumer is a Martha Stewart enthusiast, that will be the white used. All in all, her color range includes 80 colors.

Ralph Lauren's approach is to appeal to the consumer who is interested in fashion, but is not willing to pay Stewart's higher prices. Under an arrangement with Sherwin Williams, Lauren features more than 400 colors from $20 per gallon. Also he sells brushes, tools, and instructional videos about fancy finishes. Both Stewart and Lauren group colors that work well together, leaving out the guesswork of matching.

With a large segment of the population enthralled and motivated by designer names, these new paint endeavors will probably be successful.

In addition to paint labels and color selection, the paint market has expanded with the introduction of unusual **faux paint finishes.** The finishes are quite unique, with faux marble heading the list. By applying different layers of paint in different colorations and distressing them with such devices as sponges, unusual effects are achieved. The novice may accomplish a number of different finishes with the purchase of paint kits that include everything necessary to achieve the desired results. Professional painters, using their own techniques, have come up with a wide range of faux finishes. Stores like Home Depot hold regular seminars for the do-it-yourselfer, while the more daring individuals use trial-and-error methods until they come up with the pattern they want.

Wall Coverings

Papers and fabrics are available as **wall coverings.** Many are inspired by apparel designers, others are available from companies that have been in the business for years. Some wall coverings are made to match the curtains, draperies, and upholsteries used in home design, giving unity to a room's appearance. The styles range from very formal to the simple, contemporary patterns; price ranges from as little as $10 per roll. For those who wish to install their own wall coverings, many are available in prepasted versions that make adherence easier. For the professional, pastes appropriate to the type of covering are applied separately.

While the wall covering industry is still flourishing, it is losing some ground to the faux painters. Painted walls, when faded or past their prime, can easily be repainted. The removal of wall coverings is considerably more costly.

Decorative Ornaments

In addition to accessories already mentioned, home furnishings include decorative ornaments. Among them are **bifold screens** that may attractively separate two areas in a small apartment or hide something that the apartment dweller does not want to be seen. They come in many varieties, including those that are fabric covered, louver constructed, and hand painted. The **wine rack** is another functional item that also adds interest to a room. Multilevel stands that sit on the floor or on tables, hold numerous objects such as plants, flowers, fruit, or small decorative items. They are often made of wrought iron and come in a variety of heights. **Draw pulls** and **decorative hooks,** used for towel displays, also add excitement to a setting. Both are also functional as well as pleasing to the eye. **Wall plaques** and **sconces** add excitement to any room. The plaques come in any material from cement that has been casted to rich handmade glass. The sconces are glass containers that hold bulbs to light a staircase, hallway, or accent a part of a room, such as a fireplace. It is the imagination of the designer that often comes up with ornaments that others would never think of using.

Examples of apparel designers successfully making the transition from apparel to home fashions.

LICENSING ARRANGEMENTS

Names like Ralph Lauren, Bill Blass, Joseph Abboud, Gianni Versace, Alexander Julian, Adrienne Vittadini, Todd Oldham, Guess, and Liz Claiborne of the fashion apparel world are now producing home fashions in record numbers. More than one time, Bill Blass has said that it is the sheets, and not the suits and dresses, that have made him a millionaire. Alexander Julian, men's wear designer, has extolled the benefits of home fashions. Beginning with a collection of sheets, Julian now offers, under the Home Colours label, a selection of lithographs, case goods, upholstery, and lamps. He says it is the biggest success he has enjoyed in years. Not to be left behind, Adrienne Vittadini has also expanded into home fashions. In addition to a line of sheets, wall coverings are sold through the Schumacher Company in New York City. Her home fashions are marketed in much the same manner as her apparel designs, with coordinated patterns and colors the central focus. The significant growth in this industry, which has minimal risks when compared to the clothing market, and increased consumer interest can bring significant profits to a company. As a result, Donna Karan, Calvin Klein, and Mary McFadden have joined the growing list of apparel home fashion designers.

For many years, home product lines were marketed by company names. For example, in the bedding field, the appearance of such names as Martex, Westpoint Stevens (a merger of J.P. Stevens and Westpoint Pepperel), and Dan River on labels were important to sales. In dinnerware, Rosenthal and Lenox, with their famous designs, were all that was advertised. The same was true of other home products. Today, brand marketing is more important than ever. Advertising constantly encourages consumers to look for specific brands.

To further sales, these companies are entering into **designer licensing** agreements with well-known apparel fashion designers, so they can capitalize on their names and reputations. Every consumer who has ever been satisfied with a Ralph Lauren outfit, a Bill Blass dress, or a Gianni Versace creation is likely to buy the same label when in the market for bedding, dinnerware, and other home items.

Unlike a designer's involvement in the manufacture of fashion apparel and accessories, where they generally participate in decisions concerning fabric purchases, production, marketing, and so forth, the designers merely create the patterns and designs used on sheets, tablecloths, dishes, and glassware. The production and marketing are left to the licensors.

For their roles, the **licensees**—the designers whose names will be associated with the products—receive payment in the form of a percentage or commission on sales.

The degree of participation by a designer varies from agreement to agreement. In some, the designer provides the company with design sketches that will eventually be used in the products. In others, the designer oversees a staff that produces the design, with the right to eliminate those that do not meet his or her approval.

No matter which route is taken, the name of the designer takes center stage in the marketing of the product. In many stores, home fashions products are featured on the selling floors as collections, in the same manner as apparel. Ralph Lauren, for example, requires that his bedding collections occupy a particular part of the selling floor, not to be mixed with other brands, exactly as he merchandises his apparel collections.

Some of the major agreements include Springs Industries, which manufactures the Liz sheets and Bill Blass bed linens, and Fieldcrest Cannon, which produces Adrienne Vittadini's home collections. These "marriages" have been so successful that many companies have several agreements with designers to create different collections.

Entertainment Licensing

Not all licenses are designer related. There is a growing trend for characters in the entertainment industry to be featured on all types of home fashions. The majority of these products are directed toward the children's market and include cartoon characters, as well as television and film properties.

Barbie Doll®, for example, is a winning name in young girl's bedding; Harley Davidson© attracts the boys. It is the Disney organization, however, that provides the most important of these entertainment licenses. Mickey Mouse©, for example, has had an enormous influence for many years and never fails to appeal to the young set.

Entertainment licensing agreements for entertainment characters are somewhat different from those for designers. With the exception of The Walt Disney Company©, licensors have little, if anything, to do with the designs, except to have the right of approval. They are paid royalties by the manufacturers for the use of their names.

Sports Licensing

Manufacturers of sports apparel and equipment have also joined the licensing explosion, creating lines that bear the names of celebrity athletes. The Palmer Home Collection, introduced in 1995, benefits from the Arnold Palmer name. These licensing agreements are with Lexington Furniture for furniture and Guildmaster for decorative accessories. This **sports licensing** not only takes advantage of the allure of the Arnold Palmer name, but also the design background of Winnie Palmer, Arnold's wife.

Museum Licensing

The popularity of museum reproductions has opened the way for licensing arrangements among famous museums, manufacturers, and retailers. An example of a major entry into this type of licensing is Museum Treasures by Andrew Cymrot. Beginning first with a few pieces from New York's American Museum of Natural History, the company now licenses products from London's Victoria and Albert Museum, and the Royal Ontario Museum in Canada. The designs of Daniel Chester French, who designed the Lincoln Memorial, are just some of the items that will be marketed. These **museum licensing** arrangements bring a great deal of money to the museums, which otherwise depend on donations, grants, and admission fees to cover their operating expenses.

RETAILING HOME FASHIONS

As with apparel and accessories, a variety of retailers are in the home fashions market, including department stores, specialty stores, manufacturers, freestanding shops, and catalog companies.

One of the people responsible for developing home fashions merchandising is Terence Conran of Great Britain, who revolutionized retailing by applying the principles of high fashion at low cost in the Main Streets of the world. After a stint as a textile designer and furniture maker, he set up a design conservatory in 1956. He opened his first retail shop in 1964. Its instant success spawned an international chain across the United Kingdom, Belgium, the United States, Iceland, Martinique, Singapore, and Japan. His visual merchandising of the products appealed to the consumers. Before long, many were lining up to purchase home furnishings in a different manner. His early inventiveness led to such operations as Crate & Barrel, IKEA, Pier 1, and Urban Outfitters.

Department Stores

Ever since department stores opened their doors, there has been a department in which shoppers could choose from a selection of dinnerware, bedding, and other home fashions. These items, however, rarely brought the same attention to the store as did its fashion apparel and accessories.

Today, this is changing, and department stores are paying greater attention to home fashions. They are enlarging the selling floors that house this merchandise and are using promotional efforts to publicize them. At Macy's in New York City, table settings are created by celebrities as part of the store's annual Flower Show extravaganza. Personalities from stage, screen, television, and the design world are invited to **dress tables** with dinnerware, glassware, table linens, and silverware. The promotion is very successful and generates a great deal of business for the store.

With all of the attention being paid to home fashions, Macy's has opened its first free-standing store that exclusively features products for the home. This 100,660 square foot store in Las Vegas is the prototype for others to come. Burdines, the Miami-based department store that primarily concentrates on fashion apparel and accessories, has also answered the growing market for more home furnishings with separate stores for such products.

Specialty Stores

Many shops that exclusively feature home fashions are opening across the United States. They range from the small independent variety to such major operations as Crate & Barrel, Williams Sonoma, Linens and Things, Bed Bath & Beyond, Urban Outfitters, This End Up, The Bombay Company, and Pottery Barn.

These stores specialize in a limited assortment of merchandise, such as bedding, table linens, bath products, dinnerware, glassware, silverware, and related items. One of the keys to their success is the assortment that they offer to the customer. At Bed Bath & Beyond, for example, the merchandise assortment in bed linens is far greater than any department store can offer. The customer is able to choose from a wealth of designs and price points.

Exciting visual merchandising has also been a major factor in attracting customers. Instead of lining the shelves with merchandise in an ordinary manner, stores like Crate & Barrel and Williams Sonoma produce magnificent displays that immediately transform mundane items into treasures.

Exclusivity is also an approach taken by many of these stores. Instead of relying on merchandise that may be seen at many different stores, some, such

Bed, Bath & Beyond, here on New York's Sixth Avenue, is a home furnishings megastore.

as Crate & Barrel, are combing the globe to bring back goods for their exclusive sale. In this way, the customer cannot comparison shop to get the lowest possible price. Crate & Barrel is featured in a World of Fashion Profile.

Free-Standing Manufacturer Outlets

There is a trend in this industry for manufacturers to open shops that only feature their collections. Companies such as Mikasa, Villeroy & Boch, Waterford, Sheridan, and Royal Doulton operate stores all across the country that sell company-produced products. By doing so, a customer may see the entire line of merchandise under one roof. Although these manufacturers also sell to department and specialty stores, none of these has the space or need to feature every item in a single manufacturer's line. Instead, they select specific designs from a host of companies in the hope that the assortment will motivate the shoppers to buy at least one.

By entering the retail business, the companies eliminate the competition from other lines and offer a full assortment of everything they manufacture.

Catalogs

More and more catalogs that feature home fashions are delivered to households everyday. The Bombay Company, Spiegel, Sharper Image, Garnet Hill, Ballard Designs, Crate & Barrel, and the Company Store are some examples. Some catalogs are from traditional department and specialty stores; others are from catalog companies whose method of operation is direct mail. Saks Fifth Avenue, known for its high fashion apparel and accessories, has entered the home fashions market with a catalog called Folio Design for the home. It is published three times a year, and features silk throws and pillows from Gianni Versace, Calvin Klein's Home Collection, and Ralph Lauren's decoratives for the home. With such a large market for in-home purchasing, catalog sales are constantly growing. Soon, video catalogs will be available for customers to see

Crate & Barrel

When people enter Crate & Barrel stores, a visual shopping experience greets them. Unlike the typical stores that sell dinnerware, glassware, giftware, and other products for the home, their selling floors immediately impart a feeling of fashion excitement.

Crate & Barrel began uneventfully in the kitchen of its founder, Gordon Segal, in 1962. As he was washing the dishes, he wondered out loud why nobody in Chicago was selling the type of dinnerware he had just brought back from the Caribbean and New York. At that very moment he decided to open a store to fill this gap in the marketplace. From its initial opening in 1962, the company has expanded to a 50 store chain in 10 markets with more than 2,000 full-time employees.

The first store was a renovated 1,800 square foot space in an old elevator factory. By nailing up crating lumber on the walls and spilling products out of their packing crates and barrels, the perfect environment and company name was born. Prices at Crate & Barrel were also better than anywhere else in Chicago. The merchandise assortment was exciting and innovative.

Although he knew little about running a retail operation in the beginning, he did have a feeling for good design. The concept was that design didn't need to be expensive, but the products had to have a standard of excellence that was evident in showrooms, factories, and stores in Europe.

A Crate & Barrel ad targets their customer with a perfect setting and challenging copy

After the success in the first store, a team of designers developed the now famous display method that is widely imitated. The concept is to create a "vignette" for specific items to attract attention. And attention and excellent sales it did get.

In addition to the store operations, Crate & Barrel entered the catalog business in 1973, and turned it into a venture that grossed $21 million in 1994.

home furnishing lines. The scope of the home fashions industry may be quickly understood by examining all of the places from which merchandise may be procured and the size of the offerings. A visit to High Point, North Carolina, the home fashions answer to Seventh Avenue for apparel, reveals the level achieved by this market.

*IKEA and The Bombay
Company market products
through extensive catalogs.*

Chapter Highlights

- Fashions for the home are now reaching all-time highs.

- The home fashions have developed from the elaborate ornamentation of the Victorian Period to the trendy products of the 1980s.

- The products of the home fashion market continue to grow, with the use of exciting bedding, tableware, decorative enhancements, and other decorative ornaments in varieties never before available.

- Special licensing agreements with designers and well-known personalities and characters dramatically increase sales.

- Terence Conran, the British home fashions designer, is considered responsible for the retailing of low-cost, exciting furnishings. His vision spawned new operations, such as Crate & Barrel, IKEA, Pier 1, and Urban Outfitters.

- Although home fashions were once marketed primarily in department stores, many different outlets now exist for their sale. They include catalogs, specialty stores, and free-standing designer shops, each of which offers unique merchandise.

Important Fashion Terminology and Concepts

accent pillows
bedding
bedskirts
bifold screens
carpeting
china
cocooning
crystal
decorative hooks
designer licensing
dinnerware
draw pulls
dress tables
duvet cover
entertainment licenses
faux paint finishes

flatware
floor coverings
footed tumblers
glassware
hardwood flooring
kilim rug
lead glass
licensees
museum licensing
muslin
paint
percale
Persian rug
pillow sham
place settings
sconces

silverplate
soda-lime glass
sports licensing
stemmed pieces
sterling silver
stoneware
table settings
tableware
thread count
trial apartment
tumblers
valance
wall coverings
wall plaques
wine rack

For Review

1. Define the term home fashions as it is used in this chapter.

2. Describe the characteristics of home furnishings during the Victorian era.

3. Contrast the Arts and Crafts movement with the Victorian era.

4. Why did William Morris begin a new direction in home fashions, and what was it?

5. Describe some of the highlights of Art Nouveau design.

6. What were some of the highlights of twentieth-century modernism?

7. What is Art Deco?

8. What changes in the various segments of the home furnishings industry have resulted in increased sales?

9. List the names of five apparel designers who have entered the home fashions arena.

10. Under what type of arrangement do most apparel designers create bedding and dinnerware?

11. What is meant by the term "entertainment licensing?"

12. How have department stores addressed the growing interest in home fashions?

13. Discuss the impact made by Terence Conran on home furnishings retailing.

14. Currently, which specialty retailers are the leaders in fashion-oriented products for the home?

Exercises and Projects

1. Visit the bedding department in a major department store. Compare the various collections of bed linens in terms of those that feature only the manufacturer's names with those that promote designer labels. With the information gathered, determine the percentage of each category in the department.

2. Write to a dinnerware company, the names of which may be found in any store that specializes in that product line, asking for information about the products it sells. The information requested should concern construction techniques, methods of decoration, price points, and anything else that would be of interest. Photographs of the products should also be obtained. The photos should be mounted on a board according to the classifications they belong to. For each, the benefits afforded the user should be given.

3. Write to an apparel designer who also creates home fashions, asking for a press kit. A report should be prepared telling about the designer's background, and how he or she made the transition from clothing to home fashions.

The Case of the Designer Dilemma

One of the mainstays of the bedding industry for forty-five years has been T.J. Contours, Inc. Its collections have been regularly marketed through stores that cater to people in the upper-lower and lower-middle classes. Sears and Montgomery Ward are typical of the retailers it supplies.

Its strength has been the traditional types of patterns, such as flowers and stripes, which sell at modest price points. The actual designs are created by a team of "unsung heroes," who spend endless hours turning out the patterns. Its packages highlight the names of the company rather than the names of those responsible for the designs.

Alan Santos has been the president of T.J. Contours for the last ten years. He regularly studies the trade papers for new industry directions and to feel the pulse of the market. In recent years, he has noticed that more and more bedding collections bear designer signatures. While this had never been considered as an option for his company, he believes the time is right for such a move.

Betsey Peters, the executive vice-president of the company, thinks that the move to designer collections would be a mistake. After all, she states, "We've been successful for all of these years without the benefit of designer labels, and the change would be too costly for the company."

At this point in time no decision has been made.

Questions

1. With whom do you agree? Why?

2. Are there any other methods by which the company might gain further recognition?

point of view

Theater a la King

Francy Blackwood

Well before department stores had embraced the concept, Sue King latched onto the idea of retailing as theater.

Since 1978, her San Francisco shop, Sue Fisher King, has featured what King described as a "changing panoply of merchandise." The show includes bed linens, table linens, furniture, decorative accessories, tableware and gifts. The staging features artful cross-category vignettes enlivened by a steady influx of the European imports that are King's specialty.

Selecting merchandise for the 1,500-square-foot store "is like buying Armani," King said. "It's ever-changing. It's fashion. We change things all the time. . . . Maybe too often," she observed wryly one morning as her staff hauled furniture in and out of the shop.

Bed and bath linens are King's largest category, accounting for about 60 percent of sales. Ever since her days as a buyer at I. Magnin, "I've always liked bed linens," King noted. "I used to say that if I ever got my own store, I would do some really exciting stuff with bed linens."

That's one reason she turned to European suppliers. "The Europeans are very adventurous in the use of color," she said. "They cater to a smaller market, and use very expensive fabrics . . . very sophisticated jacquards with an incredible hand."

The focus on rich, elaborate mixes of pattern and color helps to distinguish King's assortment from the luxury linens at department stores. "The high thread counts department stores carry tend to be whites and creams, and they don't have many jacquards," she said.

In general, King steers clear of the popular domestically produced high-end linens carried in growing numbers by department stores. "There's no way a small store can compete in that arena," she said.

Instead, King scours international markets for unique, niche-oriented designs. She shops Pitti Casa in Florence, Macef in Milan, the Bed, Bath & Linen Show in New York, the gift show in Paris and the furniture fair in Verona. Exclusivity is high on King's agenda. "The only thing we carry that's everywhere is Palais Royal," she said.

Lacking the clout of big-volume merchants, King sometimes struggles to land the merchandise she desires. Case in point: For years, she tried unsuccessfully to get the Frette line. She might still be knocking on Frette's door were it not for a program the big-name Italian supplier launched a few years ago. "They decided to do boutiques in existing stores, and we got the exclusive for San Francisco," she said.

King has about eight key bedding suppliers, including Sferra Bros. and Frette, as well as several smaller Italian design houses. She displays the merchandise on distinctive imported furniture pieces, which are for sale. A $19,000, wooden bibliotheca, custom-made in Florence, holds Frette linens and $1,200 Emilia Bellini sheet sets. A day bed made of cherry with poplar-burl overlay is piled high with hand-blocked velvet pillows from Mirella Spinella in Venice, priced at $275 to $650.

Another bed features putty-colored striped shams of cotton sateen from Cotti Maryane and a Loro Pina throw of cashmere reversing to suede, priced at $2,800. A window display highlights the recent arrival of a collection by Italian designer Gimmo Etro.

The price points at Sue Fisher King suggest an affluent customer. And indeed, the shop draws heavily from its well-heeled Pacific Heights neighborhood. But King said her clientele is defined more by taste level than by demographics. Her customers are attracted to the store's eclectic, cross-category assortment. "They like the mixture of stuff," she said. "They're interested in things that aren't completely traditional."

At the same time, she said, "We do have a basic program of white and cream jacquards in classic styles that our customers won't let us give up." King gets the basics from a supplier who does private-label lines and linens for Harrods. Given King's bent for exclusivity, she's not about to reveal her source. "I live in fear that someone will find him," she said.

When King set up shop on Sacramento Street 16 years ago, she was attracted by the cozy, neighborhood feeling of the locale. The area is still charming, and in the years since Sue Fisher King opened, it has become a mecca for home furnishings stores. Shabby Chic is next-door, and the street is lined with antique shops and home boutiques that attract both retail shoppers and interior decorators. "We do a lot of work with decorators, and I'm trying to build that business," King said. "It's a wonderful way to get your merchandise shown."

King does very little advertising. To attract new customers, she relies primarily on semi-annual promotions. Twice a year, she rents a vacant storefront a few blocks from the shop and fills it with manufacturers' samples, discontinued styles and overstocks—all at bargain prices. For two weeks last March, she featured linens.

She announces the sales in local newspapers and attracts people throughout the Bay Area.

Many of the sale-shoppers become regular customers at Sue Fisher King. And since King buys special stock for the low price promotions, they don't cannibalize her regular volume. The sale items, "have nothing to do with any regular inventory," she said.

When her furniture sale ends, King moves the leftover pieces into the shop. She does a brisk business in chairs and side tables, and the furniture is an important element in the theatrical appeal of Sue Fisher King. "It makes it look like a home," King said.

Mood, ambiance and ever-changing presentation remain corner-

stones of King's merchandising strategy. A few months ago, she revamped the display of table linens, which used to be stacked on flat shelves. Now they're hung over dowels in an eyecatching, color-coordinated array that fills a side wall. The new display "paid off from the get-go. There was an immediate increase in sales," King reported.

"Now," she said, looking at the display with the practiced eye of a retail-stage designer, "all I need is about $1,000 worth of spotlights."

HFD, November 28, 1994.

Fashion Designers Go Home

Sharon Overton

Once we were content to wear the occasional designer label on our T-shirts or jeans.

Then we discovered the joy of sleeping on designer sheets.

Now everything from soap dishes and cereal bowls to wall paint and mattress covers comes with a designer label. In the '90s, nesting had replaced social climbing and haute couture had led to home couture.

No longer are fashion designers content simply to fill our closets. They're out to fulfill our domestic fantasies as well.

Do you long for a home with the patina of Old Money? To his extensive line of home furnishings—all designed to make you look as if you belong on the social register—Ralph Lauren has recently added wall paints. With names such as Spinnaker Blue and Dressage Red, these Sherwin-Williams hues promise

that your walls will bespeak gentility even if you weren't born with a silver spoon in your mouth.

Prefer a sort of stripped-down minimalism that conjures up images of a monastery or Zen rock garden? Check out Calvin Klein's new home collection: austere wooden bowls, sublimely simple china, Italian linen sheets and woven cashmere throws so exquisitely serene, and expensive, you'll have to take a vow of poverty to own them.

Other fashion designers are expanding into the home as well. Alexander Julian's moderately priced Home Colours collection for Universal Furniture Industries features traditionally styled furniture with subtle fashion details, such as argyle-patterned wood veneers and wingtip-style flourishes.

Gianni Versace, whose over-the-top clothing is favored by rock idols

and movie stars, does baroque-style home furnishings that might appeal to the Mick Jagger in all of us.

Even Donna Karan has announced that she'll offer a home collection sometime in 1997. (Picture little form-fitting matte jersey slipcovers and cozy chairs that cradle you like a cashmere wrap coat.)

In the meantime, everyone from Joseph Abbound to Liz Claiborne, it seems, has come out with a line of bed sheets and bath towels.

While fashion designers have long lent their names to other types of products, often with mixed results, never before have so many crossed over so completely, extending their aesthetic vision to nearly every corner of our domestic lives, says Richard Martin, director of The Costume Institute of the Metropolitan Museum of Art in New York.

"It's a particularly 1990s kind of phenomenon," says Martin, who has written about Versace's Miami Beach mansion.

As the couture business has slumped, designers have had to look elsewhere for markets to feed the enormous empires they built during the '80's.

"People do spend more money on shelter now than on clothing," Martin says. "It's very logical to move into that area."

Also, fashion designers have attained an unprecedented celebrity status that gives them greater power to influence the way we think and live.

"I suspect that Donna Karan, Calvin Klein and Ralph Lauren are names that are as familiar as Bill Clinton," Martin says.

"Every street kid now knows the names Giorgio Armani [one of the few designers, it seems, who doesn't have a home collection]. We've come to the point where fashion designers are looked upon with an enormous sense of Faith in a society that doesn't give faith to its political figures or even its spiritual figures."

Naturally, anything that exalted is bound to be ridiculed as well.

Newsweek has poked fun at the idea of pricey designer wall paint as a new "lifestyle fetish."

Starting at $21 a gallon for basic white, Ralph Lauren Paints come in 400 colors grouped in categories such as Thoroughbred, Country, Safari and Santa Fe, which complement his furniture designs. Custom finishing kits are available that will instantly age your freshly painted walls with a patina of "sun-fade, tea-stained, smoke and tobacco effects," according to a Lauren press release.

Perhaps it's not surprising in this age of mind-boggling choices that we look to designers for validation of how we dress and how we live.

Even the Gap, which created a national uniform out of khaki pants and denim work shirts, is said to be considering an expansion into home furnishings. Just imagine: Sofas that are as familiar as a pair of faded jeans and rugs, dishes and lamps all bearing that comforting, generic navy blue label.

The fact that the "Gap Home" rumors persist without confirmation from the company itself shows how eager many shoppers are for the validation of a brand name.

"People are so insecure about what to wear, how to identify themselves," says Deborah Shinn, assistant curator at the Copper-Hewitt National Design Museum in New York. "It gives you a sense of security to wrap yourself up with a name that's sort of sanctioned by the press and popular taste. The same thing goes for the home."

But do the skills that make someone good at shaping a jacket, for instance, necessarily translate into making tables and chairs?

"I think it works when fashion designers have a very, very strong sensibility," Martin says. "But I have a feeling it's the kind of thing that probably will be taken to excess. . . . Do you really need to have Marc Jacobs designing your home?

Digs. Sharon Overton. *The Times-Union.* August 24, 1996.

PART FOUR

Designing and Manufacturing Fashion Apparel and Accessories

Before most designers and manufacturers create their product lines, they consult with fashion forecasters. These specialists explore the fiber mills and other resources to learn about trends that they can pass on to the clients.

Armed with this information from forecasters and their knowledge of elements and principles of design, manufacturers begin the creative process. One of the most important elements of design is color. To choose the right color combinations, it is necessary to understand color theory. The Prang System is the most widely used.

After the designer has created the initial samples or drawings for new styles, it is time to begin production. A schedule is established that begins with the creation of a production pattern. Today that pattern is most often produced by means of a computer-aided design or CAD system. After the necessary patterns are developed, garments are cut and assembled, either by an inside shop or through outside contractors. Those products that are favorably received by retail buyers continue on to production.

Each accessory follows its own manufacturing plan. Accessory buyers must understand the many manufacturing methods in order to accurately assess the quality of the final product.

Once the garments and accessories are produced, they are ready to be sold to the stores and then to the consumers.

CHAPTER 14

Fashion Forecasting for Designers and Manufacturers

After you have completed this chapter, you will be able to discuss:

• The various ways the fashion forecaster aids the designer, product developer, and the retailer.

• The process by which the forecasters ultimately make their predictions.

• Why those who forecast fashion must begin as early as eighteen months prior to the selling season.

• Why the fiber producers use fashion shows as part of their forecasting campaigns.

Manufacturers and designers are very knowledgeable about their industry, but they must also be attuned to changes that will shape their future design decisions. At one time, designers did not need to be familiar with lifestyles, social values, culture, ecology, and other aspects of living to produce a new line. Consumers were followers, not leaders in the world of fashion. Today, designers and manufacturers must understand the needs and values of consumers before they begin to create a design. Consumers are better educated than ever, and they no longer follow the dictates of manufacturers and designers. They accept or reject fashion for a variety of reasons. Although the haute couture runways in Paris still feature innovative and extreme styling, the shows are held more to garner attention than to sell fashion. How many consumers enjoy a lifestyle in which these extravagant designs will find a place? It is the prêt-à-porter collections in France and Italy and the ready-to-wear lines in the United States that are profitable to their companies.

Those in the industry who are responsible for deciding what should be produced must be aware of consumer preferences and determine which materials best serve their needs. Major companies often employ stylists, merchandisers, colorists, and other experts to research the markets and inform their companies about what's hot and what's not. Although this is a solid approach to learning about the latest in fabrication, coloration, and other trends, the globaliza-

Fashion forecasters meet regularly to discuss the trends that they will ultimately transmit to their clients.

tion of the fashion industry makes it impossible for a few employees to adequately explore the market, discover everything that is available, and fully inform the creative teams who design the merchandise. As a result, a growing number of fashion manufacturers, designers, and product developers of private label collections are employing **fashion forecasters.**

This service is so important, that many segments of the industry operate their own forecasting divisions. In addition to independent firms that forecast women's, men's, and children's wear trends, forecasters in the home products industry, the fiber industry, resident buying offices, color associations, and other specialized areas advise manufacturers on a more limited range of products. Each provides a variety of services for its clients.

Because fashion is such an international business, forecasters are often based throughout the world so that they can bring a broader perspective to the industry. Many companies, no matter where they are headquartered, operate branches in important fashion capitals. For example, Promostyl, one of the major players in the forecasting game, has offices in Paris, London, Tokyo, and New York, each interfacing with the others so that clients will be informed immediately about fashion news throughout the world. By working with textile fiber producers, weavers, colorists, and fashion researchers, and by observing the people on the street wherever there is potential for a new fashion direction, forecasters digest what they have learned and transmit the information to the clientele they serve.

Forecasting companies offer a variety of services ranging from one to unlimited consultations. Each company uses a specific format to disseminate the information it has garnered. Such formats include forecasting publications, fabric and color libraries, slides and videos, and individual conferencing.

FORECAST REPORTS

Fashion forecasters may use reports to keep their clients informed. These reports may range from a one-page flyer or brochure to entire books, with supplements added throughout the year. Major companies publish these books twice a year. Some companies offer one all-purpose edition that discusses important developments in each segment of the fashion industry. Others take a more specialized approach and prepare individual books that concentrate on specific segments of fashion. Promostyl uses the latter approach. Through the

Silhouettes, fashion trends, and other important newsworthy predictions are presented to clients in trend books. Here are four spreads from Promostyl.

publication of **trend books,** it alerts its customers to color direction, prints, silhouettes, and style eighteen months in advance of each season. To keep abreast of any new developments that occur between the publication of editions, Promostyl prepares supplements that are sent directly to its subscribers. Because fashion is an ever-changing business, new ideas must be properly communicated in a timely fashion to those responsible for design and manufacturing. A skilled fashion forecaster can adapt an idea that might be extreme, such as the designs of Gaultier, into a product that serves a specific market, manufacturer, or retailer.

The basic format of fashion reports, such as Promostyl's trend books, is a series of **fashion directions** for the season. Drawings created by the company's artists accompany photographs from which the design inspirations were taken.

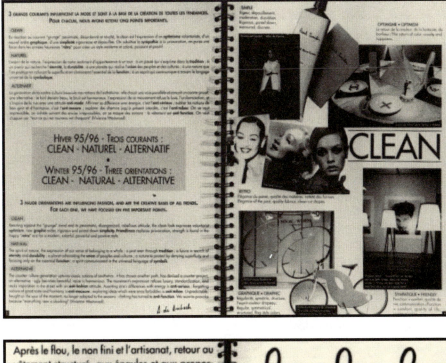

Color swatches and fabrications accompany and enhance each presentation for such apparel and accessories classifications as women's wear, men's wear, and children's wear. They clearly outline the direction in which they feel that industry segment is headed.

Promostyl is the subject of a World of Fashion Profile.

Fabric and Color Libraries

The textile industry is truly international. No manufacturer or designer can research all of the world's fiber and fabrics. Of course, they travel to many global fiber shows a year, but often they need reinforcements and reminders of what they saw, what is available, and what they might have missed at these expositions.

Promostyl

In 1966, Promostyl began what has become one of the most successful global fashion forecasting organizations. With main offices in Paris, London, New York, and Tokyo, and agents in such places as Australia, Belgium, Brazil, California, Italy, Germany, and Spain, it has been able to keep its clients informed of news on the international fashion scene. The company's client list numbers more than 2,500 designers, apparel and accessories manufacturers, fiber producers, and major retailers.

Through the use of trend books, clients are able to learn as far as eighteen months in advance of a coming season what styles, colors, silhouettes, and fabrics have the potential for success. Twice a year, clients also receive specialized books that provide invaluable information for merchandise planning. These publications fall into two categories—Premiere Books and Shape Books.

The Premiere books are offered under the following titles:

- **INFLUENCES** A compilation of what will be the up-and-coming trends in design, fashion, and interior decoration.

- **COLORS** An analysis of color ranges and harmony suggestions for the women's, men's, and children's sectors, complete with swatches and international color references.

- **FABRICS** An overview of the future of wovens, knits, and prints, illustrated with samples and developed by theme, photos, and references.

- **ACTIVE SPORTSWEAR** A study on this dynamic sector offering beachwear trends in summer and skiwear in winter, plus an overview of the outdoor wear and running gear markets.

The Shape books include the following titles:

- **GENERAL TRENDS FOR WOMEN** Individual stories are developed that include shapes, color, and fabric predictions. An important part of this book is the inclusion of fabric samples.

- **GENERAL TRENDS FOR MEN** The format focuses on the various masculine types and the shapes appropriate for each. Special attention is paid to urban, sportswear, and casualwear trends, offering suggestions on detailing and fabrication for each.

- **GENERAL TRENDS FOR CHILDREN** The book addresses the shapes and trends for children aged four to twelve. Ministories are offered and are accompanied by fabric suggestions.

- **FABRIC UPDATE** The latest in fabric innovation and suggestions for incorporation into the client's lines.

- **SHOES** Men's and women's shoe trends are featured, along with material swatches and theme strategies.

- **ACCESSORIES** An overview of bags, belts, and other accessories, and how they should relate to the fashion silhouettes.

In order to anticipate the fashion trends, Promostyl undertakes research in the following areas:

- lifestyles, attitudes, values
- leisure and sports
- street fashion, as well as designer fashion and haute couture
- architecture, design, painting, literature
- music, film
- shops, catalogs
- media
- sports
- ecology

With the broad range of services offered to its clients, Promostyl's place in fashion forecasting continues to gain international recognition.

Major fashion forecasters offer complete libraries of the fabrics and fibers available to the fashion industry. By subscribing to these services, designers can review the materials as often as they like and can compare the offerings of different fabric producers to determine which ones better suit their needs. Because the fabric is often the inspiration for a particular style, it is the **fabric library** that is most valuable to designers.

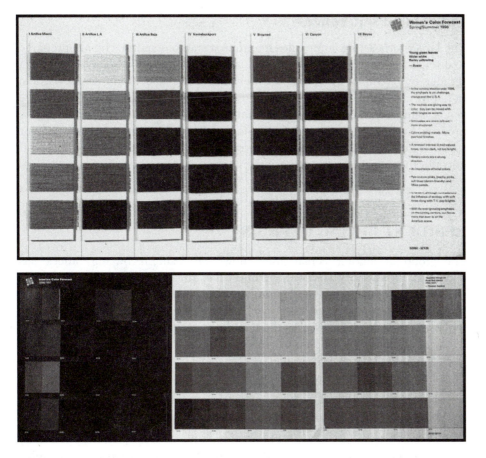

Fabric swatch cards help clients assess availability.

Design Services

Many major retailers develop their own private label merchandise. Unlike the traditional design houses and manufacturers, who are primarily engaged in creating lines of merchandise for their clients, the retailers focus on buying and merchandising. Those who enter the private label arena might choose to use a team of in-house product developers. Macy's does this for a great many of the items featured under its own labels. Others, however, find an alternative approach best serves their needs. They contract with a **forecaster design service** that designs entire collections for a fee. In this way, the retailer is assured that knowledgeable people are creating new merchandise, without the need to maintain year round, in-house creative teams.

Audiovisual Packages

To communicate the latest developments for each season, some fashion forecasters develop slide and video packages that cover trends in silhouettes, styles, colors, fabrications, and patterns. Each client receives a visual program of each season's predictions, along with a narration. For those clients too far from the forecasting company's headquarters to come in for individual conferencing or for those who need to review what was learned from personal meetings, these packages are excellent tools.

Another advantage is that the presentation may be seen by a host of viewers. For retailers interested in private labeling, the entire merchandising team can use these presentations to learn about industry trends.

Individual Conferences

The larger forecasting companies maintain a staff of experts who are prepared to discuss a client's specific problems and needs at an individual conference. A retailer, for example, who plans to enter the private label arena, might want an in-depth conference to determine the best route for producing the desired goods. Similarly, a designer might want to learn more about the best way to promote his or her line. Material sourcing might yet be another area that needs special attention. As part of their contractual arrangements, fashion forecasters offer these special consulting conferences.

RESIDENT BUYING OFFICES

The group of market consultants known as **resident buying offices** has expanded its advisory services. At one time, these agencies dealt primarily with bringing retail buyers and manufacturers together. Because many of their retail accounts now develop their own merchandise, these offices provide fashion forecasting services to assist them in determining what items to produce.

One of the major resident buying offices in the forecasting arena is Henry Doneger Associates. A profile of The Doneger Group appears in Chapter 17. The services offered by resident buying office forecasting divisions include:

- **Color Forecasts.** Seasonal color charts group specific colors into merchandise palettes. Dyed yarns and color photos generally accompany the color forecasts.

- **Trend Forecasts.** Design trends are usually depicted with photographs, drawings, colored yarns, and fabric swatches to help the user get an overview of the market.

- **Personal Consultations.** Whether it is to plan a new merchandise collection, choose specific colors and fabrics for incorporation into a line, plan promotions and visual presentations, or make any fashion-related decisions, these companies have trained staffs ready to answer questions and solve specific problems.

- **Newsletters.** One method used to convey information to clients is newsletters. They may concentrate on news on fibers and fabrics, shapes and silhouettes, the importance of a new color, hot items that should help generate future business, and color updates.

- **Workbooks.** In-depth publications that cover the designs of haute couture are presented so that designers and manufacturers at lower price points can use the styles as guides for their own creations.

- **Slide Library.** A complete collection of slides of all of the major collections are kept for each season so that they can be used for research.

- **Multimedia Presentations.** At the beginning of each season, slides, video, in-person fashion shows, and other tools are used to bring a broad fashion prospective to the customer.

- **In-person Reviews of Street Styles.** With so much of today's fashion based on what people are wearing in the street, many companies visit cities to record their observations.

David Wolfe, a leading international fashion forecaster is featured in a World of Fashion Profile.

David Wolfe

Everybody in the world wakes up naked and decides what to wear. That decision, conscious or subconscious, is the result of a great many factors and it is those factors that interest me." That is how David Wolfe explains his life-long interest in fashion, which he describes as "a fascinating mix of style, economics, history, politics, weather, science, sex and a sense of humor."

David Wolfe has gained international fame in the fashion industry, in which he is known as "America's Foremost Fashion Forecaster." Thirty-five years of experience have earned him this title.

A native of Ohio, Wolfe began his fashion career in a small town department store, where he worked in a position that combined the responsibilities of fashion coordinator, buyer, copywriter, illustrator, and advertising manager. After gaining considerable experience in these aspects of fashion retailing, he

spread his wings and tried his hand at an area for which he had great fondness, fashion art. Because London was an exciting fashion city in the 1960s, he made his way abroad and soon established himself as a leading fashion artist. His sketches appeared in *Vogue, Women's Wear Daily,* and *The London Times.* Before long he was sought by and worked for Galeries Lafayette, Liberty of London, Harvey Nichols, and Selfridges. In 1969 he became one of the first to enter the fashion service industry. As Creative Director of I.M. International, he became one of the world's leading fashion forecasters and authorities. In his tenure at that company, he was among the first to discover such talents as Armani, Lagerfeld, Montana, and Versace. Returning to America in the early 1980s, Wolfe helped to form The Fashion Service (TFS) and served as president of the New York operation for a decade.

Today, Wolfe is Creative Director of D3 Doneger Design Direction, the fashion trend and color forecasting service for women's wear, men's wear, and children's wear. His other activities include serving as Senior Fashion Consultant to *Video-Fashion,* whose weekly programs of fashion news and designer interviews are broadcast via satellite to 30 million viewers worldwide. He regularly contributes articles to fashion publications through his affiliation with the Overseas Fashion Press Association and is International Fashion Editor of *Men Men,* and *Mode Couture* magazines, high-fashion publications of the Far East.

Rounding out his busy schedule is the delivering of informative and amusing lectures, slide presentations, and television appearances that make him a popular personality on the fashion scene.

FIBER PRODUCER FORECASTERS

Traditional fashion forecasters cover every aspect of the fashion industry; forecasters in fiber and fabric production specifically provide research on fabric. Because many designer creations begin with appropriate fiber and fabric selection, they must receive fabric information as much as twenty-four months before a line actually reaches the selling floor. As with fashion forecasters, those in fiber business use a variety of publications to disseminate information. DuPont, for example, publishes booklets and bulletins about its Lycra spandex fiber. The booklets list the different properties of the fiber and how Lycra might be used in fashion products.

In addition to the standard written materials, the fiber industry regularly uses the fashion show format to feature designs made with the fibers they are promoting. Invited to these events are fashion designers who hopefully will be inspired to use the fiber in their own collections.

FIBER ASSOCIATION FORECASTERS

Forecasting has become a major function of associations in the fiber segment of the fashion industry. Through printed material and fashion shows, they present the latest news on fabric innovations, color trends, and uses of these fibers to their clients.

Groups such as Cotton Incorporated and The Wool Bureau represent producers of natural fibers. It is their responsibility to promote their respective industries and to show how their fibers may be used to serve the needs of the apparel industry and the ultimate consumer.

Cotton Incorporated, for example, utilizes a unique program of designer collections made exclusively with cotton. At such fashion events as Seventh on Sixth, designers, merchants, and the editorial press are treated to full-scale fashion shows featuring lines created specifically with cotton. The purpose is to inspire designers to consider cotton in future collections.

Forecasting programs traditionally include creatively designed books of color photographs that are used to extract color palettes for swatches of fabrics and yarns. These books also include fashion drawings and **forecast collages** that combine style, fabric, and color.

COLOR FORECASTERS

Because appropriate color selection is one of the more important aspects of fashion design and merchandising, information about color trends is needed by almost everyone. Although many fashion forecasters offer color predictions, few deal exclusively with that element of fashion design.

Color forecasters include The Color Association of the United States (CAUS) and The Color Marketing Group. The goal for these associations is to predict color at least two years in advance of the retail selling season. At CAUS, a forecasting committee meets to select the shades that it thinks will attract the American consumer.

Color forecasters meet to predict color trends at least two years in advance of the selling season.

Manufacturers of women's, men's, and children's fashion who subscribe to these services receive swatched color forecasts; interior designers and home fashions creators receive custom silkscreened charts and color chips. To provide up-to-the-minute fashion news, subscribers also receive newsletters and bulletins. In addition, fashion designers regularly consult the color libraries of these companies, which often date back seventy-five years for inspiration in creating new products.

As with all fashion forecasting agencies, those specializing in color maintain hotlines for quick answers to color-related questions and offer individual consulting sessions for clients.

SPECIALIZED FORECASTERS

As the fashion industry continues to grow, general industry forecasters find it difficult to cover every product classification. All too often, they focus on apparel first, with only a secondary emphasis on accessories. To better serve the needs of manufacturers and designers of accessories, a number of fashion forecasters have been established.

One of the more important is The Committee for Colour & Trends, an international forecasting service specializing in footwear, hats, hair ornaments, jewelry, watches, handbags, belts, and hosiery. Its clients include designers, manufacturers, importers, wholesalers, buying offices, and retailers.

As with other forecasters, the Committee tracks the colors of the fiber industry, which is so important in making fashion predictions. However, it does not stop there. It uses these color forecasts to develop color harmonies for leather and shoes, as well as other leather accessory industries.

Color is so important to the leather industry, that The Committee for Colour & Trends produces semiannual books that provide examples of new textures in leather and offer specific color recommendations for each merchandise category.

These specialized forecasters also offer individual conferences to discuss such matters as the way in which color trends relate directly to the client, how deliveries should be timed to coincide with those of the apparel industry, and which products might be best emphasized for the next season.

Chapter Highlights

- The fashion designer's creativity no longer dictates style and silhouette. Because the consumer has become more independent, fashion manufacturers and designers need accurate and up-to-date information before creating a new line.

- Product developers must learn about the newest fabrications in the marketplace, the colors that are likely to have the greatest customer appeal, and the silhouettes that merit consideration. Although many companies have staffs that research these areas, others use outside sources to gather pertinent merchandise information.

- This role is filled by different types of fashion forecasters, including the general fashion merchandise forecaster, the fiber association forecaster, a division of a resident buying office, and specialized forecasters in such areas as fiber and color selection.

· Fashion forecasters present their findings in trend books, fabric and color library facilities, the design of a complete collection, audiovisual presentations, individual conferences, and fashion shows.

Important Fashion Terminology and Concepts

color forecasters	forecaster design service	specialized forecasters
color library	multimedia presentation	trend book
fabric library	newsletters	workbooks
fashion forecaster	product developer	
forecast collages	resident buying offices	

For Review

1. Why is it important for a designer to use the services of a fashion forecaster?

2. Why are more and more retailers using fashion forecasters?

3. Describe the merchandise classifications usually researched by the general fashion merchandise forecasters.

4. How does the fashion forecasting company come up with its predictions?

5. How far in advance of a selling season is information from the forecasters available to designers?

6. What is a trend book?

7. What purpose does the forecaster's color library serve for the designer?

8. Does a fashion forecaster ever actually design a collection?

9. Why are "street" fashions sometimes used by fashion forecasters in their predictions?

10. Describe a program that Cotton Incorporated uses to show the fashion world how its fabrics may be employed.

11. What is meant by a "forecast collage?"

12. Define the term specialized forecaster.

Exercises and Projects

1. Select a theme of your own choice as a possible concept for a children's wear collection. Using photographs, drawings, fabric swatches, and color chips, prepare a collage on foamcore board as would a fashion forecaster who is about to present the idea to a client.

2. Create a workbook that features haute couture designs. The photographs may be obtained by writing directly to the major fashion houses or from the various fashion publications such as *Vogue* and *Harper's Bazaar*. Prepare an oral report discussing the styles you have selected, and how they might be translated into lower priced merchandise.

3. Write to a fiber producer such as DuPont for information on their fashion forecasting techniques. Using the material provided, prepare a report for oral presentation to the class about how the producer disseminates the information to the industry.

The Case of the Undesigned Collection

Barbara Allen and Brett Williams have both worked for Encore, a manufacturer of moderate priced women's sportswear, for the past three years. She has primarily been engaged in fabric acquisition, he as the top showroom sales rep.

Last month, the two learned that Encore was going to move its operation from New York City to Los Angeles. Each was invited to follow the company westward, but because of family obligations declined the offer. With the imminent closing of the company, both Barbara and Brett are seeking other employment in the fashion business. Although they have been offered positions with an Encore competitor, they are entertaining the possibility of beginning their own business. Experienced in moderately priced sportswear, they believe this would be the best arena for them to enter. With some money of their own and commitments from family members, they have sufficient capital necessary to get started.

Barbara will handle purchase of materials and trimmings; Brett will be responsible for sales. Neither of them, however, is an expert in the all-important area of design. Yet they recognize that to enter this highly competitive field, a solidly designed line is a requirement.

Barbara believes that they should employ a designer to create the lines. Although people with creative ability are highly paid, she thinks it is the only way to make their new company competitive. Brett would like to use an in-house designer too, but is afraid that the expense would be too great in the beginning. His suggestion is to comb the market for exciting styles and copy them in fabrics of their choice. That would save the expense of a designer.

At this time, they cannot decide if either approach warrants further consideration or if a third approach might better solve their problem.

Questions

1. Do you think either approach is a sound one? Why?

2. What other arrangement could the new company make? Would it be a better approach?

point of view

Style Gazing

How does it happen? When you walk into a store and everything seems to look the same, do you wonder how such a fashion coincidence could possibly occur? It is no coincidence. What is really afoot almost amounts to a conspiracy.

The mystique of fashion striking like creative lighting within the imagination of a designer in an ivory tower in Paris is the kind of image that the industry wants perpetuated. It makes fashion more valuable and helps to justify the high cost of dressing. But designers do not live in ivory towers and there is not much of a market for genuine, one-of-a-kind, bolt-out-of-the-blue creativity. The real process is, in fact, much more fascinating.

Revealed! The secret starting point of many trends. Fashion forecasting companies are mostly based in Paris, London and Milan, and as might be expected, there are several major firms in New York City. The key players, some of the most important forecasting companies, are Promostyl and Peclers in Paris, Design Intelligence in London plus D3 Doneger Design Direction and Here and There in New York. There are lesser firms around the world too, but not that many. It is a small, very specialised segment of the industry and its purpose is to help designers and manufacturers make the right thing at the right time.

It is important to remember that as far as the business is concerned, the right thing is not necessarily the most fashionable, but it is the most saleable. A 'forecast' is not the result of gazing into a crystal ball, but an analysis of what already exists, what has already been created, that will sell in greater quantities in the future. So much of what is passed off as forecasting is nothing more than business guidance that is based on someone else's creativity (usually a 'hot' designer like John Galliano or Anna Sui).

If this is spring, next autumn is already over for forecasters. It is Autumn/Winter 1996 right now as far as fashion forecasters are concerned. These savants of styles are way ahead of the rest of the world. Just as the brand new merchandise for Spring/Summer 1995 is being unpacked in the stores, forecasters are three seasons ahead, predicting the colours and fabrics and even the exact garment designs that will eventually be stocked in shops 18 months from now. They take their work very seriously and are taken equally seriously by their clients who pay dearly for a clear vision of the future. Millions and millions of dollars ride on decisions and plans that have to be made far in advance if fibres are to be dyed, fabrics printed and patterns programmed for mass production. One manufacturer describes his company's faith in their forecaster as "a kind of insurance policy."

Self-fulfilling prophecies make predictions come true. How can anyone be certain of what is going to happen so far in the future? It is impossible to be 100 percent accurate, but the fashion business is so precarious that almost any guidance is worth considering. Here's a typical scenario, one that is repeated over and over again, season after season.

First the staff of the forecasting company meet to formulate their vision of things to come, be it colours or a fabric or even a skirt length. They present that vision to their clients who in turn produce the goods according to that vision. Thus, the prophecy is fulfilled. It is a very simple system. Of course, there is a major glitch possible at the end of this chain. What if the forecasted vision does not sell? What if customers don't want to buy that particular colour or fabric or style? If that happens several times, then the forecasters are soon searching for new, more gullible clients. But, as is usually the case, when the customer is confronted by a confident presentation of something—almost anything—he or she becomes a believer in the validity of the presentation and will buy.

Haute couture used to act as the world's fashion forecast. Forecasting was not always a part of the fashion system. Decades ago one only needed to see what was being presented in the present, in the salons of haute couture designers in Paris. Twice a year, a dozen or so very important designers of customer-made creations showed their collections. Christian Dior, Balenciaga and Givenchy were the stars then. The premieres of their collections were totally different to the media frenzies today's fashion shows have become. They were refined little affairs; there was no music, just a voice reading the number of each garment as it was paraded.

The couture collections were kept a deep, dark secret. Several weeks after the shows the world's press were allowed to show the designs to the public. Before that 'release' date, only the women who were customers and manufacturers who paid a 'caution' (a high fee that allowed them to see the show) were given access. Of course, after the press showed the designs, then anybody could copy the new looks and they did, as closely as possible. But the delayed release date meant that the couture customers could rest assured that copies could not be made before their costly originals had been worn in an aura of expensive exclusivity.

There was a well-established trickle-down theory of fashion in those days. It was said that it took exactly two years for a Paris fashion to reach the masses. It was a system that worked perfectly as long as everyone played fair. (And any manufacturer or reporter who did not was ostracised once and for all.) It was John Fairchild, publisher of *Women's Wear Daily*, the influential New York fashion trade paper who brought the system down. He refused to abide by the release dates and was, of course, denied entry. Undaunted, he had his reporters and artists waiting outside in the streets and after each show, they would whisk buyers to a cafe and quickly get a first hand report from their informants. Those sketches and reports appeared instantaneously and copyists the world over got to work.

How times have changed. Today the couturiers are anxious for publicity, eager to cash in on the sales that can be generated when their fashion shows are hyped in newspapers and magazines as well as seen on television. And besides, most couturiers today copy themselves, making cheaper versions of their creations in 'diffusion' ranges.

Street style set the stage for the birth of fashion forecasting. Another force came into play to upset the haute couture applecart and set the stage for the birth of fashion forecasting. A new generation was making street style into fashion news early in the 1960s. Young designers like Mary Quant, John Bates and Emmanuelle Khan who were not couturiers suddenly became important. Young people wanted to wear the same styles their idols wore and manufacturers realized that haute couture was not the only game in town.

But how was a company in Hong Kong or Los Angeles or Tokyo to know what was happening in the fast-paced youth market when there was a new trend every week appearing on London's Carnaby Street? They needed on-the-spot informants, people with a trained fashion eye. Soon a little subculture of style spies came into being. They would haunt the streets and trendy boutiques, secretively sketching the newest cut or detail and then speeding off their efforts to the trend-hungry manufacturers far away.

That worked for a time until the naturally competitive manufacturers decided they had to get their versions of the new trends out before their competition. They then started asking their London and Paris-based correspondents to second-guess what the next new trend would be. And that is how fashion forecasting began. But it is not the end of the story, it is only the beginning.

How forecasting works. Colour is the starting point of any season, and every forecaster begins by creating a range of colours specific to the season. The colours are brand new each and every season, meticulously dyed and redyed until they meet the exacting specifications of the colour specialists. At D3, Gae Marino, the managing director, is also the chief colour creator, working with a small team of experts. Her colour sense is so uncanny that many of the world's leading retailers regard her colour choices as a sure route to commercial success. She is said to have an 'eye' in the same way that parfumiers have a 'nose'.

Colourists travel to the world's fashion capitals and attend fashion shows. They also research carefully the colours that are currently selling. Once colours have been selected, then the fabrics and designs quickly follow suit. The information that forecasting firms accumulate in order to project fashion forward comes from many diverse areas.

Equally vital in the formation of trends are forces such as the entertainment industry, politics, science, weather, and of course, economics. What is currently being worn has to be taken into account. Shifts in population patterns and demographics changes all influence the movement of fashion.

First hand observations are important, so forecasters are a travelling tribe, roaming Paris, London and Milan, but also venturing to far flung destinations like Lapland or even Disneyland with sketchbooks and cameras at the ready. They also go to the theatre and films, attend concerts and hang-out in clubs constantly. They read all the best-selling novels and even watch TV to check how the public pulse is coursing. A creative director assimilates all these different aspects and forms them into coherent trends that are then sketched and circulated seasonally. Trend books are big 'idea' books, loaded with photos and designs and meticulous fashion illustrations.

Were colour charts and trend books all that they did, forecasters would be more akin to magazine publishers. However, the New York based D3 Donegar Design Direction claims, "the published products are just 50 per cent of what our clients buy—the other 50 per cent is a relationship." And every forecasting firm aims to create a close working relationship that will guarantee ongoing fees and prevent notoriously fickle clients switching from one forecaster to another in their feverish race to get to the right trend fast—and first.

Where next? The future of fashion is certainly not an uncertainty to forecasters. They complete their work on Spring/Summer 1995 (the styles seen in this issue) way back at the end of 1993 and most of them cannot even 'remember' that far back. What do they see ahead for you? For Autumn/Winter 1995?

Couture, Spring/Summer 1995.

The Titans of Tint Make Their Picks

Deborah L. Jacobs

The titans of tint came to town this month.

Dressed in hues they describe as firethorn, cornmeal and purple haze—or just in suits of plain old grey flannel—the men and women of the Color Marketing Group gathered at a New York hotel for their spring ritual of secret caucuses and swatch exchanges. Their mission: to determine which colors will be big sellers on the nation's clothing racks, showroom floors and supermarket shelves the next two years.

The group, based in Alexandria, Va., is a powerful trade association whose 1,400 members include in-house color marketers at Fortune 500 companies as well as color consultants who charge tens of thousands of dollars for a two-week assignment. But the group is just one part, albeit a highly organized one, of an elite industry of colorists. Their job is to help steer multimillion-dollar marketing decisions using colors and their psychological undertones. Specific goals range from building corporate images to improving sales.

The marketers say they forecast the popularity of colors rather than force their choices upon a helpless public. But just try to find a pink this year that isn't peachy. And

good luck getting away from green—and a weathered brick color called Smithsonian, named last year at a Color Marketing Group meeting in Washington, which also seems to be everywhere.

The 15 new colors identified in workshops during the Color Marketing Group's latest meeting will start to appear next year and, the group predicts, will flourish in 1996. Announced with fanfare at the close of the three-day gathering, the new colors include three shades of gray—wet gray (like the sky on a cloudy day), highway (reminiscent of the interstate) and purple veil (lavender-tinted)—and yellowy greens named plantain (like an unripe banana) and winter moss (evergreen with a yellow tinge).

Does this mean yet more of the earth tones that now permeate the stores? Yes, said Nada Napoletan Rutka, a color consultant in Pittsburgh who is president of the Color Marketing Group. During the affluent 1980's, colors in the marketplace were considerably brighter and changed quickly as conspicuous consumers snatched up new hues, said Ms. Rutka, who attended the recent Color Marketing Group meeting dressed in a suit of "purple passion" (or was it "plummet?").

Given today's economic uncertainties, consumers spend more cautiously and look for colors that don't shift drastically each year, she said. Concern about the environment is another influence on current and future palettes.

Using information gleaned at past Color Marketing Group meetings, Reebok International has toned down the trim of its sneakers, phasing out the bright reds, oranges and yellows of the 1980's, said Pamela Boucher, a trend and color forecaster at the company, which is based in Stoughton, Mass. To match the back-to-nature colors that people are wearing from the ankles up, the company is also offering shoes of "blackened green," Ms. Boucher said.

Color Marketing Group palettes are not models for exact imitation, in house color advisers say. "Those colors are just directions," said Linda Trent, director of the color and design marketing department at the Sherwin-Williams Company, the Cleveland paint manufacturer. The company relies on them "to develop paint colors that are going to be responded to positively in the marketplace."

Still, industries that are tightly linked will strive to coordinate their palettes, so that car manufacturers, for instance, can find exterior paint that matches the upholstery inside their latest models.

While color "plays a role in creating momentary appeal," color marketers also address more long-term goals, said Anita Hersh, president of Lister Butler Inc., a New York consulting firm in corporate and brand identity. When color is part of a brand's identity, it "needs to be selected with longevity in mind," she said.

Since 1987, for example, the Owens-Corning Fiberglas Corporation, in Toledo, Ohio, has owned a trademark on the pink used in its insulation.

Then there is the case of Best Western International Inc. As part of a continuing $1.3 billion effort to upgrade the quality of its hotels, Best Western considered the effect of color on the company's image. Among the conclusions of its two-year research effort: people associated the stark colors of the company's logo—a bright yellow and black emblem—with budget hotels, fast-food chains and convenience stores. The old signs were "telling the customer that we were lower quality than we really were," said William S. Watson, senior vice president for worldwide marketing at the Phoenix-based company. The new logo features refined golden letters against a deep blue background.

Fiskars Inc., which introduced its popular orange-handled scissors in the late 1960's, has stuck with the color in succeeding decades. Since the scissors were initially designed for industrial use, the company chose "safety orange" to make them visible in factories. During the decades since then, Fiskars had become "so synonymous with orange" that it hasn't made sense to change, said Sandra Cashman, a spokeswoman for the Wausau, Wis., company.

Fiskars' strategy defies the popular assumption that orange—along with chartreuse and sulfur—is one of the colors people most dislike. These are colors commonly associated with "bodily functions," said Leatrice Eiseman, a color consultant in Seabek, Wash., who has studied the psychology of color.

Blue is still America's favorite color, Ms Eiseman said. And the current popularity of soft, pastel shades reflects the quest for calm during volatile social and economic times.

But color consultants caution against looking for a "magic bullet" to bolster sales. "Everyone has an opinion about what color means," Ms. Hersh said.

Indeed, the willingness of consumers to try new colors varies. The Cooper Marketing Group, a research company in Oak Park, Ill., has surveyed consumers the last several years and divided them into three color personalities. [See chart.]

Such studies suggest that marketers should keep their customers in mind when choosing palettes. Lands' End Inc., for instance, knows that many of its customers prefer brighter colors, rather than the dusty shades that now seem popular, said Andrea Sapon, a manager in the brand integrity group of the mail-order clothing company. The company has recently added some terracotta clothing, but kept the old standby reds and blues that its audience expects.

Color is more than an abstract preference for some consumers. "People who are fair skinned with dark hair don't look good in the new colors," said Lori Solinger, a television journalist in Providence, R.I., who reports on health and fitness. Limited by the options on a recent shopping trip, Ms. Solinger came home with a jacket of pale yellowy-green—a shade color marketers might describe as "romaine" or "green tea." When Ms. Solinger wore the jacket to work, colleagues asked her whether she was feeling ill. She has since relegated the item to the back of her closet.

"Stores will lose revenues from people who cannot wear those colors," Ms. Solinger said. "Designers and forecasters are totally shutting them out."

Marketers say the new palettes offer something for everyone, but acknowledge that if the goods don't sell, the consequences will be costly.

Color is "like a seed," said James King, a researcher at DuPont Automotive in Troy, Mich., one of the largest producers of top-coat paint for cars. "It has to fall on receptive ground."

The New York Times, May 29, 1994.

Elements and Principles of Design for Developing a Fashion Collection

After you have completed this chapter, you will able to discuss:

- The elements and principles of design on which apparel and home fashions are based.

- The numerous color harmonies available to designers.

- The individual stages of developing a designer's line or collection.

- A typical timetable that begins with the design concept and ends with delivering the merchandise to the store.

There is nothing mysterious about how ideas and concepts take shape to become the next season's line or collection. Each new product represents the collaborative efforts of a team and a plan of activities that will hopefully receive the attention and recommendations of the press, the store buyers, and the public.

As we have already studied, there are numerous avenues taken to assure that those responsible for product development and design are on the right track. They interact with the fashion forecasters, study the various influences of current fashion, and comb the fiber, fabric, and trimmings markets. To create a distinctive line or collection that is suited for consumer use, designers must apply the elements and principles of successful designing. The elements of design include the silhouette, color, texture, and details and trimmings. The principles are balance, proportion, emphasis, rhythm, and harmony, and how they relate to each other.

Once all of these considerations have been addressed, it is time to develop and design the products.

ELEMENTS OF DESIGN

When designers begin work on a new line or collection, they may be motivated by any number of factors. A particular geographic region, such as the South Seas, may provide an inspiration. A trend in movies or theatrical productions, as discussed in Chapter 4, Ever-Changing Fashion and Its Acceptance, or fabrication might provide the stimulus.

Newly developed fibers continue to inspire and direct designers. When nylon was first introduced in 1938, it gave the fashion industry something new to play with. In the 1950s and 1960s, polyester motivated designers to produce garments that would behave perfectly during travel. Not long after, spandex, with its stretch properties, gave designers a new material that provided comfort to the wearer. More recently, Micromattique®, a microdenier polyester fiber with the fineness of silk, has offered designers yet another material for their creations.

No matter where the inspiration or motivation comes from, all designs involve shapes or silhouettes, colors, textures, and details and trimmings. How each is manipulated and interrelated with the others is the designer's challenge.

Silhouette

As described briefly in Chapter 4, Ever-Changing Fashion and Its Acceptance, women's apparel has five basic silhouettes—tubular or straight model, A-line, hourglass, wedge and bell. In men's tailored clothing, there are fewer silhouette choices—the American or classic cut or the European model.

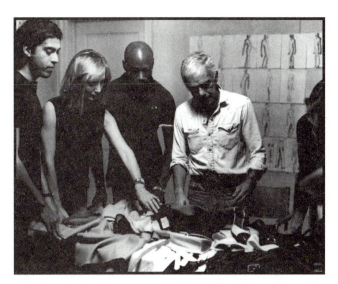

Ralph Lauren discusses the elements of a potential design with his staff.

(left) Women's clothing is based on one of four silhouettes. Here, Gianni Versace chooses the straight silhouette, adding his sensuous and sexy touch.
(right) The classic or European cut are the basics in men's tailored clothing.

Working with these shapes, each women's wear designer chooses one, or perhaps two, that will dominate a collection. In the men's industry, one silhouette appears in a collection. It is the other ingredients, such as fabric and trim, that differentiates one garment from the other.

Details and Trimmings

In women's apparel, a basic shape is individualized by various collars and sleeves and the shortening or lengthening of the hemline. In men's clothing, it might be a notched collar or the six-button, double-breasted closure that differentiates one classic silhouette from another. Other detailing might include shoulder pads, puffed sleeves in a leg of mutton fashion, or patch pockets on a jacket.

After deciding on the silhouette, detail, texture, and color of a product, the designer must choose the functional and decorative additions that will transform the garment into something unique and observably different from those with similar characteristics.

Although belts, buttons, and zippers may be classified as functional trimmings, they are often selected for decorative reasons. A plastic button may serve the same purpose as a pearl one, but the latter gives the garment a richer

quality. Similarly, zippers are most often functional, but those that are conspicuously oversized and visible might add to the design's character.

A variety of decorative trim serves to embellish and enhance a garment. Intricate beading, fine appliqués, unique embroidery, piping in contrasting colors, hand-made flowers, rhinestones, lace edging, and others all "dress up" the basic styles. A complete examination of these various details and trimmings were discussed in Chapter 11, Details and Trimmings.

Textures

Many designers will choose an identical silhouette and details for several pieces in the collection, the only variation is **texture.** Texture, the look and feel of fabric, plays an important role in a garment's appearance. Bulky yarns, for example, when used in woven goods or knits will make the wearer look heavier. Flat knits or wovens, when applied to the same silhouettes, will give a lighter, more flattering image to the same figure.

Texture also affects how the fabric may be manipulated. A stiff felt does not provide the drapability of a soft chiffon. Tweeds are perfect for rugged sportswear, but do not fit the bill for feminine evening wear.

Claude Montana mixes leather and mohair for this fashionable textured look.

A shiny satin's surface brilliantly enhances its color because of the way the light reflects off the surface, but a corduroy fabric, employing the same coloration, does not provide the brilliance because of its textural ridges or wales. Color, therefore, is also affected by the fabric's texture.

The knowledgeable designer must be well versed in textures before selecting fabrics for a particular model or design.

Color

The single element that contributes the greatest visual impact without affecting the price is color. The choice of specific design details, fabric choice, and trim can considerably increase a garment's cost, but the color changes the appearance without adding expense. Color provides excitement, mood, and emotion to a design. To maximize color's effect on apparel, accessories, and home fashions, some basic **color theories** and concepts must be understood by those responsible for design.

Color Theory

Designers must choose from a wide assortment of available colors. They must decide which colors work best with their creations and in what harmonies they should be used.

Color combinations may be chosen by understanding the most basic concepts of color or by instinct, which breaks all rules and sometimes provides fantastic results. Although most designers have a sense of which combinations are appropriate, that sense is based on an understanding of color systems.

An understanding of these color systems requires familiarity with terminology associated with color. Hue, value, and intensity are three frequently used terms in the color vocabulary.

HUE   The technical term for the name of a color. Thus, red, green, yellow, and violet are hues.

VALUE   The lightness or darkness of a color. The lightest colors are achieved by different amounts of white and are called **tints.** The darkest are achieved by the addition of black. The greater the amount of black, the darker the color. These darker colors are referred to as **shades.**

INTENSITY   Refers to the color's saturation or purity, brightness or dullness. A color may be dulled by adding gray, or its complement, a term that will be discussed later in the chapter.

Color Combinations

Various hues, whether pure or in tints or shades, are combined to add unlimited color interest to fabrics.

Combinations are based on one of two systems: the Prang or the Munsell. The **Prang System** is the better known and is used extensively by fashion professionals. Developed by David Brewster, it employs a color wheel based on the three **primary colors,** yellow, blue, and red, which are used to produce other colors. **Secondary colors,** also called secondaries, are produced by mixing two primary colors. For example, a mixture of red and yellow, two primaries, produces orange, a secondary color; blue and red result in purple, and yellow and blue provide a green hue. With the three primaries and the neutrals, black and white, an endless color array can be achieved.

Although fabrics are generally shown to designers and manufacturers in a wide assortment of color harmonies, those responsible for product development can also suggest different arrangements.

The most commonly used color combinations are as follows:

MONOCHROMATIC COLOR SCHEME   In this arrangement, one basic color is selected for a design. Interest in the design can be achieved by arranging different values and intensities of the color and highlighting it with such **neutrals** as black and white. Thus, a red pattern, with pink (a tint of red) and burgundy (a shade of red) and markings of white or black (neutrals) is considered a monochromatic harmony. Only one actual hue is being used.

ANALOGOUS COLOR SCHEME   Colors that are adjacent to each other on the color wheel are used to form analogous schemes. That is the use of yellow, yellow-orange, and orange, or blue, blue-violet, or violet are examples of this color combination. As with the monochromatic arrangement, neutrals may be used to provide additional interest.

COMPLEMENTARY COLOR SCHEME   Two colors directly opposite each other on the color wheel are referred to as complementary. Red and green or yellow and violet are examples of this arrangement. When designers are looking to enhance the colors in a pattern they often choose the complementary harmony. By placing complements next to each other, the eyes visualize the color as more intense.

SPLIT COMPLEMENTARY COLOR SCHEME   A variation on complementary harmony is one that features a basic color along with the two colors on either side of the basic color's complement. Thus, yellow might be used with both blue-violet and red-violet, each of which appears on either side of yellow's complement, violet.

DOUBLE COMPLEMENTARY COLOR SCHEME   Another variation on the complementary approach employs two sets of complementary colors. For example, yellow-orange and its complement, blue-violet, may be featured along with -yellow-green and its complement, red-violet. Interesting prints often use double complementaries.

TRIADIC COLOR SCHEME   In the triadic scheme, three colors, each equidistant from the other two, are used. For example, the three primaries, red, yellow, and blue, are often used in exciting patterns for children's clothing and furnishings.

To understand the various colors, their relationships to each other, and the various combinations or harmonies that can be achieved, see Color Plates .

Psychology of Color

Although the basic color theory has a scientific foundation, color selection often involves other considerations. Psychological factors play an important role in the appropriate selection of a particular hue and how it is used in design.

The sense of warmth and coolness projected by color are factors to consider in selecting a color scheme. Although a particular color imparts neither heat nor cold, its presence can create a feeling of warmth or coolness. Blue, green, and violet are considered the **cool colors**; red, orange, and yellow are **warm colors.** A pale blue dress, for example, imparts a cool feeling, while the same dress in red gives off a feeling of warmth.

Yves Saint Laurent

Yves Saint Laurent gained immediate prominence when he succeeded the legendary Christian Dior.

A legend in his own time, Yves Saint Laurent has been one of the most innovative fashion designers. Unlike many designers, Saint Laurent has no single design element as his trademark. He is a master off all design elements.

Born in 1936, he was 17 when he showed his drawings to the editor of *Vogue,* who then selected several for the magazine. After winning his first prize in fashion in the Concours du Secretariat de la Laine for a cocktail dress design, he was introduced to Christian Dior. His initial collection at the House of Dior, which featured the now-famous trapeze design, made him an international success.

In 1961, Saint Laurent left Dior to establish his own fashion house. Since that first collection, the company has grown considerably. Not only does he produce haute couture, but he is responsible for worldwide distribution of many products bearing his signature, such as hosiery, scarves, ties, shoes, furs, men's wear, millinery, handbags, jewelry, belts, and fragrances. His work has been recognized by numerous awards, including the Neiman Marcus and *Harper's Bazaar* awards.

He entered prêt-à-porter in 1966

with the opening of Rive Gauche in Paris. All of the styles sold in the store are designed by Saint Laurent. Today there are more than one hundred Rive Gauche shops throughout the world, in such places as the United States, Europe, Canada, Japan, and Australia.

In addition to the much heralded trapeze, Saint Laurent has received accolades for his famous peacoat, his use of the tunic, the abstractions of his Mondrian collection, his pop art dresses, beaded minidresses,

Russian peasant look, see-through look, and his dramatic, extravagant ball gowns.

While couture for an adoring public has occupied a significant amount of his time, Saint Laurent has designed costumes for the theater and for movies. His endeavors include costumes for numerous ballets choreographed by Roland Petit, for whose production he also designed the stage sets, Edward Albee's *A Delicate Balance,* and the revues of the French star Zizi Jeanmaire. His movie credits include costumes for Sophia Loren in *Arabesque,* Claudia Cardinale in *The Pink Panther,* and Catherine Deneuve in *Belle de Jour.*

His achievements have been recognized in the exhibition "Yves Saint Laurent, 28 Annees de Creation" at the Museum of Soviet Artists in Moscow and in The Costume Institute of the Metropolitan Museum of Art in New York, by the publication of *Yves Saint Laurent par Yves Saint Laurent* in Russian, and by a retrospective in the Art Gallery of New South Wales in Sydney, Australia.

Such an illustrious career is reserved for very few designers.

Another psychological consideration is the emotional effect color has on its observers. Typical reactions to colors include red as a warm, exciting choice, orange as one that provides an earthy feeling, and blue, the favorite of most people, as one with a calming effect. Green generally exudes restfulness, purple drama, and yellow a cheerful atmosphere.

It is up to the product designer to choose from the color combinations available in fabrication that will best serve their designs and the effects they would like to achieve for their collections.

The intricate manipulation of the various elements creates designs of distinction. Blending fabrics with the right feel and appearance with specific silhouettes, detailing the timely skirt lengths and waistline treatments, perfectly accenting them with decorative enhancements, and coloring them in attractive combinations, all contribute to motivating the consumer to purchase.

Designers have always tried to package these various elements creatively. Some have succeeded; others have failed. A few have been lucky enough to create signatures that are immediately recognized by consumers. For example, Fortuny's pleated fabrics made his designs immediately recognizable. Few fashion enthusiasts required label verification for a Fortuny. Of course, not many have achieved such distinction. Yves Saint Laurent has ingeniously employed all of the elements. A World of Fashion Profile outlines his achievements. Table 15.2 (pages 378-380) features a selection of designers and the specific elements that have brought them recognition.

It is the talent of the designer that helps create individuality that will meet with approval from the consumer.

PRINCIPLES OF DESIGN

Whether designers are developing a collection of dresses or suits, footwear or jewelry, or fashions for the home, they must be properly schooled in the principles of design. To capture the eye of the observer, the product must be properly executed in terms of balance, emphasis, proportion, rhythm, and harmony. Each design must effectively use these principles to create a successful product.

Balance

In its strictest sense, **balance** is the equal distribution of weight on two sides. Absolute balance, however, sometimes leads to produce designs that lack creativity. Of course, some designs benefit from this approach.

To achieve balance, create a central line for the design. This line may be a real dividing point as in the case of a man's shirt that is open down the middle and uses button closures, or one that the designer's eye imagines as the center. In either case, trim or ornamentation may be used to formally or informally balance the item. **Symmetrical balance,** most often used in apparel design,

(left) These buttons are symmetrically placed. (right) The skirt features an asymmetrical hemline.

Contrasting fabrics in designs for haute couture and ready-to-wear.

uses two identical objects on either side of the design, such as patch pockets of equal size. **Asymmetrical balance** might be achieved by the garment's pattern. For example, one side of a sweater might use a single large flower, while the other side uses several smaller flowers. If properly used, the eye sees it as a balanced arrangement.

In home furnishings, bedding displays might use two identical pillows to achieve a basic formal balance, with other shapes, more casually placed on either side of the imaginary line, to provide interest. Ralph Lauren, in room designs that feature his bedding collections, uses different sizes and shapes of pillows to create an asymmetrical balance.

Emphasis

Drawing attention to a particular area of a product is central to its success. Designers generally choose one area of a garment to feature. This is known as the focal point. If too many areas of interest are given equal attention, the eye will not know where to focus and attention will be lost.

Emphasis is achieved in a number of ways. It might be the neckline or the back of a dress that captures the eye. For example, British designer Vivienne Westwood recently added bustles to her dresses. It could also be the fullness of a skirt, enhanced with petticoats that causes attention, or some trimming, such as intricate beading. Often, emphasis is achieved through coloration, alternating stripes, or the use of an unusual pattern or print. Contrasting fabrics might provide the necessary emphasis or focal point—for example, the collar on a jacket might be in a different fabric than the overall fabric.

A successful designer must know how to achieve this emphasis without too many confusing elements.

Proportion

The various elements in the design should be scaled in size to fit its overall **proportion.** For example, the size of the trimmings should be in proportion to the dress they are enhancing. A flower that is too large for a dress may detract from the silhouette, neckline, or other detailing. A belt that is too wide or narrow to suit the garment becomes a disproportionate accent that ruins the silhouette.

In room settings, home fashions are used to enhance a setting. Their proportion must be in line with the furniture in the room or the overall appearance suffers. A mirror that is very large and placed over a very small chest will appear disproportionate.

The polka-dot pattern moves the eye over the garment.

Rhythm

While focal point is an important part of any design and is used to attract attention, the consumer must observe and evaluate the entire product. If the details and embellishments have been carefully placed, a sense of **rhythm** will move the eye from one element to the other. Rhythm can be achieved through numerous techniques.

ALTERNATION When light and dark colors are contrasted or when stripes of two colors are employed, alternation in rhythm is the result. The eye manages to focus on the alternating colors, eventually leading the observer to view the entire product.

RADIATION Using a sunburst effect, the eye moves from the central point of the sunburst to the outer portions of the design. Imagine a circular ornament that is centered on a handbag. The viewer is first attracted to the ornament, and then the eye moves to the outer edges of the design.

PROGRESSION The use of a single color that is featured in a gradation of the darkest to the lightest tone imparts rhythmic progression. The eye will automatically move from the darkest to the lightest tones, or the reverse, and draw attention to the complete item. Sometimes a design will use a specific shape for its trim in a variety of sizes. The gradation of the shapes will tend to bring the eye from one to the other, and eventually to all of the garment.

REPETITION Repetition involves moving the eye in any direction through the placement of many of the same shapes. Dots in a polka-dot fabric, for example, cause the viewer to move throughout the design. Repetition of some enhancements, such as rhinestones, throughout the garment also tends to make the eye examine the entire object.

CONTINUOUS LINE When some of the elements of the design are connected by a linear device, continuous line rhythm is accomplished. Flower ornaments that are part of a design, for example, and are connected to each other with vining makes the eye move from flower to flower and throughout the garment.

Karl Lagerfeld

Lagerfeld designs under his own label, for Chanel and Fendi.

Karl Lagerfeld has achieved distinction as the creative force behind numerous collections. In addition to his own signature collection, Lagerfeld designs for Chanel and furs for Fendi.

Lagerfeld came to the attention of the fashion world by winning the first prize for women's coat design in a contest sponsored by the International Wool Secretariat. With that achievement, he was hired as an apprentice to Pierre Balmain, where he stayed until he became the chief designer for Patou. He became prominent with his affiliation with Chloë, who produced ready-to-wear with an air of haute couture. Completely in charge of design, he created clothing with an airy look, many of which were hand painted. It was the femininity of his designs that captured the fashion world's attention.

Leaving Chloë after many years, he established a company bearing his now-famous signature, while still designing for some of the most prestigious fashion houses.

His personal charm and extraordinary presence when coupled with his creative genius make Lagerfeld one of fashion's leaders. How many designers are capable of creating simultaneous collections, each with a different focus?

Harmony

Achieving a unified effect requires a degree of cohesiveness among all of the elements in the design project. The relationship of the appropriate shapes in the fabric's pattern or the trimmings, for example, must be in **harmony** with the rest of the elements. Although there is safety when the absolute rules of harmony are followed, it sometimes results in a dull design. This can be avoided by adding elements that lend excitement. A simple black dress might receive more attention if it is trimmed with gold braid rather than black piping. Karl Lagerfeld is a master at introducing surprise elements in his collections. A focus of this designer is featured in a World of Fashion Profile.

Creatively using variety or an element of surprise transforms the mundane into something more exciting. A basic blazer, for example, is considered to be a classic in any woman's wardrobe. Although these garments are extremely serviceable, they are not very exciting. In the early 1990s, designer Joannie Criscione transformed the blazer into a high fashion item and catapulted her company to success. She unconventionally scattered rhinestones on a woolen blazer and made fashion headlines. The item ran for several years, bringing significant profits to her company, and was eventually knocked off at many lower price points. Although this design treatment might not fit the traditional concept of harmony, it proves that creativity often adds appeal to the product.

DEVELOPMENT OF THE LINE OR COLLECTION

In developing every collection, a designer must follow various stages to bring a concept to market. These stages include creating the design, costing the garment, and preparing a timetable for production that begins with selecting fabric and concludes with filling the orders.

TABLE 15.1

CAD COMPANIES AND SYSTEMS USED BY THE FASHION INDUSTRY

Company	Systems	Uses
Animated Images, Inc.	Style Manager	Apparel, footwear, home furnishings, merchandising.
AVA CAD/CAM, Inc.	AVA	Printed fabrics, apparel, draping, woven fabrics, wall coverings.
AVL Looms	AVL	Dobby, jacquard, prints, knit, apparel.
Barco, Inc.	Arabesque	Textile printing, designing.
CADTEX Corporation	PRIMAVISION	Print and knit design, apparel, hosiery, accessories.
CIS GRAPHICS, Inc.	Design3	Dobby design, apparel and yarn, design, home furnishings.
Dacal, Inc.	ScotWeave	Comprehensive textile design system.
Gerber Garment Technology (GGT)	GERBERsuite	Design and merchandising; product development; grading and marking; cutting room; assembly/sewing room
Lectra Systems, Inc.	Instinct	Design, pattern and marker making, fabric spreading and cutting.
Monarch Design	Monarch Computex	Textile design, woven and knit design, screen printing, surface design.
	Envision	Photo-realistic renderings.
	Pointcarre	Dobby and Jacquard designs.
NedGraphics, Inc.	IGOS	Jacquard design, carpet design.
TCS USA, Inc.	Custom software	Design and color for textiles.

Stages of Development

The designer or design team prepares numerous sketches for the line. Many are rejected, but the surviving ones are eventually transformed into patterns and then into samples. After each sample has been constructed, it becomes part of the initial or preliminary line.

The actual designs may be rendered by hand or increasingly by means of a CAD system. These systems enable designers to create, color, recolor, and modify the designs in a fraction of the time that it takes to do this by hand. There are numerous companies and CAD systems to choose from. Table 15.1 lists some of those currently available.

At this point, the line is shown to store buyers. Those items that receive favorable attention and are ordered by the buyers head for the production line. Patterns are made and graded and items that do not generate orders are eliminated. Once the items have been cut and assembled, they are trimmed and prepared for shipment to retailers. If an item is particularly successful, reorders are placed and filled. Items that sell initially, but are not reordered, are pulled from the line. As production continues during a season, the development of next season's collection is taking shape, and the cycle starts all over again.

In the development of the line, each garment must be costed by determining the expenses of factors such as materials, trimmings, labor, packaging, production, sales, and freight. Only then will the company know how much to charge to turn a profit. The various stages, briefly discussed here, are fully examined in the next chapter.

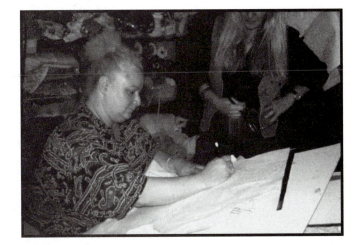

Sketches are the basis for every designer's collection.

The Timetable

The time it takes to develop a line varies from company to company. Those who create original designs spend more time in the development stages than those who specialize in knockoffs, or copies of items that are already in the marketplace. Such factors as location of production, whether it is domestic or offshore, and fabric sourcing affect the time it takes to produce a line and ship it to the retailers.

A typical interval from design inception to store delivery is six to nine months for domestically produced merchandise. In the case of offshore production, the timetable may be considerably longer.

Working six months or two seasons ahead, a typical calendar for a domestically produced line for the fall season is as follows:

JANUARY Fabrics are selected for the new season. Designers prepare their sketches and have them translated into sample garments.

FEBRUARY Samples are adjusted and improved. New designs might be created to broaden the line, others might be deleted. The new designs are produced as samples.

Many designs are often created on CAD systems.

MARCH Final decisions are made on fabric selection and the full line is readied for buyers. The actual time of store purchasing varies. Some accounts buy early during market week to get the company's first shipments; others wait until the lines have been narrowed and the slow selling items have been eliminated.

APRIL   Early production of ordered garments begins. Sales to the buyers continue in the showrooms and on the road.

MAY   This is the heaviest period for placement of orders by buyers. Production continues to fill orders that indicate early delivery dates.

JUNE   The major period for production is now in progress. The first orders for early fall delivery are shipped to the stores.

JULY   Production is at its peak, and more stores are receiving the merchandise.

AUGUST   This is the major shipping period. Production activity varies according to particular style activity. Slower selling items are taken from the line, the remainder of the production shifts into full swing for reorders.

SEPTEMBER   Reorder activity dominates the production schedule. Most initial orders have been shipped to the stores.

OCTOBER   The season ends, and the last store reorders are completed.

Quality Control

One of the major problems faced by manufacturers during the production stages involves **quality control.** If the finished product varies from what was initially expected, customer returns are inevitable. This significantly affects the company's profits. Such elements as construction specifics, material quality, and finished product measurements must be carefully assessed.

The quality control process involves three phases. They are:

1. Defining the quality requirements of the company's products in terms of what the customer's expectations will be.
2. Determining the methodology used in the assessment of the goods.
3. Setting specific goals and measuring the outcome.

Whether the system employed involves 100 percent inspection, spot checking, or some other technique, it is imperative that checking be an ongoing process. In the aforementioned timetable, quality checking is undertaken during each month that production takes place.

Characteristics of the Line

Designers and manufacturers must determine the scope of their collections. That is, how many individual items should be featured for each season, whether or not a theme will be featured throughout the line, will specific colors be exclusively used, and so on. Each company has its own direction for the characteristics of the line. Some of the considerations include:

Themes

A theme is sometimes depicted in terms of the silhouettes that will be featured, a particular color range, or fabric usage. Each season, haute couture as well as lower price point collections generally rely on an overall theme. Carole Little, for example, always uses prints as the theme for her collections and has established this as her trademark.

Often, there are several themes within a line, which are presented as groups. Several items, generally six to ten, are shown together in a specific fabrication, color, pattern, or shape. In this way, the company is able to appeal to a broader group of buyers.

Fashion Direction

In the fashion industry, a designer rarely appeals to every segment of the market. He or she must decide on a fashion direction. For example, the emphasis might be on a fashion-forward innovation or a more classic design. While fashion forward ideas often generate excitement, the more classical components of the line generally bring long-term profits.

Single Items

Throughout the industry, many manufacturers produce copies of items that were best sellers at higher price points. These items are called **knockoffs.** No relationship exists among the various items on the line. Because these individual styles have proven themselves in terms of sales, the manufacturer is generally assured of winners. The basic style is faithfully copied, using less expensive fabrics and lower quality production. Companies that specialize in these clones often employ a merchandising stylist who scouts the market looking for hot items. After the stylist selects the style, they research the textile and trimmings suppliers for less costly materials that can be used in production.

The absence of a highly paid designer and the elimination of the costs involved in producing unproven items, makes this type of operation relatively low in risk.

Coordinated Items

In the sportswear industry, designers create a variety of items that may be worn together. The separates concept enables the store buyer to select those pieces that best suit their customer's needs. Each group of coordinates might feature two skirt silhouettes in different lengths; two or three pant styles in different widths, a variety of waistbands, with or without pleats; several tops, and one or two jackets.

Designer Spec Sheets

Once the designer has selected all of the elements that will be used in his or her design, the final step before production begins is to complete a **spec sheet.** This is a compilation of all of the costs required to transform the design into a finished product.

The form usually contains a flat sketch of the design and the costs of the fabrics and trimmings that will be used. Most spec sheets are now computer generated. When the forms are completed, they are sent to management, which establishes the wholesale prices.

"Computer Spec Sheets Cut Down on Paperwork and Errors" examines the use and benefits of today's computer spec sheets (see pages 383 – 384).

TABLE 15.2

SELECTED DESIGNERS AND SIGNATURE DESIGNS OR DESIGN ELEMENTS

Designer	Designs or Design Elements
Adolfo (1933–)	Chanel-inspired knit suits
Armani, Giorgio (1934–)	Men's wear tailoring; easy shapes; use of neutrals such as taupe, beige, black, and gray
Balenciaga (1895–1972)	Architectural construction; cocoon coats; chemise; semifitted suit jackets
Barnes, Jhane (1954–)	Intricate fabrics; innovative details
Beene, Geoffrey (1927–)	Emphasis on cut and line; innovative use of fabrics and textures
Blass, Bill (1922–)	Refined cut, expert tailoring
Cardin, Pierre (1922–)	Nude look; metal body jewelry; unisex astronaut suits
Cashin, Bonnie (1915–)	Layered separates; use of jersey, leathers, tweeds
Chanel (1893–1971)	Chanel suit (collarless jacket, trimmed with braid); wool jersey dresses with white collars and cuffs; pea jackets; bell-bottom trousers; fake stones; multiple strands of pearls and gold chains; quilted handbags with shoulder chain; beige sling-back pumps with black tips; flat black hairbows
Courrèges, André (1923–)	Short, white boots; industrial zippers; sunglasses with slit "tennis ball" lenses; squared-off dresses ending above the knee
de la Renta, Oscar (1932–)	Romantic evening clothes in opulent fabrics; sophisticated daywear
Dior, Christian (1905–1957)	New Look (rounded shoulders, tiny waists, voluminous, spreading skirts); H-, A- and Y-line silhouettes
Ellis, Perry (1940–1986)	Use of natural fibers; hand-knitted sweaters
Ferré, Gianfranco (c. 1945–)	Sculptured and fluid evening gowns
Fortuny (1971–1949)	Pleated fabrics; Delphos dress; Peplos (two-piece version of Delphos dress)
Gaultier, Jean-Paul (1952–)	Mix of fabrics; overscaled garments
Gernreich, Rudi (1922–1985)	Stark cuts; striking color combinations; bold graphic patterns; "No-bra" bra; topless bathing suit; multiple cutouts on swimsuits
Grès, Alix (1903–1993)	Draped silhouette; often cutouts at midriff; jersey day dresses with cowl necklines; deep-cut or dolman sleeves; kimono-shaped coats

(continued)

TABLE 15.2 (continued)

Designer	Designs or Design Elements
Halston (1932–1990)	Long cashmere dress with sweater tied over the shoulders; combination of wrap skirt and turtleneck; evening caftans; long, slinky haltered jerseys; introduced Ultrasuede
Johnson, Betsey (1942–)	Body-conscious clothes; clinging T-shirt dress; clear vinyl slip dress
Julian, Julian (1948–)	Unusual and intricate fabrics in multiple colors (as many as sixteen in some designs)
Kamali, Norma (1945–)	Body-conscious clothes; giant removable shoulder pads; use of sweatshirt fabrics; draped and shirred jumpsuits in parachute fabrics; down coats
Karan, Donna (1948–)	Simple silhouettes; classic sportswear looks with stylish edge (well-cut pants; strong coats; sarong skirts; easy dresses)
Kawakubo, Rei (1942–)	Asymmetric shapes; cotton, canvas and linen fabrics; torn and slashed; neutral tones; some subtle touches of color
Klein, Anne (1923–1974)	Recognized suitability of sportswear to life style of American women; interrelated wardrobe pieces of blazers, skirts, pants; sweaters with slinky jersey dresses
Klein, Calvin (1942–)	Spare, sportswear-based shapes; luxurious natural fibers; leathers, suedes; earth tones and neutrals
Lacroix, Christian (1951–)	Theatrical, witty clothes; fantastic accessories; pouf silhouette
Lagerfeld, Karl (1939–)	Removes clothes from their usual context (elaborated embroidery on cotton for couture); mixes wearable clothes with dash of wit (silk dresses with tennis shoes)
Lauren, Ralph (1939–)	Classic silhouettes, superb fabric; fine workmanship; creates upper-crust lifestyles
McCardell, Claire (1905–1958)	Simple, functional clothes with clean lines; men's wear detailing; topstitching; rivets, gripper fastenings; cotton denim, ticking, gingham, and wool jersey; monastic dress; popover; draped bathing suit; ballet slippers worn with day clothes
McFadden, Mary (1935–)	Fine pleating and quilted fabrics
Missoni (Rosita: 1931–) (Ottavio: 1921–)	Geometric and abstract knit patterns; bold and multiple color combinations
Mizrahi, Isaac (1961–)	Young and inventive clothing; unexpected use of fabrics and colors; inspired by McCardell
Montana, Claude (1949–)	Wedge-shaped silhouette, leathers
Norell, Norman (1900–1972)	First to show long evening skirts topped with sweaters; cloth coats lined with fur for day and evening; smoking robe; jumpers and pantsuits; long, shimmering sequined evening dresses
Oldham, Todd (1961–)	Unconventional colors, prints, beading, and embroidery; whimsical; mix of commercial and offbeat

(continued)

T A B L E   1 5 . 2   (*c o n t i n u e d*)

Designer	Designs or Design Elements
Poiret, Paul (1879–1944)	Introduced first straight-line dress; invented the harem and hobble skirts (narrow at hem that walking was almost impossible); minaret skirt
Pucci, Emilio (1914–1992)	Brilliant signature prints inspired by heraldic banners; chemises of thin silk jersey (wrinkle-resistant)
Quant, Mary (1936–)	Initiated ideas that are now commonplace (denim, colored flannel, vinyl); miniskirts
Rabanne, Paco (1934–)	Dresses made of plastic discs linked with metal chains; plastic jewelry and sun goggles in primary colors; fur and leather patches
Rhodes, Zandra (1942–)	Soft fabrics (chiffon, tulle, silk); handscreened prints; edges finished with pinking shears; glamorized Punk designs; flounced hems finished with uneven scallops
Rykiel, Sonia (1930–)	Sweaters and sweater looks cut close to the body
Saint Laurent, Yves (1936–)	Fisherman's shirt; trapeze silhouette; Mondrian dress; see-through blouse; longuette; evening tuxedo; peacoat; Russian peasant look, pantsuits
Sander, Jil (1943 –)	Pure and sensual; highest quality in materials and craftsmanship; expert tailoring in suits and coats
Snyder, Maria	Hand-painted patterns
Schiaparelli, Elsa (1980–1973)	Workclothes fabrics for evening wear; colored plastic zippers as decorative features; ceramic buttons in the shape of hands or butterflies; shaped hats in lamb chops or a pink-heeled shoe; avant-garde sweaters with tattoo or skeleton motifs; glowing phosphorescent brooches and handbags that lit up or played tunes when opened; fastened clothing with colored zippers, jeweler-designed buttons, padlocks, clips, dog leashes
Sui, Anna (c. 1955–)	Maintains a moderate price structure; mix of hip and haute couture
Tyler, Richard (1948–)	Custom tailoring; graceful cut
Ungaro, Emanuel (1923–)	Soft fabrics; several and different prints in a single outfit; layers; body-conscious clothes
Valentino (c. 1932–)	Simple, elegant; well-cut sophisticated sportswear; entrance-making evening clothes
Versace, Gianni (1946–)	Vivid, imaginative, sexy clothes
Vionnet, Madeleine (1876–1975)	Eliminated high, boned collars from dresses and blouses; bias-cut, eliminating need for fastenings; seams finished with fagoting
Westwood, Vivienne (1941–)	Designs evidence of fierce rejection of polite standards of dress
Yamamoto, Yohji (c. 1943–)	Asymmetrical hems and collars; holes and torn edges
Zoran (1947–)	Limited color range (black, gray, white, ivory, and red); prefers not to use buttons and zippers; avoids extraneous details

Chapter Highlights

- After the designer has been inspired to move in a particular direction, he or she must focus on selecting the appropriate fabrics and other materials.

- Designers must be fully knowledgeable in the elements that constitute well-designed merchandise. These elements include the silhouette, color, texture, details, and trimmings.

- The designer must also be concerned with the principles of design, including balance, proportion, emphasis, rhythm, and harmony.

- For each individual style, samples must be constructed and evaluated before the product is readied for production.

- A production timetable is established that begins with the selection of fabrics that will be used in the samples and ends when the last reorders are filled.

Important Fashion Terminology and Concepts

alternation

analogous color scheme

asymmetrical balance

complementary color scheme

balance

color theory

color wheel

continuous line

cool colors

double complementary color scheme

emphasis

knockoff

harmony

hue

intensity

monochromatic color scheme

Munsell Color System

neutrals

Prang Color System

progression

proportion

quality control

radiation

repetition

rhythm

shades

spec sheet

split complementary color scheme

symmetrical balance

texture

tints

triadic color scheme

value

warm colors

For Review

1. What are some of the elements that constitute a collection's theme?

2. What are the four silhouettes on which women's apparel designs are based?

3. Define the terms, hue, value, and intensity and explain their impact on a design.

4. What is the difference between a tint and a shade?

5. How can a monochromatic color scheme add interest to its coloration?

6. Which color combination utilizes two hues that are adjacent to each other on the color wheel?

7. If a designer wants to use two colors that will intensify when adjacently placed, which type of combination should be used?

8. Explain and compare the different color schemes used by designers.

9. What is meant by the term triadic color arrangement?

10. How do symmetrical and asymmetrical balance differ from each other?

11. Describe why it is important for a design to have a focal point.

12. By what means may rhythm in design be achieved?

13. How long is the timetable for domestically produced fashion merchandise?

Exercises and Projects

1. Design a color wheel using color-aid paper or paint chips that are available at any commercial paint store. An alternative would be to use colored markers.

2. Bring a man's, woman's, or child's garment to class and present an oral discussion on the various elements that were used in that product's design.

3. Using fashion magazines, select two items that utilize symmetrical balance in their design and two that use asymmetrical balance. Mount the pictures on foamcore board and describe to the class the reasons why these designs do or do not work.

4. Bring three pieces of fashion merchandise to class that represent different color combinations. Describe their effects to the class.

The Case of the Undecided Manufacturer

Amanda Gallop has been working in the fashion industry for ten years. When she graduated from college, she remained with the company at which she had served an internship. The company, Litt, Inc. has been in business for thirty-five years and has regularly shown a profit. Its forté was producing knockoffs of best selling items at significantly lower price points.

Gallop came up through the ranks, beginning as an assistant to the stylist and assuming the stylist role when her supervisor retired. The job involved scouting the marketplace for best selling products and transforming them into items that could be sold at lower price points. Her daily routine included visiting high fashion stores that would most likely feature the latest in fashion at upscale prices, calling on the fabrics and trimmings houses to avail herself of materials that would be used in the production of the knockoffs, and the rearrangement of some of the design elements to give the products some individuality. She was extremely successful in the position and was responsible for many of the "winners" in the Litt, Inc. line.

Three months ago, Gallop inherited a significant amount of money. Her immediate reaction to the inheritance was to open her own manufacturing company. With her experience in the field, she might be a success.

Question

Which direction should Amanda take, and why?

Although her experience was exclusively in the area of cloning best sellers, she thought that she had sufficient expertise to design original collections. After all, she knew how to recognize good design, had a complete knowledge of the fabrics and trimmings arenas, and knew about manufacturing procedures.

After many discussions with professionals in the industry about the direction the new company should take, she still has not reached a final decision.

point of view

Computer Spec Sheets Cut Down on Paperwork and Errors

Alison Grudier

In order for a designer or product developer to convey a design idea to a manufacturer, a specification form has to be generated detailing everything from the concept sketch to measurements to fabric and trim information. A new generation of computer software is giving apparel companies the ability to make the process of communication clearer and faster.

The key element in these informational computer-aided design programs is a relational database for recording and recalling the particular details of a garment. Programs also include basic drawing and coloring tools for garment illustrations as well as spreadsheets for capturing and calculating graded measurements.

Where once designers and assistants would spend hours drawing and photocopying sketches and writing measurements, now they are able to recall similar styles from past seasons, make the necessary modifications and transmit the new information electronically to the manufacturer. All of the necessary information can be captured in one location for access by anyone who needs it.

"We have seen greater standardization of information," said Kevin McIntosh, costing manager at the Gap. "It has helped the vendors know where to find the right information on a form whether it is for the Gap, GapKids, Banana Republic or Old Navy divisions."

Bill McMeley, director of product development and production control at Glen Oaks Industries agreed.

"By using a common database, we can quickly populate a new form and get the order in the system faster. We can pull information from our pattern making system to calculate finished garment measurements."

Gui Baltar, designer and program manager at Tail, Inc., a golf and tenniswear manufacturer, notes that his company has been saving time "by a factor of four."

"Before, we had to fill out four forms for each style," he said. "Now, we fill out one set of data and it quickly generates all four forms with more accuracy than our manual methods."

Whether manufacturing domestically or abroad, the ability to transmit data quickly is an absolute necessity. At the Gap, quality assurance inspectors use laptop computers in Hong Kong to call in from the factory to receive the latest version of a spec sheet. The inspection results are available immediately to the merchandiser in San Francisco.

"This has been a tremendous benefit that was only a vision when we started the project four years ago," McIntosh said.

In private-label manufacturing, managing the communications between the customer and the manufacturer can create a huge paper trail. At Glen Oaks, all communications from the customer are scanned in and maintained in the computer specification file.

"Any time we need information on a style, it is immediately available in one central place," McMeley said. "We're eliminating redundan-

cies. The majority of the copies that were distributed on paper were never looked at; only 10% were really needed."

Despite its benefits, users of product data management software say the conversion to the technology is far from painless. Converting from paper files to electronic files can be a long and tedious process. Deciding which information is necessary, how to organize it and doing data entry takes many meetings and manhours.

"A company is being optimistic if they think they can do it in less than two years," McIntosh said.

McMeley agreed.

"We want to create a database of technical 'how-to' drawings but just haven't had the time," he said.

"The first season, we had to work with both hand and computer information," Baltar explained. "This season, we hope to have everything done on computer."

Companies like Reebok, Charming Shoppes and Mast Industries have experimented with developing their own spec sheet programs with varying degrees of success. With off-the-shelf computer programs like Lotus 1-2-3 and Aldus Illustrator, users can create computerized forms. However, these are sometimes little more than typewritten forms. Though they look more professional, they are no faster or easier to create. Programs written for the apparel industry have easy-to-use features such as topstitching, drawing tools and grade rule tables for measurements in fractions instead of decimals.

Regardless of how the information is computerized, the change is a great management tool, users said.

"This is an ideal time to take a very critical look at what you are doing. We probably changed 50 percent of what we had been creating. Not because we had to, but because when we really looked at it, a lot of what was being done was unnecessary. It's easy to get comfortable in an established system and the computer was just a good excuse to examine those systems."

While the programs are paring paperwork for users, use of paper is up.

"We're actually using more paper. We just have so much more capacity to provide information," Baltar said. "Before, we didn't have a fabrication form. Now, we do. We never gave full measurements on every style. Now we do."

"Merchandisers are reluctant to give up their paper files, but we're hoping that as they grow more used to the electronic files, we can stop printing so much," McIntosh said.

Users are generally pleased with the product specification programs. The programs, they say, make labor-intensive tasks prone to human error much easier to manage.

"Speed is what it's about these days," added Andre Bernard, systems analyst for Reebok. "We can't keep up without using computers to manage all this information."

PDM: Simplifying Product Development

David Moin

With retailers growing their private label assortments, the demands on manufacturers are mounting.

They have to speed production, raise quality standards and work closer with buyers who, during the production cycle, often direct changes in design, whether it's replacing a fabric or a trim, altering a sleeve or giving new instructions on folding garments for packaging.

Communicating this myriad information can be a dilemma, leading to miscommunications, mistakes in production and the dreaded chargeback.

But product data management systems, provided by such companies as Gerber Information Systems and Animated Images, are making life easier for a growing number of apparel suppliers and retailers. Some apparel firms have devised product management systems through their own MIS departments.

In any case, such systems collate all the product data on a single pro-gram, forming an "electronic filing cabinet" of a few dozen forms that can be viewed by anyone who needs to have access.

For example, Gerber's Product Data Management (PDM) is a package with easy-to-read forms, including designer illustrations and notes, grading sheets, cost sheets, cutting tickets, confirmation letters and photographs. The forms are stored in a windows environment, neatly organizing all the fabric, sketch, pattern and labor information.

In the apparel/retail industry, the automation of product development is a relatively new phenomenon. Last September, Gerber Garment Technology acquired Microdynamics, which started developing PDM around 1989. The Gerber Informations Systems division was formed after the acquisition.

It's only been in the past two years that PDM has really caught on, and it's now considered the standard in the industry and an important element of Quick Response.

PDM has been embraced by Macy's, the American Retail Group, the GJM division of Cygne, J. Crew, Eddie Bauer, Bugle Boy and Talbots, among other companies. According to Gerber, roughly 150 companies, with a total of about 2,000 workstations around the world, use PDM.

OshKosh B'Gosh recently bought the system and has installed it in product development, merchandising and design areas, and plans to expand it to factories and contractors. However, many apparel companies still operate manually, with paper spec sheets and other documents that get photocopied and covered with whiteout, as instructions change, and eventually become illegible.

"PDM amounts to accurate and speedier communication, combined with E-mail," said Ken Winer, vice president of MIS, for Winer Industries, a Paterson, N.J.-based $80 million private label supplier to JCPenney Co., Ann Taylor, The Limited and several other retailers.

"There's no paper, no phones, no faxes," Winer said, while noting that PDM files can be printed and faxed to companies that are not on the system. He compared PDM to EDI, which triggers reorders when retailers and suppliers communicate sales data "computer to computer," but added, "PDM communicates person to person through E-mail."

As part of its business, Winer ships blazers, skirts, pants and dresses to the Express division of Limited, which is constantly pushing to develop new products, resetting its selling floors and demanding faster deliveries. Information, including silhouette or fabric changes, sometimes arrives piecemeal, but the data, as Winer notes, can be sent automatically to all people in the production process, whether it's the pattern maker or a costing executive, giving Winer Industries better control and insuring that the retailer gets what the market demands.

"In a conventional setting, revisions result in duplicate and triplicate copies of paper forms being hand-delivered or faxed, creating a mountain of paper and turning decision makers into file clerks, particularly in the private label business, where the key to success is being flexible to the retailer's demands," Winer said. "PDM handles this by keeping lists of people to notify automatically when a form is changed. If the retailer decides to alter the design, the PDM form affected would be updated by a person. PDM would then automatically send an E-mail to the pattern maker, the purchasing department, the production planning department, etc. The key point is that it's done automatically. No one picked up a phone or made a photocopy or

faxed something somewhere. This is 21st-century product."

Discounters, including Wal-Mart, which is expanding its private label Kathie Lee Collection, haven't signed on to PDM. Neither has Dillard Department Stores, May Department Stores, or Sears, Roebuck & Co. Calvin Klein is reportedly phasing it in, but generally major designers are not tuned into the program.

Steve Fineman, director of sales for PDM, said the company expects to double its revenues over the next year, though he wouldn't specify the division's volume.

"What we are trying to accomplish is to speed up the product development cycle, and reduce the time it takes to bring products to market," Fineman said. "In the past, when we talked about Quick Response, that meant faster sewing machines. It takes 10 minutes to sew a garment, but typically it's an eight-month cycle from conception to going into production."

He contended that PDM can cut weeks out of the cycle.

"We also want to improve the quality through reducing mistakes. Every apparel firm lives in fear of chargebacks," he added.

PDM offers a digital camera, built by Kodak, and priced around $2,000. It provides color snapshots.

Videos can also be transmitted demonstrating how measurements should be taken based on a retailer's preference and other functions.

Penney's tested PDM last year in its men's division, but first installed it in children's wear, after waiting for PDM to make a windows version available. The chain plans to phase it into women's, men's and home divisions this year. That involves about 100 workstations. On average, it costs $4,000 to $5,000 per workstation, plus ongoing and upgrade costs.

Eric Blackwood, Penney's director of merchandising operations and communications, described the advantages of PDM:

"At Penney's, when our CAD [computer-aided design] fabric, print and design work is done, we put it on the PDM system, filling in the specifications on the preset forms in the system based on type of merchandise. Once that is done, we attach a drawing of the item and also [a picture of] its print, and PDM takes all that information and puts it in one package, which can be transferred by fax or electronically to the supplier. One reason we chose PDM is because it is a PC IBM compatible system, so we can work in most of our main frame systems with PDM.

"The biggest advantage we see right away is the lack of errors," says Blackwood. "There use to be a lot, when things were faxed or handwritten. On PDM, when a designer makes a correction, they can immediately fax it.

"We might be working with three different companies to produce the same garment or sample. Basically with a punch of a button, a change from a designer can automatically go to those companies. This is a quantum leap forward. It's a tremendous time saver for designers. This keeps the information correct and flows it to who you want. It used to be done on homemade forms that got faxed. That involved a lot of cutting and pasting."

Blackwood continues, "It also gives our technical designers more capabilities to do more things than in the past. Before it was the pen and pencil method. Now they can go into the system and retrieve previous designs and make alterations on them quicker.

"We hope to have some of our leading partners around the world own this package."

CHAPTER 16

Apparel and Accessories Manufacturing

Before developing a new line or product, a designer researches the concept and takes advice from fashion companies, specialized groups of merchandise fashion forecasters. Once the initial design concepts have been developed, it is time to transform the ideas into salable merchandise.

Each apparel and accessories classification has its own stages of development. Some are fundamental procedures that run across most merchandise products; others are specific to a particular product type. Men's, women's, and children's apparel, for example, generally include the same stages of production, while items such as jewelry and shoes require different and specific manufacturing techniques.

The first section of the chapter, focuses on the standard procedures used in apparel production. The second section examines the specialized construction techniques used for the production of accessories.

APPAREL MANUFACTURING

The largest segment of the fashion industry produces apparel. To be profitable, manufacturers and designers pay attention to costing the product, the methods used in procuring materials, and the manufacturing process.

Costing the Product

After the designer creates the styles that will make up a collection, the costs of transforming these ideas into products must be determined before any production may begin. Costs for each and every component of the item must be carefully assessed, so that the garment can be properly priced and a profit realized. The slightest error in determining the costs of such items as a garment's linings, and its decorative or functional enhancements could result in losses to the company. At first, costs are estimated based on the original sample. Once the decision has been made to go ahead with production, the estimated figures must be transformed into actual costs. In addition to the prices of materials and trimmings, the expenses incurred in production and distribution must also be assessed. Only when these exact figures are calculated will the producer know how much to charge the retailer for the merchandise.

Fabrics

Whether it is the fabric for a dress, leather for a coat, or skins for a fur garment, the exact amount needed for each unit of production must be determined. Very often, several types of materials are used for a garment. In such cases, each must be individually assessed and figured into the total materials cost. In the case of a ballgown, not only will the cost of the primary material be figured, but also other fabrics and the lining. The cost of the gown's materials might break down as follows:

6 yards chiffon for skirt ($22.00 per yard)	$132.00
¾ yard brocade for bodice ($16.00 per yard)	12.00
4 yards rayon lining ($1.75 per yard)	7.00
Total Cost of Materials	$ 151.00

Trimmings

Trimmings or adornments must be individually priced. Such items as buttons, zippers, hooks and eyes, beading, appliqué, flowers, and so forth must be included in the costs. Using the same ballgown as a model, the following trimmings are also figured into its cost:

½ yard satin piping for bodice ($4.00 per yard)	$ 2.00
3 rhinestone buttons ($2.30 each)	6.90
1 14-inch zipper	8.00
Total Cost of Trimmings	$16.90

The designer selects the appropriate fabric and manipulates it for the proposed design.

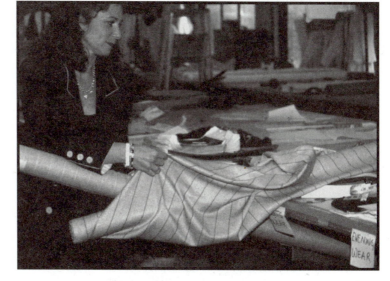

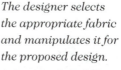

Production Labor

The next step is to calculate the production labor costs. These include making, grading, and marking the patterns and cutting and assembling the garment. If the entire process is accomplished in-house, and costs are based on hourly wages, the computation is relatively simple. This approach to production, however, is less frequently used in the industry. Most manufacturers supply some of the production tasks and engage outside contractors for the remainder of the operations. Cutting, for example, may take place in an **inside shop** that the company owns. Sewing and finishing, however, might be sent to an **outside contractor,** who is paid for services rendered. When an outside contractor is used, the cost is generally based on a predetermined schedule that is specified in a contract that is negotiated for a specific number of garments. To determine the real cost of one garment, the total cost must be divided by the number of pieces to be sewn. Continuing with the example of the ballgown, production labor costs would be as follows:

inside cutting ($28.00 per hour) ¼ hour	$ 7.00
contracted sewing (500 pieces at $15,000)	30.00
finishing ($30.00 per hour) ½ hour	15.00
Total Cost of Production Labor	$52.00

Garment assembling is a key production cost.

Transportation

The cost of freight must also be included for each unit of production. When an entire garment is produced in-house, the expense of moving it from one contractor to another is eliminated; this brings down the cost. As noted earlier, however, this is the exception rather than the rule.

The distance from one production point to another and the time needed for production dictate the type of transportation that will be used. In some cases, American manufacturers use a combination of domestic and offshore production. This results in considerable transportation costs. Manufacturers negotiate contracts with freight companies based on the number of units that will be transported. The actual cost of transportation for each unit is then calculated, so that it can be accurately figured into the final cost of the product.

Distribution

Once the product has been completed, the manufacturer must sell it to the retailer. In the garment industry, two methods are generally used. One involves the maintenance of an **in-house sales staff**; the other the use of **manufacturer's representatives** who sell the goods in their own facilities. No matter which approach is taken, the cost of selling each product must be figured.

The Wholesale Price

Once all of the costs have been assessed, the manufacturer must decide on a markup that covers any additional expenses of doing business, such as rent, utilities, and advertising, and still bring a profit to the company. The markup is the difference between the cost and the **wholesale price:**

wholesale price – cost = manufacturer's markup

$100.00 – $60.00 = $40.00

The markup is expressed as a percent of the wholesale price. Thus, in the above example, the markup percent would be 40 percent.

If expenses are not carefully determined, the actual profit will be less than anticipated. Even when the proper calculations are made, other factors may reflect anticipated profits. For example, some items might not sell as well as expected and might warrant being sold below regular wholesale prices. Bearing this in mind, manufacturers are always at risk, hoping that their initial planning proves accurate.

Materials Procurement

Once samples have been produced and their manufacturing costs calculated, the materials must be purchased. Based on the actual yardage needed for each item, the manufacturer will determine the number of items that need to be sold before a profit is realized. This number is called a **cutting ticket.** The amount of each cutting ticket varies from product to product and manufacturer to manufacturer. A company will begin to earn a profit when the number of items on the cutting ticket is sold. Some companies do not cut a single piece until orders have reached the cutting ticket. Others take chances by cutting and assembling before orders are received.

The size of the manufacturing company and its potential volume determines how materials are purchased. Large companies buy fabrics directly from the major textile mills, so that they can get the lowest prices. Smaller companies, unable to satisfy the minimum ordering requirements of major textile companies, are usually restricted to smaller textile producers or wholesale fabric suppliers. Other factors that determine which suppliers to use include delivery time, reliability of supply, and methods of payment.

Trimmings must also be purchased. Most of these purchases are made through wholesalers who deal specifically with decorative and functional enhancements.

The Manufacturing Process

The designer creates a pattern for each garment either through draping or flat patternmaking. Some companies adjust or correct these standard patterns and use them in actual production. In most cases, however, individual production patterns are created.

The Production Pattern

The process for creating **production patterns** is similar to that used to design actual garments. A production pattern has all of the exact details (sizing) of the sample pattern; sample patterns do not. Production patterns may be rendered by hand or prepared with the use of computer-aided design (CAD) systems (see Table 15.2 CAD Companies and Systems Used in the Fashion Industry). Manufacturers of mass-produced items prefer CAD systems because of their efficiency and accuracy. At this stage, strict adherence to size standardization is important. Anyone who has tried on sev-

Patterns are created with the use of computers.

eral dresses or suits of the same size made by different manufacturers will quickly notice that they often do not fit exactly the same way. Some feature narrow cuts, while others might be fuller fitting. While all refrigerators that offer twenty cubic feet have the same holding capacity, all size ten dresses do not fit the same way. The patternmaker must address the needs of the manufacturer's clientele before any patterns are prepared.

Grading and Marking the Pattern

After the production pattern is completed, it must be graded to fit the range of sizes in which the garment will be produced. Although the samples of missy size dresses are often made to fit size 8, a complete assortment of sizes for the garment might range from sizes 6 to 16.

Grading is accomplished manually or by computer. The operator creates the full range of sizes by increasing or decreasing the sample pattern. To satisfactorily perform this procedure manually, the grader must have specific skills—it is the hand that performs the actual calculation for each size. However, computer programs use a **digitizer** to mark the key points on the pattern for each size in the range. Once the key points of each design are set in the computer's memory, an accurate pattern for each size is automatically produced. Computerized grading saves so much time that manual grading is being phased out.

Once grading is completed, **production layouts,** or **markers,** as they are called, are constructed from a piece of paper that measures the same width as the material that will be used for the garment. The purpose is to minimize fabric costs by determining how to cut the maximum number of garment parts from a single piece of fabric. A separate marker is traced from the pattern boards for each of the garment's components, including the bodice of the dress, the skirt, and sleeves. Each of the parts is placed as closely as possible to the next to eliminate fabric waste. Every wasted scrap of fabric contributes unnecessarily to the cost of the garment.

Computers are used for both grading and marking. Some of the vendors for such programs include Assyst Inc., Lectra Systems Inc., and Polygon Software and Technology.

Cutting the Garment

After the patterns and markers have been generated, the fabric must be cut. The procedure depends on the number of identical items needed to be produced. In couture manufacturing, one-of-a kind garments are individually cut by a skilled craftsperson whose trained hands and eyes manipulate the fabric.

In most cases, however, where the key to success is in mass production, the layer upon layer of fabric is spread on a cutting table, and cut as if it were one piece. As many as 500 layers of material may be cut at one time, either by hand or by the use of a CAM (computer-aided manufacturing) system.

In hand cutting, the cutter guides a vibrating blade around the edges of the marker. A vertical blade is better than a circular blade because it more accurately follows the curves of some designs. The fineness or coarseness of the blade depends on the thickness and density of the material.

Although traditional hand cutting is still found in many factories, more and more companies use a computer, sometimes to direct a laser beam, to cut the garment. Its speed and accuracy significantly improves production.

If a style is a **staple** item, such as men's dress shirts, dies are developed to cut the pieces of the garment. The dies are constructed of sharp steel edges that easily cut through all of the fabric layers. **Die cutting** is similar to a cookie cutter.

Because manufacturers are always looking to lower costs, they constantly explore new ways to improve the accuracy of speed of the cutting stages.

Assembling the Garment

Manufacturing a fine men's suit, for example, might require as many as 250 separate assembling operations. Although this is not typical of all apparel manufacturing, it does indicate that the cost of sewing a garment together can be a significant factor in the cost of production.

Two approaches are used to assemble garments. A garment can be assembled by one individual or by an assembly line. The latter is the more common approach in the fashion industry because it is a less expensive way to mass produce apparel. Each individual performs just one task and then passes the garment to the next individual, who performs the next task. This process continues until the garment is completed. Factories using this approach generally locate individuals performing the same task in one area. After a batch of the pieces have been completed, it is moved to the next production area.

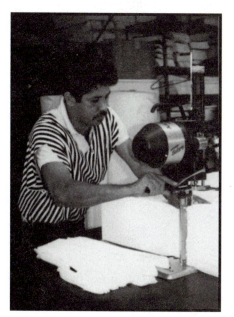 

Cutting is accomplished in numerous ways, the method being determined by the desired quantities. A cutter carefully cuts the fabric into the necessary component parts.

Assembling the garment may require as many as 250 steps.

Only very expensive garments are now hand assembled. The majority of apparel is completed with a variety of power sewing machines. Handwork, if used at all, is reserved for the application of decoration or trimmings.

There are several types of machines, including the lock-stitch that sews a straight seam; the chain-stitch that produces a looped effect; the overlock that sews one seam over another to enhance appearance; the blind-stitcher that is used to hem garments; and the buttonhole machine that automatically sews buttonholes.

As with every other stage of production, sewing is increasingly automated. This reduces costs by significantly reducing the time needed for sewing. In the manufacture of inexpensive apparel, computer-driven machines are replacing the individuals who previously sewed garments together by hand or machine.

Another time-saving technique is fusing, in which two pieces of fabric are bonded together. In the men's wear industry, for example, less expensive suits are being produced by fusing rather than sewing parts together. Although, costs are reduced, the long-range serviceability of the garment is diminished.

Finishing the Garment

After the garment is assembled, it needs to be finished. This might involve sewing buttons, setting-in zippers, applying beading or appliqués, or hand stitching for ornamentation. These finishes can be performed by hand or machine.

Once these finishes have been applied, the garment is ready to be pressed. Not only does this set the fabric, as in the case of men's suits, but also readies it for inclusion in a retailer's inventory.

Labeling the Garment

The final stage involves labeling the garment. One label identifies the manufacturer or designer. It tells the consumer who was responsible for the garment's creation. If the name is well known, the consumer may make certain assumptions about quality and the retailer may be able to charge a higher price.

Other labels include information on laundering and general care. If not accurately explained, the item might be improperly laundered and ruined, causing unnecessary returns to the vendor. Finally, if merchandise is produced offshore, the country of origin must be identified on a permanently sewn label.

Quick Response

Quick Response, as outlined by the Management Systems Committee of the American Apparel Manufacturers Association, is "a management philosophy since it embraces actions by all functions of a business, working in concert with each other. It also involves working in concert with suppliers and customers in meaningful, in-depth trading partner alliances using uniform, standard procedures. The alliance has mutual objectives of increased sales and profitability and reduced inventory for all the partners." It is a combination of techniques that a business uses during all stages of production from the procurement of raw materials to the delivery of the finished product to the consumer.

The goals of quick response include a reduction in production time, lowering of inventories, and increasing profitability. Two technologies that help achieve these goals are: **bar coding** and **electronic data exchange (EDI)**. They improve the communication process among manufacturers, materials suppliers, and retailers. Bar coding has simplified the recording of **point-of-sale (POS)** information, which can be quickly sent to those businesses involved in shipping the goods from the production point to the consumption point. EDI has improved communication among all of these businesses. Because information can be conveyed quickly to everyone from producer to retailer, inventory replenishment is fast and accurate. Ultimately, quick response results in smaller and more frequent orders, eliminating the necessity to overstock an abundance of goods. It provides the same advantage for all other segments of the fashion industry.

Garments making their way through the street of New York City's garment center.

There are many steps required to manufacture footwear—from the design sketch to the creation of the last and model shoe to transforming the last to the pattern to cutting the material and stitching the final product.

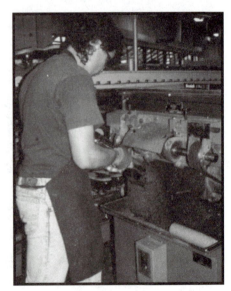

ACCESSORIES MANUFACTURING

Most people take for granted the number of different fashion accessories available to enhance their wardrobes. Few however, are informed about how these goods are produced. How many consumers, for example, could guess that it takes as many as 300 individual operations to construct a single pair of fine men's shoes! Is it no wonder that companies like Cole-Haan charge as much as $500 for a single pair of oxfords.

Although accessories and apparel manufacturers address many of the same problems including costing the items, the actual construction of some accessories require specialized production techniques. The lasting of shoes, full-fashioning of hosiery, the hammering of metals in jewelry pieces, piqué seaming of gloves, and hand-blocking of millinery are just some examples of the individual needs of accessories manufacturing.

Understanding the manufacturing techniques for accessories, when added to the information in the apparel section of this chapter, is beneficial for both industry professionals and consumers. It better enables those who sell the products to justify the prices by a commanding knowledge of production techniques. For the consumer, familiarity with the different stages of production helps them spend their dollars more wisely. Chapter 10 described all of these fashion accessories; this chapter explains how they are produced.

Footwear

From fine intricately detailed leather shoes to the various canvas models, there are literally several hundred types of shoes available for sale. Within each of these classifications, the price can vary greatly. A man's pair of business shoes may be purchased for as little as $50, or as much as several hundred dollars. The difference is based on the cost of materials and the production techniques.

Parts of the Shoe

Basically, each shoe is composed of three parts: the upper, the soles, and the heel.

1. The **upper** is broken down into three separate pieces: the *vamp*, which covers the toes and the front portion of the foot and includes the *tongue*, and the two quarters that encompass the back portion.

2. The **sole** is more than one layer of material. It consists of the *insole*, which is found on the inside of the shoe closest to the foot; the *midsole*, which lies between the insole and the outermost sole of the shoe; the *outermost-sole*, which is the thickest of the sole's components. The thickness is necessary because of the significant amount of friction caused by the shoe touching the ground.

3. **Heels**, or bottoms as they are technically referred to in the trade, are available in a variety of styles and heights. They are the last pieces to be attached to the body of the shoe.

After each part has been constructed, shoes are assembled.

Production

From original design concept to finished product requires many steps. As with other products, the complexity of construction is a significant component in the price of the final product. In some aspects of shoe production, the same operation may be completed by hand or machine. If the former is used, the final price will be higher. The shoe manufacturer must choose the production methods necessary to manufacture a shoe that addresses such factors as fit, comfort, and price.

The following stages of development are basic to traditional shoe construction.

- **DEVELOPING THE DESIGNER LAST**   Once the designer has sketched the style, a form or **last** is created on which the model shoe is constructed. Each last conforms to the style, size, and fit characteristics of the finished footwear. The last is generally sculpted from wood by skilled craftspeople. When a last is considered worthy of inclusion in the manufacturer's line, it is then transformed into a *production* or *development last.*

- **CREATING THE DEVELOPMENT OR PRODUCTION LAST**   Every style and size that is to be produced requires a separate last. These final lasts are made of polyethylene logs that are placed on duplicating lathes that turn and copy the designer's last. With the tremendous range of sizes and widths for each style, it is not unusual for as many as fifty individual production lasts to be created. After the lasts have been turned out, they are transformed into flat patterns. Today, this is often accomplished with the use of computer aided design (CAD) programs, such as MicroDesign and Artworks.

- **TRANSFORMING THE LAST INTO PATTERNS**   The three-dimensional last or form is transformed into flat patterns—a different one for each part of the shoe. To be certain that the end parts will fit when assembled into a shoe, each pattern's part must be perfectly constructed. The parts include the different pieces that constitute the upper portion of the shoe, the various soles, the heels, and various decorative embellishments.

In one method of pattern production, the last is wrapped with adhesive tape. The design and reference points are marked by pencil. The tape is then cut along the design lines and peeled away from the last. It is then flattened on paper and cut into the various pieces. At this point, some manufacturers grade the patterns into the different sizes needed for production.

- **CREATING DIES**   To mass produce shoes, many layers of material must be cut at one time. To do so, dies that resemble cookie cutters are produced. Sharp steel strips that will cut through the material are bent to conform to the various shapes needed.

- **CUTTING THE MATERIAL**   The material is cut either by hand or by dies. In the case of synthetic or manufactured goods, an automated die technique is used so that expenses can be reduced. When leather is used, the cutting process is generally performed by hand. This more costly procedure allows the skilled craftsperson to avoid parts of the leather that have blemishes and other unsightly markings.

- **FITTING AND STITCHING THE SHOE**   The largest number of individual operations are performed in an area called the fitting room. Here, all of the com-

TABLE 16.1

TECHNIQUES FOR LASTING SHOES

Technique	Description
Goodyear Welt	One of the finest methods of lasting uses two seams to attach the upper shoe to the sole. The first is a hidden chain-stitched inseam that holds a strip called the welt and the inseam together. The second is a lockstitch outseam that attaches the outersole.
Mackay	A method that uses tacking, stapling, or cementing to attach the upper to an insole. The entire piece is then attached to the outersole.
Littleway	A method by which the sole is stitched directly to the upper.

ponents of the shoe are stitched together. Some highly detailed shoes require as many as sixty individual processes during this stage of production. Linings, for example, must be attached to such parts as the vamp and quarters; the quarter is then sewn onto the vamp; the tongue, if used, is attached; "eyelets" are made; and decorative stitching applied.

- **LASTING**   This stage of construction may be performed by a number of different techniques. Basically, they all require that the fitted upper is pulled over the last in a series of operations that makes the upper conform to the shape of the last. The decision to use one lasting technique or another depends upon such factors as quality, appearance, and function.

  Some of the commonly used methods, including the Goodyear Welt, are listed and defined in Table 16.1.

- **ASSEMBLING THE REMAINING PARTS OF THE SHOE**   As the upper is being assembled, various other parts, such as the counters, sock linings, shanks, and heels, are also being assembled.

- **BOTTOMING**   The lasted upper receives the shanks and fillers, and is ready for **bottoming,** the permanent attachment of the outer sole to the shoe upper. The heels are then nailed through the insole for strength.

- **FINISHING THE SHOE**   The final operations include buffing the bottoms to achieve a smooth finish, polishing the shoe to enhance its luster, and *treeing,* which is placing the shoe on a form to make certain that it is properly shaped. If laces or ornaments are part of the design, they are attended to at this time.

Hosiery

Full-length stockings, knee-highs, pantyhose, and socks are both functional and decorative accessories for all individuals. All of these items are knitted to conform to the shape of the legs and feet. Dress hosiery may be made of microfibers or Lycra, while socks are usually made from a variety of natural fibers such as cotton, wool, and cashmere, and manufactured fibers such as rayon, acrylic, and polyester.

Production

Although the introduction of new knitting machines has made production faster, the construction techniques used in the hosiery industry are much the same as they have been for years.

Some stockings are manufactured using the **full fashioned technique,** which produces a flat form in the desired size and shape. A back seam is then used to finish the product. After the basic hosiery has been completed, it is dyed, placed on forms, and heat set for shape retention.

Seamless hosiery, a mainstay in the industry, uses a one-piece construction arrangement that forms the hosiery with the use of circular knitting machines. As with full-fashioned hosiery, it is made according to size and shape, then dyed and heat-set.

Pantyhose, the largest selling type of dress hosiery, may be made in one of two ways. One method sews individual stockings to a panty to form the product. The other creates a one-piece item on special machines. In both cases, the products are dyed and heat-set.

Socks follow the same general principles of construction as stockings and pantyhose. They are knitted on circular machines, usually in a natural color that may be dyed at a later time when the fashion colors have been decided upon. If patterns are to be used in the design, different colored yarns are used at the time of construction to generate the desired motif.

Jewelry

The cost of jewelry ranges from a mere dollar or two to several thousands for a single piece. Obviously, the materials used in its construction significantly contributes to the final price. However, cost is also affected by different production techniques.

Production

Metals are transformed into materials for use in jewelry by a number of methods. Some are accomplished by machine; others are the work of skilled craftspeople. The various techniques for producing jewelry, including **annealing** and **casting,** are listed and defined in Table 16.2.

Once the metals have been processed, they can be used alone or combined with stones to create various types of jewelry.

Gloves

The type of construction used in making gloves depends on the materials used, the desired appearance, and the final price of the product. The easiest gloves to produce are knitted. Because the entire product is generally one piece, little assembly is needed. The only sewing required is to close the tips of the fingers and to add enhancements. It is the construction of leather gloves that requires a series of different operations.

Parts of the Glove

Generally, gloves are comprised of four parts: **trank, fourchettes, quirks,** and **thumb.**

TABLE 16.2

VARIOUS TECHNIQUES FOR PRODUCING JEWELRY

Technique	Description
Annealing	Heating the metals to make them more pliable.
Antiquing	Applying chemicals to darken the metal so that an old look is achieved.
Casting	Liquefying and pouring metals into casts that represent different designs.
Die-striking	Reproducing many of the same pieces through the use of a mold or form. They are placed between the dies and squeezed into shape by means of a hydraulic press at extreme pressures.
Drawing	Softening and forcing metals that are to be woven into designs through a series of holes, each slightly smaller than the previous one, until the desired thickness has been achieved.
Embossing	Applying a three-dimensional effect to a metal with pressure.
Engraving	Scratching a design into metal by hand or machine.
Etching	Producing a design by applying acid to certain areas of unprotected areas of a metal.
Florentining	Producing a series of fine scratched lines by engraving.
Forging	Heating and then hammering metals to achieve a desired shape.
Fusing	Joining two pieces by liquefying the metal under extreme heat.
Rolling	Pressing metals into sheets so that they can then be cut or bent to required shapes.
Soldering	Joining two metals by using a third metal that has a lower melting point. The solder must be of the same color and strength as the two metals to be joined, so that it will be undetectable on inspection. The two pieces to be joined are held in place by wire, steel pins, or plaster, depending on the type of solder to be used.
Repoussé	Hammering a flat piece of metal into a three-dimensional piece.
Welding	Using heat and pressure to join together two or more metals.

1. The *trank* is the rectangular shape that constitutes the front and back portion of the glove.
2. The *fourchettes* are the narrow oblong pieces that are inserted between the fingers to improve the wearer's comfort.
3. *Quirks,* small triangular inserts that are used at the base of the fingers, provide extra comfort and movement.
4. The final part is the *thumb,* of which there are two varieties. The *bolton* is a bulky design that provides freedom of movement; the *quirk thumb* is a sleeker style that allows for a snug fit.

Production

To construct gloves composed of leather or woven goods, there are two stages—cutting the material into its various components and then sewing them together.

- **CUTTING**   The method used for cutting leather depends on its quality. For finer gloves, a skilled cutter dampens and stretches the leather to assure proper fit and cuts each piece one at a time. It is called *table-cutting.* In lesser quality leathers and woven fabrics, the glove is constructed by the pull-down method. This involves using dies that cut the material in a cookie-cutter fashion.

- **ASSEMBLING**   Basically the following four techniques are used to assemble a glove.

    1. **Inseaming.** The least expensive technique. The seams are sewn together on the outside of the glove and then turned inside out. This leaves no visible seam.
    2. **Outseaming.** The opposite of inseaming. The seams are stitched along the edges and left exposed.
    3. **Overseaming.** A technique that involves stitching over the edges.
    4. **Piqué Seaming.** The most expensive technique, **piqué seaming** requires a special machine that sews one edge of the material over the other, both on the front and back, exposing only one raw edge. It is used for sleek-glove production.

    In some constructions, a third stage called *pointing* is applied. This is the application of decorative stitching on the back of the glove.

Handbags

Handbags serve both functional and decorative purposes. They have become one of the more important parts of a wardrobe. They range in prices from a few dollars to thousands of dollars for the most intricate designs discussed in Chapter 10.

Parts of the Handbag

Using as few as three or four parts, or as many as thirty, the basic components are the *frame,* or *body,* over which the design is constructed; the *gussets* which are side panels that allow for expansion of the piece; the *lining,* which covers the stitching or gluing that has been used; the *handles,* which come in a variety of lengths and make carrying easier; and closing devices, such as zippers, clasps, locks, snaps, and drawstrings.

Although all of these components are necessary to create the handbag, it is the material that gives each item its individuality. The different types include leather, which still dominates the marketplace, vinyl, plastic, wood, straw, lucite, and metallics. Finally, ornamentation further distinguishes one product from another. It might be appliqués, fringe, buttons, sequins, beads, stones, or flowers.

As with other apparel and accessories classifications, the process begins with the designer. Most often, the design is created on paper.

Production

After the design has been completed, it is first assembled in a material such as muslin or felt and fitted with the necessary closing devices and enhancements.

Quality control is assured at all levels in a Louis Vuitton factory. Here Vuitton products are assembled.

Each style is then assessed in terms of potential sales. Those deemed to have the best chances for success will enter production.

Initially, a pattern is constructed for each part of the design. This may be done by hand, or by the use of a CAD system. In either case, the completed patterns are used as the guides over which the materials will be cut. In the case of fine leather handbags, each part is individually cut to avoid scars and blemishes. Skilled craftspeople are well paid to perform this hand-cutting task. The actual cutting may be accomplished by means of a sharp knife or, in some cases, with dies that stamp out the pieces. When fabric bags are produced, the fabric is generally layered so that many pieces may be simultaneously cut, saving time and money.

The pieces are assembled by hand or machine. They are then ready to receive any stiffening materials that might be used between the body of the bag and the lining to lend support. In soft bag construction, stiffening materials are unnecessary. Other parts, such as plastic strips or stays might provide support. Foamlike fillers can give the product a softer feel. The body is now fitted to the frame and readied for the addition of closures, handles, and any decorations indicated on the original design.

After the bag is finished, it is ready for inspection. In cases such as the Judith Leiber handbags and other high-quality products, the inspection process is carefully carried out for each item. When customers are asked to spend large sums of money for such products, only the finest quality makes it to the stores. In the case of costly bags, each one is individually boxed. For lower-priced items, bulk packing is typical.

Belts

As with many other fashion accessories, belts are enjoying new popularity. Apparel designers are now creating belts in styles that are expensive to produce. Although the final products take on many different appearances, the methods of belt construction are rather simple. It is the choice of fabric and ornamentation that creates the interest.

Production

Many different materials are used to construct belts, such as leather (still the most popular), fabric, straw, metal, vinyl, lucite, and elastic. The fabrication generally dictates the method of construction.

For leather belts, each piece is cut to the desired length and width either by hand or a strap-cutting machine. If a shaped belt is required, such as one that fits the contour of the body, a die is usually produced that stamps out the shape. In producing quality leather belts, the cutter needs to avoid unsightly markings.

Some belts are then affixed with a backing, which is attached either by means of a walking-foot machine, which sews the two pieces together, or by gluing. When fabric belts are produced, layer upon layer is stacked so that the fabric can be cut in batches by means of dies. Because the materials are manufactured, blemishes are not a problem.

After the body of the belt has been completed, decoration such as stitching or nailhead inserts, are applied. If holes are needed, they are punched into the pieces by hand or machine. Finally, the buckles are inserted and closed by sewing or gluing.

Cinch or elasticized belts are constructed by a different method. The material is cut to size and sewn around the edges. Closures such as snaps or hooks are then attached. For chain belts, the links are fastened one to another, until the desired length is achieved; a final link is used as a closing device. The easiest belt to construct is the sash. It merely requires cutting fabric to the appropriate length and width, and sewing the edges. Since there are no formal closing devices, the process is quickly completed.

Hats

Although the number of men and women who wear hats today pales by comparison with years ago, some people still consider them essential parts of a fashionable wardrobe. Of course, in cold weather, hats are a popular form of functional attire. For those who want to wear hats, a few manufacturers continue to produce them.

Production

As with all accessories, the method of production for hats is based on the ultimate selling price and the various materials required for each style. The less expensive variety is machine made; the finer entries are crafted by hand.

After the designer sketches the model, it is transformed into a sample. The basic components of each sample include the body of the hat and the ornamentation with which it will be enhanced. After the samples have been evaluated in terms of their sales potential, production is ready to begin. Sometimes, milliners are called upon to create one-of-a-kind hats that cost several hundred dollars, but most often, the items are mass produced.

For the fall and winter months, felt hats are still the mainstay of men's and women's collections. The felt is cut, either by hand or machine, and then shaped by using cones. The felt is repeatedly steamed under pressure, on the cones. The **crown,** or body, of the hat, and the **brim** are then formed. After another round of steam is applied, the brim of the hat is trimmed until the desired width is achieved. Hats are now ready for trimming. Men's hats usually include a fabric band around the crown and sometimes a small feather for decoration. Women's hats are trimmed following the designer's concept.

In the spring and summer, straw is the most popular material for hats. Sometimes these hats are made of woven mats that are shaped on wooden forms called **blocks.** Each style has its own block. The straw material is repeatedly steamed on the blocks until the shape of the hat has been achieved. Once the moisture from the steaming has been removed, a stiffening material called *buckram* might be added underneath to help maintain the hat's shape. In some straw hat designs, the construction involves overlapping narrow strips

of straw until the appropriate shape is achieved. This plaiting process is accomplished with the use of sewing machines. After the plaiting has been completed, the material is placed on blocks for shaping and is stiffened for shape retention.

Other hat styles that have less rigid formations use soft materials, such as velvet, velveteen, and velour. To produce these unstructured models, the operator cuts the fabric to size and shape, drapes it, and sews it into a soft style.

Knitting, by machine or hand, and crocheting are also used to construct many of the functional hats worn by children and adults seeking protection from the cold weather. The production is generally a one-piece affair without the need for any sewing.

A final touch that distinguishes one model from another is ornamentation. Feathers, flowers, veils, bows, ribbons, appliqués, and beads can be applied either by sewing or gluing.

The finished products are then either individually boxed or shipped in bulk cartons to the store.

Scarves

Scarves are made in a variety of sizes and shapes. Once considered only as a functional product, scarves have become a favorite fashion accessory.

Fashionable hat designs are important elements in today's fashion scene. The designer putting finishing touches to his design.

Production

The construction of scarves is simpler than that of other fashion accessories. They may be made from rolls of fabric that are cut to the appropriate sizes and shapes, and then hemmed either by machine or hand. Hand-rolling is reserved for the more expensive varieties.

Designer scarves are usually made as individual pieces. They begin with solid colors that are then silk-screened to create a pattern. Some of these scarves have become collectibles and command hundreds of dollars.

In addition to the exquisite colorations and silk-screened motifs, decorative elements such as fringe, beading, and sequins are used as enhancements.

Watches

Although watches are basically functional timepieces, many styles are now available to serve different fashion purposes. Men and women often have more than one, with each serving different wardrobe needs.

Production

The oldest variety is the mechanical model that uses jeweled movements for precision. Jewels are inserted into tiny holes to act as friction points. Although expensive watches use precious jewels, today's inexpensive variety substitutes synthetic stones.

When the electronic watch was introduced, it was quickly accepted as a more functional product. The mainspring barrel used in mechanical watches is replaced by a power cell that usually lasts for approximately a year. Instead of the common "ticking" generated by mechanical watches, the electronic watch features a soft hum. With fewer parts than the other watches, it is more serviceable.

By substituting solid-state components for the moving parts used in the mechanical and electronic models, a new generation of watches was born. Instead of hands that moved to indicate time, digital numbers were displayed whenever a button was pushed. Before long, anyone could own a reliable **digital watch** for as little as $15.

With the use of quartz crystals, the watch industry was further revolutionized. The quartz timepiece is ten times more accurate than conventional models. With the addition of microcircuitry, these watches also display dates and days of the week. Other features include stopwatches, temperature readings, and information storage capabilities.

Watch casings, which are designed to protect the mechanisms, serve as attractive bracelets. Made from precious metals, such as gold and platinum, and functional materials, such as stainless steel. They are the work of specialty designers.

Chapter Highlights

- Many of the production operations used in the manufacture of apparel goods are basic to all products. Specialized procedures become necessary, however, in the production of accessories.

- Before production begins, each product must be costed so that an appropriate wholesale price is established.

- Fabrics are bought in quantities that reflect the predetermined sales potential for each garment or accessory item.

- Apparel manufacturing requires the creation of a production pattern, grading and marking the pattern, cutting the fabric, and assembling the garment.

- Many operations are now computerized to increase accuracy and profits.

- Each garment or accessory is finished with functional and decorative embellishment and then labeled to indicate the company's name, product care, and country of origin if produced offshore.

- Many accessories require specialized manufacturing techniques.

Important Fashion Terminology and Concepts

annealing

bar coding

blocks

bottoming

brim

CAD (computer-aided design)

CAM (computer-aided manufacturing)

casting

crown

cutting ticket

die cutting

digital watch

digitizer

electronic data exchange (EDI)

full-fashioned technique

grading

heel

in-house sales staff

inseaming

inside shop

last

manufacturer's representatives

marking

outseaming

outside contractor

overseaming

piqué seaming

quick response

quirks

point-of-sale (POS)

production pattern

soles

staple

thumb

upper

wholesale price

For Review

1. What is the first step that must be considered before actual production takes place?

2. List the various factors that determine a product's cost.

3. Differentiate between inside shops and outside contractors.

4. In what ways do manufacturers sell their goods?

5. Define the term cutting ticket.

6. How have computers affected the manufacturing process?

7. Why must patterns be graded?

8. Describe the two methods of assembling garments used in the fashion industry.

9. What purposes do labels serve on fashion products?

10. What are the three basic parts of a shoe?

11. Describe the role played by lasting in shoe production.

12. What are two methods used to produce pantyhose?

13. List and define four techniques employed in jewelry construction.

14. Why is it easy to produce a cinch belt?

15. On what type of form is a felt hat shaped?

16. Differentiate between the two types of watches.

Exercises and Projects

1. If you live in the vicinity of an apparel manufacturer, inquire about the possibility of visiting the plant to learn about production. Take a camera along to record the various operations. The photographs should be mounted on a foamcore board and used in an oral report that outlines the various stages of production at the company you visited.

2. Carefully take apart a garment you are ready to dispose of and try to assess the following:

- the yardage of material used
- the functional and decorative trimmings
- special finishes

Then, determine the approximate costs of each of the elements by visiting a materials and trimmings supplier. Try to determine the actual cost of the goods in the product.

3. Consult a watch manufacturer about the different production techniques used in watchmaking.

4. Disassemble a used shoe to uncover all of its basic components. Each component should be mounted, labeled, and described in terms of the purpose it serves.

The Case of the Production Dilemma

Jan Rogers and Peter English are considering forming a partnership to manufacture moderately priced women's dresses. Each has had previous experience in the field. Jan was the production manager for Artway, a dress company that has been in business for forty years; Peter was the assistant production manager for Bell Sportswear, makers of inexpensive skirts, pants, and tops. Jan used in-house production and Peter used outside contractors.

For a designer, they have agreed on Renée Philips, who while carrying the title of assistant designer, actually created many of her own styles. She is capable of preparing both the design and production patterns, and is familiar with computer-aided design technology.

Question

Which approach would you suggest the new company take in terms of contracting versus in-house production? Why?

The new compnay has limited financial resources, but nevertheless the principles want to see their dreams come true. They expect to begin their year with four collections, one for each season.

Together with Renée, the two are planning their production methodology. Jan believes the "in-house" approach is the most appropriate, while Peter favors the use of outside contractors. Renée is not certain which route would be most beneficial to the fledgling company.

point of view

The Private Label Gold Mine

Samantha Conti

Private label manufacturers are among the best-kept secrets of Italy's fashion industry, supplying millions of pieces of clothing each year to major retailers in the U.S., Europe and Asia, and helping to determine the way many American women dress.

For more than 30 years, little-known manufacturers whose identities are jealously guarded by their top-drawer clients have been producing private label collections for the U.S., European and Asian markets.

Companies such as The Limited Group and Federated Department Stores, retail chains like Talbots and The Gap and catalogs like Lands' End do a vigorous business here, especially in knitwear and leather accessories.

U.S. retailers meet regularly with their Italian manufacturers swapping sketches, choosing fabrics and surveying samples. They also work closely with buying offices which act as liaisons between Italian companies and their foreign clients.

Industry experts say Italy's private label business is changing rapidly because clients around the world, and especially in the U.S., have become more demanding: increasing their private label orders and asking for more sophisticated, diverse products.

As a result, manufacturers and buying offices say they are working harder than ever to increase their productivity, creativity and cost-efficiency in what is becoming a highly competitive market.

"The business has changed considerably in the past 10 to 15 years. Today, there is more interest in pri-

vate label than ever before and more hard work involved in producing collections," said Francesco Diaco, owner of the Florence-based buying office IBS Italia, which represents The Limited Group.

"It used to be that buying offices just made sure the merchandise was ordered and delivered to the client on time. Today we work very closely with the client and the manufacturer and do everything from scratch. We start with the fabric and yarn fairs and follow the process through to the end," he said.

Diaco does 75–80 percent of his business with The Limited Group, which IBS has been working with since 1963. "We have a very solid history with The Limited Group— ever since Leslie Wexner came here in the 1960s, we have been coordinating their private label collections in Italy," he said.

Diaco has teams dedicated to each of the Limited stores he represents, including Henri Bendel, The Limited, Express, Victoria's Secret, Lane Bryant and Lerner's. When they are working on a collection, Diaco's teams meet at least once a month with their counterparts from The Limited stores to review fabrics, sketches and samples.

The Henri Bendel team works chiefly on accessories, knitwear and jackets. The Limited team helps create accessories, skirts, shirts, pants and knitwear, and the Victoria's Secret group spends much of its time researching fabrics that might then be cut and sewn in another country.

Diaco said he is optimistic about the future of the private label busi-

ness in Italy. "Each year, for example, Bendel's increases its volume of private label items sourced here. But it is not alone. In general, I think department stores are moving increasingly toward private label because it sets them free. They can market and manage the collections the way they want, and they can express their individuality through a private label collection," he said.

Bloomingdale's, which produces cashmere sweaters in Italy, is one store that is looking to boost its private label production here. "We'll be looking at Italy with an eye to increasing our private label business," said Kalman Ruttenstein, senior vice president of fashion direction at Bloomingdale's.

Manufacturers say they are willing to go to the ends of the planet to make their customers happy and drum up more business.

Quadro, a manufacturer based in Montale, Italy, makes knitwear for The Limited Group in collaboration with IBS and for May Co., in addition to producing three of its own labels for the Italian domestic market.

In 1995, some 60 percent of its turnover, which the company would not divulge, was generated by private label business with U.S. customers. "About three years ago, the U.S. market all of a sudden became very interested in private label, and each year our clients increase their volumes," said Cosetta Innocenti, who oversees production of private label collections.

Last year, Quadro turned out more than 600,000 units for shipment to the U.S. About one-third of those were twinsets destined for the shelves and racks of The Limited stores. Among the rest were classic merino wool sweaters for May Co.

Innocenti said her company works hard to please its demanding U.S. clients. "Americans often want to place their orders late and want delivery as soon as possible, and we are willing to meet those needs. If it means working on Saturday and Sunday, then that's no problem," she said. "The Limited stores ordered 130,000 twinsets in September, and the delivery was made by November."

Alberto Danti, the owner of Maglificio Fiesole, another Tuscan knitwear manufacturer, said his American clients, which include Federated Department Stores, Talbots and Lands' End, have become pickier and more demanding over the years.

"They have become more demanding because the market is so much more difficult today. "The Made in Italy label just isn't enough anymore," he said. "Today, we do a lot more research on color, styling and fabrics because our clients want their products to stand out. For example, we pay a lot of attention to padding, stitching and collars."

Danti said he is convinced the key to success in the U.S.—which generated 60 percent of his company's $40 million turnover last year—is developing close working relationships with clients. Fiesole has an office in New York to keep an eye on the market and react quickly to clients' needs.

Italian manufacturers and the buying offices say that while competing with the Far East is becoming increasingly difficult because of Italy's high labor costs, they are confident about the future.

"Italians can compete with the prices in the Far East because they are willing to lower their prices and make a deal," said Maureen Skelly Bonini, who owns one of the biggest buying offices in Italy and has been in the business for 25 years.

"For the manufacturers, continuity and loyalty are very important. Relationships are important, and once you have those, you can work well over here. Italy is also the strongest country for fabrics. In many cases, it's just easier to do the work over here," said Bonini, whose U.S. clients include The Gap, Banana Republic and Old Navy.

Diaco of IBS Italia agreed. "Outside competition is becoming more

and more important, and even some Italian companies are choosing to move some of their operations outside the country because of labor costs," he said.

"But, in the end, what saves this market is Italians' knack for inventing new styles, finishes and fabrics. Foreign clients need Italians for fresh ideas," he added.

The private label business is becoming just as popular inside Italy as it is outside—increasing numbers of Italian companies want to get in on the act.

"There was a time when many well-established companies turned their noses up at the idea of producing private label collections," said Armando Branchini, vice president of InterCorporate, a consulting firm here.

"But that began to change in the early 1990s, when manufacturers began to reevaluate their priorities due to the changing economy. Now, producing private label is no longer an embarrassment. If companies already have the manufacturing muscle, they know they can boost their turnover considerably by producing private label," he added.

Women's Wear Daily, Italia '96, February 1996.

Producing Custom-Made Clothes for the Masses

John Holusha

About half of all Americans buy off-the-rack clothing that does not fit well, said researchers at the Technology/Clothing Technology Corporation, an apparel industry group. Half of those pay to have their clothing altered; the rest just wear

ill-fitting clothes.

To promote a more stylish nation and to preserve some of what is left of the domestic apparel industry, the research group, which is based near Raleigh, N.C., is spending $8.5 million a year to

develop a method to make three-dimensional body scans of customers that could be used to produce custom-made clothes.

If manufacturers used the body dimensions of individual customers, standard sizes, which vary from maker to maker anyway, would become obsolete. Along with a custom fit, there would be a premium on speedy delivery of garments. This, the theory goes, would drive manufacturers to keep their plants in the United States rather than waiting months for goods to arrive from factories in East Asia.

The desire for relatively inexpensive custom-made clothes is clear. When Levi Strauss & Company introduced a computer-assisted measuring system for women's jeans in 1994, the response was sharp, even though such jeans cost $15 more than the standard retail price. A recent survey by Prof. Nancy Casill of the University of North Carolina at Greensboro found that customers were willing to pay extra for the scan, if it would insure properly fitted clothes.

But the Levi system was cumbersome, requiring women to try on several pairs of stock jeans with built-in measuring tapes.

When the new system is tested at a retail store later this year, the scanner is expected to produce a full-body profile in about two seconds, with the measurements encoded on a portable data card or entered into a central depository. Whenever that customer orders clothes, the data can be retrieved to produce a custom-fitted product.

"We are simply trying to do what a professional tailor would do, but without the time and expense," said Joseph W.A. Off, managing director of the technology research company, which calls itself TC². "Even now, there is $20 to $40 built into

the cost of men's suits to cover the cost of alterations."

To use the scanner, a person would strip down to underwear and step into a booth equipped with six light projectors and six video cameras.

Light would be projected through a grate to produce a pattern of horizontal black and white lines on the subject. The projectors would flash four times each, producing 24 images in the video camera. The grates would move after each pass, producing changes in the patterns. The cameras would record height and width; the changing patterns, along with some extrapolation, would produce depth information.

The result would be almost 1.4 million data points in three-dimensional space—more than enough to define an individual's shape.

Then the numbers would be refined to shape a figure on a computer, from which the essential measurements for clothing would be selected.

"The bicep is the largest part of the arm, so we take the bicep circumference to get the sleeve measurement," said Judson H. Early, the director of research. "But others are not as obvious, which is why we are still working on critical-measurement extraction."

The measurements would be linked to a garment pattern, which would then be modified. The resulting information would be sent to a laser, which would cut the cloth that would be sewn into the final garment.

TC² officials concede that any move to automated custom clothing would be a struggle against established apparel industry procedures. Cutting a single thickness of cloth for one garment might seem inefficient to companies that cut dozens of layers of cloth at the same time.

But the researchers said, the automated system could cut inventory costs for retailers and prevent many of the steep end-of-season markdowns that erode their profit margins.

"Everyone looks at the cost of direct labor in apparel," said Peter N. Butenhoff, president of TC². "But direct labor is only 11 percent of the cost of the garment delivered to customers. Non-value-added handling after manufacture accounts for 27 percent. That is what we are going after."

The researchers envision a much smaller retail space, where most of the stock would consist of samples that customers could examine and touch before placing orders for custom garments based on their body scans. Tied to agile factories, able to switch rapidly from one product to another, the retailer would be able to deliver the custom garment in a few days.

And, because everything would be sold before it was made, steep discounts to clear out inventory would not be necessary.

"The vision is pretty clear and the technology is almost here," Mr. Butenhoff said. "As always, the culture change will be the hardest."

The New York Times, February 19, 1996.

PART FIVE

Merchandising Fashion

Before retailers purchase merchandise, many look for expert assistance from outside sources. The largest of these information and advisory services are called resident buying offices. They provide information to the buyers, who can then make educated buying decisions.

There are many fashion retailers, including department stores, specialty stores, and direct merchants, who sell through catalogs. They operate from a variety of locations, including downtown, central districts; malls; festival marketplaces; and high-fashion centers. Each store provides services in order to gain a competitive edge on its neighbors.

To differentiate their operations from their competitors and to attract more shoppers into their stores, many retailers engage in advertising, special events, and visual presentations. Each segment of the fashion industry promotes themselves through a variety of means; the fashion show is the most typical for designers. If their methods of operation are in line with customer's needs and if the right promotions are undertaken, success will probably follow.

CHAPTER 17

Resident Buying Offices and Other Fashion Information Sources for Retailers

After you have completed this chapter, you will be able to discuss:

- Terms resident buying office and commissionaire.

- How a private office is different from an independent office.

- The services resident buying offices provide to their clients.

- Trade associations and trade publications as sources of fashion information and the roles they play in the fashion industry.

- The importance of trade exposition to designers and manufacturers.

Decision making in the world of fashion is an ongoing process. Those involved must understand the consumers' needs and how best to accommodate them. At every stage of the process, fashion professionals need accurate information on fashion trends and consumer preferences. Chapter 14, Fashion Forecasting, discussed how designers and manufacturers acquire such information. This chapter focuses on sources for retailers.

The road from the point of production to point of consumption is long and complicated. Successful fashion decision makers do not operate in a vacuum or make decisions on a whim. They rely on countless resources to gather accurate information so they can meet their goals.

The fashion industry has many institutions that provide information and advisory services to retailers, including resident buying offices, fashion consultants, trade associations, and trade publications.

The astute fashion retailer uses the services of many of these resources as much as possible before purchasing merchandise. Some services require annual membership contracts; others require relatively inexpensive dues.

RESIDENT BUYING OFFICES

In Chapter 14, Fashion Forecasting, we discussed the relationship of **resident buying offices** to designers and manufacturers. Resident buying offices also provide the *fashion retailer* with a significant number of services. They are located in wholesale fashion markets, where they have representatives who help store buyers with purchasing decisions.

The Doneger Group

Henry Doneger began his business in 1946, serving the needs of the fashion retailer. Today, The Doneger Group, located in New York City's Garment Center, is the largest resident buying office and market consulting firm in America.

Doneger's team of experts stands ready to solve the merchandising problems of small retailers as well as such giants of the fashion world as Nordstrom. The concept has been extremely successful because of the way Doneger's custom tailors and personalizes their services to fit individual needs.

In order to accomplish the many different tasks required by its clients, The Doneger Group is organized into several different divisions, including:

- Doneger Buying Connection. Emphasis is placed on the purchase of sportswear, apparel, and outerwear for the large size woman.
- Doneger Kids. Focus is children's wear in all price categories.
- Doneger Menswear. Men's tailored clothing and sportswear in all price points is their emphasis.
- Doneger Home Connection. Home furnishings of every type is researched.
- Doneger Tall Buying. For the increasing market in tall women's apparel, this division researches trends in sportswear, dresses, and outerwear.
- Price Point Buying. Focuses on the off-price retailer.

- *Thompson/Auer.* A specialized newsletter targeted towards better women's merchandise.
- D3 Doneger Design Direction. Actively involved in fashion forecasting.
- HDA International. This import–export division addresses the major global markets.

Each division communicates with their clients in many ways. Typical are newsletters that give clients a look at current and future fashion trends, private label announcements, seasonal planning guides, and trends booklets.

With experts in every aspect of the company's operation, Doneger's has become the hallmark of the industry.

Most offices are independent, serving the needs of their retail clients for an annual fee and commission. Those that are classified as store-owned, provide services exclusively to their retail owners.

Independent Offices

There are a few hundred resident buying offices in the United States and abroad. In the United States, most are based in New York City. The larger ones have branch offices in regional wholesale markets; some also maintain branches in the more important global fashion centers. With so many to choose from, retailers must decide which office best suits their needs.

Selecting an Independent Office

If a company does not manage its own office, it must choose from the **independent offices** by analyzing a number of factors.

First is the roster of stores already represented by the office. Because the fashion business is highly competitive, it is unlikely that two competing merchants would want market representation by the same company. With information regularly disseminated to member stores on such topics as merchandise recommendations, new resources, and fashion direction, it is easy to

The resident buyer communicates with clients concerning decision-making policies.

TREND

Silhouette starts to shift back towards structure with shapes somewhat exaggerated. Seams, fullness and drape shape-up structural lines. Bias effects and stretch shape-up body consciousness. Structured fabrics form strong shapes. Color keeps a low profile.

Form follows fashion!

SHAPE-UP or stay soft; the two silhouette alternatives of the season. Soft silhouettes offer continuing comfort, but somewhat more exaggerated shapes are starting to look more exciting. In the '80s, shoulder pads shaped-up the ideal fashion form that took on a masculine line. Now the ideal fashion form is ultra-feminine, all curves.

Garment Design emphasizes that ideal by adding shape to accent breasts, diminish waists, define derrieres.

Details accentuate the shape...

FALL 95

DONEGER MENSWEAR

Fashion gets dressed-up again in optimistic colors and high profile fabrics for dressy designs worn with outstanding accessories and maximum grooming.

What the world needs now is some Feel-Good Fashion!

...itive attitude for fashion. It is a violent reaction ...ownbeat, dreary, depressing and dressed-down ...ight of fashion. That mood may have been a ...reaction to the excesses of the Eighties, but *enough*, ...for some feel-good fashion. It's all uphill from here.

...stically bright and pretty, put together in

...rofile stand-outs in stunning textures and ...ed with 'nary a care.

...Dressy even though the items themselves ...well as special occasions. In fact, that is the

...and decorative.

...ion-getters, sometimes even obviously

...cent bad attitude problem and provides a style ...frivolous

...ting dressed-...ion with a ...ring lots of ...and stand-out

...positive attitude ...violent reaction against all the recent downbeat, dreary, depressing and dressed-down images presented as the height of style. Kidswear really bottomed-out with "Grunge" and it's all uphill from here. Good news!
...UP TO OPTIMISTIC COLORS, the bold and daring brights, the beautiful mid-tones and the fiery new neutrals.
...UP TO SHARPER STYLES for everything from casual clothes and jeanswear to serious special occasion outfits, now cut with emphatic shape and bold deal details.
...UP TO HIGH PROFILE FABRICS like faux furs and super synthetics, novelty knits and new plaids.
...UP TO ECLECTIC COORDINATION that puts everything together in a young, modern manner with accessories that stand-out in a crowd.

No more bad fashion attitude!

UPBEAT

FALL/WINTER 1995 TRENDS

THE DONEGER GROUP

color

DONEGER KIDS INTRODUCES FOUR FRESH FASHION PALETTES FOR BACK-TO-SCHOOL/FALL 1995.

All fashion colors for the season look lighter and brighter. Dreary color is dead. Even the traditional darks are more saturated with enriched color.

GLOBAL GAMES:
The Global Games is a not-quite-classic palette of basic darks popped with bold and daring bright accents. The basis for some exciting color combinations in solids, prints and patterns. Classic or active applications.
...basic blues, greys, burgundies and dark greens.
...hot orange, lime, lemon.

GAELICS:
The Gaelic group gathers colorful heathers from the highlands of Scotland ...painting a pretty palette of lively mid-tones that are rich ...soft and plaids.

NEWSLETTER
Doneger Design Direction
November 1994

BODY SWEATER & SILKY SKIRT!

The new "Fashion Uniform" for Spring 1995.

FLASH! It's the outfit that was in almost every designer collection in Europe and America. Destined to become the new "Fashion Uniform" of the season. An easy-to-understand outfit that suits every age and many figure types.

...BODY-FIT PULLOVER.
...BODY-FIT CARDIGAN.
...KNEE-LENGTH SOFT SKIRT.
...SATIN, SILK OR SILK JACQUARD.
...WORN WITH A NARROW BELT.
...WORN WITH STRAPPY HIGH HEELS.

David Wolfe, D³ Creative Director
Gae Marino, V.P. Fashion/Marketing

D³ Doneger Design Direction 463 Seventh Avenue   New York, NY 10018 Phone (212) 564-1266

NEWSLETTER
Doneger Design Direction
November 1994

THE SHINE SYNDROME
SHINE! SHIMMER! SPARKLE! GLISTEN! GLIMMER! GLOW!
Satin and Synthetics turn the fashion spotlight onto shiny surfaces for all sorts of apparel and accessories.

FLASH! Everything that shines is in ...e for Spring '95 (and that means ...lutely everything) from shirts and ...and suits and shorts to shoes and ...t shine like vinyl).

...SATIN.
...TURED SATIN.
...CHARMEUSE.
...SEY.
...QUARD.
...TE.
...PLASTIC.
...VINYL.
...SEQUINS.
...LUREX KNITS.
...METALLIC LEATHER.
...PATENT LEATHER.
...CIRE.

David Wolfe, D³ Creative Director
Gae Marino, V.P. Fashion/Marketing

D³ Doneger Design Direction 463 Seventh Avenue   New York, NY 10018 Phone (212) 564-1266

The Doneger Group is the industry's largest resident buying office, utilizing numerous materials to inform store buyers of pertinent fashion information. Examples of newsletters and pages from trend booklets are illustrated here.

understand how competitors could simply become clones of one another and eventually present the same fashion image. If care is taken to choose a market representative that has no competing stores as clients, ideas and information can be freely exchanged without concern for direct competition. This exchange of ideas is commonplace during market week, a period when merchants travel to their wholesale markets to preview the new lines at the resident buying office facilities.

Second, the cost of membership must be considered. The expense involved in market representation is based on a number of factors, including the size of the office, number of branches available, scope of global representation, types of services, and amount of direct purchasing undertaken for the client.

A review of typical contracts and fee schedules of numerous resident buying offices indicate that the following expenses are charged to the member stores:

1. an annual fee, generally paid in equal monthly installments, for the services provided by the office;
2. a percentage of all merchandise purchased by the resident office for the store;
3. a flat charge for postage.

Finally, the prospective client should be certain that the services provided truly fill his or her needs. Not every retailer has the same requirements. Some might merely want a representative to place reorders or special orders, check delivery dates, and follow-up on orders. Others, who deal in off-price merchandise, might only want to be directed to those vendors who have closeouts. Others might want the full complement of services, including handling complaints with vendors, direction in fashion forecasting and promotion, and suggestions on visual presentation. The section on store-owned offices is followed by a discussion on resident buying office services.

Store-Owned Offices

Some major department stores in the United States enjoy the advantage of having an office that works exclusively for them or a small group of affiliated stores. Because they require considerable attention, their needs cannot be served by an independent who represents many clients. Within the store-owned office classification, there are three types of resident buying offices.

1. The Private Office
2. The Cooperative Office
3. The Corporate Office

THE PRIVATE OFFICE Few companies are large enough to warrant an office that works exclusively for them. If, however, the company is sufficiently large or its degree of specialization is sufficiently unique, it might choose to establish an office for its exclusive use. This is known as the **private office.** Montgomery Ward and Sears have private offices because of the size and complexity of their business operations, Neiman Marcus, always in search of unique merchandise, also maintains a private office.

THE COOPERATIVE OFFICE In cases where private offices are too costly and where membership in an independent office would not afford the necessary attention, the **cooperative**, or semiprivate, **office** is the best approach.

A group of stores that are not competitive, but are affiliated in some manner, may establish a cooperative office or, as it is sometimes called, an *associated office*. The retailers in these groups own the resident operation, control its activities, and share in the cost of operating the venture. AMC, the Associated Merchandising Corporation, is an example of a cooperative venture. Representing the Federated Stores that include Bloomingdale's and Burdines, it covers the market to better serve the exclusive needs of its owners.

THE CORPORATE OFFICE Some retail organizations are complex businesses that operate a number of store operations with different names. R.H. Macy's, for example, not only manages the group of stores that bears its name, but also runs several spinoffs, such as Aeropostale and Charter Club. To better handle its merchandising needs, the company's overall operation includes an office that is known as Macy's Corporate. Because Macy's has been acquired by the Federated Stores, only time will tell if the corporate resident office will be maintained, or if Macy's will use the services of the AMC office as do the other stores in the group.

In any case, the **corporate offices** provide a host of services similar to those afforded by the independents. They also play a major role in the development of private label merchandise. At Macy's, where such private brands as Jennifer Moore, Christopher Hayes, Charter Club, Alfani, and others form part of the merchandise mix, product development is a major task.

Buying Office Services

The types of services provided by the resident buying offices vary from company to company. Some, such as the world's largest, Henry Doneger Associates (which is the subject of a World of Fashion Profile), offer every service that might possibly improve the performance of their member stores. The smaller establishments often restrict their services to market representation that places special orders and reorders, checks on the status of orders already placed, and makes recommendations on best-selling items.

The following discussion represents the scope of resident buying office operations and explains how they assist retailers to become more profitable.

Purchasing Merchandise

Although the store buyer is responsible for the purchase of merchandise, the resident office may be called on to place reorders or special orders, or in some unusual cases, may be the sole purchasing agents for the store. For example, a store might have numerous requests for $150 white dresses and not have any in stock. With the store buyer far away from the market tending to store duties and responsibilities, he or she may authorize the resident buyer to scout the market for appropriate white dresses.

Reorders are merchandise requests that need immediate attention. Because the merchandise might also be reordered by other stores, its availability might be limited to just a few retailers. With time the essence, the reorders are often placed by the resident buyers, who, because of their clout in the market, get better delivery time than the store buyer could.

Resident buying office staff work very closely with buyers during market week.

Whenever an order is placed by the resident buying office, the client is charged a commission for the service.

Preparing for Market Week

The busiest time for resident buying offices is the period preceding and including **market week.** A market week is a time when manufacturers in a specific industry introduce their new collections to retailers. Buyers and merchandisers visit the wholesale market to purchase for the coming season.

Because the store buyers come to town for such short periods of time, every hour must be carefully spent. The resident buying office plays an important role by researching the market before the store buyer's arrival. The resident buying office staff prescreens the lines, investigates new resources, determines styling and color trends, and does any preliminary work necessary to make the store buyer's visit more productive. Some offices prepare fashion presentations during market week so that their clients will know what to expect in the market. Representatives often accompany store buyers to the manufacturer's showrooms to help formulate purchasing plans.

Product Development

With the enormous growth of private label merchandise in major retailers' merchandise assortments, they have been able to sell items that are unique to their stores. For a retailer to develop a private label, there must be a need for a large quantity of the merchandise. Thus, only the largest of merchants have been able to participate in such programs.

Today, many resident buying offices are in the business of offering the same opportunity to their members. By employing **product developers,** the offices design and produce specific styles for the exclusive use of their customers. Because the membership of the office is restricted to noncompeting stores, the use of this private label merchandise will, in effect, be available only at the stores represented by the office. Under this arrangement, the smaller retailer can now purchase private label merchandise in small quantities, something he or she was unable to do alone.

Best-Seller Notification

When the season opens, retailers hope for a few items that will generate constant reordering. It is difficult to predict which, if any, of the original purchases will become a best seller, or hot item. Through their constant interaction with manufacturers and their member stores, resident buying offices are made aware of the season's best sellers. Most offices regularly communicate such news to their customers through information brochures and flyers. In this way the retailer is made aware of what's "hot" and can purchase that merchandise. Most retailers will agree that it takes only a few best sellers to make a season profitable.

Importing

Examination of the labels on apparel and accessories will reveal that much merchandise is manufactured offshore. Major stores regularly visit foreign markets and purchase goods that ultimately yield a higher profit than domestically produced goods. Small retailers, by virtue of their size and sales potential, cannot avail themselves of this source of purchasing. Because the outlay of cash necessary for such an undertaking is out of their reach, they generally purchase their merchandise from the manufacturers' standard offerings. Most of the larger resident buying offices, however, now put such purchasing within the reach of the smaller merchants. With branches in foreign countries, or through affiliation with *commissionaires* (foreign resident buying offices), the procurement of imported items is made easy.

Group Purchasing

Many vendors have minimum order requirements that are too high for the smaller retailer. Some resident offices make such merchandise available by pooling these smaller orders into one that complies with the purchasing regulations of the vendors. Not only does the retailer now have access to otherwise unavailable goods but might even receive a discount if the group order totals enough to qualify for a quantity discount. The end result is desirable merchandise at a discounted price.

Promotional Activities

An important key to success for any retailer is recognition. Few if any stores can boast freedom from competition. To attract attention and motivate shoppers to visit their stores, major retailers spend large sums on sales promotion and advertising. Without the advantage of an in-house staff or the dollars needed for participation in promotional activities, most smaller retailers are unable to participate in such sales campaigns.

Some of the full service resident buying offices have sales promotion departments to plan and develop brochures that can easily be adapted for store use, provide expertise on advertising layouts, recommend directions for every aspect of visual merchandising, and prepare mailers for insertion into customer monthly billing statements.

Off-Price Purchases

Vendors must often dispose of merchandise in their inventories to make way for next season's goods. They might have styles that did not sell as well as anticipated, colors that did not seem to capture the consumer market, or broken size ranges. Much like their retail counterparts, vendors run sales to turn over their inventories. One of the best deal makers in these situations is the resident buying office. It negotiates with the manufacturers for a rock bottom price and make the goods available to member stores. Many retailers take advantage of the situation by buying **off-price** and mixing the recently acquired goods with their regular merchandise. They might choose to sell these new items at regular prices, actually reflecting a very high markup for a while, reaping the benefits from the reduced prices they pay, or may sell them quickly at bargain prices. Many promotional retailers perceive this as the most important service offered by resident buying offices. In fact, some offices have separate off-price divisions and some are strictly organized as an off-price resident buying office. By utilizing this type of merchandise procurement, the smaller retailer can compete more easily with the giants in the industry, who are able to negotiate these closeout deals for themselves.

Checking on Delivery

Once an order has been placed, it is never safe to assume that the shipment will be delivered by the specified time. Manufacturers are notorious for shipping goods after the order's completion date. Their excuses run the gamut from employee slowdowns to late delivery of the materials needed for production. Although these might sometimes be valid explanations, they are frequently just excuses. Some manufacturers simply make promises they cannot keep or even sell merchandise earmarked for one store to another.

Whatever the reasons for the delays, retailers are the ones who suffer. They buy according to specific purchase plans and must have sufficient goods on hand to do business. Otherwise, customers will simply go elsewhere to satisfy their needs.

Most resident buying offices constantly check on the status of their customers' orders. In fact, this is one of the major duties of the resident assistant buyer. Because the offices have considerable clout by virtue of the number of stores they represent, they can apply pressure to have the goods shipped on time. If they discover that the merchandise will not be delivered as promised, they can attempt to find replacement goods for their clients.

Making Adjustments

Substitution shipping is as commonplace in the fashion industry as late delivery. Manufacturers sometimes substitute another color for the one that was ordered, send sizes that were not ordered, use a different fabric in the construction of a garment, or even send styles not ordered in place of those that were.

These occurrences are not just bothersome, they can cause serious problems for the store. The retailer now has merchandise that might not suit the store's needs. Merchandise that has been substituted for other items may be returned, but that leaves the retailer with a void in the inventory. Resident buyers are always called upon to handle such adjustments. They might persuade

Resident buyers, busy at their desks, are always ready to communicate market news to the stores.

the vendor to give the store a discount on the unordered merchandise they keep or make arrangements for price reductions on the next order. Whatever the solution, the resident buyer can represent the store in such negotiations.

Other adjustments for problems such as minor damage, returns for discoloration in laundering, shrinkage, and improper fit are often handled by the resident office. Whereas an individual retailer might receive unsatisfactory responses, the resident office is usually successful.

Merchandising

Although the store buyer is ultimately responsible for quantities, promotional endeavors, and visual presentation on the selling floor, outside help is always needed to solve some of these problems. Resident offices are generally available to assist with specific problems. Because they deal with so many manufacturers who make suggestions on how to merchandise their lines and so many clients who address these problems on a daily basis, they are excellent resources for such advice.

Making Available Store Supplies

The initial establishment of a retail operation and the improvement of an existing one involves the planning of store designs, acquiring fixtures, planning and procuring of proper lighting, purchasing of props and mannequins, developing appropriate packaging needs, and purchasing of everyday supplies.

In this complex field, merchants, who are more attuned to merchandising and management decisions, use full service resident buying offices to address and solve such problems.

Direct-Mail Programming

Retailers are increasing their sales volume through catalogs. Although larger merchants have the facility for such endeavors, the smaller retailer is often

(top) Resident buyers and store buyers regularly cover trade shows all over the world.
(bottom) Manufacturer's booths are featured at trade shows so that buyers can view the lines under one roof.

unfamiliar with the direct mail arena. More and more full service resident offices are developing catalogs for their clients. They might be specific merchandise booklets directed at a specific market or more general merchandise catalogs. These catalogs feature the merchandise the office believes will generate the most business. The office makes arrangements to have the proper assortment delivered to the store in anticipation of customer orders.

FOREIGN RESIDENT BUYING OFFICES

With fashion truly a global industry, merchandise is now produced in every part of the world. The fascination with foreign-produced goods is no longer limited to the prestige and quality associated with them. Now, lower prices coupled with excellent design also make merchandise imports desirable.

Major fashion retailers regularly visit international markets in pursuit of merchandise. Many have corporate or cooperative resident buying offices that maintain foreign branches to purchase merchandise. Some of the larger independent resident offices also have representation through their own foreign branches.

In addition to these arrangements, countries all over the world have independent resident buying offices known as **commissionaires.** While the word *commissionaire* is French, it is used wherever foreign offices function.

As with their American counterparts, commissionaires are service specialists. Working either on a fixed fee or for a percentage of the purchase cost, these agents provide the expertise needed for Americans to participate in the fashion importing arena. Not only do they make arrangements for merchandise selection, but they are also knowledgeable about quotas, tariffs, shipping arrangements, price negotiations, and storage. Because the acquisition of such goods is more complicated than that of goods domestically purchased, the store buyer must provide detailed information about the items to be imported. Dealing with a foreign vendor is often complicated by poor communications. The commissionaire's ability to speak the country's language often results in better terms for the American purchaser.

Just as domestic resident buyers assist their clients with market visits, commissionaires also accompany buyers to visit manufacturers abroad. They can make any purchasing visit more productive by screening lines and taking buyers directly to the most promising vendors.

REPORTING SERVICES

Retailers interested in keeping informed about developments on the fashion scene may subscribe to a **reporting service.** These companies are in business only to provide industry-wide information in a variety of reports.

One of the major companies in this field is the Retail Reporting Corporation. It publishes a number of informational pieces that assist the fashion retailer in merchandise planning and acquisition. Among their offerings are the following regular reports:

- *New Resources.* Published weekly, it alerts buyers to new companies and the merchandise they produce.

- *Hotline.* This weekly presentation highlights merchandise that appears headed for success.

- *Retail Executive Digest.* This weekly analysis of retailing covers every aspect of the business.

- *Editor's Overview.* An analysis of the market highlighting resources of importance, designer collections, accessories information, and retailers of distinction.

- *Reorder Report.* A compilation of the week's hottest items and the names of retailers experiencing success with these items.

- *Merchandise Report.* An individual analysis of a particular item, complete with resource, price, and store that is featuring the item, and where it has been advertised.

- *Accessories.* This weekly publication covers the latest in shoes, hosiery, jewelry, hats, gloves, and handbags suggesting where selected styles may be purchased.

TRADE ASSOCIATIONS

Throughout the fashion industry, at home and abroad, organizations have been formed to serve specific fashion groups. Their goals are primarily to publicize the specific industry component they serve to those who have the potential use for their products. Collectively, they plan seminars, prepare informational reports, conduct studies, confer awards, and disseminate information on trends.

Most segments of the fashion industry are served by these **trade associations**. Among the better known are the Chambre Syndicale, The Council of Fashion Designers of America (CFDA), The Fashion Association (TFA), The National Retail Federation (NRF), Cotton Incorporated, The Wool Bureau, Fashion Group, the Fashion Footwear Association (FFANY), the Footwear Industries of America, and the Leather Apparel Association. CFDA is featured in a World of Fashion Profile.

The scope of specific activities performed by two of the trade organizations underscores their importance to the industries they serve.

National Retail Federation

The largest of the trade associations representing the retail industry is the National Retail Federation, headquartered in Washington D.C., and previously known as the National Retail Merchants Association (or NRMA).

Representing the major department stores and specialty chains in the country, it holds its annual national meeting every January in New York City. At that time, the industry leaders make presentations examining the vital areas of retailing. Regional meetings are also held throughout the year to deal with specific areas of retail concern. The various meetings provide fashion merchants, as well as others, with information on trends, pricing considerations, offshore sources of supplies, consumer motivation, and visual merchandising. In addition to professional topical seminars, numerous trade suppliers are on hand to introduce the retailing industry to the latest available technology and products for the merchandising, management, and operations of their stores.

In addition to informative meetings, the NRF publishes a variety of journals and periodicals that enable retailers to get a glimpse of the market. Of particular importance is *Stores* magazine, which presents articles on retailers, designers, product development, and innovative trends. The magazine provides information that readers can adapt to their own situations.

The National Retail Federation is the largest retail trade association.

The Fashion Association

The Men's Fashion Association (MFA), which expanded its market representation to include women's fashions, is now known as The Fashion Association (TFA). Designed to serve as the public relations arm of the industry, it represents hundreds of firms from the design, manufacturing, textile, and retail world.

Its activities include the development of press kits that inform its members and the media of the latest innovations in fashion design. The information is disseminated using the standard media kit format, which includes slides and

The Fashion Association is the public relations arm of the fashion industry.

photographs, and a new concept called the **electronic press kit,** which was initiated in 1995. The latter is a videotape that features design trends for the upcoming season. TFA also distributes newsletters, called *Currents,* and holds an annual event at which they award design leaders with *Aldos.*

Other trade associations from which fashion retailers learn about specific trends include those in the fiber field, such as Cotton Incorporated, the Textile Association of Los Angeles, and The Wool Bureau; FFANY (The Footwear Association of New York), which explores the shoe industry; NAMSB, which deals in men's wear; The Leather Association; The Fashion Group, an organization founded by a group of women to improve women's role in fashion; and Fédération Françáise de la Couture, a French organization that has many couture houses as members.

TRADE PUBLICATIONS

One of the best sources of information about the fashion industry is the **trade publication.** Published on anywhere from a daily to a monthly basis, trade publications provide up-to-the-minute details on what is current in the industry and what can be expected. For a nominal cost, designers, manufacturers, retailers, and anyone with an interest in fashion can quickly learn about the industry. Some periodicals are directed toward a specific market segment; others provide a general market overview.

INSIDE THE BARNEYS/SAKS DEAL/2 DESIGNERS REACH FOR CANDIE'S/10

FN

FOOTWEAR NEWS JULY 29, 1996 VOL. 52 NO. 34 $1.50

Digging Sandals

Atlanta Retailers'
Gold Hopes Dashed
At Olympic G...

Salon

The Magazine for Salon Owners

Sportstyle

July 1996

children's BUSINESS

A FAIRCHILD PUBLICATION

Shoe-ins for ...

West Coa...

The Bes...

Decorative Home

THE RETAILERS' GUIDE TO DECORATIVE ACCESSORIES AND HOME GIFTS

CREDITORS' PANEL GETS OK FOR BIGGER ROLE IN BARNEYS TALKS/3

Women's Wear Daily • The Retailers' Daily ... October 14, 1996 Vol. 172, No. 72 $1.50

WWD MONDAY

...ssories/Innerwear/Legwear

Love Stream

PARIS — Love is in the air for
designers this spring. With wispy
chiffons fluttering on every runway
and more florals than the Tuileries
Gardens, designers have flirted with
the trend to the hilt. But at his
Sunday show, Valentino put his own
stamp on the style with a parade of
beautiful, delicate chiffon print
dresses that were every bit as chic
as they were racy. Here, one of his
best, with lace insets and
undershirt. For more on the Paris
collections, see pages 4 to 11.

**Strong Sept. Results
First Sign of Rebound
By Revived Ann Taylor**

By Sharon Edelson

NEW YORK — Things could be looking
up for Ann Taylor.
    After enduring problems ranging
from a string of poor monthly sales
to the resignation of its chief
executive officer, the company
bounced back with a 15.5 percent
increase in comp-store sales in
September, a month that was
disappointing for most other
retailers.
    While reluctant to say the
increase signals a turnaround, retail
analysts were impressed, and some
said Ann Taylor's performance in

See Ann, Page 23

...ury:
...kay again

...are back, and eventu...
...of the pie.

*Periodicals for every
segment of the fashion
industry are published
by Fairchild Publications,
the major trade publisher.*

The principal player in fashion-oriented trade publications is Fairchild Publications. Based in New York City, it publishes such influential newspapers as *Women's Wear Daily* (*WWD*), which covers both the domestic and international scene on women's and children's clothing, accessories, and textiles. *Daily News Record* (*DNR*), is another Fairchild publication for the men's wear and textile industries. Other American produced trade periodicals include *Fashion International, Fashion Showcase Retailer,* and the *California Apparel News.*

An excellent monthly publication for retailers is *Stores* Magazine, which features every aspect of retail management and merchandising from industry trends to current interests. It is published by the National Retail Federation.

VM&SD (*Visual Merchandising and Store Design*) is a monthly publication of particular importance to people responsible for visual merchandising and display programs. It features articles on display innovation, prop acquisition, new materials, and lighting and general store design.

Trade publications from abroad help decision makers in the United States keep abreast of what is happening all over the world. Excellent sources of information about the international fashion scene include: *Style* from Canada; *Gap* from France; *Textile Forecast, Fashion Forecast, Fashion Update, Fashionews, Fashion Record, Fashion Weekly,* and *Fashion Extras* from Great Britain; *Femme Elégante* from Spain; *Mode* from Australia; and *Italian Design Fashion* and *Sposabella* from Italy.

CONSUMER PUBLICATIONS

Some fashion magazines, such as *Harper's Bazaar, Elle, GQ, Essence, Vogue,* and *Glamour* are produced for consumers. *W* is bimonthly Fairchild publication that explores the fashion scene from the designer's collections to whose wearing what fashions for the consumer. Because buyers, manufacturers, and designers should be aware of what fashion news the consumer is being fed, they regularly study these **consumer publications.** Editors of consumer fashion publications wield considerable power in the industry because their readers often follow their suggestions. A knowledgeable fashion buyer can evaluate the fashion emphasis for a particular season in these publications and adjust inventory to reflect what the consumer is being shown.

In addition to the domestic consumer magazines, more and more foreign publications grace this country's newsstands. Such magazines as *Linea Italiana, L'Official,* and *Paris Vogue* are read consistently by the American fashion industry for inspiration and information.

CHOOSING INFORMATION RESOURCES

The fashion professional can choose from a wide range of information and advisory resources. If there are no budgetary restraints, the route to take is the-more-the-merrier one. Everyone connected with fashion is constantly seeking newer and better ways to reach as many customers as possible. By subscribing to these resources, a total overview of the fashion market can be developed.

Companies with less to spend on information must be more selective in choosing resources. Is the resident buying office a better choice than the reporting service? Only careful exploration of individual needs will provide the appropriate answer.

If financial resources are very limited, the best route to take is the trade publication. For very little money, a subscription to a publication such as *Women's Wear Daily* will bring relevant information that can be used in making retail decisions. One trade paper, supplemented by the consumer periodicals, could supply just enough to keep those in the industry aware of what is happening.

Chapter Highlights

- One of the keys for success in the fashion industry is current information. It takes only a few errors in judgment to lead a company into bankruptcy.

- Knowledgeable fashion practitioners seek as much industrial advice as possible before making fashion decisions.

- The sources available for information and advisory services include the resident buying office, reporting services, trade associations, and trade publications.

Important Fashion Terminology and Concepts

commissionaires	group purchasing	product developers
consumer publication	independent office	reporting service
cooperative office	market week	resident buying office
corporate offices	National Retail Federa-	store-owned office
electronic press kit	tion (NRF)	substitution shipping
The Fashion Association	off-price	trade association
(TFA)	private office	trade publication

For Review

1. What advantage does the private resident office afford its stores that independent affiliation does not?

2. Briefly describe the costs of resident buying office membership.

3. To what extent do resident buying offices perform actual purchasing services?

4. Describe market week.

5. How important is the best-seller notification by resident offices to their members?

6. How can resident offices make available goods that are otherwise unavailable to retailers whose requirements are comparatively small?

7. Why have foreign resident buying offices become increasingly important?

8. What is a reporting service?

9. How does a trade association help retailers learn about industry trends?

10. Discuss some of the activities undertaken by The Council of Fashion Designers of America that have benefitted the fashion industry.

11. How can a consumer publication help fashion buyers improve their positions?

Exercises and Projects

1. Write to an independent resident buying office requesting information on its operation and the forms it uses for client communication. Prepare an oral presentation on the information received, highlighting such aspects as costs for members, services available, and markets served.

2. Select a trade publication, such as *Women's Wear Daily, DNR,* or *California Apparel News.* Discuss the publication's various features. How much space is devoted to trend columns, hot items, manufacturer advertising, and classified advertising?

3. Make an appointment with a fashion buyer or assistant buyer from a large department store to learn about the information and advisory resources they use in the selection of merchandise. Present the information in a report to the class.

The Case of High–Fashion Competition

The Female Connoisseur is a specialty retail organization that epitomizes haute couture. Designer collections from all of the world's fashion centers grace its selling floors. The company has grown. In its present position, it operates a flagship store and six branches. The clientele for The Female Connoisseur is extremely affluent and is willing to pay any price for unusual fashion designs.

In its quest for high-fashion merchandise, the store utilizes a resident buying office specializing in upscale merchandise. The office assists the store buyers, who have the actual purchasing responsibility. The office has excellent coverage of the American and international fashion market. The ever-increasing annual profit margin is indicative of the store's acceptance by the high-fashion consumer.

With the emphasis on international fashion merchandising, the store has started to feel competition never before experienced. In particular, Raleighs, a major department store, has just expanded its designer offerings. Because Raleighs and The Female Connoisseur flagship stores are located opposite each other, the newly expanded fashion collection at Raleighs is resulting in intense competition. What was once an ideal, unique retail situation has now become a challenge to maintain. The Female Connoisseur is being aggressively challenged.

Questions

1. Is a high-fashion couture private label a reasonable approach?

2. Do you agree with management's decision not to hire a design team and build a design facility? Explain.

3. How would you suggest that The Female Connoisseur confront this new competition?

Amanda Baker, the store's fashion director, believes the time is ripe for the introduction of an exclusive private label collection of designer quality dresses and sportswear. If quality and design could be the hallmark of their own line, they could slowly motivate their customers to buy private label merchandise and concentrate less on lines that both stores feature. Her suggestion that the retailer hire its own design staff to create its own line has met with opposition from management, which contends that, "We are retailers and should stick to what we know best." Furthermore, the experiment could be extremely costly, requiring a large capital expenditure for workrooms and equipment.

While the challenge of producing private labels still intrigues the company, no one has come up with a plan that satisfies management.

point of view

Doneger: Tailored to Fit the Times

Susan Reda

By now the tale is familiar. Dogged by anemic sales, continued consolidation, Chapter 11 filings and obstinate consumer malaise, apparel retailers are searching for solutions and pursuing every opportunity for growth.

Not so familiar, however, is the role that some buying offices are performing as they attempt to help mitigate retail acts that in the past were fresher in terms of bottom-line results. Much like accounting firms, which no longer simply keep the books and have in fact become broad-based business consultancies, buying offices are attempting to play bigger parts in their customers' businesses.

"The term 'buying office' is limited in scope," stresses Abbey Doneger, president of The Doneger Group, a New York-based resident buying group. "Our services extend far beyond what a buying office traditionally provides. We delve into all areas of merchandising and marketing. Our objective is to help retailers generate increased sales and profits, gain market share and realize their full potential."

With an extensive client list that runs the gamut from high-end department and specialty stores to middle-market mass merchants and one-price budget formats, The Doneger Group operates from a unique perspective. Management is able to assess opportunities and obstacles from both a broad industry-wide outlook and a narrow vertical view.

"We use them [The Doneger Group] in certain areas a lot. Before we go out into the market, we go to Doneger first for trend information and vendor direction," says Mark Minsky, senior vp. gmm, Caldor.

"When we started a dress business a few years back, we were able to soak up a lot of information from them. For this fall, they helped us by recommending resources and honing in on key items for ladies' leather outerwear, a new category for us," Minsky adds.

With pricing more important than ever in today's market, it is not surprising that Price Point Buying, Doneger's off-price service, has taken on a more critical role at the company.

This division, formed in 1988 and now headed by merchandise manager Marvin Goldstein, specializes in opportunistic buying of overruns and merchandise made available because of canceled orders.

The scope of Price Point Buying has been amplified recently as mass merchants test new programs, plug up holes in their assortments and work to keep the selling floor stocked, despite the squeeze of skittish factors that have become somewhat overprotective of their accounts receivable.

"Large-scale retailers typically do not have the flexibility to react to the opportunities of off-price purchasing because the size of their businesses dictate that product development and orders be set well in advance," explains Thomas Burns, senior executive vp and gmm of The Doneger Group.

"The current retail environment has, however, opened some new doors for us. With retailers planning inventory much closer to the vest than in previous seasons, they sometimes find themselves on the short end of supply," says Burns. "We have the capacity to go into the market, find what they're looking for at the price they want to pay and deliver it to them in an efficient time frame."

Among the items Goldstein and his staff of eight have been chasing for fall are denim jumpers and vests. Typically, Goldstein relies on both his buyers and those in the women's sportswear area of Doneger to piece together a working list of vendors who have product available at the right price.

"For retailers, the name of the game is right product, right price and right time. They have to have something when it's hot—particularly since key items have been few and far between," says Goldstein. "For us, it's a question of synergy— of working with the other divisions under the Doneger umbrella of services to respond to a retailer's needs."

In the wake of several Chapter 11 filings at a number of retail chains across the country, Doneger's Price Point Buying team has been called upon to help fill in some gaps on the selling floor. According to Burns, once a factor puts up a red light, merchants have to seek out new resources that are willing to be supportive. Merchants, overwhelmed by the task of finding manufacturers that meet their quality, value and price parameters, rely on Doneger's expertise. Rose's, which successfully emerged from bankruptcy protection in May, was one of the companies that utilized

Doneger's sourcing skills when it needed help stocking its shelves.

Selling is of course a two-way street. A red light at one chain translates into manufacturers being left with fast-depreciating inventories. Vendors call on the Price Point Buying division to rid themselves of the merchandise quickly and cut their losses.

"Price Point Buying is essentially a push and pull business," says Burns. "The push comes from the market side as manufacturers look to sell off in-season product, which tends to lose value every day. The pull comes from retailers who have specific needs and are looking to secure product."

When recent changes in quotas and issues surrounding labor resulted in the canceled parts of retailers' product development programs, merchants looking for immediate sourcing—Montgomery Ward and Pamida, for instance— tapped Doneger's services.

Price Point Buying is also used by retailers attempting to better serve particular demographic and/or ethnic customer bases via micromarketing. According to Burns, the company has worked with a number of regional discounters who believe this is a critical component of differentiation.

"Different items surface in different parts of the country, and it's very difficult for a buyer who is making broad purchasing decisions for 200 or more stores to hone in on small pockets of opportunity. Still they [retailers] recognize the importance of developing these unique portions of their businesses," says Burns, who expects retailers to pursue micromarketing more aggressively as time goes on. "We can call upon the network of resources and information we have here to help them succeed."

According to Goldstein, the fuel that drives the engine when it comes to Price Point Buying and the other services provided by The Doneger Group is communication.

"The more buyers share with us about what they're trying to accomplish, who their customers are and what their specific business objectives are, the more we can focus our expertise on helping them to attain their goals."

In one form or another, that tenet has run throughout The Doneger Group since the company was founded in 1946 by Abbey's father Henry. Today, the company consists of 10 specialized divisions serving 850 retail clients.

On a simplified level, the diversity of Doneger services includes three tiers: long-term fashion direction and product development, seasonal market analysis and presentations and the chance to fill-in via incentive buying in-season.

To actualize these objectives, the company's services include the Doneger Information Network, which provides newsletters, merchandising concepts, market overviews and new resource information to clients. Retailers working with The Doneger Group can also tap into the buying group's direct mail prowess and into the worldwide sourcing opportunities and administrative support provided by HDA International, the company's import/export division, which serves both domestic and international retailers.

Doneger is especially proud of the D3 Doneger Design Direction division, which specializes in color trend forecasting. Like every service at Doneger, D3 is used by clients dealing at all price point levels.

"D3 is the fashion service for realists who regard fashion as a

business instead of an art form," says Doneger. "Our merchandising experts travel the globe gathering information and soaking up emerging trends. Then they package their findings in the 'D3 Box.' Complete with color charts, yarn and fabric swatches, and fashion sketches, the D3 Box becomes their tool caddie."

While much of what The Doneger Group does revolves around assessing trends and recommending and buying products, retailers sometimes look to the company for advice or to act as a sounding board, according to Doneger.

Recently, Doneger executives spent time with discount stores such as Hills and ShopKo to give them some direction on how to develop a career business.

"These retailers are casual-driven, but they're beginning to realize that they have an opportunity in unconstructed careerwear because of the sheer volume of women shopping in their stores and the fact that 75 percent of them are in the work force," says Burns.

With one discounter, Burns recommended that the long skirts and knit tops, which the retailer already had on the selling floor, be pulled together to create "outfit dressing" in a cohesive setting.

"Discounters are starting to realize that they don't have to relinquish the career business to other retailers. By having a few key items on hand that shoppers can buy for work, retailers will reduce the amount of cross-shopping and keep shoppers in the store for a longer period of time," explains Burns.

Perhaps one reason why The Doneger Group understands its retail clients so well is that it shares some formidable challenges. The first is dealing with a shrinking marketplace. The second is adapting to the changes that have become so much a part of daily retailing.

"We're constantly adapting to this changing marketplace and to new ways of doing business," says Doneger. "Since 1946, we've been reinventing our services to be more in sync with the needs of our retail clients, and we continue to do that today."

Looking ahead, Doneger feels that technology, with its ability to gather information with speed and accuracy, will play an increasing role in the buying group's services. The bottom line is that Abbey Doneger, an aggressive, energetic executive, and his team want to stay on the cutting edge.

Discount Store News, October 16, 1995.

CHAPTER 18

The Fashion Retailer

The hopes and dreams of fashion designers are ultimately in the hands of the fashion retailers. The design team can create an exciting new silhouette or coloration, but it is their retail counterparts who determine which products will be offered for sale. Retail buyers and merchandisers screen all available merchandise deciding which lines to display.

Fashion retailers are motivated by the needs of their specific consumer markets. Some stores concentrate on fashion-forward merchandise at very expensive price points. Others cater to the fashion-conscious consumer, who wants the latest designs at affordable prices. Between these extremes, there are shoppers with other motivations. Because fashion is an ever-changing industry, retailers must determine which new ideas and concepts will satisfy the needs of specific consumer groups.

These retailers are responsible for the successful distribution of fashion. What organizational structures govern their activities? In what types of settings are these fashion retailers found? How do these retail operations confront increasing competition to gain their fair share of the market? These are some of the questions addressed in this chapter.

CLASSIFYING THE RETAILERS

Present retail organizations bear little, if any, resemblance to the trading posts and general stores of early American history. In the highly specialized and very competitive environments of today, retailers with fashion orientations cannot rely on the techniques of their predecessors.

Today, there are many types of retailers, each with a specific formula for attracting customers. Some are industrial giants; others small entrepreneurs. Although there are specific classifications of stores, consumers are often confused by the groupings. For example, Saks Fifth Avenue and Macy's are both department stores, The former, however, is technically a specialty department

(top) Bergdorf Goodman epitomizes upscale American retailers. (bottom) Fashion oriented malls are among the most successful venues for retailers.

store because its merchandise is primarily concentrated in one major category—apparel. Macy's, on the other hand, is a traditional department store. It carries a wide assortment of both apparel (**soft goods**) and nonapparel (**hard goods**) lines, such as electronics and furniture. The following discussion describes the different types of retail classifications, based on merchandise assortment and methods of operation.

Department Stores

An outgrowth of the general store, which featured an assortment of merchandise in a casual or, more accurately, a disorganized array, **department stores** present a wide range of merchandise in defined areas or departments. As described above, traditional department stores sell hard goods and soft goods; specialized department stores sell only one major type of merchandise. Both groups operate from a **flagship,** or **main store**; they expand their operations by opening **branches** that carry a representative sampling of the flagship's offerings. Many department stores are starting to compete with specialty stores by opening smaller units that restrict their assortments to one, narrow type of merchandise. They are called **spinoff,** or twig, **stores.** Macy's is a leader in such operations, with spinoffs of some of its more successful lines. For example, Aeropostale stores and Charter Club operations, both of which carry private label merchandise, can be found across the country. This trend appeals to customers, who increasingly prefer to shop in smaller surroundings. By selling products that have already proven successful, these spinoff stores satisfy many shopper's needs and earn profits for their companies.

Even if a department store features both soft goods and hard goods, consumers are mainly attracted by fashion merchandise. For example, Sears, which built its reputation on appliances and tools, has undertaken promotional campaigns to underscore its shift toward more fashion merchandise. Profitability is the major factor in the disproportionate assortment of fashion items to hard goods.

Department stores with strong fashion orientations are the most aggressive in terms of advertising and promotion. Macy's, Bloomingdale's, and Marshall Field have almost daily fashion promotions in newspapers to capture the customer's attention. The final chapter of the text explores the department store's concentration on promotion.

Macy's annual Flower Show is just one major event sponsored by the department store.

Nordstrom

A Seattle-based department store, Nordstrom is becoming the envy of department stores across the nation. After opening its doors in 1901 as a shoe store, it initially expanded its merchandising mix by adding apparel to its offerings. The philosophy of carefully assisting shoe customers at the time of purchase was carried over to the store's newer divisions. With service becoming the benchmark on which it would build a reputation, sales per square foot rose to a level twice the national average.

At a time when many department stores are closing down their operations, Nordstrom is moving ahead with opening after successful opening. Not only is the company expanding in the west, where it is based, but also on the East coast. The latest store will serve as an anchor in the Roosevelt Field shopping mall in Long Island, New York.

Although Nordstrom carries exciting merchandise, that is not the only reason for its success. Most industry professionals agree that their attention to customer convenience is what separates Nordstrom from the rest of the field. In many of the stores, a formally attired pianist sets the tone by playing a grand piano in the center of the selling floor. Many departments have upholstered chairs for tired customers, changing rooms for parents tending to babies, and tables where children can use coloring books. These are just some of the touches that make Nordstrom unique.

Attentive selling is also a Nordstrom forté. Paid on the basis of straight commission, sales associates do everything to make the customer's experience a pleasant one. Shoppers may be assisted throughout the store by one salesperson instead of having to search for a different one in each department. This gives the shopper a feeling of personal attention. Little extras, such as snacks for the shopper, are also commonplace. This superlative personal shopping service makes the Nordstrom sales associate one of the highest paid in retailing, with annual earnings reaching as much as $75,000 per year!

Nordstrom's merchandising borrows from the past. Markdowns occur only three times a year—two at the season's end and one for its anniversary celebration. The constant markdown philosophy subscribed to by most American department stores tends to confuse shoppers, but Nordstrom's customers know exactly when prices will be lowered.

All of these factors, plus a positive image that seems to improve year after year, makes Nordstrom one of the world's most dynamic retail operations.

Nordstrom is considered the nation's most service-oriented fashion retailer.

Department stores generally feature a category of apparel at many price points, each presented in a different area of the store. Thus a store might sell sportswear in three different locations—main floor, third floor, and sixth floor—but each concentrates on a separate price range or price point. In the past, stores differentiated departments by such terms as better, moderate, or budget. Today, the progressive retailer has eliminated these obvious price designations and has assigned catchy names to each area. Consumers, however, soon come to understand what prices each name stands for. Bloomingdale's, for example, houses its moderate dress collection in Boulevard Dresses.

Many department stores are now involved in a new concept of separation called **collection merchandising.** More and more shoppers are looking for mer-

Designers, such as Ralph Lauren, merchandise their collections in retailer's "special shops."

chandise from the collections of specific designers. Therefore, instead of grouping merchandise by product category, stores are establishing departments that feature the merchandise of a well-known designer. DKNY, Tommy Hilfiger, Giorgio Armani, Liz Claiborne, and Ralph Lauren are merchandised in this manner. Sometimes, the designer makes this arrangement mandatory and may also determine how the collection will be visually presented on the store's selling floor. Ralph Lauren, for example, requires that his merchandise be featured in separate shops that utilize the Lauren "lifestyles" approach in fixturing and props.

In a related trend, some department stores are leasing floor space to outside businesses. **Leased departments** often include the cosmetics, furs, and fine jewelry departments. If the merchandise warrants specialized retailing ability, it is better to lease the space to an outside expert for a portion of the profits. To the consumer, it is another department in the store; to the department store, it is a department that follows the store's rules, but operates independently.

Cosmetic departments are generally leased arrangements between retailers and manufacturers.

Department stores are a global phenomenon, but the majority are in the United States. While London boasts Harrods, and Paris, Printemps, the United State's entries are significantly more numerous. Examples include Blooming-dale's and Macy's all over the country, Filene's in the Northeast, the May Company on the west coast, Strawbridge & Clothier in Philadelphia, Marshall Field in Chicago, and Burdines in Florida.

Specialty Stores

As merchandise became more varied, some early retailers moved away from the general merchandise concept and pioneered the first limited line stores, which concentrate on one merchandise classification. Today, these **specialty stores** are a major force in retailing. And specialize they do! Whether it is the upscale Ann Taylor or the downscale The Limited, specialty store retailing captures the attention and money of fashion-minded consumers.

This type of retail organization has two advantages. Because merchandise is restricted to one classification, the stores often feature the widest assortment available. In addition, shopping is faster and more convenient. With more people holding full-time jobs, the quick purchase has become a necessity.

The specialty store designation indicates nothing more than a merchandising philosophy. This store might be a single unit operation or part of a chain organization. Physically, specialty stores run the gamut from under 1,000 square feet to those that have several thousand square feet. So successful were the early specialty store entrepreneurs that many opened additional units in other locations. Thus, the concept of the chain was developed. Chains are retail organizations with two or more units operating from a central headquarters or home office. In the present retail environment, they continue to expand. The largest of the fashion apparel chains is The Limited, Inc. Beginning as a four-unit chain in Columbus, Ohio, it has developed into a major retailer through expansion and the acquisition of such names as Express, Victoria's Secret, Structure, Cacique, Lerner New York, Henri Bendel, and Lane Bryant. The Limited's roster now boasts more than 4,000 units!

Two members of The Limited organizations: Victoria's Secret (top) and Express (bottom).

At the same time, however, there are independents who compete successfully by carving out a share of the market.

Specialty store operations are so successful that a number of designers and fashion manufacturers have opened retail specialty shops to feature their own designs. These include Liz Claiborne, Adrienne Vittadini, Ralph Lauren, and

Designers, such as Calvin Klein (top) and Chanel (bottom) operate individual specialty shops in stores.

Nine West. Even couture designers, such as Armani, Chanel, Miyake, and Missoni are operating their own specialty stores.

Whether they are independents or parts of chain operations, specialty stores have become the major force in fashion retailing.

Boutiques

A variation on the typical specialty store is the **boutique.** It is most often a one-unit operation that features upscale, fashion-forward merchandise. The assortment is generally restricted to just a few pieces of each item, with custom-tailored apparel sometimes featured. Customers frequent boutiques because they are usually guaranteed the latest in fashion innovation and are individually assisted by trained salespersons. In many of these operations, success depends on individual salespersons, who develop their own clientele. They call customers when special merchandise arrives, notify them of special sales, and act as personal shoppers for those who want such attention.

Off-Price Retailers

Among the most successful retailers are the **off-price** merchants. The off-pricers buy late in the season, when manufacturers are forced to close out their lines at reduced prices, and can sell the merchandise at reduced prices to consumers.

Companies like T.J. Maxx, Marshall's, Loehmann's, Syms, and Burlington Coat Factory are continuously expanding to meet the needs of the consumer who looks for fashion bargains. Many prestigious labels are found in the off-price stores. In fact, the most successful are those that feature such renowned names as Jones New York, DKNY, Calvin Klein, Kenar, August Silk, and Liz Claiborne.

Factory Outlets

All across America, fashion manufacturers are opening their own units to dispose of season leftovers and current, slow-selling items. In places like St. Augustine, Florida, North Conway, New Hampshire, Freeport, Maine, and Secaucus, New Jersey—at distances that are significantly far from the traditional stores—top fashion names are liquidating their inventories. Stores bearing such prestigious fashion names as Coach, Geoffrey Beene, Calvin Klein, DKNY, Anne Klein, and Tahari are clustered in centers that group as many as 100 or more stores.

These **factory outlets** attract not only individual families, but busloads of people who come on shopping sprees arranged by the center's merchants.

Direct Retailers

As increasing numbers of women work full-time outside of the home, they have less time for in-store shopping. Their shopping needs are often satisfied by **direct retailers.**

As a result, catalog companies have proliferated, selling every conceivable fashion item at numerous price points. Joining them is the traditional retailer. Both department stores and specialty chains regularly reach their customers through direct mail. Whether it is store catalogs from Macy's, Neiman Marcus, Marshall Field, Lord & Taylor, Ann Taylor, J.L. Hudson, or Filene's, or catalogs from houses such as Horchows, Lillian Vernon, and Lands' End, consumers are inundated with catalog offerings.

In addition, companies that are not really in the business of selling goods mail catalogs to their clients. American Express, for example, sends its cardholders a catalog that features a large assortment of fashion merchandise, including precious jewelry, apparel, watches, and accessory items. The airlines include catalog offerings within their in-flight magazines. While customers are waiting to reach their destinations, they are shown many different items that may be ordered, in-flight.

Off-price retailers, such as Marshalls (top) and Burlington Coat Factory (center) are excellent outlets for manufacturer overruns and closeouts. Loehmann's (bottom) is credited with being the first women's off-price specialty operation.

Category Killers

Stores like Toys R Us, Kids R Us, and Bed Bath and Beyond are known as **category killers,** or specialty discounters. They carry large selections of one merchandise classification, and generally sell at discount prices. With the attention they generate, category killers take a great deal of business away from other stores who carry some of the same merchandise. Some department stores have found it financially sound to eliminate some of the merchandise categories, such as toys and home fashions, and concentrate on fashion apparel.

Subspecialty Stores

A new breed of retailer, the **subspecialty store,** is making a significant impact on consumers. As with specialty stores, they restrict their offerings to one classification, but the classification is even narrower. For example, the typical men's specialty store carries an assortment of tailored clothing, sportswear, activewear, and accessories. The subspecialty store selects only one of these products to sell. The Knot Shop, a store that carries only ties, is an example of subspecialty retailing. Its rapid expansion across the country indicates that this is yet another retail direction for the future.

Flea Market Operations

All across America, shoppers are flocking to **flea markets.** They can be found in outdoor locations, such as movie parking lots, and in indoor facilities that once housed single retail operations. Many operate only on weekends; others, such as one of the nation's largest, The Swap Shop in Sunrise, Florida, are open seven days a week.

The emphasis in these places is price! Merchandise runs the gamut from household to fashion-oriented items. For manufacturers seeking to dispose of leftovers and sometimes seconds, the flea market is a perfect venue. Flea markets have many vendors, each with comparatively limited retail space and

All across the United States, flea markets attract great numbers of shoppers seeking bargains. They often operate in outdoor parking lots and other large spaces.

lower operating costs than traditional retailers. Vendors work on very low markups and are able to sell at considerably reduced prices.

Many a manufacturer has been saved by being able to dispose of unwanted merchandise to flea market vendors.

Franchises and Licenses

Many companies prefer to expand their retail operations by inviting qualified individuals to open their own franchises or licensed units. The company often provides specialized training for the individual, who benefits by opening a unit with an established name and recognized product line. In return, the company receives a fee, a percentage of sales, and the individual's guarantee to buy all merchandise from the parent company. Unlike a franchising agreement, licensing arrangements do not include an initial fee for participation.

Although these agreements have long been used by fast-food vendors, such as McDonalds, Burger King, and Carvel, fashion retailers, including Lady Madonna, Benetton, Ralph Lauren, and Bellini, are now offering similar arrangements.

Mass Merchandise Discounters

Perhaps the greatest impact on retailing today has been the **mass merchandisers**, including Wal-Mart, Kmart, and Caldor. While they sell much more than fashion merchandise, their role as fashion merchandisers continues to expand. With the enormous volume they do, manufacturers find these outlets very attractive.

The emphasis is on price and value. There are few frills and limited personalized sales help. Customers generally make their own selections. The

Wal-Mart is the largest mass merchandiser.

reward is lower prices. With the increasing cost of living, more and more people are heading for these stores. These companies are now expanding into other parts of the world in impressive numbers.

Interactive Retailers

Traditional retailers, who operate from stores and through catalogs, are confronted by a number of new types of competition. Most important are the cable television stations and the ever-expanding computerized on-line shopping services. Both are known as **interactive retailers,** because sellers and consumers may talk to each other and discuss the purchase.

Cable Television

Everyone who subscribes to cable television has witnessed the growth of channels that sell merchandise. The biggest of these are the Home Shopping Network and QVC, each boasting as many as twenty thousand transactions per hour!

At first, these channels limited merchandise to lower price point items, generally in jewelry and accessories. Today, they sell high-fashion apparel at every price point. Traditional giants in retailing, such as Saks Fifth Avenue and Macy's, are now getting ready to enter the field. They hope that the upscale consumer is ready to embrace this method of purchasing fine merchandise.

On-line Shopping Services

Everyday, more and more consumers are ordering products through **on-line** services. Customers who subscribe to these services may spend their leisure time shopping at what is called **Web Malls.** Much like traditional malls, these services feature scores of different stores with a host of merchandise. Users may skip from store to store, without leaving the comforts of their home. The merchandise may be selected and paid for either with a check or a credit card. Because of problems with credit card fraud, on-line credit card purchasers are required to telephone their numbers into the company from which the purchase is being made. In the future, credit card use will become simpler and such calls will not be required.

Companies who previously restricted their selling to retail outlets or catalogs have gone on-line. They include Abercrombie & Fitch and Gap. As more people subscribe to on-line services, this form of purchasing is expected to increase significantly.

Cable shopping networks, such as QVC, attract huge audiences.

As we move towards the twenty-first century, only time will tell which type of retail organization will become the most important, which will decline in popularity, and what new methods of doing business will surface.

RETAILER LOCATIONS

At the beginning of the twentieth century, the only viable place to establish a retail operation was in a downtown area. Together with community general stores, found mostly in rural areas, and mail-order catalogs, these were the only retail outlets for customers. Times have certainly changed! Malls of every size, shape, and image now serve the needs of consumers. Some are enclosed, others open; some are vertically constructed, others expand horizontally. Festival marketplaces, which revitalize urban areas, are also very much in fashion. Abandoned places that were once thriving seaports, breweries, railroad terminals, or historical districts are developed into combination tourist attractions and retail centers. In more affluent areas, centers have been developed that cater exclusively to the upper-class shopper. While downtown is still a vital retail location, retailing is no longer relegated to the traditional downtown shopping district.

Marshall Field is a major department store anchored in a central downtown district.

Downtown Central Districts

Most major department stores still operate from their downtown flagship stores. The executive headquarters for Macy's is in Herald Square, New York City, a downtown shopping area. Likewise, Marshall Field is headquartered in downtown Chicago, and Filene's in downtown Boston. Not only are most merchandising and policy decisions made in these locations, but the parent stores generally account for a significant part of the company's sales volume.

From the 1950s through the 1970s, the downtown areas of many cities underwent significant changes. As people moved to the suburbs, flagship stores experienced declining sales. The middle class was now shopping at suburban branches. Although this was a serious situation, most retailers maintained their main stores.

In the past fifteen years, cities across America have been gentrified. Large sums have been expended to revitalize urban America. Once again, downtown is alive and well and doing considerable retail business.

Shopping Malls

Across the United States, shoppers find that enclosed shopping facilities are the perfect places to satisfy their needs. In the 1950s, the first malls were built as outdoor shopping arenas. One of the first enclosed **shopping malls** in the United States to be built was the Walt Whitman in Huntington, New York. It was so successful that it became the prototype for future malls. Outdoor malls reacted by enclosing their facilities to offer a climate-controlled shopping environment. Today, the **enclosed mall** is the dominant type of retail location. The majority are horizontally constructed in suburban areas where land is plentiful and less expensive than in the downtown urban areas. To accommodate the large number of consumers, many have added additional floors, doubling and tripling their original size. An example of the magnitude of this type of expansion is obvious at Roosevelt Field, a suburban shopping center outside New York City. Originally built in 1957 as an outdoor center, it first enclosed its facilities and then added another level to become the nation's fifth largest center. By 1997, with the completion of another extension that will include Nordstrom's, it will become one of the largest malls in the United States.

Based on the success of suburban malls, developers have begun creating downtown malls in urban centers. Because real estate costs are significantly higher and land is often less available, the direction has been toward the **vertical mall.** An early example is Chicago's Water Tower on fashionable North Michigan Avenue. Flanked by a prestigious hotel, the Ritz Carlton, and movie theaters, this shopping facility boasts an atrium and seven selling floors occupied by such major stores as Marshall Field and Lord & Taylor. In addition to the **anchor stores,** there are 125 specialty shops, including Gap, Louis Vuitton, Banana Republic, Henri Bendel, and The Limited.

Another type of mall combines an entertainment center with shopping facilities. The Mall of America in Bloomington, Minnesota, has attracted record crowds to its premises. With shops surrounded by rides and attractions, the entire family can enjoy the experience.

Since the 1950s, malls have expanded to include restaurants, department stores, specialty shops, and entertainment facilities.

Old malls, such as Roosevelt Field, are modernizing and expanding to meet consumers needs.

Festival Marketplaces

South Street Seaport in New York City, Inner Harbor in Baltimore, Quincy Market in Boston, and Union Station in St. Louis are just a few examples of **festival marketplaces.** These centers are built on abandoned properties that have been resurrected and transformed into tourist attractions boasting a considerable number of fashion operations. Through the creative genius of numerous developers, including The Rouse Company which transformed Boston's historic landmark building, Faneuil Hall, into Quincy Market, these areas have become exciting and profitable places for tourists to satisfy their shopping needs.

*Faneuil Hall became
the centerpiece for
Quincy Market in
Boston and the first
festival marketplace in
the United States.*

Unlike other shopping facilities, festival marketplaces are not anchored by giant department stores; they are basically clusters of specialty stores. Typical tenants are Gap, Structure, Express, Talbot's, The Sharper Image, and Banana Republic.

Clearance Discount Centers

A number of extremely large shopping facilities are springing up all across the United States. Some are outdoor facilities that include outlets of traditional retailers that sell unwanted items at greatly reduced prices. Several, however, have been built as enclosed environments. They feature as many as two miles of store fronts under one roof! The most famous of these are called the **Mills,** Sawgrass Mills, in Ft. Lauderdale, Gurnee Mills, outside of Chicago, Franklin Mills, near Philadelphia, and Potomac Mills in northern Virginia are examples of these complexes.

The tenants of these super shopping arenas, whose forté is bargain merchandise, include giants like Saks Fifth Avenue, Nordstrom, Spiegel, and Macy's, and chains such as Ann Taylor, Nine West, Lillie Rubin, and others, which were unable to sell out their inventory in traditional stores. With prices reduced as much as 75 percent, the cumulative sales are astounding.

High-Fashion Centers

Many major cities boast fashion centers that are not located in malls, congested downtown areas, or festival marketplaces. These are generally shopping streets dotted with upscale fashion retailers. Their target markets are affluent consumers who seek the latest in both domestic and international styles, with price not a factor. Some of these areas feature branches of such well-known fashion organizations as Neiman Marcus, and Saks Fifth Avenue, but the majority of the shops are small, boutique-like operations that feature designer

Outlet malls are excellent arenas for manufacturers to sell leftover merchandise. Potomac Mills in Virginia (top) regularly attracts throngs of shoppers.

merchandise from Yves Saint Laurent, Ungaro, Armani, Sonia Rykiel, Louis Vuitton, Hermès, Norma Kamali, and Calvin Klein.

These high-fashion centers include Madison Avenue in New York City, Rodeo Drive in Beverly Hills, Worth Avenue in Palm Beach, and Oak Street in Chicago.

Power Centers

Throughout the country, there are small shopping arenas known as **power centers.** They offer customers merchandise at highly discounted prices. The stores are usually very large retailers, known for competitive pricing, and capable of drawing large crowds. Many are fashion-oriented retailers such as Filene's Basement and Burlington Coat Factory. In these cavernous facilities, they dispose of merchandise purchased from other retailers and manufacturers. The one limitation is that a power center must be located sufficiently far from traditional malls so as not to plague them with unfair competition.

High fashion centers, such as New York's Trump Tower, attract upscale consumers.

Miscellaneous Centers

Other types of shopping environments include **mixed-use centers** that combine shopping, office space, hotels, and permanent residences; **strip centers** that feature about twenty stores, with a few fashion-oriented retailers interspersed among the grocers and service-oriented retailers; and **transportation terminals.** The latter group is gaining in importance in America. Taking their cue from London's Heathrow Airport, where fashion shops such as Harrod's and Bally serve the crowds waiting to make connections, places like USAir's Pittsburgh air terminal and Washington D.C.'s Union Station offer waiting travelers an abundance of fashion merchandise retailers.

RETAIL ORGANIZATIONAL STRUCTURES

No matter how large or small their operations are, retailers must establish organizational structures that maximize efficiency. The structures employed vary from company to company. Small stores are often negligent in this area. Many of the duties and responsibilities performed by the employees are not specifically assigned, and the actual tasks required of store personnel are accomplished in an unstructured format. This haphazard approach often leads to confusion on the part of the employees and lower profits for the company.

Larger stores, on the other hand, subscribe to a more formal, structured approach. In department stores, a divisional plan divides the store into major functions or divisions of the operation. The plan typically is a four or five function arrangement; the major areas are merchandising, management, operations, advertising and promotion, and control. Each division is supervised by a manager who often enjoys the title of vice-president and supervises numerous mid-management subordinates. In addition to the heads of these divisions, who are the major decision makers for the company, and the people who work for them, other employees function primarily as advisory or support people. Technically, this organizational structure is known as **line and staff.** The line people are the decision makers; the staff personnel serve in an advisory capacity.

TABLE 18.1

SELECTED MAJOR RETAIL CORPORATIONS

Carson Pirie Scott & Co
P.A. Bergner
Carson Pirie Scott
Boston Stores

Dayton Hudson Corporation
Target
Mervyn's
Dayton's Minneapolis
Hudson's Michigan
Marshall Field

Dillard's
Dillard's

Federated Department Stores Inc.
Bloomingdale's
The Bon Marche
Burdines
Lazarus
Rich's/Goldsmith's
Stern's
Macy's East
Macy's West

The Gap, Inc.
Gap
Banana Republic
GapKids
Old Navy Clothing

Harcourt General, Inc.
Neiman Marcus
Bergdorf Goodman

Kmart
Kmart
SuperKmart
Builders Square
Borders-Waldenbooks

The Limited, Inc.
The Limited
Limited Too
Express
Structure
Victoria's Secret
Victoria's Secret Bath Shops
Lane Bryant
Lerner New York
Henri Bendel
Abercrombie & Fitch
Cacique

The Limited, Inc. (continued)
Bath & Body Works
Galyan's Trading Co.
Bath and Body Works at Home

May Department Stores
Meier & Frank
Robinson-May
Famous-Barr
Foley's
Kaufmann's
Hecht's
Lord & Taylor
Filene's
Payless ShoeSource

Melville Corporation
Marshall's
Thom McAn
Wilson's
Kay-Bee
Linens 'N Things
This End Up
Foot Action
Meldisco

Nordstrom
Nordstrom
Nordstrom Rack

JCPenney
JC Penney

Sears
Sears

Spiegel, Inc.
Eddie Bauer
Honey Bee

Toys "R" Us
Toys "R" Us
Kids "R" Us

US Shoe Corporation
Casual Corner
Petite Sophisticate
Career Image
Capezio
August Max
Lenscrafter
Footwear
Cabaret
Caren Charles

(continued)

TABLE 18.1 (*continued*)

Wal-Mart Stores, Inc.	**F.W. Woolworth**
Wal-Mart	Woolworth
Sam's Club	Kinney/Footlocker
Hypermart USA	Richmond Brothers/Susies
Super Saver Warehouse Club	Kids Mart/Little Folks
	ZCMI

Chain organizations are similar in structure, but operate from a home office or central headquarters, away from the individual stores. They often have more divisions than department stores because of frequent expansion. This necessitates new locations, centralized warehouses, and constant research and development.

Although most retail operations have a formal structure that delineates lines of authority, an informal structure may also exist within a company's framework. Thus, certain key people have a greater voice in the management of a company than do others.

Whatever the structure of the company, it should be regularly assessed and changed to make the organization function more efficiently.

SERVICES OFFERED BY THE FASHION RETAILER

Few retailers believe customers shop in a particular store solely because of its merchandise assortment. The retail business is highly competitive; merchants must distinguish themselves from the competition in order to attract enough customers to turn a profit. One way to achieve this goal is by providing customer services. The nature of the company and its philosophy dictate the types of services that should be offered. As a rule, those with price as the chief attraction offer the fewest services; those with traditional, fashion retailing operations, provide the most.

Personal Shopping

Every upscale fashion emporium offers some kind of **personal shopping.** Every major retailer has its own program that includes a number of different approaches. Most provide telephone assistance for shoppers who call the store with merchandise requests. The caller might ask the personal shopper to assemble items from different departments to be reviewed by the customer at a designated time. This is the concept followed by the Macy's By Appointment (MBA) program. At Bergdorf Goodman, an upscale fashion retailer, customers are invited into a salon to view and try on merchandise. Lunch and refreshments are also served to each client. In Bloomingdale's men's department and at Nordstrom, the personal shopper may visit the customer's home or office with the merchandise in hand.

Corporate Purchasing

Many upscale retailers have consultants who assist businesses in the purchase of presents for employees and clients. At peak gift-giving times, such as Christmas, this is an excellent program for generating increased sales. Popular items sold through these **corporate purchasing** programs include perfume, silk scarves, small leather goods, and home products. The store wraps the gifts and sends them to designated clients with very little customer involvement.

Interpreters

Tourists are a major source of revenue for retail establishments. To attract their business, retailers in the major cities employ interpreters to accommodate foreign-speaking visitors.

Gift Registries

People who are engaged to be married and those who are prospective parents are excellent markets for fashion retailers. To eliminate the purchase of unwanted or duplicate merchandise by gift givers, these individuals select the items they would like to receive and register their preferences with an appropriate store.

Service is the key to success for many retailers.

Large department stores and specialty stores have established such **gift registries.** The store records the selections on a computer so that well wishers may purchase one of these gifts on a visit to any branch store. Purchasers outside of the store's trading area may handle the transaction by phone. Items ranging from bed and bath linens and dinnerware for the bridal couple to layette items for the expectant parents are bought in this manner. Gift registries are advantageous for the retailer, because the potential for returns is minimized.

Beauty Salons

Many retailers include a beauty salon on the premises. Although this service is a leased department, its purpose is to bring shoppers into the store. Once there, they might be motivated to make an unplanned purchase. Some fashion retailers provide informal modeling in the salons, so customers can view the range of the store's apparel and accessories. Because shopping time is at a premium, this hour or two can generate business for the store.

Travel Services

Some retailers also operate leased travel departments. While this does not directly sell merchandise, it does provide an opportunity to familiarize potential travelers with the store's merchandise. As with beauty salons, these departments attract additional consumers to the store. Sometimes, the travel department works in conjunction with the store's personal shoppers, who are able to tailor selections to traveler's needs in a short period of time.

Restaurants

Dining facilities do more than feed hungry shoppers. They give shoppers an opportunity to relax within the store's environment. Many retailers provide a variety of dining services from snack bars to elaborate restaurants. In Bloomingdale's New York City flagship, *Le Train Bleu,* a fine French restaurant, is a popular place for upscale shoppers to satisfy their appetites. During the meal, some retailers offer modeling of store merchandise. Afterward, the refreshed customer may be sufficiently motivated to continue to shop.

Gift Wrapping

Most major fashion retailers provide gift wrapping services. Some are free; others cost the customer a minimal amount of money. A gift that is beautifully wrapped always makes a positive impression. Not only does the recipient feel special, but he or she will remember the store when in need of a gift for someone else.

Executive Retreats

Busy executives are often a store's best customers. However, the store must first motivate them to come and shop. Some upscale fashion retailers have set aside part of their premises to specifically lure such customers. At these **executive retreats** the store provides a staff of secretaries to take dictation, send faxes, and serve food while busy executives wait to be fitted. The ultimate feature of a retreat is a putting green for golf enthusiasts who wish to sharpen their skills. This type of special environment may tempt even the most reluctant shopper to visit the store.

Alterations, delivery of merchandise, charge accounts, child care, and other services are provided by the retail industry. Each store must decide which services will generate enough business to warrant their inclusion, and which will help distinguish them from their competitors.

PURCHASING FASHION MERCHANDISE

While all merchants make buying decisions, none are as complex as the purchase of fashion merchandise. Just deciding what skirt length will be acceptable to customers is enough to drive most buyers crazy. Making the decision six months or more in advance of sales complicates matters further. In addition, the buyer must evaluate color decisions, price points, silhouette preferences, and fabrication selections.

Responsibility for the Purchase

At the helm of the fashion merchandising hierarchy is the store's **general merchandise manager (G.M.M.).** This person determines dollar allocations for each division's purchases and heads the team that will create the store's fash-

Fashion images are often established by constructing elegant premises.

ion image. Major stores divide the merchandising responsibility into divisions, each having a **divisional merchandise manager (D.M.M.)**. For example, stores may have divisions for men's wear, fashion apparel, accessories, and other products. The D.M.M.s are responsible for dividing their purchasing budgets among the various departments within their jurisdiction. Men's wear, for example, might be divided into tailored clothing, sportswear, activewear, outerwear, and haberdashery. Each department has a buyer who actually purchases the merchandise. Most stores have a check on their buyers and require that significant purchases be approved by the appropriate D.M.M., but it is the buyer who plays the major role in the store's purchasing.

Merchandise Selection

The actual selection of specific styles is the result of research and planning. Qualitative and quantitative decisions are based on such sources as sales records, trade publications, shopping the competition, various advisory services, fashion show presentations, and trade associations. Each buyer must carefully study all available information before making purchasing commitments. Decisions concerning specific merchandise selections, which resources are most suitable, and when goods should be delivered are then built into a purchasing plan that evaluates styles, colors, sizes, and fabrics in the right quantities at the desired price points. In practice, this is known as the development of a **model stock.**

Today's fashion buyers face more complicated challenges than their predecessors. With the enormous amount of competition and the recent growth of off-price merchants, the buyer can no longer purchase only nationally advertised labels. Although the fashion customer still purchases designer and brand name merchandise, they can easily find this merchandise at greatly reduced prices in off-price stores. As a result, retail giants have called upon many of their buyers to become product developers and help create **private label** merchandise exclusive to their stores. A seasoned buyer knows the proper mix of well-known fashion brands and private label merchandise to satisfy customer needs.

A major contribution to determining merchandise selection can be made by a fashion director. Those stores with fashion-forward images often employ these highly paid individuals to help buyers with fashion decisions. They often carry the title of vice president, indicating the importance of the position. The multifaceted job includes researching the industry before the buyer makes purchasing decisions. They typically visit the fiber mills to learn about what's new on the textile horizon, consult fashion forecasters to learn about new trends, attend fashion events that give an overview of the coming season, and meet with the editorial staff of influential fashion publications to "pick their brains." The information is then disseminated to the buyers, who are now better equipped to make purchasing decisions.

DEVELOPING A FASHION IMAGE

A retail organization's image can be determined from a review of its ads in newspapers and magazines. If every retailer had the same image, it would be difficult for the shopper to decide which one to patronize.

A major responsibility of the fashion-oriented retailer is to develop an image that will motivate shoppers to become customers. Those who successfully do this become the major players in the game of fashion.

In the past ten years, many stores that were household fashion names have disappeared. Although it is difficult to assess what went wrong with each one, the lack of a fashion image that met with customer approval certainly played some role. Stores like Gimbel's, Bonwit Teller, and B. Altman & Company, all giants at one time, are now just memories. They have been replaced by retailers who have done a better job in relaying their fashion messages to the public. Only those who continue to properly assess their customer's needs will be around to reap the benefits and rewards.

Retailers advance their fashion images through promotion. Using a variety of techniques that include fashion shows, special celebrity appearances, fashion workshops, and visual presentations, the retailer tries to motivate the customer to come and see what all the excitement is about. The next chapter focuses on how the retailer makes use of special promotional tools.

Chapter Highlights

- Traditionally, fashion retailers operate department and specialty store organizations.
- An increasing number of retailers function as off-pricers, flea market vendors, discounters, subspecialists, franchisees and licensees, mass merchandisers, direct merchants, and interactive salespeople.
- The most popular of the traditional shopping areas was usually the downtown central district. These stores are now experiencing a revival.

- The most preferred shopping environment is currently the enclosed shopping mall.
- Other types of retail centers include festival marketplaces, outlet centers, and notable fashion streets.
- To overcome increasing competition, retailers offer such services as personal shoppers, corporate purchasing, interpreters, gift registries, gift wrapping, and executive retreats.
- Merchandise selection is typically accomplished by a team headed by a general merchandise manager, but the ultimate purchasing decision is in the hands of the buyer.
- Retailers of apparel and accessories must develop fashion images that distinguish them from their competitors.

Important Fashion Terminology and Concepts

anchor stores
boutique
branch store
category killer
collection merchandising
corporate purchasing
department store
direct retailer
divisional merchandise
  manager (DMM)
enclosed mall
executive retreat
factory outlet
fashion image
festival marketplace
flagship store

flea market
franchised unit
general merchandise
  manager (GMM)
gift registries
gift wrapping
hard goods
interactive retailers
leased department
licensed unit
line and staff
main store
mass merchandiser
mills
mixed-use center
model stock

off-price
on-line services
personal shopping
power center
private label
shopping mall
soft goods
specialty store
spinoff store
strip center
subspecialty store
transportation terminals
vertical mall
Web Malls

For Review

1. In what ways are department stores competing with specialty stores?
2. How have the early malls been transformed to meet the needs of today's shoppers?
3. Why do some fashion retailers subscribe to collection merchandising?
4. What is a leased department?
5. How does the boutique differ from the specialty store operation?
6. Explain the principle reason for the popularity of direct retailing.
7. In what way does the subspecialty store differ from the specialty shop?
8. Differentiate between franchises and licenses.
9. What is a festival marketplace?
10. Describe the "Mills" operations.
11. What is meant by the term interactive retailer?
12. Distinguish between line and staff people.

13. Why has the personal shopper become such an important part of the fashion retailer's staff?

14. Define corporate purchasing.

15. Explain how an in-store restaurant helps the retailer.

16. Why has product development become so important for some buyers?

Exercises and Projects

1. Visit two retail operations in your community, one a traditional store and the other an off-price retailer. Compare their operations in terms of services offered, merchandise available, and price points.

2. Write to a major fashion-oriented department store or, if possible, visit one in order to determine the scope of its personal shopping services.

3. Interview a fashion buyer, store manager, or department manager. Prepare a report on their company's involvement in private label merchandise.

4. Visit a festival marketplace and a traditional shopping mall to compare the environments. Photographs should be taken of both and mounted on foamcore board. Identify and list their differences.

The Case of the Friendly Competitors

The downtown area of a major midwestern city has been home to two large department stores for more than fifty years. While each has a core of regular customers, they are in competition with each other. Both have fashion orientations, but Goldens is a little more fashion forward than the more traditional Baker & Foster. Like most fashion retailers, both organizations feature services for their shoppers and initiate regular promotions and special events to increase customer traffic. While they do not share company secrets with each other, their relationship has been amicable. Although several lines of merchandise are featured in both stores, they never seem to be involved in pricing disputes. Each works on the traditional retail markup, reducing prices only when items fail to sell or at the conventional sales periods.

Yesterday's lead story in major local newspapers centered on the ground-breaking for a new retail operation. Lamberts, a well-known off-price retailer announced that it will be opening a new unit three miles from the downtown area. Although the new business is not within walking distance of the old-line department stores, it is within easy reach via public and private transportation. Known for their shrewd merchandising practices, Lamberts features well-known fashion merchandise at 20 to 50 percent below regular retail. Although Goldens and Baker & Foster receive their goods early in the season and Lamberts purchases later to gain a price advantage, Lamberts does pose a threat to the traditional retailers.

Management at both Goldens and Baker & Foster have called senior staff meetings to discuss plans for dealing with this potential new competitor. Several possible approaches have been suggested:

Question

Which of the possible solutions should be employed to meet the challenge of the new retailer? Defend your answers.

1. Merchandise bearing the same labels should be discounted to meet the competition.

2. New services should be offered to capture the customers' attention.

3. Service should be curtailed so that prices could be reduced throughout the store.

4. Private labels should be increased.

5. Lines carried by Lamberts should be discontinued.

point of view

America's Hot Tourist Spot: The Outlet Mall

Edwin McDowell

Strolling past the Saks Off Fifth outlet, Dress Barn and a camera store in the vast corridors of the Potomac Mills discount mall, three college students from France smiled with anticipation as they spotted a shop that sold athletic wear.

When they emerged with their purchases, including the New York Yankees baseball caps that were high on their list, one student, Philippe D'Haucourt, said, "Now that we've seen the tourist sights, we can go home."

His quip held more than a kernel of truth. Potomac Mills and many other discount outlet centers have become so popular with foreign and American tourists that they are now bigger attractions than the Liberty Bell, the Jefferson Memorial, the Alamo and many other traditional tourist treasures.

Of the 17.2 million shoppers who spent $358 million last year at Potomac Mills, 30 miles south of Washington in Virginia's historic Prince William County, at least 4.5 million were tourists, according to a survey of mall visitors.

The travel industry defines a tourist as someone who travels at least 100 miles or stays in a hotel or motel overnight.

Under a somewhat looser definition, as many as six million of the visitors could be considered tourists, said Patrick McMahon, director of the Virginia Department of Tourism.

The gigantic enclosed mall, with its 225 shops, is far and away the most popular tourist destination in this tourism-rich state—well ahead of Arlington National Cemetery, with four million total visitors a year; Colonial Williamsburg, with 2.5 million, and Mount Vernon, 10 miles or so distant, at one million. The only attraction in the region that rivals Potomac Mills in drawing tourists is the Air and Space Museum on the Mall in Washington. It draws 8.4 million visitors a year, although many of those are from the surrounding region.

To be sure, many people combine shopping with visits to historic sites, amusement parks, beaches or family and friends. But many just want to shop, planning vacations solely around that passion.

And that is not unique to Virginia. From Maine to Hawaii, bargain hunters flock to discount outlets, turning what was once an obscure corner of retailing transacted in mostly out-of-the-way locales into a booming industry. With sales at the 331 outlet centers in the United States projected to exceed $14 billion this year, up from $6.8 billion at 186 centers in 1990, outlets are the fastest-growing segment of the retail industry—and, it turns out, one of the fastest-growing of the travel industry as well.

The trend includes Potomac Mills and 10 other discount megamalls that feature not just manufacturers' outlets, but also big discounters like Wal-Mart and Ikea and "off-price" stores like Marshall's that typically offer overstocked brand-name merchandise from a broad range of manufacturers and department stores.

Whatever their names, the outlets draw huge numbers of tourists.

In northeastern Philadelphia the 215-store Franklin Mills outlet, which opened in 1989, drew an estimated 17.8 million visitors last year, including almost 6 million tourists. That is four times the 1.5 million total visitors to the Liberty Bell, for decades the state's top tourist attraction.

In San Marcos, Tex., the estimated 4.2 million tourists last year at two outlet centers combined far exceeded the total of 2.9 million visitors drawn by the Alamo in San Antonio.

And Pigeon Forge, Tenn., a hamlet of fewer than 3,330 people with 200 outlet shops, drew 10 million visitors last year, a million more than visited the Great Smoky Mountains National Park nearby, the nation's most heavily visited destination park.

George Ku Tours in New Castle, Pa., 55 miles north of Pittsburgh, runs three-day shopping tours to the Williamsburg Pottery Factory near Williamsburg, Va., with a stop at Potomac Mills. "We don't stop at Colonial Williamsburg, since this is an all-shopping tour," said Joan George, an owner of the family business. Buses sometimes return so loaded with packages, she added, that the toilet is used as a storeroom.

Even at Niagara Falls, which has two big outlet malls, shopping often takes precedence over falling water. "You'd be surprised how many bus tours come here for shopping," a spokesman for the visitors' bureau,

Tom Darro, said, "and couldn't care less about seeing the falls."

The Travel Industry Association of America recently said shopping was the most popular activity of vacationing Americans last year, and Mr. McMahon has an inkling of the reasons. "The only time many people have to shop," he said, "is when they're on vacation."

To keep tourists flowing in, outlet centers participate in package tours with nearby hotels, golf courses and casinos. In Washington the Gray Line tours feature a daily excursion to Potomac Mills, less than 45 minutes away.

Some conventional malls also draw millions of shoppers. But they tend to be in major urban centers, charge full price and cater overwhelmingly to local shoppers.

The Mall of America in Bloomington, Minn., a behemoth with more than 400 stores, 50 restaurants, 9 nightclubs and a roller coaster in a space that could fit seven Yankee Stadiums, is one of a kind. Last year it drew 40 million visitors, including at least 12 million tourists, more than Walt Disney World, the Grand Canyon and Graceland combined.

But outlet centers, even spick-and-span Potomac Mills, are usually no-frills places. And no developer today would dream of picking a spot for one without careful regard for tourists. It was not until about 1988, three years after Potomac Mills had opened in what was a largely wooded area, that tour buses and out-of-state cars made their presence felt.

"That's when we began an all-out push to be included in Virginia and Washington's familiarization tours for tour operators, travel agents and travel writers," said L. Kathy Pelino, director of tour and travel for Potomac Mills. That is also when

developers who had not already done so began locating outlet centers with tourists in mind.

Yet for all the glass and chrome of the newer malls, the 300 outlet stores in restored factories and buildings in Reading, Pa., are thriving. Credited with being the first multitenant manufacturers' outlet center, Reading's outlets, which started to open in 1974, attract eight million visitors a year, including millions of day trippers from the Philadelphia region, as well as hundreds of thousands who arrive on 10,000 tour buses.

Although outlet shops have been a godsend for Reading, some tourism officials regard them as a mixed blessing. They provide jobs and tax revenue, yes, but critics say they also contribute to sprawl, traffic jams and one-industry economies.

The economic effects are considerable. Potomac Mills provided $3.4 million in retail sales taxes in the 1995 fiscal year, or 20 percent of Prince William County's total sales tax, along with 2,400 jobs.

But Jerome L. McElroy, a professor of economics at St. Mary's College in Notre Dame, Ind., who has written widely on the economic effect of tourism, said the benefits of outlet malls and shopping centers were often exaggerated.

"They basically deal in merchandise that is marked up, but to which only a small amount of local value is added, unlike, say, dollars spent touring historic grounds," Professor McElroy said. Switching the emphasis from history to shopping, he said, will inevitably change the mix of visitors and risk eroding the character of a state's tourism appeal.

Almost all outlet centers belong to local and state tourism bureaus. Potomac Mills also belongs to Capital Region USA, a cooperative

encompassing Virginia, Washington and Maryland that advertises in Europe.

For as the students from France who are visiting here demonstrate, not only American tourists love to shop. Two German exchange students arrived after a two-hour drive, ready to do some serious shopping.

"I have a large shopping list from my roommates for at least 10 pairs of Levis," said Melanie Roehm of Cologne. Her companion, Christel Orth of Frankfurt, said Germany's few outlet stores were so scattered that "you have to travel all over the country to visit them."

A United Airlines advertising campaign in Europe, intended to promote the carrier's hub at Dulles International Airport, features Potomac Mills prominently. In one advertisement asking "Why Washington?" the airline answered by listing Potomac Mills first, ahead of Capitol Hill and the Smithsonian Institution.

"Our foreign passengers love to shop," Milton Perry, a bus driver for the Gray Line tour to Potomac Mills, said. "They come here from all over, and when they go back to Washington they're loaded down."

Last year 5 of the 4,200 tour buses to Franklin Mills in Philadelphia were filled with Kuwaitis. Gurnee Mills in Illinois attracted groups from Ukraine and Tanzania.

Sawgrass Mills near Fort Lauderdale, Fla., which draws an estimated 5.7 million tourists among its 19 million visitors a year, is a magnet for Latin American visitors. Speaking of their free-spending ways, Anne Lipscomb, vice president of marketing for the Mills Corporation, which owns Sawgrass and Potomac Mills, said, "I've never seen so many teenagers with gold cards in my life."

The New York Times, May 26, 1996.

Outlet Malls Look to Lure Male Shoppers

Eileen Courter

Outlet developers are taking Phillips-Van Heusen Corp.'s mass closing of 200 stores (DNR, Sept. 14, Page 1) as a wakeup call that it's time to do more to attract men to their off-price centers.

And they're doing something about making them more user-friendly for men.

Outlet operators are already fine-tuning their mix of tenants to sign on more high-visibility sportswear designer names and brands. And the developers are adding special perks to lure men into existing and new outlet malls—sporting goods stores, electronics, putting greens, and more.

Their reason for arranging their building blocks this way is pure and simple: Men's wear is among the top performers in outlet centers nationally. They want to keep it that way.

As for the P-VH situation, the giant dress shirt and sportswear manufacturer/retailer, which currently has close to 1,000 outlet units, will reportedly balance the store closings with new openings in the same period. What's more, the shuttering of the 200 stores will take time.

P-VH's impending move could actually turn out to be a wash, according to outlet developers. They have been told by P-VH executives that the outlets to be closed within the next few years will be replaced by new units with possibly new names and merchandise.

But the closings aren't being taken lightly and developers admit they signal the fact that outlet centers certainly aren't immune from the lumps that other retail formats are taking.

Discussing P-VH's plans to close stores, William Carpenter Jr., president and chief operating officer, Prime Retail, the Baltimore-based outlet developer, says he is "keeping the move in perspective."

"Look, the entire picture of men's wear outlet retailing must be tucked into proper context." As for the P-VH closings, Carpenter stresses that, over the years, P-VH has closed 40 to 50 stores a year, "but continues to do an enormous amount of business." "I met with Walter Rossi [chairman, P-VH retail group] the day the closings were announced. From what he indicated to me, it has little or no effect on our portfolio. They have nearly 1,000 stores. When they finish this, and you add on the new stores opening with us, I venture to say it will probably be a wash. I think what they're doing is cleaning up their portfolio. But nobody really knows because they have not pinpointed that yet." J. Dixon Fleming Jr., board chairman of Factory Stores of America, which merged last summer with Charter Oak Group Ltd., a subsidiary of Rothschild Realty, reports P-VH has been Factory Stores' single-biggest men's wear tenant. The newly combined operation is the largest factory-outlet real estate investment trust in the U.S. and Ralph Lauren is one of the hot names added to the Factory Stores tenant roster with the merger.

As for the P-VH cutbacks, Fleming states, "My guess is some of that is a result of the move toward casualwear. And the company's primary focus, of course, has been men's dress shirts. Those guys who have

been in the casual business, as some of our tenants are, have done fairly well."

The executive indicates that even before the cutbacks, P-VH had discussed with his company plans to convert some outlets to the Izod and Gant units, brands P-VH recently acquired from Crystal Brands. Those conversations were discussed some six months ago during lease negotiations. Factory Stores agreed to allow P-VH to close eight stores, notes Fleming. Five have already been replaced. And this could be indication of what the future will bring.

One developer who refuses to mention P-VH by name is Gary Geisler, vice-president, chief operating officer, HGI Realty Inc., Muskegon, Mich., which was formed earlier this year when Horizon Outlet Centers Inc. merged with McArthur/Glen Realty Corp., McLean, Va.

Like Carpenter, Geisler states he wants to put men's wear sales in perspective.

"We haven't analyzed all our numbers, but the first quarter was quite strong for the 'Tommy Hilfigers' who have gotten in the outlet business recently. Without a certain tenant [Geisler shies away from identifying the tenant but doesn't deny the tenant's initials are P-VH] that has been having troubles across the board—and if we pull those numbers out—the first quarter was up about 12 percent against last year."

Geisler suggests that the tenant he doesn't want to name could dramatically improve its sales by changing how it's presenting its product lines. He understands the closings will actually take place over three years, with no closings in HGI malls for at least two years. Turning to men's business at HGI centers, he states, "I don't have the analysis of the second quarter yet. But it's my perception, from what I've seen from the stores doing well, men are looking for newness and more fashion. They're tired of the same polo-shirt look. They're looking for fresh colors and styling."

Geisler states that homewear has been the top performer, "thanks to the cocooning influence. Women's wear continues to be the weakest category, although manufacturers tell me they're looking for a strong fall season." Commenting on the state of men's wear outlets at the Prime centers, Carpenter asserts, "Even in a traditional retail setting, the pure men's wear category is relatively small in the overall mix." But he points out that this slice of Prime's portfolio has been performing fairly well. "Through July, which was one of our bigger months, we were running about 7.6 percent ahead in the men's wear category over the same period and same store a year ago. However, from January through July, the stores were running about 2 percent below last year." Most retailers do the major portion of their business in the second half.

Carpenter is confident that with the kinds of sales trends happening and the amount of traffic shopping at Prime's centers, business may be solidly in the black by the end of the year. He adds, "That would be better than the women's popular-to-high-priced business throughout the country, not only in regular-priced stores, but also in the outlet side of the retail business." Why will men's wear beat the overall sales trend line? Carpenter credits the shift to corporate casual for boosting men's wear sales at outlet centers. He considers these stores the perfect environment for men to piece together new workday wardrobes. Prime Retail itself offers employees casual Fridays.

"I know when I'm out buying I'll think about our casual dress Fridays. The garment I'm looking for may not be a polo shirt, but it might be a casual/dress type of shirt. I'm looking at different things than I did a few years ago. And so are our employees," Carpenter explains.

He adds that his own search for more relaxed apparel that still fits into an office setting extends to shoes and accessories. "I'm looking for something between Dockers and Allen Edmonds." Men's wear retailers and manufacturers operating outlet stores—including Brooks Brothers, Polo/Ralph Lauren, J. Crew and Liz Claiborne with its Claiborne for men—refused to comment on trends in their outlet operations. But it's clear from current successes at outlet centers that Tommy Hilfiger or Bugle Boy labels will ride the dress-down trend more readily than a store showing suits.

Fleming at Factory contends he's "cautiously optimistic" approaching the holiday season. He suggests consumer optimism has already boosted big-ticket sales such as cars and houses. "Electronics sales have also been robust. Those categories may have lured dollars away from men's wear. But if consumer optimism remains strong, some money will likely shift back into soft goods as the Christmas season approaches.

"The summer itself was pretty good. We saw sales up 4 to 5 percent. Back-to-school, as best as I can tell, was a little disappointing. Sales were pretty flat. As for expectations for the fall, most folks think they can perhaps make up what they missed during the back-to-school season.

"We are fortunate in our portfolio in that for the most part we have anchored projects. We have some larger stores that have continued to do well, and they pulled along some of the other guys." Addressing one of the core problems facing all developers, Carpenter at Prime Retail mentions the problem of bringing men into outlet malls, especially those who avoid shopping whenever they can. Prime just opened the Arizona Factory Shops in New River, Ariz., its 16th venture, and the focus was to create attractions for men.

"Outlet shopping is a family affair," Carpenter indicates.

"We're looking for things men like to do. As a company we're putting in Black & Decker, Sony, Bose—some of the hard goods names men would be attracted to in addition to the men's wear shopping they may do. "We're installing putting greens. In San Marcos, Texas, we're adding a sports court where you can buy golf clubs, then go out and drive balls to try the clubs. We're exploring that as a venue to enhance the shopping trip.

"In our sports courts we're looking at building almost clubhouse-type places where men can sit down and watch sports on television. We're the only outlet mall developer who builds large food courts with 500 to 600 seats. "You don't necessarily want to put television sets in there because you need to turn tables over. But we're almost creating rest stops for the male consumer so he's not bored."

Especially those with an appetite for new sportswear.

Advertising, Special Events, Publicity, and Visual Merchandising

Capturing the attention of potential customers, whether individuals in the trade or household consumers is the responsibility of fashion promoters. The most beautifully designed and manufactured product is a success only if it finds a receptive audience. Promotional teams develop marketing strategies and events designed to motivate consumers to buy.

Everyone in fashion recognizes the importance of effective promotion. Designers, manufacturers, and retailers of fashion merchandise pay as much attention to promoting their products as they do to designing and merchandising them. Elaborate runway shows, video presentations, and multimedia advertising campaigns are just some of the methods that can be used to introduce new collections, seasons, styles, and designs to an eagerly awaiting audience. The cost of these promotional undertakings sometimes run into the millions. Calvin Klein, for example, spent forty million dollars to launch a new fragrance.

Many fashion organizations take a four-pronged approach to promotion: advertising, special events, publicity, and visual merchandising.

ADVERTISING

"That paid for form of nonpersonal presentation of the facts about goods, services, or ideas to a group" is the American Marketing Association's definition of **advertising.** It uses both broadcast and print media to get the message across. In the fashion industry, advertising sponsors include trade organizations, mills, designers, manufacturers, and retailers. Each sponsor attempts to address the target market for his or her products.

The development of a new yarn, the opening of a designer's collection, the introduction of an innovative fashion concept, or the personal appearance of a designer all require some form of promotion. Advertising is often the form cho-

---

After you have completed this chapter, you will be able to discuss:

- Some of the promotional methods used in the fashion industry.

- How manufacturers and retailers approach advertising.

- How designers, manufacturers, and retailers use consumer publications.

- The differences between promotional and institutional advertising.

- The benefits of cooperative advertising to the manufacturer and retailer.

- Five types of special events and how they help their sponsors.

- The differences between advertising and publicity.

- The role of the visual merchandiser in promoting fashion.

sen by the fashion industry. A timely, carefully crafted advertisement usually gets the message to the appropriate audience. Each company establishes an advertising budget and chooses the media best suited to its particular product. A new women's apparel manufacturer hoping to capture retail store buyers' attention would probably select *Women's Wear Daily* for advertising, a men's furnishings company would probably concentrate on *DNR* for its advertising to potential trade purchasers, and a retailer, hoping to capture a share of the market, would select the consumer newspaper that best typifies the market in which the store operates.

Eye-catching displays are a retailer's silent salesperson.

The responsibility for advertising varies from company to company. Those with significant sales volume usually have separate in-house advertising departments responsible for such activities as campaign preparation and production. Small companies may simply rely on agencies as the need arises. Others might assign the chore to a marketing executive who has numerous other tasks to perform. There is no industry norm. Each company meets its advertising needs in the manner that best suits its particular operation.

Fashion Advertisers

The industry is segmented into numerous parts. Each establishes its objectives and then attempts to gain the attention and respect of potential purchasers. The group to which each addresses its offering dictates the format and outlets to be used in advertising.

Designers

Many designers have advertising needs that are twofold in nature. One is to make the trade aware of their creations—that is, to capture the attention of the store buyers and merchandisers who make selections for their particular clienteles. The other is to reach the ultimate consumer. By informing the ultimate purchaser of their designs, they are attempting to presell their lines to those who will wear them. Thus, designers advertise in particular trade periodicals to motivate store buyers and in consumer magazines and on television to appeal to ultimate users.

In the era of licensing, many world-famous designers have their own promotional divisions that coordinate the advertising of all their licensed products. It is not unusual for a designer, such as Donna Karan, to have a ten-page spread in a fashion magazine featuring many of the products he or she makes available through licensing arrangements.

Manufacturers

The producers of fashion merchandise spend significant sums on advertising. Their targets are generally the retailers who are their potential customers. Advertising of this nature usually appears in trade papers and magazines or through direct marketing. Many manufacturers secure the names of potential accounts from marketing research organizations and then mail brochures, flyers, and videos that depict their offerings to them. Those with nationally recognized labels might take the same route as designers and place ads in consumer fashion magazines, such as *Harper's Bazaar, GQ, Elle, Ebony,* and *Glamour,* to keep their names in the public eye.

Retailers

The major share of the retailer's promotional budget is earmarked for advertising; the major portion of the advertising budget is spent on newspaper ads. A review of any newspaper will quickly underscore this medium's importance to the retailer. For comparatively little cost per reader, a store can quickly announce a sale, promote its image, notify customers of an impending promotion, or communicate any messages that might motivate customers to buy.

Many of the major retailers have large staffs that are responsible for advertising. Specialists in copy, artwork, production, layout, and research work together to produce the scores of advertisements that appear in newspapers. The giants in the industry have additional personnel who specialize in direct mail catalogs, television, and radio advertising. Many retailers have invested in computer hardware and desktop publishing software, so they can create their own catalogs. This has cut production expenses considerably in this area of advertising.

Preparing ads requires the skills of many individuals.

Many designers use trade advertising to reach their retailers. This ad from Eileen Fisher appeared in WWD.

Trade Associations

These groups or organizations use advertising to alert members to its special events. The National Retail Federation will use direct mail to notify members of meetings, the National Association of the Display Industry might use an ad in a trade publication to announce an industrial show, and the Larkin organization might use *Women's Wear Daily* to advertise its International Women's Boutique Show, a trade presentation. These organizations are only concerned with trade members and utilize the media most closely associated with the trade represented.

Media

Selecting the appropriate print and broadcast media in which to advertise requires careful assessment of the product and its target audience. While the newspaper wins hands down for retailers, many stores choose from a number of media to spend their advertising dollars. Each fashion advertiser must examine all of the choices within each medium before deciding where to advertise most effectively.

Newspapers

The newspaper allows an advertiser to reach most readers on a daily basis. It gets its point across quickly and efficiently. Retailers, to establish customer continuity, use newspapers as their chief means of communication. With very little notice, a store can quickly capitalize on an event. A sudden accumulation of snow, for example, might tempt the footwear buyer to do a spread on the latest styles in water-resistant boots. The **lead time** needed for magazines or television advertising eliminates them as a source of last-minute advertising.

Many fashion retailers develop a style or signature for their newspaper advertisements. A particular type of fashion illustration or photography might catch the reader's attention. If used regularly over a period of time, it could be a device customers will look for when reading the paper.

Trade associations advertise upcoming shows in trade journals.

Placement of ads also plays an important role for advertisers. Many papers charge additional money for locations the reader is more likely to see. For example, some companies have contracts with newspapers that reserve a **regular position** (that is, the same place in every issue) for their ads, so that their customers can quickly locate the ad. Others pay for **preferred position**, placement in a particular part of the paper. The least expensive placement is **run of press,** a term used to indicate placement wherever the publisher decides. It does not, however, offer the advantages of the other types of placement.

Although newspapers offer such advantages as diversified readership, low ad cost per reader, ease of acquisition, and leisurely reading, they also present some drawbacks to the advertiser. The life of the message is limited, only last-

"We were looking for a refrigerator."

"But I found something much cooler."

B.B. Dakota faux leather trench $29.99

Come see the softer side of **SEARS**

An eye-catching style or signature attracts consumer readership.

ing until the next issue is published. The poor quality of the paper stock does not provide for attractive reproduction, and color is sparsely used except in magazine supplements.

Magazines

Unlike newspapers, which cover relatively regional areas, magazines are excellent for national exposure. For that reason, most manufacturers and designers prefer them for their ads. In addition, the fashion industry has magazines in which offerings can be promoted. Some are trade publications such as *Style,* produced in New York, and *Gap,* published in France; these give producers exposure to wholesale purchasers. Designers, manufacturers, and retailers opt for national advertising in consumer-oriented magazines such as *Harper's Bazaar, Mademoiselle, Glamour, Vogue, Ebony,* and *Seventeen.*

The magazines offer the finest quality reproduction in both black and white and color, an audience that generally reaches from coast to coast, although regional editions are available, and a readership life that surpasses every other medium. Unlike newspapers, readers often keep magazines for extensive periods of time or pass them to others. The latter makes them even more valuable.

Some limitations on magazine ads are the high cost, geographically dispersed markets, and the long lead time necessary between preparation of the ad and its publication.

Direct Mail

One of the most effective methods of reaching a particular market segment is direct mail. Manufacturers often send press kits, brochures, or pamphlets that

Direct mail catalogs are reaching more and more consumers each year. They capture the reader's attention.

feature their newest offerings to their regular accounts or potential customers. Retailers are the primary users of direct mail. Whether it is catalogs that alert customers to the company's new merchandise or flyers inserted with end-of-the-month charge account statements, direct mail generally brings significant additional revenue to the retailer.

At one time, the dominant direct mail piece was the Christmas catalog. Today, however, large numbers of retailers accept orders by mail, and fax.

Some retailers are even offering merchandise in their catalogs that they do not stock in the stores. Victoria's Secret, for example, limits its store inventory to intimate apparel and some fragrances, but sells an abundance of sportswear in its catalog.

Unlike other ads, direct mail earmarked for a particular household or company receives the reader's undivided attention and can be examined at the reader's leisure. One important requirement of a good direct mail program is the updating of the mailing list. If customers have moved, or the list incorrectly states the address, the mailer serves no purpose.

Television and Radio

Although these media lend themselves to advertising such products as foods and automobiles, neither the garment industry nor retailers use them as advertising mainstays. Some companies have incorporated television in their promotional programs, but only to a limited extent.

The major exception is in the cosmetic and fragrance industry. Calvin Klein's many fragrances are marketed on television, as is White Diamonds, with the messages delivered by Elizabeth Taylor. The drama and sexual appeal of these products coupled with television's ability to create a mood, has resulted in increased sales.

One advantage of television is its ability to quickly expose vast numbers of people to a particular message. Some companies, however, find that the tremendous production costs and air-time expenses are too high for a message that disappears in a matter of seconds. To make the ad worthwhile, it must be shown many consecutive times.

Some retailers use limited amounts of television time. Because their trading areas are relatively small, they generally opt for **local spots**—ads that are aired only in specific geographical areas. This significantly reduces the cost of the commercial and delivers the message to those who are within reach of the store.

Because radio must rely solely on sound to capture an audience's attention, the fashion industry is not a big customer. In cases where a store wishes to announce a sale or publicize a special fashion event, radio is sometimes used.

Advertising Classifications

There are two distinct types of advertisements used to gain customer attention. Whether the ads are trade oriented and directed toward the industry or consumer based and focused on the ultimate consumer, the formats are either promotional or institutional. **Promotional advertising,** or product advertising as it is sometimes called, is used to sell specific items. **Institutional advertising,** on the other hand, directs its efforts toward projecting a particular image, achieving goodwill, or announcing special events.

(left) Retailers sometimes combine both promotional and institutional messages in one ad. (right) A product ad features one or more items the store needs to promote.

nm presents

stanley marcus,

in person

Meet our renowned chairman emeritus October 11 from 1 to 3 at NM Paramus as he signs copies of his latest book, *The Viewpoints of Stanley Marcus — A Ten-Year Perspective*.

Neiman Marcus

THE WESTCHESTER AT WHITE PLAINS NEW YORK 914 428-2000
THE MALL AT SHORT HILLS NEW JERSEY 201 912-0080
GARDEN STATE PLAZA PARAMUS 201 291-1920.
FOR STORE EVENTS CALL TOLL-FREE 1-888-NM EVENTS.

Institutional ads promote a store's image and goodwill or announces special events.

Fashion organizations often use both formats. A manufacturer might wish to alert store buyers to a particularly hot item and will focus advertisement specifically on that style. When the aim is to advance the company's image or reputation, the institutional approach is used.

Similarly, retailers may elect to sell specific goods or to improve their fashion images. If the former is the goal, a particular item or group of items is carefully presented. If image building is the objective, then attention might concentrate on the store's roster of designer resources, its commitment to service, or anything else that will present it in a good light.

Sometimes the advertiser uses a combination of both approaches. At Lord & Taylor, for example, ads very often call the customer's attention to its loyalty to American designers. In the same advertisement, the store features specific designs by these people. The emphasis on American designers is the institutional portion of the combination ad, with the specific styles the promotional portion.

Promotional or product advertising far outweighs the use of institutional advertising. Its positive effect can be quickly measured by increases in sales for the advertised items. Institutional results cannot be measured as scientifically or as quickly. Because the store's image is the focus of such ads, success can only be judged over a long period of time.

Cooperative Advertising

When two companies share the cost of an advertisement, they are participating in **cooperative advertising.** Fiber producers who wish to motivate a designer to use their fabric in apparel collections often provide promotional assistance to the designer for the product's advertisement. Retailers are often the recipients of advertising allowances when their ads feature a particular manufacturer. In both situations, the end results should be beneficial to both participants.

With the cost of advertising always increasing, businesses increasingly look to their suppliers for promotional dollars. The cooperative arrangement makes the cost of advertising a dual responsibility. Each party generally pays 50 percent of the cost, based upon a predetermined formula. For example, a manufacturer may establish that he or she will give a retailer an advertising allowance based upon up to ten percent of purchases. This allowance will then be used to cover one half of the cost of the ad.

In addition to producing an incentive to purchase from a particular resource, such cooperation also gives the user the potential for more advertising space than the company can afford on its own.

Advertising Agencies

Although many fashion organizations maintain their own advertising staffs, they often utilize the services of experts for special campaigns. They, along with those who do not have in-house staffs, may employ an **advertising agency** to handle their print and broadcast advertisements.

Advertising agencies employ professionals who are expert in every aspect of advertisement preparation and also have a complete understanding of the media. The agency receives a commission—usually 15 percent of the cost of the ad—from the media in which they place their clients' advertisements. For specialized services, agencies may charge their clients an additional fee.

Ad agencies use professionals to create eye-catching advertisements.

The choice of an agency depends on the needs of a client. Some agencies specialize in fashion layouts for manufacturers; others in retail-oriented work; and still others in only one medium. The user should carefully select the agency that best meets his or her needs.

SPECIAL EVENTS

To bring attention to the fashion organization, many schedule happenings—**special events** that are not typical day-to-day operations. Retailers, manufacturers, designers, trade associations, and mills each have many avenues for reaching both regular audiences and potential users of their products or services. These special events may be major attractions that cost significant amounts and last for several weeks, or they may be less costly one-day affairs. Fashion shows, celebrity appearances, theme parades, demonstrations, charitable celebrations, and special sales are just some of the events in which the fashion industry participates.

Fashion Shows

Few special presentations offer the drama and excitement of **fashion shows.** Whether the audience is composed of professional industrial purchasers or consumers, the live production seems to excite everyone. The fashion industry features shows that run the gamut, from the runway show to informal modeling.

Budgeting considerations, space, audience size, and purpose play a role in deciding the format of a fashion show. Once these factors have been addressed, the production will follow one of two forms.

The **runway show** is the most elaborate type of fashion show. These shows require music, either live or recorded, choreography, scripts, and models. **Informal modeling** is the second format used. As the name implies, models

The runway show is a major industry promotion used to generate excitement.

walk among customers showing off selected outfits. In store restaurants and beauty salons, models parade the latest fashions in the hope that consumers will be motivated to buy the merchandise.

At one time, formal productions were commonplace in the fashion industry. Fiber producers, such as Monsanto, staged elaborate productions that rivaled the most original theatrical events. Original musical scores, special choreography, creative stage sets, imaginative lighting, and scripted dialogue were used in these industrial extravaganzas. Professional actors, dancers, musicians, and models spent countless hours rehearsing for the big event. Today, however, this type of show has disappeared from the fashion scene. Although it did generate a great deal of excitement in the industry, the expense outweighed the benefits.

Many segments of the fashion industry use the fashion show as one of their special events. Some use their own premises for the event; others contract for grand ballrooms, restaurants, theaters, or other arenas. In addition to selecting the proper environment, care must be exercised in inviting the members of the audience. Fashion shows are usually sponsored by the fiber industry, garment manufacturers, retailers, trade associations, and trade expositions.

Fiber Industry

The runway show has replaced the earlier extravaganzas. Companies like DuPont, for example, rent auditoriums or other arenas for the presentation of fashions that utilize their fibers. Their Lycra® spandex show is a major event to which apparel designers are invited to inspect garments made from the fiber.

Garment Industry

Seasonal shows are the norm for the garment industry. During market week, in particular, the major garment producers kick off the season with a fashion show. Many designers regularly feature runway productions on their own premises or in rented spaces. These shows concentrate primarily on the merchandise, not on the scenic backdrops. Most often, the only prop is a back wall that features the designer's name or logo.

The runway is either cluttered with several models displaying a particular design group or has only one or two models at a time. Some productions use commentary, but the trend is to use printed programs to identify each style. In most shows, manufacturers carefully accessorize each garment with compatible shoes, hats, millinery, and jewelry.

A trend in the middle price range point is to have in-house fashion shows. Showrooms are now designed so that the selling may be transformed into open spaces that can be utilized for fashion shows. Liz Claiborne's men's wear showroom can quickly hide the partitions and racks that generally fill the room to make way for its runway presentations.

Many manufacturers of men's and women's apparel are choosing unusual, off-premises, centralized facilities to present their shows. The tents at Bryant Park in New York City have been the successful home of many runway shows for women's wear. Places such as Sony's sound stage have become a venue for featuring men's fashions.

Garment industry productions are directed toward two specific groups. One is the professional buyers and merchandisers, who actually purchase the garments for their stores. The other is the editorial press, whose positive comments in their columns and on the air can bring enormous attention to a line.

Trunk Shows

Many designer and upscale manufacturer's lines are promoted through **trunk shows,** which bring a designer's entire collection to a store for a day or two for customers to view. The designer or a company representative accompanies the collection to answer questions from consumers. Because stores rarely carry a vendor's entire line, it is an opportunity for customers to view an entire collection and special-order specific items. Sometimes, shoppers are able to have certain styles customized for their special needs. A color not usually offered, a longer length skirt, or a different trim might be made available. The St. John Knit stores' trunk shows offer customizing at no additional cost to customers.

Ads in the newspapers and direct mail brochures are used to notify potential attendees of such events.

Retailers

Many store organizations also use fashion shows to motivate customers. The shows might be regular features at the store's restaurant or special productions that highlight a particular manufacturer, designer, charitable event, or promotion.

A number of the retail operations jointly sponsor fashion shows with garment manufacturers. Generally, these are informal in-house runway shows that feature a particular company's collection. The production's costs are usu-

Trunk shows are used to show a designer's entire collection to interested consumers. Here Cynthia Rowley (center) is surrounded by her models and customers during a trunk show in her boutique in New York's Soho area.

ally divided between the store and the sponsoring vendor. In cases where the retailer is a significant client of the manufacturer, the designer may be on hand to attract more attention.

Shows of this nature usually take place in or near the selling area of the department that features the show's merchandise. In this way, at the event's conclusion, immediate sales might take place.

Trade Associations

Most of the fashion industry's components have a trade organization or association for its members. The Fashion Association (TFA), for example, is the publicity arm of the fashion industry. One of its main promotional events is a fashion show that tells the press and other industry participants of the season's newest directions. In hotels and convention centers, TFA presents other major shows. The fashion show format is also used by the Chambre Syndicale in Paris, which sponsors the couture and prêt shows in a centralized environment, and Hair America, the fashion branch of the National Hairdressers and Cosmetologists Association. The trade associations use the shows to make the press aware of their field's latest offerings and to enable their membership to view the fashion directions being taken by their colleagues.

Trade Expositions

Throughout the world, producers of fashion show their new collections to the retail market in large arenas. Such groups as SEHM, which features European men's wear in Paris, The Kid's Show, and NAMSB, which is the major trade show for American men's fashions, all participate in trade expositions. These informal shows are directed toward the press and the retail buyers. The merchandise is a representation of some of the lines featured at the trade show.

Resident Buying Offices

When buyers visit the garment center during market week, many first visit their resident buying office. These offices use fashion shows to make buyers aware of trends for the season. Buyers are given programs that list the names and addresses of the featured resources, so that the buyers can visit them to see entire collections.

Sally Jesse Raphael promotes a store event in a personal appearance.

Fashion Magazines

Some magazines sponsor shows for fiber producers, retailers, manufacturers, designers, and the press. One of their goals is to develop industry relationships that can result in the purchase of advertising space.

Personal Appearances

One of the surest ways to bring an audience to a store is to advertise a personal appearance by a celebrity. Each industry, including the fashion industry, has charismatic personalities whose very presence will guarantee large crowds. Whether it is Calvin Klein or Karl Lagerfeld promoting a fragrance, Betsey Johnson talking about her newest collection, or Anna Sui showing her latest line, the results are usually successful.

In addition to the celebrities associated with fashion, popular entertainers also draw crowds. Talk show host appearances, such as the one Sally Jesse Raphael made in connection with Macy's Flower Show, bring the people into the store. Although the customer's initial intention is to get a glimpse of the celebrity, the increased traffic usually translates into sales throughout the store.

Parades

The most famous of all retailer-sponsored parades is Macy's Thanksgiving Day Parade in New York City. Not only does it provide enjoyment for the people who line the parade route, it is enjoyed by people across the country on national television. The parade signifies the official opening of the Christmas shopping season. The parade has been so successful for Macy's that stores all across the nation now have parades in their own cities.

World of Fashion Profile features Macy's and its use of special events.

Demonstrations

Capturing the shopper's attention sometimes necessitates a **demonstration** of how a product may be used. The cosmetic industry often uses the demonstration technique to entice customers to purchase its products. Cosmetics manufacturers periodically send a cosmetologist to demonstrate proper use of their products on the faces of willing participants and to explain the procedures to the audience that has gathered. Not only does the participant generally buy some of the items, so do those who watch the demonstration.

Sampling

This type of promotion requires giving away products to prospective users. As with demonstrations, the cosmetics and fragrance manufacturers use this type of promotion most often. In the retail stores where their products are sold, the manufacturers provide sample items or kits that are given free with a purchase or provided at a minimal cost.

This practice is particularly prevalent from the period between Thanksgiving Day and Christmas, when the stores are the busiest. If the sample meets with positive results, the customer may be motivated to become a regular user of the item.

The Macy's Thanksgiving Day Parade is one of the store's major annual attractions.

Macy's

One of the reasons for the enormous interest in Macy's is the wealth of promotions it produces. As a leading world fashion retailer, its fashion shows range from introducing a new designer collection to charity benefits. The company, however, does not stop there. It is Macy's institutional promotional events that separates the store from most others.

By now, the Thanksgiving Day Parade is legendary. With helium-filled balloons floating toward the sky, the marching bands making their way through streets lined with thousands of spectators, the celebrities who are regular participants, and the ultimate arrival of Santa Claus, it is a sight for both the eyes and ears. The treat is extended to millions of television viewers all across America who faithfully watch the extravaganza each year. Produced by Macy's own Special Productions Department, which works an entire year on its preparation, the parade involves 3,000 employees, who volunteer to march as clowns, dancers, and balloon handlers.

Macy's Fourth of July Fireworks is another exciting event that is viewed by thousands of people from New York City's waterfront or on board local boats. Eleven thousand display shells and effects are exploded to create more than a million bursts of color and light, playing against a specifically written musical score. Like the parade, it is syndicated on television to 150 stations. This production brings Macy's a great deal of publicity.

For two weeks every spring, the Flower Show has become another Macy's tradition. Its Herald Square flagship main floor of 265,000 square feet is filled with the exotic plants. A major spectacle, it is planned more than one year in advance. Floral experts throughout the world collect their finest specimens for showing. As an additional feature, table settings designed and created by such celebrities as Liz Smith, Bernadette Peters, John Tesh, and Sally Jesse Raphael are displayed.

Tap-O-Mania is an event that grows in size every year. For one Sunday each August, a time when shoppers are not akin to enthusiastically filling the store, Macy's puts on the largest tap dancing festival in the world. Participants, with or without tapping experience, are invited to join in the fun. Each year, the event attracts more than 6,000 tap dancers, who perform in front of the flagship's entrance, attracting scores of shoppers. Unlike the other promotions, which cost large sums of money, this one is relatively inexpensive.

Through such unusual undertakings, Macy's has established itself as the country's premier retail promoter.

Premiums

Sometimes the fragrance and cosmetic vendors reward purchasers of their products with **premiums** that are free or comparatively inexpensive. The items include umbrellas, luggage, carrying cases, T-shirts, and other items that generally bear the vendor's name. In this way, the recipient will continue to publicize the vendor name whenever the premium is used.

Personal Improvement Sessions

Many fashion retail operations present seminars on personal grooming and proper dress. These events are usually held in a store's special events center or community room and features a fashion consultant who discusses the "do's and don'ts" of appropriate dress. What to wear to the office or to that special occasion is often the main topic. Preselected outfits are shown during the presentation in the hope that shoppers will decide to purchase them. Beauty experts who talk about everything from skin care to hairstyles are also featured. These talks and demonstrations turn lookers into purchasers.

PUBLICITY

The goal of any designer, retailer, manufacturer, or trade organization is to make itself known to its public. As we have learned, enormous sums are spent on advertising and promotional events to turn potential customers into real purchasers. Most major fashion organizations hope that these paid promotional activities will earn them additional recognition from the press. Such coverage is the most cherished form of promotion, free **publicity.**

Technically, the term free publicity is correct. The media prints or airs on radio or television, without cost to the company, newsworthy stories about a company's accomplishments. For example, the New York City tent shows provide an additional boost for those designers lucky enough to be singled out for their creations by a television show, a consumer newspaper, or a trade periodical. Sometimes, the publicity is negative. A glaring headline on the fashion pages might also spread information about a disappointing collection!

While the term free is used, such publicity usually results from a company's expenditure on a special event or promotion. A designer's expenses for producing a special fashion show could reach as much as $100,000. Thus, although the publicity is free, it comes as a result of a real dollar investment.

People who are responsible for liaising with the fashion press or media are known by a variety of titles such as publicists, public relations people, marketing specialists, promotion directors, and fashion directors. They, and their staffs, are responsible for exploring all possible avenues for publicizing their companies, but they generally use two major tools—press releases and press or media kits.

Press Releases

Most companies use **press releases** to communicate with the media about interesting fashion activities. The standard format is letter size paper bearing the company's logo, name, address, telephone and fax numbers, and the contact person for additional information. The first page indicates the date the company wants the information to be disseminated. Often the word "immediate" is used.

The text of the release should have a headline in bolder type than the body of the narrative. The information should be factual and free of the writer's opinion. It should also include enough information so that the newspaper, magazine, or broadcast media can utilize all of the piece or that part it finds most appropriate for its audience. Because copy writers carry a heavy workload, the press release can save a great deal of time.

If a photograph or drawing is appropriate for the release, it can be incorporated in the narrative or sent along as a separate piece to be used at the fashion editor's discretion.

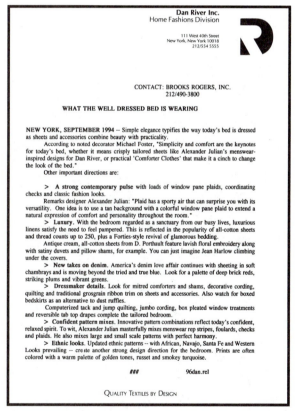

Press releases are excellent vehicles for communication in the fashion industry.

Press Kits

The major publicity tool a designer, manufacturer, retailer, or trade association uses is the **press** or **media kit.** Press kits are used to entice media coverage and alert the potential market to a special event or happening.

To attract the press to an opening of a designer's collections, in-house publicists or public relations specialists develop press kits and coordinate the activities that are necessary for its production. Included in the typical designer kit is a biographical sketch that emphasizes the designer's past achievements, a release highlighting the theme or emphasis of the collection, and photographs representative of the designer's latest efforts. Copywriters, photographers, artists, and graphic designers work together to make certain that the kit will motivate attendance and provide enough factual information to make the media's task easier.

Retailers use press kits to announce the opening of a new department or a new branch store, introduce a philosophical change in the company's direction, or publicize a special event or celebration.

When Macy's announces its many special events, such as its annual Flower Show, the Thanksgiving Day Parade, the Tap-o-mania promotion, or its fireworks display on the Fourth of July to the media, it does so with a press kit. Replete with photographs, statistical figures of the event, and written information, its purpose is to encourage favorable publicity.

Trade associations, such as TFA, the NRF, and NAMSB, need to inform their markets about special meetings or market openings. They too produce press kits in hopes of motivating the fashion media to cover their events.

Visual merchandising helps sell merchandise.

VISUAL MERCHANDISING

If a company's advertising and special events have been on target, potential customers should be motivated to examine the products available for sale. Upon arrival at a retail operation or a manufacturer's showroom, customers should be greeted with an environment carefully designed to further arouse their interest. Designed to capture on-premises attention, visual presentations enhance a company's selling and display areas by establishing a climate in which sales will be made. This is an integral part of the areas of promotion already explored.

While retailers play the dominant role in **visual merchandising,** manufacturers are also capitalizing on the favorable impressions made by visual presentations. Manufacturers of apparel, accessories, and home products carefully display their products in their showrooms in a manner that will immediately put the professional buyer in a positive shopping mood. Westpoint Stevens, in its 20,000 square foot showroom, features products in various room settings that express different lifestyles. Sheets and towels are no longer routinely stacked, but are displayed in bedrooms and bathrooms adorned with beds, furniture, and other attractive household accessories.

Interior displays show customers what the store is featuring.

The design and execution of visual presentations may be coordinated by full-time company teams headed by visual merchandising directors, many of whom carry the title of vice-president, an indication of the position's importance. The presentation can also be produced by consultants, who are paid by companies to design settings and execute display installations, and freelancers, who periodically install visual presentations.

In retailing, visual merchandising is generally broken down into two areas—windows and interiors.

Window Displays

The silent sellers for many retailers are the windows that line the streets and malls. In the downtown flagships, careful attention is paid to **window displays.** Usually changed once a week, the themes might include a holiday such as Christmas, a special salute to a designer's new collection, a specific sale period, the introduction of a store's new private label, or anything that might attract the attention of the passersby. These visual stories range from the unique, such as the animated presentations at Christmas time, to the traditional settings. Whatever the event or occasion, they must be executed with props and lighting that will enhance the display.

The major department stores plan their window presentations many months in advance. The visual merchandising director develops a *window*

Mannequins often generate interest for the merchandise they feature.

schedule which outlines, week by week, the window displays that will be executed. Stores such as Lord & Taylor, Neiman Marcus, Tiffany & Co., Henri Bendel, Bloomingdale's, and Marshall Field prepare these calendars for six-month periods and spend considerable sums that will hopefully generate in-store traffic.

Interior Displays

Inside the stores, visual merchandisers are regularly installing displays, and improving the general appearance of the store. With the enormous cost of retail rentals, many merchants are reducing the amount of space for formal windows. Particularly in malls, the windows are often merely glass fronts. In these cases, **interior displays** are given greater attention.

One of the trends in interiors is the elimination of props that depict particular seasons or holidays. For example, Gap merely changes its merchandise displays in the store, without using any holiday or seasonal symbols.

In meeting the challenge of visual presentation, both the participants, who engage in the actual installations, and company management that must approve the expenditures, must be fully versed in the company's policies and practices. Just as apparel designs must be based upon sound elements and principles of design, so must visual presentations.

Adel Rootstein

When Adel Rootstein mannequins appeared on the fashion scene, the world of visual merchandising was reshaped. Although display mannequins were readily available in a variety of materials and designs at a wide range of prices, none provided the uniqueness and quality of a Rootstein. It is not simply putting new makeup and a new wig on the same old form; her figures always reflect the changes that take place from one decade to another. The shapes of the bodies, the poses, and the facial expressions are details that reflect today's individuals.

The painstaking process begins with finding a real person from whom a model can be fashioned. Theatrical stars, celebrated personalities, beauty queens, internationally famous models, and anonymous people have all served as models for Rootstein mannequins. Next, a staff sculptor shapes a clay replica of the individual chosen. From the clay form, a mold is prepared from which forms are cast. Skin texture, color, makeup, and wigs are then fashioned to complete the mannequin. Although the company manufactures traditional as well as stylized models, the realistic form is the company's forté.

A visit to most mannequin showrooms reveals a series of unadorned forms available for purchase. Not so at Rootstein's. In keeping with its individuality, the company stages a new mannequin presentation twice a year in its showrooms. Each season's presentation is the equivalent of a new Broadway production. A theme is developed, a special costume collection is designed specifically for the mannequins, and the display is magnificently illuminated. It is visual merchandising at its best.

With more than 300 mannequins in its collection, this London-based company provides visual merchandisers all over the globe with a particular fashion image.

Elements of Visual Presentation

First and foremost, the merchandise must take center stage in any visual presentation. The excessive use of props may detract from the merchandise, making the displays less effective than originally intended. By carefully employing fixtures, props, mannequins, lighting, signage, materials, and color as enhancements of merchandise, the visual effort should be successful.

The choice of these enhancements must be left to the experts. Selecting the appropriate mannequins, for example, is a difficult decision. Not only must those in a position to purchase them have an understanding of the available varieties, but must also know which type best serves their specific needs. At the top of the mannequin field is Adel Rootstein, the London-based company that is the subject of a World of Fashion Profile.

Professional display houses offer visual merchandisers a wealth of **props.** Those with special talents also look to unusual places for their props. The "junkpile" often turns up interesting pieces that may be restored with some ingenuity and paint. Household items such as chairs and ladders, also make useful merchandise holders. A creative visual merchandiser can produce a display for a minimum of dollars.

Color is also important to the visual team. Without any additional expense, the use of the right colors in a presentation transforms the ordinary into a showstopper.

A knowledge of lighting is also necessary in order to maximize its benefits. Today's visual merchandiser has access to new forms of lighting, such as HID and halogen/quartz lights, in addition to traditional light sources. Few elements are as effective at quickly transforming unimaginative presentations into exciting ones as lighting.

Signs and **graphics** have also become more varied. They are available in a host of materials and are used to identify specific departments as well as describe the merchandise. One of the more exciting types is the backlit transparency, which incorporates light with the sign. It gives a three-dimensional effect and draws attention wherever it is used.

A great deal of signage is now produced in-house, with the aid of computer software. As a result, signage is available more quickly and less expensively than ever before.

Visual merchandising is not used merely to describe formal displays. The way in which merchandise is featured on the selling floor is equally important. Many retailers have created customer interest by the use of attractive visual merchandising. Crate & Barrel and Williams-Sonoma, both in the home products arena, use exciting visual presentation throughout their stores. By artistically arranging typical merchandise in an eye-appealing manner, they have increased their sales volume. Others, like The Disney Store, Aeropostale, and Warner Brothers, have also made enormous gains with imaginative visual presentations. It is that aspect of promotion that turns lookers into buyers.

Only when all of the components of a fashion promotion program are carefully executed will successful results be achieved. In this era of stiff competition, fashion organizations must pay as much attention to promotion as they do to product design and merchandising.

Chapter Highlights

- Fashion organizations of every type and size develop a variety of promotional programs to enhance their images and sell merchandise, including advertising, special events, publicity, and visual merchandising.

- Manufacturers, designers, trade organizations, and retailers use all of the media to advertise, with retailers making the newspaper its greatest tool.

- Special events are periodic presentations, such as fashion shows, personal appearances, demonstrations, premiums, and sampling.

- If a special event is enthusiastically received by the press, free publicity may be an eventual by-product.

- Visual merchandising chiefly is used by retailers to give their offerings more eye appeal and to motivate purchasing.

Important Fashion Terminology and Concepts

advertising	local spot advertisements	regular position
advertising agency	media kit	run-of-press
cooperative advertising	preferred position	runway show
demonstration	premium	signs
fashion shows	press kit	special events
graphics	press release	trunk show
institutional advertising	promotional advertising	visual merchandising
interior displays	props	window displays
lead time	publicity	

For Review

1. Describe the four components of fashion promotion.

2. How does advertising differ from publicity?

3. In what way does the fashion designer's advertisement differ from the fashion retailer's?

4. For what purpose do trade organizations participate in advertising campaigns?

5. Of all of the available media, which is most extensively used by fashion retailers and why is it their choice?

6. What advantages does the magazine afford the advertiser that the newspaper does not?

7. Why is direct mail such a positive force in advertising?

8. Differentiate between promotional and institutional advertising.

9. To which market is the manufacturer's fashion show directed?

10. Briefly describe the typical press kits created by fashion designers, retailers, and trade associations.

11. What is a trunk show?

12. Which fashion component makes the most use of visual merchandising?

Exercises and Projects

1. Contact a designer, manufacturer, or retailer and request a company press kit. From the materials obtained, prepare an oral report on the particular kit and use the elements as visual aids when presenting the information. If an overhead projector is available, use it to show the parts of the press kit.

2. Using fashion magazines as a resource, select one designer's clothing and prepare a press release for that designer's collection. Make sure that all of the essentials of a good press release, as discussed in the text, are utilized.

3. Make arrangements with a local store to use its merchandise for a school-sponsored fashion show. Small committees should be formed and given separate responsibilities for the show's production. One could work on coordination, another on publicity; another on music and commentary; and so on.

4. Visit a shopping mall to photograph five of their tenant's windows. Using the photos as visual aids, discuss the various elements that comprised each display.

The Case of the Cost-Free Advertising Campaign

Major manufacturers and retailers set aside large sums of money promoting their merchandise and their companies. They recognize the value of such investments and make certain that their budgets are sufficient to reach potential customers.

Barbara Simms fully understands the need for promotion. In college she learned all about the benefits, and she witnessed, firsthand, the returns realized from such activities when she worked for a major department store. The store, Atlees, Ltd., spent a great deal of money on advertising and extravagant special events. It reaped extra benefits from the publicity derived from the special presentations. The company not only invested heavily, but they had a large in-house staff that could create professional ads, build props, and create exciting promotional themes.

Recently, Barbara left Atlees, Ltd. and opened a small neighborhood fashion boutique. The initial costs of opening the shop were more than she anticipated and little was left for promotion. She would like to spend her limited resources wisely for a good advertisement and also present a cost-free special event that would make her trading area aware of her boutique. Her problem is how to coordinate an ad and special event without straining her budget.

Question

Describe a special event that would be virtually cost-free and an advertisement that would be inexpensive and compatible with the event.

point of view

Pacific Rim Ad Spending: Strong Growth Ahead

In 1986, J. Walter Thompson set out to introduce the concept of brands to China. JWT launched a major ad campaign promoting the International Wool Secretariat's three-spiral wool logo, one of the first international corporate symbols marketed to the Chinese people. The pitch was successful, alright. Within two years, the Wool-mark logo had higher recall than Coca-Cola, and all over China manufacturers began stamping the wool logo on everything—plastics, leather, even polyester.

"They didn't understand the meaning of the symbol obviously. But they knew it meant quality," laughs Grace Atkinson, JWT chairman of Greater China/Korea. "Before, people in China didn't even know what a brand was. They couldn't name a bar of soap. But once the big multinationals came in and talked about brands, the Chinese caught on quickly. They began to know Pierre Cardin and Yves Saint Laurent. Suddenly, labels and brands became very important to them."

From the bustling streets of Shanghai—where men often leave brand labels on the outside of their suits—to the sleepy tea-and-rice growing towns of rural China, consumers not only differentiate among brands these days, they demand them. When Westerners think about the potential of Asia, it's usually in boxcar numbers—the hundreds of millions of TVs and washing machines yet to be sold in countries like China. But the human face of Asia's modern assimilation is far more subtle. Thanks in large part to De Beers, for instance,

85% of Japanese brides now wear a diamond ring—a new expression of love in a culture accustomed to arranged marriages. In China, consumers are increasingly filling their tea cups with java, making Nescafé the No. 1 coffee brand. Perhaps the most improbable sign of change comes from Vietnam, where this week John Denver kicks off a concert tour, playing to crowds in the Hanoi Opera House.

For J. Walter Thompson, its long and continuous investment in the region has positioned it to cash in on that change. "Timing is absolutely critical," says Alan Fairnington, the president of JWT Asia Pacific, who oversees 43 offices in 24 cities. "We got into Korea too early and lost $3 million a year. At the same time, you can't afford to be late."

The timing seems just right for JWT these days. In 1993, JWT Asia Pacific accounted for 17% of the agency network's $876 million worldwide revenue. This year that contribution is expected to grow to 20%, with the region's offices boasting higher profit margins than their European counterparts. While other agencies like McCann-Erickson and Saatchi & Saatchi have individual market strongholds in Asia, JWT's offices rank among the top three in China, Hong Kong, Indonesia, Taiwan, Singapore, the Philippines, Pakistan, Vietnam and Sri Lanka. In the semi-closed markets of Japan and South Korea, Thompson is listed among the top three foreign agencies as well. JWT once was the biggest agency in Australia and New Zealand, where it set up shop in 1929 to service General Motors. It

had slipped badly in recent years, but under Peter Steigrad's new leadership, the offices have moved back up, from 12th place to seventh in the market.

"Consistency has been absolutely critical to our success," says Fairnington, a 46-year-old Brit who first arrived in the region in 1980 to take over JWT's Malaysia office. "As clients move more toward global advertising, they want to feel as if they're dealing with the same agency around the world. We either own or operate all of our offices here. With affiliates, clients complain, 'They don't speak my language, they don't understand my brand.' We realized that in the early '80s and set out to make JWT the best agency in every market."

Fairnington certainly knows his way around the diverse parts of the Pacific Rim. Last year he spent 230 days out of his Hong Kong headquarters, tending to clients that range from such glittering names as De Beers to the mundane likes of Lux soap. The peripatetic pace helped JWT add $178 million to its Asia Pacific billings last year, a gain of 26%. And 1994 is off to a strong start. Among JWT's wins this year are the national airlines in Philippines and Sri Lanka, San Miguel beer in Hong Kong and Foster's breweries in China.

"This area is extremely critical to us and to our clients," says Peter Schweitzer, president/chief operating officer JWT Worldwide. "It's the fastest-growing region, and the pace of change in many countries is unbelievable. It's like where the pioneers in our industry were at the turn of the century."

If Asia has become synonymous with marketing opportunity, the reality of implementing those efforts are far more complex in a region with the world's richest countries and its poorest. JWT divides it into four levels of consumer development: affluent markets (Japan, Hong Kong and Singapore); growth markets (Taiwan and South Korea); emerging markets (Thailand, Malaysia, Philippines, Indonesia) and untapped markets (China, India, Vietnam).

The more mature, affluent economies, with wealthy and well-educated consumers, are similar to those in the U.S., with their taste for Western goods and quality products. The "growth markets" of Taiwan and South Korea are spawning a middle class hungry for household items and leisure-time diversions; by the end of the decade, some 20–30% of their households should have incomes of more than US$30,000. Emerging countries still are held back by low spending power, but promise a significant future: They have large youth populations that are rapidly changing consumption behavior. (By the year 2000, the Asia/Pacific region will gain 80 million consumers aged 29–39, while the U.S. and Europe will show declines in that demographic.) The most long-term prospects are the giant landscapes of China and India, with hundreds of millions of poor, uneducated consumers—most of them aspiring to emulate their neighbors.

The range of markets and needs in Asia has long attracted JWT clients like Unilever and Nestlé, which can sell their packaged goods and consumer staples across most countries and classes. They have been followed by other multinationals on JWT's roster, such as Ford, Kodak and Citibank, who are offering more sophisticated products or services. JWT now has the region's largest direct marketing operation, for instance, driven by Citibank's plunge into credit cards, retail banking and financial services. JWT also handles some of the region's largest local advertisers, like Hong Kong Telecom, Singapore Telecom and the Australian Travel Commission.

Perhaps most surprising is the marketing prowess of De Beers, which has become JWT Asia Pacific's third-largest client. JWT, which claims to have created the "engagement ring" concept for De Beers in Japan, says Asia now accounts for six of the 10 biggest markets for diamonds. The agency is even working for De Beers in China and Vietnam.

"Asia Pacific has become the most important part of the world for De Beers," says Marc Capra, JWT vp/De Beers regional account director in Hong Kong. "The potential out here is incredible, especially since ownership is still low. You have fantastic cultures with a history of jewelry, places like Indonesia and Thailand. There are such young populations out here and, of course, status symbols are very important to people with new money."

In fact, De Beers has developed market strategies unique to the region. The South African mining consortium has targeted young Asian women with a pitch for jewelry made from lower-grade diamonds. Women are responding, not only as a way to flash their new financial status, but also as a sign of modernity. (Their mothers wore only gold.) In a mature market like Japan, JWT's ads encourage women to buy diamonds for themselves, as a sign of their increased self-confidence and importance in society. In China, De Beers' ads simply teach them about diamonds as an enduring symbol of marriage. One spot shows a couple, from childhood through teenage years to their wedding, graduating from flowers to a diamond ring as a gift.

"In the Asia Pacific area, there's a great preoccupation with luxury brands and logos in general, says JWT evp/worldwide new business director Brian Johnson. "People see it as a fast badge of success. There's a good market there for Rolex, cognacs, fine liquors." A recent study of Chinese consumers found that Rolex was the most recognized brand of watch—even though Rolex does not advertise in China.

No country in the region captures marketers' imagination like China, with its 1.2 billion consumers and their pent-up demands. The Mao suit is being replaced by Dior; "to be rich is glorious," as chairman Deng Xiaoping recently crowed. "Assimilation in China has accelerated unbelievably," notes Atkinson, whose family fled the mainland in 1948 for Hong Kong; she returned after growing up in the U.S. and joining Thompson in the mid-'70s. "There is a lot of product leapfrogging. You have a country of no phones going to cellular; a country with no typewriters moving straight to computers. People have gone from washing their hair with a bar of soap to using four-in-one shampoo/conditioning products."

The standard Western impression of China is fading, she says, as its economy gains strength. "The masses in China are not so poor. Housing, medical care, food, even personal care products are provided by employers, so a lot of people are saving 30–50% of their salaries, which are rising. Some people even save 60%."

For marketers, tapping into that buying power isn't limited to new products or constricted by existing rivals. "In the West it could take years for a company to establish a shampoo brand, but in Asia it can take off right away," says Johnson.

With huge populations like those on offer in China and India, it's easy to see how sales can expand dramatically. The share potential is staggering. Consider telephones: Only 1–2% of Chinese households have one currently. Hooking up just another 1–2% of the country adds 12 million new phones. Even ordinary retail statistics take on larger-than-life dimensions. On an average weekday in Shanghai, 400,000 people visit its First Department Store.

The power of such numbers is magnified by the region's Confucian ideals, which value hard work, savings and reputation. " 'Face' is an important concept over here. You should always look respectful, good, rich" says Sattar Khan, a JWT regional client account director in Singapore.

JWT client Warner Lambert, for instance, wouldn't sell Asians much Listerine if the marketer told them outright that mouthwash was good for them. Instead, Listerine woos them with promises of confidence and social poise.

Khan, who was head of JWT Asia/Pacific's strategic planning in 1990–91, says that while some traditions remain, many past impediments to commercial change are gone. "Religion used to be a barrier. But money has transcended religion." And unlike Europe, Asia's political ideologies seem not to get in the way of productivity and entrepreneurship. "The difference between Asia and Eastern Europe is that Eastern Europe has some fundamental economic problems as those countries move from communism to capitalism," says JWT new business exec Johnson. "Consider the hold of Stalinism in Europe and the number of years people have lived with cradle-to-grave support from the state. Despite its politics, the Asia Pacific region has always had a fierce capitalistic work ethic.

There's more of a tradition of hard work, aggressiveness and affluence."

Not that politics is an inconsequential factor for multinationals doing business in Asia. The Chinese government's crackdown after the Tiananmen Square protests scared off many marketers in 1989. The current specter of North Korea's arms buildup also serves as a sober reminder of regional tensions. No one knows fully what to expect when Hong Kong, the region's banking and trading center, is absorbed into mainland China in 1997.

Even some of the region's biggest boosters are cautious in their predictions. "If political systems don't evolve fast enough to keep up with economic progress, things could get out of balance and you might see political leaders pull back," says Atkinson.

The 52-year-old Shanghai native has bridged JWT's two worlds in the region. She lived in the U.S. for 20 years, earning her college degree and becoming fluent in Western culture. And she has spent 18 years working for JWT Asia Pacific, establishing regional offices in countries like Indonesia. Her current office in Hong Kong is designed according to the Chinese practice of *fung shui,* which holds that certain objects and their positioning in interiors can ward off misfortune. JWT has a *fung shui* expert on retainer; he visits Atkinson's office three or four times a year and is consulted before important presentations. (A lute placed in her office is meant to bring harmony and serenity; frogs on her window sill are to "help capture money from the sea.")

Such traditional customs are married to Western-style business practices. Under Fairnington, who became JWT's area director for South and East Asia in 1988 and assumed responsibility for the

entire region four years later, the agency has prospered, becoming the fastest-growing part of the agency network. Since 1988, JWT Asia Pacific billings have increased 130%, or 15% on an annualized basis, compared to the 4.5% annual gain eked out by the company's U.S. operations. Billings jumped from $370 million in 1988 to $873 million in 1993, and the upward trend shows no sign of slowing.

"The success and principles of JWT in this part of the world are largely driven by Alan," says Peter Steigrad, JWT area director of Australia and New Zealand. Fairnington, who first worked for JWT in Toronto, made the Malaysia office No. 1 in its market in three years, then built up JWT's newly-acquired Hong Kong shop into the leading firm there. He also established JWT divisions in China and Taiwan before taking on the top regional posts.

Along the way, Fairnington stressed the importance of having up-to-date practices and production values in place. "JWT has really distinguished itself with its media expertise here," says Atkinson. "Early on Alan saw that media could give us a cutting edge. We've established media systems that do post-buy analysis."

Even without such elaborate research data bases, agency investment in the region can be considerable. In densely populated Hong Kong, for instance, commercial rents for a modest office can run up to $25,000 a month. Poor countries like Vietnam, where America's trade embargo was just lifted last year, can nonetheless come at a stiff price because of the lack of commercial infrastructure.

In addition, the cost of recruiting management talent in the Asia Pacific, both locals and ex-pats, is high. JWT has one of the most rigorous training programs in the region, which has yielded good results. The majority of senior staff were developed within the agency, and only two of its offices have foreign managers. "Executive costs can be so expensive here," says Fairnington. "It pays to get a good local manager."

That extensive local know-how has paid off in dealing with government red tape associated with restrictions that limit foreign business ownership. JWT is one of the few international agencies to have wholly-owned offices in Korea and Japan, where its 38-year-old office was started before ownership limitations were implemented. In countries like Indonesia, where foreign companies aren't allowed to have equity in local concerns, JWT has resorted to some novel business practices. The agency operates an Indonesian-owned firm, called Ad Force, as a JWT office and pays the local owner 2.5% of income.

Local governments have also gotten in the way of regional media development. But that bureaucrat's stranglehold on broadcast outlets is coming to an end. "Media in Asia is changing faster than anywhere else in the world. "It's the last frontier," says Sue Johns, JWT's executive media director for Hong Kong and China. "We're seeing the free-up of government control. Cable is making inroads. When everything was government owned, it was a seller's market, and you couldn't get into quality programming."

In some cases, JWT clients—which in countries like China are the biggest purchaser of airtime—couldn't get into any programs, quality or otherwise. "These governments didn't care about profit and loss and rates were kept artificially low," says Fairnington. "In places like Korea, the government charges the same rate for 4 p.m. as they did for 8 p.m. It was so hard to get time because anyone could get

on the air. You'd be competing with the local shopkeeper for time."

With Rupert Murdoch's takeover and expansion of Star TV, the startup of dozens of private TV channels in Asia, and the birth of a professional cable industry, media opportunities are opening up to meet advertiser demand. Agencies like JWT can leverage their clients' considerable media clout, although measurement remains a problem in several countries. "We have good quantitative research, we have people meters," says Johns. "It's the qualitative research that's lacking."

That will surely come, as a consumer consciousness takes hold, reinforced by modern programming and advertising. "Countries like China have gone too far down the road," says Atkinson. "People have had a taste of spending money and making their own choices. There's no turning back."

ADWeek, May 2, 1994.

Stepping Out

Rosemary Feitelberg

Apparel, fragrance and cosmetic companies are storming the streets with ads on buses, billboards and telephone kiosks.

"Fashion as a category has never been more bold. The format is, 'Hey guys, here it is—look at this,' " said Chris Carr, vice president of the Gannett Outdoor Group. "How else can companies make a seasonal statement overnight and get the message out to everybody?"

For 1995, Gannett expects outdoor advertising sales for fashion,

fragrance and cosmetic companies to grow 20 percent over last year, according to Carr.

At TDI, meanwhile, second-half bookings for outdoor advertising for fashion are running 10 percent ahead of last year's $14 million business. And additional growth is expected, according to Jodi Yegelwel, senior vice president of TDI, the largest diversified out-of-home media company in the U.S.

"There was a time when out-of-home advertising was made for

tobacco and liquor companies," she said. "Now the fashion industry is putting excellent, creative magazine-type advertising on the streets. The perception of the medium is turning around."

Men's and women's products each account for 30 percent of the category, and generic campaigns such as those for CK One, Banana Republic and Champion comprise the remaining 40 percent, she said.

Yegelwel pointed to Calvin Klein's underwear ads featuring

Christy Turlington, DKNY's Hollywood campaign and Banana Republic's skin care shot as lasting images in advertising.

The Gap, Barneys and Daffy's have also waged eye-catching campaigns, she said.

Gannett's Carr cited ads for Nike, Levi's for Women and CK One as some of the most effective campaigns on the street.

With Nike, Reebok, and Gilda Marx already in the outdoor advertising game, the category should be the most competitive in the months ahead, he said. The interest in activewear has triggered some beverage makers such as Evian to advertise outdoors, Carr noted. The market for watchmakers is also opening up, he said.

According to Yegelwel, in recent years retailers have entered the outdoor market somewhat cautiously. While Barneys, Banana Republic, Brooks Bros., Coach, Daffy's and The Gap are now squaring off in the streets, the category should become more important in the years ahead, she said, adding that cosmetic makers should also tap into the outdoor market.

Fragrance ads, which accounted for about $1.5 million of TDI's overall volume, have become a hot category, Yegelwel noted. In the last year, Tommy Hilfiger, Calvin Klein and Ralph Lauren have introduced ads for their scents.

"First they put all their efforts behind the core of their business. Now they're having so much success with their apparel that they're looking to invest in their fragrances," she said. "If you really like a restaurant for dinner, you might give it a shot for lunch."

The focus of outdoor advertising has shifted from billboards to buses because they penetrate urban centers from shopping districts to upscale residential areas, Yegelwel noted.

"With buses, advertisers are able to reach people who are too busy to read a magazine," she explained. "Buses are a quick read and they should be visually pleasing. They're very different from a magazine ad that allows you to hold the impression eight inches away from your face to really examine it."

Women's Wear Daily, June 1995.

You Oughta Be In Pictures

Merle Ginsberg and Lisa Lockwood

Remember when all any big model *really* aspired to was a serious acting career? For Andie MacDowell, Renee Russo, Isabella Rossellini and Geena Davis, it worked out. For Cindy Crawford, it hasn't been so easy. But Cindy may be luckier than she realizes, because it seems as if every star in Hollywood wants to follow her into modeling.

Suddenly dozens of actors and actresses, from ingenues to Oscar nominees, are angling for and appearing in major fashion and beauty ad campaigns, in print and television. Fashion is hotter in Hollywood at the moment than Tom Hanks, tornadoes or drag queens. And that isn't all-Hollywood habitués are so anxious to be associated with the New York Fashion Flock, they've moved from comfortable front-row seats at shows to actually walking the runways.

Fashion designers have always been smitten by Hollywood, by movie stars, by directors, by the international exposure afforded by the Oscars. But it wasn't long ago that advertising of any kind was considered "beneath" most stars. Their agent warned that if they were too conspicuous in commercials or print ads, audiences wouldn't pay to see them on the big screen. Hollywood logic has it that Cher stopped being a movie draw when her infomercial came directly into bedrooms night after night. And the stigma of "selling out" was always attached to advertising and commercials.

But along came the supermodels. They got the press, the glamour, the cachet, the boyfriends, the exposure, the lifestyle and, in some cases, the money that movie stars are used to. Designers like Karl Lagerfeld and Isaac Mizrahi announced that Linda, Claudia, Cindy and Naomi were much more glamorous than the current crop of screen sirens, who were making the scene in ponytails, flowered dresses and combat boots.

And with the supermodels came the glamorization of the fashion industry-through mediums like MTV, VH1, "Entertainment Tonight" and "Extra." Fashion magazines are doing more commentaries than ever on the way celebrities dress, while entertainment magazines are now doing fashion spreads and stories on designers and models.

"Everything's cyclical," claims Cari Ross, vice president of publicity for Susan Geller & Associates, which represents Anjelica Huston, Meg Ryan, Claire Danes and Fran Drescher, among others. "There used to be a big music crossover with Hollywood. Now it's fashion. Next year, it will be something else. I think it had a lot to do with Isaac [Mizrahi] doing a movie—a really good movie—and the attention all those Calvin Klein ads have gotten. Stars want to horn in on the cultural trends."

A lot of stars. Melanie Griffith and Halle Berry are doing Revlon; Elizabeth Hurley is the Estée Lauder woman; Gabriel Byrne was featured in a Donna Karan campaign; Tim Roth is in Prada's ads; Juliette Lewis did a commercial for Guess; Drescher and Tina Turner are in Hanes campaigns; Antonio Sabado Jr. just stripped down to Calvin Klein skivvies; Juliette Binoche is the Lancôme face; Madonna did a Versace campaign; Natalie Portman has appeared in Mizrahi's ads for Isaac, and Diane Lane will be in the fall Isaac campaign. Elisabeth Shue is in the current Gap campaign, Chloe Sevigny and Drew Barrymore appeared in Miu Miu ads, and Claire Danes and Molly Ringwald modeled in Cynthia Rowley's show.

Meanwhile, the grandmother of all the new pitch people, Elizabeth Taylor, has been starring in her own ads since she got into the fragrance business. Prada has just announced that it will feature Willem Dafoe in its fall men's ad campaign to be shot by Glen Luchford, and Versace has nabbed big daddy Carlos Leon—whose sole claim to celebrityhood is that he fathered Madonna's child—

for a new campaign to be photographed by Bruce Weber. But the big clincher came this spring with the news that two of Hollywood's biggest stars, Demi Moore and Bruce Willis, will be the only models in Donna Karan's fall collection print campaign, which will be done by Peter Lindbergh.

Even the children of celebrities are getting into the act. In a fall campaign for Tommy Jeans, Tommy Hilfiger will feature the progeny of the famous, including Ivanka Trump and Kidada Jones (daughter of Quincy Jones), Balthazar Getty, Kimberly Stewart (daughter of Rod and Alana) and Mark Ronson (Mick Jones' son). Meanwhile, Sofia Coppola, Donovan Leitch and Zoe Cassavetes have already appeared in a number of fashion ads and shows.

While Hollywood's fascination with fashion is a relatively new phenomenon, fashion's fascination with Hollywood isn't. Back in the Thirties and Forties, stars were routinely featured in all sorts of ads, among them campaigns for clothes, cold creams, perfumes and cigarettes. The idea of stars wearing fashion has gone in and out of vogue as much as the stars themselves have. In 1968, Blackglama launched its "What Becomes a Legend Most?" campaign, which spotlighted Bette Davis, Lauren Bacall, Barbra Streisand, Judy Garland and Melina Mercouri. Scores of stars went on to be photographed in Blackglama mink coats.

The incentive for those stars was a mink coat; today's celebrities have their own reasons for "selling out."

"Initially, I think actors think it's money for old rope [easy money] to get an advertising/beauty contract," says Elizabeth Hurley. "It sounds easier than making movies or performing in a play. Actually, it's incredibly difficult to concentrate for long periods of time on a still image and it is exhausting—quite as

much as filming. But for me, it seems to have been a good career move: It ups your visibility, which makes you more marketable. So far, so good."

"It's a way of [getting] exposure without telling your life story to a reporter all over again," says Liz Rosenberg, spokeswoman for Madonna. "Fashion people are rock stars now; they've become big celebrities, and now they're all in the same club. Doing ads doesn't have the same stigma it once had.

"When Versace approached Madonna," Rosenberg continues, "she was advised it might be tacky to do the ads. But all the feedback we've gotten is how beautiful she looked. If it's a clever ad with a great photographer, why not? Basketball stars do very hip commercials and ads. You can have control over an ad shoot, but not an editorial one, and that's what artists want. Plus, five or 10 photos in the major magazines is always good—Warner Bros. Records is never going to take out an ad campaign that big. For the right product, it can enhance your image."

Many in Hollywood concur that the real fashion/film crossover kicked in several years ago when Giorgio Armani began to woo stars to wear his clothes to the Oscars and other high-profile events.

"His aggressiveness in the marketplace convinced the other designers to go for it," says one top Hollywood public relations executive.

Versace and Valentino followed, and, for this year's Oscars, Calvin Klein, Isaac Mizrahi, Badgley Mischka, Donna Karan, Ralph Lauren, Dolce & Gabbana, Richard Tyler, Escada, and Pamela Barish all courted the nominees by hiring public relations reps to go get 'em and dress 'em. Word has it Gucci and Prada are also planning to hire "star coordinators" for their West Coast offices.

And some of the stars still need all the help they can get.

"Just because they're actors doesn't mean they know how to dress," says Cari Ross. "Claire Danes decided to do Cynthia Rowley's runway show because she just loves her clothes—and if you have to look good all the time, it's easier to do with a designer in your corner. Fran Drescher's a different case; she really knows her own look and doesn't need help. She did the Hanes ads because they paid her a lot of money. But if the campaign wasn't classy, if the concept wasn't cool—we would have told her not to do it."

According to Anne Jardine, vice president of marketing at Hanes, "Fran was perfect. She has such humor; that was great for Smooth Illusions. We had good increases in sales when she appeared."

"Remember, it's not a one-way street," says Pamela Barish, who has dressed many a Hollywood star. "Yes, designers get exposure—but actors get a glamorous image and free clothes. We enhance their image. It's a fair exchange."

But stars do bring something to fashion photography that models don't—the memory the audience has of them from the big—or little—screen. "Actors bring so much, they add a narrative from their collective movie images," says Miuccia Prada. "They add character to the clothes, and an intensity. I chose people who are not mainstream, people with edge, whose work I admire—it's a very personal choice. And the consumer always has a strong opinion about the actor. Plus, I don't think men buying clothes relate at all to male models."

Star photographers, who often shoot celebrities for editorial pages, have certainly helped seduce the stars into advertising. Greg Gorman, for example, started shooting the LA Eyeworks campaign with the tag line, "A face is like a work of art: It needs a great frame," in 1982. Since then, he has photographed Drew Barrymore, Sharon Stone, James Woods, Melissa Etheridge, Ian McKellen and many others. "One day, Raquel Welch called up and said she loved the campaign," says Ruth Handel, LA Eyeworks' director of advertising. "About an hour later, she was over at Greg's studio shooting the next one." Another star photographer, Matthew Rolston, helped enlist Ashley Judd and Vanessa Williams in a new campaign for Carmen Marc Valvo.

After all, major photographers such as Rolston, Lindbergh, Weber, Ellen von Unwerth, Mario Testino and David Sims make far more money on advertising than on editorial shoots, and ads can often be equally as arty. The stars, for their part, seem to enjoy hanging out with photographers.

But the photo studio isn't the only place to get a taste of the fashion life. Some actresses have headed straight for the runway. Nicole Miller used eight young actresses, Gina Gershon, Maxine Bahns, Rachel York and Rebecca Gayheart among them in her spring '95 show. Even Miller was surprised by the results.

"I did it to just have fresh faces, but the actresses really added a human element: They weren't perfect, they don't walk perfectly, and it's less intimidating to real women," Miller says. "And, boy, did the press snowball—the actress element outshined the clothes."

Designers' relationships with stars are also getting increasingly more intimate. Calvin Klein nearly landed Gwyneth Paltrow, who has been wearing him exclusively and ubiquitously, to do his fall ad campaign—until she got a movie that filled her schedule. Ralph Lauren has been dressing Julia Ormond for every occasion, and brought her along to last year's "Seventh on Sale" in New York. More recently, she presented him with a CFDA award—wearing his dress, of course.

Donna Karan landed Demi Moore because the two became friendly through their association with spiritual leader Deepak Chopra. "They share a Deepakian sensibility," says Demi's production partner Suzanne Todd. "That's a big bond. There were no agents involved with the decision—Donna and Demi agreed over it personally. Donna created a cold-shoulder dress for one of Demi's dolls in her collection years ago, and they've been friends ever since."

And for Moore, the highest-paid woman in Hollywood, it is yet another form of self-expression.

"She's into all kinds of formations of beauty," says Todd. "Dolls, sculptures, even the human form she's showed on *Vanity Fair*. A Peter Lindbergh fashion photograph is an art form she gets to be part of. Modeling is a chance for actresses to wear beautiful clothing and just emote glamour."

Many companies report that an association with a celebrity has not only heightened awareness of their brand, but had a positive effect on sales.

Elizabeth Hurley has been doing wonderfully for us," says Leonard Lauder, chairman of Estée Lauder. "It was a good decision, and the easiest one we ever made. We were looking for someone who was beyond being a supermodel. She's been very effective for us and has subtly repositioned the company for the 21st century. It's made the company more youthful. Everyone identifies Estée Lauder as a classic beauty; [Hurley] is a contemporary beauty." Lauder called Hurley's contract "an evergreen."

Of course, there can be a downside to linking a well-known face with a company, especially when the star—or his or her significant other—runs into trouble, as stars are wont to do.

For example, last year, when Hurley's boyfriend, Hugh Grant, was arrested with a prostitute, it put Hurley smack in the limelight. "It's one of the risks that you take," says Lauder. "If Christy Turlington's boyfriend got into the same kind of trouble, she'd be on the front page, too."

Another Lauder division, MAC Cosmetics, has RuPaul and k.d. lang as spokespeople. RuPaul appears in the ads, but Lang will only be a spokeswoman.

Kathy Dwyer, president of Revlon Cosmetics USA, says the company added Melanie Griffith and Halle Berry as spokespeople for the brand [which already featured Cindy Crawford, Claudia Schiffer and Daisy Fuentes] because "we select women who have a recognizable accomplishment in what they do."

When Griffith started appearing in Revlon's Age-Defying makeup ads in 1994, "it was a major breakthrough, and we became the number-one brand in eight months," said Dwyer. Griffith is now in her third year of an exclusive multiyear contract. Dwyer recalled that, when Revlon started looking for a new face in 1993, it considered a lot of people. "We found people could relate to [Griffith] and like seeing women who are real, and who have overcome difficult things that have happened to them."

When Donna Karan started advertising her collection 10 years ago, she used one model, Rosemary McGrotha, to embody the Donna Karan woman. Since then, the campaign has evolved to include all types of women, including some well-known and not-so-well-known faces.

"To me, it's not even celebrities, it's just finding interesting people," says Trey Laird, senior vice president of creative services and advertising at Donna Karan Co. "We've used people who are really famous, such as Demi Moore and Bruce Willis and Diana Ross, but we've also used Francesco Clemente and Anouk Aimee. It's more than the appeal of their style.

"We sit down and brainstorm. Donna will have her friends, and we'll speak to agents. We have specific people in mind. For example, we chose Gabriel Byrne because Donna had just seen The Usual Suspects, and Donna loved the way he looked. When we used Fred Ward, he had such an emotion that came through. But for other campaigns, models are perfect."

"We don't have written rules, but we will use celebrities when there's an exceptional character," says Paul Marciano, president of Guess? "It worked with Tom Skerritt. It was the best thing for the men's campaign. I saw him in Top Gun, and we used him for several seasons. It helped his career, too.

"In women's, we never used a celebrity until we hired [photographer] Wayne Maser, and then he chose Drew Barrymore. She did two major campaigns, and after that got four movies in a row. Drew was extremely good, and we got a good response. It was very unusual. She has such an amazing presence, and the camera really captures her."

Earlier this year, Guess ran a commercial called "Cheat" that starred Traci Lords, Juliette Lewis, Peter Horton and Harry Dean Stanton. "Juliette just thought it was cool," says her spokesperson, Paul Block of Rogers & Cowan.

The key to a successful association, says observers, is the comparability of the celebrity and prod-

uct. Take the upcoming Tina Turner campaign for Hanes.

"It's all about her legs. In a national survey, she came up as the number-one pair of legs people aspire to," says Peter Arnell, chairman of the Arnell Group, which created the Hanes campaign.

"Fashion advertising lends itself naturally to great promotion in a stylized way for these celebrities. It's a terrific association for them," says Arnell. Turner will appear in TV, print and outdoor ads shot by Lindbergh.

Some modeling agencies, such as Elite and Ford, have even set up separate divisions to handle celebrities. Elite Celebrities represents for commercial work such stars as Drew Barrymore, Brooke Shields, Eric Roberts, Shannen Doherty and Natasha Kinski. Ford has Ali MacGraw, Faye Dunaway, Twiggy, Betty Buckley, Sela Ward, Shari Belafonte, Marlo Thomas, Maud Adams, Tippi Hedren, Carey Lowell and Elizabeth Berkley.

They [fashion companies] all want to use actors," says Olga Liriano, head of the celebrity division at Ford Models. "Photographers find it more interesting. Supermodels are waning and they're spent. Photographers feel actors can give more."

But whether or not that's actually true, it seems that actresses are more believable than supermodels who, as Liriano puts it, are "so skinny and almost flawless. Even Demi Moore—people can relate to her. She's been so open about how she got in shape. [Actresses have] done interviews about their regimes. When you hear Kate Moss say, 'I eat hamburgers,' people say 'sure.'"

Appendices

Selected Examples of Color and Fashion Trend Forecasting Services

The Color Association of
the United States (CAUS)
409 West 44th Street
New York, NY 10006
(212) 582-6884
Fax; 212 757-4557

The Doneger Group
463 Seventh Avenue
New York, New York 10018
(212) 564-1255
Fax: (212) 564-3971

Here & There
1412 Broadway
New York, NY 10018
(212) 354-9014
Fax: (212) 764-1831

International Colour Authority
(for American agent, see
Color Association of the United States)
Amsterdam

Margit Publications
1412 Broadway, Suite 1102
New York, NY 10018
(212) 302-5137
Fax; (212) 944-8757

Pantone Color Institute
590 Commerce Boulevard
Carlstadt, NJ 07072
(201) 935-5500
Fax: (201) 896-0242

Pat Tunsky Inc.
1040 Avenue of the Americas
New York, NY 10018
(212) 944-9160
Fax: (212) 764-5105

Promostyl (Paris (headquarters,
with subsidiary offices in NY,
London & Tokyo)
80 West 40th Street
New York, NY 10018
(212) 921-7930
Fax: (212) 921-8214

RTW Review
P.O. Box 27688
Milwaukee, WI 53227
(414) 425-6503
Fax: (414) 425-2501

The Tobé Report
40 East 42nd Street
New York, NY 10017
(212) 867-8677
Fax: (212) 867-8602

Selected Trade Publications
for the World of Fashion

APPAREL

Newspapers

Women's Wear Daily: Published Monday through Friday by Fairchild Publications. Covers national and international news in the fashion industry. Focus is on women's and children's apparel and fabrics. Special accessories supplements, Monday issues feature accessories/innerwear/legwear industry news. Friday issues feature cosmetics and fragrances.

Daily News Record: Published Monday through Friday by Fairchild Publications. Covers national and international news in the men's wear and textile industries.

California Apparel News, Dallas Apparel News, Atlanta Apparel News, Chicago Apparel News: Published weekly. Covers fashion industry news with a focus on regional companies and markets. Includes classified advertisements.

Children's Business Published monthly by Fairchild Publications for retailers of children's products including apparel, footwear, toys, entertainment, and juvenile products for infants through preteens, boys and girls.

Salon News: Published monthly by Fairchild Publciations for salon owners.

SportStyle: Published by Fairchild Publications, 18 times a year, for retailers and manufacturers of sportswear and sports equiment.

Footwear News: Published weekly by Fairchild Publications on Monday. Focuses on the fashion, retailing, manufacturing, and financial segments of the international shoe industry.

Hosiery News (published by the National Association of Hosiery Manufacturers)

APPAREL

Magazines

Apparel Industry Magazine: Published monthly by Shore-Varrone, Inc. Covers all facets of the apparel manufacturing industry.

Bobbin: Published monthly by Bobbin Blenheim Media. Bobbin is the "premier news and information source of the global sewn products industry."

Earnshaw's Infants, Girls, and Boys Wear Review: Published monthly by Earnshaw Publications. Earnshaw's is the "business/fashion magazine of the children's wear industry."

Textiles

America's Textiles International: Published monthly for managers in the textile industry; includes information concerning textile business, finances, and manufacturing.

American Dyestuff Reporter: Published monthly; covers textile wet-processing.

Daily News Record: Published Tuesday through Friday by Fairchild Publications for men's fashion, retailing and textiles.

Fiber World: Published quarterly for fiber producers.

Knitting Times: Published weekly; covers business conditions, technical developments, and forecasts for knitted fabrics and apparel.

Nonwovens Industry: Published monthly; covers manufacturing processes, distribution and end use applications of nonwoven textile products.

Textile Hi-Lights: Published quarterly by the American Textile Manufacturers Institute; statistical study of all aspects of the textile industry.

Textile Organon: Published monthly; market data for natural and manufactured fibers.

Textile Technology Digest: Published monthly; abstracts of periodicals, books, and patents related to the textile industry.

Textile World: Published monthly; covers technical developments in the textile industry.

Retailing

Advertising Age, the international newspaper of marketing: Published by Crain Communications, this trade publication includes articles on domestic and international advertising news and trends.

Chain Store Age Executive: A Lebhar-Friedman publication, this trade magazine focuses on information of interest to managers and executives of chain stores, such as finance, sales, new products, and chain store news.

Discount Merchandiser: Published by Schwartz Publications, this publication addresses all aspects of discount merchandising including manufacturing, retailing, advertising, and other industry information.

Discount Store News: the international journal of retailing: Published by Schwartz Publications, this trade newspaper focuses on timely news related to discount stores. Articles cover new products, licensing, visual merchandising, and industry trends.

Marketing News: reporting on the marketing profession and its association: A publication of the American Marketing Association, this newspaper covers information and news of interest to marketing professionals including marketing strategies, retailing, market research, and trends.

Retail Control: retail business review: A publication of the National Retail Federation and National Retail Dry Goods Association, this bi-monthly magazine focuses on retail trade and accounting issues in retailing.

Retailing Today: Published by Robert Kahn & Associates, a monthly newsletter for retail managers focusing on trends, sales, and issues in the retail industry.

Stores: A publication of the National Retail Federation, this monthly trade magazine includes information of interest to retailers in general. The July issue includes a ranked listing of department stores; the August issue includes a ranked listing of specialty stores.

VM&SD: Published by ST Publications Inc., a monthly magazine focusing on merchandise presentation and store planning.

Home Fashions

Bedtimes: Published monthly by International Sleep Products Association, monthly. Focuses on mattress manufacturing industry and its suppliers, and other sleep products trades.

Decorative Home: Published monthly by Fairchild Publications as a guide to retailers of decorative accessories and home gifts.

FDM - Furniture Design and Manufacturing: Published monthly by Cahners Publishing Co. Covers the furniture, bedding and upholstering industries.

Floor Covering Weekly: Published weekly by Hearst Business Communications in a tabloid format.

Flooring: The Magazine of Interior Surfaces: Published monthly by Douglas Publications. Covers in-depth feature stories, as well as the latest industry new, and information on all the latest products and services in areas such as: wood flooring, ceramic tile, carpet, vinyl flooring, and accessories.

Home Accents Today: Published by Cahners Business Newspapers, 8 issues per year is a merchandising and fashion news magazine of the home accent industry. Aimed at the decorative accessory, specialty home accent, and major gift buyers shopping the major furniture markets in High Point, Dallas, Atlanta, and San Francisco; and gift markets in New York, Los Angeles, Atlanta, Dallas, and Chicago.

HFD (previously *Home Furnishing Network*): Published weekly by Fairchild Publications. Covers furniture, bedding, floor coverings, giftware and housewares for retailers, wholesalers, manufacturers, and suppliers.

Home Furnishings Executive: Published monthly by Pace Communications for the home furnishings retail trade.

Home Furnishings Review: Published monthly by the Home Furnishings International Association. Covers business information drawn from a variety of publications and other sources, digested into brief articles aimed at helping the home furnishings retailer operate a more profitable business.

Home Textiles Today: Published weekly by Cahners Business Newspapers for the marketing, merchandising and retailing of home textile products.

Homemarket Trends: Published by Lebhar-Friedman, Inc, 6 times per year. Coverage includes furniture, bed and bath, table top and window treatments.

Interior Design: Published by Cahners Publishing Co., 17 issues per year. Provides information on trends and new products to the professional designer.

LBD Interior Textiles: Published monthly by Columbia Communications, monthly for retailers of home furnishings, textiles and bath products, including linens.

The Decorative Rug: Published monthly by the Oriental Rug Auction Review, Inc. Covers new oriental rugs at the wholesale and retail levels.

Upholstery Design & Manufacturing (UDM): Published monthly by Cahners Publishing Company. Covers information related to the design and manufacturing of upholstery textiles and upholstered furniture.

Wallcoverings, Windows, and Interior Fashion: Published monthly by Publishing Dynamics Inc.

Selected Trade Associations for the World of Fashion

APPAREL

American Apparel
Manufacturers Association
2500 Wilson Blvd.
Arlington, VA 22201
(705) 524-1864

Associated Corset & Brassiere
Manufacturers Inc.
1430 Broadway, Suite 1603
New York, NY 10018
(212) 354-0707

Clothing Manufacturers Association
1290 Avenue of the Americas
New York, NY 10104
(212) 757-6664

Council of Fashion Designers
of America (CFDA)
1412 Broadway
New York, NY 10018
(212) 302-1821

Crafted with Pride in the USA
1045 Avenue of the Americas
New York, NY 10018
(212) 819-4397

The Fashion Association (TFA)
475 Park Avenue South
New York, NY 10016
(212) 683-5665

The Fashion Group International Inc.
597 Fifth Avenue
New York, NY 10017
(212) 593-1715

Infant's, Children's & Girl's Sportswear &
Coat Association, Inc.
225 W. 39 Street
New York, NY 10018
(212) 398-2982

International Association of
Clothing Designers
475 Park Avenue
New York, NY 10016
(212) 685-6602

International Swimwear & Activewear
Market and the Swimwear Association
110 East 9th Street
Los Angeles, CA 99079
(213) 239-9347

The Intimate Apparel Council
150 Fifth Avenue
New York, NY 10011
(212) 807-0878

Men's Apparel Guild of California
(MAGIC)
100 Wilshire Blvd.
Santa Monica, CA 90401
(310) 393-7757

National Association of Men's
Sportswear Buyers (NAMSB)
500 Fifth Avenue
New York, NY 10110
(212) 391-8580

National Knitwear & Sportswear
Association
386 Park Avenue South
New York, NY 10016
(212) 447-1234

Uunderfashion Club Inc.
347 Fifth Avenue
New York, NY 10016
(212) 481-7792

United Infant's & Children's Wear
Association
1328 Broadway
New York, NY 10001
(212) 244-2953

Young Menswear Association
47 West 34th Street
New York, NY 10001
(212) 594-6422

ACCESSORIES

American Leather Accessory Designers
(ALAD)
c/o Marcia Sherrill
Kleinberg Sheriff
392 Fifth Avenue
New York, NY 10018
(212) 971-0906

Fashion Footwear Association of
New York (FFANY)
870 Seventh Avenue
New York, NY 10019
(212) 247-4660

Fashion Jewelry Association of America
Regency East
1 Jackson Parkway
Providence, RI 02903
(401) 273-1515

Headwear Institute of America
1 West 64th Street
New York, NY 10023
(212) 724-0888

Jewelers of America
1185 Avenue of the Americas
New York, NY 10036
(212) 768-8777

National Association of Fashion and
Accessory Designers
2180 East 93rd Street
Cleveland, OH 44106
(216) 231-0375

National Association of Hosiery
Manufacturers (NAHM)
200 N. Sharon Amity Road
Charlotte, NC 28211
((704) 365-0913

National Association of Milliners,
Dressmakers, and Tailors
157 West 126th Street
New York, NY 10027
(212) 666-1320

National Fashion Accessories Association
330 Fifth Avenue
New York, NY 10001
(212) 947-3424

National Women's Neckwear and
Scarf Association
1350 Avenue of the Americas
New York, NY 10019
(212) 708-0316

Neckwear Association of America
151 Lexington Ave., #2F
New York, NY 10016
(212) 967-3002

Sunglass Association of America
71 East Avenue
Norwalk, CT 06851
(203) 852-7168

TEXTILES

Acrylic Council
1285 Avenue of the Americas
New York, NY 10016
(212) 554-4040
Fax: (212) 554-4042

American Association for
Textile Technology, Inc.
347 Fifth Avenue
New York, NY 10016
(212) 481-7792
Fax: (212) 481-7969

American Association of Textile Chemists
and Colorists
P.O. Box 12215
Research Triangle Park, NC 27709
(919) 549-8141

American Fiber Manufacturers
Association
1150 17th Street NW
Washington, D.C. 20036
(202) 296-6508
Fax: (202) 296-3052

American Fur Industry
363 7th Avenue
New York, NY 10001

American Printed Fabrics Council
45 West 36th Street
New York, NY 10018
(212) 695-2254
Fax: (212) 947-0115

American Textile Machinery Association
7297 N. Lee Highway, Suite N
Falls Church, VA 22042
(703) 533-9251

American Textile Manufacturers Institute
1801 K Street NW
Suite 900
Washington, D.C. 20006
(202) 862-0500
Fax: (202) 862-0570

American Wool Council
6911 South Yosemite Street
Denver, CO 80112
(303) 771-3500
Fax: (303) 771-8200
New York Office:
   50 Rockefeller Plaza, Suite 830
   New York, NY 10020
   (212) 245-6710
   Fax: (212) 333-560

American Yarn Spinners Association
P.O. Box 99
Gastonia, NC 28053
(704) 824-3522

Camel Hair and Cashmere Institute
of America
230 Congress Street
Boston, MA 02110
(617) 542-8220
Fax: (617) 542-2199

Carpet and Rug Institute
P.O. Box 2048
Dalton, GA 30722
(706) 226-3877

Cotton Incorporated
1370 Avenue of the Americas
New York, NY 10019
(212) 586-1070
Fax: (212) 265-5386

Eastern Mink Breeders Association
151 West 30th Street
New York, NY 10001

Fur Farm Animal Welfare Coalition, Ltd.
405 Sibley Street
St. Paul, MN 55101
(612) 293-0349

International Linen Promotion
Commission
200 Lexington Avenue
New York, NY 10016
(212) 685-0424
Fax: (212) 725-0438

International Silk Association
c/o American Silk Mills
41 Madison Avenue
New York, NY 10010
(212) 213-1919
Fax: (212) 683-2370

Leather Industries of America
1000 Thomas Jefferson Street NW
Suite 515
Washington, D.C. 20007
(202) 342-8086
Fax: (202) 342-9063

Mohair Council of America
36 W. Beauregard Street
Room 516, FNB Bldg.
San Angelo, TX 76903
(915) 655-3161
Fax: (915) 655-4761

National Cotton Council of America
P.O. Box 12285
Memphis, TN 38182
(901) 274-9030

Polyester Council
1675 Broadway
New York, NY 10019
(212) 527-8941
Fax: (212) 527-8989

United Textile Association
386 Park Avenue South
New York, NY 10016
(212) 689-3807
Fax: (212) 889-6160

Wool Bureau Inc.
330 Madison Avenue
New York, NY 10017
(212) 986-6222
Fax: (212) 557-5985

RETAIL

American Management Association
135 West 50 Street
New York, NY 10019
(212) 586-8100

Footwear Industries of America
1420 K Street NW
Washington, D.C. 20005
(202) 789-1420

National Mass Retail Association
1901 Pennsylvania Avenue NW
10th Floor
Washington, D.C. 20006
(202) 861-0774

National Retail Federation
100 West 31st Street
New York, NY 10001
(212) 244-8780

National Shoe Retailers Association
9861 Broken Land Parkway
Columbia, MD 21046
(410) 381-8282

Shoe Retailers League
275 Madison Avenue
New York, NY 10016
(212) 889-7920

HOME FASHIONS

American Furniture Manufacturers
Association
P.O. Box 2436
High Point, NC 27261

Association of Interior Decor Specialists,
Inc. (AIDS INTERNATIONAL)
2009 N. 14 Street #203
Arlington, VA 22201

Carpet and Rug Institute
P.O. Box 2048
Dalton, GA 20720

Decorative Fabrics Association (DFA)
950 3rd Avenue
New York, NY 10022

International Home Furnishings
Representatives Association (IHFRA)
666 Lake Shore Drive
Chicago, IL 60611

National Association of Decorative
Fabrics Distributors (NADFD)
6022 West Touhy Avenue
Chicago, IL 60648

National Association of Floor Covering
Distributors (NAFCE)
13-186 Merchandise Mart
Chicago, IL 60654

National Home Fashions League, Inc.
(NHFL)
107 World Trade Center
Dallas, TX 75258

National Home Furnishings Association
(NHFA)
900 17th Street NW, Suite 514
Washington, DC 20006

Upholstered Furniture Action Council
(UFAC)
Box 2436
High Point, NC 27261

Index

Picture Credits

The authors and publisher wish to thank the following for supplying photographs and granting permission to use them.

Chapter 1: UPI/BETTMANN: 3, 5; BETTMANN: 4; Marshall Field, State Street: 6 (left); CORBIS-BETTMANN: 6 (right); The Mall of America: 10; *WWD*: 12, 16; *NYTimes* Pictures: 15 (Al Grillo); The Kobal Collection: 18.

Chapter 2: UPI/BETTMANN: 24, 31 (left) 37, 38, 39 (top), 40, 42; The Cincinnati Museum of Art: Fortuny (1871-1949) Dress (pleated silk) and belt, 1920-30, Gift of Mrs. James Morgan Hutton by exchange. Jacket (silk velvet), 1931, Gift of Mrs. Charles Fleischmann, in memory of Julius Fleischmann: 26; CORBIS-BETTMANN: 27, 31 (right), 33 (bottom), 34-36, 39 (bottom), 44; THE BETTMANN ARCHIVE: 28; *WWD*: 29, 41 (profile), 43, 46, 48; Los Angeles County Museum of Art (LACMA): 30; Bonnie Cashin: 32; Time Inc.: 33 (top); *NYTimes* Pictures: 41 (William E. Sauro), 47 (Philip Greenberg); The Kobal Collection: 45.

Chapter 3: American Demographics, Inc.: 59 (bottom); VALS2. SRI International: 60; *NYTimes* Pictures: 62 (Naum Z. Kazhdan); *WWD*: 64, 67, 68; AP/Wide World Photos: 69 (Wilfredo Lee); UPI/BETTMANN: 71; Focus Suites of Philadelphia: 77.

Chapter 4: Nina Ricci, 89; *WWD*: 93; CORBIS-BETTMANN: 94; Springer/BETTMANN Film Archive: 95; The BETTMANN Archive: 96 (profile); The Kobal Collection: 96 (bottom), 97 (top); ABC, Inc.: 97 (bottom, left); MPTV: 97 (bottom, right); AP / Wide World Photos: 98 (George Nikitin); UPI/BETTMANN: 110; Reuters/BETTMANN: 111.

Chapter 5: Hong Kong Trade Development Council: 112, 123; *WWD*: 117-119, 125; Zandra Rhodes: 120 (Polly Estes).

Chapter 6: Christopher Everett, 151; *WWD*: 153, 157.

Chapter 7: Fairchild Books: 175, 180 (top), 185 (top), 186 (bottom); National Cotton Council: 178, 183 (right), 184 (top); International Linen Promotion Commission: 179 (top), 195; The Wool Bureau: 179 (bottom); American Fiber Manufacturers Association, Inc.: 180 (bottom), 185 (bottom), 188; Steve Bidman: 183 (left); Burlington Industries,

Inc.: 184 (bottom), 191 (bottom); Bassett-Walken, a division of VF Corporation: 186 (top); Hendorfer: 187; Cotton Incorporated: 194.

Chapter 8: *WWD*: 204, 206, 213; UPI/BETTMANN, 205; North Atlantic Fur Auction: 207; Seidel Tannery: 209, 216 (Ellen Diamond); Reuters/BETTMANN: 211; Leather Apparel Association: 214, 219; Andrew Marc: 215.

Chapter 9: *NYTimes* Pictures: 233; *WWD*: 232, 233 (right), 234, 236, 237, 240, 247; Liz Claiborne: 238 (Paul Lange); Seventh on Sale (CFDA): 242; UPI/BETTMANN: 245; The Fashion Association: 246, 248, 249; Reuters/BETTMANN: 251; Tickle Me!: 253.

Chapter 10: The Fashion Association, 265; The DuPont Company, 267; Barry Kieselstein-Cord: 268 (top) 271, 274 (top) (Albert Watson); Tiffany & Co.: 268 (bottom); Robert Lee Morris: 269 (Teresa Misagal); *WWD*: 272, 273 (bottom), 274 (bottom), 275 (bottom); *NYTimes* Pictures: 273 (Mohin); OGAN / DALLAL Associates Inc.: 275 (top).

Chapter 11: Lola Hats: 282 (Ellen Diamond); Illustrations by Kichisaburo Ogawa: 283-286; Joanne Criscione, 292 (Ellen Diamond); *NYTimes* Pictures: 290 (top) (Rebecca Cooney); The DuPont Company: 291.

Chapter 12: *WWD*: 297, 305-307; *NYTimes* Pictures: 303 (Marilyn K. Yee), 308 (John Maier Jr.); Marc Rosen Associates: 304.

Chapter 13: Colours by Alexander Julian for Dan River: 323, 327; *NYTimes* Pictures: 325, 332 (Barbara Alper), 329 (Andrew Lichtenstein); *WWD*: 338.

Chapter 14: The Doneger Group: 349 (Ellen Diamond); Promostyl: 350, 351; Color Association of the United States (CAUS): 353, 356.

Chapter 15: *WWD*: 365 (top and bottom left), 366, 369, 370-373; Sal Cesarani, Fineberg Publicity: 365 (bottom right).

Chapter 16: Gerber: 389, 392 (Robert A. Flynn, Inc.); *WWD*: 393, 401; Alan Edmunds: 394 (Ellen Diamond).

Chapter 17: The Doneger Group: 413, 414, 417; *WWD*: 421; National Retail

Federation: 423; The Fashion Association: 424; Fairchild Publications: 425.

Chapter 18: Bergdorf Goodman, J.T. Kakaoke Associates, Architects, L.A.: 433 (top), 453 (Jaime Ardiles-Aece); Melvin Simon: 433 (bottom); Macy's Publicity Department: 434; *WWD*: 435, 436, 438, 440, 442; Marshall Field, State Street: 444; Roosevelt Field: 445 (Bruce Bennett Studios); The Rouse Corporation: 446; *NYTimes* Pictures: 447 (top) (Scott Robinson); F.W. Thorlton Photographics, Woodbridge, N.J.: 447 (bottom); Bloomingdale's, Chicago: 451 (Ellen Diamond); ACA Joe: 453 (left).

Chapter 19: *NYTimes* Pictures: 471 (Steve Goldstein), 478 (Don Hogan Charles); UPI CORBIS-BETTMANN: 473.

Photographs by Ellen Diamond: 7 (bottom), 59 (top), 73, 90, 116, 126, 127, 142-147, 149, 152, 154-156, 190, 264, 288, 289, 290 (bottom), 328, 375, 387, 388, 391, 403, 420, 437, 441, 448, 462, 463 (top), 469, 470, 472, 476-478.

Color Plates: (1) Evening gown decorated with Art Nouveau scroll design. Formerly belonged to Elizabeth Drexel. Lady Decies. Label: Worth, Paris. Gift of Miss Eva Drexel Dahlgren, 1976. (2) Theater coat, 1912. Designer; Paul Poiret. Purchase. Irene Lewisohn Trust Gift, 1982. (3) Designer: Coco Chanel. Left; Ensemble, ca. 1927. Dress of printed silk chiffon; coat of wool tweed lined in dress fabric. Gift of Diana Vreeland, 1994; Center: Suit, 1937. Blue linen. Gift of Mrs. Stephane Groueff, 1976. Right: Suit, ca 1955. Black, blue and azure tweed. Isabel Shults Fund, 1984. The Metropolitan Museum of Art; photographed by Sheldan Collins. (4) and (5) Hong Kong Trade Development Council. (6) Gianfranco Ferré; (7) Mariuccia Mandelli for Krizia; (8) Giorgio Armani; (9) Donna Karan; (10) Bill Blass; (11) Jean Paul Gaultier. (6-11, from *W*.) (12) Nautica; (13) Dolce & Gabbana; (14) Giorgio Armani. (12-14 from *DNR*.) (15) Baby B'Gosh; (16) Boo; (17) Guess. (15-17 from *Children's Business*.) (18 and 19) Image Bank; photographer, C. Irion. (20) Tyson's Corner, VA. Lendorff Group, Dallas; (21) Bloomingdale's, PGA. (22) Marshall Field, State Street. (21 and 22 from FRCH Worldwide.) Photos of accessories from *W*.